NEW
DIMENSIONS
IN
ADULT
DEVELOPMENT

NEW DIMENSIONS IN ADULT DEVELOPMENT

ROBERT A. NEMIROFF, M.D.
AND
CALVIN A. COLARUSSO, M.D.

EDITORS

92-526

Basic Books, Inc. Publishers

NEW YORK

Library of Congress Cataloging-in-Publication Data
New dimensions in adult development / Robert A.
    Nemiroff and Calvin A. Colarusso, editors.
        p.   cm.
    Includes bibliographical references.
    ISBN 0-465-05010-7
    1. Adulthood—Psychological aspects.
I. Nemiroff, Robert A.   II. Colarusso, Calvin A.
BF724.5.N47   1990
155.6—dc20   89-43165
                                              CIP

This book is dedicated to our colleagues, fellow adult developmentalists, who have encouraged, supported, and inspired our work.

CONTENTS

CONTRIBUTORS

Judith M. Bardwick, Ph.D.
Clinical Professor of Psychiatry, University of California at San Diego

Stanley H. Cath, M.D.
Medical Director, The Family Advisory Service and Treatment Center, Belmont, Massachusetts

Bernard Chodorkoff, Ph.D., M.D.
Associate Professor of Psychiatry, Wayne State University, School of Medicine

Bertram J. Cohler, Ph.D.
William Rainey Harper Professor of Social Sciences, The University of Chicago

Calvin A. Colarusso, M.D.
Clinical Professor of Psychiatry, University of California at San Diego

Robert M. Galatzer-Levy, M.D., S.C.
Lecturer in Psychiatry, The University of Chicago

Marcia Kraft Goin, M.D., Ph.D.
Clinical Professor of Psychiatry, University of Southern California Medical School

Louis A. Gottschalk, M.D., Ph.D.
Professor of Psychiatry and Social Science, University of California at Irvine

Roger L. Gould, M.D.
Associate Clinical Professor of Psychiatry, University of California at Los Angeles

Brian P. Griffin, Ph.D.
Associate Professor of Psychiatry, Department of Psychiatry and Behavioral Sciences, Northwestern University Medical School

Jerome M. Grunes, M.D.
Associate Professor, Department of Psychiatry, Northwestern University Medical School

David Gutmann, Ph.D.
Professor of Psychiatry and Education, Northwestern University

H. Peter Hildebrand, Ph.D.
Top Grade Clinical Psychologist with Greater Responsibility, Tavistock Clinic

Jordan Jacobowitz, Ph.D.
Assistant Director, Older Adult Program, Northwestern Memorial Hospital

Doryann Lebe, M.D.
Assistant Clinical Professor of Psychiatry, University of California at Los Angeles

Robert Jay Lifton, M.D.
Distinguished Professor of Psychiatry and Psychology, John Jay College of Criminal Justice, City University of New York

Wayne A. Myers, M.D.
Clinical Professor of Psychiatry, Cornell University Medical Center

Carol C. Nadelson, M.D.
Professor and Vice Chairman, Department of Psychiatry, and Director, Training and Education, Tufts–New England Medical Hospitals

Robert A. Nemiroff, M.D.
Clinical Professor of Psychiatry, University of California at San Diego

Nancy Newton, Ph.D.
Associate Dean/Director of Clinical Training, Chicago School of Professional Psychology

Leo Rangell, M.D.
Clinical Professor of Psychiatry, University of California at Los Angeles.

John Munder Ross, Ph.D.
Clinical Associate Professor, Cornell Medical College

G. Mark Schoepfle, Ph.D.
Research Associate, Oak Ridge National Laboratory

Calvin F. Settlage, M.D.
Clinical Professor of Psychiatry, University of California at San Francisco

Estelle Shane, Ph.D.
Faculty, Department of Psychiatry, University of California at Los Angeles

Morton Shane, M.D.
Associate Clinical Professor, University of California at Los Angeles

Sheila A. Sharpe, Ph.D.
Adjunct Faculty, California School of Professional Psychology, San Diego

Judith Stevens-Long, Ph.D.
Professor of Psychology, California State University, Los Angeles

Martin D. Topper, Ph.D.
National Indian Program Coordinator, United States Environmental Protection Agency

ACKNOWLEDGMENTS

We are most grateful to the colleagues who joined us in this undertaking and thank them for their efforts, ideas, and contributions to the field of adult development.

As with our two previous books, we could not have brought the project to fruition without the invaluable help of our friend and editor Barbara Blomgren, upon whose talents and conscientiousness we have come to rely for many such projects.

Jo Ann Miller, Senior Editor and Director of Professional Books at Basic Books, was enthusiastic about this project from its inception to completion. She expressed thorough appreciation of the value of adult developmental concepts and provided valuable insight and guidance.

Our colleagues in the Department of Psychiatry at the University of California, San Diego, and at the San Diego Psychoanalytic Institute were, as always, a major source of encouragement and support.

We give special acknowledgment to Phyllis Baumgart, Administrative Coordinator of the Residency Training Program in Psychiatry at the University of California, San Diego. With cheerful competence, she performed myriad tasks that greatly facilitated our efforts.

Once again we thank our wives, Barbara Nemiroff and Jean Colarusso, who graciously sacrifice a good deal of their own increasingly precious adult developmental time for our projects.

INTRODUCTION

When I was younger, there was much talk about the century of the child. Has it ended? We hope it has quietly joined the era. Since then we have gone through something like a century of youth. But when, pray, is the century of the adult to begin?

—Erik Erikson
Dimensions of a New Identity

We have been privileged for the past ten years to be part of the emergence of an exciting new field of study, "adult development." This new field studies the adult years, that is, the span of life of approximately fifty years or more between adolescence and senescence. As Judith Stevens-Long points out in her *Adult Life* (1988), the study of human development focused almost exclusively on the first few years of the life span until the 1960s. Prior to the 1960s, the first half of the century, driven by the spread of compulsory education and the exclusion of children from the labor force, led to a great thirst for information about the development of children and adolescence. As research progressed, we learned that childhood and adolescent learning and maturation were complex and could be divided into predictable stages. Interestingly, for a long time there was little comparable interest or research of the adult years. In fact, most social scientists tended to view the adult years in a static, almost negative fashion, devoid of a development of its own, concerned with only "adjustment" to the burdens of being an adult. For many, adulthood was seen stereotypically as an inevitable two-stage process. The first segment of adulthood was involved with stability: that is, one got married, settled into a career, and then waited quietly for the decline and degeneration of the second stage, old age. In recent years we have been part of the educational and investigatory process that has demonstrated the dynamic complexity of the adult years and its enormous significance in understanding the entire life cycle and treating our adult patients.

In our first book, *Adult Development: A New Dimension in Psychodynamic Theory and Practice* (1981), we presented a model of normal adult functioning and began to formulate a psychodynamic theory of development during the second half of life. We first demonstrated how ideas about the life cycle have existed since antiquity. From the very dawn of literate time, each culture in its most ancient writings has put forth its own complex chronology of an individual's progress through the life cycle. We then set forth seven hypotheses, as a part of a new psychodynamic theory of adult development. Hypothesis I asserted that the nature of the developmental process is basically the same in the adult as in the child. We disputed the common idea that, compared with the child, the adult is relatively free from environmental influences, and suggested instead that for the achievement of new and phase-specific developmental tasks in adulthood, the individual is as dependent on the environment as is the child.

In Hypothesis II, in contradistinction to the notion that the adult is a finished product, we suggested that development during the adult years is an ongoing, dynamic process. To differentiate child from adult development, we proposed in Hypothesis III that whereas child development is focused primarily on the formation of psychic structure, adult development is concerned with the continuing evolution of existing psychic structure and its use. Hypothesis IV deals with the relationship between childhood and adulthood, positing a continuous, vital interaction—the fundamental issues of childhood continuing in altered form as central aspects of adult life. In our opinion, attempts to explain all adult behavior and psychopathology in terms of childhood events is reductionistic. We proposed in Hypothesis V that developmental processes are influenced by the adult past as well as childhood. Psychoanalysis has emphasized the influence of the body on mental development in childhood and adolescence but has virtually ignored the body after that, until dealing with the climacteric and old age. Our Hypothesis VI speaks to the effects of physical processes on psychological expression after adolescence and to the profound influences of the body and physical changes on development in adulthood. Finally, with Hypothesis VII, we addressed a paramount issue affecting the developmental process in the second half of life: namely, the growing awareness of death, suggesting that a central, phase-specific theme of adult development is a normative crisis precipitated by the recognition and acceptance of the finiteness of time and inevitability of personal death. Physical signs of aging, the deaths of parents and friends, the maturing of children, and the growing understanding that not all of one's life goals will be realized force upon the adult in middle age an unwanted awareness of temporal limitation that clashes with our ever-present wish to deny death. We see this conflict as universal, containing within it the possibility of developmental progression or regression and arrest. In our own chapter in this book, we update these seven hypotheses by integrating new data. It is gratifying to find much confirmation of these original hypotheses in the work presented here by our colleagues. In our discussions of their chapters we have in many cases been able to make connections between our hypotheses and their creative work.

In *Adult Development* we applied the preceding themes to issues of narcissism in the adult development of self, myths about the adult body, male and female midlife crises, parenthood, and alternative lifestyles. Finally, in the clinical section, we presented a novel method of adult developmental diagnosis and demonstrated the importance of adult developmental concepts on a variety of psychotherapeutic interventions. We attempted to translate these theoretical concepts into practical clinical strategies that enable us to understand and to treat patients with a wide variety of psychopathology. For instance, recognizing that the fundamental developmental issues of childhood continue as central aspects of adult life focuses the therapist's attention on three goals: (1) defining the relationships between infantile experience and adult symptom; (2) elaborating the effects of the infantile experience on all subsequent developmental tasks, from childhood to adulthood; and (3) relating the insights to current, phase-specific arrests in development, leading to a re-engagement of the adult development process.

In *The Race Against Time: Psychotherapy and Psychoanalysis in the Second Half of Life* (1985), we expanded on the adult developmental model by presenting additional theoretical concepts, such as the concepts of adult developmental lines and adult developmental arrests; but our primary intent, aided by clinical contributions from eleven experienced therapists, was to apply these ideas to the clinical situation. This goal was accomplished through the presentation of detailed case histories of psychotherapy and psychoanalysis in patients from ages forty through eighty. Based on those case studies and clinical data from our own practices, our overall conclusion was: *Psychodynamically oriented psychotherapy and psychoanalysis are valid clinical techniques for selected patients in the second half of life, regardless of age.* Specifically, we were able to demonstrate (1) the complexity of the developmental process in the second half of life; (2) the vitality and resourcefulness of the human mind in regard to sexual and aggressive impulses and the capacity for introspection and self-analysis; (3) the great variety of diagnostic and therapeutic techniques usable with older patients, from psychoanalysis to a wide range of supportive techniques—despite the many biases some therapists hold against working with older patients; and (4) the effect on therapists of work with old patients. We found much creativity and flexibility in evidence in these case histories, including a striking degree of honesty about the transference and countertransference reactions in work with older patients.

The clinical issues discussed in *The Race Against Time* may be summarized as follows. (1) Older patients need not be treated superficially. Selected individuals are suitable cases for dynamic psychotherapy and psychoanalysis, regardless of age. (2) An adult developmental orientation, as expressed through adult developmental lines and tasks, and a developmental history of the life cycle add new dimensions to the diagnostic process and therapeutic effort. (3) Symptoms are a condensation of experience from all phases of development, not a simple expression of infantile conflict in the adult present. (4) The aging body, time limitation, and personal death are central themes in the treatment of every adult patient: that is, the therapist must always start with the patient's concern about his or her aging body. (5) Sexual thoughts, feelings, and activity remain powerful, dynamic issues until death—and older patients wish to resolve their sexual problems. (6) In the second half of life, transference is a more complex phenomenon, taking several multigenerational forms. Special attention should be paid to the adult past as a source of transference. (7) Similarly, countertransference responses to the older patient are complicated, since they are reflections of the therapist's infantile and adult experience with his or her parents and other significant figures.

Our intent in this book is to stimulate further the growth of this new field, adult development, by entering into a dialogue with creative scholars and clinicians who we know are working on the cutting edge of the field. We selected the leading exponents of many different facets of adult developmental theory and practice and asked our contributors to write a chapter describing their current ideas about adult development. Developing a multidisciplinary focus, we invited authors from such diverse disciplines as anthropology, child development, psychology, psychoanalysis, and sociology.

We were most fortunate to receive a collection of highly original and creative chapters, filled with new ideas and exciting directions. We hope that the reader will expand on the dialogue initiated with each contributor in the brief discussions we have appended to each chapter.

The chapters are organized into four main sections. In part I, "Transition to Adulthood," child developmentalists and psychoanalysts describe transitions to the adult stages by elucidating late adolescent phenomena and individual entries into adulthood. Part II, "New Concepts in Adult Development," includes an article summarizing our own latest thoughts about the frontiers of adult development theory and practice. Other contributors suggest new concepts and original ways to advance the theory. Part III, "Clinical Perspectives," describes primarily the clinical situation of treating the older patient in psychotherapy and psychoanalysis. These chapters suggest exciting and innovative ways to approach the clinical situation with a patient in the second half of life. Part IV, "Applications of Adult Developmental Theory," demonstrates how broad and heuristic the concepts of adult development can be and includes applications of adult development theory to anthropology, biology, dream psychology, literature, political science, and self psychology.

Our hope in composing this volume of exploration of the breadth, extent, and evolution of this new field of adult development has been largely realized. We are in considerable debt to this remarkable multidisciplinary group of original and creative colleagues. With them and others, we hope to continue the work of understanding what it really means to be an adult, in all its wonderful complexity and multifaceted dimensions.

Robert A. Nemiroff
Calvin A. Colarusso

NEW
DIMENSIONS
IN
ADULT
DEVELOPMENT

PART I

TRANSITION TO ADULTHOOD

1

Seventeen:

The Approach to the Portal of Adult Life

LEO RANGELL

As my contribution to this volume on adult development, I choose to write not on a phase, or a stage, or an age group, but on a specific age, the age of seventeen. It is a year of life that approaches the portal to adulthood, a time near the end of gestation for the adult. Psychic and somatic structures and their derivative traits and characteristics are beginning to assume form and unite into a cohesive whole. Physically, one can begin to see the face and body of the adult. Psychologically, the self, the character, and the nature and attributes of the person are gradually becoming visible. By the seventeenth year, the process is well on its way.

It is surprising that in psychoanalysis—a paradigm that examines the past in the present, that sees life as a series of unfoldings, and that exposes repetitive cycles—we have not tended to think the first succession of developmental phases (oral, anal, phallic, preoedipal and oedipal, latency, puberty) is typically repeated in the adolescent years. Yet between the ages of thirteen and twenty, maturation traverses the same sequences it recently crossed for the first time. Oral taking-in from the environment, anal-independent self-sufficiency, phallic, vaginal, genital exchanges with objects (now as a more total sexual and aggressive entity)—all evolve in accordance with a combination of constitutional givens, maturational characteristics, and experiential inputs. Every aspect is recapitulated: drive pressures, old and new, a steady expansion of ego development, superego characteristics in more definitive forms, both similar to and different from

3

earlier ones—all leading again to separation-individuation and changed object relations. Unlike the drama, suddenness, and violence of the original birth, or the burst of physical changes at adolescence, the birth of the adult slips in quietly. It is my impression that this birth is easily overlooked.

Just as progression culminates in a new whole at puberty after the first unfolding, so the young adult emerges after the adolescent second sequence. The initial phasic, yet continuous, development has repeated itself, the original forms either consolidating their structures and characteristics, or acquiring new content and shape. The next nodal point, the appearance of a significantly new level of personhood, finds the physical and psychological still intimately related. Perhaps it is in accord with man's phylogenetically developing sense of time and cognition that changes and new forms in the first third of life lend themselves to numerical division into decades: childhood, the teens, and the twenties.

Margaret Mahler's (Mahler et al. 1975) felicitous reference to "the psychological birth of the human infant" during the first year of life shows us that the concept of birth need no longer be confined to the physical; it can be applied to psychological achievements as well. Indeed, it leads to a general principle: life after birth is a succession of births as well as deaths or passings of stages and organizations. If we distance ourselves from conventional generalizations, we see at once that just as life begins not at birth but at conception (political debates about the morality of abortion follow from biological theories), so is birth not limited to that dramatic moment when the newborn traverses the border between the intrauterine and the external environments. Birth as inception occurs at conception. The term *maturation* was formerly limited to the organic, and the term *development* to the psychological, a distinction introduced by Heinz Hartmann (1939). But both are to be taken into account in understanding all stages of the life cycle. Late adolescence is no exception.

Some distinctions need to be made. *Congenital* is not the same as *constitutional.* Congenital characteristics are *already* a product of constitution and environment, and contain somatic and psychological potentials. The earliest intrauterine environment is determined by both those elements of the maternal surround. In addition to somatic factors, psychological anlagen and potentials are already present, according to Hartmann's (1939, 1950) ego-id matrix, innate ego apparatus, and possible ego energies; Rapaport's (1953) inborn discharge channels; and the innate releaser mechanisms of Konrad Lorenz (1950), Nicholas Tinbergen (1951), and other ethologists. Affect attunement (Stern 1983), object synchrony and mutuality (Erikson 1950), active reciprocity (Winnicott 1957)—all observed from birth on— and Freud's (1896; Breuer and Freud 1893–95) descriptions of affects as deriving phylogenetically from inherited hysterical attacks, render aca-

demic any distinction between psychic and somatic. The acrimonious debate between nature and nurture is clearly outmoded. Constitutional and
acquired characteristics, psychic and somatic structures are united and
reciprocal. Borders and overlaps are both operative and important; distinctions and continuities together are necessary for scientific apprehension of
the data of development.

I have had for many years nascent, not so latent thoughts about the
individual's arrival not just at late adolescence, but precisely at the age of
seventeen and the dynamics operative at that moment in life. From more
than four decades of clinical and theoretical psychoanalytic work, I have
concluded that this critical and formative developmental period has a
nodal significance that has not commanded the attention it deserves.

Following Freud's early emphases, psychoanalysis has pinpointed the
oedipal period, ages four through six, studying, discussing, and constantly
rethinking its apical position. Secondarily, perhaps even reactively, attention shifted to what were first called the pregenital years. When the genital
was discovered to antedate the oedipal (Roiphe 1968; Roiphe and Galenson
1972; Galenson and Roiphe 1974), the term became *preoedipal.* From this
phase of discovery, intense interest now focused on mother and child and
finally on the earliest mother-infant relationships. The literature on each
is prodigious. My experience in confronting psychoanalytic issues has
been that turning to an unfamiliar or neglected area is usually met by a
defense of the familiar or preceding areas of interest and attention. That
response is not necessary here. Everything gained previously still stands.
But new veins, as Sándor Ferenczi (1930) put it, can be found in old mines,
which need constantly to be explored.

Puberty begins around eleven or twelve, visibly, with surface changes
and glandular activity. The adolescent to come has been expected. The
ensuing intergenerational activity is intense, strained, and determined, but
usually good-natured. Exasperating problems come and go with wide oscillations. The patience of all is tested and honed. Characteristics are
demonstrated across the spectrum of actions and affects: good, bad, acceptable, horrid, predictable, surprising, steady, changeable, and chaotic. This
is the most action-oriented period of parent-child relations, but I pass over
it to focus on the age I have selected for discussion here.

The junior year in high school, the year before graduation and the move
to bigger things is known to students and faculty as the most decisive year
in a young person's life. Decisions about further education are made at the
end of the junior year; the senior-year grades count relatively little in
comparison to those of this crucial year. All that has preceded leads to a
series of critical choices. Until now, life has mainly provided one's necessities. The young person applies or does not apply to college or for another

activity, whatever or wherever it may be. Equipped usually with only surface knowledge, each moves in social, occupational, and geographic directions, appearing to choose but being directed by deeper, unconscious elements. Where will one go to college, if at all? Near family or away from them? Perhaps to stay? What goals will one reach for, who will be one's friends and loves, and how will one relate to them? From these choices, made with all levels of the psyche participating, later occurrences will derive and be attributed to "chance." These choices will determine the adult's enduring states in love and work.

Seventeen may strike one as a young and tender age to be given such decisive importance; but just as in a horizontal sense, major conscious decisions are preceded by long unconscious preparatory stages, so in longitudinal development, crucial and active periods of decision are prepared and shaped by preliminary formative periods that may encompass years. The self and its mental representation within the ego are reaching a fairly formed or crystallized stage at seventeen. A characteristic of the self that will be applied more and more regularly is its image of where it fits or belongs in the pecking order of life. The nature of object relations begins to be seen and to be predictable. I recently returned from the fiftieth reunion of my medical school class, which had been preceded some six years earlier by my high school reunion. In each case, I was struck by how little, rather than how much, everyone had changed.

It is surprising, in clinical practice and in life, how many roads lead back to the age of seventeen without commensurate attention having been paid to it. Clinical reconstructions and direct observations have pointed to, and reinforced with convincing regularity, the crucial nature of this age. As in all things psychological, I am not speaking of a sharp demarcation and would not wish to be held to an expectation of such precision. All psychoanalysts grant this fluidity unambivalently. In the kaleidoscope of human life, the oedipal period can be at age four, five, six, or seven; puberty between ten and fourteen. Here I am speaking of ages fifteen or sixteen in some and nineteen to twenty-one in others. I would still, however, single out age seventeen, and the points I am making can be tested there.

The observations from which my reflections are drawn come from both sides of adolescence, from outside as well as inside the psychoanalytic situation, and from personal experience—namely, my children and my grandchildren. All patients past adolescence were once seventeen and reproduce critical material from that period, material that is too often overlooked. My patients report about their adolescent children, and now some are bringing in thoughts about their grandchildren as adolescents. I also hear and read about grandchildren of former patients whom I knew when they themselves were younger.

At the end of late adolescence, the adult is "born"—albeit metaphorically. In many ways, young adults are as raw for their new roles and new functions as the newborn were for the challenges of the world into which they arrived. Presumably, the adolescent's mental functions have grown or are growing to be "mature." At least the world is getting ready to expect and demand of the young adult as if these mental functions were mature. The id and derivative affects have been tamed; the superego has been tried, tested, and shaped, and is supposedly reliable. The ego has had time to institute an effective inventory of defenses and is experienced enough to differentiate impulses that can be directed toward appropriate action from those that need to be deflected or defended against. Mastery is sufficient to deal with internal instinctual demands and pressures and over external limiting stimuli, so that the ego executor and moral agent are at the brink of being accountable for the person's deeds. All is close to being in order.

Or so the script goes. But at this, as at all ages, regressions and progressions are intermixed; the achieved state is stable in name only. Every stage of development, from the earliest to the end of the life cycle, bears imprints of former phases and portents of stages to come. David Rapaport (1959) points out that in the stages of development of psychoanalytic theory, as in ontogenetic development itself, each phase borrows from the past and looks to the future. Regressions and progressions are the norm, not exceptional or pathological. Freud (1937) wrote that "portions of the earlier organization always persist alongside of the more recent one, and even in normal development . . . residues of earlier libidinal fixations may still be retained in the final configuration" (p. 229).

For a report that can stand alongside clinical observations of this simultaneous backward and forward look, I quote not from another psychoanalyst but from the novelist Booth Tarkington's novel, *Seventeen* (1916). The subject is hapless Silly Willy Baxter, to whom love has come for the first time during the summer of his seventeenth year:

In the elder teens adolescence may be completed, but not by experience, and these years know their own tragedies. It is the time of life when one finds it unendurable not to seem perfect in all outward matters: in worldly position, in the equipments of wealth, in family, and in the grace, elegance, and dignity of all appearances in public. And yet the youth is continually betrayed by the child still intermittently insistent within him, and by the child which undiplomatic people too often assume him to be. Thus with William's attire: he could ill have borne any suggestion that it was not of the mode, but taking care of it was a different matter. Also, when it came to his appetite, he could and would eat anything at any time, but something younger than his years led him—often in semisecrecy—to candy-stores and soda-water fountains and ice-cream parlors; he still relished green apples and knew cravings for other dangerous inedibles. But these survivals were far from painful to him; what injured his sensibilities was the disposition on the part of people—especially his parents, and frequently his aunts and uncles—to regard him as a little boy. Briefly, the deference his soul demanded in its own right, not from strangers only, but from his family, was about that which is supposed to be shown a Grand Duke visiting his Estates. Therefore William suffered often. (P. 20)

Times have changed, but not human psychology or development. Although this description is dated, it is also timeless. The affects and their contents can be the same. Even soda-water fountains and ice-cream parlors, among other things, have reappeared.

In spite of the new "birth's" being metaphoric, a new form has emerged, one that is stable enough (to borrow Winnicott's [1951] phrase regarding mothering). For the first time the self can be viewed as semipermanent: "permanent" because it can be expected to endure, yet "semi" because it remains open to change and evolution. There will still be many surprises. It is a time of integration and consolidation, of decisions, of directions. Unconscious choices have hardened into character attitudes at major crossroads of behavior: a position on the spectrum of activity-passivity, a characterologic attitude toward objects, a turn toward an exclusive or at least a dominant sexual orientation and identity. Theodore Jacobs (1987) refers to this age as a "discrete developmental phase." Deep unconscious patterns take shape in the relations between ego and superego, attitudes toward success or failure, achiever-nonachiever, leader-follower, winner-loser. To Freud's (1905) statement that the heir of the oedipal complex is the superego, Peter Blos (1962) adds that the heir of adolescence is the self.

Like the new form that has emerged, the separation that ensues at this stage is real. In the movement from child to adult celebrated at the entry to adolescence, at bar mitzvah, bas mitzvah, or any confirmation, the declaration "Now I am a man" (or "Now I am a woman") was an *as-if* anticipation of things to come. At age eighteen, however, the passage is no longer symbolic. The boy becomes a man; the girl, a woman. If anyone thought that separation-individuation of the mother and child at age one and a half was uniquely traumatic for both, one has but to view the affective reactions at this new and more final separation. It is not atypical for the young person to leave for college and never return to live at home. On both sides, reactions of anxiety, mourning, and a gamut of related emotions may be conscious or may reveal themselves by indirect symptomatic or other sequelae. During this ambiguous time, it is hard to say which of the participants in the separation has taken the active role and which the passive; the child-adult and the parents play both roles.

The legal age recognizing maturity and responsibility is indistinct, perhaps unconsciously reflecting the psychological ambiguity. In different
states, license to drive may come anywhere from ages fifteen to eighteen,
to vote at eighteen, to drink alcohol at twenty-one, to register for the draft
and be inducted into the military at eighteen. Girls can be given the pill
in their early and midteens, but cannot have their tubes ligated legally until
age twenty-one. Sexual activity is also now real for this age group, con-
summation having taken place sometimes years earlier. The possibility of
parenthood is also more acknowledged and expected. Acceptance of adult
responsibility is becoming more common in young males, for whom it has
always been biologically less obligatory than for females. Besides the fate
of sexual impulses, the ego's status vis-à-vis the vicissitudes of the aggressive as well as the sexual drives is a determining factor in the intrapsychic
and (reflectively) the interpersonal activities of the newly established and
independent self.

A woman in her fifties has an obsessive preoccupation with anxiety
over social interaction, to the point of suffering from a social phobia.
Every actual or potential social exchange, whether with the most mild
and innocuous or the most authoritative individuals, is regarded as a
confrontation involving possible attack, humiliation, and traumatic
helplessness. The patient reacts with severe anxiety over aggression,
fearing first that her own ever-present anger will come out and be
visible, and that the inevitable retaliation will reduce her to a state of
crumbling and collapse.

The severe pregenital mother-child psychopathology upon which this
syndrome was built had been held in abeyance during her childhood by
a psychological withdrawal, a shyness, and a reticence. She held back
from all but the most necessary contacts. She was saved, she felt, from
exposure and punishment only by her loved and loving father, whose
positive attitudes toward her sustained her in daily life although he was
mostly absent. The character stance of quiet, submissive withdrawal,
covered by a social pseudocompliance, took definitive and stable form
during her late adolescence when she left home for a boarding school
and assumed what were to be lifelong interpersonal patterns. A pseudo-
compensation prevailed until college. When marriage imposed increased
social contacts, which could no longer be staved off, her defenses of
withdrawal and avoidance were undone. Since then she has been subject
to social anxiety toward any and all of her displaced objects.
During the waning of adolescence, as in other periods of life, an important
formula for the status of self-esteem is the relationship between the
ego and the ego-ideal. The distance between the ego-ideal and the self-
representation within the ego, with regard to superego functioning and the

status of object relations, is crucial for mental well-being, as described by Edith Jacobson (1953, 1964), Joseph Sandler (1960), and Sandler and Bernard Rosenblatt (1962). This relationship has also been stressed, although differently, by Heinz Kohut (1971, 1977), John Gedo (1979), and in most nonanalytic theoretical systems (e.g., Nathaniel Branden, 1971), but without the role of the id and the interrelationships of all the psychic structures. Jacobson (1953) described self-esteem as the gulf between or concordance of the wishful concept of the self and the self-representations.

Striking to any observer can be the almost universal discrepancy between such an inner self-representation and achievements in "actuality," to use Erikson's (1962) term. The formative years, preoedipal and oedipal, coming to a consolidated position in late adolescence, produce an internal conceptual image of the self that ignores, distorts, or alters reality and that lives an independent existence with almost no relation to one's actual significance and status in the outer world. Ongoing achievements in adult years only minimally affect or counteract a negative self-image formed and hardened from childhood through adolescence. Case after case confirms this in a way that never ceases to impress and surprise me. Empirically, such a negative self-image also can occur where parental input has been satisfactory. The opposite, a grandiose self-image, also occurs, but less often, and is almost always the result of reaction formation. Arrogance is usually due to insecurity.

The goal of psychoanalysis is to undo the impermeability of a pathologically structured self-representation, and to allow subsequent events to influence and correct it. I have the feeling with some patients that at a deep formative ego level they took care of "actual" reality first, built up a solid physical and material base, and unconsciously decided to take care of the self-image later. To repair their self-image in analysis, they discover, is not always an easy task. It may, however, be easier than the other way around, where the image comes first, the reality perhaps never.

It is impressive, when one determines to be aware of it, how often a definitive event in neurosogenesis involves the period of passage through the seventeenth year.

A patient in treatment for many years refers repeatedly to the onset decades ago of his obsessive, ruminative pan-neurosis, which he remembers as having started at age seventeen while visiting his grandfather in another city and studying there for his college entrance exams. His grandfather, who like his parents always expected big things from him, was especially doting and loving. An A student until then, the patient remembers studying late at night, with his grandfather asleep in the next room, when the thought suddenly struck him that he would fail and that his whole life would be ruined; he felt that he was going crazy.

That was the first panic attack of many he was to suffer over the years. The charged and fertile background of his formative years, with the gradual buildup of increasingly less controllable sexual and aggressive impulses, has become known during the analysis in all its traumatic quality. And the vicissitudes of his severe neurosis, often reaching borderline severity, have been lived, experienced, and treated, with variable and unstable success. But the time of onset has always had its own meaning along the lines I have described. In relation to the total neurosis, it is akin to the day-residue that is the precipitating stimulus of a dream.

During occasional overviews of her life development, another patient invariably returns to the time at age seventeen when she left her homeland and her family to come to the United States to study. Although she had not planned to make a permanent move, she never returned to live abroad. Not only her career but her further character development, with the anxiety and symptoms that enveloped it, stemmed from that decision and action, a major focal point in her life. As her oldest son approaches that same age, the patient is even more acutely aware of that period in her own life and of the crucial directions to which it led.

References to age seventeen come up clinically with remarkable frequency. Another patient reports two dreams, both featuring the number seventeen. In one dream the patient arrives at his analytic hour seventeen minutes early. He walks in without waiting to be admitted and sees the analyst lying on the couch with the covers over him. He has probably just received a massage. In the second dream, a pretty girl is making advances to the patient. He is tempted but upset, feeling she is too young, probably seventeen. If she were eighteen it would be okay to respond, but seventeen is dangerous. Both dreams relate to incestuous conflicts in the patient's early life, repeated in the transference. The dream about the analyst points to primal scene oedipal material, displaced to the transference. The patient is in his forties, having conflictual and frustrating times with women. These problems go back to oedipal wishes, conflicts, and fears. He is also chronically worried about certain possibly illegal financial actions. If he were below the legal age, he could be excused. Up to seventeen, oedipal fantasies and other crimes can be entertained with some excuse. As an adult, however, their derivatives cannot be tolerated by his superego without severe anxiety and guilt. Seventeen is the last year of innocence and protection.

The perception that all roads seem to lead to and from age seventeen stems from an apparently wide unconscious acknowledgment of the nodal point it represents. In Arthur Miller's *Death of a Salesman* (1949), seventeen-year-old Biff comes upon his errant father in a hotel room. Crushed and exposed, the father tells the story of his failed life to his son: that when he was seventeen, he lay down, and never did anything again. In a television program about being young again, a forty-year-old expresses the wish to be seventeen. In Nazi Germany, the storm troopers looked for youths of seventeen, old enough to do the job but young enough to be indoctrinated.

In Steven Spielberg's film *Back to the Future* (1986), which touched a receptive nerve in a large audience, a boy of seventeen reacts with dismay as he is caught in a crisis of identification with a weak, cowering, and ineffectual father. "I am no good at confrontations," the father laments as an excuse for his recurrent disgrace and humiliation. Through a series of magical interventions, the boy is catapulted back to the year when his father was seventeen.

Through some zany incidents, the boy maneuvers to have his father take a different position and character trait on the scale of activity-passivity in relation to the town bully who mistreats and humiliates him. At the last moment, when the father, then wooing the mother, was submitting to the aggressive acts of his constant tormentor as he had in reality in the past, the son, turning down an oedipal seduction by the mother on the way, peps up the father and exhorts him to fight back. The scene shows the cowardly father begin to tighten and expand his fist almost like Popeye, and suddenly gaining strength and stature, he strikes the bully down with one blow.

With this one turn from passivity to aggression, the father's subsequent life is totally altered. He wins his wife, not by the accident of being there, but by his heroic act. When time is re-reversed, the father appears as a confident, potent, and aggressive male. The erstwhile bully is working for him, polishing his car (ass) in an obsequious role. Rather than being an alcoholic as in the original development, the mother becomes an attractive, active, successful, and proud woman. The boy now has two positive parents to identify with as he proceeds with his own development. The course of life has been altered by the seventeen-year-old redirecting his father at seventeen!

In a recent paper (Rangell 1986), I summarized the course of behavioral events and their outcomes as being brought about by a combination of psychic determinism, autonomous ego will, and chance. Spielberg altered the original brew and the ratio of those ingredients and changed the courses of his characters' lives.

The seventeen-year-old is king of the hill among the teenage crowd. All things being equal, he is the big man on campus of that cohesive age group. Of course, things are never equal. A rough fifteen- or sixteen-year-old can easily dominate a passive ("wimpy") seventeen-year-old in the pecking order. But at fourteen, fifteen, or sixteen, the youth is looking upward; and at eighteen, the big man leaves his position behind and is at the bottom of the heap among the young grownups.

The magazine *Seventeen* is read mostly by girls twelve and older. They avowedly want the boys; boys do not openly admit the opposite at that young age. The twelve- and thirteen-year-old girls are prematurely "making up and making out." The magazine is a source of instruction for those who would study the status of impulses, defenses, and group organization at that age. Intimate questions are laid out and answered there for all to see: To have sex or not to?; how to walk, sit, and talk," concerns about the body, thoughts, appearance, and affects; fear of herpes, vaginal infections, odors, and so forth; problems of body ego, of object relations, and of comparisons on the social scale. One ad proclaims "Playboy tampons." The first open flowering appears of internal dilemmas of the kind that are put more resignedly by older adults for advisers of the lovelorn to answer.

Times change, yet they do not. In the columns of *Seventeen,* girls are told, as their mothers told them, that you can still say no. Alongside is an article on how to deal with embarrassing parents; another describes how the most stylish dress one girl could find for a dance was one of her mother's that had been buried under mothballs in a chest in the attic. She wore it proudly. Twelve- and thirteen-year-olds take the pill, and some become pregnant. The magazine debates the pros and cons of abortion. The choice is no longer automatically for it. Boys are taught, and are beginning to accept, the responsibility of parenthood. Clothes change from skin-tight pants and the "sweater-girl" look to their fathers' shirts or coats and the baggy look—or to Guess?, or Benetton, or Salvation Army—and back to tight-fitting clothes again. The symbols have changed, but not the conflicts, inner goals, or psychological mechanisms.

Although adolescents seem to strive fiercely for independence, the tendency to cling, to each other and in groups, is still apparent. Dependence is manifested as much now as at any earlier or later period in life. Although separation-individuation has taken place in the early years, object attachment remains forever, as Mahler (1972; Mahler and Furer 1968; Mahler et al. 1975) pointed out with regard to reapproachement and beyond. Before her, Freud (1937) wrote about the "adhesiveness of the libido," which at times makes analysis interminable. John Bowlby (1969, 1973, 1980) pointed to the same phenomenon of attachment behavior, as did Kohut (1971, 1977) writing about self/object, and as I have done in terms of figure-ground (Rangell 1954, 1955) or the derivative universal "need to belong" manifested in the psychology of groups, small and large (Rangell 1975, 1976, 1980). A prototype for these was the classic work of Imre Hermann (1936) on clinging.

Fads, including the most dangerous cults, have always drawn heavily

upon the vulnerable teenage group. Styles, fashions, and tastes change—
uniformly and together. Hair becomes long, then short on all young people, not one alone. There is protest outwardly against family closeness, but
closeness with others is sought as much. Where the goal is to shock by
being different, they become conforming to each other. One lad told his
mother he is embarrassed that his parents are still together; all his friends'
parents are divorced. His friends have two homes to go to; he has only one.
Those with Mohawk haircuts walk around together. Music styles change
in unison. Once the Beatles reigned over adolescents; now the Boss fills the
stadium. But still, underlying mechanisms are more stable. The music may
change from the Charleston to rock-and-roll, jazz, or country, but all play
to the chords of the body and the id. Producers know that the biggest
money-making films are those directed toward the teenage audience and
that it is the most cohesive and predictable group. The tough, the cool, the
loose, and the soft porn (sex and aggression) sell the most.

As an apt description of the social affinity of young adults for the group
and of their banding together against the common enemy or the outsider,
I quote another excerpt from Tarkington's *Seventeen*. Note the importance
of body size, and body movements, the stress upon actions and their effects
on others. Willy has just been introduced by Johnnie Watson to his "big
fat lummox of a cousin," who comes on too strongly to the magical girl
everyone wants:

> This severe phrase of theirs, almost simultaneous in the two minds, was
> not wholly a failure as a thumb-nail sketch of Mr. George Crooper. And
> yet there was the impressiveness of size about him, especially about his
> legs and chin. At seventeen and eighteen growth is still going on, some-
> times in a sporadic way, several parts seeming to have sprouted faster
> than others. Often the features have not quite settled down together in
> harmony, a mouth, for instance, appearing to have gained such a lead
> over the rest of a face, that even a mother may feel it can never be
> overtaken. Voices, too, often seem misplaced; one hears, outside the
> door, the bass rumble of a sinister giant, and a mild boy, thin as a cricket,
> walks in. The contrary was George Crooper's case: his voice was an
> unexpected piping tenor, half falsetto and frequently girlish—as surpris-
> ing as the absurd voice of an elephant.
>
> He had the general outwardness of a vast and lumpy child. His chin
> had so distanced his other features that his eyes, nose, and brow seemed
> almost baby-like in comparison, while his mountainous legs were the
> great part of the rest of him. He was one of those huge, bottle-shaped
> boys who are always in motion in spite of their cumbersomeness. His
> gestures were continuous, though difficult to interpret as bearing upon
> the subject of his equally continuous conversation; and under all circum-

stances he kept his conspicuous legs incessantly moving, whether he was going anywhere or remaining in comparatively one spot.

His expression was pathetically offensive, the result of bland confidence in the audible opinions of a small town whereof his father was the richest inhabitant—and the one thing about him, even more obvious than his chin, his legs, and his spectacular taste in flannels, was his perfect trust that he was as welcome to every one as he was to his mother. This might some day lead him in the direction of great pain, but on the occasion of the "subscription party" for Miss Pratt it gave him an advantage.

"When do I get to meet that cutie?" he insisted, as Johnnie Watson moved backward from the cousinly arm, which threatened further flailing. (P. 130)

Self-centered and asocial actions coexist with the noble and altruistic. The intrapsychic balance is a tug between two poles. The id is on one side, pressing always to be heard. But the superego at the opposite pole can be as strong. Idealism has always been the stamp of youth, the same young people who are also prey to drugs or to other paths of immediate expression and satisfaction. The ego between the two psychic structures can be effective as well as overwhelmed. One young man, a student arbitrator and a member of the ethics committee at his school, judges and makes decisions about others in trouble because he is considered to be the most "fair." A patient tells of a crucial time in his life that occurred when he entered junior high school. After feeling anxious, depressed, and rejected for a number of years (probably during his whole latency), he remembers, when he moved into the new school, deciding almost consciously—or preconsciously and probably unconsciously, too—that people would be nice to him if he was nice to them. His efforts to "be nice" to others were at first self-consciously deliberate and then became automatic. Not long afterward, he became president of the class in his early teens, a feat he repeated when he became student body president of a large college some years later. He has since gone on to a successful political career! It will be no surprise to hear that in analysis he was dealing with a "jelly-center," a core of unconscious anxiety that obstructed all his upward moves.

In a period that calls for massive integration, the ego can be overwhelmed as easily as it can rise to its task. As Blos (1962) states, "Late adolescence is a decisive turning point, and consequently is a time of crisis" (p. 130). Since the work of Erikson (1950, 1956), this turning point has been known as an identity crisis. Just as with psychic trauma (Rangell 1967), the outcome now depends upon the ratio between ego capacity and the stimuli and demands impinging upon it from three sides: the instincts, the superego, and the external world. Fragility of the ego vis-à-vis the pressures upon it makes breakdown and decompensation at this age common experiences. These pressures have accelerated, not decreased, with technological advance, in which the human dimension becomes lost rather than furthered. Surveying the sweep of civilization through a psychoanalytic lens, Robert Waelder (1967) described history as an alternation of excesses and noted that progress has as many victims as beneficiaries.

Trygve Braatoy (1934) has emphasized the high psychic mortality of the postadolescent period. The suicide rate among fifteen- to twenty-four-year-olds increased more than 50 percent between 1970 and 1980 and has become a serious public health concern. The dynamic backgrounds for this increase are complex, as the act occurs as often in times of apparent success as in states of obvious material and psychological deprivation. Choices made may be not for the child (a term no longer appropriate chronologically, but psychologically still valid) but for the father or mother. Good grades in college, admission to a professional school, a promising start, a seemingly ideal situation, and then suicide from an undiscovered and undisclosed depression form a not-uncommon sequence. The son has been living out the parents' ambitions, not his own. I have seen this kind of tragedy happen suddenly in a seemingly successful medical student. A similar syndrome, but with a less drastic outcome, was seen in a young professional tennis champion, fulfilling his father's frustrated wishes, until analytic treatment succeeded in altering the course of his life to more ego-syntonic goals.

Again, as at age two, intergenerational rifts and a clash of interests between parents and child assume major proportions. Now as always, interpersonal conflicts are internalized into intrapsychic ones. The prospect of a more definitive external separation and its accompanying intrapsychic fantasies and anxieties are dominant issues requiring urgent and current solutions. Separation now will no longer be symbolic or metaphoric but will connote an air of actuality and an intention of finality. These conflicts can lead either to satisfactory resolutions by adaptive choices or to successful compromises—or, during unfavorable conditions, to unresolvable impasses with pathological or even malignant results.

Problems of love, work, and ideology are in the balance, the most crucial decisions that will determine future life. The directions taken and paths unconsciously chosen are determined by current internal and external conditions grafted upon the character, by formative intrapsychic modes, and by interstructural relations operative since the earliest years, added to by inputs from the gamut of development thus far. Again, the psychological and the somatic are merged, and early structural determinants of a psychic and somatic nature are operative. Recently I saw a photograph of a young man whom I had not seen since he was a child and I thought the picture was of his father as I had known him years ago. Identical features of voice, posture, attitudes, and affect accompany similar, sometimes identical body frames, all coming together at successive maturational phases. Nurture and nature continue to act reciprocally even in their later derivatives and effects.

Will there be integration and synthesis, Heinz Hartmann's (1939, 1950) and Herman Nunberg's (1931) main criteria for normality and mental health? Or will the ego's efforts result in pathological splitting and fragmentation? Besides separation and depression, the gamut of etiologic anxieties can be at work. Oedipal castration anxiety plays a central role in the onset of psychopathology at this as at any other period. In fact it can be revived with great intensity. Even in choices of illness, the tendency to cling and to identify with others reveals itself. Hysteria, the contagious mental illness in *fin-de-siècle* Vienna, has been replaced in today's culture by anorexia or anorexia-bulimia, particularly in young girls. As Freud (1896) showed with hysteria, the root of the contagion is unconscious identification. Although manifestly oral, the etiology of the eating disorder syndrome today is determined by the entire spectrum of oedipal and pregenital fixations and regressions (Fischer 1985; Ritvo 1983).

With respect to sexual choices and pathology, homoerotic activities and relationships in the early teens are not as significant for future psychosexual solutions as are the sexual preferences that take definitive shape and recur with regularity in later adolescence. Sexual identity and patterns that become evident then acquire a more stabilized and enduring state. In one of my patients a decisive direction of enduring homosexuality took place at seventeen. Another young man underwent a homosexual crisis and panic at the same age from which he seems now to be moving to a heterosexual choice.

What I have said about relative finality or psychic constellations during this period of life does not, of course, mean that conditions and relationships will not be continually open to change. Development and maturation have a long way to go. Sexual as well as other conflicts or unfinished tasks have a lifetime ahead. Masturbation fantasies during adolescence, considered by Moses and Egle Laufer (1976, 1984) as centrally indicative of the status of both intrapsychic life and object relations, presumably have opportunities beyond adolescence to be carried over from fantasy to reality. That such a transposition is never completely accomplished is well known to writers and is a common observation of psychoanalytic clinicians. A gulf between unconscious fantasy and reality is a given of psychic life. This gap might also be credited with playing a major role in creative urges and achievements. Or there can ensue the "syndrome of prolonged adolescence" (Blos 1954).

Evolution, gestations, and even new later constellations continue throughout the life cycle, as described by Erikson (1950) and by others since then. Changes, surprises, and unexpected outcomes occur at any time. A newly appointed college president describes how he was disturbed and involved with drugs during adolescence. A man under forty who is already a legendary business and financial success, returns to a reunion at his high school where he was a "loser" and an underachiever. There was a well-known song after the Second World War about the private who after the war became president of the New York Stock Exchange. Indeed, psychoanalysis is relevant and can be effective only because of our continuous if not permanent openness to change.

Early conditions and determinants will out. A patient has twin sons now in their thirties. From birth, the first-born was physically less robust than his twin, but was nevertheless the leader and the aggressor of the two. The second-born, who could knock over the first twin and could outperform his brother in any activity requiring physical strength, merely "tagged along" and was always the passive follower. The first twin became a successful rock-and-roll star. The second-born led an inadequate, drifting life and has recently been hospitalized as a schizophrenic. The mother, who suffered from frequent migraine headaches, was reserved and withdrawn and addicted for years to sedatives and pain-relieving medication. The rock star gradually slipped into a severe and chronic cocaine addiction and is in as serious trouble as his more decompensated younger twin. They now have emotional disabilities of different forms but of comparable intensity.

Freud himself did not arrive at monumental achievements until his thirties and forties. Early indicators, however, were not absent. In a remarkable group of letters (the earliest to be preserved and the latest to be discovered), Freud (1969), then sixteen to eighteen years old, describes his feelings to his friend Emil Fluss upon returning to Vienna after having visited his birthplace, Pribor in Moravia, which he had left when he was three years old. To illustrate the connections between Freud at seventeen and at forty, I quote my own earlier observations on these letters (Rangell 1972), which annotate several remarkable characteristics already at home in this searching young mind:

(1) He is already seen to subject his affective stirrings, his feelings and excitements, his "first love" (Gisela, his friend's sister), to introspection and to describe them in terms of the secondary process. (2) He seeks to convey his thoughts in a communication that is private, special, unlike any other. The opening letter addressed to "Dear new friend" is marked confidential. (The recipient changes some years later from Fluss to Fliess!) (3) His communication is characterized by a search for the truth: "I shall

confess the unvarnished truth to you—but to you alone." (Already the basic element of psychoanalysis.) (4) But there also needs to be complete trust, the basic trust. "I trust that no one will be allowed to see what was not meant for him to see," or else. (5) There is another, more usual type of communication: "All you would hear would be smooth-tongued platitudes that won't tell you anything."

There are already some profound harbingers of things to come. (6) "I enjoy tracing the closely knit web of connecting threads which chance and fate have woven around us all." Or (7) "How admirable is the fine instinct with which nature has endowed us." Or, discounting the role of accidental circumstance when his friend and the latter's girlfriend happen to meet, he is (8) convinced of "the inscrutable workings of a divine power."

Even more prophetic, and in keeping with a central theme of this paper: (9) "I have a good deal of reading to do—among them Sophocles' *Oedipus Rex.*" (His paper on this was rated "good," the only one in the class.) And recognizing already the complicated results of such knowledge, (10) "You deprive yourself of much that is edifying if you can't read all these, but on the other hand you retain that cheerfulness which is so comforting about your letters."

Even a sense of his own destiny does not escape him. (11) "So now I would counsel you (about these letters) preserve them—bind them together—guard them well—you never know!" And finally there is a more ominous reference to the future, which comes back to our subject [aggression]: he refers to a recurrent toothache: (12) "It was a last feeble eruption of an erstwhile mighty crater. The last quiver from a region of my body that has for a long time been in open rebellion against peace and order in my system. I am referring to my teeth. Where others live to eat, I live to ruin my teeth. And where others eat to live, I suffer from toothache to live. Thus my life is inextricably bound up with toothache which will consequently stay with me for as long as I live."

It was precisely there, pinpointed with uncanny accuracy at that tender age, that Freud half a century later was to begin his long, silent struggle against pain and inner destruction which was to continue for the last sixteen years of his life. And it was here again, from looking into the processes of his own inner life struggles, that Freud came up with insights with which all men could identify and which applied to all mankind.

All this was already there. Today, a hundred years and twenty-seven International Congresses later—the promise of that sixteen-year-old youth did not go unfulfilled. The cohesive theory of human behavior that proliferated from his enjoyment in "tracing the closely knit web of connecting threads" has become the common heritage of the intellectual world. (Pp. 3–4)

Thinking of Freud, one is reminded how much can happen long after one's teens and one's twenties. These excerpts, however, also demonstrate how the age of seventeen continues into the rest of life.

REFERENCES

Blos, P. 1954. "Prolonged Adolescence: The Formulation of a Syndrome and Its Therapeutic Implications." *American Journal of Orthopsychiatry* 24:733–42.
———. 1962. *On Adolescence: A Psychoanalytic Interpretation.* New York: Free Press.
Bowlby, J. 1969. *Attachment and Loss. Vol. 1: Attachment.* New York: Basic Books.
———. 1973. *Attachment and Loss. Vol. 2: Separation, Anxiety and Anger.* New York: Basic Books.
———. 1980. *Attachment and Loss. Vol. 3: Sadness and Depression.* New York: Basic Books.
Braatoy, T. 1934. *Manner swischen 15 und 25 Jahren.* (Men between 15 and 25 Years of Age). Oslo: Fabritius and Sonner.
Branden, N. 1971. *The Psychology of Self-Esteem.* New York: Bantam.
Breuer, J., and Freud, S. [1893–95] 1957. "Studies on Hysteria." In *Standard Edition,* ed. J. Strachey, vol. 2, pp. 3–251. London: Hogarth Press.
Erikson, E. H. 1950. *Childhood and Society.* New York: W. W. Norton.
———. 1956. "The Problem of Ego Identity." *Journal of the American Psychoanalytic Association* 4:56–121.
———. 1962. "Reality and Actuality." *Journal of the American Psychoanalytic Association* 29:179–219.
Ferenczi, S. [1930] 1955. "The Principle of Relaxation and Neocatharsis." In *Final Contributions to the Problems and Methods of Psychoanalysis. The Selected Papers of Sándor Ferenczi,* ed. M. Balint, vol. 3, pp. 108–25. New York: Basic Books.
Fischer, N. 1985. "Anorexia Nervosa and Unresolved Rapprochement Conflicts—A Case Study." Paper presented at the International Symposium on Separation-Individuation, Paris, November 3.
Freud, S. 1896. "The Aetiology of Hysteria." In *Standard Edition,* ed. J. Strachey, vol. 3, pp. 189–221. London: Hogarth Press.
———. 1905. "Three Essays on the Theory of Sexuality." In *Standard Edition,* ed. J. Strachey, vol. 7, pp. 125–245. London: Hogarth Press.
———. [1937] 1957. "Analysis Terminable and Interminable." In *Standard Edition,* ed. J. Strachey, vol. 23, pp. 211–53. London: Hogarth Press.
———. 1969. "Some Early Unpublished Letters of Freud." *International Journal of Psycho-Analysis* 50:419–27.
Galenson, E., and Roiphe, H. 1974. "The Emergence of Genital Awareness During the Second Year of Life." In *Sex Differences and Behavior,* ed. R. C. Friedman, R. M. Richart, and R. L. Van der Wiele, pp. 223–31. New York: John Wiley & Sons.
Gedo, J. E. 1979. *Beyond Interpretation: Toward a Revised Theory for Psychoanalysis.* New York: International Universities Press.

Hartmann, H. [1939] 1958. *Ego Psychology and the Problem of Adaptation.* New York: International Universities Press.

———. [1950] 1964. "Comments on the Psychoanalytic Theory of the Ego." In *Essays on Ego Psychology: Selected Problems in Psychoanalytic Theory,* pp. 113–41. New York: International Universities Press.

Hermann, I. 1936. "Sich-Anklammern Auf-Suche-Gehen." *Internationale Zeitschrift für Arztliche Psychoanalyse* 22:349–70.

Jacobs, T. J. 1987. "Chairman's Address." Panel on Psychoanalysis of the Young Adult: Theory and Technique. J. F. Chused, reporter. *Journal of the American Psychoanalytic Association* 35:175–87.

Jacobson, E. 1953. "Contribution to the Metapsychology of Cyclothymic Depression." In *Affective Disorders,* ed. P. Greenacre, pp. 49–83. New York: International Universities Press.

———. 1964. *The Self and the Object World.* New York: International Universities Press.

Kohut, H. 1971. *The Analysis of the Self.* New York: International Universities Press.

———. 1977. *The Restoration of the Self.* New York: International Universities Press.

Laufer, M. 1976. "The Central Masturbation Fantasy, the Final Sexual Organization, and Adolescence." *Psychoanalytic Study of the Child* 31:297–316.

Laufer, M., and Laufer, M. E. 1984. *Adolescence and Developmental Breakdown.* New Haven: Yale University Press.

Lorenz, K. 1950. "The Comparative Method in Studying Innate Behavior Patterns." Symp. Soc. Exp. Biol. 5.

Mahler, M. S. 1972. "Rapprochement Subphase of the Separation-Individuation Process." *Psychoanalytic Quarterly* 41:487–506.

Mahler, M. S., and Furer, M. 1968. *On Human Symbiosis and the Vicissitudes of Individuation: Infantile Psychosis.* New York: International Universities Press.

Mahler, M. S., Pine, F., and Bergman, A. 1975. *The Psychological Birth of the Human Infant: Symbiosis and Individuation.* New York: Basic Books.

Miller, Arthur. 1949. *Death of a Salesman.* New York: Viking.

Nunberg, H. [1931] 1961. "The Synthetic Function of the Ego." In *Practice and Theory of Psychoanalysis,* pp. 120–36. New York: International Universities Press.

Rangell, L. 1954. "The Psychology of Poise—With a Special Elaboration on the Psychic Significance of the Snout or Perioral Region." *International Journal of Psycho-Analysis* 35:313–33.

———. 1955. "The Quest for Ground in Human Motivation. Address, First Western Division Meeting of the American Psychiatric Association and West Coast Psychoanalytic Societies, October 29.

———. 1967. "The Metapsychology of Psychic Trauma." In *Psychic Trauma,* ed. S. S. Furst, pp. 51–84. New York: Basic Books.

———. 1972. "Aggression, Oedipus, and Historical Perspective." *International Journal of Psycho-Analysis* 53:3–11.

———. 1975. "Man in a Group." Third Robert Waelder Memorial Lecture, Philadelphia Association for Psychoanalysis, October 17.

———. 1976. "Lessons from Watergate. A Derivative for Psychoanalysis." *Psychoanalytic Quarterly* 45:37–61.

———. 1980. *The Mind of Watergate. An Exploration of the Compromise of Integrity.* New York: W. W. Norton.

————. 1986. "The Executive Functions of the Ego. An Extension of the Concept of Ego Autonomy." *Psychoanalytic Study of the Child* 41:1–37.

————. 1987. "Historical Perspectives and Current Status." In *The Significance of the Interpretation of Dreams in Clinical Work,* ed. A. Rothstein, pp. 3–24. Workshop 3, American Psychoanalytic Association. New York: International Universities Press.

Rapaport, D. 1953. "On the Psychoanalytic Theory of Affects." *International Journal of Psycho-Analysis* 34:177–98.

————. [1959] 1960. *The Structure of Psychoanalytic Theory.* New York: International Universities Press (Psychological Issues Monograph no. 6).

Ritvo, S. 1983. "Eating Disturbances in an Adolescent Girl." Presentation, panel on The Child and Adolescent Psychoanalyst at Work with a Focus on Female Sexuality: Adolescent Case. 33rd International Psychoanalytic Congress, Madrid, July 26.

Roiphe, H. 1968. "On an Early Genital Phase: with an Addendum on Genesis." *Psychoanalytic Study of the Child* 23:348–65.

Roiphe, H., and Galenson, E. 1972. "Early Genital Activity and the Castration Complex." *Psychoanalytic Quarterly* 41:334–47.

Sandler, J. 1960. "On the Concept of Superego." *Psychoanalytic Study of the Child* 15:128–62.

Sandler, J., and Rosenblatt, B. 1962. "The Concept of the Representational World." *Psychoanalytic Study of the Child* 17:128–45.

Stern, D. N. 1983. "Affect Attunement: Mechanisms and Clinical Implications." Presentation, Second World Congress on Infant Psychiatry, Cannes, March 29. Reprinted in *Frontiers of Infant Psychiatry,* ed. J. D. Call, E. Galenson, and R. L. Tyson, pp. 3–14. New York: Basic Books, 1984.

Tarkington, B. 1916. *Seventeen.* New York: Harper & Row.

Tinbergen, N. 1951. *The Study of Instincts.* London: Oxford University Press.

Waelder, R. 1967. *Progress and Revolution.* New York: International Universities Press.

Winnicott, D. W. [1951] 1974. "Transitional Objects and Transitional Phenomena." In *Collected Papers. Through Paediatrics to Psycho-Analysis,* pp. 229–42. New York: Basic Books.

————. 1957. *Mother and Child: A Primer of First Relationships.* New York: Basic Books.

DISCUSSION

From several standpoints, it is appropriate that Leo Rangell's contribution, "Seventeen: The Approach to the Portal of Adult Life," is the first chapter in this multidisciplinary collaboration. For many years, Rangell has been among the most creative psychoanalytic scholar-clinicians on both the national and international scenes. Along with Erikson, he was one of the first to recognize the importance of the paradigm of lifelong development. As early as 1953 he wrote:

The Oedipus complex has a continuous and dynamic line of development, from its earliest origin through various phases in the life of man, and the described phenomena are but stages in the continual moving stream. By no means is it an event which plays a tumultuous but short-lived role limited to the phallic scene of the play of life, but it is rather a constantly reappearing character which comes across the stage in new and changing ways progressing with the ages of man. (P. 13)

He proceeded to describe the effect of oedipal themes on various phases of parenthood, from the birth of the first child to reactions to a new son- or daughter-in-law, thus allowing us to appreciate the oedipal complex as a dynamic developmental process evolving throughout life.

In the present chapter, he continues his exploration by describing the events and dynamics that occur around age seventeen. He writes, "Unlike the drama, suddenness, and violence of the original birth, and the burst of physical changes at adolescence, the birth of the adult slips in quietly. It is my impression that it is easily overlooked." From more than four decades of clinical and theoretical work in the field and from personal observations as well, Rangell has long recognized the nodal significance of this particular developmental period. More important, he endeavors here to remedy the lack of attention it has received.

The seventeen-year-old is usually a junior in high school. In our culture, the junior year is the preparatory year before one moves beyond the world of adolescence. Crucial decisions are made during or soon after that year; and the youngster must, perhaps for the first time, make *active* choices about social, occupational, and geographic matters. Everything is a question: college? work? family? sex? friends? goals? lovers? In the matrix of these choices, the beginnings or outlines of the adult self can be seen.

Rangell describes the emergence of new forms and functions and the ways in which the self can be regarded as both tentative and permanent, as an entity that will endure, but is bound to change as well. Seventeen is unarguably a major psychological crossroads where unconscious choices are hardening into attitudes and behavior patterns revolving around questions of activity (versus passivity), relationships, sexual orientation, and so forth. Further deep unconscious patterns take shape in the relations between ego and superego, attitudes toward success and failure, achievement and disappointment, leading or following, and winning or losing.

As he earlier described oedipal phenomena throughout the life cycle, Rangell does the same for some of the preoedipal issues, specifically matters of separation-individuation. Mahler and colleagues (1975) described the separation-individuation process by which the human infant gradually emerges as a separate, distinct being, aware of its own existence and nature and of its relationship to others. Neither Mahler nor Rangell sees the separation-individuation process as limited to the first three years of life. In an important panel of the American Psychoanalytic Association (1973),

Mahler described separation-individuation as a lifelong process because of the inherent threat of loss in every stage of independence. The *absolute* dependence on the mother, which is characteristic of infancy, becomes a *relative* dependence in later life. There is an adult need (Mahler 1973) to redefine oneself and one's relationships to significant people at such critical, affect-laden junctures as marriage, parenthood, grandparenthood, the climacteric, retirement, and senescence. Rangell states that "if anyone thought that the separation-individuation of the mother and child at age one and a half was uniquely traumatic for both, one has but to view the affective reactions at this new and more final separation." This separation gives rise to reactions of anxiety, mourning, and a gamut of related emotions, which may be conscious or unconscious, and reveal themselves by indirect symptoms or other sequelae.

After many years of analytic experience, Rangell is impressed with how a definitive event in neurosogenesis involves the period of passage through the seventeenth year—particularly in the creation of a pathologically structured self-representation. Drawing on an array of clinical examples, illustrations from literature, teen culture, magazines, and the movies, Rangell demonstrates how "all worlds seem to lead to seventeen" (p. 11) and that seventeen is the last year of innocence and protection. He describes it as a period that calls for massive intrapsychic personality integration; a dangerous period when the ego can be overwhelmed as easily as it can develop and progress. Since Erikson (1950, 1956), late adolescence has been known as a time of potential identity crisis. Blos (1962), too, has stated that "late adolescence is a decisive turning point." In structural terms, Rangell describes how fragility of the ego vis-à-vis the pressures upon it make breakdown and decompensation at this age a common experience. This has been accelerated, not decreased, with technological advance, in which the human dimension becomes lost rather than furthered.

Rangell's wide-ranging chapter summarizes persuasively several of the crucial events for adult development that center around age seventeen. As his closing example of how experiences at the "portal of adulthood" continue with us throughout our lives, he cites Freud himself, tracing from adolescent letters themes that reverberated through Freud's life and work.

REFERENCES

Blos, P. 1962. *On Adolescence: A Psychoanalytic Interpretation.* New York: Free Press.
Erikson, E. 1950. *Childhood and Society.* New York: W. W. Norton.

———. 1956. "The Problem of Ego Identity." *Journal of the American Psychoanalytic Association* 4:56–121.

Mahler, M. 1973. "The Experience of Separation-Individuation . . . through the Course of Life: Infancy and Childhood; Maturity, Senescence, and Sociological Implications." Panel Reports, American Psychoanalytic Association. *Journal of the American Psychoanalytic Association* 21:135, 633.

Mahler, M., Pine, F., and Berman, A. 1975. *The Psychological Birth of the Human Infant.* New York: Basic Books.

Rangell, L. 1953. "The Role of the Parent in the Oedipus Complex." *Bulletin of the Menninger Clinic* 19:9.

2

Childhood to Adulthood:

Structural Change in Development toward Independence and Autonomy

CALVIN F. SETTLAGE

Introduction

This chapter was motivated by the idea that the definition of adulthood could be sharpened by a new understanding of the development of psychic structure.

Various frames of reference have been used to delineate adulthood. These include (1) the societal granting of adult privileges, such as the right to vote; (2) the assumption of adult responsibilities, such as parenthood; (3) the fulfillment of developmental tasks, such as the achievement of intimacy and mutuality in a gratifying sexual relationship; (4) the transformation of adolescent into adult psychological characteristics, such as gaining an objective view of the self; and (5) the attainment of adult-level structural development, such as an ego ideal attuned to reality (see, e.g., Staples and Smarr 1980; Adatto 1980). It is apparent that some of these criteria are more reliable indications of functional adulthood than others. Because I see it as defining adulthood in the most fundamental and reliable way, my frame of reference is structural development.

As conceived by psychoanalytic theory, *psychic structure* constitutes the internal organization of the components of human personality, namely, the needs, the regulatory defensives, the adaptive capacities, and the governing value system. In Sigmund Freud's terms, psychic structure consists of the *id* embodying the sexual and aggressive drives, the *ego* embodying

26

the functional capacities, and the *superego* embodying the conscience and ideals. Psychic structure thus underlies and regulates manifest behavior and defines the attained level of development.

The new understanding of structural development derives from contemporary object relations theory, which focuses on the role of the human object relationship in psychic development. Contemporary object relations theory stems from direct observational research on development during the first three years of life, from the clinical exploration of pathology from those years in the treatment of narcissistic and borderline disorders, and from direct observational and clinical studies on adult development.

Developmental studies during infancy and adulthood suggest that psychic structure formation occurs throughout the life course. Attaining adulthood is the outcome of the early formation and continuing evolution of the regulatory structures of human personality. Mature adulthood is an ideal toward which we strive in a lifelong developmental progression.

Central to my structural definition of adulthood is the new understanding of the psychoanalytic concepts of libidinal object constancy (Hartmann 1952) and self constancy. In clinical work with adolescents and adults, as it involves the application of emerging concepts of early development, I have been increasingly impressed by the problems that inadequately or pathologically developed object and self constancy pose for the move from adolescence to adulthood, and for truly adult functioning. Object and self constancy embody gradually established, lasting, predominantly good representations of the parent and the self as shaped by experience in the developmental relationship. They serve, respectively, the formation, regulation, and maintenance of relationships, of self-esteem, and of the sense of self and identity.

The defining idea is that becoming and functioning as an adult involves the *intrapsychic* integration, the "owning" for oneself, of these regulatory structures at an adult level of autonomy of function. This adult level rests initially on adolescent development, as it adds a new increment of independence from the parents and from the sexual and aggressive drives. The independence from the parents is both from them in actuality and from their internal representations (Blos 1967, 1977).

The Nature of Human Development

In exploring the structural definition of adulthood, I found myself thinking about human development generally. I became aware that this generalized thinking reflected a need to synthesize old and new understandings of the development from childhood to adulthood. The following discussion provides the broader context for that synthesis.

The evolutionary perspective

Human development is defined in its most basic sense by evolution. From an evolutionary perspective, individual development reflects the development of the species. As Heinz Hartmann (1939) observed, evolution leads to an increased independence of the organism from its environment. Reactions that originally occurred in immediate response to the external world "are increasingly displaced into the interior of the organism" (p. 40). The more differentiated the organism, the more independent from immediate reaction to environmental stimulation. Through evolution, human adaptation involves a temporary suspension of response to the external world and trial activity internally before a response is made. The development of ego modulation of the instinctual drives, of internal regulatory values as structured in the superego, and of thought interposed between stimulus and response are examples of the evolutionary process of interiorization.

The largely inherited, instinctive behaviors that serve regulation and adaptation in other animals are thus superseded in the human by generic instincts or drives, by intelligence, by learned adaptive behaviors, and by developed rather than inherent regulatory structures. Hans Loewald (1978) characterized the human central regulatory structure as more highly organized, more complex, and more versatile than that of other species, ordained, as it were, by the laws of evolution.

Human phylogenesis has important consequences for individual development that bear ultimately on adult functioning. The combination of adaptive behavior and psychic structure that are to be learned and developed and the helplessness of the human infant require an extended dependency. Because of the vital role of environmental influence during this dependency, development can be exposed to highly favorable or highly unfavorable influences. That human behavior and its governing structure are developed and do not preexist accounts not only for the great flexibility and effectiveness of human adaptation as a species but also for the vulnerability of individual development to arrest and pathological deviation.

Because our regulatory structure is developed and is subject to environmental influence, it can vary widely among individuals. Whereas the stage and phase progression of development is determined by universals in biological maturation and life experience, such as puberty, parenthood, and generativity (Erikson 1950; Benedek 1959), their familial and cultural processing can vary considerably (Settlage et al. 1968). For example, partial dependence of the adult offspring on the parents and family is officially sanctioned in some cultures and eschewed in others.

The variability and social importance of individual behavior account for *the uniquely human function of morality:* the expectation of behavior in accordance with shared values. Erik Erikson (1980) termed this unique function *the evolutionary principle of morality.* Hartmann (1960) observed that every individual, as well as every culture, possesses a moral potential as a psychological given. He also noted that Freud's main contribution to the study of morality is the understanding that moral valuation and moral conduct are necessary attributes of "natural man." Looking to the future, Erikson (1964) speculates that the effective hierarchical development of morality could move toward an evolutionary advance. This hierarchy embodies the imperative morality of the oedipal-level superego, the aspirational morality of the adolescent-level ego ideal, and the overarching ethicality of the mature adult ego and superego.

Moral development has two aspects, both of which normally culminate in adulthood. One is the formation of the involved governing structures, and the other is the specific values they embody. Structuring can be either normal or impaired by pathology and developmental arrest. Although the governing structures are common to all human beings, the differences among their value content are striking because of the variation in values among cultures and subcultures and among families and individuals within the same culture. Value content also varies from generation to generation within the same culture due to changing technology and mores (Settlage 1973).

A major problem and concern stemming from the evolutionary vulnerability of individual development is that of "taming" the instinctual drives, particularly aggression. In this regard, Erikson (1975) introduced the concept of *pseudospeciation* as applying to the human species. Most animals have a built-in constraint against destroying members of their own species. No such constraint is guaranteed by the processing of aggression in human development; hence, pseudospeciation.

Hartmann (1939) quotes Freud's statement that, "Given our drive dispositions and our environment, the love for fellow men must be considered just as indispensable for the survival of mankind as technology." From today's perspective, Freud's then reasonable view of technology as indispensable for survival is grimly ironic. But the necessity of love for our fellow beings is a truly prophetic observation. Freud saw the interiorization of aggression in the formation of superego as a main trend in the development of civilization: conscience is a necessity for the individual and for society (Hartmann 1960). But a natural value hierarchy, valid for all humans, does not exist (Hartmann 1960). Hartmann also underscored

Freud's observation that the control of aggression in individual development can result in an unrealistic, tyrannical superego, which interferes with the integration and effectiveness of the moral system.

The developmental perspective

The nature of human development is reflected also in developmental theory. Newly appreciated and relevant to the attainment of adulthood, as defined by truly adult functioning, is the concept of adult development (Settlage et al. 1988).

Historically, development was originally considered a childhood phenomenon ending with the attainment of adult sexual capabilities during puberty and adolescence. Freud's (1905) theory of psychosexual development is thus anchored in the biologically predetermined, maturational progression from birth through the adolescent stage of psychosexual development.

Psychoanalytic thinking later defined development as being initiated not only by biological but also by experiential and psychological factors. Development was thus extended to include adulthood (Erikson 1950; Benedek 1959; Bibring 1961). Freud's theory of psychosexual development has been significantly extended by Margaret Mahler's separation-individuation theory. In complement to psychosexual theory, its focus is primarily on the development of ego and self and on the roots of adaptation as it begins in the matrix of the early mother-child relationship (Mahler et al. 1975). Although focused on the first three years of life, separation-individuation theory has life-course applicability (Winestine 1973; Marcus 1973; Sternschein 1973). Such application is illustrated in Peter Blos's (1967) conceptualization of the second individuation process of adolescence. Recent studies of "lifespan psychology" have generated data confirming and adding to the proposition that development continues actively throughout life and that structural change does not stop with adolescence (Emde 1985).

The concept of structure formation in adulthood gave me a clearer appreciation that the further structuring of existing structure is inherent in development. This awareness led in turn to consideration of structure formation from three perspectives of psychoanalytic developmental theory.

In *stage and phase theory*, new and different developmental influences are brought to bear on the same structures in successive stages and phases. These influences include (1) changes resulting from biological maturation or decline; (2) changes in developmental relationships; (3) changes in familial-cultural expectations associated with developmental advance; (4)

generational changes in the familial-cultural and intercultural or societal environments; and (5) consequent changes in the phase-specific developmental challenges posed to and embraced by the individual.

Anna Freud's (1963) *line-of-development theory* offered an organized conceptualization of the continuity of development, a continuity that both partakes of and transcends stage development. As indicated by her references to structuralization and specifically to ego, superego, and object constancy, line-of-development theory clearly embraces structure formation. But this theory focuses more on the hierarchical development of functions than on the details of structure formation. It is of interest to our topic that Anna Freud's prototypical line of development progresses from infantile dependency to emotional self-reliance and adult object relationships.

The *theory of developmental process* (Settlage 1980a; Settlage et al. 1988) conceives structure formation to be based upon the developmental interaction. Initially, developmental process rests on the mother-child interaction, but it can occur potentially in any two-person relationship embodying a developmental potential or gradient (Loewald 1960). This potential is determined by the difference between the functional abilities and structural level of the individuals involved. Because of the gradient, the developmental interaction results in the formation of structure and the "lifting" of it to a higher-level of organization. Through internalization and identification, the regulatory and adaptive functions and the governing values of the developmental partner become a part of one's own structure. Developmental process is generic to all stages of development. Unless the development of a particular structure has been arrested or closed by pathology, developmental process is open-ended (Emde 1980), and structuring can continue.

Together, these complementary psychoanalytic theories of development support the view of human development as a lifelong process. The regulatory structures of adulthood have their beginnings in earliest childhood, evolve through the childhood stages, achieve an initial level of adult capability in the transition from adolescence to young adulthood, and continue to evolve throughout adult life.

The Regulatory Structures

In the order of their developmental emergence, the human regulatory structures, as postulated by psychoanalytic theory, are the *ego ideal, the ego, the self, object and self constancy,* and the *superego.* In their full development, these structures account for the independence and autonomy as well as the integrity of adult functioning.

Each of the regulatory structures has its beginning in early childhood. The ego ideal is conceived to arise during the second half of the first year in response to the sense of loss associated with the infant's earliest conscious awareness of separateness from the mother (Freud 1914; Jacobson 1964; Settlage 1973). As strongly amplified by recent studies of infant development (Stern 1985), ego development begins essentially at birth. With body-self precursors, the knowing sense of self has its beginnings at about four months of age in the differentiation phase of separation-individuation (Mahler and McDevitt 1982). Object and self constancy have their origins in the earliest emotional experiences in the mother-child relationship, are forged during the rapprochement phase, and reach an initial level of integration at about thirty-six months of age at the end of the object-constancy phase (Mahler et al. 1975). With precursors derived from the disciplinary experiences of the second year of life, the superego undergoes its initial structuring during the oedipal stage from about thirty-six months to five or six years of age.

Because of their centrality to a structural definition of adulthood, object and self constancy will be discussed in the context of an evolving, life-course development of psychic structure and will be illustrated by the example of *trust,* a prime ingredient of object and self constancy.

Life-course structural development

Basic trust, as conceptualized in Erikson's psychosocial theory, is the desired outcome of the child's experience of the constancy of the mother's love during the oral stage of psychosexual development (Erikson 1950). With regard to evolving structure, Valenstein (1972) conceives the earliest mother-child relationship to be the primary organizing experience of morality.

As conceived by separation-individuation theory, during the second year of life this internalized trust is threatened by the anger and aggression mobilized by disciplinary experiences and by fear of loss of the love object created by acute awareness of separateness and relative helplessness. Successful resolution of this rapprochement-phase crisis affirms and restructures basic trust. But the resolution now has the added significance of mastery of this early developmental surge of aggression.

During the third year of life, the affirmed sense of trust is instrumental in the initial integration and consolidation of object and self constancy. The view of structuring as a continuing process was conveyed by Mahler in her term for this phase: *on the way to object constancy.*

connecting threads" has become the common heritage of the intellectual world. (Pp. 3–4)

Thinking of Freud, one is reminded how much can happen long after one's teens and one's twenties. These excerpts, however, also demonstrate how the age of seventeen continues into the rest of life.

REFERENCES

Blos, P. 1954. "Prolonged Adolescence: The Formulation of a Syndrome and Its Therapeutic Implications." *American Journal of Orthopsychiatry* 24:733–42.

———. 1962. *On Adolescence: A Psychoanalytic Interpretation.* New York: Free Press.

Bowlby, J. 1969. *Attachment and Loss. Vol. 1: Attachment.* New York: Basic Books.

———. 1973. *Attachment and Loss. Vol. 2: Separation, Anxiety and Anger.* New York: Basic Books.

———. 1980. *Attachment and Loss. Vol. 3: Sadness and Depression.* New York: Basic Books.

Braatoy, T. 1934. *Manner swischen 15 und 25 Jahren.* (Men between 15 and 25 Years of Age). Oslo: Fabritius and Sonner.

Branden, N. 1971. *The Psychology of Self-Esteem.* New York: Bantam.

Breuer, J., and Freud, S. [1893–95] 1957. "Studies on Hysteria." In *Standard Edition,* ed. J. Strachey, vol. 2, pp. 3–251. London: Hogarth Press.

Erikson, E. H. 1950. *Childhood and Society.* New York: W. W. Norton.

———. 1956. "The Problem of Ego Identity." *Journal of the American Psychoanalytic Association* 4:56–121.

———. 1962. "Reality and Actuality." *Journal of the American Psychoanalytic Association* 29:179–219.

Ferenczi, S. [1930] 1955. "The Principle of Relaxation and Neocatharsis." In *Final Contributions to the Problems and Methods of Psychoanalysis. The Selected Papers of Sándor Ferenczi,* ed. M. Balint, vol. 3, pp. 108–25. New York: Basic Books.

Fischer, N. 1985. "Anorexia Nervosa and Unresolved Rapprochement Conflicts—A Case Study." Paper presented at the International Symposium on Separation-Individuation, Paris, November 3.

Freud, S. 1896. "The Aetiology of Hysteria." In *Standard Edition,* ed. J. Strachey, vol. 3, pp. 189–221. London: Hogarth Press.

———. 1905. "Three Essays on the Theory of Sexuality." In *Standard Edition,* ed. J. Strachey, vol. 7, pp. 125–245. London: Hogarth Press.

———. [1937] 1957. "Analysis Terminable and Interminable." In *Standard Edition,* ed. J. Strachey, vol. 23, pp. 211–53. London: Hogarth Press.

———. 1969. "Some Early Unpublished Letters of Freud." *International Journal of Psycho-Analysis* 50:419–27.

Galenson, E., and Roiphe, H. 1974. "The Emergence of Genital Awareness During the Second Year of Life." In *Sex Differences and Behavior,* ed. R. C. Friedman, R. M. Richart, and R. L. Van der Wiele, pp. 223–31. New York: John Wiley & Sons.

Gedo, J. E. 1979. *Beyond Interpretation: Toward a Revised Theory for Psychoanalysis.* New York: International Universities Press.

confess the unvarnished truth to you—but to you alone." (Already the basic element of psychoanalysis.) (4) But there also needs to be complete trust, the basic trust. "I trust that no one will be allowed to see what was not meant for him to see," or else. (5) There is another, more usual type of communication: "All you would hear would be smooth-tongued platitudes that won't tell you anything."

There are already some profound harbingers of things to come. (6) "I enjoy tracing the closely knit web of connecting threads which chance and fate have woven around us all." Or (7) "How admirable is the fine instinct with which nature has endowed us." Or, discounting the role of accidental circumstance when his friend and the latter's girlfriend happen to meet, he is (8) convinced of "the inscrutable workings of a divine power."

Even more prophetic, and in keeping with a central theme of this paper: (9) "I have a good deal of reading to do—among them Sophocles' *Oedipus Rex.*" (His paper on this was rated "good," the only one in the class.) And recognizing already the complicated results of such knowledge, (10) "You deprive yourself of much that is edifying if you can't read all these, but on the other hand you retain that cheerfulness which is so comforting about your letters."

Even a sense of his own destiny does not escape him. (11) "So now I would counsel you (about these letters) preserve them—bind them together—guard them well—you never know!" And finally there is a more ominous reference to the future, which comes back to our subject [aggression]: he refers to a recurrent toothache: (12) "It was a last feeble eruption of an erstwhile mighty crater. The last quiver from a region of my body that has for a long time been in open rebellion against peace and order in my system. I am referring to my teeth. Where others live to eat, I live to ruin my teeth. And where others eat to live, I suffer from toothache to live. Thus my life is inextricably bound up with toothache which will consequently stay with me for as long as I live."

It was precisely there, pinpointed with uncanny accuracy at that tender age, that Freud half a century later was to begin his long, silent struggle against pain and inner destruction which was to continue for the last sixteen years of his life. And it was here again, from looking into the processes of his own inner life struggles, that Freud came up with insights with which all men could identify and which applied to all mankind.

All this was already there. Today, a hundred years and twenty-seven International Congresses later—the promise of that sixteen-year-old youth did not go unfulfilled. The cohesive theory of human behavior that proliferated from his enjoyment in "tracing the closely knit web of

In the oedipal stage, the issue of trust in human relationships is recon-fronted and reworked in developmental competition with the parent of the same sex because of the now-erotized love of the parent of the opposite sex. Here exist the imagined threats of punishment and castration. Resolu-tion of this conflict involves relinquishment of the erotized love in favor of tender love and the establishment of a predominantly loving identifica-tion with the parent of the same sex. In both relationships, trust is again affirmed.

In the latency stage, the development of trust continues to involve the parents but also moves beyond the relationships with them, as well as beyond those with parent surrogates and siblings, into the broader sphere of relationships with peers and new adults. Here, the further structuring of object and self constancy depends upon the adequacy of trust, as already represented in structure, and the trust-affirming or disaffirming potential of the first loving and aggressive encounters in the larger world.

The adequacy of the internal representation of trust is particularly cru-cial in adolescent development. The biological maturation of sexual, ag-gressive, and intellectual capabilities to the adult level propels the adoles-cent to move away from dependence on parents and family. With this shift, the influence of the parents as represented in the superego is dimin-ished, and structural integration is loosened. Structure is thus opened up for the characteristic, culturally important adolescent revision of values and ideals in relation to generational changes (Settlage 1973). An important outcome of these changes, which supports the move to independence in young adulthood, is a new level of trust in oneself. This trust results from the transformation, and "owning" for oneself, of trust as it has been developed in relationships with others.

Trust, and the object and self constancy structures that embody it, can be built, or further modified, by developmental relationships in adulthood. This can involve adult development in its own right (Settlage et al. 1988) or the resumption of arrested childhood development, notably through effective therapy. A recently conceived process model of development has the specific aim of delineating criteria for adult development (Settlage et al. 1988). Based on the concept of developmental process, this process model supplements the stage and phase model.

The process model postulates a sequence of developmental process lead-ing to the formation of a given self-regulatory or adaptive function. The sequence includes (1) a *developmental challenge,* revealing the need for a new skill or a revision of values; (2) *developmental tension,* serving as a motivating force; (3) *developmental conflict,* reflecting the normal uncertainty about change and anxiety about the consequences of success or failure; (4) *resolu-tion of developmental conflict* through mastering the challenge, and internalizing and integrating the new function; and (5) a corresponding *change in the self-representation,* altering the individual's sense of self and identity.

A sequence of developmental process results in one or more of the following accomplishments: (a) the formation of a new function; (b) the elaboration or refinement of an existing function; (c) the further integration of an existing function toward greater autonomy and structural stability; and (d) the reorganization of psychic structure to a higher level of function.

The challenges in adult development stem from two sources: the characteristic life events, such as marriage, parenthood, retirement, biological decline, or the loss of loved ones through death; and the possibility of achieving a new and better mode or level of function and adaptation.

Object and self constancy

Libidinal object and self constancy are outcomes of separation-individuation. Mental representations of the mother as the primary love object and of the self are initially closely intertwined. They are sorted out through the process of self-object differentiation prompted by advancing cognitive development. These differentiated representations are conceived to be organized by the child's subjective sense of emotionally charged, contrasting, good and bad experiences in the mother-child interaction. At this early level of cognitive development, the child is thus seen to have a disjunctive sense of unintegrated good and bad representations of the mother and the self. The subsequent amalgamation and blending of these good and bad representations results in unified representations of the mother and the self as separate entities, each encompassing both good and bad features. Ambivalence is a consequence of this integration.

The attainment of object constancy means that the parent, figuratively, is now within the child and therefore ever-present. Separation can take place without the former overwhelming anxiety. The amalgamation of object images into object constancy means also that the child expects that the love relationship will survive hostile feelings and episodic angry confrontations. The internal presence of the parent tends further to diminish the external presence of the parent in support of the regulatory functions being developed through internalization and identification. Early psychic structure formation has thus culminated in a definitive step toward independence and autonomy.

Self constancy is developed through entirely similar, codetermined processes and has analagous outcomes. In addition to the sense of a single integrated self, there is the confidence that the self will survive separation from the love object. There is also the expectation that the integrated predominantly good self will survive a temporary resurgence of the bad self. The sense of self and self-esteem can thus be regulated and maintained.

The effective structuring of object and self constancy takes place under the aegis of a predominance of love over anger and hostility in the child-parent relationship (McDevitt 1975). The predominant representation of love in these structures is the glue, if you will, of their integration.

With regard to hierarchical development, there is a particularly important functional relationship between object constancy and the superego. Both effective integration of object constancy and, later, of the superego occur within a mainly loving relationship with the parents. Since this loving relationship is represented most basically in object constancy, it provides the intrapsychic aegis for the maintenance of superego function. Impaired object constancy thus has the potential to undermine the functional integrity of the superego. Undermining can occur, in childhood or adulthood, when the structure of object constancy is disrupted by anger resulting from feeling betrayed or abandoned by an important current love object.

Pathogenesis and object and self constancy

The basic structuring of object and self constancy is a function of the early mother-child relationship: Good experience promotes healthy structuring and bad experience interferes with it. An important factor in pathogenesis is the young child's utter dependency upon the parent for survival. The relationship with the parent is sometimes maintained at the cost of impaired development.

The attempt to avoid severe conflict with the parent can result in the abrupt, unmodulated internalization of the threatening parental attitudes and the associated "bad" representations of the parent. Although serving adaptation in the relationship, such internalizations often exist as unintegrated "foreign bodies," contributing to a negative sense of self and object. The rage, destructive impulses, and fantasies associated with the child's hostile aggression toward the parent also threaten the relationship. They are, therefore, likely to be repressed in avoiding conflict with the parent. Such repression can be pathogenic and can result in intrapsychic conflict.

The repression of hostile aggression, as distinguished from its control and modulation, has several undesirable consequences. Excluding these feelings from consciousness also excludes them from the developmental interaction that could process them toward mastery. They are subjectively sensed to be a potentially uncontrollable, even explosive internal liability. Moreover, they contribute to a bad sense of self.

By interfering with the amalgamation of aggression with love, repressed aggression also impairs or arrests the structuring of object and self constancy. The failure to amalgamate good and bad representations of the object and the self lends itself to splitting as a defense. In this reality-distorting defense, the good and bad images of the object and the self are split and displaced onto others in an attempt to deal with problems in the object relationship.

In addition, the defenses of idealization, grandiosity, and omnipotence fantasies tend to be evoked to counter feelings of helplessness and vulnerability. The lack of a well-defined sense of object and self tends to cause problems for intimacy and separation, with attendant merger and abandonment anxieties. Commonly there is a defensive flight into a pseudo-precocious self-sufficiency. The formation of gender identity may be confused as a part of the conflicted, ill-defined, unintegrated sense of self (Settlage 1980b).

Structural impairment of object and self constancy is often a circumscribed psychopathology. Although pathologically determined, the continuing excessively dependent relationship with the parent nevertheless permits an interaction that can effectively serve cognitive development and ego development generally. In the closeness of family relationships, the dependency may go unrecognized until it is unmasked in adolescence. Such unmasking and its symptomatic consequences occur most strikingly in the context of a pending or actual geographic move away from the family, such as going off to college.

The Hallmarks of Adult Functioning

The life-course development of the regulatory structures of the human personality culminates during adulthood. As distilled from the thinking of analysts, the hallmarks of adult functioning are:

1. *identity,* a persistent sameness within self and in relationships with others

2. *responsibility* and *accountability,* with regard to oneself and others

3. *loyalty,* allegiance to one's friends and loved ones

4. *fidelity,* faithfulness to one's chosen work, beliefs, and causes

5. *morality,* compliance with the imperativistic values of the superego and with the goal values of the ego ideal

6. *ethicality,* a higher-level commitment transcending moral restraint and encompassing idealism.

tient's problem with closeness. She desperately yearned for intimate love and equally feared reaching out for it. Her overriding concern was that she would not be able to form a close, loving, lasting relationship with a man, and would never marry.

In the latter half of the analysis, she confronted her extreme difficulty in feeling and expressing anger and hostility. She was intellectually aware that her withdrawal reactions were based on hurt and anger. But feelings were at first absent. When she began to feel anger, she could not express it. She feared that a destructive loss of control would result in the end of any relationship, including the analytic relationship. The experiencing and interpretation of her repressed anger and aggression in the transference were the most difficult and most crucial aspects of the therapeutic work. This problem reflected the postulated early childhood repression of aggression in order to maintain the indispensable relationship with the parent.

Paradoxically, the severity of the patient's problems was matched by the strength of her will and her determined effort to solve them. She refused to give up. In addition to presumed good experience during her first year of life, a developmentally intriguing basis for her hope and persistence was discovered in the treatment. In talking about her childhood, the patient noted that everything she recalled was as vivid and real now as when it had originally happened. In exploring the reasons for her unusual recall, she became aware that it was her way of keeping the door to the past open for change. She had the prevailing expectation that her mother would one day change and become the wished-for, all-good mother. Fulfillment of this wish meant that past hurts would be undone and that the patient, too, would change. Development would thus be resumed.

Toward the end of the analysis, it became apparent that this expectation was interfering with the patient's continuing development. Analogous to the block resulting from failure to confront and mourn the painful loss of a deceased loved-one, the patient was blocked by not confronting and mourning the painful loss of the wished-for mother of childhood. Because she had not gone through the "mourning-liberation" process (Pollock 1976) as conceived originally by Freud (1917), she was not fully free to develop in other relationships. Confronting that childhood loss in the context of analysis proved to be essential to her late-adolescent move into adulthood. As would be expected, the mourning of the childhood loss was admixed with the loss of the analyst during the process of termination.

Following the termination of analysis, the patient took a position in her chosen field in a community far from home. At intervals of months, she telephoned the analyst. These calls affirmed that the analyst still cared about her and thus provided support for the continuing integration of her psychic structure. Her reports on her progress indicated that she was consolidating the gains achieved in therapy.

At age twenty-five, she reported a further step in her development toward independence and autonomy. This step reflected change in her relationship with her father. The oedipal and preoedipal determinants of this idealized, dependent relationship, and its interference with her development, had been recurrently in focus in the treatment. With a mixture of humor, chagrin, and sadness, she noted that she was finally letting go of the idealization. She continued to love and value her father but also allowed herself to recognize and accept emotionally his shortcomings. She was thus confronting and mourning her loss of him, too, as the parent of childhood. She was moving into an adult-to-adult relationship with him and freeing herself for close relationships with other men. This young woman was approaching full responsibility for herself.

This important index of adulthood was recognized and soberly characterized by another woman, one in her late fifties, during the termination phase of her analysis. The feeling of being accountable to herself as never before both exhilarated and moved her. In her words, "It's between me and me, and it is none of your business. I am taking myself seriously. I also am shaken by the realization that I will be tough on myself. I won't throw away the rest of my life. I not only feel accountable to myself but feel I will achieve my goals. Not only is my work here done, but I am ready for my future."

Summary and Conclusions

Against the background of a discussion of human development, I have attempted to convey the relevance of psychic structure to the definition of adulthood. The particular focus is on the object and self constancy structures underlying independence, autonomy of function, and trust and commitment. Independence and autonomy result from integrating and owning for oneself the regulatory and adaptive functions acquired largely through internalization and identification with the parents. The structuring toward independence and autonomy is impaired by an ongoing pathological dependence on the parent, which can result from an anger-evoking disruption of the developmental relationship. Repressing this anger, instead of mastering it in the relationship, impairs structure formation and disrupts the achieved integration and functional integrity of the existing structure. Through interference with the involved amalgamation of aggression and love, the repressed anger impairs the capacity for trust and commitment.

The transition from adolescence to young adulthood and the subsequent achievement of full adulthood are placed in the context of structural development as a lifelong process. In this process, the formation of basic regulatory structure begins in earliest childhood, evolves through successive stages, and continues in adulthood. The hallmarks of adult functioning are the result of the culmination of lifelong structural development.

That young adulthood is not the same as full, optimally mature adulthood is not a new realization. What is new, or newly understood, is the vital fact of adult development, which provides a positive and hopeful perspective on individual human development. If the door to the past can be kept open, or be reopened, to new developmental relationships, the highest possible levels of adult morality, ethicality, and commitment remain attainable. If ways can be found to enhance the potential for adult development, the quality of individual life could be much improved.

If these newfound ways, and new ways of enhancing child development as well, can be embraced in enough of our human societies, the general human condition could be much improved. Perhaps humankind can yet move toward Erikson's evolutionary advance in morality.

REFERENCES

Adatto, C. P. 1980. "Late Adolescence to Early Adulthood." In *The Course of Life: Psychoanalytic Contributions Toward Understanding Personality Development. Vol. II; Latency, Adolescence, and Youth,* ed. S.I. Greenspan and G.H. Pollock, pp. 463–76. Washington D.C.: U.S. Government Printing Office, DHHS Publication No. (ADM) 80-999.

Benedek, I. 1959. "Parenthood As a Developmental Phase: A Contribution to Libido Theory." *Journal of the American Psychoanalytic Association* 7:389–417.

Bibring, G. L.; Dwyer; T. F.; Huntington, D. S.; and Valenstein, A. F. 1961. "A Study of Psychological Processes in Pregnancy and the Earliest Mother-Child Relationship." *Psychoanalytic Study of the Child* 16:9–72. New York: International Universities Press.

Blos, P. 1967. "The Second Individuation Process of Adolescence." *Psychoanalytic Study of the Child* 22:162–86. New York: International Universities Press.

———. 1976. "When and How Does Adolescence End? Structural Criteria for Adolescent Closure." *Journal of the Philadelphia Association for Psychoanalysis* 3(3):47–58.

Emde, R. N. 1980. "Ways of Thinking about New Knowledge and Further Research from a Developmental Orientation." *Psychoanalysis and Contemporary Thought* 3:213–35.

———. 1985. "From Adolescence to Midlife: Remodeling the Structure of Adult Development." *Journal of the American Psychoanalytic Association* 33:59–112.

Erikson, E. H. 1950. *Childhood and Society.* New York: W. W. Norton.

———. 1964. *Insight and Responsibility.* New York: W. W. Norton.

———. 1975. *Life History and the Historical Movement.* New York: W. W. Norton.

———. 1980. *Identity and the Life Cycle.* New York: W. W. Norton.

Freud, A. 1963. "The Concept of Developmental Lines." *Psychoanalytic Study of the Child* 18:245–65. New York: International Universities Press.

Freud, S. [1905] 1953. "Three Essays on the Theory of Sexuality." In *Standard Edition,* ed. J. Strachey, vol. 7, pp. 135–243. London: Hogarth Press.

———. [1914] 1957. "On Narcissism: An Introduction." In *Standard Edition,* ed. J. Strachey, vol. 14, pp. 69–102. London: Hogarth Press.

———. [1917] 1957. "Mourning and Melancholia." In *Standard Edition.,* ed. J. Strachey, vol. 14, pp. 243–58. London: Hogarth Press.

Hartmann, H. 1939. *Ego Psychology and the Problem of Adaptation.* New York: International Universities Press.

———. 1952. "Mutual Influences in the Development of the Ego and the Id." *Psychoanalytic Study of the Child* 7:9–30. New York: International Universities Press.

———. 1960. *Psychoanalysis and Moral Values.* New York: International Universities Press.

Jacobson, E. 1964. *The Self and the Object World.* New York: International Universities Press.

Loewald, H. 1960. "On the Therapeutic Action of Psychoanalysis." *International Journal of Psycho-Analysis* 41:16–33.

———. 1978. *Psychoanalysis and the History of the Individual.* New Haven: Yale University Press.

Mahler, M. S.; Pine, F.; and Bergman, A. 1975. *The Psychological Birth of the Human Infant: Symbiosis and Individuation.* New York: Basic Books.

Mahler, M. S., and McDevitt, J. B. 1982. "Thoughts on the Emergence of the Sense of Self, with a Particular Emphasis on the Body Self." *Journal of the American Psychoanalytic Association* 30:827–48.

McDevitt, J. B. 1975. "Separation-Individuation and Object Constancy." *Journal of the American Psychoanalytic Association* 23:713–42.

Marcus, I. M. 1973. Panel Report: "The Experience of Separation-Individuation in Infancy and Its Reverberations throughout the Course of Life: 2. Adolescence and Maturity." *Journal of the American Psychoanalytic Association* 21:155–67.

Pollock, G. H. 1977. "The Mourning Process and Creative Organizational Change." *Journal of the American Psychoanalytic Association* 25:3–34.

Settlage, C. F. 1973. "Cultural Values and the Superego in Late Adolescence." *Psychoanalytic Study of the Child* 27:74–92. New York: Quadrangle Press.

Settlage, C. F. 1980a. "Psychoanalytic Developmental Thinking in Current and Historical Perspective." *Psychoanalysis and Contemporary Thought* 3:139–170.

Settlage, C. F. 1980b. "The Psychoanalytic Theory and Understanding of Psychic Development During Second and Third Years of Life." In *The Course of Life: Psychoanalytic Contributions Toward Understanding Personality Development, Vol I: Infancy and Early Childhood,* ed. S. I. Greenspan and G. H. Pollock, pp. 523–39. Washington D.C.: U.S. Government Printing Office, DHHS Publication No. (ADM) 80-786.

Settlage, C. F.; Gadpaille, W. J.; Hawkins, M. O.; Noshpitz, J. D.; Rakoff, V.; and Wermer, H. 1968. Group for the Advancement of Psychiatry Report: *Normal Adolescence: Its Dynamics and Impact.* New York: Charles Scribner and Sons.

Settlage, C. F.; Curtis, J.; Lozoff, Marjorie; Lozoff, Milton; Silberschatz, G.; and Simburg, E. 1988. "Conceptualizing Adult Development." *Journal of the American Psychoanalytic Association* 36:347–69.

Staples, H. D., and Smarr, E. R. 1980. "Bridge to Adulthood: Years from 18 to 23." In *The Course of Life: Psychoanalytic Contributions Toward Understanding Personality Development. Vol. III: Latency, Adolescence, and Youth,* ed. S. I. Greenspan and G. H. Pollock, pp. 477–96. Washington D.C.: U.S. Government Printing Office, DHHS Publication No. (ADM) 80-999.

Stern, D. N. 1985. *The Interpersonal World of the Infant: A View from Psychoanalysis and Developmental Psychology.* New York: Basic Books.

Sternschein, T. 1973. Panel Report: "The Experience of Separation-Individuation in Infancy and throughout the Course of Life: 3. Maturity, Senescence, and Sociological Implications." *Journal of the American Psychoanalytic Association* 21:633–45.

Valenstein, A. F. 1972. "The Earliest Mother-Child Relationship and the Development of the Superego." In *Moral Values and the Superego Concept in Psychoanalysis,* ed. S. C. Post, pp. 63–73. New York: International Universities Press.

Winestine, M. C. 1973. Panel Report: "The Experience of Separation-Individuation in Infancy and throughout the Course of Life: 1. Infancy and Childhood." *Journal of the American Psychoanalytic Association* 21:135–54.

DISCUSSION

In this chapter, Settlage explores how the formation and evolution of psychic structure occur throughout the life course, particularly in the adult years. He helps chart new territory, because the body of developmental psychoanalytic theory has concentrated on childhood and adolescence. He brings new data and information that support a hypothesis we first formulated a decade ago (Colarusso and Nemiroff 1979).

Our hypothesis was as follows: *Whereas childhood development is focused primarily on the formation of psychic structure, adult development is concerned with the continuing evolution of existing psychic structure and with its use.* We felt that part of the reason the adult has been conceptualized as static, as opposed to dynamic, in psychological development has been the failure to recognize the scope and subtlety of psychic change in adulthood. We described the formation of psychic structure in the child as similar to broad strokes painted on a bare canvas, whereas the evolution of psychic structure in adulthood was equated to fine, nearly invisible strokes on a complex background. Likewise, the appearance of new and basic mental functions in childhood is easier to notice than the internal refinements in these structures that occur in adulthood.

One of our favorite examples of the difference was presented by William Binstock (1973) in a comparison between adolescent infatuation and mature love:

> The state of being in love completes the lover's identity as part of a male-female duality. It is a structure-forming state in the ego which aspires to genitality. Whereas infatuation is an exercise in identity formation along the lines of sexual differentiation and sorting out of issues about activity and passivity, the gratifying love relationship, by contrast, puts into practice the structuring that has already occurred. *Whereas infatuation ends with being in love, genital love begins with it.* Of course, neither of these generalizations applies in pure form. If the infatuated lover obtains no gratification, his pursuit is a dreary and depressing one. If the adult lover undergoes no further development in the gratifying relationship, the life gradually goes out of it. Love involves a continuing securing and refinement of identity, else it will not endure. (P. 104, *italics added*)

Thus Binstock has aptly described how adolescent infatuation builds structure and how adult love refines it by stimulating a continuous evolution in identity and other processes. Adult love is thus an expression *and* a modifier of existing structure.

A major mechanism for the lifelong evolution of psychic structure and formation is the continued possibility for identification. Adult developmentalists are demonstrating that the process of identification is *not* limited to childhood or adolescence, but occurs regularly in adult life as well. During the course of a marriage, for example, spouses may take on each other's attributes and will often know what the partner is thinking without a word having passed between them.

The mentor relationship is another striking example of an opportunity for new internalizations and identifications during adult life and consequent formation and modification of psychic structure. For many creative scientists a close relationship with an older mentor during their formative young adult years is crucial. This new identification is central to scientific commitment and to ways of working that eventually lead to new discoveries. Although partly based on earlier infantile identifications, such adult processes should not be seen as mere replications of parent-child relationships. The identification with the original objects is the means by which the child's psychic structure forms and becomes like that of the adult, whereas later identifications provide *specificity* to the adult personality—in this example, the choice of profession and the quality of work achievement. The capacity for creativity, the legacy of childhood, can be directed into specific areas by adult identifications.

In *Adaptation to Life,* George Vaillant (1977) described the results of the Grant Study, a seminal longitudinal study of ninety-five male Harvard graduates that began in 1939. The investigators found that in individuals who were able to master conflict gracefully and to harness instinctual strivings creatively, adaptive styles—their mechanisms of ego defense (an important indicator of psychic structure)—continued to mature throughout their lives. With the passage of years they used mature defenses with increasing frequency. As adolescents, they were twice as likely to use immature defenses as mature ones; as young adults they were twice as likely to use mature mechanisms as immature ones. By midlife they were four times as likely to use mature as immature defenses. This research convincingly demonstrates how the ego, as measured by its mechanisms of defense, evolves, changes, and transforms during the life cycle.

In the embryonic tradition of psychoanalytic adult development work, Settlage wishes to sharpen the definition of adulthood by reexamining the development of psychic structure from childhood to adulthood. His work is derived from contemporary object relations theory, which is defined by its focus on the role of the human object relationship in psychic development. His ideas stem from observational research on development during the first three years of life, from clinical exploration of pathology from those years in the treatment of narcissistic and borderline disorders, and from direct observations and clinical studies on adult development.

Focusing on the psychoanalytic concepts of libidinal object constancy and self constancy, he describes how, in clinical work with adolescents and adults, he has been increasingly impressed by the problems that inadequately or pathologically developed object and self constancy pose for the move from adolescent to adult function. Object and self constancy embody gradually established, lasting, predominantly good representations of the parent and the self as shaped by experience in the developmental relationship. They serve respectively the formation, regulation, and maintenance of relationships and the regulation and maintenance of self-esteem and the sense of self and identity.

Settlage's central idea is that "becoming and functioning as an adult involves the *intrapsychic* integration and 'owning' for oneself of these regulatory structures at an adult level of autonomy of function. This adult level rests initially on adolescent development as it adds an increment of independence from the parents and from sexual and aggressive drives. The independence from the parents is both from them in actuality and from their internal representations (Blos 1967, 1977)" (p. 27).

Settlage makes an important contribution to adult developmental theory in his description here of a process model of development, which he offers to supplant older "stage and phase" models: "The process model postulates a sequence of developmental processes leading to the formation of a given self-regulatory or adaptive function. The sequence includes (1) a *developmental challenge,* revealing the need for a new skill or a revision of values; (2) *developmental tension,* serving as a motivating force; (3) *developmental conflict,* reflecting the normal uncertainty about change and anxiety about the consequences of success or failure; (4) *resolution of developmental conflict,* through mastering the challenge and internalization and integration of the new function; and (5) *a change in self-representation,* altering the individual's sense of self and identity" (pp. 33–34).

Clearly and precisely, Settlage spells out how this sequence of developmental processes results in the following accomplishments or changes in psychic structure and functions: "(a) the formation of a new function; (b) the elaboration or refinement of an existing function; (c) the further integration of an existing function toward greater autonomy and structural stability; and (d) the reorganization of psychic structure to a higher level of function" (p. 34).

Summarizing his ideas about the start of a developmental process, he writes, "The challenges in adult development stem from two sources: the characteristic life events, such as marriage, parenthood, retirement, biological decline, or the loss of loved ones through death; and the possibility of achieving a new and better mode or level of function or adaptation" (p. 34).

We predict that Settlage's integration of psychoanalytic structural theory and object relations theory, particularly in the elaboration of his process model of development, will be heuristic in the future of adult developmental theory.

REFERENCES

Binstock, W. 1973. "On the Two Forms of Intimacy." *Journal of the American Psychoanalytic Association* 21:93–107.

Blos, P. 1967. "The Second Individuation Process of Adolescence." *Psychoanalytic Study of the Child* 22:162–80.

———. 1977. "When and How Does Adolescence End: Structural Criteria for Adolescent Closure." In *Adolescent Psychiatry,* ed. S. C. Feinstein and P. L. Giovachini, vol. 5, pp. 5–17. New York: Jason Aronson.

Colarusso, C. A., and Nemiroff, R. A. 1979. "Some Observations and Hypotheses about the Psychoanalytic Theory of Adult Development." *International Journal of Psycho-Analysis* 60:59.

Vaillant, G. E. 1977. *Adaptation to Life.* Boston: Little, Brown.

3

The Eye of the Beholder:

On the Developmental Dialogue of Fathers and Daughters

JOHN MUNDER ROSS

It is fifteen years since I began to study fatherhood (see Ross 1975, 1979 a, b). The inspiration for this undertaking came from a rather unlikely source—the woman's movement, at its height then, demanding a disciplined reconsideration of the nature and sources of sexual identity in both women and men. In that climate, my initial interest resided in a boy's and man's envy of woman, particularly her capacity to make and feed babies. Only gradually, when juxtaposed with phallic strivings, was this initially maternal set of aspirations and identifications transfigured into a paternal identity. Subsequently I joined other analytic researchers, like Abelin (1971, 1975, 1977) and Herzog (1980, 1982), in conducting research on "fathering" proper. Through observation and clinical inquiry, I explored the gender-specific contributions a man actually makes to his children's upbringing—a man, I would add, whose paternity precipitates him into a protracted adult developmental crisis in its own right.

With this chapter on fathers and daughters, a topic which in the past I have eschewed for fear of trespassing on feminist terrain, I find myself returning to the original themes that seized my interest. I do so after having diverted my attention for some time from examining fatherhood to reflecting on the erotic life of men—in literature and in reality—reflections which have persuaded me to reassert that the urge to be *at one with woman*, in sexual union with her and otherwise, figures preeminently in a man's basic heterosexual quest, his "object love" (Ross 1985, Kakar and Ross

1987). Moreover, this pursuit is nothing less than a "soul-searching." Man's longing to possess woman evokes the image of Cupid's chasing after his immortal Psyche. Like parenthood, romantic and sexual love are suffused with mystery and with the ambisexual paradox.

These are generalizations, of course. Over the past decade and a half, to the contrary, I have become more and more impressed by *individual variations* on universal lines of development—specifically by the *dialogues* taking place between parents and children through the course of the life cycle. The references here to guiding theoretical overviews are obvious: Spitz's (1965) notions about basic object relational exchanges that usher in love and self-sufficiency and Erikson's (1963, 1964) notion of the ongoing evolution of an individual's psychosocial identity within the generational cycle. Early on, the transactions between the primary caregivers (the mother of infancy, the two parents of toddlerhood) and the child are fundamental, fairly direct, evident in behavior. As psychic structures accrue, however, much of what takes place becomes unconscious, defended and distorted on both sides, so that "derailment of the dialogue," in Spitz's felicitous metaphor, "mismatching," and the simple *malentendus* of everyday life become "par for the course." Thus, a parent may be instinctually moved in some manner toward his child but may act quite differently for defensive purposes. He will find that his or her actions and manifest communications are filtered through and apprehended according to a child's age-specific cognitive equipment. Those perceptions then are further distorted by fantasy and developmental imperatives as they are finally internalized by the child. All this occurs within an evolving cultural context, which shapes each generation's images of the other. Perhaps nowhere is this tangled web of latent meaning and subliminal interpretation more evident than in the misunderstandings between father and daughter.

We are used to searching out the starker truths of adult psychological life by going backward, relying on their genesis in the longings and conflicts of the child. In this chapter, however, I shall reverse direction and proceed to old age in order to discover the vulnerable and regressed father's *needs* of his daughter in a literary preamble with Lear at its heart. Following that, I will join several analysts, critics, and ideologues in reexamining the responses of a middle-aged Freud at the height of emergent power to the adolescent Dora (Freud 1905a), to the appeals she makes to him, and to answers she seeks to retrieve in this "fragment" of a psychoanalysis. We may recall that Freud discovered "transference" in this case, while inadvertently revealing for later readers his own countertransference reactions. Most important for our purposes, this first emotional drama between analyst and patient recapitulates and, when interpreted, adumbrates hidden agenda in the more archaic psychological dance of fathers and daughters.

Following a vignette from the analysis of a newborn father of a baby daughter and an observational anecdote, the chapter then focuses on those early exchanges. Subsequently, brief excerpts from treatments of adult women illustrate their reliance on the exhibitionistic supplies tendered by men who find themselves playing the roles of preoedipal as well as oedipal-paternal transference figures. Such gratification remains necessary, I argue, if these women are to sustain individuation of their body images from those of their mothers (whose pull toward reimmersion never fully abates) as well as a physical sense of self-esteem and well-being. Being admired in adult life revives the "eye-vulva" object relational and libidinal dialogues of father and daughter—interchanges that begin during a little girl's second year and continue, becoming reciprocally conflict-laden as she progresses through the oedipal era into adolescence.

Wheels of Fire: A Second Childhood

Akira Kurosawa's film *Ran* (1986) is an adaptation of Shakespeare's *King Lear,* transfiguring what may be the greatest of Western dramas into a more recognizably Japanese saga. The director succeeds in retaining the prototypic existential angst of the original, the sublime and excruciating solitude of Lear's imperious disinheritance of himself. But does the film capture the pathos of the parent bereft, of the warrior grown fond and foolish, in need of succor more than success, who is cruelly savaged by the sharp "serpent's tooth" of a "thankless child?" Deferring no doubt to the cultural context for the workings of Japanese martial masculinity and their aftermath, Kurosawa changes the story's cast of characters in one dramatic particular. Instead of daughters, the old king is betrayed and redeemed by sons, one good and two bad, as in Shakespeare's original drama. In Japan, patriarchs keep their distance, formally at least, from females of all generations, although Kurosawa's movie tells us, the latter may exercise their feminine wiles and work forcefully through their men to gain their ends.

In fact, the sex change has made for an effect quite different from that of *Lear.* For instance, the good son Jiro, dying on the battlefield beside his aggrieved and guilty father, touches us yet does not evoke the same pity as the tender Cordelia, her corpse cradled in the old father's unsteady arms. *Ran* has *misread* his sons, overestimating or belittling them. Still, he has not demanded, in addition to their filial fealty and protection, their nurturing, sensuous love—the sort of comfort one might expect and ask only of a woman, albeit a daughter. The vulnerability, the dependency, and the distinctive ironies are not there.

In *Lear,* the drama of the father deluded and misled by a son is the subsidiary plot, the story of Gloucester, Edmund, and Edgar. The king's plight—that of the exiled parent—is captured in his use of Edgar, disguised as Poor Tom o' Bedlam, the naked madman, as a foil for his abandoned and regressed self. Cast out by Goneril and Regan and pelted by the storm, Lear greets the bereft beggar:

> What, have his daughters brought him to this pass?
> . . . . Wouldst thou give 'em all?   (3.4.65–66)
> . . . Thou art the thing itself; unaccommodated man is
> no more but such a poor, bare, forked animal as
> thou art.   (3.4.110–14)

Earlier robed as tyrant benefactor, Lear has demanded of his daughters professions of their love, to which the elder two, hitherto eclipsed by their younger sister, the favored Cordelia, have given their seemingly capacious but hollow, hypocritical assent. In contrast, she responds truthfully according to her filial bond—"no more, no less." Indeed, Cordelia wonders, why have her sisters husbands if the father is preeminent in their affections? Stung by what we analysts today would deem a sort of counteroedipal rejection (common enough as a late adolescent girl approaches marriage), by Cordelia's "nothing," the once worldly monarch is precipitated toward infancy, confessing:

> I loved her most, and thought to set my rest
> On her kind nursery.   (1.1.125–26)

It is an apt sentiment, culturally sanctioned in the West then, as it has continued to be until recently in Asia—the expected conversion of tended progeny into the caregivers of one's old age. Yet Lear's sentiment is a double-entendre; his wishes reach beyond the hope of easeful retirement in the future and circle *back* to his oedipal and preoedipal origins. Like many great achievers today, the leader has his analyst, guru, or Fool, who confronts and interprets this regression, ascribing his own sobriety to the fact that:

> . . . thou mad'st thy *daughters* thy *mothers;*
> for when thou gav'st them
> the rod, and put'st down thine own breeches . . .
> I for sorrow sung.   (1.4.187–94)

The implication of this ambiguous, paradoxical metaphor is that in ceding generational authority and direction, Lear has committed a grave indiscretion, a sort of incest. In so doing, he abdicates not only his kingly mandate but also his masculinity. "Bound upon a wheel of fire," he becomes a raging infant. In the process of thus empowering his children to care for him, he opens Pandora's box, releasing truths concealed by dissembling and defense—sibling rivalry, penis envy, and the castrative vindictiveness of woman scorned—all the narcissistic ragings and hostilities leveled by daughters at a once commanding and/or indifferent patriarch. In the dialogue of father and daughter, the hoary warrior casts himself as the hapless, vulnerable baby, the dear girl as the puissant viper, the "bad" and "phallic" mother.

Later, having banished Cordelia, Lear gazes fiercely at these treacherous daughters and specifically curses their fecundity, damning their *wombs*, which he would make barren and ugly—more testimony to his Fool's reading of the unconscious. He descends in his own private reflections into an abject, naked dependence, one which confounds the boundaries between a disintegrating sense of self in desperate and almost wantonly unreasonable "need" (Reason not the need!) and her, the woman, who might answer it:

> O, how this mother wells up toward my heart!
> Hysterica passio [the disease of the womb], down,
> thou climbing sorrow,
> Thy element's below. Where is thy daughter?
> (2.4.56–59)

In his progressive "dedifferentiation" (Jacobson 1964, Mahler et al. 1975), the erstwhile monarch yields his sceptre for "women's weapons," the tears that scald his cheeks, the cries of the newborn with which, he tells blind old Gloucester, we have all greeted the world for the first time. His testing of his adult self, the yielding to psychological truths, and the regressing are heroic and teach us about ourselves. His is a conquistador's courage that confronts helplessness head on, leaving Lear, as always, "every inch a king," but now, to borrow from Freud, his "majesty the *baby!*" (Freud 1914c, p. 239–44)

Stung by old hurts, Goneril and Regan know nothing of and care less about the old man's existential tempest, hellbent as they are on acquiring sexual love and secular power. Only the wronged Cordelia feels for his condition and returns from France, which has granted her asylum, to rescue her father with her love and with the repose prescribed by an Elizabethan physician.

A BBC television film (1985) featured Laurence Olivier as Lear, in a long-overdue effort to essay the role but he was, ironically, too enfeebled by the ravages of age and illness to sustain the senile relentlessness required by the mad scenes on the heath. Nonetheless, Olivier conveyed lyrically the pathos of the father's rediscovery of Cordelia, his true daughter. In an earlier version of the crudely constructed production, the film editor's lapse permitted an eerily invasive insight into the imperious patriarch's infantilization and loss of self-identity, an inadvertent image imposed upon the complex language of the play.

The audience hears a high-pitched singing voice. Before we actually see the bizarrely garlanded king devouring a raw rabbit (as I recall), we are confronted by a naked breast, its reflection glinting in the eddying waters of a stream, which further reflect Olivier's more familiar face. For a moment we imagine it must be Cordelia's and half expect Lear to suck the nipple. But, as the camera pans up and away, we learn to our horror and our embarrassment, that this is Sir Laurence's soft, fleshy chest, last exposed to public view in the darkened muscularity of his Othello twenty years earlier. Estrogenized by illness and medication, the pectorals have been blanched and denuded. Has he willingly, we wonder, exhibited his "naked frailty," the ravages and reversals of a man's senescence in the spirit of the great actor, offering himself up to us as the androgynous, indeed effeminized, child that Lear becomes? Has he found Cordelia—his vulnerability, her care, youth's promise of infinite potential, in other words, the world of childhood—has he found her, it, all in himself? No, the meaningful montage was mere mischance; so much for illusions of intent. The final version of the film, haphazardly put together, omitted the breast in deference to the great actor's privacy before proceeding to the daughter's and father's rapprochement and their piteous love-death, with which *King Lear* concludes.

With the exception of Gloucester, or possibly Henry and Hal, Shakespeare, by Freud's admission the greatest of psychoanalysts, never dealt directly with the dialogues of *living* fathers and sons. When he did ponder this relationship, in Hamlet's ghostly soul-searching, the perspective was unilaterally that of the son. Perhaps it was—and Shakespeare pathography is a dubious enterprise—that his only boy Hamnet died at eleven, leaving his two daughters to survive into their adolescence and his middle age. In any event, the hearts of fathers, old ones mostly, doting on or cruelly possessive of their daughters (who were about to leave them and marry), occupied much of Shakespeare's imagination. The abiding ties between them, heartwrenching and redemptive, are portrayed repeatedly as quintessential expressions of the generational cycle. Again and again the daughter represents the aging man's hope of sensuous and spiritual renewal: Lear and the three sisters, Shylock and Jessica, Prospero and Miranda, Cymbeline and Imogen, Leontes and Perdita (the lost one).

In most cases, interestingly, mothers are absent from the scene, deceased, implying an oedipal and counteroedipal triumph, a realization of implicit incest. The purely dyadic interplay, moreover, allows Shakespeare the psychologist to reach behind and beneath the intersystemic tensions of the Oedipus complex to plumb the exchange of identities taking place between father and daughter. Narcissistic disappointment and jealousy provoke hostilities and breaches of empathy for needful daughters until the dust of intrapsychic conflict clears to reveal the child as mother, mother to the children of one's future after the grave.

In his middle age, Shakespeare seems to have intuited the enduring truths revealed in an old man's sense of loss and depletion (Cath 1962). In his daughters, a man looks for the mother (wife) who was once his better half.

Freud: Daughters Masquerading as Sons

So, too, with early Freud. Notwithstanding the phallocentric (Jones 1961) accent of his overarching theory, his original subjects are daughters. From *The Studies in Hysteria* (1895) to Dora (1905a), Freud portrayed the uneasy, often neurotic efforts of young women to come to terms with the fathers who seemed inevitably to betray and forget them. Most often exploitative and sometimes downright licentious (Katarina's father, for instance, subjected her to incest), these fathers had seduced their girls with the promise, at the very least implicit, of an unhallowed love and oedipal victory and then abandoned them as cast-off pawns to other lordly desires, lusting after women their own age, after all. How both odd and predictable it is, then, that Freud, and we after him, should construct a general "son psychology" (see Mahl 1982) with Oedipus at its core, and not Electra or Iphigenia, the devoted daughterly lover and the victim of paternal pride and ambition. Even when we, father researchers, have attempted to correct a false dichotomy between the preoedipal mother and the father of the Oedipus complex by tracing the male parent's presence back to its delineation at least as early as the rapprochement subphase (Abelin 1971, 1985)— even then the tendency has been to concentrate on sons, not on daughters.

What are our resistances all about? Is it something frightening, merely elusive, or both about daughters and in ourselves that makes these relationships hard to conceptualize? In the hope of essaying these "counterreactions," oedipal and otherwise, I will turn now to Freud's evident countertransference responses to the transference he discovered in his first fully reported psychoanalytic case history, *The Fragment of a Case of Hysteria*, written in 1901 and published four years later.

Dora: a daughter's dreams

When Ida Bauer was referred to Felix Deutsch in 1922 (Deutsch 1957) by her physician to explore possible psychological factors in her bout with Meniere's syndrome, she confided that she had been Freud's famous patient "Dora," the protagonist in the first fully reported analysis, which was broken off after eleven weeks some two decades earlier. Of all the material in her abortive treatment, Ida, or Dora, singled out for recall and reconsideration Freud's interpretations of her two equally renowned dreams. In the one instance, Freud had underscored the eighteen-year-old girl's erotic desires for the infamous Herr K, her would-be corrupter. In the other dream, he highlighted her wish for revenge against all the older men who, she felt, had insidiously seduced and abandoned her—Herr K, of course; her father; and by extension of the transference, Freud himself. These notions had stuck in her craw, for something was not quite right or complete about them, and Dora could not take them in. Accenting her unconscious intentions, Freud's formulations ignored both her horror at the loss of authenticity and protection on the part of her various father figures (as Erikson 1963 has noted), and their actual failures truly to requite her love. And thus his formulations probably contributed to Dora's flight from the analysis and to the deterioration of a young girl of engaging good looks and promising intelligence, in Freud's original estimation, into a middle-aged woman later described by one of Deutsch's colleagues as one of the "most repulsive hysterics" he had ever encountered (see also Marcus and Francis 1975; Glenn 1980).

When she had consulted Freud (for a second time) a quarter century earlier, symptomatic and critical of the adults around her, Dora had become a burden to the father she once lovingly nursed. To return to that clinical encounter: Dora threatens the father's liaison with Frau K. by openly protesting the advances of Herr K. at the lake (and in the privacy of his office four years earlier, when he rashly kissed her and pressed his erect penis against her). Dora senses that she has been palmed off to the dirty not-so-old man as a sop to assuage his cuckoldry and buy his silence.

Freud takes her seriously and does not collude with the father's disclaimers of the reality of these would-be seductions by deeming them mere "fantasy" (Masson 1985 to the contrary). Indeed, he finds intimations of the truth in Dora's little hysteria—the displacement, for instance, of the genital contact and of her arousal during Herr K.'s embrace, which she has tried to disavow but which reappears in the form of a cough. He does, however, deemphasize the role of current reality in the girl's neurosis. Instead, Freud aims immediately to ferret out her unwanted erotic wishes and their childhood origins, her love for both K.'s along with her father (she utterly repudiated her obsessive-compulsive mother even while identifying with her), and Dora's earlier history of furtive masturbation and enuresis in latency. Precipitated by the demands and disappointments of her burgeoning adulthood, Dora is impelled regressively and defensively to revive her oedipal drama—its frustrations and satisfactions—and to occupy herself symptomatically with unconscious fantasy.

What better way to link the two, present and past, than through the dream? Indeed, one of Freud's major agenda in the first case history is to illustrate the principles set forth in the dream book (1900), which appeared about the time the analysis was being conducted. (It took four years before he felt ready to publish the case history.)

In the process of reconstructing this unknown past, however, Freud acts in himself, betraying the middle-aged man's nostalgic and various response to youthful femininity and the defenses marshalled to contain yet express his longings for renewal. All older men are fascinated by daughters and other young girls—by their purity, wantonness, and their vitality. We are all of us Herr K., Humbert Humbert (Nabokov, *Lolita*), Van Veen (Nabokov, *Ada*), as we seek to pinion that which we envy, admire, and pursue endlessly in women—the butterfly, our immortal soul. Even an upright man, like Freud in his prime, cannot escape the allure. Rather than heed her tacit cautionaries and demur (by his own admission naive as yet about the forces of transference), Freud will find himself confronting Dora and teasing her according to the dictates of *her* unconscious desires for him. (No wonder he has taken such pains to liken the analytic to a *dispassionate* but gynecologic exploration!)

In this context, Dora reports her famous "first dream," its manifest content a recurrent one, but dreamt again as if this time for her analysis:

A house was on fire. My father was standing beside my bed and woke me up. I dressed quickly. Mother wanted to stop and save her jewel case; but father said: "I refuse to let myself and my children be burnt for the sake of your precious jewel case." We hurried downstairs, and as soon as I was outside I woke up. (1905a, p. 64).

Freud enjoins Dora to associate to the dream's various images and verbalizations, in the process now familiar to us all. He thereby demonstrates the connection between the "daytime thought," a sort of "entrepreneur," and the "capitalist" or unconscious wish, rooted in childhood desires, which energizes it, moving the day residue to empower the images of the night. Fearful at L. that Herr K. would surprise her while dressing, Dora has responded to the present sexual danger with references to the female genitalia (the jewel case) and allusions to her masturbation and enuresis (fire) as a child. Rivalry over her father's gifts of jewelry to her mother in her associations further tells of current and past oedipal triangles (not fully conceptualized as such at the time, of course). Sexual indiscretions on her father's part—his syphilis—had led to her mother's vaginal catarrh, an affliction also suffered by Dora as a child in identification with her mother.

On the verge of completing his dream interpretation, Freud tries a "little experiment." He alludes to the matches on his table. In children, playing with fire, he suggests, is a euphemism for and a displaced expression of autoerotic activity that excites urethral urges and leads often to bedwetting.

Now Freud's experiment, a shared fantasy or daydream, elicits responses in the patient similar to his own. Just as the interpretation of the dream seems nearly finished, Dora, in a tertiary elaboration, introduces an addendum that ties the dream to the analytic situation. She remembers the smell of smoke upon awakening. As Freud has noted, this afterthought, the forgotten detail, betrays an especially heartfelt effort at repression (1905a). In particular, he continues, this aroma pertains to Herr K.'s smoking and to his own. It is Freud now whose interpretations and innuendoes threaten to undress and molest her, violating Dora's *psychic* privacy and innocence.

In association to the conflict Freud's teasing has evoked, Dora has already reacted with wordless daydreams of her own making. Like the smell of smoke, these are actions that elude verbalization, the cognitive lexicon of the adult, and therefore, the fully conscious verbal representation, recall, and reflection.

Freud will treat this act merely as "symptomatic," indeed symbolic, not as a thing in itself conveying a specific and highly structured longing of one person for another. He has already conveyed meaning in action, rather boyishly. He has "played secrets" as if he had been poised to play with matches himself. The allusion to the derivatives of masturbation is, of course, an ingenious one, an intuition into the particulars of childhood play. Unfortunately, Dora, it becomes clear, does not embrace Freud's sagacity but, rather, reacts unconsciously to the mode in which the interpretation is couched and to the interpreter as if he were a Peeping Tom of a brother who had no business titillating her. Later critics have underscored the literal manner in which unconscious apperceptions transliterate what we consciously dismiss as mere metaphor or wit. How well Freud might have heeded not only the dream book, which the Dora case was intended to substantiate, but his joke book (1905c) as well.

In the opening reverie, Dora has played with her purse—opening and closing her now infamous reticule, putting her finger in it and then withdrawing it. Later she conceals in it an innocuous letter from her grandmother. Freud confronts her coquettish communication by saying that *she* is playing secrets with him and revealing how she once played with herself. True enough, but the verbal reading of the act and of the dream is incomplete and, as a result, is more provocative of resistance than conducive to insight. The intervention omits Dora's identifying with Freud's titillation, his implicit playing with fire, his penetrating her psychic privacy, his subsequent withdrawing into neutrality and mere commentary, and his provoking her by suggesting and then reneging on half-wanted promises of intimacy.

And there is something more to this evidence of countertransference, to the vague, unwanted lasciviousness, and to the sibling sadism and incestuous rumblings whispered in Freud's banter with the girl whose tender years elude his articulation (if not his sensibility). In tickling her fancy and in scaring her, Freud has entered Dora's domain, the postoedipal province, the night of her enuretic latency. At one level, as I have implied, he has enacted the role of cousin and brother, tutoring her in the mysteries of masturbation and bedwetting. More significant, when he pinpoints the opening and closing of the little purse, he reveals, I believe, his unconscious and *trial identification with her feminine anatomy.* He feels for her acts, as if they were his own, much as a male onlooker is unconsciously intrigued by his vicariously positioning himself in the place of a female stripper. Most latency-age children are still at heart ambisexual, whatever their protests to the contrary (Blos 1962; Bettelheim 1954). Both Freud and his patient reverberate with this secret knowledge of each other. Later Freud speaks of his underestimating the "masculine" and "gynecophilic" currents in *her* psychic life, cross-sexual trends that find a counterpart in his own.

Moreover, Freud's understanding seems not to encompass the totality of Dora's reverie in motion. At one level, hers is an unconscious fantasy of penetration, an admission of her earlier autoerotic or self-penetration, most probably accompanying masturbatory scenarios of being invaded. Still, at another level her fantasy is the very wish from which she has fled. The playing with the reticule is, like the manifest dream contents, a by-product of both impulse and defense—an expression of psychic compromise. More important, her behavior is also a sensorimotor daydream, a further regression to preoedipal days, when a daughter might revel in the exhibitionistic pleasures afforded by the father's gaze without the complications of oedipal and postoedipal desire and conflict. Moreover, her behavior sheds light on the potentially paradoxical meaning of the dream. Dora does not really seek a genital encounter but, rather, hopes to be rescued from her mother's claustrophobic hold by the attentions of her father and those of Freud. She wishes to be left poised on the threshold of a future and to be released from the invasive and exploitative narcissism of all the adults around her. Her wish is appropriate to adolescence, as it is to the preoedipal genital (phallic) narcissism of a girl in quest of optimal distance and a manageable seductiveness from all her love objects. It is a wish ideally answered in the transference and its well-timed interpretation.

The theme recurs in the second dream and, during the course of her associations, in allusions to another of Dora's wordless reveries. Once again modes of apperception *other* than the verbal are telling:

> I was walking about in a strange town . . . streets and squares . . . were strange to me. Then I came into a house where I lived . . . my room . . . and found a letter from Mother. She wrote saying that as I had come home without my parents' knowledge. She had not wished to write to say that Father was ill. Now he is dead, and if you like you can come. I then went to the station and asked about a hundred times [where it was]. . . . I always got the answer: "Five minutes." I then saw a thick wood before me which I went into, and there I asked a man whom I met. He said to me: "Two and one half hours more." He offered to accompany me. But I refused and went alone. . . . I had the usual feeling of anxiety in dreams when one cannot move forward. Then I was home. I must have been travelling in the meantime, but know nothing about that. I . . . enquired for our flat. The maidservant opened the door and replied that Mother and the others were already in the cemetery . . . (1905a, p. 94)

Even more than the first dream, the manifest content of this second report comes to life in a rich web of associations that ultimately lead to the latent dream itself. Freud emphasizes that the funereal theme points to Dora's wish for revenge against those who have falsely professed their love and care for her. Through the transference, these objects of unrequited love have come to include Freud. Thus, these two-and-one-half hours are a reference to the sessions remaining in her analysis and as Dora's associations reveal, the allusion to a fortnight's notice that a governess gives her employer is to Herr K.'s peccadilloes with the nursemaid on whom he practiced the same Svengalian wiles he used on Dora. The mother's presence is a further signal of oedipal rivalry and prohibition in Dora's longing for the father.

As in the first dream, however, sensation indicates another meaning. Dora is anxious because she feels she cannot move forward, yet discovers she has traveled all the while, progressing unawares. In one of her associations she finds herself, like her wandering male guest, standing and gazing two hours upon the Sistine Madonna—associations that Freud aptly analyzes in reference to Dora's fascination with the purity of the virgin mother. Like the olfactory registration of the smoke, however, the kinesthetic sense of immobility and stillness—both waking phenomena—akin to daydreams, further pertain directly to the transference. Dora wants smoke, not fire. She wishes to move without moving, without her own conscious agency. She yearns once more to be looked at herself, to be seen, even studied but not invaded, not yet; she does not want any man to enter the thick wood of her genital or her psyche. Her development, her true progress, requires calm and composure. Without this stance on the part of her objects, she loses the representation of paternal protection, a safe alternative necessary if she is to be lured and wrested from the hold of her tainted but obsessively clean mother. Without this guarantee of protection, her father does indeed "die," fading as a father, and she must dress quickly and fall back into angry and embittered self-absorption. To accent only the vindictive ingredients in Dora's oedipal constellation, in its both positive and negative dimensions, is to overlook the structure in which the unconscious fantasy has already become conscious—at the level of sensation verging on perception—and to sidestep a developmental imperative. I believe that these omissions contributed to the fragmentation and interruption of Dora's analysis.

At the moment of the analysis's "fragmentation," both Freud and Dora have pulled back, she fleeing in characteristically hysteric and reactive fashion, Freud retreating behind his physician's role. He has already distanced himself by interpreting solely her wishes, slighting her fears and her conscience—all in a kind of psychic rape. As she prepares to leave, he shifts to the side of the superego and finds himself indirectly judging her, unconsciously spurning her for defensive reasons—accenting her wish for revenge and perhaps ignoring his own. When she then returns to pay homage unconsciously to his narcissistic, we would say phallic, pride, he fails to hear her hidden request for a similar admiration and affirmation. Freud's accent on Dora's vindictiveness may even betray his unconscious fear of retaliation for having invaded her psyche. Undoubtedly, her earlier flight has undone his analytic work. Having been left by young Dora, he summons up his authority, the stature of the extraordinary professor, to conceal and impel his own embitterment. Concluding that she is not now in earnest, he tells her to leave again, for good.

Thus, Freud helps reenact a variation on the traumas of seduction and abandonment that Dora has repeatedly suffered in her real life. Moreover, the oscillation between innuendo and psychological closeness verging on violation, on the one hand, and an abrupt remoteness when challenged or found out, on the other, are reminiscent of the typical ambivalence and inconsistencies of fathers in responding to an adolescent girl's emergent sexuality.

To return to the other side of the dialogue: Dora responds to the advances and rebuffs of her various father figures with terror, hurt, and rage, afraid of the loss of generational boundaries and stung by their repeated, almost deliberate failures to honor her love for them. Her father's inability to reciprocate her devotion finds a stark denouement in his casting her off, as if selling her into prostitution by exposing her to Herr K.'s self-serving, lewd sexuality. With Freud she probably feels that she suffers an oblique and subliminal repetition of these insensitivities.

Brilliant as his reconstruction of the course of her symptoms is, especially during her postoedipal development, Freud inevitably omits the earliest forms of overstimulation and damage possibly done at the father's hands and repeated in adolescence. In a developmental and object relational context, as I have said, Dora's opening and closing of the reticule not only intimates conflicting impulses but may signify the roots of her adolescent ruminations in interactions and/or longings from her preoedipal years. Indeed, it seems that she is exhibiting her genital to Freud's view, as he suspects, but not merely for (symbolic) gratification. The enactment is also a communication, a preverbal appeal, no doubt repeated many times over (Freud had not yet conceptualized the repetition compulsion), in her behavior, her memories, and her recurring dreams. Dora yearns to be admired, but from afar—to have her selfhood made vibrant and clear. It is the sort of quest one sees in the coquettishness of the two- or three-year-old flirt, to whom I turn shortly as she wrests herself from her mother's hold and searches out male admirers, above all wooing her father, thereby seeking images of other objects and of a self apart from the dual unity whence she came.

Dora's identification with the male wanderer and onlooker in her concluding dream has invited Freud, and by extension her father, to put himself once again in her place and to intuit the delicate balance sought among her competing needs and wishes. Look at me lest I leave, Dora the dreamer seems to say; wordlessly, look but don't move, don't touch like Herr K! I need the safety and the pleasure at once. I need your gaze and, as much as a baby and penis in fantasy, I *wish to be seen in reality.* Lure me gently into your universe, allowing both of us composure and containment in intimacy.

Dora's need for optimal distance from both primary objects becomes the father's and the analyst's prime task. Without such relatedness, in fact, her father and analyst abdicate their parental role, further compromising the femininity of the daughter's self-representation. At the oedipal level, she is robbed of the initiative to reach forward and so collapses into an angry and immobilized self wedded to the worst aspects of unity with her mother, and of their shared representation. Like her mother's, Dora's vagina seems sullied. Indeed, we learn later that she has been forced to participate in her mother's psychotic house cleaning.

Freud had chosen the pseudonym Dora as a reference to his sister Rosa's nursemaid (1905a). A servant without much say in her employer's home, she had been compelled by her employer to change hers from Rosa lest she confuse the household by challenging the prerogative of her mistress, the real mother. A serving girl of sorts, nursemaid to her father—identified with the K.'s governess—Dora had also been similarly disinherited.

The Eye-Vulva Dialogue

I am reminded of a recent episode from the analysis of a father of an infant girl, one that reveals similar conflicts to those of Freud in reacting to the mere promise of Dora's femininity. Contemplating the treatment's forthcoming termination after many years, the patient succumbed to the irritable bowel syndrome long ago analyzed and largely resolved. As is typical in termination, the resurgence of the symptom represents an effort to undo the work and to cling to the analyst. He does not want to lose the analyst, who, he feels, has substituted for volatile and defective parents, providing him with the stability necessary to deal with the demands of his own fatherhood. In the past, he remarks, identification with his mother as the aggressor and his defensive misogyny, which masked his wishes to be a mother, would have distanced him from his baby girl or possibly moved him to act abusively. Now his impatience and hostility are more than counterbalanced by his love for "my little girl, Sara." In the midst of his musings, he pauses to visualize the intestines plaguing him. He thinks of two spots and imagines them for a moment to be ovaries, of all things! "I wonder," he continues, "do I want to be a baby like Sara or a girl for once? Do I want to start all over like her and be anything I could—it took me so long to realize that I wanted to be like a woman sometimes. When I saw her vulva after she was born, my feelings were different from before. I used to think of girls as the have-nots, but her crack seemed to reach up forever. It doesn't scare me, it's beautiful." He remembers getting angry, foolishly, at the "little twat when she puked all over me this morning. Then I remembered I had just shat my brains out, like her. Come to think of it, maybe there's a new twist to this G.I. crap. Maybe I want to be her."

Another anecdote: Fourteen years ago I was doing research in nursery schools on the evolving wishes of little boys to bear and rear babies. On one occasion, I found myself alone in an elevator with an adorable four-year-old girl with raven curls, navy knee socks, and a Black Watch kilt skirt. She didn't take her eyes off me as we traveled up from the basement to the sixth floor, smiling unabashedly slyly from beneath the curve of her cheeks. The elevator was a slow one and our solitude uninterrupted by any further passengers. By the third floor she had begun to fidget. Between four and five, just short of the journey's end, she could no longer contain herself. Lifting up her skirt to expose her underpants, she grinned and squealed, "Aren't I pretty?!" She let it drop gaily, the doors opened, and we went our separate ways—Oh yes, I had said, "Yes"—never seeing each other again.

Related but more systematic observations of young girls and their fathers have been made by Herzog (1980). Especially from the second half of the second year, it is the father, in these studies, who sanctions and affirms from afar a toddler's masturbation involving labia, vulva, and, to some extent, the clitoris. Mothers, in contrast, tend to be either overtly repelled or quietly disapproving. At least their flirtation's "ocular relationship," to borrow from Nabokov, is the ideal. Other fathers from a less savvy sample of my own (see Ross 1979b) did tend to retreat from their daughter's genitals and from the girls themselves, probably because of the castration anxiety stirred by the daughter's anatomy and by some of the conflictual longings dealt with earlier in the chapter. Nor can one ignore a daughter's equally prepotent and simultaneous desires to see her father's penis and to watch him urinating. These desires are both fierce wishes and universal behaviors, according to Galenson (1982) and colleagues. Moreover, when juxtaposed with a daughter's average and expected exhibitionism, the wishes demonstrate once more the ready interchangeability of subject and object in all instinctual vicissitudes—a seeming paradox first illuminated by Freud in his paper on the subject (Freud 1911).

The instinctual paradox is solved, as Freud implied and as we now know, in understanding the tenuous and incomplete differentiation of self and object representations early in development. A daughter's intense wishes to see and to be seen both derive from this developmental immaturity and bespeak a striving to get beyond it, namely, to get away from her mother. They arise first of all within a complex context of the rapprochement subphase (Mahler et al. 1975) characterized by a number of cognitive object relational and libidinal achievements: the emergence of representational thinking and the symbolic function; object constancy; an awareness of anatomical difference; the establishment of core gender identity from eighteen to thirty months (Stoller 1968); an early genital phase, particularly pronounced for girls. During this time, the child's unreliable and meager language repertoire is not yet sufficient to ensure affective distance from the mother or to invite others to relate to the child. Instead, as the "ambitendent" comings and goings of the toddler suggest (Mahler et al. 1975), locomotion—approach and avoidance—provides the major means of engaging with and disengaging from objects. However, in girls, often more visually inclined from infancy on, and possibly predisposed by anatomical destiny toward taking in, according to Erikson (1964), looking toward and showing may very well offer alternatives to cruder motorics or to evolving verbal skills.

In that inceptive mode a daughter begins to turn to her father as her first distinct "other" object; contact and cuddling are not yet critical. Indeed, quite the contrary, the space inherent in their ocular relatedness is desirable in itself—contrasting with the tactile, enveloping transactions with her mother—and helps to crystallize a separate and individuated body image. Her eye and vulva are equated as the little girl stares at her father while inviting him to look upon her genital and herself. Pleasure is discovered not as much in the self-stimulation often accompanying the behavior as it is in the act and emerging idea of *seeing onself being seen*.

Perhaps the same prototypic rivalry noted by Abelin (1975) for boys but not for girls pertains here. One objective of the female toddler is to wrest her father's attention from mother and focus it on herself. More to the point, however, this gender-specific figure, whose penis she has either sensed or seen outright, provides a counterpoint to her mother's diffuse presence and a mirror for a self-representation difficult to define. Whereas a boy will ultimately disidentify from mother by finding his body and himself in his father, a girl, by virtue of her anatomical similarity to the primacy and quasi-symbiotic caregiver, remains wedded to her, stuck in a "dual unity" forever.

In fact, the near ubiquity of precociously flirtatious behaviors like these lead me to disagree with Abelin's notion that, in contrast to boys, girls are not significantly affected by paternal insufficiency during the rapprochement subphase, or more generally, the preoedipal era, and are not vulnerable to their fathers' absence until the subsequent oedipal phase. The observational studies to which I have alluded, further confirm the existence of early triangulation and sex-specific relatedness in the ontogeny of the girl's self-identity. In private, at least in study groups, James Herzog (pers. comm.) has spoken of the "penis-to-penis" dialogue of fathers and sons. With daughters, the preverbal (and ongoing) discourse becomes one between eye and vulva, "an eye-vulva dialogue" cast in a more or less incorporative and subsequently gender-specific inceptive modality.

Later in life, many girls and women are driven to seek male "admirers" in order to affirm and delineate their very existence. Indeed, long after the oedipal period, a daughter will remain erotically affiliated with her father, using him and his proxies to draw her out of her structureless beginnings.

This progressive thrust, more than any structural deficit and more than an inadequate superego (Freud 1924, 1925, 1931, 1933), is what probably underlies the persistence of incestuous, and quite specifically exhibition-istic, wishes in girls. For boys, in contrast, the paternal castration threat conspires with the dangers of reengulfment and total regression, to make mothers off limits. In becoming close to another woman, a young man may discover that the terror of being engulfed is exactly what he yearns for, and finds some measure of, in the erotic little death.

This dialogue of father and daughter becomes an ongoing intrapsychic exchange, it seems. With the advent of words and with progressive inter-nalization, fathers continue to whisper in their daughters' minds and hearts about how wonderful they can be (see Tessman 1982). Long after a father's presence has become a memory, a daughter continues to cleave to him in various incarnations. Nor, as I have noted, does the oedipal father pose the same threat to a daughter's individuation as does a mother to a son's. Hence the omnipresent potential of father-daughter incest which, failing to challenge society's generational order, is far more common than inter-course between mothers and overreaching sons. Moreover, even in the face of potential transgression, father and daughter, through much of their lives, can exchange many tolerable intimacies of the sort denied to mothers and sons.

To summarize, I suggest that it is the gaze, the look, of the father—itself a convergence of conflicting vectors—to which daughters respond above all. Although they seek their fathers' affirmation of the beauty of their vaginas and thus of their feminine selves, daughters are not merely making restitution for their lack of a penis. Penis envy alone is not responsible for the intense exhibitionistic excitement and anxiety we see in many female patients, most of whom have significant screen memories and fantasies organized around their fathers' seeing or almost seeing their vulva. The wish to be gazed upon does not result *only* from a defensive compromise-formation in the face of more frightening, guilt-ridden urges to be pene-trated and impregnated, but from even more primal aspirations and imper-atives.

As I have stressed, this quest for admiration is also an appeal to be wrested from the mother's hold, the grip of her imagined vagina-womb, her orbit. At a higher level, it is also a yearning to be penetrated visually, to be plumbed beneath the surface vulva and to know therefore that one has a vagina and a womb of one's own, which takes in as it is taken in—a desire to be a powerful mother oneself. These wishes are wordless, cast in images, felt, and enacted in sensorimotor corollaries: the feeling of being seen and of watching all the while, as if surveying the two separate actors in the dyadic drama—self and father.

Later in the Life Cycle: Crazy about Their Bodies

The desire to be admired by a man lies, as Ethel Person (1983) has noted, at the very core of a woman's heterosexuality. The disjunction between a woman's central desire and the primary motives in a man's erotic life—to conquer mother, woman, and then to unite with her (Ross 1985), accounts for the derailment in romantic and everyday relationships between men and women of all ages (Ross and Kakar 1987). Without the affirmation that comes with feeling loved by a man, many women tell us, they become incapable of distinguishing themselves from images of their mothers—often at their worst. Without a man to look longingly upon them, in fact, their body image, even their reflection in the mirror, especially when they are most anxious, tends to collapse into amorphism, merging or becoming overladen with the diffuse picture of the mother's physical form. And these are not psychotic women, who exhibit signs of dedifferentiation in the absence of exhibitionistic supplies.

For example, a colleague from Boston describes the following case. An accomplished and very pretty, obsessive-compulsive woman, a lawyer in her mid-thirties, had sought analysis with her because of a history of aborted marriages and love affairs, which had left her childless. A recurring daydream from adolescence had her cast as a freedom fighter in Spain, a wife of a handsome man, and a mother to his beautiful daughter, who looked just like her. In the end, the husband and child were blown up in the war. She later returned to Spain to pay homage to La Passionaria, the woman guerrilla chieftaine. Masturbation fantasies involving a sister pointed to the erotic dimensions of this strong tie, evident as well in her verbatim reports of any exchange with her mother. These scenes were etched in bolder relief than those with her lover or the powerful men and women with whom she did business.

Now, Ms. K. had long outstripped her mother in work, and after losing weight in adolescence, she had become much prettier than her mother. Her one comparative shortcoming was her barrenness, a symptom, to be sure, but also a sacrifice to her stellar career. Her men had seemed more charismatic than her own father, a dentist with a flabby body like her mother's. She said that she had never seen him naked, though the outline of his penis had once been discernible through his briefs. Her controlling mother's body she did recall, however, along with her repulsion at the obesity and the small sagging breasts. Having never felt good enough about herself—though by no means a hard-core narcissist—she was compelled to seek approval from people, men in particular, and to work to the breaking point in order to satisfy her own standards.

At one point, her boyfriend of two years became ill and sexually disinterested for several weeks. At first, the patient succumbed to jealously obsessional thoughts about being betrayed that had plagued her throughout her adult life. She rationalized her jealousy because of J.'s history of many affairs before meeting him, but her self-torture, in the long run, revealed her erotized attachment to a mother who had invaded and controlled her body's private parts when she was little. Now and then she also evoked the masturbation fantasies disguising the same terrifying negative oedipal wishes. Her weak body image regressed to its depths as she anticipated her Canadian parents' visit for the weekend. She stared at her face and nude torso in the mirror, hard put to distinguish her sharply defined features, trim body and well-shaped breasts from the pudgy, sagging figure of the older woman. For a moment, this highly organized woman seemed to see her mother's image imposed on her own.

Now, as a child, she had been fat and big-nosed, both defects corrected (through will power and surgery) when she was in her midteens. To some extent she lived with an outworn "body ego." More important, however, her young and emotionally vulnerable mother had discouraged her flirtations with the patient's father. Thus, in one screen memory she remembered herself at age four, wearing a pretty dress (not the pants her mother gave her) as she prepared to be taken on a date by her father to see Cinderella. At the last minute, her mother had intruded and aborted their plans. Associations led predictably to her mother's rivalry with her for her husband's attentions. Beyond these positive oedipal (and counteroedipal) motives, however, the patient reconstructed her mother's competition with her father for *her*. Discouraging their intimacy and constantly criticizing both the daughter's and father's appearance, she had laid claim to the former's body—punishing her for early fecal play, penetrating her anus with thermometers and enemas, later entering her vagina with a suppository on the occasion of her first vaginal infection. The girl and her father had not been free to adore each other, and thus the patient had never escaped her mother's hold. Even as a heterosexual and highly successful adult, she was doomed to abort her relationships and repeatedly to return to pay homage at the lesser woman's throne.

Penis envy and castrative urges did appear in this woman's associations from time to time, but *not* in the context of her exhibitionistic strivings. Rather, they were most evident when her lovers, as her father, disappointed her expectations, proving less resourceful, powerful, and generous than she had hoped or had initially perceived them to be. Releasing her rage, she retaliated by saying that they had failed her: they lacked the wherewithal, the "balls," to fight her mother for her. Indeed, this transferential struggle—this constant testing of Dr. A's resolve—was what the patient's analysis was all about.

Conclusions

I have highlighted a few of the many conflicts that can either dim or enlighten the eye of the father as he beholds his daughter. Out of her elemental dance before "daddy" emerges a view of herself that will be internalized according to her own fantastical imperatives and her complex, unfolding psychic structure, determining the nature and quality of a woman's sexual and self-identities, her self-love, her expectations of others and, to some degree, even her initiative in work.

In analysis, our task is, as always, not only to open the portals to the patient's unconscious fantasy but also to liberate his or her imaginings, speculations, intuitions, and perceptions regarding the parents' inner lives and often disavowed agenda (Ross 1982, 1985). Daughters must allow themselves insight into their fathers' unconscious or veiled intentions and reactions to them if they are not to be wounded forever by what their parents have revealed and what they have felt.

Thus, one woman, en route to a raging, positive oedipal transference and to a reconstruction of her long forgotten eroticism, made a telling parapraxis when she recalled her father's fury at her makeup and short skirts during her teenage years. She had meant to say that he went "apeshit" but found herself uttering "bullshit" instead. With this slip and its analysis, the image of her father as merely an austere ogre faded to reveal oedipal and even earlier scenes between the two. Indeed, he proved to be the most tender of parents—having filled in for her mother. The recollected encounters were suffused with a tender sensuousness—being bathed and dried, sitting in his lap, creeping into his bed, riding in his car—memories that had become frighteningly realistic with the sexual possibilities promised by the changes of early adolescence. Maybe she had known their true feelings for each other all along, striving to protect both him and herself from dangerous truths by colluding in shared defensive stereotypes and hostilities, and by conforming to our culture's false truism that fathers and daughters—in contrast to sons—do not matter as much to one another.

REFERENCES

Abelin, E. 1971. "The Role of the Father in the Separation-Individuation Process." In *Separation-Individuation,* ed. J. McDevitt and C. Settlage. New York: International Universities Press.

———. 1975. "Some Further Comments and Observations on the Earliest Role of the Father." *International Journal of Psycho-Analysis* 56:293.

———. 1977. "The Role of the Father in Core Gender Identity and in Psychosexual Differentiation." Read to the American Psychoanalytic Association, Quebec.

Bettelheim, B. 1954. *Symbolic Wounds.* Glencoe, Ill.: Free Press.

Blos, P. 1962. *On Adolescence.* New York: Free Press.

Cath, S. H. 1962. "Grief, Loss and Emotional Disorders in the Aging Process." In *Geriatric Psychiatry,* ed. M.A. Berezin and S.H. Cath. New York: International Universities Press.

Deutsch, F. 1957. "A Footnote to Freud's 'Fragment of an analysis of a case of hysteria.'" *Psychoanalytic Quarterly* 26:159–67.

Erikson, E. H. 1962. "Reality and actuality." *Journal of the American Psychoanalytic Association* 10:451–74.

———. 1963. *Childhood and Society.* New York: W. W. Norton.

———. 1964. *Insight and Responsibility.* New York: W. W. Norton.

Freud, S., and Breuer, J. [1895] 1955. "Studies on Hysteria." In *Standard Edition,* ed. J. Strachey, vol. 2, London: Hogarth Press.

Freud, S. [1900] 1953. "The Interpretation of Dreams." In *Standard Edition,* ed. J. Strachey, vols. 4–5. London: Hogarth Press.

———. [1901] 1960. "The Psychopathology of Everyday Life." In *Standard Edition,* ed. J. Strachey, vol. 6. London: Hogarth Press.

———. [1905a] 1953. "Fragment of an Analysis of a Case of Hysteria." In *Standard Edition,* ed. J. Strachey, vol. 7, pp. 7–122. London: Hogarth Press.

———. [1905b] 1953. "Three Essays on the Theory of Sexuality." In *Standard Edition,* ed. J. Strachey, vol. 7, pp. 135–243. London: Hogarth Press.

———. [1905c] 1953. "Jokes and Their Relation to the Unconscious." In *Standard Edition,* ed. J. Strachey, vol. 8. London: Hogarth Press.

———. [1910] 1957. "A Special Type of Object Choice Made by Men." In *Standard Edition,* ed. J. Strachey, vol. 11, pp. 163–76.

———. [1911] 1958. "Psychoanalytic Notes upon an Autobiographical Account of a Case of Paranoia. In *Standard Edition,* ed. J. Strachey, vol. 12, pp. 1–84. London: Hogarth Press.

———. [1914a] 1955. "Some Reflections on Schoolboy Psychology." In *Standard Edition,* ed. J. Strachey, vol. 13, pp. 239–44. London: Hogarth Press.

———. [1914c] 1957. "On Narcissism: An Introduction." In *Standard Edition,* ed. J. Strachey, vol. 14, pp. 69–102. London: Hogarth Press.

———. [1915c] 1957. "Instincts and Their Vicissitudes." In *Standard Edition,* ed. J. Strachey, vol. 14, pp. 111–40. London: Hogarth Press.

———. [1924] 1961. "The Dissolution of the Oedipus Complex." In *Standard Edition,* ed. J. Strachey, vol. 19, pp. 173–79. London: Hogarth Press.

———. [1925] 1961. "Some Psychical Consequences of the Anatomical Distinction between the Sexes." In *Standard Edition,* ed. J. Strachey, vol. 19, pp. 243–58. London: Hogarth Press.

————. [1931] 1961. "Female Sexuality." In *Standard Edition,* ed. J. Strachey, vol. 21, pp. 221–43. London: Hogarth Press.

————. [1933] 1964. "New Introductory Lectures on Psychoanalysis." In *Standard Edition,* ed. J. Strachey, vol. 22, pp. 1–82. London: Hogarth Press.

Galenson, E., and Roiphe, H. 1982. "The Preoedipal Relationship of a Father, Mother and Daughter." In *Father and Child,* ed. S. Cath, A. Gurwitt, and J. Ross, pp. 151–62. Boston: Little, Brown.

Glenn, J. 1980. "Freud's Adolescent Patients: Katharina, Dora and the 'Homosexual Woman.' " In *Freud and His Patients,* ed. J. Glenn and M. Kanzer, pp. 23–47. New York: Jason Aronson.

Herzog, J. 1980. "Sleep Disturbance and Father Hunger in 18- to 28- Month-Old Boys: The Erlkonig Syndrome." *Psychoanalytic Study of the Child* 35:219.

————. 1982. "On Father Hunger." In *Father and Child,* ed. S. Cath, A. Gurwitt, and J. Ross, pp. 163–74. Boston: Little, Brown.

Jacobson, E. 1964. *The Self and the Object World.* New York: International Universities Press.

Jones, E. 1961. "Early Female Sexuality." In *Papers on Psychoanalysis,* pp. 485–95. Boston: Beacon Press.

Mahl, G. 1982. "Father-Son Themes in Freud's Self-Analysis." In *Father and Child,* ed. S. Cath, A. Gurwitt, and J. Ross, pp. 33–64. Boston: Little, Brown.

Mahler, M.; Pine, F.; and Bergman, A. 1975. *The Psychological Birth of the Human Infant.* New York: Basic Books.

Marcus, I. M., and Francis, J.J. 1975. "Masturbation: A Developmental View." In *Masturbation from Infancy to Senescence,* ed. I. M. Marcus and J. J. Francis, pp. 9–52. New York: International Universities Press.

Masson, J. M. 1985. *The Assault on Truth: Freud's Suppression of the Seduction Theory.* New York: Farrar, Straus & Giroux.

Nabokov, V. [1969] 1981. *Ada or Ardor: A Family Chronicle.* New York: McGraw-Hill.

———— [1955] 1982. *Lolita.* New York: Berkley Books.

Person, E. S. 1983. "The Erotic Transference in Women and Men: Differences and Consequences." Keynote address to the winter meeting of the American Academy of Psychoanalysis, San Juan, Puerto Rico. Panel Report: American Psychoanalytic Association, December Meetings, New York, 1985.

Ross, J. M. 1975. "The Development of Paternal Identity." *Journal of the American Psychoanalytic Association* 23:783–817.

————. 1979a. "Fathering: A Review of Some Psychoanalytic Contributions on Paternity." *International Journal of Psycho-analysis* 60:317.

————. 1979b. "The Forgotten Father." In *Psychosexual Imperatives: Their Impact on Identity-Formation,* ed. M. Nelson and J. Ikenberry, pp. 261–303. New York: Human Sciences Press.

————. 1982. "From Mother to Father: The Boy's Search for a Generative Identity and the Oedipal Era." In *Father and Child,* ed. S. Cath, A. Gurwitt, and J. Ross, pp. 189–204. Boston: Little, Brown.

————. 1985. "The Sins of the Father." In *Parental Influences in Health and Disease,* ed. E. J. Anthony and G. Pollock, pp. 477–510. Boston: Little, Brown.

Ross, J. M., and Kakar, S. 1987. *Tales of Love, Sex and Danger.* New York: Basil Blackwell.

Shakespeare, W. [c. 1605] 1942. *King Lear.* In *The Complete Plays and Poems of William*

Shakespeare, ed. W. A. Neilson and C. J. Hill, pp. 1136–1179. Cambridge, Mass.: Houghton Mifflin.

Spitz, R. 1965. *The First Year of Life.* New York: International Universities Press.

Stoller, R. 1968. *Sex and Gender,* New York: Science House.

Tessman, L. 1982. "A Note on Father's Contribution to the Daughter's Ways of Loving and Working." In *Father and Child,* ed. S. Cath, A. Gurwitt, and J. Ross. Boston: Little, Brown.

DISCUSSION

In an earlier volume (Colarusso and Nemiroff 1981), we described fatherhood, not as a biological event or a psychological state limited to one phase of life, but rather as a complex developmental task that extends throughout the life cycle. We suggested that midlife (ages thirty-five to sixty) is particularly formative in the evolution of paternal identity because of phase-specific interactions between the developing middle-aged father and his developing adolescent children. Parental response was characterized not only as a reaction to adolescent behavior and development but also as a result of equally (or more salient) developmental forces *within the parent* that are impinged upon by the adolescent or child.

We find strong affinity between our work and that of John Munder Ross. During the past fifteen years he has published a number of cogent studies of fatherhood (Ross 1979, 1982, 1985), stressing the subtle interplay and evolution of the dynamics between fathers and their sons and daughters.

In this chapter he continues his creative investigations into the lifelong vicissitudes of the paternal identity and role as, in his term, a "protracted adult developmental crisis." He notes how psychoanalysts are used to searching out the starker truths of adult psychological life by going backward, looking for their genesis in longings and conflicts of the child. Then he reverses direction and proceeds directly to middle and old age to discover the vulnerable and regressed *father's need* of the daughter, giving as vivid examples King Lear, Freud's relationship with his patient Dora, and instances from his own psychoanalytic practice.

He also presents brief excerpts from treatments of some adult women, illustrating their lifelong reliance on exhibitionistic supplies tendered by men who found themselves acting as preoedipal and oedipal paternal transference figures. One of Ross's central theses is that such gratification is necessary if these women are to sustain *individuation* of their body images and senses of self of distinct from their mothers (the pull toward reimmersion never fully abating), as well as a physical sense of self-esteem and well-being. He describes how being admired in adult life revives the "eye-vulva" object relational and libidinal dialogues between father and daughter. These interchanges begin during a little girl's second year and continue, becoming reciprocally conflict-laden, as she progresses through the oedipal era, into adolescence, and through adult life.

He discusses how Shakespeare intuited the enduring truth of an old man's sense of loss and depletion (Cath 1962). In his daughters, an older man looks for his mother/wife, who was once his "better half," and thus hopes for restoration and youthful revival.

Focusing on the father-daughter interaction, Ross reanalyzes Freud's analysis of Dora and notes that through the countertransference Freud betrays the middle-aged man's nostalgic response to youthful femininity by expressing his own longings to be younger. Frequently, older men are fascinated by daughters and other young girls—their purity and wantonness, and by the vitality that they seem to proffer. Ross captures that yearning beautifully:

> We are all of us Herr K., Humbert Humbert (Nabokov, *Lolita*), Van Veen
> (Nabokov, *Ada*), as we seek to pinion that which we envy, admire, and
> pursue endlessly in women—the butterfly, our immortal soul. (P. 55)

Unwittingly then, Freud helped reenact a variation on the trauma of seduction and abandonment Dora had suffered in her life. Ross maintains that the oscillations between Freud and Dora, between innuendo and psychological closeness verging on violation, on the one hand, and abrupt distancing when challenged or found out, on the other, are typical of the ambivalences and inconsistencies in the responses of "fathers" to the emergent sexuality of adolescent girls.

Ross sensitively describes the little girl's wish to be admired by her father. He reexamines the concluding dream of Dora's treatment, pointing out her identification with the male wanderer and onlooker, and her invitation to Freud, and by extension to her father, to put himself in her place, to intuit the delicate balance she was seeking among her competing needs and wishes:

> Look at me lest I leave, Dora the dreamer seems to say; wordlessly, look
> but don't move, don't touch like Herr K! I need the safety and the
> pleasure at once. I need your gaze and, as much as a baby and penis in
> fantasy, *I wish to be seen in reality.* Lure me gently into your universe,
> allowing both of us composure and containment in intimacy. (P. 60)

Ross feels that what the Doras want is optimal distance from both primary objects, and providing that distance is the father's and the analyst's prime task. Despite the wish for distance there is also a need for appropriate relatedness, and in his opinion both father and analyst abdicated the parental role in Dora's case, further compromising the femininity of the girl's self-representation. Moreover, at the oedipal level, she was robbed of her motivation to reach forward—her "initiative" and "purpose"—and thus regressed into an angry and immobilized self, fused in symbiotic union with her mother.

Particularly with his introduction of the concept of the "eye-vulva dialogue" between fathers and daughters, Ross has made an important contribution to our perception of the way that the early father-daughter interaction affects the lifelong tasks of separation-individuation and identity formation for both parties.

REFERENCES

Cath, S. H. 1962. "Grief, Loss and Emotional Disorders in the Aging Process." In *Geriatric Psychiatry,* ed. M. A. Berezin and S. H. Cath, pp. 21–72. New York: International Universities Press.

Colarusso, C. A., and Nemiroff, R. A. 1981. "The Father at Midlife: Crisis and Growth of Paternal Identity." In *Adult Development,* pp. 315–27. New York: Plenum.

Ross, J. M. 1979. "Fathering: A Review of Some Psychoanalytic Contributions on Paternity." *International Journal of Psycho-Analysis* 60:317.

———. 1982. "From Mother to Father: The Boy's Search for a Generative Identity and the Oedipal Era." In *Father and Child,* ed. S. Cath, A. Gurwitt, and J. Ross., pp. 189–203. Boston: Little, Brown.

———. 1985. "The Sins of the Father." In *Parental Influences in Health and Disease,* ed. E.J. Anthony and G. Pollock, pp. 477–510. Boston: Little, Brown.

4

Origins and Evolution of Narcissism through the Life Cycle

LOUIS A. GOTTSCHALK

In psychoanalytic theory generally, the roots of narcissism have been placed in the preoedipal or pregenital phase of development. Some authors (Klein 1932; Heimann 1951) emphasize that early precursors of oedipal behavior and emotional responses occur at the age of two or even earlier. Although I agree that the origins of narcissism can be traced to a very early stage of development, I believe that narcissism has no necessary relationship to the oedipal phase. Moreover, the developmental lines influenced by narcissistic orientations may or may not influence thoughts, emotions, and behaviors that are recognized as having oedipal characteristics.

Sándor Ferenczi's (1913) description of the stages of the development of the sense of reality focuses on the infantile period during which narcissism exists normally. The infant's environment is experienced as nearly unconditionally supporting, nurturing, and accepting. A state of near-omnipotence and unconditional self-worth is evoked as a result of the child's complete dependence on external milieu for such necessities as warmth, food, and the maintenance of cleanliness. As long as there is not serious deprivation resulting from untoward events, the infant's experience of his surroundings is similar to his intrauterine experiences. The evolving capacity to appraise its surrounding gives the neonate repeated signals that the environment is good and caring. Feeling loved and protected without reservation, he begins to feel capable of generating this evidence of loving care when he wills it. For a period of time ranging from months to years, the emerging child acquires the impression that he can easily shape and mold ambient people and their nurturing behavior in his own behalf. This state of inner satisfaction, self-confidence, omnipotence, infallibility, and consummate entitlement can prevail for several years. The natural, nonpsychopathological self-perception of a well-cared-for child has been called the stage of "primary narcissism" in contradistinction to later stages of life when the child and the adult realize that love and praise are earned.

The word *narcissism* has been used in diverse ways (Hinsie and Shatzky 1940). Freud (1914) distinguished Havelock Ellis's (1928) use of the term "to denote the attitude of a person who treats his own body . . . in the same way in which the body of a sexual object is ordinarily treated" from his own concept of "primary and normal narcissism"; namely, "the egoism of the instinct of self-preservation, a measure of which may justifiably be attributed to every living creature" (p. 31). Crediting Ferenczi (1913), Freud acknowledged that the primary narcissism of the developing child is characterized by *megalomania,* an overestimation of the power of wishes and mental processes; the *omnipotence of thought,* a belief in the magical virtue of words; and a *method of dealing with the outer world*—the art of "magic"—which appears to be a logical application of these grandiose premises (1914). What, then, constitutes normal versus psychopathological narcissism during subsequent phases of development?

The Course of Normal and Psychopathological Narcissism through the Life Cycle

Age zero to five

Events that challenge the state and trait of primary narcissism may evoke protests from the child. Examples are abrupt withdrawal of loving care by the parent or other caregiver, the birth of a sibling, parental separation, a family move, or a physical illness suffered by the child. Going to nursery school and kindergarten place the child in milieus that force him to share limited bounty with children who have similar grandiose notions of their own place and worth in the (center of the) universe. When these challenges occur in a timely and reasonably distributed fashion, they do not incur serious narcissistic injury. In fact, they contribute to acculturation and expose the child to the reality that love and nurture are not unconditional and are more likely to be forthcoming when he performs in ways that are approved by the parents and other caregivers.

If these challenges to the child's grandiose self-conception occur at a very early age or in clusters that severely test the capacity to cope, various manifestations of narcissistic injury may appear: anxiety, phobias, depressions, sleep or eating disturbances, and psychosomatic disorders like peptic ulcer, hypertension, or colitis. Further, the very young child's ability to cope with sudden or overwhelming challenges to normal narcissism is limited to autoerotic activities like thumb sucking or dependence on transitional objects.

Overwhelmingly rejecting, cruel, or exploitive parenting can produce serious narcissistic injuries that result (through imprinting and/or defensive adaptation) in later maladaptive behavior such as early and unwanted pregnancy, child abuse, rape, multiple personality disorder, robbing, murder, and the various drug addictions including alcoholism. These patients may not be perceived by others as having a narcissistic personality disorder according to the American Psychiatric Association's DSM-III classification (1980), but they reveal their narcissistic injuries by acting out their sense of entitlement and grandiosity when they steal, murder, or otherwise engage in antisocial behavior.

At the other extreme, children who are greatly wanted and highly indulged by their parents develop a self-concept that reinforces a profound sense of their own specialness, uniqueness, and lovability. Eventually they, too, must learn that unconditional approval and love are not immediately forthcoming from everyone, although their parents may remain doting and indulgent.

Ages five to ten

The term *latency* implies that the oedipal desire to love and marry the parent of the opposite sex has been resolved and that vigorous claims to compete with a parental or other rival are temporarily quiescent. Children in this age range are generally tractable and open to the educational processes to which they are exposed. In school and at home, adults expect children to acquire knowledge according to progressively higher and more stringent standards of performance. Unconditional positive regard is minimized, and societal standards of achievement are rewarded.

Religious education, on the other hand, tends to emphasize that the individual is special, elect, and preferentially recognized by the godhead and his entourage. Such belief systems help the child, and later the adult, tolerate disappointments and frustrations resulting from minor and major narcissistic blows, and provide a sense of continuity in the face of the existential anxieties faced by everyone.

Countless stresses and vicissitudes affect an individual's sense of importance, omniscience, omnipotence, and grandiosity. Family intactness and size, the quality of parental modeling and rules, race, sex, socioeconomic factors, intelligence, physical appearance, and religion are only some of the factors that influence one's feelings of worth in our society. No one has successfully defined universal parameters of healthy self-regard and narcissism for this age range or others; perhaps it should only be attempted for specific social groups or societal subsets.

Ages eleven to twenty: adolescence

Most societies require that pubertal and adolescent youth engage the following developmental tasks:

1. Develop the capacity to understand and accept peer group customs and standards.

2. Demonstrate an understanding and appreciation of the sexual roles and responsibilities dictated by the society.

3. Acquire knowledge and skills that can be used in the pursuit of a vocation or profession.

4. Establish an identity as an individual within adolescent/adult society.

5. Learn how to love others and be loved in socially acceptable ways.

6. Develop standards for the maintenance of physical and mental health.

7. Begin to evolve a socially workable and self-respecting belief system.

The maintenance of an appropriate and healthy level of self-love is directly related to the degree of success or failure that youth encounter in engaging and mastering these developmental tasks. The permutations and combinations of favorable and unfavorable events are legion, and no attempt will be made to detail them here. At least in the Western world, adolescence is typically fraught with wide fluctuations in the expression of narcissistic claims, particularly when the goal is to gain "heaven on earth" and a durable state of unchallenged bliss (a perfect reunion with an all-giving mother). Through repeated frustrating encounters in reality, adolescents seek but fail to recapture the paradise of early childhood when they felt like the center of the universe.

The risk of self-destruction increases during adolescence as vulnerable individuals, propelled by a lack of realistic self-worth, try to leave a world that seems to ignore their unique virtues and qualities, or attempt to take masochistic revenge on caregivers and erstwhile lovers who are seen as having withheld or withdrawn support and love.

On the other hand, successes at attracting external commendation, applause, and recognition through achievements that society values can lead to a solid sense of self-confidence or, in some arenas like sports or the performing arts, to temporary overvaluation of the self and regression to the grandiosity that was normal in infancy and early childhood.

Ages twenty-one to fifty: early and middle adulthood

During the stretch of time from young adulthood to middle age, a number of themes typically enhance or impair the sense of self-importance:

1. Choosing a vocation and earning a living.

2. Pairing with another individual, usually of the opposite gender, and learning how to have comfortable intimate relations.

3. Deciding whether to have and raise children.

4. Trying to maximize one's skills and productivity in selected pursuits, for example, domestic, familial, vocational, avocational, economic, social, political, existential, etc.

5. Finding an acceptable position in one's local or larger community.

The relative success or failure of negotiating these and other such hurdles influences the individual's self-concept. An accumulation of more successes than failures fosters a sense of self-confidence and proficiency, whereas a preponderance of failures promotes an attitude of despair and adverse self-criticism. Such a person is inclined to develop a chronically depressed mood, which may increase the use and abuse of illicit drugs or lead to abuse of prescriptive psychoactive drugs. Various types of psychotherapy may be sought. Depressed individuals who feel defeated by life's trials are more susceptible to physical illness, which further aggravates the loss of self-esteem.

People who have experienced smooth transitions from the infantile and early childhood state of primary narcissism (when it was appropriate to be loved and cared for unconditionally) to the more adult state of stable self-esteem (when it became understood that love from others would more likely be conditional on one's behavior and achievements) are less vulnerable than others to minor and major physical and mental disorders. The poor in self-love get poorer and the rich in self-love get richer. Those who are extravagantly and excessively loved by others may be temporary exceptions to this rule; they may be unduly susceptible to narcissistic injury when the adulation suddenly diminishes or disappears.

Ages fifty-one to eighty: maturity and later adulthood

The ages of late maturity and senescence bring new obstacles to the preservation and evolution of an adaptive sense of self:

1. Providing economic support and educational opportunities for dependents and carrying out other parenting functions.

2. Responsibilities associated with other goals when one has no offspring to rear and support.

3. Coping with the problems associated with retirement from work.

4. Maintaining a sense of usefulness and a self-respecting place in the community after retirement.

5. Mourning the loss of members of one's kinship and social network to illness and death.

6. Compensating for increasing mental and physical debilitation.

7. Facing the inevitability of one's own death.

It seems humans have always been intent on maintaining their being and coexistence with certain others in one form or another. Our utter dependence on caring others during infancy and childhood produces a profound attachment to them, which continues after their deaths and contributes to preoccupation with and hope for some form of immortality for ourselves and others.

Most people believe that some immutable portion of the self survives death. Despite such beliefs, frequently staunchly held, people often approach death with considerable protest, manifesting temporary rage at their deity or themselves because they have not been made an exception, for example, miraculously cured of an ordinarily fatal illness. There is perhaps more resignation in the face of fatal illness among those who do not believe in immortality or resurrection. Even among those who accept death's inevitability and finality, however, are some who express rage when confronted by life-threatening illness or an accident. These kinds of protests are often lingering expressions of primary narcissism with which we begin our existence. A variation on the theme of finitude is one in which cognitive impairment due to organic causes may relieve an individual of knowing he faces the end of life while giving him free play to remaining memories and self-concepts that have qualities of grandiosity and omnipotence.

I have traced the characteristics and evolution of the narcissistic dimension of human life through the phases of the life cycle. Natural, normal manifestations as well as pathological excesses or deficits in narcissism can occur at any phase. The word *narcissism* has acquired negative connotations, possibly because of its origin in the Greek myth of the youth who pined away for love of his own reflection and was transformed into a narcissus. The narcissus, however, is a beautiful flower and it merits a modicum of recognition. Metaphorically speaking, no special justification or exception need be made to include the dimension of self-love, self-respect, and self-esteem in our concept of healthy narcissism. It may be difficult for behaviorists and social scientists to agree on the bounds of normal narcissism, but there is no need for therapists of any persuasion to try to eradicate the self-respecting, age-appropriate aspects of narcissism in their clients.

The Detection and Treatment of Excessive Narcissism

Narcissistic manifestations during psychoanalysis

Pathologic degrees of narcissism are encountered frequently during the conduct of intensive psychotherapy, particularly in psychoanalysis. The strategies to consider when confronted with such manifestations depend on the patient, the nature of the problem that brought the patient into psychotherapy, and the therapeutic context in which the narcissistic symptoms and signs appear. Let me discuss the subject in terms of various psychotherapeutic situations.

Training psychoanalysis of "normal" candidates. Max Gitelson (1954) wrote about the psychoanalysis of the "normal" psychiatrist whose psychoanalytic education included a personal training analysis. He noted that among such "normal" trainees are individuals who have remnants of infantile or childhood neurosis that reemerge during the transference neurosis and transform the analysis into something more than an intellectual learning experience or exploration of "normality." Gitelson's observations have been corroborated by my own experience as a training analyst. Moreover, without exception, the training analysands with whom I have worked were professionally competent and gifted individuals who had been lovingly cared for and nurtured, usually by both parents. It was not surprising that at some stages of our work they transiently experienced themselves as special and displayed grandiose and self-aggrandizing perspectives. At such moments they expressed desires to please me by mimicking my identity (i.e., mirroring) and to fuse with me. The psychoanalytic process is likely to re-evoke and re-create such states in the transference to the analyst, states which may arise gradually without apparent provocation, as the analysand experiences less and less shame about making personal revelations and gains trust in the analyst and the psychoanalytic situation. Such states may occur also after a particularly empathic or helpful comment by the analyst or when the analyst or the psychoanalytic process reminds the analysand of some parameter of reality that frustrates an overt or covert dependent desire. For example, the analyst may suggest a schedule change at a time when the patient wants no time limitations, or otherwise deny some wish-fulfilling orientation or fantasy. The emotional poignancy of reexperiencing oneself in a variety of precipitated psychodynamic circumstances provides the analysand with new insights and intellectual comprehension of unconscious mentation and forgotten steps from his or her early development.

With this group of atypical patients such narcissistic manifestations require little psychotherapeutic comment from the analyst. I agree with Heinz Kohut (1971, 1984), who suggests that the training analyst need give only a sign of empathic understanding. Other training analysts may wish to say more, depending on their predilections and perceptions of the patient. I believe that in most training analyses, regardless of variations in technique, the results will be similar because of the common denominator of respect for, and understanding of, the origins, evolution, and variability of the analysand's narcissism.

Training psychoanalysis of the "not-so-normal" analysand. Some candidates present with more severe psychopathology, which is associated primarily or secondarily with conflicts involving narcissistic parameters. These parameters usually include impaired primary or achievement-oriented narcissism side-by-side with some degree of overvaluation of the self.

Those difficulties are amenable to classical psychoanalytic therapy. Narcissistic problem areas in analytic trainees surface early, often in relation to inordinate expectations for recognition or wishes to be given special consideration in extra-analytic and intra-analytic situations. When such wishes and expectations are not immediately gratified, responses typically range from overt to covert rage to depression and withdrawal. There may be long silences or incomprehensible free associations, even an episode of extra-analytic alcohol or drug abuse. Consistent neural acceptance of such phenomena with timely interpretations of the unconscious psychodynamic and psychogenic ramifications is indicated. The patient's dreams and the joint interest of the analyst and the analysand in understanding them serve as intellectual stabilizers, providing a good measure of emotional distance and insight into the narcissistic phenomena. In every individual, the origins of such narcissistic problems are multiple. Among them are the birth order (e.g., the analysand may have been the first boy in a family desirous of male offspring); a transient grief and bereavement reaction in the mother when the analysand was very young; an unexpected parental separation or divorce when the analysand was in puberty; an unresolved and symptomatic neurosis, in one or another parent or grandparent (who functioned as a caregiver) and so on.

As with all psychoanalyses, the analyst needs to be open to self-analysis and self-scrutiny of his or her countertransference, including continual study of reactions that may facilitate an understanding of and appropriate response to the analysand's problems, and those which are empathically disparate and unrelated to the experiences that the analysand is undergoing.

Psychoanalysis of patients with narcissistic problems. A host of mental disorders classified in the DSM-III are presented there as unrelated to narcissistic problems. Yet in one way or another, either primarily or secondarily, they are indeed associated with psychopathological deviations in narcissism. All the depressive disorders, including dysthymic reactions, major depression, and affective disorders with or without psychosis, involve narcissistic manifestations, as do the phobic disorders, secondarily if not primarily, and the schizophrenias. The addictive and the sociopathic disorders can be understood as narcissistic disturbances in which deviant behaviors represent lifelong efforts to defend against and cope with early narcissistic injuries. Even the large group of cerebral organic disorders is associated with narcissistic manifestations in the sense that early in the course of these conditions the patient is usually aware of failing intellectual capacities, and as a consequence, self-worth and self-esteem are significantly decreased.

The Assessment of Narcissism

One might conclude that such broad use of the term *narcissism* makes it as ubiquitous as anxiety or depression or hostility and that as such it loses its specificity and its relevance for describing and understanding the pathogenesis of mental disorders. To the contrary, I believe broad application of the word *narcissism* can enhance our knowledge of pathogenesis. Before describing in detail the ways in which narcissistic problems suffuse many well-recognized psychiatric disorders, let me elaborate on the measurement of narcissism.

The psychobiologic dimensions of anxiety, hostility, and depression have long had descriptive value for the fields of mental health and abnormal psychology. These dimensions have also been of heuristic value when applying to psychiatry the burgeoning discoveries of the neurosciences. A growing body of knowledge involves the ways in which changes in the presence and availability of various neurotransmitters at the receptor synapses in the brain influence the arousal as well as the inhibition of anxiety-fear, hostility, and depression. The discovery and development of psychoactive pharmaceutical agents have been based on their antianxiety and antidepressant effects in animals and in humans. In some instances, a new psychoactive drug's known effects on the norepinephrine, serotonin, or gamma aminobutyric acid (GABA) available at neuroreceptors have suggested and promoted its trial as an antianxiety, antihostility, antidepressant, or antischizophrenic drug.

There is no known brain-behavior equivalent with respect to narcissism and pertinent neurotransmitter substances. More is known about the psychosocial factors influencing narcissistic manifestations than about the biomedical ones. It is likely that narcissistic needs and fixations are also influenced by hereditary determinants but those issues have not been investigated. There can be no fruitful integration of biomedical and psychosocial research with respect to narcissism until it can be defined and measured. Some such measures have been developed (Mayman 1967; Exner 1969; Urist 1977; Raskin and Hall 1979; Harder 1979; Blazer 1981; Collins and LaGanza 1982; Solomon 1982; Millon 1982; Auerbach 1984; Prifitera and Ryan 1984) or are in the early stages of development (Russell 1989). Meanwhile, the diagnostic criteria for narcissistic personality disorder in DSM-III (1980) provide a model definition that has enough general acceptance to specify one kind of psychopathological narcissism: excessive narcissistic claims. As mentioned above, other DSM-III categories are associated with narcissism without so specifying. In some instances these are derivatives of narcissistic injury, for example, anxiety, phobia, and depressive disorders; in other instances the derivative involves a substitute way of gratifying unfulfilled narcissistic requirements, for example, alcoholism, drug abuse, sociopathic or antisocial personality.

Depressive reactions are generally associated with increased shame, guilt, or separation anxiety—all derivatives of damaged self-esteem. Individuals suffering from depression may also have overly strict and punishing superegos and ego ideals, as well as conscious old memories and recent experiences in which they felt rejected or repudiated by another. From this perspective, the depressed mood can be understood as an affect that derives from impaired normal narcissism, and the conscious decreased self-worth as a direct consequence of decreased self-assurance. Anxious and phobic patients are apprehensive of the prospect of socially inadequate performance or fearful of potential emotions that will lead to the loss of support and love from others. Hence the symptoms are both a direct expression of precarious self-respect and a defensive warning and maneuver to prevent the loss of any remaining narcissistic supply. The alcoholic, the drug abuser, and the person with an eating disorder has despaired of receiving from others the satisfaction of narcissistic needs, usually as a consequence of frustrations in their emotional needs earlier in life, which prompted them to depend on food or chemical substances to change their level of consciousness and awareness and to provide "comfort."

Individuals susceptible to the schizophrenias suffer from a variety of disruptions in the normally gradual transition from neonatal narcissistic dependence to the establishment and maintenance of a sense of self-worth based on successful behaviors and achievements. That certain inherited traits may predispose people to schizophrenia (for example a low threshold to personality disruption when supplies of support and love are withdrawn, or an inherited pessimistic view of the reliability and constancy of others) appears to be a distinct possibility (Kety et al. 1968, 1978; Kinney et al. 1986). Certainly there appears to be a fragile and disorganized capacity to maintain an integrated valuation of the self. The psychotic episodes and hospitalizations of those individuals—with society eventually labeling them as "schizophrenic"—secondarily detracts from an adequate self-concept and stable identity. Much the same can be said about so-called borderline and narcissistic personalities, who appear to have been less severely damaged than people who develop schizophrenia.

Some Comments on the Psychoanalytic Treatment of Narcissism Phenomena

Most psychoanalysts agree that classical psychoanalysis is highly effective for patients who are intelligent, psychologically minded, have good reality-testing ability, and are not excessively alienated from themselves and others. A fair amount of psychoanalytic literature deals with criteria for analyzability (Diatkine 1968; Lower et al. 1972; Waldhorn 1967; Huxster et al. 1975), and I have no argument, in general, with the opinions expressed there.

Active and continuing alcohol and drug abuse are deterrents to successful psychoanalysis. The more serious mental disorders, including the depressive and schizophrenic psychoses and the borderline and narcissistic personality disorders, are questionable indications for classical psychoanalysis, although psychoanalysts who have specialized in treating such disorders claim to have good results. They admit to using variations in the standard procedure, for example, having the patient sit and face the therapist, giving psychotherapeutic advice, and using pharmacotherapy. Although it is conceivable that these modified analytic approaches (sometimes called "psychoanalysis with parameters") are effective, no further review and evaluation of them will be attempted here.

All psychiatric patients coming for treatment reveal shame and feelings of inferiority and/or embarrassment about their disorder. These secondary reactive manifestations of narcissistic conflict are common and natural in individuals who have evolved a conditional concept of the value of their identities. They perceive mental and physical illness as a weakness and a disadvantage and have come to believe that sickness is not likely to win them approval and love. Hence they suffer from narcissistic symptoms of loss of self-respect and self-worth. Such symptoms generally are not based on a disturbance of the position of primary narcissism.

One exception to this presentation is encountered in patients who have evolved a defense of dramatic helplessness and dependence, people who appeal to others for sympathy, even pity, to secure and maximize a steady source of attention and care. Feelings of shame are suppressed for the sake of obtaining more desperately needed reassurances that one is lovable and worth caring for. Such patients have usually undergone earlier and/or sudden insults to their normal primary narcissistic position (ages zero to five). Within the usual time parameters of psychoanalysis (five or six sessions per week, including occasional double sessions), it is useful to make a serious attempt to accommodate the dependent demands of a patient who presents with a markedly urgent appeal. The intention is not to provide an external replacement for the sense of loss and deprivation that the patient signals, for there is an insatiable quality to such hunger, but to acknowledge the urgent emotional needs being expressed. Invariably after a while, the patient is able to recognize the analyst's commitment and will experience small amounts of shame at the magnitude and insatiability of his or her needs. The patient then becomes more ready to collaborate in explorative and interpretive work with the analyst, studying and understanding the painful origins and ramifications of the early narcissistic injuries.

Accordingly, although patients come to psychoanalysis with feelings of shame about their problems that are within normal limits and have learned that narcissistic gratification is permissible through one's achievements, *relentless* self-recrimination over having any emotional conflicts or problems reveals a psychopathological internalized conscience.

With healthier patients, the analyst needs to empathize with a well-established narcissistic self so that society's requirements and the related shame can be acknowledged and understood. These patients need help in understanding that no one solves all of life's problems easily, particularly those with strong unconscious determinants. Working through such experiences is integral to the analytic work, and the analyst may make subtle inquiries to evoke memories of experiences that contributed to the patient's problems, thus making them available for analysis.

Psychoanalysis can proceed in the usual fashion with such patients.

tic status and the psychopathogenesis of the problems along this developmental line.

The Use of Psychopharmacological Agents

The impaired reality testing of patients with major mental disorders—with or without psychosis—interferes with the effectiveness of all psychotherapies, except those that focus strictly on reality issues. The antipsychotic drugs have proved to be successful in suppressing the psychotic ideation manifested in two-thirds to three-fourths of patients diagnosed as having schizophrenia or a major depression (Cole et al. 1964; Goldberg et al. 1965; Davis 1976; Gottschalk 1979). Lithium treatment effectively inhibits mania in a larger percentage of patients with affective disorders of the manic type (Gerbino et al. 1978). Minor tranquilizers like the benzodiazepines effectively relieve the symptoms of anxiety and depression secondary to anxiety (Gottschalk 1978). These and other psychoactive drugs have significantly and favorably influenced the success of psychiatric treatment by relieving the incapacitating effects of serious mental disorders. For the most part these drugs improve the integrative mental capacity, normalize emotional function, and stabilize sleep patterns. In so doing, they enhance feelings of well-being and self-esteem and render the patients accessible to the psychotherapies.

Two kinds of problems affect the narcissistic balance of psychiatric patients on psychoactive drugs. (1) Some psychoactive drugs impair some of the finer aspects of cognitive function. For example, the benzodiazepines can impair short-term memory consolidation and the smoothness of intellectual function (Gottschalk 1977, 1988); lithium may have some adverse cognitive effects (Agulnik et al. 1972); and neuroleptic and antidepressive drugs may cause a degree of mental confusion (Haefner et al. 1965; Sovner and DiMascio 1978; Schatzberg et al. 1978). Such unfavorable effects on cognitive function also adversely affect a patient's level of self-esteem.

(2) Many psychiatric patients maintained on one or another psychoactive drug begin to conclude they are not capable of functioning without the drug. Further, they are inclined to regard achievements and successes as expressions of the drug's action rather than of their own efforts. This chronically adverse and depreciated self-concept is difficult to eradicate as long as use of the drug is continued. The attempts of some psychiatrists to ease the minds of their patients by telling them they suffer merely from a "chemical imbalance" of the brain does not relieve the plaguing sense of inferiority and damaged self-esteem of those patients. For these reasons,

rapid or gradual weaning from the chronic use of such drugs is advisable whenever possible.

Summary and Conclusion

Narcissism has become a major focus in mental health over the past fifteen years and has generated interesting and useful theoretical and conceptual contributions stimulated especially by the psychoanalytic writings of Kohut (1971, 1984) and Kernberg (1975, 1980).

This chapter synthesizes certain definitions and perspectives about narcissism to illustrate how primary narcissism and achievement-oriented narcissism pervade most, if not all, of the psychopathological disorders of our psychiatric classification system as well as many aspects of mental health. I have tried to link some threads of thought about narcissism and, at the same time, provide a broad framework for viewing the origins, development, and treatment of pathological narcissism. The emphasis has been on psychoanalytic psychotherapy, not because other schools of psychotherapy lack relevance, but because most of the theoretical and clinical contributions on narcissism have come from psychoanalytically oriented writers.

REFERENCES

Agulnik, P.L.; DiMascio, A.; and Moore, P. 1972. "Acute Brain Syndrome Associated with Lithium Therapy." *American Journal of Psychiatry* 129:621–23.

American Psychiatric Association. 1980. *Diagnostic and Statistical Manual of Mental Disorders*, 3d ed. Washington, D.C.: American Psychiatric Association.

Auerbach, J. S. 1984. "Validation of Two Scales for Narcissistic Personality Disorder." *Journal of Personality Assessment* 48:649–53.

Blazer, D. G. 1981. "Narcissism and the Development of Chronic Pain." *International Journal of Psychiatry in Medicine* 10:69–77.

Cole, J. O.; Goldberg, S. C.; and Klerman, G. L. 1964. "Phenothiazine Treatment in Acute Schizophrenia." *Archives of General Psychiatry* 10:246–61.

Collins, J., and LaGanza, S. 1982. "Self-Recognition of the Face: A Study of Adolescent Narcissism." *Journal of Youth and Adolescence* 11:317–28.

Davis, J. M. 1976. "Recent Developments in the Drug Treatment of Schizophrenia." *American Journal of Psychiatry* 133:208–14.

Diatkine, R. 1968. "Indications and Contraindications for Psychoanalytic Treatment." *International Journal of Psychoanalysis* 49:266–270.

Ellis, H. 1928. "The Conception of Narcissism." In *Studies in the Psychology of Sex,* vol. 7, chap. 6. Philadelphia: Davis.

Exner, J. 1969. "Rorschach Responses As an Index of Narcissism." *Journal of Projective Techniques and Personality Assessment* 33:324–30.

Ferenczi, S. 1913. "Stages in the Development of the Sense of Reality." *International Zeitschrift für Arztliche Psychoanalyse* 1:124–38.

Freud, S. [1914] 1948. "On Narcissism: An Introduction." In *Standard Edition,* ed. J. Strachey, vol. 14, pp. 30–59. London: Hogarth Press.

Gerbino, L.; Oleshansky, M.; and Gershon, S. 1978. "Clinical Use and Mode of Action of Lithium." In *Psychopharmacology: A Generation of Progress,* ed. M.A. Lipton, A. DiMascio, and K. F. Killam, pp. 1261–1276. New York: Raven Press.

Gitelson, M. 1954. "Therapeutic Problems in the Analysis of the 'Normal' Candidate." *International Journal of Psychoanalysis* 35:174–83.

Goldberg, S. C.; Klerman, G. L.; and Cole, J. O. 1965. "Changes in Schizophrenic Psychopathology and Word Behavior as a Function of Phenothiazine Treatment." *British Journal of Psychiatry* 11:120–35.

Gottschalk, L. A. 1977. "Effects of Certain Benzodiazepine Derivatives on Disorganization of Thought as Manifested in Speech." *Current Theories in Research* 21:192–206.

———. 1978. "Pharmacokinetics of the Minor Tranquilizers and Clinical Response." In *Psychopharmacology: A Generation of Progress,* ed. M.A. Lipton, A. DiMascio, and K. F. Killam, pp. 975–86. New York: Raven Press.

———. 1979. "A Preliminary Approach to the Problems of Relating the Pharmacokinetics of Phenothiazines to Clinical Response with Schizophrenic Patients." In *Pharmacokinetics of Psychoactive Drugs, Further Studies,* ed. L. A. Gottschalk, pp. 63–81. New York: Spectrum.

———. 1988. "Affective and Cognitive Problems with the Benzodiazepines." *Journal of Clinical Psychopharmacology* 8:223–25.

Haefner, H.; Heyder, B.; and Kutscher, I. 1965. "Undesirable Side Effects and Complications with the Use of Neuroleptic Drugs. *International Journal of Neuropsychiatry* 1:46–58.

Harder, D. W. 1979. "The Assessment of Ambitious-Narcissistic Character Style with Three Projective Tests: The Early Memories TAT and Rorschach." *Journal of Personality Assessment* 43:23–32.

Heimann, P. [1951] 1957. "A Contribution to the Re-Evaluation of the Oedipus Complex—The Early Stages." In *New Directions in Psychoanalysis,* ed. M. Klein, P. Heimann, and R. Money-Kyrle, pp. 23–28. New York: Basic Books.

Hinsie, L. E., and Shatzky, J. 1940. *Psychiatric Dictionary.* New York: Oxford University Press.

Huxster, H.; Lower, R.; and Escoll, P. 1975. "Some Pitfalls in the Assessment of Analyzability in a Psychoanalytic Clinic." *Journal of the American Psychoanalytic Association* 23:90–106.

Kernberg, O. 1975. *Borderline Conditions and Pathological Narcissism.* New York: Jason Aronson.

———. "A Theory of Psychoanalytic Psychotherapy." In *Internal World and External Reality: Object Relations Theory Applied.* New York: Jason Aronson.

Kety, S. S.; Wender, P. H.; and Rosenthal, D. 1978. "Genetic Relationships within the Schizophrenia Spectrum: Evidence from Adoption Studies." In *Critical Issues in Psychiatric Diagnosis,* ed. R. L. Spitzer et al., pp. 213–23. New York: Raven Press.

Kety, S. S.; Rosenthal, D.; Wender, P. H.; and Schulsinger, F. 1968. "The Types and Prevalence of Mental Illness in the Biological and Adoptive Families of Adopted Schizophrenics." In *The Transmission of Schizophrenia*, ed. D. Rosenthal et al., pp. 345–62. Oxford: Pergamon Press.

Kinney, D. K.; Jacobsen, B.; Bechgaard, B., et al. 1986. "Content Analysis of Speech of Schizophrenic and Control Adoptees and Their Relatives: Preliminary Results." In *The Content Analysis of Verbal Behavior in Clinical Medicine and Psychiatry*, ed. L.A. Gottschalk, F. Lolas, and L. L. Viney, pp. 197–205. Heidelberg: Springer-Verlag.

Klein, M. 1932. *The Psychoanalysis of Children*. London: Hogarth Press.

Klein, M. [1921] 1957. "The Psychoanalytic Play Technique: Its History and Significance." In *New Directions in Psychoanalysis*, ed. M. Klein, P. Heimann, and R. Money-Kyrle, pp. 3–22. New York: Basic Books.

Kohut, H. 1971. *The Analysis of the Self*. New York: International Universities Press.
———. 1984. *How Does Analysis Cure?* ed. A. Goldberg and P.E. Stepansky. Chicago: University of Chicago Press.

Lower, R.; Escoll, P.J.; and Huxster, B. 1972. "Bases for Judgments of Analyzability." *Journal of the American Psychoanalytic Association* 20:610–21.

Luborsky, L.; Chandler, M.; Auerbach, A. H.; Cohen, J.; and Bachrach, H. M. 1971. "Factors Influencing the Outcome of Psychotherapy: A Review of Quantitative Research." *Psychology Bulletin* 75:145–85.

Luborsky, L.; McLellan, A. T.; Woody, G. E.; and O'Brien, C. P. 1985. "Therapist Success and Its Determinants." *Archives of General Psychiatry* 42:602–11.

Luborsky, L.; Singer, B.; and Luborsky, L. 1975. "Comparative Studies of Psychotherapy. Is It True That Everybody Has Won and All Must Have Prizes?" *Archives of General Psychiatry* 32:995–1008.

Martin, J. 1985. "Clinical Contributions to the Theory of Fictive Personality." *Annual of Psychoanalysis* 33:267–300.

Mayman, M. 1967. "Object-Representations and Object-Relationships in Rorschach Responses." *Journal of Projective Techniques and Personality Assessment* 32:303–16.

Millon, T. 1982. *Millon Multiaxial Clinical Inventory Manual*. Minneapolis: National Computer Systems.

Prifitera, A., and Ryan, J. J. 1984. "Validity of the Narcissistic Personality Inventory (NPI) in a Psychiatric Sample." *Journal of Clinical Psychology* 40:140–42.

Raskin, R. N., and Hall, C. S. 1979. "A Narcissistic Personality Inventory." *Psychobiological Reports* 45:490.

Russell, S. 1989. "The Measurement of Narcissism Through the Content Analysis of Verbal Behavior." Ph. D. diss. in progress, Division of Social Sciences, University of California at Irvine.

Schatzberg, A. F.; Cole, J. O.; and Blumer, D. P. 1978. "Speech Blockage: A Tricyclic Side Effect." *American Journal of Psychiatry* 35:600–601.

Solomon, R. S. 1982. "Validity of the MMPI Narcissistic Personality Disorder Scale." *Psychological Reports* 50:463–66.

Sovner, R., and DiMascio, A. 1978. "Extrapyramidal Syndromes and Other Neurological Side Effects of Psychotropic Drugs." In *Psychopharmacology: A Generation of Progress*, ed. M. A. Lipton, A. DiMascio, and K. F. Killam, pp. 1021–1032. New York: Raven Press.

Urist, J. 1977. "The Rorschach Test and the Assessment of Object Relations." *Journal of Personality Assessment* 41:3–9.

Waldhorn, H. 1967. *Indications for Psychoanalysis.* New York: International Universities Press.

DISCUSSION

The concept of narcissism has emerged in recent years as a most important theoretical and clinical issue. Groundbreaking work has been contributed by Kohut (1971, 1977) and Kernberg (1975), and their writings have stimulated a focus on the structure of the self and the crucial role of self-esteem and its psychopathology. From a developmental perspective, Gottschalk examines here the definitions and perspectives involving narcissism and provides a framework for viewing the origins, development, and treatment of pathological kinds of narcissism in the context of modern psychotherapy and psychopharmacology.

He traces the characteristics and evolution of the narcissistic dimension of human life through the phases of the life cycle, showing how self-esteem and self-concept are dynamic, evolving entities. He describes how natural, normal manifestation as well as pathological excesses or deficits in narcissism *can occur at any phase,* not just during the preoedipal or oedipal stages. In so doing, he constructs a comprehensive picture of lifelong vulnerability to narcissistic injury and the subsequent formation of psychological illness.

In 1981 we reviewed the few studies of narcissism then available, including Lichtenberg's (1975) description of the child's sense of self in terms of three lines of development related to narcissistic issues: (1) self-images based on body experiences associated with instinctual need satisfactions; (2) self-images that emerge as entities having discrete differentiation from others; and (3) self-images that by virtue of idealization retain a sense of grandiosity and omnipotence shared with an idealized person, such as a mother. In describing how the self becomes cohesive, Lichtenberg wrote of a lifelong "blending and balancing" of these three clusters of self-images.

Kernberg (1977) noted how normal narcissistic gratifications in adulthood increase self-esteem. When they are closely linked to relationships with others, such gratifications strengthen inner representations, shaping the adult self in the process. The self is further modified by narcissistic gratifications that come from work, creativity, and "an internal build-up of the nonpersonal world of nature and things" (p. 10).

Building on the preceding concepts, we (1981) also described the relationship between the adult self and narcissism as an evolving and dynamic interplay throughout the life cycle. We delineated how each individual must engage the narcissistic issues involved in the major developmental tasks of adulthood, and we agree with Gottschalk that such issues are absolutely central to the development of the adult self. It is not enough simply to resolve the narcissistic issues of early life; adult life brings *new* ones into play, and these must be engaged if growth and development are to continue.

Like Gottschalk, we find that forces modifying the adult self are fueled by narcissistic gratifications and disappointments *in adulthood.* We assume those gratifications to include the self-nurturing fantasy process, which in the integrated person is closely related to reality and often leads to realistic action. Our term for that is *healthy self-aggrandizement,* and it is akin to Kohut's "healthy narcissism." Narcissistic disappointments affecting the evolution of the self often occur when realities do not fulfill idealizations—for example, the differences between one's idealized infant and the real child who emerges with increasing clarity over time.

Although we emphasize the effect of narcissistic issues in adulthood because they have been largely ignored until recently, narcissistic issues from earlier developmental phases also have a major effect on the evolution of the adult self. Just as the adolescent relied upon the accomplishments of latency to bolster him against the regressive and narcissistic injuries of adolescence, so, too, the adult gains sustenance from the gratifications provided by the accomplishments of young adulthood, such as the attainment of intimacy and career goals.

Gottschalk makes an important clinical contribution when he argues for broad application of the term *narcissism* as essential to an understanding of many psychopathological disorders. He feels that an appreciation of the narcissistic elements in various disorders can considerably increase our knowledge of pathogenesis. In DSM-III-R numerous mental disorders are classified and presented as being unrelated to narcissistic problems, yet "in one way or another, either primarily or secondarily, they are indeed associated with psychopathological deviations in narcissism" (p. 9). For instance, the depressive disorders, including dysthymic reactions, major depression, and affective disorders (with or without psychosis) involve important narcissistic manifestations. The narcissistic involvement holds true for the phobic disorders, secondarily if not primarily, and the schizophrenias as well. Further, the addictive and the sociopathic disorders can be understood as narcissistic disturbances in which deviant behaviors represent lifelong efforts to defend and cope with early narcissistic injuries. Gottschalk makes the point that even for the large group of cerebral organic disorders, narcissistic manifestations play an important role because early in the course of those conditions, the patient is usually aware of failing intellectual capacities and may feel that his "self is shattering." As a consequence, his self-worth and self-esteem are significantly impaired.

Clinicians, in either their evaluations or actual psychotherapeutic or psychoanalytic work, are well advised to gain as clear an understanding as possible of their patient's underlying narcissistic injuries, as this greatly helps in understanding and eventually resolving the manifest symptomatology, no matter what the disorder.

In a particularly useful clinical section on the treatment of patients with early narcissistic injury (years zero to five), Gottschalk discusses patients who have evolved a defense of dramatic helplessness and dependence. These are individuals who appeal to others for sympathy to gain a steady source of attention and care. Gottschalk describes how their feelings of *shame* are suppressed for the sake of obtaining more desperately needed reassurances that they are lovable and worth caring about. Here he strongly suggests that the key therapeutic intervention is to appreciate the sense of loss and deprivation that the patient signals and to acknowledge the urgent emotional needs being expressed—particularly the hidden shame. This appreciation allows the patient eventually to form a strong therapeutic alliance with the therapist.

Returning to the central issue of narcissism throughout the life cycle, Gottschalk describes how evidence of excessive or deficient narcissistic expectations recurs in the transference and will be tied directly to events and memories dating to ages zero to five, six to ten, eleven to twenty, twenty-one to fifty, or fifty-one to eighty, but *not necessarily related to such landmark paradigms as oedipal or preoedipal positions.* He outlines helpful criteria for orienting the therapist and for evaluating narcissistic phenomena:

1. Are they appropriate or inappropriate for the stage of life from which the memories and mentation are retrieved?

2. Are they excessive, reasonable, or deficient in what they request for the self?

3. Are they essentially originating from the stage of primary narcissism or achievement narcissism?

4. Has the stage of primary narcissism been cut short or prolonged, and if so, why?

5. Do they indicate whether the quality or the stages of primary or

achievement narcissism have been influenced by excessive or deficient erotic or aggressive drives and by excessive or deficient degrees of conscience?

REFERENCES

Colarusso, C. A.; and Nemiroff, R. A. 1981. *Adult Development: A New Dimension in Psychodynamic Theory and Practice.* New York: Plenum.

Kernberg, O. 1975. *Borderline Conditions and Pathological Narcissism.* New York: Jason Aronson.

———. 1977. "Pathological Narcissism in Middle Age." Presentation, American Psychoanalytic Association, Quebec, May 1977.

Kohut, H. 1971. *The Analysis of the Self.* New York: International Universities Press.

———. 1977. *The Restoration of the Self.* New York: International Universities Press.

Lichtenberg, J. D. 1975. "The Development of the Sense of Self." *Journal of the American Psychoanalytic Association* 23:453.

PART II

NEW CONCEPTS IN ADULT DEVELOPMENT

5

Frontiers of Adult Development in Theory and Practice

ROBERT A. NEMIROFF AND CALVIN A. COLARUSSO

In 1979, Judith Stevens-Long characterized the knowledge of adult development in the following manner:

The study of the life span is reminiscent of a fifteenth-century map of the world. Europe, the origin of the map, is carefully detailed. All the shapes and proportions are recognizable in the context of current knowledge. Like the study of childhood, the territory looks familiar. On the other side of the world, China—like the psychology of later life—is partially mapped. In the middle, however, stretch vast unexplored territories. Odd shapes and sizes, fanciful names, and vague outlines are everywhere.

Those who study adulthood quickly discover the limits of our information as did those early cartographers. Little is known about adulthood, and especially the middle years, from the twenties to age sixty-five. But the unknown lures us and we have a sense of adventure. It is exciting to be among the first to explore the area. We know enough to realize that there is much more to learn—enough to motivate the most energetic and imaginative among us! (Pp. 5–6)

Since then, there have been several multidisciplinary studies of the normal developmental processes in the adult. Sufficient interest has been generated that adult development has emerged as a distinct field of study. Building on the pioneer efforts of Sigmund Freud (1905), Arnold Van Gennep (1960), Carl Jung (1933), and Erik Erikson (1963), and contemporary investigators like Roger Gould (1978), David Gutmann (1977), Daniel Levinson (1978), Bernice Neugarten (1979), George Pollock (1961), and George Vaillant (1977), we (1981, 1985) have been working to increase our understanding of the second half of life and integrating data with what is known about child development. In this chapter, we present new theoretical concepts in adult development and explore the clinical implications for treating patients in the second half of life.

Definition of Development

First, what do we mean by *development?* We cite a statement by Rene Spitz (1965) in which he defined development as the emergence of forms, of functions, and of behaviors that are the outcome of exchanges between the organism, on the one hand, and the inner and outer environment on the other. We have found this definition to be most useful because *both* biological and environmental factors are considered. Development, then, may be seen as the result of the *lifelong* interaction between the two.

As our first point, we submit that this definition of development has a particularly heuristic value in contemporary psychiatry and psychoanalysis. With the rise of biological psychiatry in the medical schools, we have witnessed an unsophisticated polarization of adherence to biological variables on the one hand or to psychological variables on the other. Recently, outstanding scholars of both disciplines have called for true integration of the biological and the environmental. In reviewing Reiser's important book, *Mind, Brain and Body* (1984), Kandel (1986) said:

> Among the most important tasks facing psychoanalysis as an evolving intellectual discipline is to develop an effective interaction with the behavioral and biological sciences: with cognitive psychology on the one hand, and with cell and molecular neurobiology on the other.

In a similar vein, writing from the vantage point of psychoanalysis in an article for the *American Journal of Psychiatry* entitled "Will Neurobiology Influence Psychoanalysis?" Cooper (1985) stated:

> Neurobiologic research has begun to elucidate brain mechanisms of affective state and behavioral patterns. Discussions of anxiety and sexual identity demonstrate how these researchers lead the psychoanalyst to broader views of behaviors that were previously considered entirely psychological in origin. . . . Psychoanalytic theory is challenged to accord with newer findings in biology and to provide important questions for further research. (Pp. 1395–1402)

Both biologic and psychoanalytic purists have overlooked a passage in Freud's paper, *The Dynamics of Transference* (1912), in which he stated the issue clearly:

> I take this opportunity of defending myself against the mistaken charge of having denied the importance of innate (constitutional) factors because I have stressed that of infantile impressions. A charge such as this arises from the restricted nature of what men look for in the field of causation: in contrast to what ordinarily holds good in the real world, people prefer to be satisfied with a single causative factor. Psychoanalysis has talked a lot about the accidental factors in aetiology and little about the constitutional ones; but that is only because it was able to contribute something fresh to the former, while, to begin with, it knew no more than was commonly known about the latter. We refuse to posit any contrast in principle between the two sets of aetiological factors; on the contrary, we assume that the two sets regularly act jointly in bringing about the observed result. Endowment and Chance determine a man's fate—rarely or never one of these powers alone. (P. 99)

Freud never gave up the desire that psychoanalytic findings should accord with and be affirmed by findings in the other sciences and the humanities. In that spirit, we feel that in its emphasis on both the biological and the environmental, developmental theory—both child and adult—offers us an especially heuristic framework in which to understand our patients, and we attempt that integration wherever possible.

Basic Hypotheses

Building on Spitz's definition of development, we (1981) described seven hypotheses about adult development, which we now update with data and observations collected since then.

First, we propose that the nature of the developmental process is basically the same in the adult as in the child. This assertion contrasts with the commonly held conception that the adult is relatively free of environmental influences. In the achievement of new and phase-specific developmental tasks of adulthood, we see the adult as dependent as the child on the environment, which now consists of adult love objects, children, and colleagues instead of parents, teachers, and peers. Is the death of a spouse merely a "precipitating event" or is it a major upheaval in one's life, leading to potentially serious psychopathology or to significant, new adult development? Our clinical experience is clearly the latter; adult experience must be given its full import, not merely be reduced to childhood origins. Our emphasis is on integrating *both* childhood and adult determinants. The engagement and mastery of adult developmental tasks such as mature sexual functioning, intimacy, creativity, work, and coping with adult loss are as important to the adult as the mastery of bowel and bladder, formal learning, and the internalization of the superego are to the child—*all* result from the constant interaction between organism and environment throughout the life cycle.

Thus we have observed that development in adulthood is an ongoing dynamic process; yet there are some who believe the opposite. For example, Anna Freud, Humberto Nagera, and W. Ernest Freud (1965) state that the ultimate stages of development are reached in childhood. In their work on the adult profile they have written that in conceptualizing the adult we are dealing

> with a finished product in which, by implication, the ultimate develop-
> mental stages should have been reached. The developmental point of
> view may be upheld only insofar as success or failure to reach this level
> or to maintain it determines the so called maturity or immaturity of the
> adult personality. (P.10)

Essentially, their view supports the concept of the adult as a static, finished product instead of a dynamic, constantly changing and developing organism—potentially until the time of death. The difference between the two viewpoints may be reconciled by recognizing that for most theoreticians development is synonymous with the *formation* of psychic structure, such as the ego, superego, and ego ideal, in childhood. We do not propose that any new structures are added in adulthood, but we do believe that the changes occurring *within* these structures as a result of adult processes are sufficiently significant to warrant the term *development*. For instance, the term *father* is used for both a twenty-five-year-old man with a young wife, young children, and middle-aged parents and for a fifty-year-old man with a middle-aged wife, grown children, and aged or dead parents; yet the differences in psychic structure between the two are considerable. The father ego ideal of the twenty-five-year-old is quite different from the father ego ideal of the fifty-year-old. The difference is analogous to maintaining the facade of an old building for historical purposes while gutting the interior. The building looks the same from the outside and has the same name, but its internal structure is vastly different because of the continuing restorative work.

Another of our hypotheses suggests that the fundamental developmental issues of childhood continue as central aspects of adult life, but in altered form. This implies that the major developmental themes of childhood (or adulthood, for that matter) are never completely mastered or

when we begin to discuss clinical implications, i.e., what happens between two adults in the consulting room, the subject either changes completely, or it veers off inexorably into a discussion of the infantile, be it oedipal or preoedipal. In trying to understand this phenomenon I have wondered whether the more somber aspects of this [adult] developmental phase in which we all are engaged have a frightening effect on us and cause us to switch the subject. Moreover, I have wondered if there is some sort of a conceptual dissolution that takes place when we attempt to translate adult developmental theory into clinical practice. It appears easily subsumed under other issues such as infantile development, the adult reworking of infantile issues, the real relationship, the extra-analytic life of the patient, and so on (pers. comm. 1985).

Contradictory Treatment Ideas in the Literature

Freud (1906) was pessimistic about the treatment of older patients. "Near or about the fifties," he wrote, "the elasticity of the mental process, on which the treatment depends, is as a rule lacking—old people are no longer educable" (p. 264). Even if the elasticity were present, "the mass of material to be dealt with would prolong the duration of the treatment indefinitely" (p. 264). Further, such an analysis might not be cost-effective because the patient would have only a short time in which to enjoy his or her newfound health. Other early analysts, like Karl Abraham (1919) and Smith Ely Jelliffe (1925), conducted successful therapies with older patients and were optimistic about treating this age group. The struggle between the two divergent views may be observed in the literature across the decades: cautious, supportive intervention described by Otto Fenichel (1945), Marc Hollender (1952), and George Wayne (1953) versus insight-oriented techniques suggested by M. R. Kaufman (1937), Hann Segal (1958), Elliot Jacques (1965), Paul King (1980), and George Pollock (1980).

The skepticism has a much broader base than Freud's negativism. Robert Butler and M. L. Lewis (1977) relate avoidance of older patients by therapists to the following six factors: (1) the aged's stimulation of therapists' fears of their own old age; (2) conflicts about parental relationships mirrored in work with patients of the same age as that of their parents; (3) anticipated therapeutic impotence stemming from a belief in the ubiquity of untreatable organic states in the elderly; (4) a wish to avoid "wasting" therapeutic time and skills on older individuals (Freud's cost-effectiveness argument); (5) fears that the patient may die during treatment; and (6) a desire to avoid colleagues' negative comments about efforts directed toward the elderly.

Countertransference reactions may be the most important factor behind the avoidance of dynamic interaction for reasons presented clearly by Rechtschaffen (1959):

> The anxiety aroused by hostility toward a parent figure may lead to a watering down of the therapeutic process and to an exaggerated emphasis on supportive and covering-up procedures. Defending against anxiety, a therapist may propose only the most benign interpretations, and may assume an attitude of reverence toward an older patient that is out of keeping with the patient's actual readiness to examine himself. (P. 73)

In contrast, our experience and that of colleagues has led us to believe that *psychotherapy and psychoanalysis are valid, valuable forms of therapeutic intervention for many selected older patients, regardless of age.*

The relative absence of clinical theory and case reports on the treatment of older patients led us to publish *The Race Against Time: Psychotherapy and Psychoanalysis in the Second Half of Life* (1985). The belief that dynamic therapies are suitable, even preferred forms of treatment for older patients, expressed in that volume, is a point of view that is just emerging in the literature. For example, in 1983, the *Journal of Geriatric Psychiatry* devoted an entire issue to psychotherapy of the elderly. In the introduction, Martin Berezin (1983) noted that exploratory psychotherapy is used infrequently with older patients. Later, Savitsky and Goldstein (1983) comment that "recent gerontological literature offers a growing body of theory and clinical material supporting the value of systematic psychotherapy" (p. 40). The concept of adult development is beginning to be seen in articles with other focuses as well; for example, Burke and colleagues (1986) included in an article on the clinical researcher in psychiatry a discussion of major adult developmental tasks facing clinical researchers and presented a developmental perspective on the transition to research.

The Diagnostic Process

Because of the nature of development in midlife and later adulthood, an expanded diagnostic process should be considered. Among these are a developmental history of the life cycle, adult developmental tasks, adult developmental lines, and the concept of adult developmental arrest.

According to Pearl King (1980), older patients seek therapy for the following phase-specific reasons: (1) fear of diminution or loss of sexual potency; (2) fear of loss of effectivness in the workplace; (3) concerns about retirement; (4) anxieties about marital relationships in the empty nest; (5) awareness of aging, illness, and the resulting dependency on others; and (6) growing awareness of the inevitability of personal death.

When a patient in this age group arrives in our office, we find it useful to explore these issues through a *developmental history of the life cycle.* Detailed developmental histories are routine in the evaluation of children, but not of adults. This neglect may be due to the notion that developmental processes play a minor role in the adult and, until recently, to the absence of conceptual tools needed to organize the information. Now, however, by using the concepts of adult developmental stages, tasks, and lines to frame his questions and understand responses, the therapist may trace the patient's experience from the time of conception to the present. These data are then integrated with the information obtained from the history of the present illness, family history, and psychological or neurological testing to provide insight into the symptomatology and to plan the most effective therapeutic intervention. Because of the increased incidence in older patients of physical problems related to aging and disease, we pay particular attention to the influence of organic factors on normal and pathological emotional development. This concern can continue in the psychotherapy, which, in many instances, may focus on the patient's denial of organic problems or avoidance of getting proper care or of following our physicians' directions.

Adult Developmental Stages, Tasks, and Lines

The adult developmental history may be organized in two ways: first, a chronological description of adult developmental stages and tasks, providing continuity with the childhood developmental history; second, a delineation of adult developmental processes, that is, singling out major themes for more comprehensive examination. The diagnostician may conceptualize the material in both ways, integrating data as the evaluation proceeds.

Following Erikson (1963), we have divided adulthood into four broad stages: early (ages twenty to forty); middle (ages forty to sixty), later (ages sixty to eighty), and late-late (eighty and beyond). However, because of the limited knowledge of adult developmental processes (particularly those in late-late adulthood), the absence of biological demarcators to designate the beginning and end of phases, and the tendency of major tasks to overlap stages (for example, becoming a parent at eighteen, forty-five, or sixty), we find the stage framework not entirely useful in understanding adulthood. Concurring with our findings, Settlage (1985) has recently proposed the concept of *adult developmental process* to supplement the stage model. According to his hypothesis, disruption of a previously satisfactory self-regulatory and adaptive system is the stimulus for development, presenting the individual with a challenge that leads first to developmental tension and then to developmental conflict. Resolution proceeds hand-in-hand with the acquisition, mastery, and structural integration of the new function and leads to a change in self-image, marking the accomplishment of a unit of developmental process. In applying these ideas to treatment, Settlage suggests that the therapeutic endeavor can include the developmental process and that adult development is observed clinically in the interplay between the undoing of pathology and the resumption or initiation of developmental process.

Adult developmental tasks. The concept of adult developmental tasks—major, universal themes that engage the thoughts and, usually, the actions of every adult—is a flexible, open-ended way to organize diagnostic thinking. We have divided these tasks into groups corresponding roughly to the four developmental stages. To illustrate, let us consider middle adulthood in a diagnostic or therapeutic relationship with a patient between the ages of forty and sixty. The clinician who is attentive to the tasks related to that phase of development will increase his chances of understanding the patient because the patient, and perhaps the therapist as well, is undoubtedly trying to engage and master (or avoid) one or more of the following issues: the aging process in the body; the increased awareness of time limitation and personal death; the illnesses or deaths of parents, friends, and relatives; the changes in sexual drive and activity; the markedly altered relationships with parents, young adult children, and a maturing spouse; the assessment of career accomplishment and the recognition of falling short of personal goals; and planning for retirement. Many of the symptoms presented by patients in this age group are expressed in terms of these tasks or are partially caused by a failure to have engaged them successfully.

Clinical Example

A fifty-five-year-old lawyer sought help for depression. "I'm depressed. I've never felt this way before. I even thought of ending it all. . . . I take home $150,000 a year and I'm in debt. I haven't had a vacation in five years. . . . It's my wife and those damn kids."

A detailed developmental history revealed childhood problems with separation, probably caused by an overprotective, seductive mother, and significant difficulty with a developmental task of middle adulthood. Mr. J. and his wife had eight children ranging in age from twenty-nine to seventeen—all eight remained financially and emotionally dependent on him to one degree or another. Jim, age twenty-nine, had recently quit graduate school; he was living at home, interviewing for jobs. Jeff, twenty-six, a junior in a European medical school, was taking a semester off, traveling around the country at father's expense, and interviewing at United States medical schools. A third son, David, twenty-four, was in his second year at a private law school. The oldest daughter, Pearl, twenty-three, was recently married; her father was paying for both her college tuition and the couple's upcoming vacation. Two other daughters, Sara, twenty-two, and Terry, twenty, had recently returned home; Sara had abruptly quit her first job after college; Terry had not returned to college for her sophomore year; neither was working. The youngest daughter, Maggie, eighteen, had just started her freshman year at an expensive private college, while Ron, seventeen, an excellent student, was considering Ivy League schools.

The therapist used the concept of adult developmental tasks to understand the symptom, in this case, that the patient could not bring himself to separate from his adolescent and young adult children. This difficulty was recognized as a significant developmental conflict, powerful enough to cause depressive symptoms. The evaluation, particularly the developmental history of the life cycle, indicated that Mr. J. was an intact, well-functioning individual without evidence of significant past psychopathology. Consequently a recommendation was made for short-term dynamic psychotherapy focusing on the phase-specific task of separating from adult children. This separation was accomplished by emphasizing the following: (a) exploring why he was unrealistically supporting the children; (b) reemphasizing the marital relationship as a dyad apart from the children; and (c) confronting why he was not taking better care of himself physically and emotionally, and not gratifying his own needs in the process. Through an exploration of these issues, including connection with childhood dynamics, the patient achieved new understanding and resolved his anxiety and depression within weeks.

Adult developmental lines. Anna Freud (1965) introduced the concept of developmental lines for childhood, the detailed longitudinal elaboration of specific aspects of ego development across developmental phases: for example, from the freedom to soil and wet to the achievement of bowel and bladder control. Since development is lifelong, similar lines may be delineated for adulthood. We (1981) have outlined ten: (1) intimacy, love, and sex; (2) the body; (3) time and death; (4) relationship to children; (5) relationship to parents; (6) mentor relationship; (7) relationship to society; (8) work; (9) play; and (10) finances. We are working on a more detailed elaboration of these developmental lines to broaden knowledge of normal adult developmental processes and to increase the usefulness of adult developmental lines in the clinical setting.

As an example, the developmental line of intimacy, love, and sex may be summarized as follows. In the late teens and twenties, building on the base of adolescent sexual experimentation and fantasy, each individual finds, under normal circumstances, a heterosexual partner, learns to use the body comfortably as a sexual instrument, and develops the capacity for intimacy—the ability to care for the partner at least as much as for the self. Then in the twenties and thirties, the urge to invest exclusively in one partner and begin a family is engaged. Midlife brings the challenge of accepting the diminution of sexual drive in the partner and the self and a redefinition of relationships with spouse and children. In later years, many individuals face the loss of a spouse, the unavailability of sexual partners, and the need to forge sustaining ties with friends, children, and grandchildren. The use of this developmental line allows the clinician to trace the patient's experience in these areas across the adult years, relating current and past experience, and anticipating future progression or fixation. In child development, chronologic and phase markers are more clearly defined than in adulthood, which spans many more years and contains a much wider variety of experience. Consequently, significant, normal variation will be noted along each adult developmental line. Nevertheless, a certain orderliness and predictability are evident, determined by the processes of biological aging that underlie adult development.

Adult Developmental Arrest

We have also found the concept of adult developmental arrest useful in the diagnostic process. The concept of a developmental arrest has long been considered useful in child analysis (Nagera 1964; Weil 1953). Through fixation or regression, or a combination of the two, a child's progress along a developmental line may be arrested. Similarly, we maintain that phase-specific stimuli to development occur in adulthood, and development may be arrested in the face of adult developmental tasks. Important to this concept is the new emphasis on the adult past (along with the childhood past) in history-taking (Colarusso and Nemiroff 1979, 1981;

Shane 1977). In a more open-ended view of development, the genetic approach takes on a longitudinal dimension, incorporating experiences that occur in all phases of life. Thus, in addition to the patient's childhood and adolescence, the therapist must consider middle-age experience as well. The following is an example of a detailed developmental history, including child *and* adult developmental information in which an adult development arrest played a significant role.

A successful thirty-one-year-old attorney sought treatment because he felt unhappy in his relationships with women. He described a pattern of disrupting relationships when he felt too involved and "trapped." Married in his mid-twenties, Mr. B. continued to be sexually involved with women other than his wife. After several months of marriage, he abruptly divorced his wife, without external provocation. The memory of that sudden, inexplicable action continued to pain him six years later. At that time he was seriously involved with another woman, but found himself wanting to leave her. While lying with his head in her lap, he had the idea of "wanting to stab her in the vagina with a knife." He became frightened about the thought and sought analysis. The patient is the eldest son of an intact family that includes father, mother, younger sister, and younger brothers. Mr. B. was a planned, full-term baby. There were no particular problems with the pregnancy, although he was told that his mother suffered from mild depression both before and after his birth. She was involved in his care on a full-time basis. For unknown reasons, breast feeding was interrupted soon after it was begun. This was told to the analyst when the patient was describing his lifelong fascination with breasts. Physical milestones of development such as sitting, standing, and walking occurred within normal limits. Mr. B. was told that he was completely toilet trained before the age of two and, according to family lore, there were never any regressions from "this perfect toilet training." The patient reacted strongly to the birth of his sister when he was two, and he remembers many battles with her during childhood. When Mr. B. was three, his mother, who had been a constant figure in his life, was badly hurt in an automobile accident and remained hospitalized for almost a year. Mr. B. has no memory for this interval, during which the family lived with the maternal grandmother.

The oedipal years were characterized by frequent paternal absences of two to three weeks. Mr. B. remembers missing his father during that time and wishing that he could accompany him. When his father was away, his mother often invited the boy to sleep with her. The patient recalled vivid memories of lying in bed with his mother, aware of her negligee, thinking about touching or sucking on her breasts. But his mother could also be punitive. One day when he was six or seven, she discovered him involved in sex play with another boy. She told him over and over again that he was "bad" for such activity.

Although he had been able to separate easily from his mother to attend school, he was described by several of his teachers as a mildly hyperactive child who had difficulty sitting still and concentrating. The patient had some initial problems with reading, but soon he became a good student. He had many friends and was well accepted by the peer group. During latency, his relationship with his father remained difficult because his father continued to travel and considered him to be a "destructive, selfish child, only interested in himself and never taking the time to think."

Puberty occurred at thirteen. Masturbatory fantasies were centered on girls' breasts. The patient was becoming a fine student, but he also has vivid memories of continually trying to look down girls' blouses in school. He started to date regularly toward the end of high school. His father's business travel continued, but the son no longer slept in mother's bed; instead, the two of them would watch television late into the night. He remembered feeling overwhelming sexual desire for her that often culminated in masturbation, accompanied by conscious sexual thoughts about her. During those years his father developed a serious problem with alcohol. In addition to intensifying the tension between father and son, the drinking created a new bond between mother and son as they worked closely together to control the father's behavior.

Initial young adult development was quite positive. Mr. B. was accepted at the college of his choice, which was at a considerable distance from home; he greatly enjoyed himself, doing well scholastically, athletically, and socially. Eventually he decided upon law as a career and was accepted at an outstanding school. There he met his future wife. Mr. B. was very attracted to her, particularly because of her ample breasts. After a brief courtship, they married impulsively.

However, almost immediately after marriage, Mr. B. found himself obsessed with other female law students, particularly the wife of a close friend. He was hardly married a month when he started a torrid affair with the woman. Against his wife's pleading and to the dismay of family and friends, he abruptly divorced her in a callous and cavalier fashion. After finishing law school successfully, Mr. B. entered a prominent law firm. He saw many women in "Don-Juan" one-night stands, but eventually became seriously involved with an attractive female lawyer. Mr. B. felt that she was "perfect," but he was troubled by feelings of being trapped. He was drawn to her, but struggled with his wish to run. The recurrent and insistent idea of wanting to stab her in the vagina with a knife tortured him. He also found himself suffering remorse over the memory of his behavior toward his divorced wife; he felt he still loved her and could not make sense of his irrational behavior toward her.

Mr. B.'s analysis revealed considerable preoedipal and oedipal rage that interfered with the achievement of intimacy and a loving relationship with a woman. In the transference, he relived early narcissistic injuries relating to both his father and mother as is demonstrated by the following dream and associations:

In a dream, Mr. B. is called by a colleague and asked to recommend a good attorney. Mr. B. gives a name. The person is dissatisfied, so Mr. B. gives his own name and then feels agonized that he has to sell himself. He cries out in the dream, "Why do I have to be so defensive and always justify myself?"

His associations are to feelings of inferiority. Things are going well in his law practice, but it will collapse. His anxiety causes him to give his own name inappropriately and oversell himself. He associates to the injuries in his life: his mother's depression, the births of sister and brothers, and his father's alcoholism and unavailability. Mr. B. feels that the analyst always evades his questions, as did his father. He believes that his father must have held back from him because the patient was inferior. He wants to go home with the analyst and be there all the time. "What I really want is to wrap my legs around you and get inside of you. I want to have you all to myself, that there be no end to our sessions, no weekends, no vacations. But I can't stand talking to you like this." The analyst asks what frightens him about these feelings. "It would give you so much control over me. It's what I wanted from my mother, but she would completely take me over. I can't trust her. Now I see, with your help, how I have my girlfriend, you, and my mother all mixed up. You and my girlfriend are not my mother."

The patient also feared his rage, which he experienced as murderous. Closeness with the analyst and his girlfriend had to be avoided; he had to protect them from being destroyed. Mr. B. reexperienced feelings of wanting to crush his sister's head with a hammer. His mother was hospitalized, and his father went away on business trips because he was such a destructive child. He was a killer, and his parents were fragile. He had better keep his distance from people.

This patient had both significant childhood traumas and a developmental arrest in young adulthood when he began to struggle seriously with conflicts over intimacy and love. The adult developmental arrest was precipitated by the sudden divorce, which was experienced as a significant adult trauma, as was his continued inability to make a commitment to one woman. Although the analysis considered all aspects of Mr. B.'s life, the patient and the analyst decided to focus on the adult developmental arrest and the barriers to intimacy and loving relationships with women because the emphasis on both childhood events *and* adult experiences increased the analyst's armamentarium and the patient's understanding. The developmental perspective played a major role in helping to orient and organize the analysis. Although the patient dealt with many aspects of his childhood, current reality, and transference during the five-year treatment, his central problem was the inability to achieve intimacy with a woman during his young-adult years. Eventually, he gained considerable emotional perspective about the origins and ramifications of this barrier and was able to make a commitment to an appropriate woman and to progress along the adult developmental line of intimacy, love, and sex.

The following clinical case illustrates a common diagnostic problem and our approach in working with older patients.

The patient, a seventy-six-year-old widowed professor emeritus of biochemistry, came for consultation because of memory difficulties, both short- and long-term. Further, he stated, "I feel a general declining of my mental ability which affects the quality of my life. I have a great deal of difficulty in making decisions dealing with the most trivial details of life."

Even though he readily participated in the diagnostic process, he maintained, with a twinkle in his eye, a skepticism of psychotherapeutic evaluation, wondering about the ambiguity of the process, the unscientific questions about feelings, and the value of talking about feelings. Because of his complaints about memory and mental abilities, both neurological consultation and psychological testing were arranged immediately. A complete battery of tests was ordered, including the Wechsler Adult Development Intelligence Scale (SCALE), the Bender Visual Motor Gestalt Test, the Wechsler Memory Scale, and the full Halstead-Reitan neuropsychological battery. All tests revealed he was not functionally impaired; in fact, in many areas he was functioning *above* average. Neurological examination was also negative. It is our practice to review with the patient as completely as possible the results of medical and psychological reports, making sure the patient understands the results and allowing enough time to discuss fully the patient's anxieties about his or her physical condition.

A comprehensive history of this patient's life cycle was taken, including tracing the stages, tasks, and developmental lines. After feeling reassured about his mental processes, he revealed that he was having an affair with a forty-one-year-old woman who was suffering from a manic-depressive condition. He was being harassed night and day by this woman, who demanded nearly constant attention, including frequent sexual activity. When frustrated, she would call his house repeatedly and once drove her car onto his front lawn. He believed that his having sex with her made him responsible for "treating" her mental condition. The therapist explored this unrealistic demand of himself and helped him to formulate reasonable limits in the relationship. Soon his woman friend went under the care of a psychiatrist, the relationship ended, and his anxiety and depression diminished as did his difficulties with memory and indecision. It seemed as if he had been saying through his anxieties about his memory, "Stop harassing me. I'm an old man. I'm getting senile. Stop asking me for sex." Memory "performance" was substituted for anxiety about sexual performance. A displacement upward from genital concerns to concerns about the intellect seemed to have occurred.

He then entered twice-weekly exploratory psychotherapy, which uncovered an incomplete grief reaction revolving around the death of his wife four years earlier. He recognized a physical similarity between his forty-one-year-old woman friend and his wife when she had been in her forties. His punishment at the hands of the manic-depressive woman was both for unexpressed hostility toward his wife and his guilt over having sex with the girlfriend. He traced a lifetime of guilt and conflict over sex in relation to his parents' harsh and moralistic attitudes toward sex. These attitudes were also expressed in the transference, as he had difficulty discussing his sexual fantasies and masturbation with the therapist; he felt sure that the therapist thought he was an "inappropriate dirty old man." Masturbatory anxiety had again become particularly intense since the death of his wife, and the discussion of his increased masturbation brought considerable relief and decrease of anxiety.

After he and his therapist dealt with his loneliness, he made plans to spend more time with his children and his colleagues. He completed treatment, his anxiety diminished, his depression lifted, and his concern over his memory abated. Understanding more about his sexual and aggressive conflicts and feeling better enough about himself to make more appropriate contacts reduced his loneliness. In light of prevailing biases against treating the older patient in an exploratory, psychoanalytically oriented psychotherapy, this man could have received only superficial "supportive" attention and might not have achieved as much as he did.

An Adult Developmental Understanding of Transference

We believe that transference phenomena in adulthood come from three sources: (1) new editions or elaborations of infantile experience; (2) experiences from all developmental stages beyond early childhood; and (3) current midlife or late adulthood developmental conflicts. In such a framework, the adult past as well as the childhood past becomes an important source of transference. The idea that all behavior may be explained by an understanding of the first three to six years of an individual's life is ingrained in Western scientific and cultural thought. For example, at a conference on adolescence not long ago, speaker after speaker explained patient symptomatology and behavior almost exclusively in preoedipal and oedipal terms, paradoxically ignoring the latency and adolescent years. Similarly, at an interdisciplinary seminar at the University of California, San Diego, historians, anthropologists, and psychoanalysts debated whether an oedipal or preoedipal conceptualization of Homer was more useful, as though the epic should be explained fully by one or the other.

We suggest a theoretical base in which every phase of development throughout the life cycle is recognized as potentially important; each, because of its position in the life course and its relationship to preceding and subsequent stages, contributing uniquely to the evolution of the mind and to the nature of psychopathology. Childhood is the era in which psychic structure is formed and from which various psychopathology emerge. The enormous importance of this phase of life does not, however, diminish that of adulthood. The significant changes in psychic structure and the childhood tendencies toward normality and/or pathology are realized and determined by adult experiences.

Developmental Assessment of a Neurosis

The following outline, reconstructed by the patient and the analyst during a five-year analysis, illustrates our technique of taking a comprehensive life-cycle history and the manner in which symptoms are formed out of phase-specific events. The patient was a thirty-eight-year-old man who sought treatment when his cardiac neurosis and fear of going to work were nearly incapacitating.

Preoedipal years: Mother was lovingly involved in the patient's care on a full-time basis. Toilet training was early and severe. *The patient got off to a fairly solid start in life.*

Oedipal phase: The patient preferred his mother, who was seductive.

Often nude, she frequently invited him into her bed. Father was emotionally distant. A pronounced infantile neurosis was present, particularly evidenced by severe nightmares. A tonsillectomy was performed at age five. When the patient was six, his sister developed diabetes and began to take daily insulin injections. There was clear evidence of an unresolved oedipal complex and infantile neurosis. This phase is the first stage of development in which the mind is sophisticated enough to form neurotic structures in response to oedipal drives and conflicts.

Latency: At age eight the patient developed phobias (of robbers and monsters) and obsessions (addition and subtraction rituals). At age ten he underwent sudden major surgery. A few months later his father suffered a heart attack and began to take medication. When the patient was eleven, his father died of a second infarct. During this phase of development, classical neurotic symptoms occurred for the first time in response to unresolved oedipal conflict; major traumas occurred that influenced future symptom formation and the adolescent and young adult developmental tasks of choosing a career.

Adolescence: At age fourteen the patient became fearful that he and his mother would die (as a defense against the upsurge of adolescent sexual feelings toward her and as a reaction to his oedipal "victory" over his dead father). Between ages fifteen and seventeen new symptoms appeared: a sleep disturbance and depression, leading the patient to use sleeping pills (an identification with his father and sister). Other aspects of adolescent development were less problematic—fine academic performance, numerous friends, and some dating. During adolescence the neurosis was elaborated with the onset of a sleep disturbance and the beginning of a pattern of drug dependence, symptoms related to a latency event (the death of his father), and adolescent sexual maturation.

Young adulthood: The patient decided to become a physician. In medical school he had intercourse for the first time and continued to self-medicate, using tranquilizers and sleeping pills. At age twenty-five he married. Life revolved increasingly around his symptoms. Age thirty-five saw the onset of a cardiac neurosis (identification with and punishment for his father's death), followed at age thirty-seven by a work phobia. A year later he entered analysis because he was unable to work and feared that he would die in his forties, as his father had done. Phase-specific tasks were both skewed by the neurosis and determined by its elaboration. The choice of career had been strongly influenced by the death of his father and his own surgery during latency. He could trust no one but himself for his own care. The onset of the cardiac neurosis was related to the growing, phase-specific midlife preoccupation with time limitation and personal death.

Technically, it was not enough to help the patient understand the relationship between the infantile and adult neuroses, that is, the oedipal and preoedipal determinants. Therapist and patient also had to detail the elaboration of the neurosis through all subsequent developmental phases to the present. Then, as has been described by Shane (1979), the patient was helped to consider the effects of the insights and freedom gained in the analysis to his present and future development. Working through, an integral part of gaining insight, becomes a process in which new phase-specific adult developmental tasks and conflicts that were not encountered earlier in life are examined both to evaluate the effects of earlier experience on normal adult developmental processes and, conversely, to determine the contribution of adult developmental conflict to the symptom picture. Adult developmental theory provides a new framework within which to understand the effect of infantile experience on later life and a new dimension to the concept of working through.

With the life-cycle perspective in mind, let us turn to a more specific consideration of transference. Developmental views of transference have been expressed by Cohler and Coltrera. Cohler (1980) writes of development and remembering:

Consideration of the impact of psychological development across the life cycle on the experience of remembering the past shows that it is impossible to consider an objective past apart from developmentally determined views of this past which emerges successively during childhood, adolescence, young adulthood, and middle and old age. The fantasies which emerge during the oedipal phase are but prototypes of such developmentally determined fantasies which are associated with each of the phases of development across the life cycle. (Pp. 174–75)

Coltrera (1979) speaks directly about transference: "The transference neurosis is very much developmentally determined, its character and focus changing throughout the life cycle according to phase-specific developmental and conflict resolutions and their subsequent internalization" (pp. 304–305).

Forms of Transference

Clinical understanding may also be enhanced by the recognition that transference phenomena take several forms in older patients, depending on whether childhood or adult experience is the source of the transference. *Parental transference* is the most common and best understood. On the basis of past experience, patients of any age react to the therapist, regardless of age, as though he or she were a parent. In traditional terms the reference to the past is to the infantile past, the oedipal and preoedipal years, but in our conceptualization, experience with parents in adolescence and adulthood may also be represented in the parental transference.

In *peer* or *sibling transference* the patient reacts to the therapist as though he were a spouse, friend, or sibling. That persons other than the parents play important roles in every individual's development is obvious enough, but there is little recognition of their significance in the existing theory of transference, as evidenced by the dearth of literature or scientific presentations about transference objects other than the parents of early childhood. The following comment by Hiatt (1971) is an exception:

> A spouse may occupy a greater span of years than a parental figure, and children, who may be all that remain of the patient's family constellation, tend to alter the transference seen in psychotherapy. In the "replaying of the chorus" of those growing old, the therapist should try to uncover the "infantile neurosis"; however, other significant figures than the patient's parents may have an impact on the transference which the patient reflects with his physician. (P. 594)

We see the lack of reference in the transference literature to spouses and children as another example of how the exclusive emphasis on early childhood has inhibited theoretical understanding of the importance of adult experience.

The third form of multigenerational transference is *son* or *daughter transference*. Here the usual transference paradigm is reversed, and the patient reacts to the therapist as though he were the patient's child. This form of transference has infantile components, since children play at being parents and are deeply engrossed with their own progenitors, but it grows primarily out of the actual adult experience of parenthood. Drawn from multiple phases of development, parent-patients transfer their unresolved expectations and disappointments and their hostile and loving impulses toward their children onto the therapist. For example, one seventy-year-old woman, who was unnecessarily sterilized at age twenty-one and had a lifetime of difficulty with her adopted children, developed an intense, idealized son transference toward her thirty-five-year-old male therapist. He was the accomplished, attentive, loving son for whom she had always wished. As this aspect of the transference emerged, the patient became punishing and critical. Gradually her profound anger and disappointment in her adopted children and her wish for a perfect child of her own came to the fore. As these feelings emerged, they were interpreted like any other transference. The therapist understood the transference to be a central component of this woman's character, symptomatology, and life experience. By no means was the transference limited to this form; the patient developed strong paternal and sibling feelings as well. In all three forms of transference, the therapist becomes the object of powerful libidinal and aggressive feelings.

Another example of a reversed transference occurred in the psychotherapy of a woman in her early fifties.

The patient came for treatment as a result of the pain caused by watching her twenty-three-year-old son struggle to leave home. The therapist's explanation of the son's *continued* search for identity—a task she felt he should have finished in his teens—not only relieved her fears that he was severely disturbed but also stimulated her transference relationship to the therapist. Her son's verbal abuse and rudeness, a defense against dependency, contrasted sharply with the therapist's kindness, understanding, and empathy, and led to the emergence of a transference paradigm in which the therapist was seen as a good and caring son. This idealization facilitated the exploration of the *mother's* role in her son's conflict, namely, ambivalence about giving him up.

At that point the therapist became the equivalent of an adult transitional object, facilitating the mother's separation from her son. As the son actually individuated, the patient regressively tried to reestablish the relationship in the transference through attempts to control the therapist and seduce him around issues of medication and a mutual interest in literature ("Let's read Chaucer, why talk about such depressing stuff").

The resolution of the transference allowed the patient to focus on other phase-specific developmental issues such as the "empty-nest" syndrome—what to do with life now that her children were raised—as well as her changing relationship with her husband, and so on. In the process the therapist went from being "my good son" to "my good friend."

Although these three forms of transference are presented separately for the sake of clarity, we do not mean to imply that they occur in isolation. There is no simple trichotomy. All transference material has multiple meanings, determinants, and developmental sources. The therapeutic tasks remains the same, *but more complex:* to understand the meanings of the transference phenomena and eventually to convey these insights to the patient.

Countertransference Patterns in Treating Older Patients

Therapists' countertransference responses to older patients run the gamut, just as they do with younger adults or children, but in addition, there are countertransference reactions that are specifically related to adult development. To illustrate, let us briefly consider three. The first of these has to do with the therapist's reaction to aging, an issue addressed by Hassler (1985).

> For both the middle-aged (or older) analyst and his or her patient, thoughts and feelings about the finiteness of time and personal death, although disguised, are rarely absent. Both partners in the analytic process deny on various levels the clinical and developmental significance of this objective time frame. (P. 115)

Second, therapists tend to react to the sexuality of older patients with surprise, dismay, guilt, and anxiety, particularly when it is directed toward them in the transference, as illustrated by the following remarks from an attractive female therapist in her thirties responding to a male patient in his sixties (Nemiroff and Colarusso 1985).

> Early in the treatment process, Mr. D.'s sexual feelings emerged. His well-groomed appearance and adolescent-like nervousness in the first half of the sessions prompted a little discomfort on my part. My concern was how to engender respect and develop a therapeutic alliance with a patient who was old enough to be my grandfather. (Pp. 164–65)

The determinants of this attitude are likely from both infantile and adult sources. Unconscious factors may be related to the therapist's unresolved oedipal feelings about parental sexuality and adult oedipal feelings of triumph over aging or dead parents.

Lastly, the dependency needs of older patients, particularly those expressed by individuals who are alone and/or ill, take on a special prominence in treatment. The exaggerated dependency needs of the patient may stimulate the therapist's infantile wishes to dominate and control the parent/patient and may become intertwined with actual ongoing conflicts with aging parents in the present. In either event, the therapist is consciously and unconsciously forced to confront a powerful confluence of feelings about his parents from the past and present that affect the treatment process and may be expressed in countertransference reactions.

The Analysis of a Seventy-Year-Old Woman

Several ideas presented here emerged from the psychoanalysis of a seventy-year-old woman conducted recently by Dr. Eli Miller and studied in collaboration with us. Other aspects of the case have been reported elsewhere by Dr. Miller (1987).

Symptoms: The patient was a sixty-eight-year-old married female with grown adopted children. She sought treatment for anxiety, depression, and a general sense of disorganization in her life, especially related to trauma associated with her children.

The spouse: The patient's husband was a supportive, cheerful, successful, retired businessman. They were soon to celebrate their fortieth anniversary. Her relationship with him was warm, positive, and nonconflictual, although the patient desired sex more often than he.

Psychological testing: "Her memory is sharp and clear, her grasp of information intact. Judgment is unimpaired, and in general she presents a picture of a high level of ego integrity. There is no evidence of deterioration or sclerotic implications. . . . These findings place her in good stead for any kind of dynamically oriented therapy . . . while one does not often think of psychoanalysis for a person of her age" (p. 32).

Response to recommendation for analysis: When I discussed the possibility of analysis with the patient, I pointed out to her that in the past a contraindication for analysis in her age group was potential depression upon discovering all that one may have missed in life. She responded with a chuckle, saying that you did not have to be in analysis for that to happen; someone her age often did that without any other prodding.

Ability to analyze transference and infantile oedipal material: As year two progressed, Mrs. T. began to ask many questions and to express frustration when they were not answered. I asked if this repeated an interaction with her father. "Yes, my father was taciturn, but you are still stingy with words." I mentioned that she might consider my words gifts or love. She responded by agreeing and crying. She thought of someone in her childhood who had given her a lollipop and then recalled being depressed at age six while sitting in a small rocking chair. She associated these thoughts to the sadness she had experienced when her father was away. I proposed a link between the childhood depression and the relationship with her father. She said that the sadness began around age three and wondered why it was lingering.

Relationship between late adolescent and oedipal themes: She associated to a dream with incestuous themes (incest was horrible) and recalled an incident at age twenty when she had a surprisingly strong burst of intimate feelings for father. "I had had sex very recently before the episode with a very charming young man. I was fearing I'd be pregnant and that emotion hit me as I hugged my father. He was shaving, and I must have scared him."

Multigenerational transferences—oedipal father, son, young lover: Early in the third year of her analysis, Mrs. T. brought her pregnant poodle to a session. She wanted to give me one of the puppies. I asked her about the meaning of that wish. "The wish to give a baby to you would be the likely meaning (laughing). And then it could mean that I want to have sex with you. I want to give you all sorts of gifts. I want to know what kind of house you live in, and what sort of possessions you have. It's like with my children; I want them to have what they want and need." I stated, "You're feeling toward me like a son." "Yes, mentally, materially, emotionally. It's through children that one carries on. They are your immortality." Mrs. T. continued to focus on the puppies and recalled that before marriage she had wanted six children. This connected with the six puppies in the litter. Teasingly, she promised to bring me a puppy soon. "I haven't asked you yet whether you want a boy or a girl. Shouldn't we discuss the sex of the baby?" I responded, "Our baby?" She replied, "Of course, you said so (laughing). Now you're going to disclaim fathership? I'll go and have a baby anyhow . . . six of them. Having a baby is a collaboration between two people." To her surprise, the patient associated to the fifteen-year-old daughter of a friend who had committed suicide with her father's gun. Mrs. T. was deeply distressed and wondered why the girl had chosen her father's gun. "Maybe he was too close to his daughter, both physically and emotionally. Like I wanted my father and you to be," she added.

This analysis, conducted without parameters, produced considerable symptom relief, a more coherent sense of self, resolution of long-standing sexual conflict, and an optimistic outlook toward the future.

The study of adult development, as described in this book, is a multidisciplinary theoretical frontier. The clinical application of adult development theory is an outpost on that frontier. As our knowledge of the developmental processes in the second half of life increases, we should see continuous enhancement in psychotherapeutic technique and the need to revise continually existing theory of normal development and pathology.

REFERENCES

Abraham, K. [1919] 1949. "The Applicability of Psychoanalytic Treatment to Patients at an Advanced Age." In *Selected Papers on Psychoanalysis*, pp. 312–17. London: Hogarth Press.

Berezin, M. A. 1983. "Introduction to Psychotherapy of the Elderly." *Journal of Geriatric Psychiatry* 16:3–6.

Burke, J. D., Jr.; Pincus, H. A.; and Pardes, H. 1986. "The Clinician-Researcher in Psychiatry." *American Journal of Psychiatry* 143:968–75.

Butler, R. N., and Lewis, M. L. 1977. *Aging and Mental Health: Positive Psychosocial Approaches.* St. Louis: C.V. Mosby.

Cohler, B. J. 1980. "Adult Developmental Psychology and Reconstruction in Psychoanalysis." In *The Course of Life: Psychoanalytic Contributions Toward Understanding Personality Development, Vol. III,* ed. S. I. Greenspan and G. H. Pollock, pp. 149–99. Washington, D.C.: U. S. Government Printing Office, DHHS Publication No. (ADM) 81–1000.

Colarusso, C. A., and Nemiroff, R. A. 1979. "Some Observations and Hypotheses about the Psychoanalytic Theory of Adult Development." *International Journal of Psycho-Analysis* 60:59–71.

———. 1981. *Adult Development: A New Dimension in Psychodynamic Theory and Practice.* New York: Plenum.

Coltrera, J. 1979. "Truth from Genetic Illusion: The Transference and the Fate of the Infantile Neurosis." *Journal of the American Psychoanalytic Association* (suppl.) 27:289–313.

Cooper, A. M. 1985. "Will Neurobiology Influence Psychoanalysis?" *American Journal of Psychiatry* 142:1395–1402.

Crusey, J. E. 1985. "Short-Term Psychodynamic Psychotherapy with a Sixty-Two Year Old Man." In *The Race Against Time: Psychotherapy and Psychoanalysis in the Second Half of Life,* ed. R. A. Nemiroff and C. A. Colarusso, pp. 147–66. New York: Plenum.

Erikson, E. H. 1963. *Childhood and Society,* 2d ed. New York: W. W. Norton.

Fenichel, O. 1945. *The Psychoanalytic Theory of Neurosis.* New York: W. W. Norton.

Freud, A. 1985. *Normality and Pathology in Childhood: Assessment of Development.* New York: International Universities Press.

Freud, A.; Nagera, H.; and Freud, E. 1965. "Metapsychological Assessment of the Adult Personality." *Psychoanalytic Study of the Child* 20:9–41.

Freud, S. [1905] 1953. "Three Essays on the Theory of Sexuality." In *Standard Edition,* ed. J. Strachey, vol. 7, p. 125. London: Hogarth Press.

———. 1905 (1904) 1942. "On Psychotherapy." In *Standard Edition,* ed. J. Strachey, vol. 7, pp. 257–68. London: Hogarth Press.

———. [1912] "The Dynamics of Transference." *Standard Edition,* ed. J. Strachey, vol. 7, pp. 99–108. London: Hogarth Press.

Gould, R. L. 1978. *Transformations: Growth and Change in Adult Life.* New York: Simon and Schuster.

Gutmann, D. L. 1977. "The Cross-Cultural Perspective: Notes Toward a Comparative Psychology of Aging." In *Handbook of the Psychology of Aging,* ed. J. E. Birren and K. W. Schare. New York: Van Nostrand Reinhold.

Hassler, J. M. 1985. "Turning Forty in Analysis." In *The Race Against Time: Psychotherapy and Psychoanalysis in the Second Half of Life,* ed. R. A. Nemiroff and C. A. Colarusso. New York: Plenum.

Hiatt, H. 1971. "Dynamic Psychotherapy with the Aging Patient." *American Journal of Psychiatry* 25:591–600.

Hollender, M. H. 1952. "Individualizing the Aged." *Social Casework* 33:337–342.

Jacques. E. 1965. "Death and the Midlife Crisis." *International Journal of Psychoanalysis* 46:502–514.

Jelliffe, S. E. 1925. "The Old Age Factor in Psychoanalytic Therapy." *Medical Journal Records* 121:7–12.

Jung, C. G. 1933. *Modern Man in Search of a Soul.* New York: Harcourt, Brace.

Kandel, E. 1986. "Book Review." In *Psychotherapy and Social Sciences.* Northvale, N.J.: Jason Aronson.

Kaufman, M. R. 1937. "Psychoanalysis in Late-Life Depressions." *Psychoanalytic Quarterly* 6:308–315.

King, P. H. 1980. "The Life-Cycle as Indicated by the Transference in the Psycho-analysis of the Middle-Aged and Elderly." *International Journal of Psychoanalysis* 61:153–60.

Levinson, D. J.; Darrow, C.N.; Klein, E. B. et al. 1978. *The Seasons of a Man's Life.* New York: Alfred Knopf.

Mahler, M.; Pine, F.; and Berman, A. 1975. *The Psychological Birth of the Human Infant.* New York: Basic Books.

Miller, E. 1987. "The Oedipal Complex and Rejuvenation Fantasies in the Analysis of a Seventy-Year-Old Woman." *Journal of Geriatric Psychiatry* 20:29–51.

Nagera, H. 1964. "On Arrest in Development; Fixation and Regression." *Psychoanalytic Study of the Child* 19:222–39.

Nemiroff, R. A., and Colarusso, C. A. 1985. *The Race Against Time: Psychotherapy and Psychoanalysis in the Second Half of Life.* New York: Plenum.

Neugarten, B. L. 1979. "Time, Age, and the Life Cycle." *American Journal of Psychiatry* 136:887–95.

Pollock, G. H. 1961. "Mourning and Adaptation." *International Journal of Psycho-Analysis* 42:341–48.

———. 1980. "Aging or Aged: Development or Psychopathology." In *The Course of Life: Psychoanalytic Contributions Toward Understanding Personality Development, Vol. III,* ed. S. I. Greenspan and G. H. Pollock. Washington, D.C.: U.S. Government Printing Office, DHHS Publication No. (ADM) 81–1000.

Rangell, L. 1953. "The Role of the Parent in the Oedipal Complex." *International Journal of Psycho-Analysis* 42:341–48.

Rechtschaffen, A. 1959. "Psychotherapy with Geriatric Patients: A Review of the Literature." *Journal of Gerontology* 14:73–84.

Reiser, M. F. 1984. *Mind, Brain and Body: Towards a Convergence of Psychoanalysis and Neurobiology.* New York: Basic Books.

Savitsky, E., and Goldstein, R. 1983. "Psychotherapy of the Elderly: Case Reports." *Journal of Geriatric Psychiatry* 16:39–41.

Segal, H. 1958. "Fear of Death: Notes on the Analysis of an Old Man." *International Journal of Psychoanalysis* 34:178–81.

Settlage, C. F. 1985. "Adult Development and Therapeutic Process." Presentation, Denver Psychoanalytic Society and Mt. Airy Psychiatric Center, Denver, Colo., October 1985.

Shane, M. 1977. "A Rationale for Teaching Analytic Techniques Based on a Developmental Orientation and Approach." *International Journal of Psycho-Analysis* 58:95–108.

———. "The Developmental Approach to 'Working Through' in the Analytic Process." *International Journal of Psycho-Analysis* 60:375–82.

Spitz, R. 1965. *The First Year of Life.* New York: International Universities Press.

Stevens-Long, J. 1979. *Adult Life: Developmental Processes.* Palo Alto, Calif.: Mayfield.

Vaillant, G. E. 1977. *Adaptation to Life.* Boston: Little, Brown.

Van Gennep, A. 1960. *The Rites of Passage,* trans. M. B. Vizedow and G. L. Caffe. Chicago: University of Chicago Press.

Wayne, G. L. 1953. "Modified Psychoanalytic Therapy in Senescence." *Psychoanalytic Review* 40:90–116.

Weil, A. P. 1953. "Certain Severe Disturbances of Ego Development in Childhood." *Psychoanalytic Study of the Child* 8:271–86.

6

Adult Development:

Theories Past and Future

JUDITH STEVENS-LONG

> Fully to understand a grand and beautiful thought requires, perhaps,
> as much time as to conceive it.
>
> —Joubert

In the past ten years, the study of adult development has led to an explosion of grand and beautiful thoughts, and it has been my task, as an interpreter of these thoughts, to spend the time required to understand them fully. This chapter focuses on the grandest of those thoughts, the theoretical work that has appeared in the form of original theory, revival, and synthesis. If we adopt the standard definition of *theory* as a set of abstract principles that can be used to predict facts in the context of a particular body of knowledge and, ideally, to explain those facts, then the study of adulthood has not yet produced rigorous theory. Current theories offer interesting but often untested predictions about the course of adulthood, and convincing explanations exist with regard to only limited sets of behaviors rather than whole domains of development. Nonetheless, as Francis Bacon observed, "Even wrong theories may be better than chaos." Even inadequate theories can prompt one to observe more rigorously and to generate more coherent ideas. Moreover, theory organizes and integrates what we know, allowing us to order and remember and, therefore, to apply our knowledge to that which is unexplained.

Although there is no way to begin at the beginning—theories of adulthood and aging have existed since ancient times—a current intellectual history and review might begin in the late 1960s with the work of K. Warner Schaie (1967) and Paul Baltes (1968), Hayne Reese and William Overton (Reese and Overton 1970; Overton and Reese 1973), and Klaus Riegel (1972, 1975a, 1975b, 1977). Each of these works derived in part from the collision of what Riegel referred to as the American inductive paradigm and "continental European thinking," most specifically, the work of Jean Piaget.

From the point of view of an American graduate student at the time, Flavell's (1963) translation of Piaget's work had become by 1968 required reading for those of us taking a doctorate in developmental psychology, but few of us were sure where it fit into our intellectual scheme. In the years from 1967 to 1970, *Child Development* published dozens of articles in which researchers claimed that the operations Piaget had outlined could be taught in a matter of days, proving the general inadequacy of stagelike conceptions of development.

Despite the heroic efforts of these researchers, Piaget was here to stay, along with a world view that was more interactive and evolutionary than the mechanical, Newtonian view that dominated graduate training at the time. As Reese and Overton tackled those opposing world views, they turned our attention to the differing sets of assumptions that delineated what they called the *mechanical and organismic models.* The mechanists favored a metaphor of human development that emphasized the study of objective, overt responses and that suggested developmental changes were generally a function of external, objective events. Development, from the mechanist's perspective, represents the accumulation of experience, learning, or modeling and occurs along a predictable, cumulative curve. Organismic thinkers, according to Reese and Overton, saw development as the successive emergence of qualitatively different stages, marked by discontinuities. Behavior, from the organismic view, reflects change in internal structures such as cognitive operations or the components of personality. Developmental psychologists were not unaware of basic schools of thought; these had been traced for us graduate students *ad nauseum,* to Locke and Rosseau, and often to stretch a point, to Plato and Aristotle. What was refreshing in the writing of Reese and Overton, as well as Jonas Langer (1969), was the clarity and the immediacy with which they described the manifestation of these paradigms. Furthermore, although an underlying bias toward one model or the other can hardly be avoided, Reese, Overton, and Langer appeared more motivated to clarify distinctions than to promote a particular point of view.

To this thickening intellectual stew, the Europeans brought a sense of history, both as a force in shaping theory (Baltes and Goulet 1970; Baltes 1983), and as a basic dynamic in human development within and over generations (Schaie 1967; Baltes 1968; Baltes, Baltes and Reinert 1970). Furthermore, the Europeans seemed unwilling to dismiss psychoanalytic tradition, and the work of Erikson in particular. This truculence appealed to some of us graduate students and women, although we were not yet as articulate as we would become—the presence of Karen Horney, Melanie Klein, and Anna Freud representing minimal relief from the predominantly masculine intellectual world we inhabited. Finally, as graduate students in the late sixties, we were participants in the human potential movement, busily encountering each other, acting through our dreams à la Fritz Perls, and having the peak experiences described by Abraham Maslow (1968).

Throughout the 1970s, as the study of adult development became more central to developmental psychology in general, we also became more aware of how existing social and historical forces affected what we knew and the theories to which we were willing to subscribe. In other words, as we were wont to do during those years, we became increasingly aware of the politics of thought. Among those who were interested in such politics, few were more articulate than Klaus Riegel.

Klaus Riegel (1975a, 1975b) was among the first to speak of a dialectical paradigm or world view that might offer a synthesis of American and European thought. The term *dialectics* itself derives from the concept of dialogue, or to paraphrase Charles Tolman (1983), dialectic implies movement from one state (for example, ignorance) to another (for example, knowledge) by means of a process (dialogue), characterized by opposition (contradiction), and governed by internal necessity (logic). *Dialectics*, Tolman continues, refers to any method of argument or exposition that systematically weighs contradictory facts or ideas with a view to resolving apparent contradictions. The dialectical world view, as Riegel interpreted it, acknowledged the role of conflict or contradiction in human affairs. In other words, dialectics cast conflict in the role of change agent.

The model or metaphor that most closely captures the dialectical world view is the dialogue. In dialogue, the speaker affects both the listener and the self. We are affected, after all, by what we say, often more than the person who is listening. We create our own response in this way. Similarly, human beings are shaped by environmental conditions and, at the same time, are central to shaping those conditions (Riegel 1975a, 1977; Buss 1979; Reese 1983). By assuming an intense transaction between the organism and the environment, Riegel was able to synthesize important ideas found in both the mechanistic and organismic positions (E. W. Labouvie 1982).

Perhaps more than anything, a graduate education in human development circa 1968 left one with a certain respect for differences, a mistrust of intellectual monotheism, and a burning desire to synthesize the works of B. F. Skinner and Albert Bandura with Freud and Erik Erikson, with Abraham Maslow and Frederich Perls, and with Jean Piaget: a formidable task—and one, it might easily be argued, that could lead only to cognitive pablum. Still, the attempt to hold these enormously different views in the same mind and in the same lifetime, has been a central theme in the development of a life-span psychology.

Theory: A Multiplicity of Views

We owe almost all our knowledge not to those who have agreed, but to those who have differed.

—Charles Caleb Colton

At this juncture, the stew has been simmering for at least twenty years, and those most involved have generally adopted the position that a life-span treatment of human development requires a variety and a broad range of useful, workable theory. Writers like Baltes (1979) and Lerner (1983) argue that developmental patterns may differ substantially from one arena of development to another. For example, the pace and direction of perceptual development may be different from the developmental path that characterizes problem-solving behavior. Even within the same arena (e.g., intellectual development), patterns may change at different stages of the life span and, therefore, be most easily explained by different theoretical approaches.

Moreover, Baltes (1979, 1984) has become a major spokesperson for the *multicausal* approach, arguing that developmental patterns may be shaped by various forces, both internal and external, acting either in isolation or in concert. Purely mechanistic, or organismic, thinking is rare, having given way to an interactionist perspective that emphasizes the centrality of developmental transactions between person and environment. A transaction is an ecological construct that emphasizes change in both elements of an interaction. In other words, people change their environment and are, in turn, changed by it. Theorists working within antithetical frameworks, from psychoanalysis to behaviorism, have begun to assume a strong interaction between a developing organism and a changing environment. Learning theorists now speak more easily of cognition, emotion, and even self-control (Bandura 1981). Organismic thinkers pay increased attention to the influence of social and cultural factors, and psychodynamic writers have been more concerned about the role of thought and language in development, as well as environmental events.

Given the many competing theoretical constructs in the literature on adulthood, it may be best to think of developmental theories as a set of lenses, each one sharply focused on a different dimension or system of development. Psychodynamic theorists have, for instance, looked most closely at emotional or affective development, often overlooking the implications of their ideas for cognitive and behavioral development. Learning theorists appear to be talking about behavior but are often speaking of motivation (a reinforcer is a motivator, not a behavior). Cognitive theorists are interested in the development of the intellect. Somewhat arbitrarily, this review assigns theories to one of four major developmental systems: motivation, emotion, cognition, and behavior.

There are, of course, other possibilities. We might, for example, treat memory as a separate system rather than a subsystem of cognition. A more psychodynamic thinker might insist on the inclusion of defenses as a developing system. It is possible, however, to include most of the grander, more general ideas about development in this simple four-part system. Moreover, as we shall see, some telling holes appear when we begin to sort theories into systems and treat systems as developmental phases.

Theories of cognitive development

There is little doubt that the area of greatest theoretical ferment has been in the area of cognitive development. The work of Schaie (1967, 1979), Schaie and Hertzog (1985), and Baltes (1968, 1979, 1984), concerning the intellectual domain, and the study of cognition became the point of impact in the collision of American and European developmental psychology. For many, Piaget's work has served as a wellspring of ideas about adult life from the study of ego development (Kegan 1982) and moral thought (Kohlberg 1973; Gilligan 1982) to a consideration of love in long-term relationships (Stevens-Long 1988).

Probably the most elaborate theoretical work on adult cognitive development springs from the notion, orginally expressed by Riegel (1975a), that there might be a fifth, postformal stage of thinking. To understand current formulations of this stage, however, we will review several critical assumptions that Piaget made about developmental sequences.

Piaget believed that the intellectual operations emergent at each new stage of development were content free. That is, he argued that new abilities could be said to constitute only a qualitative or stage-type change if those abilities allowed one to operate on various subjects. For example, the stage of concrete operations is characterized by the emergence of an ability to classify objects along two dimensions at once. The ten-year-old concrete operator can easily identify the brown leaf in a collection containing brown objects and green leaves, but only one

brown leaf. The ability to classify is handy in the service of any intellectual subject matter.

Furthermore, Piaget contended that stages must follow one another in
an invariant sequence. In other words, everyone must necessarily go
through all stages in the same order, neither skipping any stage nor regressing. Sequence is insured only when the elements of one stage form a
logically necessary base for later stages (Commons and Richards 1982;
Richards and Commons 1982; Flavell 1963; Miller 1983).

A concrete operator is capable of classifying an object or concept with
two stable dimensions. Brown is a static trait, and leaf-shaped is stable
enough to allow one to identify confidently the intersect of brown and
leaf-shaped. At the fourth and final stage of Piaget's scheme, the stage of
formal operations, the ability to deal with variability arises. The formal
operator is able to formulate and test hypotheses methodically because he
or she understands the idea that traits or characteristics can vary in intensity or quantity. Therefore, a formal operator sees the need to hold some
elements in a problem constant while systematically changing other elements one at a time.

Obviously, the ability to think scientifically depends upon formal operations, and similarly, according to Piaget, the ability to think historically,
anthropologically, or philosophically. Formal operations permit one to
make propositions about propositions—that is, to think about events or
ideas that are counter to reality. The formal operator can grasp how things
might have been in the distant past or in the future, how they might be
in a society with different customs, or what the probable consequences of
social and moral changes might be. Formal operations allow one to infer
a general principle from specific instances or to deduce hypotheses and
corollaries from statements of general principles.

What, if any, further intellectual developments might occur over the
adult life span? By late adolescence or early adulthood, formal operations
are apparent. Do they represent an endpoint in the development of logical
thinking? Developmental psychologists Michael Commons and Francis
Richards (1982) have extended Piaget's scheme, preserving the assumptions that new abilities are content free and emerge in invariant sequences.
They have argued that, at the most basic level, formal operations allow the
thinker to understand the relationships between variables in a problem.
Beyond formal operations, they contend, lies a stage characterized as structural analytic thought, in which the thinker begins to grasp the relationships between sets of relationships. Another way to talk about this stage
is to say that one begins to understand relationships between systems.

If we see the organismic model, for instance, as a statement about the
relationships between an organism and its environment, and we see the

mechanical model as an alternative statement about those relationships, we might argue that these models represent different systems of thought about human development. Now, if we begin to compare the assumptions of these two models we also begin to look at the relationships between systems. This kind of thinking is *structural analytic.* The study of differing systems or theories is permitted by structural analytic thought (Commons 1982).

Using some of the same logic, the cognitive theorist Michael Basseches (1984) has tried to describe a stage he calls *dialectical thinking.* Like structural analytic thought, dialectical thinking allows one to analyze competing systems of relationships. Basseches maintains that a basic attribute of dialectical thinking is the dynamic of relativity. Formal thinkers, Basseches writes, focus on universals. They assume that there exists a single best answer to a problem. Postformal thinkers assume that since change is a basic characteristic of reality, there may be no finite truths.

Perhaps no one theory of human development contains the whole truth. Perhaps the truth about human development changes from one historical time to another (Gergen 1977, 1985). Such relativity of thought is characteristic of the postformal or dialectical thinker, according to Basseches. The dialectical thinker is aware that interactions between ideas and facts, as well as interactions between people and information, create what we regard as truth within a particular system of thought or a particular historical period. Certainly, looking back five hundred or one thousand years, one can see monumental changes in what is regarded as truth. It is more difficult to understand that what we now regard as truth may become outmoded.

Where are the chinks in the armor of the present truth? This question fascinates the dialectical thinker. Because he or she questions present truth, contradiction and paradox hold special interest for the dialectical thinker. Basseches believes that dialectical thought seeks contradictions among systems as a positive source for understanding change. Contradiction or paradox is not experienced as an unfortunate problem, but as an exciting opportunity for the emergence of a new idea. Basseches claims that the dialectical thinker understands how every effort to organize or systematize knowledge omits something—something that will eventually threaten the system with contradictions and create change.

Despite the strong emphasis on change, however, Basseches also argues that the dialectical thinker is able to identify certain universal forms within a changing context. That is, paradox or contradiction between systems may create a constantly changing view of the universe, but the significance of contradiction is constant. Similarly, the existence of paradox at the edges of our ability to reason is a constant.

Commons, Richards, and Basseches have found evidence for both the existence and the sequentiality of a fifth stage. Their subjects have been, by and large, young adults. Structural analytic or dialectical thinking may follow formal operations, but it seems to emerge fairly early in adult life. Other writers struggling with the issue of an adult stage of intellectual growth have focused on the meaning of changes in performance on traditional intelligence tests and problem-solving tasks as well as on tests of formal operations.

Both longitudinal and sequential research studies of intellectual performance over the adult years point to certain kinds of decline (Denney and Palmer 1982; Denney and Pearce 1982; Horn 1982; Schaie and Hertzog 1985). There is reason to believe that these declines are not as great as older, cross-sectional research once suggested, but performance on tasks that require formal operations as well as on some nonverbal and problem-solving tasks does decline, especially after sixty or seventy. Although it is possible that such changes in performance simply represent an inevitable sign of age, at least one writer has argued that such apparent decline may signal the emergence of a new, more pragmatic type of cognition arising in adulthood.

Gisela Labouvie-Vief (1982a, 1982b) argues that formal operations are appropriate only when a single, correct answer can be deduced from the premises of a problem. "All dogs are animals; Spot is a dog; therefore, Spot is an animal" is an example of formal logic in verbal reasoning. Life, however, is rarely this logical. The best solutions to social problems are seldom clear to everyone, and often the most rational solutions are impractical. Reality is fraught with uncertainty and paradox. As a function of experience in an illogical universe, Labouvier-Vief believes that some adults progress not only beyond formal operations, but also beyond a dialectical perspective (she calls it *intersystemic thought*), to the stage of autonomous thought.

Labouvie-Vief has conceptualized formal operations (what she terms *intrasystemic thought*) as the ability to analyze the relationships within a finite, closed system. Newtonian physics is an example of intrasystemic thinking. Ordinary objects in everyday life behave in accordance with Newton's laws. When we consider physical systems outside our planetary system, Newton's work fails to predict the workings of the universe. Intrasystemic thought focuses on what is universal, unchanging, predictable. At the next stage, intersystemic thought permits one to understand how certain truths are relevant only within particular systems. Intersystemic thought makes it possible to take multiple intellectual perspectives in a changing reality. On *terra firma,* Newtonian physics adequately describes the physical universe. When we are interested in objects that are light-years away, however, Einstein's formulae supercede ideas based upon Newton.

In the final or autonomous stage of development, Labouvie-Vief contends there is an "increasingly complex understanding of real-life system(s) . . ." which finally subordinates the "buoyant and naive if brilliant thought derived from 'pure logic' " (1982b, p. 76). Autonomous thinkers are able to formulate decisions that integrate logic and the irrational aspects of experience. Autonomous thinkers see not only how truth can be a product of a particular system, but also how the thinker participates in creating the truth. They understand that social and personal motivations influence one's formulation of truth and are able to discriminate between personal and universal reality. Performance on tests of formal operations may decline, in part, because older people no longer see problems of pure logic as relevant or interesting. They may be unable to accept the premises of such problems, looking for solutions that integrate practical experiences outside the problem as stated.

For instance, Labouvie-Vief illustrates her point by using an example (Cohen 1979) in which college students and older adults were asked to make inferences based on the information in the following problem:

Downstairs, there are three rooms: the kitchen, the dining-room, and the sitting-room. The sitting-room is in the front of the house, and the kitchen and dining-room face onto the vegetable garden at the back of the house. The noise of the traffic is very disturbing in the front rooms. Mother is in the kitchen cooking and Grandfather is reading the paper in the sitting-room. The children are at school and won't be home till tea time (quoted in Labouvie-Vief 1985, p. 524).

When subjects were asked to infer who would most likely be disturbed by the children upon their arrival for tea, college students almost invariably chose the grandfather. Labouvie-Vief writes that the answer "grandfather" shows "evidence of having processed the logical relationships embedded in the test: that is, about midafternoon the traffic is likely to be noisy, especially in the front rooms, and so forth. Older adults, on the other hand, do not appear to engage in this mode of analysis and thus fail to infer that it is only the grandfather who might be disturbed . . . is it not possible, however, that the adults in this study perceived *different* logical relationships from the ones of interest to the experimenter rather than none at all?" (1985, pp. 524–25). Labouvie-Vief proceeds to argue that older adults may use a qualitatively different mode of thinking—one that goes beyond or outside the information given in the problem. For example, older adults might argue that the grandfather could not possibly be the one likely to be most disturbed; otherwise, he would simply leave the sitting-room; or that the mother would be disturbed since she is most likely to interact with the children, who would probably go directly to the kitchen. In other words, older adults might assume the operation of choice. "From this perspective, the college students' behavior appears to reflect a degree of naively literal interpretation" (p. 525). College students appear to accept the task at face value, to be motivated by the need to comply with authority, and to search for the solution most likely to be considered correct by those authorities (Labouvie-Vief and Blanchard-Fields 1982).

The developmental psychologists Wolfgang Edelstein and Gil Noam (1982) have described the intellectual behavior of older adults as a reunion of logic and affect. Edelstein and Noam talk about the search for a socially adequate solution to problems rather than acceptance of the most "logical" solution. Wisdom, they argue, develops from an appreciation of the long-term consequences of action, and from the attempt to mediate between the demands of logic and emotion. The experience of responsibility in adult life is prerequisite to the development of wisdom. Responsibility, according to Edelstein and Noam, is the ability to continue to be oneself and to exercise good judgment in the face of personal disequilibrium.

Similarly John Rybash, William Hoyer, and Paul Roodin (1986) contend that the "formal thinker is infatuated with ideas, abstractions, and absolutes" (p. 31). Through young adulthood and middle age, they maintain, people learn to reconnect reason with the socioemotional realities of life. Whereas formal operations allow the thinker to analyze a closed system (one that is characterized by a finite and knowable number of variables), problems in real life are influenced by an unbounded number of interacting variables (Koplowitz 1984). Over the span of adult life, Rybash, Hoyer, and Roodin believe, thought becomes increasingly relative. Postformal thinkers understand that knowledge and reality are only temporarily true, not universally fixed, and that contradiction is a basic aspect of reality. Postformal thinkers possess the ability to synthesize contradictory thoughts, emotions, and experiences.

In yet another version of postformal operations, Allan Chinen (1984) has emphasized the mixture of logic and reason that may characterize the last stages of intellectual development. However, as he cautioned, "Enlightenment is a rare but natural virtue of old age" (p. 53). Chinen believes that this late-life potential exists in the ability to experience different modes of logic. Sometime during middle age, one experiences not only the "what" of thinking but also the "how," and an appreciation of such cognitive features as doubt, commitment, and faith emerges. This existential mode, as Chinen calls it, develops out of a resurgence of fantasy and playfulness at midlife. He argues that thinking at middle age is relative and contextual, but that the enlightenment of old age is, once again, more concerned with the universal aspects of truth.

In the final stage, the thinker develops a sense of the infinite, according to Chinen. There is an experience of mystery and transcendence, and an ability to appreciate the aesthetic qualities of one's own life, its completeness and necessity. This description is reminiscent of an early attempt by Lawrence Kohlberg (1973) to describe a seventh stage of moral judgment involving a religious orientation, although not a conventional one. Kohlberg wrote of a feeling of unity with the whole of nature, a moral sense more abstract and universal than most people ever possess. Unable to develop a more cogent description of such judgment, Kohlberg seems to have dropped the matter. However, one is reminded of Thoreau's perspective in *Walden Pond:*

Men frequently say to me, "I should think you would feel lonesome down there and want to be nearer to folks, rainy and snowy days and nights especially." I am tempted to reply to such, This whole earth which we inhabit is but a point in space. How far apart, think you, dwell the two most distant inhabitants of yonder star? Why should I feel lonely? Is not our planet in the milky way? (P. 17)

In an article written at approximately the same time Kohlberg wrote of a cosmic perspective, Van den Dale (1975) also suggested that adults develop the ability to consider the aesthetic properties of ideas and concepts rather than simply to assess their applicability to known facts. Ideas have qualities like beauty and elegance as clearly as have paintings. The work of Skinner reminds one of Japanese flower arrangement—sparse and essential—whereas Jung or Freud might be said to represent the baroque sensibility in thought.

Labouvie-Vief's autonomous stage, along with the work of Chinen, Kohlberg, and Van den Dale, suggests some swing back from the highly relativistic, contextual thinking of middle-aged postformal thought to a renewed appreciation of the universal, perhaps in the form of aesthetic or affective properties. Arguing that relativism allows us to develop a coherent system of values and to appreciate alternative value systems, Rybash, Hoyer, and Roodin (1986) quote an article by the journalist Peter Shaffer (1984) of the *New York Times Magazine:* "Great art always suggests the existence of absolutes." Although they ignore the implications of this statement for a final, less relativistic stage, these authors do suggest that postformal operations may not constitute a real stage, but a "set of styles of thinking that emerge in adulthood" (p. 56).

Whether we are looking at stages or styles, there seems to be an overarching theme that is linked with the synthesis of motivation, emotion, thought, and values in the struggle to understand reality. Chinen (1984), Kohlberg (1973), Edelstein and Noam (1982)—all refer to Erikson's concept of *integrity.* Labouvie-Vief, Rybash, Hoyer, and Roodin emphasize the integration of logic and affect. All of them suggest an increasingly strong interaction between developmental systems in adulthood, particularly among motivation, emotion, and cognition. If we begin to see integrity as a process rather than a state, the idea of strong or intense interaction among systems seems relevant; accordingly, integrity has been explored intensely as a component of motivational development in adult life.

Theories of motivational development

The study of motivational development has taken a more interactionist perspective, perhaps because the study of human goals necessarily has an almost teleological flavor, yet it is impossible to deny the effect of social circumstances and life history on motivation. In both the study of development and personality, the work of Maslow and Erikson reflects an appreciation for this interaction, but from different perspectives. Erikson's work is recognized as a starting point for a dialectical theory of life-span development (Riegel 1977), whereas Maslow—clearly a humanist, rather more an organismic thinker than Erikson—described an extensive set of environmental preconditions for the emergence of the mature personality.

A brief outline of Erikson's (1963) eight stages appears in table 6.1. Erikson believed that these stages were universal and that they emerged in an invariant sequence governed by a genetic ground plan he called the *epigenetic principle.* According to Erikson (1968a, 1982), the epigenetic principle determines the time at which certain developmental issues gain ascendance in the individual life span. This ascendant period presents a series of optimal moments for resolving the developmental conflict characteristic of each stage. If these moments pass without positive resolution, all future development is jeopardized. In biology, *epigenesis* refers to the forces underlying the development of the fetus from one stage to another. Erikson used the term to label the internal drive or force he believed produced qualitative change from one stage to the next (Kitchener 1978). Erikson conceptualized a strong interaction, not only between the person and the external environment, but among developmental systems as well: the biological, the psychological, and the social systems. Most important, Erikson clearly described the way in which the organism transforms the environment and is transformed by it. He contended that age-grading reflects the interaction between epigenesis and the social structure (Erikson 1963; Lerner 1976; Riegel 1977). Cross-cultural research convinced him that every society creates age-related institutions. Religion, for example, is viewed as both the outcome and the major environmental force behind the development of basic trust. He also maintained that weakness or deterioration of

TABLE 6.1

Erikson's Eight Stages of Life

Conflict at Each Stage	Emerging Value	Period of Life
Basic trust versus mistrust Consistency, continuity, and comfort produce a feeling of security and predictability.	Hope	Infancy
Autonomy versus shame and doubt Parental firmness allows for the experience of demand fulfillment with limits that produce self-control.	Will	Early childhood
Initiative versus guilt The development of the superego and cooperation with others support the growth of planning and a sense of responsibility.	Purpose	Play age
Industry versus inferiority Working and learning with others produces skill and the ability in using tools, and weapons, and method, as well as feelings of self-esteem.	Competence	School age
Identity versus role confusion The physical changes of adolescence arouse a new search for sameness and continuity and the need for a coherent sense of self.	Fidelity	Adolescence
Intimacy versus isolation A new ability to tolerate the threat of ego loss permits the establishment of mature relationships involving the fusion and counterpointing of identity.	Love	Young adulthood
Generativity versus stagnation The adult need to care for children and to guide the next generation produces the desire to leave something of substance as a legacy.	Care	Maturity
Integrity versus despair An accrued sense of order and meaning allows one to defend one's own life cycle as a contribution to the maintenance of the human world.	Wisdom	Old age

SOURCE: Reprinted from Judith Stevens-Long, *Adult Life* (Palo Alto, Calif.: Mayfield Publishing, 1988), p. 46.

age-related institutions hindered the positive resolution of developmental conflicts.

Although the specific institutions that Erikson placed at each developmental transaction (for example, the idea that monogamous heterosexual marriage is the institutional reflection of intimacy) have been criticized as ethnocentric, the basic notion that human development changes the structure of social institutions and is, in turn, influenced by those institutions is an intriguing example of how one might operationalize the notion of the person-environment transaction. Furthermore, Erikson has suggested that the length of developmental stages, or even the number of such stages, may be affected by changes in the length and quality of the life span over generations (Erikson and Hall 1983).

Unfortunately, Erikson leaves the mechanisms of development, as opposed to the content, essentially unexamined. He casts his stages in terms of conflict but never specifies the conditions under which conflict emerges. He has essentially ignored mechanisms such as learning or modeling and has not specifically addressed the interface between cognition and motivation, although his conceptualization of wisdom as a virtue derived from the development of integrity may touch on the matter. As Patricia Miller (1983) observed, "Erikson presents his theory as would a novelist or an artist rather than a scientist. At most, the theory is a loosely connected set of ideas and observations that could not, strictly speaking, be called a . . . theory" (p. 173).

In his own defense, Erikson (1982) has maintained that the everyday words of living languages, words like *love, wisdom, hope, and faith* "express both what is universally human and what is culturally specific" (p. 58). He believes that such terms harbor some fundamental relationship to human development and that simple, objective definitions may miss the most important aspects of their meanings.

In a similar vein, Maslow tended to rely on everyday words to express the content of development. Although Maslow's theory is not specifically developmental, nor does he use any developmental mechanism like epigenesis, it seems reasonable to argue that the higher stages of Maslow's pyramid are most likely to be at issue during adolescence and adulthood.

Figure 6.1 presents Maslow's hierarchy. At the base of the pyramid, Maslow (1968, 1970) placed the deficiency needs including biological requirements like food, water, and air as well as less immediate social needs such as the need to belong, to be loved, and to have self-esteem. The metaneeds (collectively, the need for self-actualization) appear at the apex because Maslow believed that they do not emerge until all deficiency needs are met. The metaneeds include the need for truth, for beauty, for self-

Figure 6.1

Maslow's Need Hierarchy

Needs

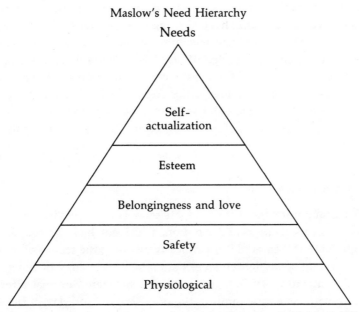

SOURCE: Reprinted from Judith Stevens-Long, *Adult Life* (Palo Alto, Calif.: Mayfield Publishing, 1988), p. 49.

sufficiency, and other abstract motives that are satisfied through *self-actualization,* which Maslow defines as the fulfillment of individual creative potential. In his attempt to describe the self-actualized person, Maslow (1970) turned to the biographies of historical figures like Abraham Lincoln, Thomas Jefferson, Albert Schweitzer, and Eleanor Roosevelt. The identification of life themes led him to conclude that the self-actualized person is more likely than other people to see the truth, better able to detect dishonesty and fakery. Self-actualized people displayed an acceptance of the self, nature, and others; were problem-centered rather than self-centered; and exhibited a strong desire to benefit others. These characteristics bring to mind Erikson's description of the generative midlife adult. Maslow also saw, however, some of the more aesthetic aspects of personality development, describing the self-actualized person as creative, discriminating, and empathic. He observed that such people had hearty appetites, enjoyed the pleasures of the world without shame or doubt, and were capable of intense, profound relationships. Again, the interaction of developmental systems, specifically affective and motivational development, seems to be a key concept.

Like Erikson, however, Maslow leaves us with examples and language drawn from common cultural wisdom, but without the specificity or particularity of definition that might be useful in operationalizing his constructs. This lack of specificity seems to be common to those theorists most interested in constructs that have a strong affective dimension. It is probably in the study of emotional development that we encounter the worst problems of definition. The definition of emotion is difficult enough, let alone the exploration of differences in content or feeling between various affective states. How does love differ from affection, shame from guilt, dislike or disgust from hatred? These are questions rarely approached by psychologists, yet they are often the questions that initally bring us to the study of psychology.

Theories of affective development

A major disappointment of the graduate school curriculum in 1967–68 was the course in motivation and emotion. I had not had the course as an undergraduate and entered it breathlessly awaiting the secrets of love and sex. I ended up spending ten weeks studying the biology of hunger and thirst. Because few psychologists actually considered normal affect the proper arena of scientific inquiry, the only serious work lay in the study of depression as a pathology—a disorder that one studied in abnormal psychology, not motivation and emotion.

The normal emotions remain immensely powerful yet are among the least understood dimensions of human development. In the second edition of the *Handbook of the Psychology of Aging,* a chapter on emotion and affect appears, but Richard Schulz (1985) admits that "emotions are . . . rarely addressed from a developmental perspective. Major textbooks on adult development and aging devote little space to it; moreover, major theories regarding the determinants of human emotions . . . have little to say about emotionality through middle and old age. It is unclear whether this neglect is due to oversight, to the unavailability of the necessary data, or the assumption that age, beyond early adulthood, is an irrelevant dimension for the understanding of emotionality" (p. 531).

The inclusion of the Schulz chapter in the *Handbook* is, undoubtedly, the result of the serious consideration that is finally being given to emotional development, spurred by the work on cognition in adult life. However, researchers have not reached any basic agreement on the nature of emotion. For instance, one group of thinkers whom we might call the *cognitive-emotional* theorists (Berscheid 1982; Fiske 1982; Linville 1982; Mandler 1982) have argued that emotional experience can be defined as the cognitive evaluation of arousal in the autonomic nervous system. In other words, thought is said to determine the quality and content of emotion;

qualitative differences between feelings are the product of intellectual interpretation. The *somatic* theorists (Leventhal 1982; Izard 1982), on the other hand, maintain that thought and emotion are independent but parallel systems. Emotions, this group suggests, may be represented in the older portions of the brain, like sensations or motor behaviors, and may not be entirely accessible to the more sophisticated cortical activity we ordinarily label cognition (Izard 1982).

Part of the problem here is that there is little agreement about whether there are basic emotional states—whether emotions come in different genetically wired flavors. Is there a biological base for feelings of joy that is different from the base for fear? Are emotions differentiated in the nervous system the way taste for salt and for sweet are? Or is all emotional differentiation learned by the attachment of a general physiological state to certain situational cues from the environment? What are the basic emotions, if any, and along what dimensions do they differ?

Those who believe there are a set of differentiated, primary affects have suggested perhaps six to twelve such independent factors. Candidates for these positions include interest, enjoyment, surprise, distress, fear, shame, contempt, and rage (Tomkins and McCarter 1964). Those who claim that emotions do not exist as discrete entitities might adopt Russell's (1980) approach. Using two simple dimensions, arousal and pleasure, Russell is able to distinguish twenty-eight different emotional concepts as they are ordinarily used by young adults.

The developmental implications of Russell's model are explored by Schulz (1985), who writes that age may be related to changes along at least six important dimensions of emotional experience:

1. *Intensity:* Does it increase or decrease with age?

2. *Duration:* Do emotions last longer with age since the physiological events that accompany them are thought to return to baseline more slowly?

3. *Variability:* Does emotional experience become more or less variable?

4. *Frequency:* Are certain emotions more or less frequent with age?

5. *Quality:* Are there qualitative changes in some emotions, like love or sorrow, with age?

6. *Elicitors:* Do different stimuli come to elicit emotional experience at different stages of the life span?

Schulz concludes that the available data do not suggest changes in the ratio of positive to negative emotions with age (Cameron 1975). However, these data do conflict with data suggesting an increase in the frequency of depression among the elderly. Perhaps, Schulz speculates, a new class of emotional events, the loss of significant others and important objects, causes new, intense, and long-lasting negative affective states. Again, however, we are dealing with the pathological aspects of emotion or emotional development, saying little about the normal, much less the optimal, course of affective development over the life span.

Probably the most persistent theme that emerges when normal development is addressed is emotional control. Because emotions are generally viewed from the perspective of pathology, American psychologists have approached emotional development as a way to understand the growth of emotional control. Their inquiry becomes a search for the features of cognition or environmental circumstance that allow one to maintain a positive, stable emotional tone. The experience of intense emotion is almost universally conceptualized as a negative event. The theme of emotional control appears in both the work of the cognitive and somatic theorists. George Mandler (1982) argues, for instance, that whether emotions are positive or negative depends upon one's knowledge of the world. In those situations where one knows how to respond, emotions are likely to be positive and relatively mild. If one's knowledge of the situation is insufficient, there is incongruity with existing response patterns, and the outcome may be positive or negative depending upon whether the accommodation one makes is successful or unsuccessful. In this way, Mandler implies, cognitive and intellectual development should produce increasing emotional control over the life span. Figure 6.2 presents Mandler's scheme for predicting the intensity and value of emotional experience. From this point of view, we might also predict, however, that new situations like the bereavement associated with age and the interruptions of normal response patterns caused by illness or loss of resources would produce strong negative emotional experiences. Over time, however, bereavement and grief will usually be experienced less strongly as one has more experience with important losses. These kind of specific predictions would make interesting tests of the cognitive positions vis-à-vis affect.

Studies of cognitive complexity do support Mandler's position (Linville 1982). People who possess more complex self-concepts show fewer, less intense mood swings than those with relatively simple self-concepts. In this research, complexity of self-concept was defined by the number and variety of clearly distinguishable roles in which the person appeared to function. Linville arued that complexity of self-concept has a stablizing effect on emotional experience because a negative event in one area or role in life is less likely to spill into another area. Developmentally, complexity seems to increase through the adult years until later life when role losses through death, retirement, or illness force a person to live in a more

Figure 6.2

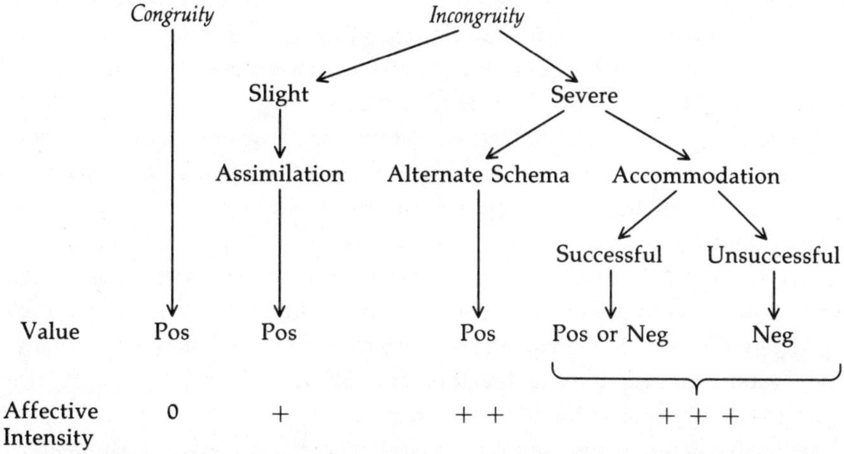

```
       Congruity                    Incongruity
           |                       /          \
           |                   Slight        Severe
           |                     |          /      \
           |                     ↓         ↙         ↘
           |                Assimilation  Alternate Schema  Accommodation
           |                     |             |          /        \
           |                     |             |         ↙          ↘
           |                     |             |    Successful   Unsuccessful
           |                     |             |         |            |
           ↓                     ↓             ↓         ↓            ↓
  Value   Pos                   Pos           Pos    Pos or Neg      Neg
                                                      _____/
                                                               Y

Affective   0          +              + +              + + +
Intensity
```

Several possible outcomes of schema congruity and incongruity in terms of both values and affective intensity. The resultant value is shown as either positive (POS) or negative (NEG). Degree of affective intensity is shown to vary from zero to +++.

SOURCE: Reprinted, by permission of the publisher, from G. Mandler, "The Structure of Value: Accounting for Taste," in *Affect and Cognition,* ed. M.S. Clark and S. T. Fiske, p. 22. Hillsdale, NJ: Laurence Erlbaum, 1982.

elementary, less complex style which, one would predict, should produce greater volatility. Yet, Lowenthal, Thurnher, and Chiriboga (1975) claim that older people tend to exhibit some decline or restriction in the flow and expression of the more "vulnerable volatile, or emotional components of person existence" (p. 64).

The somatic theorists have also pursued the issue of emotional control. In particular, Howard Leventhal (1982) has been intrigued by the idea that if emotion and cognition are, to some extent, independent systems, it may be possible to use reason and propositional thought to control emotional experience. Leventhal has argued that in time people learn to control their emotions because they are increasingly able to predict how they will respond to various environmental situations. Over the course of adult life, he contends, emotional responses cease to have an impulsive quality. The ability to predict one's own behavior produces more deliberate, controlled emotional experience.

Leventhal has been particularly interested in the emotional development of people who are dying, and has observed that, given time, they learn to cope with the terrors and can continue to experience joy and happiness even near death. From the extreme somatic view, emotional experience is completely independent of cognition and, therefore, uncontrollable. Leventhal takes a more moderate position, maintaining that affect is a form of cognition, different from abstract reasoning or perception, but capable of integration with other cognitive processes. Emotional development consists, from this view, in the growth of that integration.

Except for the notion that loss in later life may trigger some intense new emotional experience, neither the cognitive nor the somatic theorists have suggested the emergence of any new development in the affective system during adulthood. In fact, few psychologists have considered the possibility aside from Erikson's suggestion that love arises as a virtue associated with the development of intimacy, and that caring is a product of middle-aged generativity. Even Erikson switches from the emotional to the cognitive systems to describe the developments of old age, proposing that wisdom is the virtue associated with integrity.

In the past ten years, some empirical research on love has appeared, primarily from the cognitive camp (Berscheid 1982). Generally, this view dictates that *love* is an interpretation of the general autonomic arousal one feels in any exciting situation. The difference between falling in love and falling in an elevator has to do with the environmental cues. The emotion generated in the presence of a person of the appropriate sex who seems to offer certain kinds of social assets and a potential for furthering one's goals and plans can be interpreted as love. The arousal in the presence of numbers speeding by the floor indicator is interpreted as fear. As the behavior of two people who interpret their arousal as love becomes integrated into smooth, predictable chains of responses, hot emotion, the being-in-love, disappears, reemerging only when there is disruption or fear of loss. From this point of view, love in young adulthood has no special qualities associated with the development of intimacy, although emotional development might occur through the understanding and control of love experiences.

Erikson himself did little to clarify the unique qualities of love, which might arise as a virtue of intimacy. Although he implies that love in young adulthood must be different from love at an earlier stage of life because of its dependence upon a strong sense of personal identity, Erikson never treats the affective component of intimacy in any detail. On the other hand, a group of contemporary psychoanalytic thinkers, the object relations theorists, like Otto Kernberg (1976), Stanley Coen (1980), and Martin Bergman (1980), have been concerned with a definition of *mature love* as differentiated from other, earlier forms of affection. They argue that the development of mature love requires both the emergence of a mature sexual identity and couple bonding (Kernberg 1976). The unique qualities of mature love include feelings of tenderness toward the other and the ability to identify with the partner so that the interests, wishes, feelings, and shortcomings of the partner attain about the same importance as one's own. Sexually, mature love expresses itself in the ability to enjoy, even to lose oneself in the orgasm of the partner.

Kernberg (1980) has argued that mature love does not develop in the absence of certain cognitive abilities. He believes that one must be able to think abstractly enough to develop adult ethics and commitment in order to love. Furthermore, one must be able to assess the love object realistically, to understand and identify his or her interests, wishes, feelings, and shortcomings. Object relations theorists also return to a theme that has, no doubt, become familiar by now. Mature love depends upon the ability to integrate the good and the bad in oneself and in the love object, seeing the self and the partner as whole people.

There has been no empirical work on emotional development in middle age. While there is clinical description of midlife crisis and the attendant turmoil or depression, the only unique quality attributed to this period appears to be the acceptance of depression described by Vaillant and MacArthur (1972) in the Harvard studies of men at midlife. The emergence of mature caring or compassion that develops in the context of generativity has not been explored, although it has been suggested that mature empathy may depend to some extent on the growth of post-formal operations.

As for any positive emotional development in later life, the only suggestions come from the work of Carl Jung (1933, 1960). Jung argued that *maturity* consisted in the integration of conflicting tendencies or aspects of the personality. The opportunity for maturity arises, for the first time, according to Jung, at middle age, when a person turns from biological and social interests and activities to a concern for the inner, spiritual world. Jung argued that people become more religious, philosophical, and intuitive in the second half of life, and that they are increasingly able to integrate unconscious experience into everyday life.

As this intergration proceeds, Jung believed, wisdom and patience develop. The mature person tolerates, and eventually transcends conflict and opposition, even within the self. Finally, the truly mature person possesses an ability to identify with all living things in an uncritical, appreciative manner. Perhaps Jung's notion of *identification* with all living things can be used as a starting point for defining some emotional attribute of old age that has a counterpart in the object-relations notion that mature love is the ability to identify with another person. In middle age, Erikson's notion of *caring* might be clarified by the concept of identification with the larger social community, even with all human beings. The expansion of positive affect from the self to one other, then to many others, seems to be a dimension for the exploration of emotional maturity beyond the notion of emotional control as advanced by the somatic and cognitive theorists.

Notwithstanding the talk about cognitive change and the concern about changes in the nature, intensity, frequency, or quality of affect throughout the life span, there is almost no speculation in the literature, much less any data, about how behavior may vary, except as it reflects changes in cognitive or emotional life. In other words, everyone seems to assume that when cognition changes, problem-solving changes, or if emotions change, behavior will become more or less adaptive. The study of behavioral development per se has not been undertaken. Behavior is usually conceptualized as a function of environmental circumstances or cognitive intention rather than a separate developmental system with its own momentum. Even the radical behaviorism of Skinner might be considered a theory of motivation rather than a theory of behavior, since change in the nature or timing of reinforcement is thought to motivate all behavioral change.

Theories of behavioral development

Theories that emphasize the behavioral aspects of development have generally focused on how life events are related to outcomes like health and adjustment. Health and adjustment are assumed to reflect something about behavior, such as how successfully is one able to cope or how adaptive is one's behavior. Most of what we know about behavior, then, is the product of inference rather than the direct observation of overt response patterns. One such approach is illustrated by the work of David Chiriboga and Lorraine Cutler (1980). Chiriboga and Cutler have been particularly interested in how the perception of life events might affect behavior.

Beginning with an analysis of the Holmes and Rahe Social Adjustment Scale, Chiriboga and Cutler undertook the measurement and quantification of stress perception. The Holmes and Rahe Scale is presented in table 6.2. To use the scale, one simply adds up the points assigned to each life event experienced during the previous twelve months. The total number of points is used to predict the probability of stress-related illness during the coming year. The Holmes and Rahe Scale has been criticized because of its assumption that everyone will perceive the events included in the scale similarly. It is unlikely, however, that a divorce is equally stressful for everyone. Young adults, married only a few years, who own no property and have no children, may sail through a divorce with few difficulties. Middle-aged people with property and children are much more likely to have a hard time. The birth of a baby may be a blessed event for one couple

TABLE 6.2

Social Readjustment Rating Scale

Life event	Mean value
1 Death of spouse	100
2 Divorce	73
3 Marital separation	65
4 Jail term	63
5 Death of close family member	63
6 Personal injury or illness	53
7 Marriage	50
8 Fired at work	47
9 Marital reconciliation	45
10 Retirement	45
11 Change in health of family member	44
12 Pregnancy	40
13 Sex difficulties	39
14 Gain of new family member	39
15 Business readjustment	39
16 Change in financial state	38
17 Death of close friend	37
18 Change to different line of work	36
19 Change in number of arguments with spouse	35
20 Mortgage over $10,000	31
21 Foreclosure of mortgage or loan	30
22 Change in responsibilities at work	29
23 Son or daughter leaving home	29
24 Trouble with in-laws	29
25 Outstanding personal achievement	28
26 Wife begin or stop work	26
27 Begin or end school	26
28 Change in living conditions	25
29 Revision of personal habits	24
30 Trouble with boss	23
31 Change in work hours or conditions	20
32 Change in residence	20
33 Change in schools	20
34 Change in recreation	19
35 Change in church activities	19
36 Change in social activities	18
37 Mortgage or loan less than $10,000	17
38 Change in sleeping habits	16
39 Change in number of family get-togethers	15
40 Change in eating habits	15
41 Vacation	13
42 Christmas	12
43 Minor violations of the law	11

SOURCE: Reprinted with permission from [*Journal of Psychosomatic Research,* 11:-216, T. H. Holmes and R. H. Rahe, "The Social Readjustment Scale"]. Copyright [1967], Pergamon Press plc.

and an unwelcome burden for another. Chiriboga and Cutler revised the scale so that the subject assigns points to each event and indicates whether the event was experienced as a positive stressor or a negative one. Furthermore, Chiriboga and Cutler added a number of events missing from the Holmes and Rahe, including events that were more likely to occur to the elderly, like the loss of a driver's license due to failing health.

Data from the revised scale suggested the existence of at least four major behavioral patterns in response to stressful events. One group of subjects seemed dedicated to avoiding any sort of stress; another was able to increase the amount of positive stress without increasing the negative stress (these subjects were dubbed the "lucky" group). A third group was "overwhelmed" by large amounts of negative stress, and the fourth seemed to be "stress-prone" (reporting high levels of both negative and positive stress). The inference made from this information is that people probably learn to "do" something to avoid stress or to increase positive stress, and that being overwhelmed by negative stress suggests that one lacks the behaviors required to cope with or avoid negative events.

In a similar vein, Orville Brim, Jr., and Carol Ryff (1980) argue that life events may be described along three dimensions: the objective properties of the events themselves, the individual's perception of them, and the effects of those perceptions of behavior. Brim and Ryff have been most interested in how the objective properties of events might influence behavior. For instance, they believe that the *distribution* of life events is a critical predictor of behavior. Distribution is defined as the frequency with which people experience a particular event, whether the event is likely to be age-related, and how likely will the event occur within a particular person's life. Table 6.3 illustrates the distribution of various types of events. If the distribution of an event is widespread (that is, nearly everyone will experience that event) and if it takes place at the point in the life span when one's cohorts are going through the same experience, the event is much less likely to be disruptive than is an improbable occurrence. For instance, the death of one's father is a common event, especially during middle age, and is likely to occur in the life of any adult who has a father (of course, one could die before one's father, thereby avoiding this common event). When such an event occurs on time (during middle age), *anticipatory socialization* prepares people and allows them to behave in adaptive ways, according to Brim and Ryff. Anticipatory socialization includes the delivery of information and training, formally or informally. Paternal death among one's friends and information from older relatives, doctors, and so on, are part of the process.

Some events are thinly distributed, like succession to the throne of a small European country. Nonetheless, if one is in line for the throne, one

TABLE 6.3

Life Events Typology

Correlation with Age	Experienced by Many		Experienced by Few	
	High Probability of Occurrence	Low Probability of Occurrence	High Probability of Occurrence	Low Probability of Occurrence
Strong	Marriage Starting to work Retirement Woman giving birth to first child Bar Mitzvah First walking Heart attack Birth of sibling	Military service draft Polio epidemic	Heirs coming into a large estate Accession to empty throne at 18	Spinabifida First class of women at Yale Pro football injury Child's failure at school Teenage unpopularity
Weak	Death of a father Death of a husband Male testosterone decline "Topping out" in work career Children's marriages Accidental pregnancy	War Great Depression Plague Earthquake Migration from South	Son succeeding father in family business	Loss of limb in auto accident Death of daughter Being raped Winning a lottery Embezzlement First black woman lawyer in South Blacklisted in Hollywood in 1940s Work disability Being fired Cured of alcoholism Changing occupations

SOURCE: O. G. Brim, Jr., and C. Ryff, 1980. "On the properties of life events." In *Life-Span Development and Behavior,* vol. III, ed. P. B. Baltes and O. G. Brim, Jr. New York: Academic Press.

is likely to know it and to have received sufficient anticipatory socialization. On the other hand, the sudden inheritance of a million dollars from an unknown relative might precipitate quite maladaptive behavior, since one was totally unprepared. Hayne Reese and Michael Smyer (1983) note that the social desirability of an event is also a critical determinant of behavior, regardless of distribution. It is better to become king of England than to be imprisoned for espionage, although both are low probability events. Reese and Smyer also mention the importance of age-relatedness as well as cohort specificity in determining response patterns. An event can be improbable in the general population (like the damage Vietnam veterans suffered from Agent Orange), but be more frequent among members of a particular cohort.

Most theories that focus on the properties of events tend to emphasize the measurement and objectification or the perception of those events. Furthermore, such conceptions tend to be designed to predict the probability of adaptive behavior where such behavior is inferred through the collection of data on health and adjustment. Although the direct observation of behavior in everyday life is not impossible, of course, it rarely appears in the literature on adult life. Research on infancy, childhood, and even adolescence often relies on the direct observation of behavior; but tracking the behavior of adults is more difficult, because adults are not accessible through general institutions like schools. To generalize from behavior under laboratory conditions to behavior outside the laboratory is problematic; the behaviors in which we are interested are quite complex and often poorly defined.

It may be easier to study the occurrence of certain specific kinds of behavior, like reeducation in adult life or entry into therapy. One recent framework, *action theory,* has developed around the notion that it may be possible to predict and explain such *intentional behavior.* Action theorists are interested in how beliefs, plans, and expectations influence subsequent behaviors (Baltes 1984). In particular, they are interested in what intentional behavior means to the actor; how feeling effects action; how goals, evaluations, memories, and other cognitive events influence action (Eckensberger and Meacham 1984).

Jochen Brandtstadter (1984a) has written that "individual development across the entire life-span is embedded in and dependent upon a highly complex, dynamic, conflicting structure of personal goals and potentials and of social demands and opportunities" (p. 2). Action, according to Brandtstadter, is self-planned behavior under personal control, and explicable in terms of expectation, goals, beliefs, and opportunities. Action analysis reconstructs the actor's base, the cognition, values, and the like, that lead to particular behaviors.

Brandstadter (1984a, 1984b) also argues that expectations about age are particularly powerful predictors of action and, therefore, of development over the life span. If people believe that they are in control of their own development, they are more likely to create the conditions that enable change; their behavior will remain flexible and adaptive over the life span. Brandstadter refers to beliefs about one's role in one's own life as *control beliefs*. His position on the function of control beliefs has also led to the proposition that therapy ought to proceed by argumentation. That is, analysts should attempt to persuade people to believe in their own potential, and to foster the belief in personal control over the developmental process.

Two major issues have been raised with the view forwarded by action theory. First, from the psychodynamic framework, action theory fails to address why people do things that they claim they do not wish to do (Harris 1984). Why do people act in a manner that is patently destructive or masochistic? Why do they engage in actions that prevent them from actualizing their own plans and expectations? Second, intention is an extremely slippery concept, and Baltes (1984) cautions that "for many behavioral scientists the use of action and intention may initially spell a return to a 'philosophical' rather than a 'natural-science' approach to human behavior" (p. 137). On the other hand, it has been difficult for even the most dedicated behavioral scientists to talk about the interaction between person and environment without considering how people's plans, expectations, and beliefs influence subsequent behavior (Bandura 1981).

One of the less slippery suggestions of action theory, however, concerns the direction behavioral development might take over the life span. From this view, positive control beliefs about aging should produce specific attempts to create the conditions that foster change and flexibility. In other words, optimal behavior in adulthood might include reeducation, therapy, exposure to new people and experiences, and continued attempts to master new skills. These developments are thought to be a product of cognitive or emotional events. Rarely is behavior considered an independent developmental system that might change over the course of the life span, with the possible exception of the emergence of motor milestones in infancy.

Is it possible that predictable or optimal behavioral developments are both a function of, and a contribution to, the motivational, cognitive, and affective developments we have been discussing? A few suggestions exist, though little consideration has been given to that proposition. In some older case-study research, Robert White (1975) advances the notion that commitment emerges as a dimension of behavior in young adulthood; that is, for the first time, long-term perseverance can be observed. The same theme appears in Erikson's work on intimacy and the thoughts of the object relations writers on mature love. White develops the idea of *commitment*, suggesting that young adults can derive satisfaction from an activity itself. Commitment is thus fostered by the experience of competence, and behavior becomes more perserverant because it is maintained by task variables rather than by social gains, approval, and attention from others.

The work of the object relations theorists (Kernberg 1976, 1980) and Lawrence Kohlberg's (Reid 1984) thoughts on moral development in young adulthood also suggest that during this first phase of adult life, behavior becomes more ethical or principled: people begin to act in a way that is more congruent with their own judgments of right and wrong. This focus on moral development is also apparent in the world of Edelstein and Noam (1982) who have suggested that, optimally, behavior in adulthood becomes more *reciprocal*. Reciprocal is not used in the ordinary sense here. For Edelstein and Noam, *reciprocity* means that the mature adult does not use other people to achieve his or her own personal goals. The concept of reciprocity is also known as the Kantian principle.

Nowhere, however, does anyone speak of any specific behavioral qualities that may emerge at midlife. Does generativity or compassion imply anything about behavior? Is there something we consider admirable about the behavior of respected middle-aged people that might be studied in some objective way? Or is behavioral development only comprehensible in relative terms such as flexibility and adaptation? Perhaps what is most revealing about this review of developmental theories is the number and nature of unanswered, in fact, unasked questions that become apparent in a system-by-system, phase-by-phase anaysis of the available work, both theoretical and empirical.

A Matrix of Theoretical Constructs

The knowledge we have acquired ought not to resemble a great shop without order, and without an inventory;
we ought to know what we possess, and be able to make it serve us in our need.

—Liebniz

In order to summarize the ideas and research presented in this chapter, I have devised a schema in figure 6.3 that illustrates "research and theory in adult development at a glance." The four basic developmental systems we have discussed are represented by rows, the major age strata by columns. The age strata do not represent biologically fixed stages, but rather they reflect something fundamental about the way society defines adulthood in the twentieth century. Age strata may be seen as boundaries that are crudely attuned to biological, social, and psychological processes. There

Figure 6.3

A Summary of Theory and Research in Adult Development

	Young Adulthood	*Middle Adulthood*	*Later Adulthood*
Motivation	Intimacy (Erikson) Self-Actualization (Maslow)	Generativity (Erikson) Self-Actualization (Jung)	Integrity (Erikson)
Cognition	Structural Analytic Stage (Commons & Richards) Dialectical Stage (Basseches, Reigel) Intrasystemic Stage (Labouvie-Vief)	Wisdom (Jung, Edelstein & Noam) Intersystemic Stage (Labouvie-Vief)	Wisdom (Erikson)
Emotion	Love (Erikson) Mature Love (Kernberg)	Caring (Erikson) Control (Leventhal, Mandler) Patience (Jung) Responsibility (Edelstein & Noam)	
Behavior	Ethical Behavior (Kernberg) Commitment (Kernberg, White, Erikson) Principled Behavior (Kohlberg)		Reciprocity (Edelstein & Noam) (Kant)

SOURCE: Reprinted from Judith Stevens-Long, *Adult Life* (Palo Alto, Calif.: Mayfield Publishing, 1988), p. 64.

is little reason to think of stages in adult life, despite the hoopla about midlife crisis, as an invariant, inevitable sequence of qualitatively different sets of abilities or concerns. Certainly, there is no evidence suggesting that the transitions between the socially defined age strata are abrupt or discontinuous. It is, however, possible to assume that the motivational, cognitive, emotional, or behavior structures that characterize adult life change over the years, and that the structures developed at one period are gradually replaced by the structures typical of the next phase (Kagan 1983; Labouvie-Vief 1982a).

Furthermore, it is unlikely that changes in different developmental systems arrive simultaneously. Human development tends to be *asynchronous;* that is, the timing of developments in one area are not well-related to the timing of developments in another (Campbell and Richie 1983). Generally, the idea of sequence is far more useful than the idea of stage. A sequence is a series of events in which A is necessary for the emergence of B, B for C, and so on. The notion of sequence is compatible with a mechanistic, organismic, or dialectical world view, since it is always assumed that simple behaviors and cognitive skills are learned before more complex ones are mastered.

Finally, it is unlikely that the development outlined in figure 6.3 represents a universal, or even an optimal developmental path in adulthood. As the systems thinker might argue, the truth can be considered a product of a particular system. Because a particular scheme works in one context does not necessarily imply anything of interest to developmental psychologists about the universe of social and historical context. Perhaps figure 6.3 represents an ideal aging pattern, given certain social and historical forces, or it may reflect simply the logical flow of recent theoretical ideas. In any event, it presents both revealing lacunae and points of emphasis in current work on maturity and adulthood.

The overall theme that most strongly characterizes figure 6.3 is the notion that development proceeds from differentiation to integration, from embeddedness in context to awareness. To be embedded is to be unaware of the biological, social, political, or historical forces that shape one's development and are, in turn, shaped by human development. At each stage, some recognition of how one fits in a particular system is implied, along with the differentiation of a new system, and the attempt to integrate the self within that larger system. Development in young adulthood seems to be embedded in close relationships. Intimacy, love, commitment, and the analysis of relationships within a finite system—all seem related to the mastery of those relationships most immediate to personal experience. The transition from young adulthood to middle age implies a widening of concern to the larger social system. The emergence of intersystemic thinking implies the differentiation of one's own social, political, and historical system from others, appreciation of its strengths and weaknesses, and an ability to identify with, and hence feel compassion for, another human system. In young adulthood we learn to comprehend and identify with another human being, in middle age with another human system.

Little has been said about development in later life, so that it is difficult to speculate about old age. However, as a logical outgrowth of the direction suggested in young adulthood and middle age, the developments of old age may be said to appear almost ecological. Jung (1933) suggests that the most mature of us become able to identify with all living things, to see our place in the universe, and to adopt a cosmic perspective. Those ideas have been extremely difficult to develop because identification with the universe or the cosmos has never been queried empirically, but Jung's thought that wisdom is linked to that identification does suggest a moderately concrete conceptualization, despite Jung's somewhat mystical treatment.

Perhaps, at its best, development in old age brings one to an ecological perspective: the growing awareness that we are part of a large ecosystem and that our impact on the environment affects not only the development of human beings, but the development of all living things and the future of the planet. The differentiation of the human system from the other subsystems with which we share the earth, the understanding of the relationships between those systems, and the emergence of an attempt to integrate or achieve some degree of harmony between such systems may be the key to filling in some of the blanks in figure 6.3.

One of the more interesting aspects of figure 6.3 is the emergence of blank cells. Little has been written about what characteristics consititute positive behavioral developments in middle age, and virtually no work has appeared on the positive emotional aspects of later life. Furthermore, some cells contain many more suggestions than others—often a reflection of how much research was available. Figure 6.4 presents some terms that might be used to summarize the concepts offered by various researchers and thinkers. This figure is arranged to emphasize where the preponderance of data and theory exist. In the third row down, labeled "cognition," there are many explicit suggestions. A fair amount of research and theory also exists on emotional development, less on motivation, and little on the qualitative aspects of behavior. Research on issues identified in the left hand column of Figure 6.4 (young adulthood) is more fully developed than research on other age ranges. Since researchers generally focus on college students, there is more information on the development of intimacy and love, principled behavior, and formal operations than any other of the possibilities of later life.

Filling in the blanks, one might be guided by the concept of sequence (Campbell and Richie 1983; Commons and Richards 1982), by assuming that the development of an ability or characteristic listed at an early period is a logical stepping stone in a sequence that continues to unfold across the adult life span. Furthermore, one might also assume that developments in each of the systems during any phase both contribute to and are encouraged by developments in other systems.

Consider for instance, how commitment, love, intimacy, and intrasystemic or formal operational thought can be seen as contributing to one another. There seems to be strong general agreement that the ability to

Figure 6.4

Development Across the Adult Life Span (NOTE: Dark outline indicate cells where
the most research is available.)

	Young Adulthood	Middle Adulthood	Later Adulthood
Motivations	Self-Actualized Intimacy The need to resolve the conflict between individuation and fusion in the context of close relationships; to be intimate and self-sufficient	Self-Actualized Generativity The need to develop and maintain the social system and continue to individuate in the context of pressure; to be stable and responsible	Self-Actualized Integrity The need to accept one's past, one's life history as meaningful, and to continue to develop or individuate
Emotion	Mature Love The ability to identify completely with another and maintain a strong sense of self	Responsibility The ability to maintain a sense of self and exercise judgment in spite of personal and social disequilibrium; to exhibit both compassion and control	Patience The ability to tolerate conflict; to identify with opposition
Cognition	Insight The ability to analyze relationships within a system and to find logical solutions	Perspective The ability to compare relationships across systems, and to find adequate solutions	Autonomy The ability to see one's own role in the experience of reality; to mediate between emotions and cognition
Behavior	Ethical/Committed Behavior becomes ethical, driven by personal principles rather than conformity; interests deepen	Effective/Enabling One is able to meet one's own needs and to assist others without wasted effort; behavior becomes productive	Reciprocity One is able to meet one's own needs without using another person instrumentally

SOURCE: Reprinted from Judith Stevens-Long, *Adult Life* (Palo Alto, Calif.: Mayfield Publishing, 1988), p. 66.

analyze relationships within a finite system is central to formal operations.
Intimacy may be the social context in which such analysis occurs. Mature
love as defined by Erikson or the object relations theorists depends heavily
upon the ability to maintain one's personal identity (to differentiate self
from other) in relationships (the integration of self and other). Without

love, the tension between losing and maintaining the self seems unlikely to be compelling.

As Erikson has framed it, the tension between losing and maintaining the sense of identity gained in adolescence is central to the development of intimacy. The conflict, he believed, was between intimacy and isolation, with intimacy representing the optimal outcome. It is possible, however, to regard intimacy as a kind of middle ground, and to specify the extreme solutions as fusion and isolation—on the one hand, the loss of personal identity, on the other, an inability to integrate one's identity with that of another. In her presidential address to the American Psychological Association, Janet Spence (1985) recently argued that the conflict between individuation and fusion is one of the central issues of all human development.

The behavioral developments outlined by Kernberg, White, and Kohlberg echo Erikson's concern for the role of commitment in the development of intimacy, and work on the growth of personal values and political thought also suggest that adult ethics emerge at the end of adolescence (Stevens-Long and Cobb 1983). Of course, it has proven extremely difficult to research such hypotheses. The construction of a significant ethical dilemma in the laboratory that does not violate the rights of the participants to understand the research and that protects them from psychological repercussion is hard to imagine. The questions of behavioral development demand field research, and few have been willing to undertake the task.

What further expression might the developmental trends of young adulthood find at midlife? Maslow's description of the self-actualized, problem-centered person, committed to the benefit of others is similar to Erikson's conceptualization of the generative person. Movement from close personal relationships to a concern for the wider context of society may form the basis for the differentiation of the social, political, and historical system in which one's roles are played. Edelstein and Noam's definition of *responsibility* as the maintainence of self and the exercise of good judgment under stress seems to reflect the challenges of midlife and the exposure of the self to a wider context.

Middle age clearly brings increased stress. One's obligations to family, community, and work increase enormously. Emotionally, one must begin to empathize with others on a rather grand scale, as Erikson suggests. Furthermore, increased emotional control seems essential. Middle-aged people make the long-term financial, social, and political decisions that shape the future of families, organizations, and institutions.

One must be able to make comparisons across systems. What works as a parent may be poor managerial behavior at work. A good manager may be a poor politician (this was said to be Dukakis's major problem as a presidential candidate). The term *perspective* might capture what is identified here. One must be able to develop solutions that are appropriate to the changing roles, situations, and systems with which one becomes engaged.

The development of perspective permits one to design effective, productive solutions suited to context and tempered by caring. Behaviorally, effectiveness and productivity seem a hallmark of a successful middle age. In figure 6.4, behavioral development at midlife is termed effective/enabling, reflecting a gap in the language. To find a word that implies both productivity and a concern for others is difficult, but productivity without an ethical dimension is not particularly admirable. Effectiveness also implies flexibility—the ability to try another strategy if the present one seems unworkable. Enabling refers to a focus on the goals of others as well as the self. To mentor, to teach, and to lead effectively and responsibly are ways to enable or empower others to meet their own goals. The language has no single word that connotes both responsibility and effectiveness.

Finally, Erikson is the only one of our theorists who has addressed development in old age, although one might argue that Jung's description of self-actualization begins at midlife, but flowers later. Jung's thoughts on maturity seem closer to Erikson's ideas about integrity than to the social struggles characteristic of middle age. As Leopold Rosenmayr has written in the *Handbook of the Psychology of Aging* (1985), "Late middle-age is a phase of withdrawal and must perhaps be regarded as the key phase for gerontology in its classical sense" (p. 194). Much of the early work on disengagement and change in the executive processes during middle age (Neugarten et al. 1964) suggested a declining interest in the external world. More recently (Butler 1974), this observation has emerged in work on the life-review process in later life.

Rosenmayr argues that withdrawal in late middle age reflects a need to question oneself or one's behaviorally decisive principles in order to control the defensiveness and regression common in old age. As Jung describes it, the final stages of self-actualization must address tolerance for conflict within the self, the ability to question the self, and the need to integrate opposing forces. The pressure to engage with society, apparent in middle age, certainly abates. Perhaps the conflict between integrity and despair reflects a tension between continuing selective engagement with the external world and self-absorption.

Labouvie-Vief's definition of autonomous thinking suggests the emergence of an ability to see one's role in one's personal development, and to discriminate between personal and universal truth. She also argues that autonomy arises from an awareness of the genuine complexity of the social system, an awareness gained in middle age (Labouvie-Vief 1985). Basseches and Riegel spoke of an ability to deal with paradox at the final levels of adult cognitive development. Edelstein and Noam discuss wisdom in terms of the ability to mediate between emotional and cognitive truth. Kegan (1982) has written that the "recognition that values are self-constructed . . . does not have to lead to the conclusion that there is no way to compare value systems" (p. 67). Kegan argues that there is an *institutional* stage of development similar to some of the concepts of middle age we have been discussing here, during which people are embedded in personal autonomy.

All of these notions lead to the proposition that there may be some further, less relative, stage of development in which one discovers the limits of personal autonomy and relativity. As Michael Commons once commented in a class of mine, "Stages go on. People don't." If we adapt the notion that development proceeds from embeddedness to objectification, from differentiation to integration, from absolute to relative, middle-aged people are at the relative end of the spectrum. Thought in middle age is contextual and probabilistic. All truth is seen as the product of a particular system. There are no great, universal truths, only socially adequate solutions. Might there be some swing back toward a more absolute frame as one approaches the end of the life span? Perhaps an appreciation of the interrelatedness of systems, rather than an appreciation of their differences, occurs among the most mature of us.

Emotionally, Jung's concept of patience appealed to me as filler for the open cell concerned with emotional growth in later life. Although no one has spent time defining patience, it would seem that patience requires both attention and caring. However, it is more than caring; it also implies tolerance for opposition. In fact, patience might be said to require identification with the people or things that create opposition, perhaps an understanding of the interrelatedness of opposing systems.

Patience also suggests an understanding of the long-term consequences of one's own behavior, and restraint. It suggests that one has learned when to do nothing, when to go slowly. Perhaps the appreciation of one's role in personal development leads to an understanding of the importance of finding one's own way.

Finally, reciprocity stands as the only current thought about behavorial development in old age. *Reciprocity,* as defined by Kant, means never using another person as a means to one's own ends and insists upon the ability to meet one's own needs, to be effective, compassionate, and patient. It also requires great insight, knowing what one's goals are, how they differ from the goals of others, and how that knowledge is related to the larger social system. Such an achievement does seem worthy of the term *life-span development.* Furthermore, if we expand the definition of reciprocity to include an appreciation of the interrelatedness of all systems, an ecological view, and a reluctance to use any *system* to personal ends, it is indeed an achievement worthy of development over generations.

Speculating about which concepts or terms most aptly describe each cell is an exercise most people find challenging, at least for a while. Some of the fascinating suggestions I have not incorporated into the schema include courage and dignity (I found the latter exceptionally difficult to define), as well as facetiousness, which brought up the arena of humor. Facetiousness is the ability to poke a kind of intelligent fun at oneself or the outside world. Certainly humor develops over the adult life course, especially self-directed humor (Farrell and Rosenberg 1981). The psychodynamic thinkers would probably place the development of humor somewhere in the description of a fifth system, the defenses. Other thinkers might see it as a subsystem of cognition.

Courage is also difficult to define, although it seems to involve one's ability to deal with loss, even the loss of one's own life, and may develop at any point in the life span where one must face that prospect. Although the sequence outlined in figure 6.4 may represent a hierarchy, to some extent, it is likely that particularly powerful life events or choices can force certain developments earlier than the norm. For example, the decision to become a psychotherapist may force the development of patience and the sorting out of one's personal goals from the goals of others earlier than usual. The discovery that one has a life-threatening illness in young adulthood may produce early differentiation from close relationships. I tend to see figure 6.4 as a checkerboard lying flat on a table. On every square, imagine a stack of checkers, the height of which represents the degree of individual development that has emerged in that particular cell.

On most of these developmental game boards, the stacks are higher along the left hand column. For women, the stacks may be somewhat higher along the row that represents emotional development. For men, the first row may be "stacked." People who have faced emotionally traumatic events early in life have more pieces in the emotional development row. Those who have faced difficult ethical decisions early in adulthood may show more behavioral development. There is no reason to suggest that everyone will present the same pattern. Some people may evidence great gains at the end of the life cycle. Of course, the quality, the depth, and the extent of patience or wisdom may be different when they develop early or late, but that doesn't necessarily mean they can't develop at all. In this way, everyone's development has a unique topography determined, to some extent, by the logical sequences of psychological growth, but also shaped by the unique events that influence a particular life course.

Being middle-aged, I am tempted to conclude with the notion that the ideas presented in this chapter suggest a variety of interesting, exciting new hypotheses and arenas for research; but everything is relative, and what we think or discover about aging can only be probabilistic and contextual. Furthermore, our discovery is certain to change over time, and to be replaced by some other equally relative truth. But, then again, maybe not.

REFERENCES

Baltes, P. B. 1968. "Longitudinal and Cross-sectional Sequences in the Study of Age and Generation Effects." *Human Development* 11:1145–71.

———. 1979. "Life-Span Developmental Psychology: Some Converging Observations on History and Theory." In *Life-Span Development and Behavior, vol. 2,* ed. P.B. Baltes and O. G. Brim, Jr. New York: Academic Press.

———. 1984. "Discussion: Some Constructive Caveats on Action Psychology and the Study of Intention." *Human Development* 27:135–39.

Baltes, P. B., and Goulet, L. R. 1970. "Status and Issues of a Life-Span Developmental Psychology." In *Life-Span Developmental Psychology: Research and Theory,* ed. L. R. Goulet and P. B. Baltes. New York: Academic Press.

Bandura, A. 1981. "Self-Referent Thought: A Developmental Analysis of Self-efficacy." In *Social Cognitive Development: Frontiers and Possible Futures,* ed. J. H. Flavell and L. Ross. New York: Cambridge University Press.

Basseches, M. 1984. *Dialectical Thinking and Adult Development.* Norwood, N.J.: Ablex.

Bergman, M. S. 1980. "On the Intrapsychic Function of Falling in Love." *Psychoanalytic Quarterly* 69:56–78.

Berscheid, E. 1982. "Attraction and Emotion in Interpersonal Relations." In *Affect and Cognition,* ed. M. S. Clark and S. T. Fiske. Hillsdale, N.J.: Lawrence Erlbaum.

Brandtstadter, J. 1984a. "Personal and Social Control Over Development: Some Implications of an Action Perspective in Life-span Developmental Psychology." In *Life-Span Development and Behavior,* vol. 6, ed. P. B. Baltes and O. G. Brim, Jr. New York: Academic Press.

———. 1984b. "Action Development and Development Through Action." *Human Development* 27:11–19.

Brim, O., and Ryff, C. 1980. "On the Properties of Life Events." In *Life-Span Development and Behavior,* vol. 3, ed. P.B. Baltes and O.G. Brim, Jr. New York: Academic Press.

Buss, A. 1979. "Dialectics, History and Development: The Historical Roots of the Individual-Society Dialectic." In *Life-Span Development and Behavior,* vol. 2, ed. P.B. Baltes and O.G. Brim, Jr. New York: Academic Press.

Butler, R. N. 1963. "The Life Review: An Interpretation of Reminiscence in the Aged." *Psychiatry* 26:65–76.

Cameron, P. 1975. "Mood as an Indicant of Happiness: Age, Sex, Social Class, and Situational Differences." *Journal of Gerontology* 30:216–24.

Campbell, R. L., and Richie, D. M. 1983. "Problems in the Theory of Developmental Sequences." *Human Development* 26:156–72.

Chinen, A. B. 1984. "Modal Logic: A New Paradigm of Development and Late Life Potential." *Human Development* 27:52–56.

Chiriboga, D., and Cultler, L. 1980. "Stress and Adaptation: A Life-span Perspective." In *Aging in the 1980s,* ed. L.W. Poon. Washington, D.C.: American Psychological Association.

Coen, S. J. 1981. "Sexualization As a Predominant Mode of Defense." *Journal of the American Psychoanalytic Association* 29:893–921.

Cohen, G. 1979. "Language and Comprehension in Old Age." *Cognitive Psychology* 11:412–29.

Commons, M. L., and Richards, F. A. 1978. "The Structural Analytic State of Development: A Piagetian Post-Formal Operational Stage." Paper presented at the meeting of the Western Psychological Association, San Francisco, April.

Commons, M. L., and Richards, F. A. 1982. "A General Model of Stage Theory." In *Beyond Formal Operation: Late Adolescent and Adult Cognitive Development,* ed. M. L. Commons, F. A. Richards, and S. Armon. New York: Praeger.

Denny, N. W. 1982. "Aging and Cognitive Abilities." In *Handbook of Developmental Psychology,* ed. B.B. Wolman. Englewood Cliffs, N.J.: Prentice-Hall.

Denny, N. W., and Palmer, A. M. 1982a. "Adult Age Differences on Traditional and Practical Problem-Solving Measures." Unpublished manuscript, University of Kansas.

Denny, N. W., and Pearce, K.A. 1982b. "A Developmental Study of Adult Performance on Traditional and Practical Problem-Solving Tasks." Unpublished manuscript, University of Kansas.

Eckensburger, L. H., and Meacham, J.A. 1984. "The Essentials of Action Theory: A Framework for Discussion." *Human Development* 27:166–73.

Edelstein, W., and Noam, G. 1982. "Regulatory Structures of Self and 'Post-Formal' Stages in Adulthood." *Human Development* 25:407–22.

Erikson, E. H. 1963 *Childhood and Society,* 2d ed. New York: W. W Norton.

———. 1968a. "Generativity and Ego Integrity." In *Middle Age and Aging,* ed. B. L. Neugarten. Chicago: University of Chicago Press.

———. 1968b. *Identity, Youth, and Crisis.* New York: W. W. Norton.

———. 1982. *The Life Cycle Completed: Review.* New York: W. W. Norton.

———. Interview by E. Hall, June 1983. "A Conversation with Erik Erikson." *Psychology Today* 17:22–30.

Farrell, M. P., and Rosenberg, S.D. 1981. *Men at Midlife.* Boston: Auburn House.

Fiske, S. T. 1982. "Schema-Triggered Affect: Applications to Social Perception." In *Affect and Cognition,* ed. M. S. Clark and S. T. Fiske. Hillsdale, N.J.: Lawrence Erlbaum.

Flavell, J. H. 1963. *The Developmental Psychology of Jean Piaget.* New York: Van Nostrand Reinhold.

Gergen, K.J. 1977. "Stability, Change, and Chance in Understanding Human Development." In *Life-Span Developmental Psychology: Dialectical Perspectives on Experimental Research,* ed. N. Datan and H. W. Reese. New York: Academic Press.

———. 1980. "The Challenge of Phenomenal Change for Research Methodology: Implications of a Dialectical Perspective for Research Methodology." *Human Development* 23:254–65.

―――. 1985. "The Social Constructivist Movement in Modern Psychology." *American Psychologist* 40:266–73.

Gilligan, C. 1982. *In a Different Voice: Psychological Theory and Women's Development.* Cambridge, Mass.: Harvard University Press.

Harris, A. 1984. "Action Theory, Language, and the Unconscious," *Human Development* 27:196–204.

Horn, J. L. 1982. "The Theory of Fluid and Crystallized Intelligence in Relation to Concepts of Cognitive Psychology and Aging in Adulthood." In *The 1980 Erindale Symposium,* ed. F. I. M. Craik and S. E. Trehub. Beverly Hills, Calif.: Sage.

Izard, C. E. 1982. "Comments on Emotion and Cognition: Can There be a Working Relationship?" In *Affect and Cognition,* ed. M. S. Clark and S. T. Fiske. Hillsdale, N.J.: Lawrence Erlbaum.

Jung, C. G. 1933. *Modern Man in Search of a Soul.* New York: Harcourt, Brace, & World.

―――. 1960. *Collected Works,* ed. H. Read, M. Fordham, and G. Adler. Princeton, N.J.: Princeton University Press.

Kagan, J. 1983. "Developmental Categories and the Premise of Connectivity." In *Developmental Psychology: Historical and Philosophical Perspectives,* ed. R.M. Lerner. Hillsdale, N.J.: Lawrence Erlbaum.

Kegan, R. 1982. *The Evolving Self.* Cambridge, Mass.: Harvard University Press.

Kernberg, O. 1976. "Mature Love: Prerequisites and Characteristics." In *Object Relations Theory and Clinical Psychoanalysis,* ed. O. Kernberg. New York: Jason Aronson.

―――. 1980. "Love, the Couple, and the Group: A Psychoanalytic Frame." *Psychoanalytic Quarterly* 69:78–108.

Kitchener, R. F. 1978. "Epigenesis: The Role of Biological Models in Developmental Psychology." *Human Development* 21:141–60.

Kohlberg, L. 1973. "The Claim to Moral Adequacy of a Highest Stage of Moral Development." *Journal of Philosophy* 70:630–46.

Koplowitz, H. 1984. "A Projection Beyond Piaget's Formal Operations Stage: A General System Stage and a Unitary Stage." In *Beyond Formal Operations: Late Adolescent and Adult Cognitive Development,* ed. M.L. Commons, F. A. Richards and C. Armon. New York: Praeger.

Labouvie, E. W. 1982. "Issues in Lifespan Development." In *Handbook of Developmental Psychology,* ed. B. B. Wolman. Englewood Cliffs, N.J.: Prentice-Hall.

Labouvie-Vief, G. 1982a. "Dynamic Development and Mature Autonomy." *Human Development* 25:161–91.

―――. 1982b. "Growth and Aging in Life-span Perspective." *Human Development* 25:65–78.

―――. 1985. "Intelligence and Cognition." In *Handbook of the Psychology of Aging,* 2d ed., ed. J. E. Birren and K.W. Schaie. New York: Van Nostrand Reinhold.

Labouvie-Vief, G., and Blanchard-Fields, F. 1982. "Cognitive Aging and Psychological Growth." *Ageing and Society* 2:183–209.

Langer, J. 1969. *Theories of Development.* New York: Holt, Rinehart & Winston.

Lerner, R. M. 1976. *Concepts and Theories of Human Development.* Reading, Mass.: Addison-Wesley.

―――. 1983. *Developmental Psychology.* Hillsdale, N.J.: Lawrence Erlbaum.

Leventhal, H. 1982. "The Integration of Emotion and Cognition: A View from the

Perceptual-Motor Theory of Emotion." In *Affect and Cognition,* ed. M. S. Clark and S.T. Fiske. Hillsdale, N.J.: Lawrence Erlbaum.

Linville, P. W. 1982. "Affective Consequences of Complexity Regarding the Self and Others." In *Affect and Cognition,* ed. M. S. Clark and S. T. Fiske. Hillsdale, N.J.: Lawrence Erlbaum.

Lowenthal, M.; Chiriboga, D.; and Thurnher, M. 1975. *Four Stages of Life.* San Francisco: Jossey-Bass.

Mandler, G. 1982. "The Structure of Value: Accounting for Taste." In *Affect and Cognition,* ed. M. S. Clark and S.T. Fiske. Hillsdale, N.J.: Lawrence Erlbaum.

Maslow, A. H. 1968. *Toward a Psychology of Being.* New York: Van Nostrand.

———. 1970. *Motivation and personality,* 2d ed. New York: Harper & Row.

Miller, P. H. 1983. *Theories of Developmental Psychology.* San Francisco: Freeman.

Neugarten, B. L.; et al. 1964. *Personality in Middle and Later Life.* New York: Atherton Press.

Overton, W. F., and Reese, H. W. 1973. "Models of Development: Methodological Implications." In *Life-Span Developmental Psychology: Methodological Issues,* ed. J. R. Nesselroade and H. W. Reese. New York: Academic Press.

Piaget, J. 1970. *The Psychology of Intelligence.* New York: Harcourt Brace.

Reese, H. W. 1983. "Some Notes on the Meaning of the Dialectic." *Human Development* 26:315-20.

Reese, H. W., and Overton, W. F. 1970. "Models of Development and Theories of Development." In *Life-Span Developmental Psychology: Research and Theory,* ed. L.R. Goulet and P. B. Baltes. New York: Academic Press.

Reese, H.W., and Smyer, M. 1983. "The Dimensionalization of Life Events." In *Life-Span Developmental Psychology: Nonnormative Life Events,* ed. E. Callahan and K. McClusky. New York: Academic Press.

Ried, B. V. 1984. "An Anthropological Reinterpretation of Kohlberg's Stages of Moral Development." *Human Development* 27:57-64.

Richards, F. A., and Commons, M. L. 1982. "Systematic, Metasystematic, and Cross-Paradigmatic Reasoning: A Case for Stages of Reasoning beyond Formal Operations." In *Beyond Formal Operations: Late Adolescent and Adult Cognitive Development,* ed. M. L. Commons, F. A. Richards, and S. Armon. New York: Praeger.

Riegel, K. F. 1975a. "Adult Life Crises: A Dialectic Interpretation of Development." In *Life-Span Developmental Psychology: Normative Life Crises,* ed. N. Datan and L. H. Ginsberg. New York: Academic Press.

———. 1975b. "From Traits and Equilibrium Toward Developmental Dialectics." *1974-75 Nebraska Symposium on Motivation,* ed. W. J. Arnold and J. K. Cole. Lincoln, Nebr.: University of Nebraska Press.

———. 1977. "History of Psychological Gerontology." In *Handbook of the Psychology of Aging,* ed. J. E. Birren and K. W. Schaie. New York: Van Nostrand Reinhold.

Rosenmayr, L. 1985. "Changing Values and the Position of the Aged in Western Cultures." In *Handbook of the Psychology of Aging,* 2d ed., ed. J. E. Birren and K. W. Schaie. New York: Van Nostrand Reinhold.

Russell, J. A. 1980. "A Circumplex Model of Emotion." *Journal of Personality and Social Psychology* 39:1161-78.

Rybash, J. M.; Hoyer, W.; and Roodin, P. 1986. *Adult Cognition and Aging.* New York: Pergamon Press.

Schaie, K. W. 1967. "Age Changes and Age Differences." *The Gerontologist* 7:128-32.

———. 1979. "The Primary Mental Abilities in Adulthood: An Exploration in the

Development of Psychometric Intelligence." In *Life-Span Development and Behavior,* vol. 2, ed. P. B. Baltes and O. G. Brim, Jr. New York: Academic Press.

Schaie, K. W., and Hertzog, C. 1985. "Measurement in the Psychology of Adult-hood and Aging." In *Handbook of the Psychology of Aging,* 2d ed., ed. J. E. Birren and K. W. Schaie. New York: Van Nostrand Reinhold.

Schulz, R. 1985. "Emotion and Affect." in *Handbook of the Psychology of Aging.* 2d. ed., ed. J. E. Birren and K. W. Schail. New York: Van Nostrand Reinhold.

Seymour, P. and Morgan, J., eds. 1971. *Henry David Thoreau's Classic Writings: Reflections at Walden Pond.* Kansas City, Mo.: Hallmark.

Shaffer, P. "Paying Homage to Mozart." *New York Times Magazine,* 2 September 1984.

Spence, J. 1985. "Achievement American Style: The Rewards and Costs of Individ-ualism." Presidential Address, American Psychological Association Convention, Los Angeles, Calif.

Stevens-Long, J. 1988. *Adult Life,* 3d ed. Palo Alto, Calif.: Mayfield.

Stevens-Long, J., and Cobb, N. 1983. *Adolescence and Young Adulthood.* Palo Alto, Calif.: Mayfield.

Tolman, C. 1983. "Further Comments on the Meaning of Dialectic." *Human Develop-ment* 26:320–24.

Tomkins, S. S., and McCarter, R. 1964. "What and Where Are the Primary Affects? Some Evidence for a Theory." In *Handbook of Mental Health and Aging,* ed. J. E. Birren and R. B. Sloane. Englewood Cliffs, N.J.: Prentice-Hall.

Van den Dale, L. 1975. "Ego Development and Preferential Judgment in Life-Span Perspective." In *Life-Span Developmental Psychology: Normative Life Crisis,* ed. N. Datan and L. Ginsberg. New York: Academic Press.

Vaillant, G. E., and Mc Arthur, C. C. 1972. "Natural History of Male Psychological Health: The Adult Life Cycle from Eighteen to Fifty." *Seminars in Psychiatry* 4:415–27.

White, R. 1975. *Lives in Progress: A Study of the Natural Growth of Personality,* 3d. ed. New York: Holt, Rinehart & Winston.

DISCUSSION

Dr. Stevens-Long begins her chapter with a fascinating account of the complex contradictions that have coexisted in adult developmental theory over the last twenty years. Her conclusion that the contradictions were not all bad, since dialectics cast theoretical conflict in the role of change agent, is a meaningful one for us because it parallels the psycho-analytic belief that all development, normal and pathological, emerges from conflict. We also concur with her observation that "theorists work-ing within antithetical frameworks, from psychoanalysis to behaviorism, have begun to assume a strong interaction between a developing orga-nism and a changing environment" (p. 128). This vantage point incorpo-rates the three components which we, along with Spitz, believe are al-ways present in development: the biological organism, the psyche, and the external environment, coexisting and influencing each other at any point in the life cycle.

After discussing the theoretically fruitful ferment existing in the field of adult development, Dr. Stevens-Long turns her attention to cognitive development. She describes the efforts of such theorists as Michael Commons, Francis Richards, Michael Basseches, and others to extend cognitive theory beyond adolescence, and beyond the stage of formal operations, that is, beyond Piaget. Through their conceptualizations of structural analytic thought and dialectical thinking, these authors suggest that cognitive development does not end in adolescence or young adulthood, but continues into adulthood where new thinking capacities of greater complexity emerge for the first time.

A similar process seems to have occurred in psychoanalysis and cognitive science; in both realms an initial focus on childhood and adolescence and relative neglect of the adult years was generally taken to mean that there *was* no further development in adulthood. In psychoanalytic thinking, development became synonymous with the formation of psychic structure in childhood. In Piagetian thinking, the achievement of formal operations in adolescence was considered the highest and final level of cognitive development. These ideas stifled creative thinking and new theory formation about the adult years. A major important theoretical concept to emerge from the evolution of adult development theory is the hypothesis that the developmental processes in adulthood do result in major alterations in existing psychic structure and the emergence of new functions (such as structural analytic thought), which were not present in childhood or adolescence.

Stevens-Long seems to be mildly critical of Commons and Richards as well as Basseches because their data for suggesting a fifth stage of cognitive development are based primarily on the study of young adults. We have no quarrel with their approach if the fifth stage is not assumed to be fixed and finished, the standard for the remainder of the life cycle. At forty, life expectancy is approximately another forty years, years that will continue to produce change. A fine example of such change is contained in the work of Labouvie-Vief, who describes the evolution of cognitive processes beyond dialectical thought:

> Intersystemic thought permits one to understand how certain truths are relevant only within particular systems. . . . Autonomous thinkers are able to formulate decisions that integrate logic and the irrational aspects of experience. Autonomous thinkers see not only how truth can be a product of a particular system, but also how the thinker participates in the creation of the truth . . . and are able to discriminate between personal and universal reality. (P. 15)

We believe Labouvie-Vief is describing an aspect of wisdom. This capacity to understand the world and the individual's limited place in it is possible only after many years of experience in living: after the engagement and relative mastery of the developmental tasks of childhood, adolescence, and early and middle adulthood, a truly adult developmental experience.

Those of us who teach have a great opportunity—and a considerable task ahead—as we take the theories of Rybash, Hoyer, and Roodin, Chinen, Kohlberg, Van den Dale, and Labouvie-Vief on cognitive development, integrate them with other theoretical frameworks, and introduce them to our students. The systematic study of adult development in colleges and universities, including medical schools and psychoanalytic institutes, is still rare. In human development courses, the study of cognitive development is usually limited to Piaget and, therefore, to childhood and adolescence. One of the great values of Dr. Stevens-Long's contribution here is her outline of Piagetian cognitive theory for the second half of life.

Dr. Stevens-Long's ideas on Erikson's work parallel our own: in *Adult Development* (Colarusso and Nemiroff 1981), we described him as a pioneer adult developmentalist and a major theoretician in adult developmental theory. As Patricia Miller was quoted by Stevens-Long, "Erikson presents his theory as would a novelist or an artist rather than a scientist. At most, the theory is a loosely connected set of ideas and observations that could not, strictly speaking, be called a . . . theory" (p. 138). As sketchy as Erikson's ideas were, they made a profound contribution because of their relationship to and expansion of psychoanalytic theory. Erikson's lifelong series of developmental polarities rest squarely on Freud's construct of libidinal stages in childhood and express the psychoanalytic idea that all development, normal and pathologic, emerges from conflict. From an adult developmental point of view, Erikson's genius is his ability to recognize that development continues into the second half of life, beyond childhood, beyond the formation of psychic structure—ideas still contested in some psychoanalytic circles.

We are a long way from understanding affective development in general, and in adulthood in particular. Is anything new added to affective development in adulthood? If we use the framework of psychoanalytic structural theory, the answer is a tentative yes, because in adults we find (1) increased capacity to modulate and integrate affects based on enhanced object relations, namely, a sharper differentiation of self and object; (2) heightened ability to integrate positively and negatively experienced affects due to continued modification of the superego/ego ideal; and (3) enhanced capacity of the ego to accept and tolerate powerful affects based on experience with the gamut of human affect. Kernberg's concepts of mature love and

Erikson's concept of generativity and integrity are examples of the emergence of this adult ability to utilize and integrate affects.

In relation to behavior, Dr. Stevens-Long discusses the effect of the distribution of events on the adult developmental process. In essence, she suggests that if an event is widespread, that is, experienced by others in the same age group, it will be less disruptive. Developmentally, this discussion considers the mutual experience of engaging phase-specific tasks by those in the same developmental phase. Beyond early childhood, the awareness of experiences shared by peers has a significant effect on development, in a sense helping the individual prepare for the future. Brim and Ryff call this preparedness to engage developmental tasks "anticipatory socialization." An example in mid-adulthood is anticipating of the death of parents; in late adulthood, a task might be anticipating the death of a spouse or the unexpected death of a child.

Dr. Stevens-Long notes that the direct observation of adults is not described in the literature. We have also suggested that direct observation could be as valuable to the study of adults as it has been to the study of children. Just as schools, camps, and playgrounds are places for observing children, so are the workplace, sporting events, and parks fine sites to observe adults at work, at play, or in family interactions. Josefowitz and Gaden, Bardwick, and other prominent consultants to industry use techniques of direct observation to great advantage in their work, as have we in formulating adult developmental theory.

Although we basically agree with Stevens-Long's ideas about the limited value of stage theory in adulthood, the use of chronologically defined eras as characterized by phase-specific tasks remains, for the present, a remarkably useful conceptual tool because it provides a biological-temporal framework within which to place and describe psychological change. Phase theory underscores the importance to normal development of the universal experience of physical maturation and growth during childhood and physical retrogression and decline during adulthood. Fortunately, newer sophisticated methods for conceptualizing intrapsychic change in adulthood are beginning to appear. Particularly noteworthy is the work of Settlage and his colleagues on psychological process in adulthood, which we discuss elsewhere in this volume.

We especially enjoyed Dr. Stevens-Long's summary of the transition from early to middle adulthood because of its descriptive and conceptual clarity:

Development in young adulthood seems to be embedded in close relationships [such as] intimacy, love, commitment, and the analysis of relationships within a finite system. . . . The transition from young adulthood to middle age implies a widening of concern to the larger social system. . . . In young adulthood we learn to comprehend and identify with another human being, in middle age with another human system. (P. 154)

We see the obvious parallels with the oedipal-aged child's movement from the nuclear family to the latency age peer group. But there are important differences between the latency age child and the young adult, differences that must be recognized before developmental change in adulthood can be understood. The healthy young adult has a mature body, is psychologically separated from parents, can think abstractly—even dialectically, does productive work, has an active sexual life (ideally within an intimate loving relationship), and may be a parent. As a result of these young adult developmental experiences and the changes that they produce in intrapsychic structure, the emerging middle-aged adult can begin to comprehend human systems as well as individuals and to recognize his or her place in the larger scheme of human existence: one human among billions, related to a few others by blood or through association, and to all others through the universal experience of growing and maturing in the first part of life, and aging and dying in the second. The middle-aged person considers the imponderables of existence and relates them to himself and all mankind. This reflection is the essence of the dawning of wisdom in middle age, the beginning of a new developmental era.

7

Psychological Development and Pathology in Later Adulthood

DAVID GUTMANN

The Sources of Late Adult Development

In our generally sentimental psychology, almost any change in behavior or attitude that does not involve frank psychosis is likely to be vaguely eulogized as "growth," the outcome of a developmental process. In this imprecise modern view, "self-actualization" is the goal of any developmental sequence, and progress in these terms can be tracked on the "life-satisfaction" scale. But a sterner doctrine recognizes that true development has, by definition, a genetic basis; as a product of human evolution, it will have goals and consequences that go beyond individual satisfaction.

In short, development entails more than superficial shifts in attitudes or interests; it involves tectonic changes at the deepest strata of personality, revisions that change basic appetites as well as the ways in which we think about appetites and their objects. Such powers, prepotent though not necessarily conscious, can bring about new psychological structures: new executive capacities of the personality on the one hand or late-onset pathology on the other, depending on the settings—both intrapersonal and interpersonal—in which these forces are expressed.

From this dynamic perspective, we will review the linkages between development and pathogenesis in later life, with particular reference to the inner changes that are set in train by the postparental transitions of late adulthood. A model of late-onset pathology will be presented, along with

170

biographical material from a great artist who was a clear casualty of later life transitions, and a prime exemplar of the model presented here: the writer Ernest Hemingway.

The Stressful Passage toward Androgyny

My studies of older men and women in various cultures have led to this conclusion: late development and late-onset pathology are often fueled by the same forces. They are driven by energies, released in men and women, in the course of the postparental transition toward androgyny. This tendency of older individuals to become androgynous, to acquire appetites, attitudes, and even behaviors characteristic of the opposite sex—for example, the *contrasexual* transition—was first clinically identified by Carl Jung (1933) and was first studied empirically in nonclinical and non-Western populations by this author (Gutmann 1964, 1987). Confirmatory findings have been reported by several independent investigators.*

Regarding androgyny, it appears that (save for neurotic individuals) bisexuality does not become a significant problem, does not take on crisis proportions, until normal men and women stand down or demobilize from the "emergency" phase of parenthood. The gender distinctions, which emerge most sharply when young parents enter what I have termed *the chronic emergency* of parenthood, get blurred as the last children are launched, usually in the parents' middle years. Thus, when maturing children demonstrate that they can assume major responsibility for supplying their own physical and emotional security, the stringent requirements of parenthood are relaxed. Fathers and mothers can then reclaim the strivings and capacities that conflicted with the parental assignment and therefore had been either repressed or lived out vicariously, through the spouse.

Postparental men appropriate qualities of nurturance and tenderness that were once relatively alien within themselves, and only tolerable in their dependents—their wives or children. By the same token, postparental women adopt some of the ascendant, competitive qualities that their husbands are relinquishing. As each postparental spouse becomes as the other used to be, the couple moves toward the normal androgyny of later life.

Given its linkage to the generic requirements of parenthood, the so-called contrasexual transition is, like paternity and maternity themselves,

*See Atchley 1976; Benedek 1952; Brenneis 1975; Brown 1985; Feldman et al. 1981; Galler 1977; Gold 1969; Hurlbert 1962; Jaslow 1976; Leonard 1967; Lewis 1965; Lowenthal et al. 1975; Peskin and Livson 1981; Ripley 1984; Shanan 1978; Streib 1968; Tachibana 1962; and Van Arsdale 1981.

a quasi-universal event. As such, it usually precedes a developmental advance. Indeed, after some period of psychic dislocation, most men and women do accommodate to the changes in themselves and in their spouses. They gradually craft the energies liberated by the postparental reversal into new executive capacities of the personality. They do not at the same time lose their gender identities as men or women: instead, they revise their self-conception to include the new powers that accompany the mid-life transformation. The result, for most men and women, is an expanded sense of self rather than a loss of self-continuity. The contrasexual upheavals of the postparental period have brought about new constancies in the form of new structures, new ego capacities for knowing and enjoying: psychological development has taken place.

Androgyny and Pathology: A Model

Our clinical studies (conducted under the auspices of the Older Adult Program at Northwestern Medical School) show that significant numbers of men and women do become casualties of this same contrasexual reversal. Like the minority of adolescents who become disturbed following puberty, these seniors become casualties of their "allergic" reaction to their own surgent energies. In the course of working with patients in their late fifties and early to middle sixties, we have identified some predisposing characteristics. These render certain patients particularly vulnerable to their own contrasexual potentials, to the point where they convert a normal, universal transition into a pathogenic stressor.

Despite his informal study methods, Jung (1933) accurately described the pathological as well as the healthy outcomes of later life androgyny. He noted that the resulting "sharpness of mind" of the wife as well as the unexpected "softness" of the husband could lead to marital troubles for the couple and to neurotic difficulties for individuals who experience such untoward changes in themselves.

When we investigate the developmental histories as well as the clinical pictures presented by older men (aged fifty-five to sixty-five), those hospitalized for the first time with acute psychiatric illness, we find ample evidence to support Jung's original insight. We will first consider the presenting symptoms, and then the deeper pathogenic issues—the personality characteristics and formative experiences that render these men particularly vulnerable to late-onset disorders.

Taken by themselves, we find that the presenting symptoms do not tell us very much about the causes of these late-blooming disorders. The symptom pictures range across the whole DSM-III and include severe alcoholism, diffuse anxiety states, significant and often suicidal depressions, and paranoid psychosis (in which the patient believes that other men are accusing him of being gay or effeminate). Nevertheless, although the symptoms may vary they are in all cases severe, and their strength sharply contrasts with the precipitating circumstances which for the most part are relatively undramatic. In many patients it is difficult to find a clear precipitant, and those that can be identified do not involve some disastrous loss of the sort predicted by conventional, depletion-centered geropsychiatry. Rarely do we find major losses in health, work, social relationships, or finances severe enough to account for the flagrant symptoms.

Though the victims of late-onset disorders are generally located within a relatively narrow age band, they are widely dispersed across the entire social, economic, and ethnic spectrum. These disorders afflict cab drivers and executives with equal impartiality. Despite their wide-ranging symptoms and social backgrounds, these men strikingly resemble each other in the more personal sense. They tend to be intelligent; and despite some problems with success, they are driven to achieve and to feel shame when they fail. These ascendant qualities appear early in life. As boys, these patients sought out and excelled in the rougher, more dangerous sports. In their young manhood, most of these patients were in the armed services, usually as volunteers rather than draftees. They went to war as they had once gone to the playing fields: pressing to the forefront of the battle, they typically became paratroopers, submariners, or combat infantrymen.

The factors that truly characterize these late-onset patients are connected to their formative rather than their adult experience—particularly, their early experience of their mothers, in their families of orientation. All these men also report much the same kind of mother—destructively dominant. This picture of the witch-mother is not a product of clinical inference. These men state quite bluntly that the mother was a dragon and that the father was her prey, her meat. In some cases, the mother freely disparaged the father; in other cases she attacked him physically as well as verbally; and in a few instances, the mother openly cuckolded the father by bringing her lovers (in some cases, her clients) into the marriage bed, without bothering to disguise her peccadilloes from the husband or even from the future patient, her son. But where the father was openly debased, the son was often elevated by the mother, to the point where he was sometimes equated with the mother's idealized parent, his own maternal grandfather. In the patient's experience, the mother put the hopes and expectations that had been disappointed by the husband into her son; he became, in effect, the grandfather's true heir—the son that she had dreamt of having by her own father.

Despite this maternal favoritism, the sons usually split their feelings, reserving fear and grudging respect for the mother, and sympathy, even love, for the father. In a reversal of the usual triangular family drama, the son wanted to protect the father, to be his St. George against the dragon, but without knowing how to accomplish that feat. But as oedipal victors, these men also knew that they had conspired with the mother to bring about the father's defeat; and that they had drawn pleasure from it. Their oedipal victory was tainted; deep down, these men knew that the father's stolen power would ultimately turn against them. Thus, they bore through life the guilty conviction that they were doomed to share the father's fate.

But despite their distrust of her, these men inherit strong ego ideals from their mothers; and they are driven as much by shame as by guilt. They cannot accept their own victory; neither can they accept the prospect of defeat. Thus, their identification with the defeated father is counteracted by an equally strong need to deny their linkage to such a shameful, victimized man. Guilt pushed them toward the father; shame wrenched them away from him.

However, *both* guilt and shame combined to lever these patients *away* from the mother. Lacking a potent (oedipal) father to interpose between themselves and the possessive, seductive mother, these men were always in danger of remaining in the shameful "mama's boy" position. By the same token, guilt made them fear (and covertly seek) the father's fate at the hands of a castrating woman; and the mother has already shown her fitness for the executioner's assignment. The combination of guilt, fear, and shame drove these patients to distance themselves from the mother in all major spheres: physical, social, and if possible, psychological. Both avoidances, of the father as well as of the mother, were managed through the same kind of bold action. By seeking danger in a "man's world," these men rejected with one inclusive stroke the oedipal trophy, the title of "mama's boy," and the equation with a castrated father. They showed the courage that was unavailable to the father and the nonconformity that would shock, even alienate the mother.

Because they cannot achieve secure psychological separation from the mother, these men compensate by amplifying their physical and social differences. Physical separation is gained outside the domestic orbit, in the man's world of male allies, mentors, hunters, athletes, and soldiers. Social distance is gained via the kinds of rebellious and delinquent behavior that violate the mother's rigid rules and standards. In effect, they force the mother to push them away, and thus bring about the social distance that they cannot achieve on their own.

Furthermore, as these men gain sexual maturity, they finally achieve a tolerable degree of psychological distance from the mother, usually through their attachments to women who are completely unlike her: demure, soft-spoken, dependent, even adoring. Through such sexual liaisons these men distance themselves from the mother in at least two ways. The submissive wife is herself distant from the mother's character; through this so obviously feminine creature, these inwardly divided men can distance themselves from their *own* feared passivity. The dependent mate becomes the outward metaphor of their own "feminine" qualities, now decisively excised from the self and relocated externally in the wife. In effect, these men conserve the mother's strength for themselves, but they eject her "softer," feminine aspect into the psychosocial ecology or niche conveniently provided by the wife. In the family of procreation the wife assumes the passive role that was played out by the father vis-à-vis the mother in the family of orientation. The wife then becomes the linchpin, the guarantor of the husband's delicate psychological balance. Through her he can demonstrate his unlikeness to the father as well as his distance from his internal and external mothers.

As long as these men can retain this life arrangement—the psychological niche provided by their wives—they do not become patients, and they do well in the crucial realms of work and even love. Intelligent, if somewhat driven (perhaps Type A) men, they advance in a variety of careers, and they tend to become responsible husbands and fathers. These seemingly strong protectors of weak people do well as long as they can rely on dependent women and children to remove from them the stigmatized figments of their androgynous nature: the woman, the "mama's boy," the castrated father.

But children grow up, take over the responsibility for their own security, and become less dependent. And, as we have seen, after the launching period, postparental development levers even a submissive wife out of the closet to assume a more independent, sometimes a more competitive and domineering stance toward her husband. This liberation happens precisely during the period when surgent postparental tides are pushing the husband in the opposite direction: toward the weakened position of passive mastery, toward the position that the father had held in the family of orientation. In short, the wife rejects a passive stance precisely at that time when the husband acutely needs an external repository for that stance. In effect, the ascendant wife abandons the passive position and in so doing gives back to the husband the hidden aspect of his own sexuality; she forces him to confront his own masculine/feminine bi-modality. In addition, the midlife pacification of the man and the corresponding activation of the wife has a specific and catastrophic meaning for these men. In their eyes, the traumatic situation of childhood has been reconvened: The middle-aged husband is turning into his own weakened father, and the middle-aged wife is turning into a *simulacra* of the castrating mother. Thus, for most men at risk, we find that a current domestic life with a strong wife is for them the *reprise* of a traumatic past and a threat to their established lifeways and defenses, their protection against any repetition of that traumatic history. The long-avoided (but also long-awaited) sword of Damocles is about to fall.

The afflicted men react to their changed external circumstances and to their internal crisis in ways that reflect their life situation as well as their various temperaments. Wealthy men, who can afford multiple alimonies, may stave off symptoms for a while, by divorcing the aging wife and by replacing her with a young, fresh, and still adoring "father's daughter"; they find a new external vessel for the suspect feminine side of their own bi-modality.

Less affluent men, or men whose religion does not allow divorce, may try to change their wife's responses rather than get rid of her, particularly if the spouse herself feels guilty about her nascent aggression. The wife, whose guilt is reciprocal to her husband's shame, may damage herself in a last-ditch attempt to preserve her husband in the psychological sense. In order to keep the husband whole, the wife may develop a midlife depression or become a psychosomatic cripple. Thus, some women that we have studied will stay in the closet and take on for themselves what would otherwise be the husband's depression. Through this sacrifice, the wife performs a late act of nurturance toward the husband; she satisfies his unconscious requirement, of a needy, damaged wife. In those cases, the wife rather than the husband is more likely to end up as a patient.

However, the men we see clinically are precisely those who cannot change external matters—in this case, the wife—in their favor. Lacking wives who will not surrender their own newfound ascendancy, these men have exchanged outer harmony for internal conflict. They sometimes express their inner, troubling sense of sexual bi-modality through psychosomatic disease. They bring some damaged organ—a metaphor both of the wife and of the damaged, needy aspect of themselves—for medical treatment. The organ, rather than themselves, takes on the status of patient. Others turn to alcoholism, a state that permits them to live out both sides, active and passive, of their own bi-modality; one can be first a hero and then a helpless baby in the course of the same drinking bout. Others, in shamed revulsion against their own passive aspect, become depressed, sometimes to the point where they might launch a suicidal attack against this despised, alienated part of themselves. And some avoid unconscious awareness of their inner split by projecting that awareness in the form of paranoid sensitivity: Other men, they claim, are accusing them of being effete or homosexual.

Androgyny and Pathology: The Case of Ernest Hemingway

Before discussing Ernest Hemingway as a classic exemplar of the at-risk type of man, I make the usual (and decent) disclaimer. By tracing out the precursors and manifestations of Hemingway's late-onset disorders, I do not claim to account for all aspects of his complex personality, or of his literary genius. In this discussion, we limit ourselves to tracing the threads of his major preoccupation with the tragic dilemmas of manhood. We will look at the influences that underpin these concerns, as well as the ways that the aging Hemingway struggled to preserve the sense of uncorrupted masculinity. Hemingway's genius made him unique, but it did not save him from the common human fate, when in the later years his sense of manhood was fatally compromised.

As his final doom took shape, Ernest Hemingway ran the whole gamut of behaviors and symptoms—from serial divorce, to paranoia, to suicide—already noted. Hemingway had four wives, and he got rid of three of them at the point when they either lost the bloom of youth or stood up to him. Mary Hemingway, the last wife, may have preserved her marriage at the cost of chronic disability; she kept herself in a state of continuous damage through various self-inflicted accidents. Symptomatically, Hemingway, always a heavy drinker, became increasingly alcoholic to the point where his writing and even his thinking were often affected. In addition, Hemingway suffered from hypochondriasis, as well as hypertension and other psychosomatic disorders; he finally lapsed into frank paranoia and the suicidal depression that ended his life at age sixty-one. Hemingway's later writing (as well as his later behavior) reflected the themes that we have been tracking in the population of older male patients. Thus, Hemingway's novel *The Garden of Eden* (1986), a work that he began at age forty-five and worked on until his final years, is a story of a wife who becomes explicitly masculine and who attempts to destroy her husband's manhood.

Hemingway is also of particular interest because, like the majority of men in the late-onset population, his psychopathology was not prompted by objectively catastrophic circumstances. As he sank toward his final psychotic depression, Hemingway was wealthy, revered, married to an attractive and considerate wife, and not lethally ill in the physical sense. In order to understand his illness (and in order to locate the true precipitants), we have to look at the predisposing character and the roots of that character in Hemingway's early experience.

Hemingway's developmental history aptly fits our model. Grace Hemingway was a classic example of the pathogenic mother that we have already identified in the accounts of less gifted men. Trained as an operatic singer, she never accepted her domestic fate. Her children were raised by nannies; Hemingway's father, although a doctor, was responsible for the cooking; and Grace made it quite clear that she had given up a great artistic career for a man who was not worthy of her sacrifice. Apparently she was disappointed in Dr. Hemingway's ability to provide, and she may have disparaged his sexual abilities as well. As a teenager, Hemingway saw his father angrily evict from their home a woman suspected of being Grace Hemingway's lesbian lover. In these domestic wars, Hemingway clearly sided with his father.

Though disparaged within the home where he was deferential toward his imperious wife, Hemingway's father came into his own in the outdoors. As a doctor he commanded the respect of neighbors (including Michigan Indians) whom he treated; and he was an accomplished hunter and fisherman who taught those skills to Ernest. The young Hemingway seemed to have learned from his father that manhood was always at risk within the domestic world of women, but that it could be preserved and even enhanced outside the home in tests of courage, in conflict with physical nature and with other men. In the world of combat or raw nature, men could be defeated and even killed; but as long as they lived by the tragic code, their manhood was never at risk. But the trophies of war or of the hunt would not survive the transition into the home. Hemingway angrily recalled how his mother, while moving the household, deliberately burned Dr. Hemingway's prized collection of nature specimens.

His mother gave Ernest compelling reasons to sympathize with his father; they were both targets of the mother's castrating drives. Thus, while Grace regarded Ernest (the first son) as a replacement for her own idealized father and dubbed him her "precious boy," she also dressed him as a girl for the first three years of his life. Grace claimed that, of her six children, Ernest was most like her, and this sense of twinship seemingly overrode the gender differences between mother and son. Thus, as reported by Kenneth Lynn (1987), Grace dressed Ernest, longer than was customary for that era, in pink gingham gowns with white Battenberg lace hoods, fluffy, frilly dresses, black patent-leather shoes, high stockings, and picture hats with flowers on them. He was also coiffed in the manner of a girl-child of that time, with long, carefully bobbed hair. Grace Hemingway titled a picture of Ernest in this get-up (taken before his second birthday) as "A Summer Girl." Finally, Grace enacted her sense of oneness with her son through the oldest child, her daughter: Marcelline and Ernest were treated like twins of the same sex—sometimes as two boys, sometimes as two girls, but always paired. (Like Ernest and their mutual father, Marcelline eventually commited suicide.)

However, Ernest was temperamentally a dynamo, and he tugged strongly against the golden cord. At age three, he announced, "I ain't afraid of nothin!"; and in his first-grade school compositions he already displays his lifelong interest in the outdoors, in competitive sports, and in hunting. Clearly, he was gaining some precocious distance from the mother by identifying with the "sportsman" aspect of the father—the aspect that evaded Grace Hemingway's control and disparagement.

As Ernest grew up, he compensated for the lack of psychological distance by putting maximum *physical* distance as soon as he could, between himself and his mother. He went to war in his father's way, as a medic, enlisting in the ambulance corps of the Italian army, and suffered grave leg wounds. Hospitalized, Ernest fell in love with his nurse, an older woman named Agnes Von Kurowski. This choice was typical; until his later years most of Hemingway's lovers and wives were older than himself. Returning home from the war (and jilted by Agnes), Ernest again lost the necessary physical distance from his mother. But he quickly interposed social distance in its place, and became to her a sullen, provocative, and disappointing adolescent.

After his job as a reporter, Hemingway made an early marriage to his first wife, Hadley (again, an older woman) and moved with her to Paris. There he began his full-time career as an author and began to turn out the bold, realistic, and earthy writing that would be his signature. Predictably, his writing offended—as it was meant to—both his parents, but particularly his mother. Interestingly, Ernest ignored the father's criticism of his raunchy prose but expressed great bitterness about his mother's critique, and accused her of disloyalty to him. The social distance between mother and son was now entrenched. Ernest never forgave his mother, avoided her company, and in 1928 blamed her for his father's suicide by gunshot. In his later years, Ernest referred to his mother only as "that bitch," and claimed that she would be more dangerous dead than most women would be alive. General "Buck" Lanham, his wartime buddy, observed that Hemingway hated his mother more than any man he ever knew. Ernest did not attend her funeral.

During the Paris years Hemingway had established physical, social, and—via his wife, Hadley—psychological distance from his mother. But when Hadley herself became a mother, and became matronly in bearing, Hemingway enacted the typical pattern: He left Hadley for a new love, the adoring, obsequious (and older) Pauline. Ernest had once more relied on a passive and dependent woman to gain psychological distance from the maternal person. But Pauline in her turn became a mother; Hemingway subsequently kept his distance from *her* through frequent fishing trips on the *Pilar,* as well as some intense and protracted love affairs. One lover was

Martha Gellhorn, a war correspondent whom Ernest met and courted during the Spanish Civil War. He subsequently divorced Pauline and married Martha in 1939.

For the first time, Ernest had taken a wife who was younger than himself. Although she was young, Martha was also spirited; unlike his more adoring and biddable wives Hadley and Pauline, Martha was, like Hemingway, an accomplished writer and an adventerous reporter. True, during the Spanish war, Martha had been the ideal Hemingway woman. Ernest knew Spain, and he knew war; and Martha was content to be the admiring young companion of "Papa" Hemingway. But after the honeymoon, in Cuba, Martha quickly tired of the housekeeper and sex-kitten role that Ernest assigned her, and she became disenchanted with Hemingway's self-indulgent and alcoholic lifeways. Against Hemingway's bitter opposition, she took off to pursue her trade in the European theater of war. It has been said that Martha Gellhorn was the first woman, besides his mother, to stand up to Ernest, and he reacted predictably. Becoming sullen and depressed, he played, aboard the *Pilar,* at submarine- and spy-chasing around the coasts of Cuba. Back from a real war front, Martha saw through these self-dramatizing games and accused Hemingway of sitting out the war against fascism, while good men died to defend his freedom and comforts.

Finally shamed into action, Ernest became a war correspondent for *Colliers,* the same magazine that employed his wife. Hemingway was now openly competitive with Martha. He mocked her assignments and writing and never forgave her for going ashore on D-Day while he stayed offshore on a landing craft. Again, Hemingway handled the deterioration of his third marriage in typical fashion. In wartime London, while still married to Martha, he started an affair with Mary Walsh, the woman who would become his fourth wife.

Mary was in Ernest's comfortable mode: obedient, self-effacing, appreciative, and even masochistic. Even though he had found a replacement for Martha, there is solid evidence that Hemingway never really recovered from his first rejection—and a scornful one at that—by a wife. Ernest's shame was compounded by his continuing attachment. Although he ridiculed Martha publicly, he continued to carry a torch for her. Even after his marriage to Mary, Ernest kept Martha's portrait in his living room, and she appears in barely disguised form as the hero's lost love in a later book, *Islands In the Stream* (1970). In losing Martha, Hemingway lost more than a desirable woman; by her rejection he appears to have lost an essential fulcrum of his psyche. Bear in mind that this insult from an independent woman came when Ernest was forty-five years old. He was at the stage when most men, having launched their children, begin to feel stirrings from the occulted, passive side of their nature. This is the age when men with Ernest's background need a dependent wife to hold and externalize for them the dangerous internal burden. In Hemingway's case, the woman who should have been the adoring one, the repository of his softer side, had refused that assignment. She had seen through his macho posturing, she had disparaged his manhood, and, instead of holding his *anima* in escrow for him, she had returned it to him.

Hemingway's separation from his dangerous but seductive feminine identifications depended on a strong union with a needful woman; by splitting the couple, Martha had in effect handed back to Ernest the dangerous side of his nature. Once separated from Martha, Ernest was no longer separated from his feminine side, and he may have come to the shocked recognition that these dangerous qualities were part of himself and not of the woman "out there."

The foregoing comments on Hemingway's inner life are of course musings and speculations. But Hemingway did in fact begin to write *The Garden of Eden*, his long (and until recently unpublished) novel on the dangers and temptations of explicit androgyny, about a month after the divorce with Martha became final. In this novel Hemingway tries to make art out of the occult concerns of men in his life stage, particularly those with his early background and psychic constitution. *The Garden of Eden* is the story of a brief and strange marriage between two beautiful young people, Catherine and David. Their union starts as an idyllic honeymoon in southern France but ends disastrously, owing to Catherine's explicit desire to be a man and to turn David into her androgynous twin. At first a typical Hemingway woman, Catherine starts out as an adoring, passionate lover, but she soon reveals her secret wish to be manly in all possible ways: to wear her hair short, to wear men's clothes, and to take the male role in sex. Additionally, Catherine requires that David take up complementary roles: he should play sexual games in which the roles in intercourse are reversed. In addition, she requires that David cut and dye his hair in her fashion, that he acquire her deep shade of tan, and that he wear matching clothes. Moving more drastically toward masculine sexuality, Catherine brings in a very attractive young woman, Marita, to be her own lesbian lover.

Marita is the passive, hyperfeminine member of the lesbian pair, and David—like Hemingway, a war veteran and a writer—in effect saves himself through her, by seducing and converting the complaisant lesbian to passionate heterosexuality. But before she leaves the sexually reconstituted couple, the now psychotic Catherine strikes a final blow against David's manhood. She burns her husband's treasured manuscript, the record of his boyhood adventures on safari with his father.

This last vignette tells us who Catherine really is: a condensation of

Grace and Marcelline Hemingway, the two imperious older women of Ernest's childhood. Thus the fictional Catherine acts toward David as the mother had acted toward both Ernest and his father, and as the sister had acted toward her little brother. She dresses a man like a woman, she coifs his hair like a woman, she twins him with a woman, and she burns the manuscript about the male hunt, the life away from women. Catherine burns David's book about the hunt in the same manner that his mother burned the father's relics from the hunt. The witch-mother and the witch-sister returned at that point in the life cycle when most men, writers or illiterates, begin to face those demons within themselves. In our research, we find equivalent "Catherine" fantasies making their first appearance in projective test protocols of middle-aged men.

In Hemingway's case, the bad dreams did not stay within the unconscious; after Martha left, the dream of the castrating mother became the stuff of his fiction, that hidden part of his oeuvre, which remained for a long time unpublished. In that occulted body of his work, Hemingway used his genius to confront the ogre, to explore and come to terms with his own emerging sexual bi-modality. Although this effort at self-therapy through art may have delayed his breakdown, it did not finally prevent it. The myth of castrated androgyny was not finally containable within the fictional world. In the remaining fifteen years of his life, the fantasy of destruction by a fierce woman was taken over and enacted by Hemingway himself, as he moved into alcoholism, "accidental" injuries, paranoia, depression, and the shotgun blast to the head, which mimicked his father's suicide and terminated his own life.

In summary, Hemingway used *Eden* to explore and master the sexual duality that is uncovered as part of development in later life. But his courageous attempt at self-discovery failed; Hemingway had finally to kill himself in order to kill off the twin-mother that he found growing within him. In the minds of some men, death restores the mother to them; but in Ernest's troubled mind, death was the final escape, the only trustworthy separation from the "feminine," from the "Mother" emerging within "Papa" Hemingway.

REFERENCES

Atchley, R. 1976. "Selected Social and Psychological Differences between Men and Women in Later Life." *Journal of Gerontology* 31(2):204–211.

Benedek, T. 1952. *Psychosexual Functions in Women.* New York: Ronald Press.

Brenneis, C. R. 1975. "Developmental Aspects of Aging in Women." *Archives of General Psychiatry* 32:429–35.

Brown, J. 1985. *In Her Prime, A New View of Middle-Aged Women.* South Hadley, Mass.: Bergin & Garvey.

Feldman, S.; Biringen, C.; and Nash, S. 1981. "Fluctuations of Sexual-related Self-attributions as a Function of Stage of Family Life Cycle." *Developmental Psychology* 17:24–35.

Galler, S. 1977. "Women Graduate Student Returnees and Their Husbands: A Study of the Effects of the Professional and Academic Graduate School Experience on Sex-Role Perceptions, Marital Relationships, and Family Concepts." Ph.D. diss., The School of Education, Northwestern University, Evanston, Ill.

Gold, S. 1969. "Cross-cultural Comparisons of Role Change with Aging." *Student Journal of Human Development* (University of Chicago) 1:11–15.

Gutmann, D. L. 1964. "An Exploration of Ego Configurations in Middle and Later Life." In *Personality and Later Life,* ed. B. Neugarten, pp. 114–48. New York: Atherton.

————. 1987. *Reclaimed Powers: Toward a New Psychology of Men and Women in Later Life.* New York: Basic Books.

Hemingway, E. 1970. *Islands in the Stream.* New York: Charles Scribner's Sons.

Hemingway, E. 1986. *The Garden of Eden.* New York: Charles Scribner's Sons.

Hurlbert, J. 1962. "Age as a Factor in the Social Organization of the Hare Indians of Fort Good Hope, Northwest Territories." Ottawa, Ontario, Canada: Northern Co-ordination and Research Centre, Department of Northern Affairs and National Resources.

Jaslow, P. 1976. "Employment, Retirement and Morale among Older Women." *Journal of Gerontology,* 31(2):212–18.

Jung, C. 1933. *Modern Man in Search of a Soul.* New York: Harcourt, Brace.

Leonard, O. 1967. "The Older Spanish-Speaking People of the Southwest." In *The Older Rural Americans,* ed. E. Youmans, pp. 239–61. Lexington, Kentucky: University of Kentucky Press.

Lewis, O. 1965. *Life in A Mexican Village: Tepoztlan Restudied.* Urbana, Ill.: University of Illinois Press.

Lowenthal, M.; Thurnher, M.; and Chiriboga, D. 1975. *Four Stages of Life.* San Francisco: Jossey-Bass.

Lynn, K. S. 1987. *Hemingway: The Life And The Work.* New York: Simon & Schuster.

Peskin, H., and Livson, N. 1981. "Uses of the Past in Adult Psychological Health." In *Present and Past in Middle Life,* ed. B. Eichorn et al., pp. 148–64. New York: Academic Press.

Ripley, D. 1984. "Parental Status, Sex Roles, and Gender Mastery Style in Working Class Fathers." Ph.D. diss., Department of Pychology, Illinois Institute of Technology, Chicago, Illinois).

Shanan, J. 1978. "The Jerusalem Study of Mid-Adulthood and Aging (JESMA). Effects of Ecology and Culture on Stability and Change of Psychological Functions and Structures in the Transition from Middle to Later Adulthood." *Israel Journal of Gerontology* 2(8):44–59.

Streib, G. 1968. "Family Patterns in Retirement." In *Sourcebook on Marriage and the Family,* ed. M. S. Sussman, pp. 70–86. Boston, Mass.: Houghton Mifflin.

Tachibana, K. 1962. "A Study of Introversion-Extraversion in the Aged." In *Social and Psychological Aspects of Aging: Aging Around the World,* ed. C. Tibbitts and W. Donahue, pp. 655–56. New York: Columbia University Press.

Van Arsdale, P. W. 1981. "The Elderly Asmat of New Guinea." In *Other Ways of*

Growing Old: Anthropological Perspectives, ed. P. T. Amoss and S. Harrel, pp. 23–31. Stanford, Calif.: Stanford University Press.

DISCUSSION

In this recent elaboration of his seminal work on the contrasexual transition in midlife, Dr. Gutmann relates the "stressful passage to androgyny" to the end of the "emergency" phase of parenthood, to that point in middle adulthood when "maturing children demonstrate that they can assume major responsibility for supplying their own physical and emotional security" (p. 171). This shift, which Dr. Gutmann stresses is universal, produces a profound effect upon the developmental process and intrapsychic structure.

As with all developmental processes, normal or pathologic, the contrasexual transition grows out of internal conflict. We wish to underscore our agreement with that point in general and with Dr. Gutmann's conclusion that in the healthy individual conflict results in "an expanded sense of self rather than a loss of self-continuity. . . . new constancies in the form of new structures, new ego capacities for knowing and enjoying: psychological development has taken place" (p. 172). Dr. Gutmann's work on the contrasexual transition has always been, for us, a demonstrably convincing précis of evidence for our belief that, as a result of experiences in adulthood leading to significant intrapsychic change, development continues into later life. In other words, psychic change in adulthood cannot be explained on the basis of infantile experience alone.

In seeming contradiction to this viewpoint, Dr. Gutmann, through his model of androgyny and pathology and his reconstruction of the life of Hemingway, appears to emphasize the power of infantile experience. We feel that no genuine contradiction exists and that pathology in midlife is *always* the result of unresolved conflict from the infantile past, the adolescent and young adult past, and current, phase-specific developmental pressures.

He further notes that reliance on descriptive symptomatology to understand the patient is highly limited because the androgynous shift can produce symptoms that fall in a broad range of diagnostic categories. An invaluable contribution of the developmental framework is the insight it provides into motivation and psychopathology. In this case, *behind* the various symptom pictures are common personality characteristics (despite a wide social and cultural incidence) and similar childhood experience with dominant mothers and passive fathers. These men were all oedipal victors.

They "managed" their unresolved infantile conflicts in latency, adolescence, and young adulthood by avoiding their fathers and mothers and resorting to bold action. Dr. Gutmann's detailed description of the psychological mechanisms involved clearly demonstrates how the thrust of development and the addition of development themes that have never been experienced before, such as the ability to choose sexual partners and various endeavors in adolescence and young adulthood, can contain pathologic processes and prevent the onset of symptoms for long periods of time. Dr. Gutmann's attempt to understand the nature of late-onset pathology is truly a pioneering effort.

In addition to using new developmental themes to maintain symptom-free psychological equilibrium, these men also used psychological mechanisms employed in healthy development. In adolescence and young adulthood they, as their healthier counterparts, projected their feminine identifications (unusually prominent because of the intense involvement with mother) onto the women they loved and became dominant, "macho" males. Both the reliance on work and sex dominance, and those projections of feminine aspects of the self onto the partner worked as long as these men could rely on dependent women and children to remove from them the stigmatized fragments of their androgynous nature.

This defense may continue until midlife but must inevitably crumble under the power of the newly emerging development toward postparental androgyny. Then "the middle-aged husband is turning into his own weakened father, and the middle-aged wife is turning into a *simulacra* of the castrating mother" (pp. 175–76). Developmental pressures that had been used to keep the unresolved internal conflict at bay suddenly become an enemy rather than an ally, the existing defenses are unequal to the task of containing the unacceptable impulses, and symptom formation is called into play.

Dr. Gutmann's case study of Ernest Hemingway proves again that intelligence and creative genius are no protection against psychological illness. The creative artist may sublimate some of his conflict into his work, as Hemingway did in his novel *The Garden of Eden* and other works, and still suffer the onset of late-life pathology. Although our knowledge of his life is sketchy, it appears that Shakespeare, as presented in Dr. Hildebrand's chapter, experienced a more benign mid- and late-life course, undoubtedly because of different infantile experiences and character structure. His relative stability allowed him to write and think about death in the manner of Prospero's words, "my every third thought shall be of death" (p. 481); rather than to use death as an escape to "the other side of the wall."

8

Where We Are and What We Want:

A Psychological Model

JUDITH M. BARDWICK

As a nation, we have experienced profound shifts in our values in a brief time. The pendulum of change swung far to the left in the late 1960s. It was inevitable that a swing to the right would follow, and that happened in the early 1980s. The next phase, which is also predictable, is a transitional one of compromise and consolidation as the pendulum swings back through a center that is no longer where it was.

During periods of transition we try to evolve ways of living with the consequences of basic social change, but it is difficult because we lack clear norms and values. We are in a transitional phase now, and as a result, we have wider differences among groups and among people of similar ages than there were during the 1950s and most of the 1960s when only one set of norms existed: the traditional.

To clarify this legacy of complexity, I have constructed a model in which I group people according to age and gender. Those two dimensions can tell us a good deal about people's desires and their activities because most people's lives run along the schedules considered "normal" for males and females at various times. In addition, one's psychological stance is formed by individual experiences and age cohort. Especially within the past two decades, each cohort has been significantly affected by rapidly changing cultural values and economic events.

What was life like in their formative years for the different age cohorts? What impacted most on each group? People now in their twenties were powerfully influenced, for instance, by the recession of the early 1980s and the general turn toward traditional values. Today's thirties cohort was especially influenced by the feminist movement and the antiestablishment era of the Vietnam War. Those now in their forties felt the force of the chaotic decade in changes in sexual values between 1965 and 1975, after they had spent many years as Eisenhower-era Eagle Scouts. Fifty- and sixty-year-olds were adults in unparalleled good times, but born in the depression, they have difficulty taking economic security for granted.

In addition to differences in gender and age cohorts, we also note significant differences among individuals within each age group. All the important psychological stances—attitudes, values, goals, and lifestyles—are to be found within each cohort. It is not a matter of one group having a value that other groups do not have. Rather, the differences among age groups and between men and women are a matter of the proportion of individuals in any group who hold a particular view.

Differences between the Sexes

In this model, I have characterized women and men as psychologically *traditional* or *interdependent (complex)* or *nontraditional.*

Psychologically traditional men and women

The basic psychological difference between traditional men and women is fundamental and profound. Many people think of gender differences in terms of what the sexes *do.* Traditionally, she stayed home, and he went to work; today the majority of American women are in the labor force. The crucial gender difference is not a matter of what women and men do, but rather a matter of how they *perceive* themselves or *experience* themselves in relation to the world.

Traditionally, men are socialized to be self-oriented. By *self-oriented* I mean that the world is experienced with the self as its center. Self-oriented people can be psychologically healthy or unhealthy, generous or selfish, and usually make decisions based largely on how they will be affected. Most of those decisions involve work, as the psychologically traditional man is ambitious and grounds much of his identity in his career. Traditional men are not only self-oriented, they are also oriented toward action, concerned more with what they *do* than with how they *feel.* This is not surprising because traditional norms socialize males to experience only two emotions: sexual passion and aggression, the latter becoming competitive-

ness. Other emotions are considered feminine. As most American psychologists have described it, adult development is unwittingly *male*.
Becoming mature has long been regarded as becoming a self-oriented
individual.

Traditionally, women are socialized to be *other-oriented*. By *other-oriented* I
mean the world is experienced in terms of relationships. Woman's traditional values emphasize meeting responsibilities within relationships.
Other-oriented people gain identity from being in relationship with others, and they gain self-respect as they see themselves as loved and as
helpful to others. These people make decisions after considering how they
would impact on emotionally important others. Traditionally, females are
socialized to experience all emotions *except* those of lust and aggression.
Like those who are self-oriented, other-oriented people can be givers or
takers, psychologically healthy or unhealthy.

People who are self-oriented are mentally free to construct their goals
and images of themselves, and therefore make decisions in those terms.
Because of their psychological emphasis on relationships, traditional
women are not free to create dreams and make long-term decisions in the
same independent way. Women who are psychologically traditional must,
to varying degrees, keep their goals tentative because how they will live
and what they will do is often deeply enmeshed with the priorities of
others. The difference between *self-* and *other-* orientation is very basic. We
cannot assume that the same behaviors, particularly those of going to
school or to work, are based on similar core senses of the self in men and
women.

Today large numbers of women who were initially psychologically traditional have decided they need to have identities and goals of their own.
After a transition period, most of those women become psychologically
complex or what I am calling *interdependent.* Conversely, but in fewer numbers, traditional men may move from a self-orientation to a complex or
interdependent orientation. Every age cohort in this model shows that far
more women than men are interdependent, and far more men than women
are psychologically traditional.

Interdependent women and men

The most revolutionary aspect of feminism was its challenge to women's
traditional priorities and way of viewing themselves. The essential message of feminism was that psychological and economic dependence was a
woeful way to live. Men's lives and self-oriented motives were better.
Thus in the earlier and angrier years of feminism, male values became the
new model for women. But that proved unworkable; it swiftly became

obvious that two self-oriented people could not live in the same household. Thus the idea developed rather rapidly that the ideal woman and man combined the gender characteristics that had been traditionally associated with one sex, that is, that they become androgynous, from *andro* meaning male, and *gynous* meaning female. In short, they develop qualities from both the self- and the other-orientation. The new ideal was to become complex people.

The major values of interdependent women and men are essentially the same. Interdependent people have a clear sense of who they are and frequently act to enhance their self-esteem, their interests, and their self-oriented perspective. Interdependent people are also other-oriented. They acknowledge a need to be in relationships; they are aware that they are not independent, but rather, they need to love and feel loved. Because that need does not make them feel vulnerable, they are sensitive to both their own feelings and those of others. Overall they will make decisions based about equally on the effects on themselves and on the other person. The complex psychological stance can develop in any lifestyle, but it emerges most readily when people live lives of multiple commitments. Interdependent people are often ambitious in their careers, but they will compromise their self-oriented goals if those goals jeopardize the well-being of important others. The interdependent couple are peers who respect as well as love one another and therefore share decision-making power equally.

Psychological interdependence may be the most mature of the psychological stances, and it is increasingly the professional paradigm for mental health. However, relatively few young adults have these values; most people need to accomplish whatever the traditional norms require before they become interdependent. For example, it is psychologically easier for women to allow themselves to be assertive when they are secure that they are loved as women. Similarly, it is easier for men to allow themselves awareness of their emotional needs after they have achieved enough career success to feel confident as men.

Psychologically nontraditional people

A third group of people are psychologically nontraditional; they have reversed traditional values. Nontraditional men do not seek success in work as their major source of identity and self-esteem, and nontraditional women do not turn to relationships and love. Some people are consistently nontraditional. For others, probably a larger group, being nontraditional is a transition to becoming interdependent.

Nontraditional men can be self- or other-oriented. Men who are nontraditional and self-oriented relate to the world in terms of themselves but, unlike traditional men, they are not ambitious. They may say, "I don't want to work too hard; there's too much else to do in life. I don't think that success is two cars and a big house in the suburbs. For me, success means having enough to eat and clothes on my back and time to do the things I really enjoy."

Men who are nontraditional and other-oriented perceive the world in terms of their relationships. A man may become other-oriented for a few years when marriage or some other relationship is threatened or ends; frightened and depressed because of the emotional loss, he becomes aware of how much he needs love. It is not uncommon for men in middle age to become other-oriented. When they are no longer absorbed in their careers, they may become aware that the development of their relating skills and emotional sensitivities has lagged behind their competitive and achieving skills. At work they may become involved as mentors; at home they may give more emotionally to their grandchildren than they did to their children.

Nontraditional women are self-oriented. Like nontraditional men, they fall into two groups. The most noticeable characteristic of one group is ambition. Those women have decided that, for the present, they do not want the responsibilities of significant relationships because they are unwilling to compromise their freedom or ambition. The most obvious characteristic of the other group of self-oriented women is their rage. Their anger often stems from their sense that their trust and love have been betrayed, a feeling often rooted in their own or their parents' divorces.

A permanent self-centered stance in women is rare because the socialization pressures on women focus on being feminine, which means being emotionally giving and responsible in personal relationships. For most of these women, being self-oriented is a phase that may last several years, until they achieve some substantial success or recover from divorce.

The Model

There are five important simplifications in the model I am proposing: (1) the description is limited to the middle class; (2) events like college or marriage are assigned to one age group; (3) consistency is assumed, although people are rarely consistent in all spheres of their lives, particularly when they are stressed; (4) the model is a portrait of a moment in time and does not describe how people change; and (5) certain lifestyles are attributed to the different psychological stances, although people with different psychological stances can lead similar lives.

The prototypic lifestyle of psychologically traditional men and women is one in which the husband is employed, the wife is not, and the children are at home. If a traditional wife is in the labor force, she regards work largely as a way of earning money to help the family live better. Psychologically, the work she does outside the home is identical to the work she does within it because both contribute to the welfare of her family. Traditional people have one major commitment: he has his career, and she has her family.

The prototypic lifestyle of the interdependent or complex woman and man is that of the dual-career couple. In this case, each partner regards his or her own and the other's work as serious commitments. Typically, household tasks and child care are not divided equally, but they are regarded as the responsibility of both. Complex people have multiple commitments.

There is less consistency in the lifestyles of nontraditional people. Nontraditional men do not consider their work a crucial source of identity or self-esteem. Although some nontraditional women are not employed, many are. Among those in the labor force, their most compelling commitment is to achieve success in their work.

In the model I am describing, all the psychological stances and their associated lifestyles are found at every age, but the proportions within the cohort differ. Because more women than men have been affected by the feminist movement, at any age the percentages of women and men in each group are unequal. Today women are pushing for a more complex lifestyle, and men feel pushed.

The Model Organized by Age

The college years (ages fifteen to nineteen)

Despite lip service to modern values, the psychological stance of today's college generation is largely traditional for three reasons. First, we are in a traditional period both in politics and in social values. Although the peace movement, the civil rights movement, and the women's movement dominated the media during the 1960s and 1970s, at the same time there was a conservative swell in the nation. While most people were aware of the liberals in office and the radicals who dominated the media, conservatives were quietly organizing and gaining power. As a result of that organizing, Ronald Reagan was elected to the presidency in 1980. To conserva-

TABLE 8.1

Where We Are in the Mid-1980s:
Psychological Stances Attributable to Women and Men in Different Age Groups *

	Psychologically Traditional	Psychologically Interdependent	Psychologically Nontraditional
Women	Other-oriented	Interdependent	Self-oriented: ambitious angry
Men	Self-oriented	Interdependent	Self-oriented: not ambitious Other-oriented
LIFESTYLE:	Employed husband	Dual-career	Varied
Age 15–19			
Women	60%	25%	15%
Men	70%	10%	20%
Age 20–29			
Women	50%	35%	15%
Men	65%	15%	20%
Age 30–39			
Women	30%	40%	30%
Men	50%	25%	25%
Age 40–49			
Women	35%	45%	20%
Men	40%	30%	30%
Age 50–59			
Women	55%	35%	10%
Men	60%	20%	20%
Age 60 and older			
Women	65%	25%	10%
Men	55%	15%	30%

*These percentages are logical estimates only and are not grounded in data. The social and economic phenomena on which they are based are elaborated in the text.

tives, the war in Vietnam was the "liberals' war," and the economics of the New Frontier and the Great Society resulted in "stagflation." The social engineering practices of liberals—busing, antipoverty programs, gender and racial quotas—violated conservative convictions about the appropriate role of government. At the same time, the hedonism of the decade between 1965 and 1975, the "Me" generation, the drug culture, the sexual revolution, the peak in the divorce rate, and the legalization of abortion—all provoked a revival of religion, often with a fundamentalist cast. After more than a decade of convulsive upheavals in which values swung toward the left, it was inevitable that we would enter a conservative period.

Second, today's collegians' experience of the economy contributes to their traditionalism. There were three recessions beginning in 1973, the most recent being the most severe. The national debt, the balance of payments, widespread cutbacks in government programs, the October 1987 crash in the stock market, and other economic factors make the recovery feel fragile. Economic conditions contribute significantly to individual and national feelings of optimism and willingness to create change, or of pessimism and a trend toward conservatism. Today's college students are asking, "What do I need to do in order to make myself (economically) secure?"

Third, this age group's conservatism is classic; no matter how much adolescents seem to act rebelliously, adolescence is basically a conservative period. Conformity is a way of reducing anxiety. Not only are they trying to answer the question, "What am I going to do in order to be an adult?" They also ask, "What must I do in order to be a man (or a woman)?" Traditional norms answer those questions with comforting specificity: males must establish their careers; females, their families. At a time when the economy provokes fear and the culture is veering toward tradition, it is especially likely that young people will reduce anxieties by turning toward the certainties of tradition.

The majority of today's younger adults are, therefore, psychologically traditional. Because they are aware of feminist values, traditional women ($\sim$60 percent) may have evolved some sense of themselves as self-oriented, but in the main they are other-oriented and their goals are fluid. Traditional young men ($\sim$70 percent) are developing similarly, but the emphasis is reversed. Although they have some awareness that they need to form relationships, they are self-oriented, focused especially on "getting ahead."

Most young women in college realize that choosing a career is important because they know they will work. But their highest emotional priority is to create the relationship that will lead to marriage. Except for the quarter of them who may already be interdependent, in all likelihood their urges to marry conflict with pressure from parents and professors who tell them that they must make plans based on what *they* want to do.

Those issues frequently surface as realistic problems. How do two people find jobs in the same city? How do you combine a demanding career with raising children? Underlying the reality of such problems is a psychological conflict based on the fear that pursuing your ambition can cost you the relationship, while committing to a relationship can cost you your own goals. Beneath the conflict, of course, is the bedrock difference between self- and other-oriented priorities.

Although many college-age women want to combine a career, marriage, and child rearing, my guess is that only about 25 percent of them are psychologically interdependent. Because there were not many dual-career couples among their parents, relatively few developed an interdependent orientation. As I shall discuss later, the larger percentages of interdependent women *and* men in their forties and fifties typically developed those values after their children were grown.

Having postulated a higher percentage of psychologically traditional young men than women (70 percent versus 60 percent), I can assume that the percentage of males with an interdependent stance is lower than that of women. Young men are normally self-preoccupied and absorbed in preparing for their careers, and that tendency is heightened now because of their sense of economic vulnerability. While the same, say, 15 percent of young men and women may have grown up with interdependent parents, fewer men (10 percent) than women (25 percent) would have adopted those values. Young men often experience interdependence largely as the loss of male privilege. Because they have not yet achieved the career success that most men need in order to feel confident, they usually have difficulty accepting a female partner as a genuine equal.

I would estimate that around 15 percent of the women and 20 percent of the men in this cohort are psychologically nontraditional, possiby as a result of their parents having divorced. Of those women, I would guess that two-thirds (10 percent of the cohort) are probably self-oriented, refusing to be vulnerable in an emotional commitment. Conversely, I would say that about half the men are nontraditional and other-oriented because they reacted to parental divorce in the reverse way, that is, they gained a heightened awareness of their need for family. I think that only about 5 percent of the women in this age group are self-oriented for reasons of career; that proportion would have been higher in the early 1970s, but I find it relatively rare now that the era of militant feminism is past. The remaining half of nontraditional men can be counted as self-oriented, but more concerned with pleasure than with traditional success.

In sum, the most clear-cut characteristic of today's late adolescents is their traditionalism based on fears generated by economic concerns and anxiety exacerbated by fundamental changes in the roles and relative status of women and men. Still, some effects of basic value changes are apparent because roughly one in four young women has already developed an interdependent stance. These young women want a life that integrates work and love, both the self- and other-orientations. That goal will be difficult to accomplish because there are far fewer young men in their age cohort with the same orientation.

The beginning of adult commitments (ages twenty to twenty-nine)

If we take the average age of the next cohort (ages twenty to twenty-nine) as twenty-five in 1985, we recall that mainstream feminism was the majority view when they were fifteen. We were recovering from the recession of 1973–74 and the oil embargo that made our economic vulnerability painfully apparent. Between feminism and inflation, many saw their mothers enter the job market. Women's economic and psychological jeopardy due to their traditional dependence had a new reality as the divorce rate peaked around 1977 (Westoff et al. 1984). Thus when this cohort was in mid-adolescence, the feminist warning that women had better be prepared to take charge of their lives and be able to support themselves gained force. When this group entered college in 1978, the number of women with jobs was climbing rapidly.

Between 1978 and 1982, while they were in college, inflation was high, but the economy was strong. Yet upon graduation they entered the labor force during a severe recession. These people grew up in affluence and passed into young adulthood wondering if depression were imminent. Violent economic changes result in a sense that one cannot predict or control much, so one had better avoid risk and grab as much security as possible. Thus, like their younger brothers and sisters, the majority of those now in their twenties are psychologically traditional.

Nevertheless, the probable percentage of interdependent women in this cohort is substantial because these women now in their twenties grew up in a culture with both traditional and feminist values. In school they were taken far more seriously than their mothers had been. The marked increases in women's enrollment in graduate and professional schools began in 1975. Today, women make up 25 to 50 percent of the students of medicine, law, pharmacy, veterinary medicine, and business (Associated Press 1984).

Most women in their twenties who are seriously involved in their careers also want to marry and have children. I would estimate the women who are psychologically interdependent and who want to live in dual-career marriages at around 35 percent. While few of their mothers had careers, the ideal of psychological interdependence and of women combining all the major commitments is widespread and highly publicized. However, I think the percentage of interdependent men in this age group is only about

15 percent, and I suspect most of them grew up in dual-career homes and learned that an interdependent wife does not diminish a husband's masculinity.

An interdependent arrangement requires that the woman not feel less feminine because of success and the man not feel less masculine because of his partner's diminished dependence. The dual-career relationship requires that partners be confident enough to compromise their respective egocentricities, dependencies, and ambitions.

As mentioned earlier, most men do not achieve a secure sense of masculinity until they feel successful at work. That sense, as Levinson (1978) indicates, does not usually happen until they are in their later thirties. Because of the male need to assure masculinity, the fragility of the economic recovery, and the large numbers of twenty-five- to thirty-nine-year-olds competing in the world of work, the majority of men in their twenties are anxious. As a result, I would say that probably 65 percent of them are psychologically traditional.

Somewhat fewer women in their twenties are traditional. Although most of them are employed, few see themselves as independent. In some ways that view is useful because these are the years when most women bear children. An other-orientation that finds pleasure in nurturing and joy in responses from children is essential for adequate mothering. On the other hand, if there were no self-orientation, these women would be especially vulnerable; young children are totally egocentric and a young mother may feel engulfed by their demands, especially if they are joined by the self-oriented needs of her husband. Completely subordinating her interests to those of her family is likely to leave any woman feeling self-less.

Some psychologically traditional women are employed professionally but are not in satisfying personal relationships. It is easier for a woman to add an autonomous sense of self to the traditional core if her femininity is confirmed in an intimate personal relationship. Until they achieve that kind of affirmation, for some women career success actually adds to anxiety and a sense of vulnerability.

My model estimates that about a third of the 15 percent of women in their twenties who are psychologically nontraditional are absorbed solely in their careers; the others have been hurt emotionally and want to protect themselves from further injury. Some of these are divorced; some are daughters of divorce. Although most of those who divorce in their twenties will simply remarry, others will become self-oriented, unwilling to trust again, at least for a while.

Rather more men in their twenties, $\sim$ 20 percent, are psychologically nontraditional. Among this group, especially in the later twenties, some are no longer ambitious in their careers because they have experienced the frustrations of a nonexpanding economy. Their paths already seem blocked by the baby boomers in their thirties. Disenchanted, such men may turn for a while to hedonistic goals.

The majority of people in their twenties are psychologically traditional. For men, real work has begun, and they bring both ambition and energy to it. Life is also serious for traditional women in their twenties, and they bring a similar intensity to establishing the relationship that will anchor their lives as women. In this cohort, as in the younger one, the women who are interdependent in their psychological stance, more than a third, will have difficulty finding partners because only about 15 percent of men have the same values. In this phase of life, rather few men can compromise the pursuit of their self-directed goals.

The inescapably adult years (ages thirty to thirty-nine)

This is the Vietnam, Woodstock, and Haight-Ashbury generation, the youths who were caught up in the Hippie movement, communes, the drug and sexual revolutions, the anti–Vietnam War crusade, the civil rights movement, political terrorism, gay rights, and radical feminism.

This group was fifteen in 1965, twenty in 1970. Because of their age, the value changes in the 1960s and 1970s were experienced more strongly by those now in their thirties than by any other age group. When they were children, societal values were traditional. By the time they became young adults, traditional values were challenged and people were pressured to choose new, nontraditional values. Reared traditionally but liberally, as young adults these people were part of the radical and successful movements of the late 1960s and early 1970s. Now, as they are entering middle age, the nation has quieted and returned to older values. This generation successfully defied tradition, parental authority, and the law. Three major themes motivated them: (1) "The older generation has nothing to teach us." (2) For sons, "The pursuit of success was a waste of my father's life." (3) For daughters, "The domestic and dependent life of my mother was a waste of her life."

And they got their changes! The Vietnam War was ended; deserters were granted amnesty; new laws prohibited discrimination on the basis of race, gender, or sexual preference; affirmative action goals were set, and schools and employers sought blacks, women, and other minorities. It is ironic that the generation that began its adult years by successfully defying the old authorities lost its power when the Establishment incorporated their views. Unified and powerful when there was an adversary, they splintered without one.

The thirties cohort grew up in unprecedented affluence, which created a buoyant sense that anything was possible. But the major recession of 1973 in the midst of soaring inflation was followed by two more recessions and a shaky economy. There is nothing like hard times to make people lose their idealism.

The baby boomers are expected to be the first cohort since 1890 to have a lower standard of living than their parents. Yuppies, although beloved by the media, are distinctly in the minority. This generation is, in fact, downwardly mobile. In the aggregate as adults, they will not live as well as they did as children. To achieve a standard of living similar to what most of them experienced in childhood, the women must earn money. This is the first cohort of men to be economically dependent on their wives. Because of their sheer numbers, these men have had to compete all their lives—for a place on the team, for admission to college, for that outstanding first job, for the next promotion, and so on. Some in this group have already reached plateaus in their careers, which makes the likelihood painfully imminent for the rest. Elbowing one another, they look up and see the entrenched forty- and fifty-year-olds. The equally competitive cohort in their twenties is beginning to push hard from below. In the past thirty years reaching a career plateau, although almost always stressful, rarely happened in one's thirties, but for the next three decades, it will be relatively common. The psychological blow may be awful. The men will not have been successful long enough to become confident or to have reached the level of economic security they assumed would be theirs. Some, of course, will decide that the odds are too great and will pursue different objectives; but those who remain in the race will push extremely hard.

In this thirties cohort there are substantial numbers of nontraditional women who are egocentric and angry. In 1970, when they were around twenty, there was a small cadre of very influential and aggressive feminists, especially on university campuses. Radical feminism accepted no compromise with traditional feminine values and lifestyles. The enemy was not the abstraction of a sexist society; instead, the rage was directed at men. Relating to a man meant going to bed with and becoming a victim of your adversary. Women caught up in this form of feminism were ideologically committed to living nontraditionally. They identified with traditionally male values and concepts of success, which they were determined to achieve.

Now, after ten years in the labor force, with promotions slowing and the competition increasing, they have learned what can and cannot be achieved through work. Because they were pioneers, success required enormous effort and once achieved, it was exhilarating. Now, for most of them, that rush has slowed, and the implications are clear when they look ahead and see an executive level that is overwhelmingly male. Now in their mid-thirties, they are increasingly aware of aging. Psychologically, women seem to enter middle age around thirty-three, whereas men acknowledge aging as they near forty. The biological clock chimes earlier and more stridently for women because their personal time tolls in units of fertility.

Women in this group decided to be their "own" persons and to avoid commitments in which they would be expected to be other-oriented. With independence as their goal, they turned to work for fulfillment. But the pursuit of success in the marketplace is fun only as long as you are winning, only as long as there are potential triumphs. When age creates the fear that time is running out; when experience reveals that work produces money and status but not love; when work has been mastered, and promotions are rare; when competition is cruel; and when being alone is more frequently lonely than free—then such women ask themselves *why* they made the choices they did. "What have I done with my life? Am I going to be alone forever?"

Those are very difficult questions because almost all the men they see are married and are fathers. Although a substantial number of men will divorce and remarry, they will tend to choose younger women. Women's marriage and remarriage rates begin to fall at age thirty. The statistics of marriage and remarriage tell us that many single women in their thirties will never find a partner, never marry (or remarry), never have children (Morrisroe 1984; Westoff et al. 1984).

There is a quality of bitterness in some of these women. Approaching middle age, they want love and emotional commitment. Frustrated because they are unable to achieve it, they are angry at a society that appeared to promise happiness if they were "liberated"; angry at their employers because so much was required from them that there has been nothing but work in their lives. Most poignant, they are angry with themselves because of the choices they made. The intensity of their bitterness has a special source. These are the women who said, "I am going to be a New Woman. The last thing I'm going to do is be like my mother. My mother never had an identity of her own. I am going to be my own person. I love my mother, but I don't respect her." If a woman's life is based on the idea of "liberation," she will find it difficult to acknowledge that in some ways she is traditional. It will not be easy for her to face the fact that, like her mother, her highest priority is to be loved.

Some women in this group have faced their loneliness and accepted that they are, in part, other-oriented; they want to marry and may want to have children. We now have the highest rate in our history of women giving birth to a first child at the age of thirty-five or older (Naisbitt 1984). Many of these older mothers have successfully shifted from a self-oriented, career-absorbed lifestyle to an interdependent one.

Because of aging, the thirties can be a decade of crisis for women. Among today's women in their thirties, I would say about 30 percent are embittered. They had choices about how they would live and what kinds of people they would be. They idealized those choices. Now they have learned that every choice has a price. Some feel cheated because they chose a traditional lifestyle; when they compare themselves with women who pursued careers, they know they lost the decade critical for creating the opportunities for an outstanding career. But most of the women who are bitter chose a work-centered life, and now they are afraid they will be lonely forever. They tend to form friendships with other women who have similar lives, often become involved with nieces, nephews, and friends' children, and tend to pull back from work for short periods, only to return with more intense devotion. It is not really what they want, but work is the only sphere in which they can immerse and extend themselves and feel good.

Among the quarter of men in their thirties whom I estimate to be psychologically nontraditional, some are working through the pain of divorce. During their grief and loneliness, they are psychologically other-oriented. Another segment was influenced strongly by a general antitraditionalism that included a rebellion against the value that men ground their identity and masculinity in success at work. Either because of that ideological commitment or because of the ever-present threat of career plateaus, these men say, "The last thing I'm going to do is pin my self-esteem on work. No matter how hard I work, I won't make it like my father did." Another segment in this cohort postponed the usual commitments of adulthood—never began a career, never married, and never had children. Among those, some seem frozen now, stuck in the past, thirty-five-years-old and still boys.

Most women now in their thirties began adult life psychologically traditional, but they could not escape awareness of feminist values. Most are married, now the mothers of school-age children who will need less and less mothering. Their husbands are increasingly involved in work where they must make their mark by their late thirties or never. As their late thirties arrive, most of these women will probably change their lives. Many will return to work, or work more ambitiously; some will return to school; some will have love affairs.

Psychologically traditional women's stresses and needs for change normally arise as the result of changes in the family, especially the children growing up. Just thinking about what *you* are going to do is a self-oriented activity. Current values encourage women to develop spheres of activity that are self-oriented, but for some women, wanting something for themselves makes them feel selfish, and that makes them feel guilty. For many women, ease or difficulty in being self-oriented is heavily influenced by the attitudes of their families, particularly their husbands. Does *she* want to change her life at a time when *he* is particularly stressed? To be confident, men need to experience themselves as peers of men they once looked up to. That much success does not usually happen earlier than the late thirties because that level of acceptance takes many years of increasing responsibilities. Thus, many women need to change how they live and push for more self-satisfaction when it is make-or-break time for their husbands. His capacity to adapt to her growing needs for independence is affected and limited by the pressures he is experiencing at work. While 40 percent of women may be interdependent by the time they reach their late thirties, only about 25 percent of men are; the late thirties is precisely the stage at which men are most motivated by psychologically traditional needs.

The women in their thirties, especially those who are interdependent, are today's superwomen. They are stressed because no matter what other work they do, they accept the major responsibility for the emotional welfare of their families. The real core of their stress is their need to be "perfect." It is hard for them to ask husband and children to share household responsibilities because they might not be perceived as "good" enough. With the spectre of divorce very visible, they strive ever harder for perfection.

A quarter of men in this age cohort are interdependent, probably as a result of marrying women who were as educated and as professional as themselves. The need for two incomes and the growing acceptance of women with careers encouraged this development. Over the past ten years, interdependence has become easier for men to accept. While many in this group became *psychologically* interdependent because they were *financially* interdependent, those who made the transition probably have found their lives richer because of increased emotional satisfaction.

In the traditional family all the major decisions are designed to increase economic opportunities for the husband, whose earnings determine everyone's economic status. However, when both spouses earn significant amounts of money, decisions must protect both careers. Neither can afford untrammeled egocentricity.

In view of their historic privilege of self-orientation, at least 50 percent of the men in their thirties are psychologically traditional. Like some women who embraced a nontraditional ideology when they were younger, they have had to accept facets of their own traditionalism, especially the need to achieve traditional success in order to feel like "real" men.

In sum, men and women now in their thirties have less certainty about society's rules for being an adult than do their older or younger counter-

parts who have had more consistent societal experiences. They are susceptible to becoming militant adherents to "new" values as they seek certainty
in an ocean of ambiguity. The pressures and the pain of change are especially acute for the women. Some feel that they have lost any chance to
have a career; others fear they have lost any opportunity for love, marriage,
and children. Extreme competitiveness at work and early career plateaus,
combined with the need for two incomes, is making it difficult for the
psychologically traditional men to achieve enough success to be confident
of peer acceptance. The groups who are most single-mindedly ambitious—
the psychologically traditional men and the nontraditional women—are
vulnerable because of the likelihood of early career plateaus. Nevertheless,
the percentage who are interdependent and therefore less vulnerable to
leveling-off in their careers, is substantial.

The middle years (ages forty to forty-nine)

Forty is a symbolically powerful age for Americans. In addition to the
stress of aging, the forties is the decade when almost all will reach their
plateaus at work. For the majority, work will be mastered, promotions will
end, and the responsibilities of child rearing will be over. Thus the commitments made in the past no longer provide satisfaction in the present or
guidelines for the future. People ask themselves what they give and what
they gain from work, spouse, children, friends. The future is shortening.
One may have spent twenty years in an occupation and may face spending
the next twenty doing the same thing. Likewise, twenty-year-old marriages are often comfortable but rarely exhilarating, yet ending one means
losing roots and injuring a spouse whose only sin may have been being
around too long.

Although some people wither mentally, prohibited by fear from making
necessary internal changes, most do not. Many experience this decade as
their fullest and most creative. Others, who may have begun adulthood
psychologically traditional, become interdependent. Typically, men
achieve enough success to feel less tyrannized by the passions and ambitions of youth. They become more aware of their emotional selves, an
awareness which enables them to be more sensitive and responsive to
others. Typically, women experience themselves as succeeding within relationships and they become more autonomous, better able to engage the
world and pursue gratifications as individuals. By the time they reach their
late forties, I guess that about 45 percent of the women and 30 percent of
the men are interdependent.

In 1960, when this group was around twenty, the country was conservative. Over 95 percent of the population married, and 90 percent of those

who married had at least one child (Veevers 1972). The infertility rate, at around 10 percent, meant that virtually everyone who could do so became a parent. Although a substantial minority of women went to college and later worked, they usually left the labor force when their first child was born. When child-rearing responsibilities ended, many felt they had to construct a new phase for their lives. While that was both difficult and frightening, they were not angry with themselves for having made a wrong choice. Unlike those now in their thirties, those in their forties had no other choices when they made their initial commitments.

This group reached thirty-five around 1975, forty around 1980. As the major responsibilities for the women were declining, feminism was in the mainstream and offered goals for the next phase. Just when their days and weeks were no longer filled with purpose, society gave women permission to go to work. That sanction was made easier by affirmative action goals, centers for continuing education in colleges, the growth of community colleges, and the numbers of middle-aged women returning to school or the labor force. Everyone knew someone who had done it! Because they had been out of the labor force for a long time, these women paid the penalty of not being able to achieve the highest career levels of which they may have been capable. But unlike the women then in their thirties, they had played their traditional roles without ambivalence. They knew those responsibilities were important, and they gained confidence from having done them well. After twenty years of raising children, returning to work had a fresh quality for these women. In the wake of feminism and the human potential movement, people were doing things to "grow," to express themselves, and to become more independent. Women in their forties reentered the world of work with some self-oriented motives, raising the proportion of women in this age cohort with a psychologically interdependent stance.

The men in this same cohort became very successful, many achieving economic levels they had not anticipated. Some therefore became interdependent without significant struggle; confident, satisfied with their level of success, and pleased with their lifestyles, they turned to self-development. Others perhaps became interdependent after a harsh struggle when, at a career plateau, their old ambitions became a source of anguish. Psychologically they had to move on, and they did.

Most men's lives have included both major commitments of work and family; when they reach a plateau they do not have an immediately obvious alternative activity to which to turn. Middle-aged men who feel that their lives are generally set and limited by the lack of new external goals can be forced to accomplish an extraordinary transformation, to generate new values internally, in terms of who they *are* rather than in terms of what they *do.* This profound change means becoming emotionally aware and open to others because of how they make you feel rather than how they can be useful to you. In addition, relating to others supportively makes both the giver and the receiver feel good. In short, these changes mean accepting traditional female values, and in sexist societies that is not easy. Nevertheless, many men do become interdependent and find gratification in their own increased complexity and emotional responsiveness.

No age group escapes social change unscathed. While those now in their thirties were most affected by the illusion of free options, those in their forties struggled with a decade (1965–75) of egocentric hedonism in society. They are old enough to have followed society's old rules, but they are young enough to be affected by the siren-call of an abundant future that encourages risk taking and change. They may feel they are on a plateau at work when they are at the pinnacles of their careers. They are accustomed to the good life their earnings bring, yet feel the economic drain of educating their children. Feeling content and trapped at the same time, these men find it difficult to give up the secure and familiar to begin again.

The criteria for satisfaction in relationships have grown more egocentric and hedonistic. Women and men ask what they gain and what they give up, even in long-term marriages. Given these changes in criteria and the cost of every choice, and considering the increase in feelings of desperation created by career plateaus and aging, one cannot be surprised that the chances of divorce are high even after long marriages. Feeling stuck in work and at home, aware that time is running out, those in their forties may think that the marriage relationship, which can be changed, is the only commitment large enough to be blamed for life's losses. A new relationship might revive the feelings and pleasures of change and youth. Among forty-year-olds there has been a recent marked increase in divorce after decades of marriage (Keys 1975).

In their forties many women discover that their ordinary responsibilities have ended and they must learn to fill their days. Some never married or are widowed; others are divorced; most see their children leave home. The time when the children leave is usually both sad and joyful but is, overall, benign. Bitterness is predictable when marriage ends after many years. Even though a couple may feel that they are friends and not lovers— despite the discord and fights—even if both endure rather than enjoy, they have been together for so long a time that they feel as though they should stay together. Although men can feel equally bitter after divorce, bitterness is more common among women because they lose their assets faster in the sexual marketplace. Statistics say there is little probability that people divorced in their forties will find new partners (Westoff et al. 1984).

Women who are other-oriented went from being the daughters of their parents, to being the wives of their husbands, to being the mothers of their children. Their lives and self-concepts were created by relationships. Now, for those who are divorced and without their children, there are no commitments creating the obligations to fill their days. No one to cook for, or shop for, or run errands for. After lifetimes of thinking in terms of other people, they must ask, "What will *I* do today? How will *I* fill this time?" The shift in orientation from others to the self is facilitated when women can direct their anger outward rather than inward. Directed outward, anger can generate a sense of energy and purpose and is, for brief stretches of time, a useful psychological state. These women must develop a sufficiently strong sense of self to construct new goals and new lives. The task is difficult, and the journey takes at least several years. The energy for the change is created by the jolt of aloneness. Many of these women become interdependent as they draw upon their sense of reality, genuine competence, and an emerging sense of "me."

As the thirties is often the crisis decade for women, the forties is that for men. Nearly a third of men in their forties probably go through a transition during which they are nontraditional because they feel deprived of joy in marriage or significant success at work. Transitionally nontraditional men often feel distant from their wives. They may say, "We don't like to *do* any of the same things anymore," but some have begun to intuit that the essential problem is that they no longer *feel* anything in the relationship anymore. In this phase they begin to allow themselves to feel, and they become especially susceptible to love affairs, partly because of the sex and feelings of youthfulness, and also just because emotions are intense in any new relationship.

Traditional women whose lives become unsatisfactory, frequently because of divorce or widowhood, have to make a complex journey from being other-oriented, then angrily nontraditional, to eventually becoming interdependent. These women must leave their depression and work through their anger. Traditional men whose lives become unsatisfactory, frequently because their careers are stalemated, have to make an equally complex journey from being self-oriented to a transition period of feeling nontraditional and depressed, before they become interdependent. The men must leave their anger and face their depression. When those odysseys are accomplished and the emotional knots from the past are untied, both sexes are much better able to acknowledge reality and create a future. If the depressed, nontraditional phase is a transition to interdependence for half the men, then we can estimate that 45 percent of them will be psychologically complex by age forty-nine.

I would say that 35 percent of the women and 40 percent of the men in their forties remain psychologically traditional. Most people do not change in fundamental ways without a sense of crisis. To reach plateaus in work and in one's personal life has long been accepted as common in this decade of life. Thus many men remain self-oriented and absorbed in work because it is familiar and comfortable. Similarly, some women will remain psychologically traditional and other-oriented because they find that way of living satisfying and emotionally secure. Of course, some of both sexes will remain fixed in their habits even if they find life unsatisfying because they are afraid to change. The majority of men and women in their forties realize that the goals that had dominated their adult lives are no longer ahead of them. Until now their lives were guided by long-term responsibilities of pursuing success and sustaining their children. Losing the guidance of those long-term goals is often painful, but as they grapple with issues and explore possibilities, many make the transition and become psychologically complex or interdependent.

This cohort grew up without choice, and because there is no one lifestyle that is best for everyone, the introduction of choices has been a positive change. Most women who led traditional lives have been able to move into a new phase of their lives with the support of widely accepted new values. While most did benefit, change inevitably claims some victims. In the forties cohort, among the losers are psychologically traditional women who had to create new selves and new lives when they found themselves alone. For their part, the men in this group have had to accept limitations of middle age, of their careers, and of their hedonistic expectations. Often women can turn to new external activities to generate the next life phase. Because they have already participated in both major commitments of work and family, men in this age group have only the option of changing internally. Some never do.

The years of maturity (ages fifty to fifty-nine and beyond)

People who are now fifty or older grew up during the Great Depression. As a result, they never take prosperity for granted, and they bring the highest levels of commitment and discipline to work. After they went to work as adults, the economy was extraordinarily prosperous for twenty-five years. The result was rapid promotion and much more affluence and success than their parents achieved. Given their Depression-born, hard-driving scramble for security, and the probable rewards of hard work, these populations have high percentages of workaholic men, many of whom simply never learned to live any other way.

The sixties cohort were born around 1920 and are more scarred by the depression than today's fifties cohort; during the depression they were old enough to understand how poor they really were. In their early twenties between 1940 and 1945, they went to war; that is, the men went to fight and the women went into the labor force. After the Second World War, the nation "came home" to a traditionalism that had never been. We "returned" to a more restrictive and conservative concept of what people were supposed to be and do. Despite the fact that we had always had a significant percentage of adults who had never married or had children, by 1945 there was only one acceptable way to live: Men worked, women stayed home and reared children, and their sexually monogamous marriages ended at death.

The fifties cohort traversed their mid-twenties between 1952 and 1960 when Eisenhower was president. In those conservative days, there was still only one set of values so by age twenty-eight one had made the major commitments. Those fortunate enough to go to college had already graduated. A college-educated female was likely to be married at twenty-two to a man who was twenty-four, and the first of the three children was born 2.5 years later. She may have worked to earn the down payment on the three-bedroom house in the suburbs, but when the first child was born, she stayed home. Meanwhile a man's military obligation was over, and he was probably at his first or second adult job.

The imposition of such rigid norms eventually provoked the inevitable response. Major social ferment began in the middle 1960s. The challenge to Establishment values was widespread in the media and therefore unavoidable. As a result, many people began to wonder why they lived lives of duty and responsibility when everyone else seemed to be having fun. Although hedonism, narcissism, feminism, and sexual liberation were a constant inescapable presence, they were too radical for these age groups to take seriously as prescriptions for personal change. Moreover, their conservatism increased because of their experience as parents of the radical young. Some had to face their children's using drugs, running away from home, joining communes, resisting the draft, becoming radical feminists, and being sexually liberated. Because of the depression's impact on their early lives and the onslaught of their children's radicalism in their mature years, the percentage of those in their fifties and sixties who are psychologically traditional is substantial.

In 1975, when today's fifty-year-olds were in their mid-forties, their children were, say, fifteen, eighteen, and twenty-one; maybe two in college, one to go. Inflation was high, mainstream feminism and women going to work was acceptable. Husbands were not eager for their wives to work, but living was expensive and college cost a lot. The women then in their forties were among the first to return to the labor force. Because of widespread feminist values, many women entering the workplace were, un-doubtedly, self-motivated; therefore I estimate the percentage of interde-pendent women in their fifties at 35 percent.

I think about a quarter of the women in their sixties and older could be called psychologically complex or interdependent. Although they are not in the labor force in numbers as high as their younger sisters were, many achieved interdependence through confidence gained by being successful in their traditional roles. Older unemployed women tend to be ambitious and assertive within the traditional realms of their extended families, communities, churches, and so on.

Only about 20 percent of men now in their fifties and 15 percent of those who are sixty or older could be called interdependent. It is probably easier for men to regard their wives as equal partners when the women are successful in work, the sector of greatest commitment for most men—that is, when the wife demonstrates she can achieve in ways that earn her husband's greatest respect. Given the small percentage of women in these age groups who achieved careers, and the reality that many men remain traditional unless they are pushed to interdependence by their wives, the number of interdependent men is bound to be small.

Most men in their fifties (60 percent) and beyond (55 percent) are psy-chologically traditional. They have remained so even when there is noth-ing very satisfying in it, perhaps because they don't know what else to do with themselves. They have organized their lives around a self-oriented commitment to work and that is all they can imagine. As long as they continue to work hard, they can avoid thinking about aging and retirement.

The majority of women in these age cohorts are also psychologically traditional: 55 percent of those in their fifties; 65 percent of those sixty and older. When society finally approved of women's need to change, many of them felt it was too late. Partly, they felt old. They also spent a lifetime avoiding risk, never gaining the confidence to cope with its consequences. With traditional husbands, few friends who returned to college or started careers, thirty years at home, and too little experience in venturing outside, most of these women remained psychologically traditional. Because it seemed to attack their values, some even experienced feminism as a power-ful threat to their self-esteem.

About 10 percent of women in these cohorts are psychologically nontra-ditional. For many this phase will last several years because they are angry or depressed. Some find themselves divorced, and many are widowed. Being alone for the first time is particularly difficult for traditional women who have never had to take care of themselves financially.

Psychologically nontraditional men in their fifties are about 20 percent of the total; after sixty the percentage probably rises to about 30 percent. In this country and many others, a significant percentage of men stop being absorbed in the external world and turn inward in middle and old age. Cultures differ greatly in how they accept such a change. In India, for example, men in their sixties are *expected* to turn their businesses over to younger people and devote themselves to meditation. The journey into the self is esteemed and recognized as challenging. We have no comparable tradition; we have no heroes of the passive lifestyle. We do not esteem introspective men unless they succeed in transforming that interest into a book or a movement. It is very difficult for American men to feel respected if they are not active, winning, and working.

The cohorts who are fifty and older have significantly more traditional values and lifestyles than the younger ones. Affected by the depression that followed the stock market crash in 1929, they easily accepted the principle that work and duty are always more important than pleasure and play. In these populations the numbers of workaholic men are comparable to the numbers of women who extended their traditional commitments outside the home, usually in volunteerism, when their children left home. Perhaps most interesting, and the least understood, are the men who have stopped engaging the world and have become more introspective and emotionally richer. Some of the men and women in this age group have managed the transition to a new life phase successfully; others, equally dissatisfied, have not changed and are emotionally resigned; there will always remain those who find the plateau comfortable.

Conclusions

During eras of major change, enough people adhere to any particular value and lifestyle to make everyone feel that his or her own choice is correct. In the current transition, there are more differences within and among age groups, and between women and men, than there were when many of us were growing up. These changes in cultural opportunities have to be considered along with the changes that occur normally as people age.

When we are young, we imagine that when we are grown and old we will know what we want. It is unsettling to learn that nothing is settled forever. Some feel good because their lives are richer and more complex than anticipated. Others are frightened because they have lost the comfort of knowing what they should do and how they should be. Some people are in transition because they have reached plateaus and are struggling to create a new life phase that has value for them. Still others on plateaus, paralyzed by bitterness or fear, are unable to make the changes they need.

The probability of experiencing painful plateaus in work or relationships is highest among people who have only one major commitment. All commitments begin, mature, level off, and ultimately end. In every age group, a higher proportion of men than women is psychologically traditional and preoccupied with work. As harassed and overextended as women with complex lives may feel, they are relatively protected from the frustrations of reaching plateaus; men, especially in middle-age, are consistently more vulnerable.

People who feel anguish when they are stuck on a plateau are distraught because life is too discrepant from what they expected. Many who developed expectations about what they could achieve and how satisfying their lives would be paid too little attention to existential realities. Discontent is a positive state when it provokes people to change their goals and alter their expectations so that they *can* gain satisfactions. Discontent as a negative state comes when expectations create criteria for satisfaction that cannot be met.

Those of us in our fifties are the last cohort whose expectations have been molded by the despair of the Great Depression. Until recently, the cohorts who follow us have not had to wonder about economic survival. The long-term economic prosperity from 1950 to 1975 was the basis upon which people created expectations that work and life should be filled with happiness. But when their hopes have no limits, people will never be happy. Postwar youth grew up in an economic climate of optimism that created the feeling that opportunities and choices were limitless, but the economics of the 1980s are harsh. The common despair about today's early career plateaus is the first symptom of a major psychological disruption that must occur when reality requires people to alter their most basic assumptions about what their lives will hold.

Psychological change and the demand for it will never end because our lives never stop changing. All our commitments have their phases. We are students; then we are workers. At work we are beginners with promise, and later, with experience, we become experts. We are the parents of babies; then we are the parents of adults. We are our parents' children; when they are old they become our children in many ways. All the while we age, and accepting that changes us too.

I have described a model involving three psychological stances determined primarily by the ways gender and age intersect with developments in the times in which we live. I hope it has provided a helpful perspective on where we are and what we want in middle-class America in the mid-1980s.

REFERENCES

Associated Press. 1984. "Women Now One-Third of All First-Year Medical Students." *San Diego Union,* September 28, p. A16.

Bardwick, J. M. 1986. *The Plateauing Trap.* New York: Amacom.

Keys, M. F. 1975. *Staying Married.* Millbrae, Calif.: Les Femmes.

Levinson, D. J. 1978. *The Seasons of a Man's Life.* New York: Alfred A. Knopf.

Morrisroe, P. 1984. "Forever Single." *New York Magazine,* August 20, pp. 24–31.

Naisbitt, J. 1984. *Megatrends.* New York: Warner Books.

Veevers, J. E. 1972. "The Violation of Fertility Mores: Voluntary Childlessness as Deviant Behavior." In *Deviant Behavior and Societal Reaction,* ed. C. Bogdell, C. Grindstaff, and P. Whitehead, pp. 571–92. Toronto: Holt, Rinehart & Winston.

Westoff, C.; Goldman, N.; and Hammerslough, C. 1984. "Demography of the Marriage Market in the United States. Population Index." (Cited in Shearer, L. [1984] "Special Intelligence Report." *Parade Magazine,* August 5, p. 15.)

DISCUSSION

Dr. Bardwick provides us with a new framework from which to view the effect of the sweeping social and economic changes of the last fifty years on intrapsychic development in adulthood. An eminent feminist herself, with a sophisticated, temperate view of the results of the women's movement, she pointedly reminds us that most adult developmental theory is unwittingly male. "We cannot assume," she says, "that the same behaviors, particularly . . . going to school or to work, are based on similar core senses of the self in men and women" (p. 188). How true! One of our basic intentions in this book is to bring together scholars who would add new dimensions, theoretical constructs, and viewpoints to the field. Dr. Bardwick has succeeded admirably for us and has moved to correct the lack of focus on feminist thought and theory building.

Her elaboration of the term *interdependent* is an attempt to establish a new conceptualization of maturity, a *new normality* that synthesizes the economic and social changes, particularly feminism, of the recent past. We applaud this effort and value her contribution because it provides a theory that brings *specificity* to our understanding of the way in which environment affects and alters psychic structure. Over the years we have become more convinced than ever that Rene Spitz's (1965) definition of development: "the emergence of forms, of function, and of behavior which are the outcome of exchanges between the organism on the one hand, and inner and outer environment on the other" (p. 5)—is the most comprehensive one available because it emphasizes the constant interaction between biological and environmental forces. Biology, and its psychological expression, the drives, remain more constant in their effect on developmental processes than the environment, which changes rapidly, dramatically. Dr. Bardwick's concept of interdependence is valuable because it translates rapid environmental change into psychological terms and effects.

Having introduced the concept of interdependence, she then proceeds to describe the effects of social and economic changes on adolescence, young, middle, and late adulthood. Her explanation of the move toward conservatism in today's adolescents has a ring of truth to it.

Third, this age group's conservatism is classic; no matter how much adolescents seem to act rebelliously, adolescence is basically a conservative period. Conformity is a way of reducing anxiety. Not only are they trying to answer the question, "What am I going to do in order to be an adult?" They also ask, "What must I do in order to be a man (or a woman)?" Traditional norms answer these questions with comforting specificity: males must establish their careers; females, their families. At a time when the economy provokes fear and the culture is veering toward tradition, it is especially likely that young people will reduce anxieties by turning toward the certainties of tradition. (P. 193)

In addition to explaining the conservative trend in today's late adolescents, Dr. Bardwick is also describing how environmental factors influence the transition from adolescence to young adulthood. More specifically, she discusses how the fruits of adolescent development—that is, intrapsychic separation from parents and the capacity for love and independent work—become translated at any particular point in time into young adult patterns, which are adaptive to existing circumstances.

In her eloquent prose, Dr. Bardwick describes the shattering of the Woodstock generation. How heady it was:

The Vietnam War was ended; deserters were granted amnesty; new laws prohibited discrimination on the basis of race, gender, or sexual preference; affirmative action goals were set, and schools and employers sought blacks, women, and other minorities. It is ironic that the generation that began its adult years by successfully defying the old authorities lost its power when the Establishment incorporated their views. Unified and powerful when there was an adversary, they splintered without one. (P. 197)

In a developmental context the splintering was inevitable: the idealism of youth, namely, the need to transform society, was subsumed by the inordinately more powerful developmental forces of the late twenties and thirties. Swept along by the aging process in the body, commitment and parenthood, and the need to take care of themselves financially—in other words by the developmental tasks of young adulthood—they became different people, a generation removed from Haight-Ashbury. In our opinion they can look back with pride on who they were and what they accomplished because they changed society more dramatically, for the better, than most generations and sometimes at great personal expense.

The profound developmental changes that take place between twenty and forty also explain why the new freedom produced loneliness and frustration rather than happiness for some women in their thirties. Those who threw themselves into their work and neglected other aspects of life could not or did not anticipate how dramatically they themselves would change; nor did the unfulfilled realize that success along one developmental line *at the expense of several others* will often produce unhappiness. Happiness is usually based on the successful engagement of most or all major, *phase-specific* developmental tasks. Ask today's "superwomen," who successfully manage career, marriage, and family, interspersed with exercise classes. They are truly a new breed whose lives are rich, varied, and difficult!

These superwomen have also done those in the forties' and fifties' cohorts a big favor. Having already entered committed relationships and raised their children according to prefeminist standards, these women find themselves in middle age freed from traditional responsibilities. *Joyously* aware of the empty nest, they can pursue options, made possible by their daughters, that their mothers never had!

REFERENCES

Spitz, R. 1965. *The First Year of Life.* New York: International Universities Press.

9

Self, Meaning, and Morale across the Second Half of Life

BERTRAM J. COHLER AND ROBERT M. GALATZER-LEVY*

Contributions over the past two decades within both life-course social science and psychoanalysis reflect a shift away from experience-distant study of functions, mechanisms, and dispositions, toward concern with systematic study of the experience-near realm of wish, intent, and experience of self and others over time. Developmental study has shown that collection and correlation of external "facts" regarding lives over time gain significance only from the meanings people give them. A similar shift toward study of personal meaning may be observed within psychoanalysis, where concern with psychic agencies and forces has been replaced by concern with the means by which persons organize and maintain meanings across the course of life. Although there is much controversy regarding the content of such concepts as the *self* and the *origins of intersubjectivity,* there is agreement within psychoanalysis that maintenance of meaning and the experience of the self are vital psychological issues.

Study of personality and adjustment across the second-half of life provides an important means for realizing increased convergence of psychoanalytic and social science approaches. Social science findings show that

*This chapter is dedicated to the memory of Nancy Datan, one of the pioneers in the study of adulthood and aging, whose tragic early death is a personal loss for her many friends and an intellectual loss for the field. Discussions with Drs. Nathan Schlessinger and Charles Jaffe, and Professor Bernice Neugarten, were helpful in formulating this chapter.

continuing interdependence with others is important in maintaining morale across the course of life. Contemporary psychoanalysis has provided increased understanding of the significance of the manner in which others are experienced for preservation of personal integrity.

Longitudinal studies from early childhood, through middle age and into later life have produced two remarkable findings. First, discontinuity rather than continuity best characterizes lives over time. Second, chance factors are far more important than previously recognized as a means for organizing personal experience. Those findings highlight the value of a human science approach, emphasizing the manner in which persons maintain a sense of meaning and coherence through time. This approach contrasts with traditional empirical approaches emphasizing experience-distant studies, in which persons are taken merely as objects for scientific investigation that eschews teleology and motives. Because the human science approach focuses on wish and intent, psychoanalysis is able to make important contributions to longitudinal studies.

In this chapter we discuss the significance of psychoanalytic perspectives, particularly those emphasizing concepts of the self, for the study of morale and adjustment across the second half of life. We also show how a modern psychoanalytic approach can help us to understand empirical findings about development in those later years. Finally, we suggest steps toward a psychoanalytically based life-course study.

Personal Integration and Study of the Self

The study of meaning and intent provides the basis of both psychoanalytic and human science (or interpretative) approaches to the study of lives (Cohler 1982a; Neugarten 1985; Ryff 1986). Psychoanalysis is sometimes equated with metapsychology. However, Freud's elucidation of the personal, subjective world has had far greater impact than his metapsychology on psychotherapy, the humanities, and the human sciences. Metapsychology is an elaboration of the German experience-distant, scientific world view of the late nineteenth century (G. Klein 1976; Galatzer-Levy 1976). Freud's use of that world view was based on his prepsychoanalytic biological studies (Bernfeld 1941, 1949, 1951; Sulloway 1979). It neither emerges from his unique methods of investigation nor constitutes a unique contribution to psychological theorizing.[1]

The psychoanalytic approach has been particularly useful in studying how experiences with others (intersubjective experiences) lead to the development of the self. By *self* we mean an *intra*psychological attribute that includes the sense of personal integration, the preservation of a sense of meaning, and the experience of attributes of others as a source of solace at times of distress (for examples see Winnicott 1953, 1960, 1963; G. Klein 1976; Gill 1976; Schafer 1980, 1981a, 1983; Gedo 1979, 1984; and Stern 1985).

Psychoanalysis and the study of self

Among human sciences, psychoanalysis is most explicit about the contribution of the observer to the observed, and the importance of the narrative that arises from the joint constructions of the participants in the process of studying people. Since Freud's (1909, 1913, 1914) first discussions of transference, making implicit meanings in the transference explicit, and thereby accessible to understanding, is central to the curative force of psychoanalysis (Strachey 1934; Loewald 1960; Gill 1976, 1983).

The recognition that the curative factor in psychoanalysis is the interpretation of transference in the analytic "here and now" implies that a central reconstruction in psychoanalysis should be the course of the analysis itself, including the changing meanings attributed to transference enactments as the analysis progresses (G. Klein 1976; Gill 1976, 1983; Schafer 1980, 1981b, 1982). The only developmental narrative that effects therapeutic change is the interpretation of transference, that is, the narrative of the analysis itself (Novey [1968] 1985).

The process of "working through," arriving at new affective understandings experienced through their repeated examination in the analytic situation, results from the collaboration of analyst and analysand in arriving at an enriched narrative of the life course that provides greater personal comfort and lessened conflict than the preanalytic life story. The historian Collingwood ([1946] 1972) was the first to argue explicitly that general historical events gain importance only as part of a comprehensible narrative (Wyatt 1962; White 1972–73, 1980, 1987; Wallace 1985). This concept was extended to the interpretive social science—"facts" made sense only as parts of comprehensible narratives (Gademer [1960] 1975; Geertz 1973, 1983; Rabinow and Sullivan 1979).

Most recently it has become clear that elements of personal developmental histories, including the case histories of the course of analyses, derive their significance from their place within a narrative (Cohler 1980; Cohler and Freeman 1988; Neugarten 1984). These narratives are not arbitrary; rather, they represent socially constructed embodiments of shared understandings of the meaning of events and experiences, including the expectable course and duration of life (Habermas 1968; Ricoeur 1970, 1977, 1983; Crapanzano 1980). As Emile Durkheim (1912) observed, time itself is socially organized. Indeed, the meanings attributed to time and age vary dramatically across cultures (Guiteras-Holmes 1961; Geertz 1966, 1974; Marriott 1980; Kakar 1982; Lutz 1985).

Viewing psychoanalysis as a human science concerned with the study of meaning, rather than a study of mental mechanisms, does not entail, as William Meissner (1981b), Grunbaum (1984), Spence (1982), Holzman (1985), and Wallerstein (1986) assume, that systematic psychoanalytic study is impossible. However, criteria for validity in psychoanalytic study do change with this shift from study of functions and mechanisms to study of meanings. An idea is "true" within a mechanistic approach insofar as it allows prediction and control of "brute facts" (Anscombe 1957). In an interpretive approach the validity of an idea rests on its coherence and integrity within the discipline. The criteria are different but not necessarily less rigorous:

> To tell a story with narrative integrity does not mean abandoning either science or theory. The unsolved problem in applied and clinical psycho-analysis is to link method with narrative integrity. . . . Psychoanalysts should explore questions left unanswered by more obvious methods while deepening and enriching the narrative. (Zaleznik 1987, p. 314)

The interpretive approach is not a rejection of concern with issues of reasons and causes (Polayni 1949, 1958, 1965; Holt 1972; Toulmin 1979, 1981; Freeman 1985). However, it does suggest both new methods and an epistemology that differs from Freud's scientism. Ironically that scientism led to continued emphasis on experience-distant investigations of psychology and mechanisms implicit in Wundt's psychology of act (Boring 1950), which Freud had sought to replace (G. Klein 1976; Gill 1976). Bettelheim (1983) asserts that Freud's writing reflects his concern with experience-near inquiry regarding such issues as soul and self, and that Strachey's translation interposed a terminology that fosters a mechanistic approach.[2] Heinz Hartmann (1950) acknowledges the inconsistency and ambiguity in Freud's use of *self* as a term, particularly its exclusion as a concept in his metapsychology.

Theorists employing experience-distant metapsychologies have difficulty dealing with the concept of self (Jacobson 1964; Meissner 1981a, 1981b, 1983, 1986a, 1986b). In fact, no one has successfully and systematically integrated Freud's experience-near discoveries with metapsychology.[3] Over the past thirty years, the significance of the concept of "self" has increased in psychoanalysis, accompanying increased interest in the experience-near viewpoint. The appreciation of the intrapsychological use of others as a source of meaning and comfort throughout life has occurred simultaneously in the work of several contemporary theorists (Winnicott 1953, 1963; Kohut 1971, 1977; A. Green 1975, 1978; G. Klein 1976; Gedo

1979, 1984; Stechler and Kaplan 1980; Stern 1985). There are important differences among contemporary theorists of the self, particularly in their clinical techniques. However, there is agreement that as a study of meanings, psychoanalysis contributes to increased understanding of the determinants of personal integration.

Contemporary psychoanalytic theory views the self as an intrapsychological attribute, constructed through experience of and with others, and accessible to study through empathy (Fliess 1942; Schafer 1959; Kohut 1959, 1971, 1982). The most effective empathic investigations focus on the construction of a story of the relationship between remembered past and anticipated future in the context of the present analytic situation (Gill 1983). The psychoanalytic psychology of the self emerging from such collaborative study between analyst and analysand is more consistent with "postmodern" scientific method than the mechanistic, experience-distant ego psychology, which was the intellectual heir of Freud's metapsychology.

Kohut's psychoanalytic psychology of the self

Among the students of the experience-near self, Kohut and his associates have been particularly systematic in exploring the role of experience of others in creating and preserving a sense of meaning and maintaining a sense of personal integrity.[4] Kohut's (1959, 1971, 1982) descriptions of empathic observation precipitated much discussion about methods of observation in psychoanalysis (Bornstein et al. 1981; Lichtenberg, Bornstein, and Silver 1984). Kohut observed that one person can understand the experiences of another through the process of vicarious introspection which, as he continually emphasized, is entirely different from intuition, referred to by Brenner (1987), only partially in jest, as a kind of ESP.[5]

As with any other method, empathic investigation presents particular problems. Indeed, a major problem with the experience-near approach is in differentiating one's own and other's wishes and intents. The psychoanalytic method is distinctive in requiring the investigator's systematic self-knowledge as a prerequisite to exploring the psychology of others. This requirement has particular relevance for the study of later life. For example, younger investigators' difficulties in talking about the finitude of life and the nearness of death with older people often arise from the investigator's anxiety about these matters rather than the anxieties of the older interviewee. A terminally ill older woman observed she had less trouble talking about death than any of the people responsible for her care, including her physician.

In a study of the ethics of terminating heroic life-support measures for older persons, Zweibel (1987) found that elders have much less difficulty than their middle-aged offspring in discussing disconnecting respirators and in facing death. Offspring have trouble even thinking about these issues, although their parents are usually aware of the issues involved and are clear in their desire to terminate life-support systems that do not increase the quality of life. Psychoanalytic education, which increases the investigators' awareness of their own concerns and interactions with other people's concerns, complemented by a comprehension of life-span development (Cohler 1987), yields an understanding of the issues of later life that is not otherwise possible.[6]

Kohut's clinical studies showed that the experience of integration and vitality over space and time are essential for well-being, and that continuing intrapsychological experience of others is indispensable throughout life to preserve feelings of meaning, personal integration, and vitality. The value of being accurately understood is a matter of everyday observation. As has so often been noted in the study of aging and mental health, the patient's tolerance of anxiety about death and dying is greatly enhanced by feeling understood. Self psychology provides a means for conceptualizing both the significance of this understanding and the factors that may interfere with the use of others as sources of support and assistance.

Kohut's third major contribution was his description of the way involving others to support one's cohesion and vitality enters into the analytic situation (Kohut 1971). Kohut's study of the origins and course of intersubjectivity was a result of his concern with the role of empathy in the clinical situation. This concern with the manner in which persons experience others was also based on prior psychoanalytic contributions (Cohler 1981), including those of Klein (1928, 1934) and Winnicott (1953, 1963), and is consistent with both clinical observational studies and developmental theories regarding the experience of others (Wolf 1953; Sander 1975; Stechler and Kaplan 1980; Stern 1985).[7] Kohut's (1971) rejection of direct observation of children and infants as a means to understand their experience—as in his critique of Mahler's developmental theories—reflects his belief that those methods lack empathic psychological immersion. In fairness, Mahler and her co-workers do believe their method involves empathic comprehension of the subjects' experience (Mahler, Pine, and Bergman 1975), although they are less explicit than Kohut about the systematic use of empathy in clinical study.

From the observer's point of view, care provided by others is experienced initially as an aspect of the self. Somewhat later, children come to appreciate that this care reflects the caregiver's own actions. There is some controversy about the age when children can first differentiate between those kinds of care (Stern 1985). However, the distinction is clearly documented by the middle of the second year (Huttenlocher and Smiley 1988). Inevitably, caregivers sometimes fail to respond as they "should" from the baby's viewpoint. When these momentary lapses are part of generally "good enough" care, they can contribute an increased confidence by showing that tension states can be tolerated and resolved.

When the child experiences caregiving as "not good enough" over relatively long periods of time, the child develops a sense of being unable to regulate his inner states (Winnicott 1963; Stechler and Kaplan 1980; Stern 1985). This failure of development may form the basis for lifelong deficits in personal integration and maintenance of meaning, or for the introduction of compensatory methods that aim at maintaining those qualities (Cohler and Galatzer-Levy 1988a). The associated sense of deficit may initially result from difficulties in reading the child's cues (Sander 1962, 1975, 1983), maternal preoccupation, feelings of depletion and depression, and other factors. In any case, the child's experience of others as sufficient sources of solace, and in integrating goals and intentions, is disturbed.

Two aspects of this formulation of self-development should be noted. First, although early experience profoundly effects the formation of the self, no single event (either satisfying or traumatic) or age range (critical period) assumes a primary position. Intersubjectivity results from "living with" caregivers and family over long periods of time (Winnicott 1963; Stern 1985). In this context, children evolve assumptions about the limits and dependability of caregiving. Stern calls the results of this process "representations of interactions that have been generalized" or "RIGS" (pp. 97–99).

Second, there is continuing capacity to use others to foster self-regulation and to maintain a sense of meaning. This capacity imparts a sense of continuity between past and present. The experience that others may be nurturing to the self leads to increased optimism and increased facility in using others. Kohut's (1977) "selfobject," Stern's (1985) "evoked companion," and Galatzer-Levy and Cohler's (1988) "evoked or essential other," consist of attributes of another person that are initially experienced as actions undertaken by the self and remain significant in providing solace, vitality, and integration over time.

Traditionally, many of these phenomena would be understood in psychoanalytic theory as identifications, based on internalization (Schafer 1968; Miller with Cohler 1971; Meissner 1981a). From the viewpoint of internalization theory, the self is built up from attributes of others represented within oneself. From the viewpoint of self psychology, the self evolves from variations in the intrapsychological experience of others, with functions experienced from the outset as being done by and for the self. Only later does the baby come to recognize the caregivers' actions on the child's behalf as a category separate from himself (Cohler 1980).

When we speak of something experienced as part of the self, we mean that it is subject to the kind of automatic control expected of aspects of the self: The infant has no delusion that the caregiver is part of his body but rather that, as he can control his bodily movements, he can control the caregiver. One way of appreciating the subjective experience of selfobject failure is to recall situations in which the body fails to "act right," for example, a leg falling asleep or a toe getting stubbed. The best way to appreciate such "essential-other" functions is through particular instances. For example, Greenson (1971) described how a flier, downed by enemy fire and awaiting rescue at sea, virtually hallucinated (or dreamed) the comforting words of his mother's nursery song in the original Flemish, even though his mother spoke English at all other times except when singing him to sleep as an infant. The flier thus succeeded in evoking a desperately needed experience of comfort and safety associated with his mother's soothing lullaby in a time of tremendous fear. An older medical patient reported that when she felt particularly anxious about the gravity of her illness, she was reassured by her physician's comforting smile and expressions of concern and care.

A mature scholar, whose father had died many years before, was about to present novel ideas, about which he had some misgivings. He correctly anticipated that many of his colleagues would irrationally and angrily reject some innovative parts of his presentation. As he went to the meeting, he warmly recalled how his scholar-father's interests had focused exclusively on the subject under study. "Political" concerns were of little importance for his father. The scholar smiled and felt warm and secure because he now had the evoked experience of his father with him.

Although traditional psychoanalytic formulations would regard these examples as regressions from more mature psychological functioning, we believe that such views are incomplete and fail to address the manner in which adults continue to provide the solace and comfort that promote feelings of personal integration and psychological well-being. These examples show how people are able to use the care provided by others as a source of comfort because that experience is rooted in the certainty or basic optimism that such solace is possible. The interesting questions in the study of the intersubjective realm (Stern 1985) concern variation in the capacity to use the experience of others as sources of comfort and solace.

Clearly, some persons in similar circumstances experience interference in their capacity to be comforted (Horton 1981). They are less able to rely upon past experiences of solace and less able to take advantage of the empathic concern of others as a means of consolation, or are so sensitive to any lapse in empathy that they cannot sustain such comforting. Other persons feel ashamed of their need for solace from others and may indignantly reject all expressions of sympathy or offers of help from others. Psychoanalytic psychology of the self offers a description and theory of continued experience of others as a means of preserving feelings of personal integration and sense of meaning over the course of life.[8]

Self and Maintenance of Meaning in Adult Lives

As psychoanalytic thought has largely shifted from experience-distant metapsychology to concern with personal coherence and meaning, there has been a shift in the study of lives over time. One basis for this shift arises from longitudinal research showing that change rather than continuity is most characteristic of lives across periods as long as several decades. Another source of this shift comes from cross-sectional studies showing that the meaning of adverse life events, rather than the objective characteristics of the events, is the most important factor determining their impact. Finally, changing views about the nature of evidence in social science have modified perspectives about the basis of change in lives over time. Studying how people "make sense" of the course of their lives, including problems in maintaining a coherent sense of self, effects a convergence of psychoanalytic and social science research. Understanding how a comprehensible narrative is constructed in clinical psychoanalysis (Schafer 1981b, 1982) provides a plausible means for exploring how people successively revise the stories of their lives over time outside the treatment situation.

The course of development: discontinuity and management of meaning

Changing models of psychological development. Since the Enlightenment, it has been believed that early life events shape the experiential world of later life (Aries 1962). Nowhere is this view more thoroughly accepted than in the genetic point of view within psychoanalysis (Rapaport and Gill 1959) and developmental psychology (Werner 1926). Freud's study of developmental processes was undertaken in the spirit of physicalistic physiology pioneered and sworn to in 1848 by Hermann von Helmholtz, Ernst Wilhelm von Brücke, and others (Bernfeld 1941, 1949; Sulloway 1979; Cohler 1987).

The genetic approach, systematized in psychoanalysis by Karl Abraham (1921, 1924) and Erik Erikson ([1950] 1963), received apparent support from animal studies of "critical periods," or moving windows in development, when the occurrence or absence of events permanently affects functions of the evolving organism. Critical periods were clearly demonstrated for certain animal behaviors, for example, imprinting in ducks (Lorenz 1937; Tinbergen 1951). The concept was generalized to human development without empirical evidence. In the same manner, both social learning approaches and Piaget's genetic epistemology emphasize the developmental primacy of early experiences (Miller and Dollard 1941; Murphy [1947] 1966). However, although the Piagetian model shares the functionalism implicit in Freud's own mechanistic metapsychology (Wolff 1966; Basch 1977; Cohler 1988), it is at least partially consistent with contemporary views of development in emphasizing partial discontinuity of thought between earlier and later points in development.

Freud explicitly acknowledged the importance of his early neurobiological training in Brucke's laboratory as the source for the ideas that became the genetic point of view (Freud 1910, 1915–17; Bernfeld 1941; Sulloway 1979; Rapaport and Gill 1959). Experience-distant metapsychology was founded on the assumptions of developmental neurobiology; as elaborated by Abraham, Erikson, and others, this genetic point of view became the implicit model for the clinical understanding of psychological development, without, we think, sufficient critical examination.

The epigenetic model of psychological development presumes a necessary, causal connection between earlier and later states. However, this rigid connection has been questioned by both clinical and systematic empirical studies of lives over time. For example, imprinting plays a minimal role in human learning and development: ethological models are largely irrelevant to the study of human infant development (Kagan, Kearsley, and Zelazo 1978; Emde 1981; Colombo 1982; Berenthal and Campos 1987; Cohler 1987).[9] Longitudinal studies of personality from childhood through middle and late life demonstrate that lives are less continuous and predictably ordered than is assumed in epigenetic models (Neugarten 1969, 1979; Gergen 1980, 1982; Clarke and Clarke 1976; Kagan 1980; Emde 1981; Skolnick 1986; Cohler and Freeman in press).[10]

Nuclear neurosis as characteristic transformation. In contrast to the epigenetic formulation, longitudinal and cross-sectional studies show little developmental predictability over time (Clarke and Clarke 1976; Kagan 1980; Emde 1981; Skolnick 1986). The course of development might better be portrayed as a series of transformations leading to dramatic reordering of the meaning of time (Eisenbud 1956; Loewald 1962, 1972; Kafka 1973; Wessman and Gorman 1977; Colarusso 1979) and the use of memory to account for the present experiencing of a past experience (Schachtel 1947; Fine et al. 1959; Cohler 1982a; Cohler and Freeman in press)—all presenting a "crisis" (Bibring 1959) rather than a series of well-ordered stages.[11]

These transformations successively generate in persons a sense of disruption and discontinuity that requires narrative resolution in order to preserve the meaning and continuity of self. Potentially useful mathematical models of such drastic transformations are available from a branch of mathematics called "catastrophe theory" (Galatzer-Levy 1978). Apparently disorderly change often contains an underlying structure.

The view that development is a series of drastically reorganizing crises producing distress over the loss of continuity, calling for the reparation of this distress through reconstruction of the narrative of the self, is consistent with *clinical* psychoanalytic formulations about development. Many analysts regard the "nuclear neurosis" as the cornerstone of psychoanalytic thought. In resolving this epochal struggle (Freud 1900, 1909, 1910; A. Freud 1965; Shapiro 1977, 1981), a resolution that is part of a larger transformation that S. White (1965) named the "five-to-seven shift," children become amnesiac of the past and more concerned with the present and instrumental mastery (Erikson [1950] 1963). Psychoanalytic accounts of the tumultuous appearance and resolution of the infantile neurosis (Nagera 1966) are consistent with experience-near observational descriptions. For example, Piaget's description of the transformation from preoperational to operational thought includes the child's anguish as she tries to make sense of the world in new ways (Piaget [1975] 1985; Berlin 1974).

Adolescence and identity. Later transformations, including those from middle childhood to adolescence, young adulthood to midlife and, possibly, early old age to late old age—all share the common characteristic of dramatic alteration in sense of time and use of memory. The five-to-seven shift has been most extensively documented, but there is also profound reordering of time sense at the onset of adolescence (Erikson, [1950] 1963, 1959; Cottle 1977; Cottle and Klineberg, 1974). The adolescent believes the important time is the future. Memories of the personal past are now devoted to fostering goals, based on presently understood personal past and both family and community traditions, whose attainment is imagined in the future. The goal of the transformation from early to middle childhood is to forget the past with its unacceptable wishes. The task of adolescence is to anticipate the future and, at the same time, to maintain a sense of personal integrity that preserves the connection of past, present, and future. Erikson's (1959) study of Luther documents the problems inherent in maintaining a sense of personal integrity in adolescence in the face of necessary developmental reorganization of experience.

Middle age and interiority. Just as the adolescent looks forward to the future, remembering the personal past in ways that are believed to be consistent with future attainments, persons at midlife begin to use memory of the past as a guide to solving problems (Lieberman and Falk 1971). This third transformation of the life course, characteristically occurring during the sixth decade of life, is significant not just for changing the use of memory, but also for the experience of time, now felt as foreshortened with the accompanying personalization of death (Neugarten and Datan 1974) or awareness of finitude (Munnichs 1966).[12]

Increasing interest in the study of midlife over the past two decades has provided findings that support the view initially proposed by Jung (1933) regarding increased experience of midlife introversion, more recently portrayed by Neugarten (1973, 1979) as "interiority." This introversion, occurring sometime during the sixth decade of life, has an impact similar to that reported both for the "five-to-seven shift" from early to middle childhood and for the adolescent transformation. One particularly significant aspect of change in the sense of time across the second half of life concerns shared agreement about the expected duration or finitude of life (Munnichs 1966), including one's own perception of expectable longevity.[13] Neugarten (1979) and Neugarten and Datan (1974a, 1974b) have portrayed the experience, generally occurring at some point during the fifth decade of life, of realizing that there is less time to be lived than has been lived already. This crisis of finitude is a consequence of the comparison of the trajectory of one's own life in terms of shared expectations of the duration of life. Awareness of finitude is fostered by increased acquaintance of mortality through the deaths of parents and other family members and, increasingly, consociates as well (Jaques, 1966, 1980; Pollock 1961, 1971a, 1971b, 1981).

This midlife transformation is characterized by increasing preoccupation with the meaning of life, taking stock of personal accomplishments and disappointments, and diminishing interest in various interdependent ties with kindred, particularly those that are obligatory rather than voluntary (Cohler and Grunebaum 1981; Cohler 1983; Pruchno, Blow, and Smyer 1984; Rook 1984), and lessened interest in taking on new challenges. It should be noted that this transformation need not be reflected in changing patterns of social ties, as had earlier been suggested in discussions of disengagement (Cumming and Henry 1961; Hochschild 1975). The primary focus of this midlife transformation is the impact of the changing sense of time and the use of memory to maintain a sense of continuity and integrity, or coherence of self.

Lieberman and Tobin (1983) and Cohler and Lieberman (1979) have reported findings from systematic studies showing that persons in their mid to late forties, and early fifties, experience particular disharmony, lowered morale, increased concerns about health, and increased anxiety and depression. Although particularly characteristic of men, both men and women showed marked distress accompanying the transformation to midlife and increased awareness of finitude. At least in part, these heightened concerns appear to account for first experiences of psychiatric illness in midlife (Gutmann, Griffin, and Grunes 1982). With advancing age, reminiscence becomes increasingly important as a part of taking stock of one's life, in mourning dreams never realized, and in settling accounts with the past (Butler 1963; McMahon and Rhudick 1964, 1967; Coleman 1974; Kaminisky 1984; Moody 1984a, 1984b; Woodward 1986).

Findings reported by Back (1974), Gutmann (1977, 1987) and Sinott (1982) suggest, additionally, that there may be gender-related differences in the expression of interiority, the timing of the transformation to midlife, and the significance of this transformation for continued adjustment. Men at midlife become increasingly concerned with issues of personal comfort and seeking succor from others, moving away from reliance upon active mastery in solving problems at home and in the workplace. Women, on the other hand, may become more oriented toward active mastery and "instrumental-executive" activities, moving away from their earlier involvement in caring for others as wife, mother, and kin-keeper (Firth, Hubert, and Forge 1970; Cohler and Grunebaum 1981; Gilligan 1982; Gutmann 1987). Back's (1974) study suggests that with the advent of midlife, women begin to see themselves less in terms mediated through relationships such as wife and mother, and more directly in terms of present involvements beyond home and family.

As a consequence of increased awareness of the finitude of life, both men and women intensify concerns with self and display less patience for demands upon time and energy, which are acutely experienced as being in "short supply" (Back 1974; Cohler and Lieberman 1980; Cohler and Grunebaum 1981; Erikson 1980, Erikson, Erikson, and Kivnick 1987; Neugarten 1979; Hazan 1980; Kernberg 1980; Rook 1984). Realization of goals and reworking the presently understood story of one's life course in order to maintain a sense of personal coherence become particularly important in later middle age and require time and energy, which is then less available for other pursuits. The ability to mourn goals not attained and to accept the finitude of life without despair provides some evidence that this effort has been successful (Pollock 1981).

Other findings point to differences in personality organization comparing the first and second half of life. Gutmann, Griffin, and Grunes (1982) have described first episodes of psychiatric illness at midlife among persons previously not experiencing personal distress. Lieberman and Tobin (1983) have shown that assuming a more paranoid adaptation in later life predicts increased longevity among persons relocated to institutional care. Gutmann (1973) has reported that persons reporting the highest levels of morale are more likely to externalize sources of problems. Although such externalization may interfere in adjustment at younger ages, it appears to play an important role in the maintenance of adjustment across the older adult years. In midlife memory serves a new function.

Old age and the crisis of survivorship. There may be a fourth transformation: a crisis of survivorship, beginning sometime during the eighth decade of life, as persons begin to outlive their age cohort, and to replace time/space relations (Novey 1968) with memories. Accompanying the life review (Butler 1963; McMahon and Rhudick 1967; Kaufman 1986), or settling accounts with the past, there may be increased mythological activity, reconciling previous conflicts and controversies in favor of desired outcomes, which provide a particular sense of solace. Consistent with Kearl's (1980) observation regarding the importance of maintaining a sense of meaning and personal coherence across the life course, Marshall (1986) has portrayed this reworking of the personal or developmental narrative as the "legitimization of biography," justifying to oneself decisions and actions over the course of a lifetime.

Further, as both Keith (1982) and Marshall (1986) have noted, if persons can believe that time was well spent in the past, then they can hope that their remaining time will be put to good use, leading to the conviction that a sense of personal coherence and integration can be maintained, despite the recognition of the nearness of death. If persons at midlife begin to look to the past for inspiration, rather than to the future, much older persons appear to live principally within the time frame of the particular day. To date, there has been little detailed study of this crisis of survivorship. However, changing population demographics have expanded our interest in examining the second half of life.

Persons over age eighty constitute the most rapidly growing sector of the population; yet little is known of the means used by older persons to preserve a sense of personal coherence or of the significance of the experience of others in fostering maintenance of meaning (Nemiroff and Colarusso 1985). For example, while Lee (1979) has shown the presence of a few confidants is important in preserving morale in later life, Matthews (1986) suggests that different meanings may be attributed to friends known lifelong, and to those first encountered later in life. However, there has been little study of differences for preservation of coherence in later life of the stage at which confidants were first met. There is an urgent need for increased study of personality and adjustment among the frail elderly, emphasizing the struggle with problems of survivorship, which includes both feelings of guilt at having outlived a cohort—sometimes one's own offspring—and resolution of grief and feelings of loss accompanying the deaths of spouse and friends (Butler 1963; Myerhoff 1979; Kaminsky 1984; Erikson, Erikson, and Kivnick 1986; Woodward 1986).

Some of the easy empathy between elders and preadolescent children may reflect similarities in the experience of time. The sense that what is to be done must be done now can lead the creative individual to new and startling degrees of freedom and fearlessness (Russell 1987).

Life changes and maintenance of meaning

External life changes are among the most thoroughly investigated aspects of adulthood. Over the past decade, inspired by findings that indicate life-event stress plays a major role in physical and psychological illness (Holmes and Rahe 1967; Pearlin et al. 1981; Kessler, Price, and Wortman 1985), many therapists have dramatically increased their study of these life changes. Many of these studies ignore not only vital distinctions between life changes and role strain, between expectable, normative changes and eruptive, "off-time" changes, but also the meaning of life changes and the impact of those changes on the maintenance of meaning.

Chance events are more important in determining the course of life than was appreciated by psychological investigators (Gergen 1977; Bandura 1982) until very recently. Fisseni (1985), for example, reports that people think chance or unexpected events are the most potent sources of distress and adversity. A central question in the study of lives is how people cope with such unexpected adversity—how adversity can be managed so as to preserve meaning and personal coherence (Lecky 1945; Kohut 1971, 1977; Gergen 1977; Gergen and Gergen 1986; Antonovsky 1979, 1987; Cohler 1982; Sirgy 1986). Psychotherapists (and others who deal with people's responses to inexplicable adversity) often imitate Job's "comforters" who, by attempting to impose plausible but emotionally unreal meanings on awful experiences, merely increase torment or delay the process of discovering meaning or meaninglessness.

Sontag (1978) demonstrates how the need to give metaphorical meaning to illness increases the suffering of the already miserable, although she does not sufficiently recognize a patient's need for metaphorical meaning of the experience of illness. A woman in analysis, in part because of sexual inhibitions, developed a uterine mass late in her treatment. She was convinced that she had "caused the mass, probably cancer, psychologically," and promptly offered her own interpretation that it was her way of punishing herself for a new and satisfactory relationship with a man. Additional analytic study showed that her motive for this interpretation was not founded in increased self-analytic capacity to further development (a motive that was also present), but in her effort to make sense of the idea that such adversity could be a chance or accidental event.

We need to know more about how people deal with such vicissitudes of life. For example, little is known about the use of prior adversity in fostering later resilience. How do early family economic reversals (Elder 1975; Elder and Rockwell 1979), family disorganization (Garmezy 1985), parental psychiatric illness (Cohler and Musick 1983), early adulthood military service (Elder 1986), or other unexpected, adverse life changes determine later capacities for dealing with difficulties (Anthony 1987; Cohler 1987)? Why are some people psychologically fragile to the degree that minor problems overwhelm them, whereas others develop capacities to deal effectively with extreme adversity?

Changes in the social sciences' understanding of lives over time have been fostered by an emerging human science approach, which has focused on the study of meaning and intent (Weber 1905; Husserl 1954; Geertz, 1966, 1974; Habermas 1968; Taylor 1971; von Wright 1971; H. White [1972–73] 1978, [1980] 1987, [1984] 1987; Ricoeur 1977; Rabinow and Sullivan 1979; Freeman 1984, 1985). Just as within psychoanalysis, where inquiry has moved away from the world view underlying metapsychology, the interpretive or human science approach relies on narrative coherence rather than isolated facts (Anscombe 1957) as the basis for evaluating ideas about people. Such questions as "what are the effects of a spouse's death?" are understood by both psychoanalysis and other human sciences as having little significance outside the context of personal meaning.

Personal coherence and continuity are experience-near states of the self, not experience-distant mechanisms. If we are to understand how people maintain narrative integrity through life, we need to create a life-course social science based on studying experience-near issues of meaning, including the intrapsychological use of others as an essential element in maintaining personal coherence.[14] After carefully reviewing findings on life continuity and change, Datan, Rodeheaver, and Hughes (1987) conclude:

> The notion that adult development is linear and cumulative—that is, that certain personalities are more "adult" than others—underlies stage theories of adult development. There is little empirical evidence for such orderly and progressive change, nor is there any agreement on the outcome. That there seems to be no final stage toward which the adult personality evolves has led Neugarten to suggest that we liberalize the concept of development, free it from the notion of linearity, perhaps even go so far as to say we are not studying life-span development at all but rather the "course of human lives." From this perspective, life-

span development becomes individual life history, which in turn becomes a life story—an attempt by the individual to create a narrative given order and predictability only by the choices and decision making of that individual. The order in the course of lives lies, then, in the mind of the persons experiencing those lives, not in the observer. The goal of the study . . . "(is) to explicate contexts and thereby to achieve new insights and new understandings" (Neugarten 1984, p. 292). If adult personality demonstrates any order, then, it may not be the result of a developmental trajectory but instead a reflection of the individual's attempts to maintain a sense of continuity. (Pp. 162–63)

Intersubjectivity and the Maintenance of Meaning in Adult Lives

Psychoanalytic self psychology addresses questions of maintaining meaning, coherence, vitality, and solace that have also become central in the human sciences. Further, there is evidence from each discipline that the presence of others can be helpful in times of crisis. For example, simply being with others positively effects psychophysiological measures of stress (Schachter 1959). Kohut's studies of the intrapsychological use of others represents an important effort to understand the basis of such findings. The experience of being with others who are trying to understand a person's difficulties appears to be an important source of comfort.

To date, there has been little study of that issue in later life. There is some evidence from survey reports, descriptions of psychoanalytic psychotherapies, and psychoanalyses of older adults that indicate the psychological experience of others may be helpful in maintaining meaning across expected adult transformations. However, only limited conclusions may be drawn from these studies. The literature on social ties in adulthood focuses largely on the social network and functional assistance, rather than the meaning of this assistance to the recipient. There are few detailed, clinical case reports that examine how adults use their experience of the therapist in resolving characteristic transformations of middle and later adulthood.

Several factors have limited psychoanalytic investigation of adult development. Since Freud's time psychoanalysis has assumed that little substantive personality change is possible after early adulthood. As Burke (1988) observes, Freud had serious personal problems in discussing issues of aging. This bias against clinical application of psychoanalysis continues to the present. Indeed, one peer review manual for psychoanalysis goes so far as to list middle-aged and older persons as unsuitable for psychoanalytic intervention. The pessimism about analytic work with middle-aged and older adults, partly motivated by intense countertransference issues, becomes a self-fulfilling prophecy, in which the lack of analytic experience with these patients provides clinicians little clinical experience or understanding as the basis for undertaking such analyses.

Social ties, evoked others, and the maintenance of meaning

Contrasting psychosocial and intrapsychological perspectives. The perspective on the intrapsychological significance of social ties presented here differs from other formulations of social relations over the life course. Those formulations include (1) the ethological-attachment group (Bowlby 1969, 1973, 1980), which focuses on the study of adult social relations (Kahn and Antonucci 1980, 1981; Rowe and Kahn 1987; Antonucci 1976, 1985; Marris 1982, 1986); and (2) the separation-individuation paradigm formulated by Mahler, Pine, and Bergman (1975), which is based on the study of parents and their toddlers and, subsequently, the study of middle childhood, adolescence, adulthood, and aging (Panel 1973a, 1973b, 1973c).

Psychoanalytic psychology of the self focuses on the significance or the *meaning* of social ties over time, as observed through such experience-near contexts as ethnographic and psychoanalytic interviews (Kohut 1959, 1971; Geertz 1975; Watson 1976; Myerhoff 1979; Crapanzano 1980), rather than the number and frequency of social contacts or observation of time/ space relationships. Focusing on the psychological experience of others, the self-psychology perspective differs from more traditional psychoanalytic explorations first in how these issues are investigated, and second in what constitutes an adequate explanation. An adult developmental perspective demands a third change in viewpoint: the recognition that social relations change in meaning as one moves through life.

Psychoanalytic psychology of the self examines, particularly, the manner in which people use the experience of being with others as the basis of a continued sense of personal continuity and meaning, rather than merely demonstrating that adults maintain significant social ties, or that these ties are important in managing tasks of daily living. As George (1982) notes, discussions of adult social roles seldom consider the meaning of those roles to the people who enact them. Much of the recent literature demonstrating the significance of ties with others for adult adjustment, examines correlates of self-reported numbers of others available as sources of assistance and morale, without consideration of the meaning of such care and support (Antonucci 1985; Rowe and Kahn 1987).

The social network or convoy of social support is believed to reduce otherwise stressful effects of adverse life changes (Kahn 1979; Kahn and Antonucci 1981; Antonucci 1985; Caplan 1974, 1979; Dean and Lin 1977; Eckenrode and Gore 1981; Turner 1981; Aneshensel and Stone 1982; Greenblatt, Becerra, and Serafetinides 1982; Killilea 1982; Weiss 1974, 1982) but, to date, there has been little discussion of how social support provides consolation. For example, two women, each the widow of a distinguished scholar and researcher, were moved to tears by the large and enthusiastic turnout at memorial gatherings honoring their respective husbands. One felt that the response indicated that her husband's ideas would live on and that the grandeur of his life's work had not died with him. The other felt that the response proved that the many painful sacrifices she had made in support of her husband were now shown to have been worthwhile by this testament to his high professional status.

An additional problem with this social psychological approach to the study of social ties concerns the complex interplay between place in the life course and the experience of offering or receiving help. Studies about the importance of social ties for adjustment rarely consider how aging affects one's experience of others. Age-related perspectives can lead to significant misunderstandings. Kernberg (1980), for instance, fails to appreciate the role of increased interiority as an expectable concern in midlife when he ascribes the increased preoccupation with self at this point in the course of life to increased narcissism.

Much of the conflict between young adult daughters and their middle-aged mothers is caused by their different expectations for each other. Daughters often expect their mother's availability as a source of assistance in managing household tasks and baby-sitting. Young adult daughters assume caregiving as an essential element of family ties. However, many studies show grandparents rapidly become resentful of demands by their young adult offspring for assistance with baby-sitting (Robertson 1977; Wood and Robertson 1978; Cohler and Grunebaum 1981; Cherlin and Furstenberg 1986). Daughters are often surprised at the reluctance of their middle-aged mothers to provide advice, help with housework, and baby-sitting (Cohler and Grunebaum 1981). The daughter's reaction is sometimes a source of lowered morale for the middle-aged parent, who prefers "intimacy at a distance" (Rosenmayr 1977; Rosenmayr and Kockeis 1963).

Most studies focus on the benefits of receiving care rather than the cost or benefits of providing it (Cohler et al. 1988). Further, social networks and families involve *inter*dependence among their members, not unilateral reliance[15] (Cohler 1983; Cohler and Lieberman 1980; Cohler and Grunebaum 1981; Pruchno, Blow, and Smyer 1984; Rook 1984). When a family member experiences adversity, other family members are expected to provide assistance. The impact of adversity and its sequelae radiate from the immediate family to a large sphere of relatives. Providing support for others, especially several others, can become enormously burdensome.

On the other hand "invisible loyalties" (Boszormenyi-Nagy and Spark 1973), which bind people together, have important rewards, permitting family members to realize their ideals of providing care for one another at times of distress. Much of the discussion of caregiving for psychologically or physically impaired family members overlooks the enhanced sense of meaning and personal integration associated with "doing what is right" and expectable in a family or community. Isaacs (1971) found that family members who care for elders with Alzheimer's disease, despite considerable strain, overwhelmingly accept the responsibility expected of them, and often express increased satisfaction and personal integration as a result of acting according to their ideals.

Middle-aged parents, the "generation in the middle," are expected to provide help both upwards and downwards across the generations (Brody 1970, 1978, 1981, 1985) while confronting the transformation of midlife, including the personalization of death and the crisis of finitude. Caring for dependent parents, although often a source of role strain, at least in the short run, is somewhat less distressing for the generation in the middle than caring for young adults and their offspring (Cohler et al. 1988). The difference is that parents and grandparents share a view of the life course that explicitly recognizes life's finitude, which young adult offspring do not share (Bromberg 1983; Cohler and Carney 1988; Cohler et al. 1988). Young adults have difficulty viewing life as foreshortened in the way their parents do. Thus their expectations for care and support often fail to take into account their parents' feelings.

Further, parents' earlier experience of being cared for by their parents can determine their response to their elderly parents' need for assistance—a sense of equity resonates in providing care for those who once cared for you.[16] In contrast, many parents feel that they have given enough to their children, and should now receive some return on their investment—or at least be free of further demands. In addition, having finished active parenting, middle-aged mothers may return to school or start working, and feel their daughter's demands to be an intrusion on their own time and schedule. Indeed, feelings of role strain and overload may be more troublesome than are feelings of social isolation among late-middle-aged women in our society (Dunkel-Schetter and Wortman 1981).

Solitude and loneliness. Increased interiority across the second half of life is associated with changes in the way others are used for solace. In midlife people are likely to seek more time for themselves, and to become increasingly preoccupied with aging. There is a preference for solitude, which is too often mistaken for social isolation. Most older people do *not* feel lonelier than they did earlier in life (Townsend 1957; Lowenthal 1964; Lowenthal and Robinson 1976; Fiske 1980; Mancini 1979; Mancini et al. 1980). Possible exceptions to this finding include widowed men (Elwell and Maltbie-Cromwell 1981), and women who had lived with a spouse for many years, as contrasted with women who lived alone (Essex and Nam 1987). Bankhoff (1983) reports that distress is greatest immediately after widowhood.

Across middle and late life, there is a major difference between being alone and being lonely (Fiske 1980). For example, if widowhood occurs approximately "on-time," that is, at roughly the point when it is expected in the widow's culture, this loneliness appears to be less intense. As family and friends die, move, or become incapacitated, there may be diminished access to forms of social support that was taken for granted earlier in life. At the same time, with the increased use of reminiscence, first in middle age as a means to solve problems and later in life to provide comfort and preserve a sense of meaning and a continuity of experience, being alone is less disturbing and even desirable, since it allows time for reflection. Despite being foreshortened, the present becomes meaningful through its connection to the past. This connection provides a sense of personal integration. Family and friends may move away or die; memories do not.

Reflection on the past, memories of shared joys and sorrows and, above all, recollection of comforting provided by parents, spouse, children, and others—all sustain feelings of personal integration as was done by the nursery song recounted by the pilot waiting to be rescued in Greenson's (1971) case of "a dream while drowning." An older woman used to sit alone, quietly, at her bridge table. Believing her mother to be depressed, her daughter brought her to a therapist. The mother explained that it gave her comfort to sit at the table where she and her husband had spent many years of joyful activity with close friends. She can still create a bridge game in memory any time she chooses. At least part of the terror inspired by cognitive impairment, such as that associated with Alzheimer's disease, is the loss of memory and the ability to reminisce and, so ultimately, the breakdown in personal integration.

Intrapsychological use of others in later life: evidence from psychotherapy

The impact of the changing experience of life's duration is often problematic in psychotherapy, where older patients present material, at least some of which is difficult for younger therapists to understand (Nemiroff and Colarusso 1985). Although all therapists have experienced transformations from early to middle childhood, and middle childhood to adolescence, and are potentially able to respond to the patient's distress with empathy grounded in personal experience, not all therapists have experienced the transformation from the "stable adult years" (Cohler and Boxer 1984) to midlife, or even in some instances from adolescence to young adulthood.[17] For this reason, it is sometimes hard for younger therapists to understand transferences in which they are experienced, for example, as a grandchild.

These enactments should be added to the list of what Weiss (1988) calls the "neglected transferences," those transferences that are inadequately understood because the analyst has difficulty in imagining himself in the role assigned him by the patient. (A typical example of a neglected transference occurs when the patient experiences the male analyst as the oedipal phase mother. Most male analysts find it easy to picture themselves as a preoedipal mother but find it hard to imagine themselves as the object of a man's heterosexual interest.) The therapist working with an older adult may be aware of a vague discomfort at being unable to understand these reenactments; from the perspective of the older patient, the therapist's sympathetic attempts at understanding are important, but they are not the accurate mutative transference interpretations, which provide the basis of psychoanalytic change (Strachey 1934).

This perspective on the changing significance of the evoked or essential other throughout the course of life has important clinical implications. The focus shifts from adjustment in the time/space world to the intrapsychological world. It is virtually impossible to determine how people understand or use relationships with others simply by observing interpersonal relations. Many older people *appear* to have impoverished ties with others, but this appearance may not reflect intrapsychic reality. As the opportunities for concrete social ties diminish, people replace actuality with reminiscence, preserving the comfort formerly obtained from continuing interpersonal relationships with spouse, close friends, and family members. Indeed, beginning with middle age, people often seek diminished interpersonal relationships, particularly those accompanied by feelings of obligation and required reciprocity, in favor of increased time for self.

Some cultures appear to recognize this changing significance of interpersonal ties in the second half of life. Kakar (1969) describes the situation of the Indian businessman who expects to begin to withdraw from the active world in his late forties, increasingly preferring a more solitary and religious life in his fifties and sixties. Rather than viewing this change as a sign of depression or "disengagement" (Cumming and Henry 1961), it is normative and expected.

The view that increased interiority is pathological and undesirable can yield bizarre results in the hands of well-intentioned professionals. A young and enthusiastic worker at a "model" home for the aged described her job as "keeping the heart young. . . . It's an uphill battle keeping these old folks engaged." Indeed it was; the home had an almost carnival atmosphere as old people were rushed from activity to activity, each designed to replicate the social roles and interpersonal interactions of much younger people. One old man's comment, "You don't give us time to think," was met with a cheery "That's right." The profound disrespect for the psychological processes of their elderly charges reflected in the "model" home's policies bears witness to the intense anxiety stimulated in the staff. (One has only to contrast Barbara Meyerhoff's [1979] capacity to learn about old age and dying from her elderly subjects to our social worker's need to struggle against those realities to understand the need for self-understanding in research and work with the elderly.)

The changing sources and significance of interpersonal ties across the second half of life may be observed in psychotherapy. It may be difficult for the psychotherapist to understand the particular problems encountered by older persons in making use of the psychotherapeutic experience to attain increased personal integration. While often intertwined with unresolved psychic conflict derived from incomplete resolution of the nuclear neurosis, problems confronted by older persons are uniquely posed by the loss of family and friends or the recognition of having failed to achieve life goals. Further, feelings of depression accompanying cognitive impairment are often related to a diminished capacity to remember and, as a consequence, to reminisce, an activity vital to the continued use of others as sources of solace.

Conclusion

Psychoanalytic perspectives on the concepts of the self, derived from detailed clinical reports of the manner in which people use attributes of others for solace and comfort, suggest new ways to think about the study of lives over time. Many problems in the psychoanalytic study of development reemerge in traditional psychoanalytic approaches to understanding adulthood. Experience-distant, mechanistic approaches, such as Bowlby's ethological paradigm or Mahler's separation-individuation paradigm, foster inquiry more concerned with enumerating the significant social ties than with discovering the ways to preserve a sense of personal continuity and sameness in later life.

Much social science research about mid and late adulthood fails to consider the changing nature of the experience of life itself. Because the meaning of time, memory, and relationships changes across the second half of life, the significance of observable behaviors requires different interpretation at different points in the life course. Reminiscence, for example, may not be principally a regression from current reality, but a highly adaptive mode of solving problems in middle age, and, later in life, a mode of evoking experiences that fosters well-being and meaning in one's life.

In very late life, largely as a result of the crisis of survivorship, reminiscence virtually supplants time/space social ties, providing important consolation in living from day to day. Partly because of inevitable restrictions on physical mobility, a reduced concern with the future, and the inherent richness and value of past experience, very old people obtain particular comfort from reminiscence based on a lifetime of memories. Reminiscence is often mistaken for withdrawal, depression, regression, or loneliness. To date, little is known about how continuing morale and a sense of personal integration is supported through such reminiscence activity.

The clinical psychoanalytic method should be of particular benefit in understanding this maintenance of personal coherence in very late life, just as it has been important in clarifying the significance of interiority in middle age. The necessary working through of countertransference problems not only improves understanding, but also increases the clinical investigator's capacity to tolerate discussions of death and dying, which are more difficult for young and middle-aged therapists than for very old persons. The empathic method permits the investigator to experience the intrapsychological world of older persons through examining transference and transferencelike enactments—not merely those that are a result of the nuclear neurosis and the more familiar identity crisis of young adulthood, but also the subsequent transformations: the crisis of finitude as a part of the transformation from the adult years to midlife; and the crisis of survivorship accompanying the transformation from old age to very late life.

A major question in the study of older people concerns the manner in which they are able to rework narratives in order to assure continuity of self and experience, continued morale, and a sense of personal integration. The human science perspective provides an important means for the study of lives across middle and later adulthood. Use of the clinical psychoanalytic method, as informed by life-course perspectives regarding successive transformations of time and memory, enhances study of the experience-near realm of meaning, and fosters understanding of the intrapsychological significance of others as sources of meaning and coherence. Such an approach will yield an increasingly rich vision of the second half of life.

NOTES

[1]Freud constructed a metapsychology (Freud 1915; Rapaport and Gill 1959) based on mechanistic physiological analogies. Psychoanalysis has made important headway in clarifying and pruning metapsychology, particularly the economic point of view (Gill 1976; Swanson 1977; Wallerstein 1977, Galatzer-Levy 1976, 1983). But there is a continuing confusion about what parts of analytic theory derive from psychoanalytic investigation and what parts are analogies from other sciences. This is particularly true of the genetic point of view (Abrams 1977; Cohler 1987). The difficulty arises partly from attempts to preserve that status of psychoanalysis as a "science" modeled on the physical sciences (Basch 1977; Peterfreund 1978; Lichtenberg et al. 1984). More sophisticated contemporary perspectives about scientific inquiry (Habermas 1968; Taylor 1971; von Wright 1971; Polkinghorne 1983) stress what Toulmin (1981, 1986) calls "postmodern" or interpretive inquiry. In the postmodern view meaning cannot be studied apart from actions in specific contexts. Metapsychology was essential to Freud in preserving the coherence between two apparently disparate aspects of his career. We believe it has now become a major hindrance to psychoanalytic thinking.

[2]Freud was inconsistent in his use of the terms *ego, self,* and *person.* In a footnote to the translation of "The Ego and the Id" (Strachey [1923] 1961), the translators note that, in a few places, they translate "ich" as self instead of ego, thus confirming the difficulty in distinguishing the two terms. In "Civilization and Its Discontents," Freud (1930) declares "There is nothing of which we are more certain than the feeling of our self, our ego" (p. 65). Hartmann (1950), Laplanche and Pontalis (1973), and Kernberg (1982) all maintain that Freud never intended a sharp distinction between ego and self. Indeed, the translation of the German word *Ich* into "ego" preserves this systemic confusion. However, both Schafer (1976, 1980, 1983) and Bettelheim (1983) argue for a more reflective or introspective rendering of the German term as "I" or "me," emphasizing the active self as central in the psychoanalytic study of lives.

[3]There are, of course, many translations between clinical theory and metapsychology, and there are imprecise uses of metapsychological (especially energic) terms to summarize clinical theory. But it is rare that metapsychological propositions predict clinical findings or that metapsychological statements about clinical matters add anything new to what has already been said. Compare that imbalance to chemistry, in which the theory of the chemical bond explicitly predicts chemical reactions and in turn describes chemical reactions in terms of chemical bonds—a conceptualization of the phenomenon that is substantially richer than the description of the laboratory experiment alone.

[4]Although we find Kohut's views about self development to be important to the creation of a life-course psychoanalytic psychology, we are distressed that this perspective has become the focus of such extensive political controversy in psychoanalytic circles. In part, this politicization is an inevitable, delayed response to wider changes in psychoanalysis which, as we have tried to show, extend to formulations about the self, empathy, and development that extend beyond the work of Kohut and his colleagues. The development of new ideas

never occurs without institutional and interpersonal conflict (see Merton 1973 among many others.) This is particularly true in psychoanalysis. Theoretical commitments are often tied to the most profound experience of the analyst's adult life—his or her own analysis (Greenacre 1966a, 1966b; Roustang [1976] 1982).

Kohut, and to a lesser extent his colleagues, have contributed to the problem. In an effort to differentiate their views from those of psychoanalysts who approach the self and therapeutic intervention from different theoretical perspectives, they have made it more difficult to understand and integrate contributions from the large explorations of the psychology of the self tradition not only by Kohut, but also by Winnicott, A. Green, G. Klein, Schafer, Sander, and others (Cohler 1981). We recognize that there are times when investigators need to spin out their ideas in the company of like-minded researchers, unencumbered by the need to answer criticism from the larger community, and that the punctilious documentation and acknowledgment of every source of ideas is not only a large and time-consuming task but, in fact, a job that often requires levels of scholarship of the highest order (Merton 1985). We are also aware that most of Kohut's writing about the psychology of the self was done while he knew that he had a serious illness that might take his life at any time. Nonetheless Kohut's strident, and often denigrating, differentiation of his views from other researchers in the psychology of the self and his simultaneous failure to acknowledge the contributions of others have contributed significantly and unnecessarily to the controversy that surrounds his work.

[5]This assumption, which is the foundation of the clinical psychoanalytic method, has been difficult for psychoanalytic investigators to accept, because it appears to contradict many of the assumptions of natural science investigations (Holzman 1985; Wallerstein 1986). However, a postmodern epistemology of psychoanalysis goes beyond mechanistic models and positivist criteria, based on nineteenth-century ideas of description, theory, and validation. Indeed, as we have shown elsewhere (Galatzer-Levy and Cohler 1988), this empathic mode of inquiry is consistent with contemporary physical science inquiry (Holton 1973).

[6]Psychoanalysts have had a remarkable influence on psychological and particularly developmental thought in this century; especially considering their small numbers, the even smaller number of analysts who write for publication, and the unsystematic and statistically inadequate nature of their samples and methods. Whether they accept or reject analytic hypotheses, virtually all psychological investigations of motives, emotions, development, and increasingly, the neurosciences of higher mental function, take psychoanalytic concepts as their explicit or implicit starting point. Readers of the *New York Times* must be impressed that reports of new findings in psychology are almost invariably contrasted to "older" or "classical" psychoanalytic views—the need to repudiate these ideas points to their central importance. We believe that the analytic contribution is important because of the greater freedom that clinically trained analysts have in exploring internal reality.

[7]The significance of this experience-near empathic method is implicit in Winnicott's (1953) discussion of the intermediate or shared space created between parent and child and in clinical work influenced by Winnicott's views (Flarsheim 1974; Cohler 1974; A. Green 1975, 1978). Although Winnicott's work clearly

anticipated Kohut's contributions to the study of intersubjectivity (Cohler 1981), it should be noted that Winnicott's concept of the intermediate space specifically included the contributions of both caregiver and child; whereas Kohut's work on the development of a resilient self is concerned essentially with the child's experience of this caregiving as an attribute of self. To the extent that the care is "not good enough," the child experiences this deficit as his own failure to resolve tensions.

[8]The conflict perspective in psychoanalysis, founded upon study of people's responses to the discomfort stemming from conflicting wishes and intents, explores primarily the sequelae of socially unacceptable wishes and intents derived from the family romance and associated with the nuclear conflict of early childhood (Freud 1900, 1910). Inclusion of perspectives emphasizing the self and psychological development over the course of life complements and extends the conflict perspective. For example, there can be little question that long-standing fantasies of rivalry with the mother of early childhood may continue to inspire conflicted interpersonal relations among adult women and their own middle-aged and older mothers (Chodorow 1978). However, there is evidence (Low 1978; Cohler 1988; Cohler and Grunebaum 1981) that in midlife feelings of rivalry subside as mother and daughter increasingly share a common outlook on the passage of time. While the advent of the mother's widowhood may spark additional conflict as mother and daughter each attempt to deal with the feelings of loss of husband and father, the same loss may bring the generations together in mourning.

[9]This, of course, does not mean that animal studies are not useful sources of hypotheses about human behavior. Nor does it mean that ethological *methods* may not prove extremely useful in the study of humans (Wolff 1987).

[10]The failure of most longitudinal investigations to show continuity in personality over time—from the trait-oriented work of Kagan and Moss (1962) to reports from the Berkeley studies, based on standardized ratings of personality—has sometimes been attributed to so-called sleeper effects, in which a particular personality dimension may be related to another dimension at one point in time but not at another (Livson and Peskin 1981; Peskin and Livson 1981). It is not clear whether these sleeper effects are due primarily to variation in development and adjustment over time or to measurement error.

[11]In the cognitive realm Piaget explored how schemata are progressively stretched as new aspects of experience are "assimilated" until the scheme can no longer contain the new information so that the underlying organizational structure is reorganized, the structure itself "accomodates" (see, for example, Piaget [1936] 1953, [1975] 1977).

[12]Although it has sometimes been maintained that the advent of parenthood may also lead to the reordering of memory (Benedek 1959, 1973), study of the assumption of this new adult social role does not suggest that it leads to new ways in which memories are used, or to the reordering of time perspectives. While the transition to parenthood often disrupts present adjustment (Rossi 1968; Cohler 1984, 1988), it does not appear to transform the sense of self in the manner of life-course transformations such as the nuclear neurosis or the midlife crisis of finitude.

[13]Consistent with the perspective provided by Sorokin and Merton (1937), Roth (1963), Neugarten and Hagestad (1976), Hazan (1980), Cohler and Boxer (1984), Hagestad and Neugarten (1985) and Spence (1986), persons' understanding of the course of their own lives follows a socially structured, symbolic "timetable." From early childhood through later life, they continually monitor their own lives in terms of expectable milestones. While expected timing or attainment of particular transitions—graduation, marriage, advent of parenthood, work attainments, retirement, and widowhood—varies with social status, ethnicity, gender, and other factors within groups of persons defined by historical circumstances or cohorts (Ryder 1965; Elder 1974), survey studies have shown marked agreement among persons regarding the expectable structure or placement of events throughout life (Cain 1964; Neugarten and Moore 1968; Hogan 1981), as well as significant changes over historical time in the placement and distance between milestones marking the life course (Glick 1979; Uhlenberg 1979, 1980; Cherlin 1981; Hareven 1986, 1981, 1982; Kohli 1986). The nature and significance of personal experience is portrayed in the context of these shared definitions of the timing and direction of lives. Persons continually compare themselves in terms of particular attainments at particular ages, both as more or less "on" or "off" time for expectable transitions and life changes, and as experiencing these changes in a more or less "ordered" or "disordered" manner. The timing of transformations such as those portrayed here assumes the usual ordered nature of timing. However the crisis of finitude may be experienced at markedly varying points in life, depending upon timing of role changes and losses, and unanticipated adversity such as death of a spouse or a child.

[14]There are similar problems in the paradigm of adult development proposed by Levinson and his associates (1978). Their portrayal of an inevitable, age-linked series of transitions in the role of work and generativity in adult lives, aside from reflecting an unswerving developmental optimism, fails to explore the meaning of change, or even the perception of change, for the subjects of the study.

[15]Women are expected to provide care both upwards and downwards across the generations, which often leads to feelings of dissatisfaction with social ties (Rook 1984). Women have been socialized from early childhood to roles of kin-keeping and child care (Firth, Hubert, and Forge 1970). Chodorow (1977), following Komarovsky (1950, 1956), called this socialization the "reproduction of mothering." Women in the middle-aged generation are particularly likely to report feelings of being overburdened by demands of the social network or convoy and associated feelings of lowered morale. Recent survey studies (Shanas 1987) show that men are becoming more involved in caring for relatives, particularly their own parents.

[16]Not infrequently the issue of "equity" has conscious and unconscious negative dimensions, as the adult child finally gets a chance to enact hostile fantasies on many developmental levels, for example, revenge for abuse or neglect or oedipal fantasies of having the parent to himself.

[17]It is striking that many therapists who are interested in aging patients have backgrounds in work with children. To do adequate work with children demands the sustained ability to see the world, including the organization of time, the role of memory, and the function of others from a point of view not native

to the adult therapist's mode of functioning. The child therapist who has or develops this capacity is likely to be more at ease when adult patients, whether his contemporaries or elders, organize their worlds in ways different from that of the therapist.

REFERENCES

Abraham, K. [1921] 1953. "Contributions to a Discussion on Tic." In *Selected Papers in Psychoanalysis,* pp. 320–25. New York: Basic Books.
———. [1924] 1953. "A Short Study on the Development of the Libido Viewed in the Light of Mental Disorders." In *Selected Papers on Psychoanalysis,* pp. 418–501. New York: Basic Books.
Abrams, S. 1977. "The Genetic Point of View: Antecedents and Transformations." *Journal of the American Psychoanalytic Association* 25:417–25.
Ainsworth, M. 1982. "Attachment: Retrospect and Prospect. In *The Place of Attachment in Human Behavior,* ed. C. M. Parkes and J. Stevenson-Hinde, pp. 3–31. New York: Basic Books.
Aldous, J. 1987. "New Views on the Family Life of the Elderly and the Near-elderly." *Journal of Marriage and the Family* 49:227–34.
Aneshensel, C., and Stone, J. 1982. "Stress and Depression: A Test of the Buffering Model of Social Support." *Archives of General Psychiatry* 39:1392–1396.
Antonucci, T. 1976. Attachment: A Life-Span Concept. *Human Development* 19:135–42.
———. 1985. "Personal Characteristics, Social Support, and Social Behavior." In *Handbook of Aging and the Social Sciences,* ed. R. Binstock and E. Shanas, 2d ed., pp. 94–128. New York: Van Nostrand and Reinhold.
Aries, P. 1962. *Centuries of Childhood,* trans. R. Baldik. New York: Random House.
Anthony, E.J. 1987. "Children at High Risk for Psychosis Growing up Successfully." In *The Invulnerable Child,* ed. E.J. Anthony and B.J. Cohler, pp. 147–84. New York: Guilford.
Anscombe, G.E.M. 1957. *Intention.* Oxford: Basil Blackwell.
Antonovsky, A. 1979. *Health, Stress, and Coping: New Perspectives on Mental and Physical Well Being.* San Francisco: Jossey-Bass.
———. 1987. *Unraveling the Mystery of Health: How People Manage Stress and Stay Well.* San Francisco: Jossey-Bass.
Back, K. W. 1974. "Transition to Aging and the Self Image." In *Normal Aging: II,* ed. E. Palmore, pp. 207–16. Durham, N.C.: Duke University Press.
Bandura, A. 1982. "The Psychology of Chance Encounters and Life Paths." *American Psychologist* 37:747–55.
Bankoff, E. 1983. "Social Support and Adaptation to Widowhood." *Journal of Marriage and the Family* 45:827–39.
Basch, M. 1977. "Developmental Psychology and Explanatory Theory in Psychoanalysis." *The Annual of Psychoanalysis* 5:229–63.
Benedek, T. [1959] 1973. "Parenthood as a Developmental Phase: A Contribution to the Theory of the Libido" (with discussion). In T. Benedek, *Pschoanalytic Investigations: Selected Papers,* pp. 377–407. Chicago: Quadrangle Books.

Berenthal, B., and Campos, J. 1987. "New Directions in the Study of Early Experience." *Child Development* 58:560–67.

Boszormenyi-Nagy, I., and Spark, G. 1973. *Invisible Loyalties: Reciprocity in Intergenerational Family Therapy.* New York: Harper & Row.

Bernfeld, S. 1941. "Freud's Earliest Theories: On the School of Helmholtz." *Psychoanalytic Quarterly* 13:341–62.

———. 1949. "Freud's Scientific Beginnings." *American Imago* 6:163–96.

———. 1951. "Sigmund Freud, M.D., 1882–1885." *International Journal of Psycho-Analysis* 32:204–17.

Berlin, R. 1974. "A Developmental Analysis of the Coping Process." Ph.D. diss., The University of Chicago.

Bettelheim, B. 1983. *Freud and Man's Soul.* New York: Knopf.

Bibring, G. 1959. "Some Considerations of the Psychological Processes in Pregnancy." *Psychoanalytic Study of the Child* 14:113–21.

Boring, E. G. 1950. *A History of Experimental Psychology,* 2d ed. New York: Appleton Century Crofts.

Bornstein. M.; Silver, D.; et al., eds. 1981. *On Empathy.* New York: International Universities Press. *Psychoanalytic Inquiry* 1: no. 3.

Bowlby, J. 1969. *Attachment and Loss, vol. 1. Attachment.* New York: Basic Books.

———. 1973. *Attachment and Loss, vol. 2. Separation, Anxiety, and Anger.* New York: Basic Books.

———. 1980. *Attachment and Loss, vol. 3. Sadness and Depression.* New York: Basic Books.

Brenner, C. 1987. "Notes on Psychoanalysis by a Participant Observer: A Personal Chronicle." *Journal of the American Psychoanalytic Association* 35:539–56.

Brody, E. 1966. "The Aging Family." *The Gerontologist* 6:201–06.

———. 1970. "The Etiquette of Filial Behavior." *The International Journal of Aging and Human Development* 1:87–97.

———. 1981. " 'Women in the Middle' and Family Help to Older People." *The Gerontologist* 21:471–80.

———. 1985. "Parent Care As a Normative Family Stress." *The Gerontologist* 25:19–29.

Bromberg, E. 1983. "Mother-Daughter Relationships in Later Life: The Effect of Quality of Relationship upon Mutual Aid." *Journal of Gerontological Social Work* 6:75–92.

Burke, N. 1988. "Psychoanalysis and Aging." In *The Psychodynamics of Aging,* ed. N. Miller and G. Cohen. New York: International Universities Press.

Butler, R. 1963. "The Life Review: An Interpretation of Reminiscence in the Aged." *Psychiatry* 26:65–76.

Cain, L. 1964. "Life-Course and Social Structure." In *Handbook of Modern Sociology,* ed. R. Faris, pp. 272–309. Chicago: Rand-McNally.

———. 1967. "Age Status and Generational Phenomena: The New Old People in Contemporary America." *The Gerontologist* 7:83–92.

Caplan, G. 1974. *Support Systems and Community Mental Health.* New York: Behavioral Publications.

Cherlin, A. 1981. *Marriage, Divorce, Remarriage.* Cambridge, Mass.: Harvard University Press.

Cherlin, A., and Furstenberg, F., Jr. 1986. *The New American Grandparent: A Place in the Family, A Life Apart.* New York: Basic Books.

Chodorow. N. 1978. *The Reproduction of Mothering: Psychoanalysis and the Sociology of Gender.* Berkeley: The University of California Press.

Clarke, A. D. B., and Clarke, A. M. 1981. " 'Sleeper Effects' in Development: Fact or Artifact?" *Developmental Review* 1:344–60.

Clarke, A. M., and Clarke, A. D. B. 1976. *Early Experience: Myth and Evidence.* New York: Free Press.

Cohler, B. 1976. "The Significance of the Therapist's Feelings in the Treatment of Anorexia Nervosa." In *Tactics and Technique in Psychoanalytic Therapy, Vol. 2,* ed. P. Giovacchini. New York: Science House.

———. 1980. "Developmental Perspectives on the Psychology of Self in Early Childhood." In *Advances in Self Psychology,* ed. A. Goldberg, pp. 69–115. New York: International Universities Press.

———. 1981. "Adult Developmental Psychology and Reconstruction in Psycho-analysis." In *The Course of Life,* ed. S. Greenspan and G. Pollock, vol. III, pp. 149–201. Washington, D.C.: U.S. Government Printing Office.

———. 1982a. "Personal narrative and life course." In *Life Span Development and Behavior,* ed. P. Baltes and O. G. Brim, Jr., vol. 4. New York: Academic Press.

———. 1982b. "Stress or Support: Relations between Older Women from Three European Ethnic Groups and Their Relatives." In *Minority Aging: Sociological and Social-Psychological Issues,* ed. R. Manuel, pp. 115–20. Greenwich, Conn.: Greenwood.

———. 1983. "Autonomy and Interdependence in the Family of Adulthood: A Psychological Perspective." *The Gerontologist* 23:33–39.

———. 1987. "Approaches to the Study of Development in Psychiatric Education." In *The Role of Psychoanalysis in Psychiatric Education: Past, Present and Future,* ed. S. Weissman and R. Thurnblad, pp. 225–70. New York: International Universities Press.

———. 1987 "Adversity, Resilience, and the Study of Lives. In *The Invulnerable Child,* ed. E. J. Anthony and B. Cohler, pp. 363–424. New York: Guilford.

———. 1988. "The Mother-Daughter Relationship in the Family of Adulthood." *Journal of Geriatric Psychiatry.*

Cohler, B.; Borden, W.; Groves, L.; and Lazarus, L. 1988. "Caring for Family Members with Alzheimer's disease." In *Alzheimer's Disease, Treatment and Family Stress: Directions for Research,* ed. E. Light and B. Lebowitz. Washington, D.C.: U.S. Government Printing Office.

Cohler, B., and Boxer, A. 1984. "Settling into the World: Person and Family during the Middle-Years." In *Normality and the Life-Cycle,* ed. D. Offer and M. Sabshin pp. 145–203. New York: Basic Books.

Cohler, B., and Carney, J. (in press). "Developmental Continuities and Adjustment in Adulthood: Social Relations, Morale, and the Transformation from Middle to Late Life." In *The Psychodynamics of Aging,* ed. N. Miller and G. Cohen. New York: International Universities Press.

Cohler, B., and Freeman, M. 1988. "Psychoanalysis and the Developmental Narrative." In *The Course of Life,* rev. ed., ed. G. Pollack and S. Greenspan. New York: International Universities Press.

Cohler, B., and Galatzer-Levy, R. 1987. "Self Psychology and Psychotherapy." In *New Concepts in Psychoanalytic Psychotherapy,* ed. J. M. Ross and W. A. Myers. Washington, D.C.: American Psychiatric Association Press.

Cohler, B., and Galatzer-Levy, R. 1988. "Self-Psychology and Psychoanalytic Psychotherapy." In *New Concepts in Psychoanalytic Psychotherapy.* ed. J.M. Ross and W.A. Myers, pp. 204–225. Washington, D.C.: American Psychiatric Association Press.

Cohler, B., and Geyer, S. 1982. "Psychological Autonomy and Interdependence within the Family." In *Normal Family Processes,* ed. F. Walsh, pp. 196–228. New York: Guilford.

Cohler, B., and Grunebaum, H. 1981. *Mothers, Grandmothers and Daughters: Personality and Child Care in Three Generation Families.* New York: Wiley-Interscience.

Cohler, B., and Lieberman, M. 1979. "Personality Change across the Second Half of Life: Findings from a study of Irish, Italian and Polish-American Men and Women." In *Ethnicity and Aging,* ed. D. Gelfand and A. Kutznik, pp. 227–45. New York: Springer.

———. 1980. "Social Relations and Mental Health: Middle-aged and Older Men and Women from Three European Ethnic Groups." *Research on Aging* 2:454–69.

Cohler, B., and Musick, J. 1983. "Psychopathology of Parenthood: Implications for Mental Health of Children." In *Parental Psychopathology and Infant Development,* ed. J. S. Musick and B. J. Cohler. New York: Human Sciences Press. Also *Infant Mental Health Journal* 4(3):140–64.

Cohler, B., Stott, F. 1987. "Separation, Interdependence, and Social Relations across the Second Half of Life." In *The Psychology of Separation Through the Life-Span,* ed. J. Bloom-Feshbach and S. Bloom-Feshbach. San Francisco: Jossey-Bass.

Colarusso, C. 1979. "The Development of Time Sense: From Birth to Object Constancy." *International Journal of Psycho-Analysis* 60:243–51.

———. 1987. "The Development of Time Sense: From Object Constancy to Adolescence." *Journal of the American Psychoanalytic Association* 35:119–44.

Colarusso, C., and Nemiroff, R. 1981. *Adult Development.* New York: Plenum.

Coleman, P. 1974. "Measuring Reminiscence Characteristics from Conversation As Adaptive Features of Old Age." *International Journal of Aging and Human Development* 5:281–94.

Coleman, P., and McCulloch, A. 1985. "The Study of Psychosocial Change in Late Life: Some Conceptual and Methodological Issues." In *Life-Span and Change in a Gerontological Perspective,* ed. J. Munnichs et al., pp. 239–56. New York: Academic Press.

Collingwood, R.G. [1946] 1976. *The Idea of History.* New York: Oxford University Press.

Colombo, J. 1982. "The Critical Period Concept: Research, Methodology, and Theoretical Issues." *Psychological Bulletin* 91:260–75.

Cottle, T. 1977. *Perceiving Time: A Psychological Investigation.* New York: John Wiley.

Cottle, T., and Klineberg, S. 1974. *The Present of Things Future.* New York: Free Press.

Crapanzano, V. 1980. *Tuhami: Portrait of a Moroccan.* Chicago: The University of Chicago Press.

Cumming, E., Henry, W. 1961. *Growing Old: The Process of Disengagement.* New York: Basic Books.

Datan, N.; Rodeheaver, D.; and Hughes, F. 1987. "Adult Development and Aging." *Annual Review of Psychology* 38:153–80.

Dean, A., and Lin, N. 1977. "The Stress-Buffering Role of Social Support." *The Journal of Nervous and Mental Disease* 165:403–17.

Dunkel-Schetter, C., and Wortman, C. 1981. "Dilemmas of Social Support: Parallels between Victimization and Aging." In *Aging: Social Change,* ed. S. B. Kessler et al., pp. 349–81. New York: Academic Press.

Durkheim, E. [1912] 1965. *The Elementary Forms of the Religious Life,* trans. J. W. Swain. New York: Free Press.

Eckenroade, J., and Gore, S. 1981. "Stressful Events and Social Supports: The Significance of Context. In *Social Networks and Social Support,* ed. H. Gottlieb, pp. 43–68. New York: Sage.

Eisenbud, J. 1956. "Time and the Oedipus." *Psychoanalytic Quarterly* 25:373–84.

Elder, G. 1974. *Children of the Great Depression.* Chicago: The University of Chicago Press.

———. 1979. "Historical Change in Life Patterns and Personality." In *Life-Span Development and Behavior,* ed. P. Baltes and O.G. Brim, pp. 117–59. New York: Academic Press.

———. 1986. "Military Times and Turning Points in Men's Lives." *Developmental Psychology* 22:233–45.

Elder, G., and Rockwell, R. 1978. "Economic Depression and Post-War Opportunity: A Study of Life Patterns and Health." In *Research in Community and Mental Health,* ed. R. Simmons, pp. 249–304. Greenwich, Conn.: JAI Press.

———. 1979. "The Life Course and Human Development: An Ecological Perspective." *International Journal of Behavioral Development* 2:1–21.

Elwell, F., and Maltbie-Crannell, A. 1981. "The Impact of Role Losses upon Coping Resources and Life-Satisfaction of the Elderly." *Journal of Gerontology* 36:223–32.

Emde, R. 1981. "Changing the Models of Infancy and the Nature of Early Development: Remodeling the Foundation." *Journal of the American Psychoanalytic Association* 29:179–219.

Erikson, E. [1950] 1963. *Childhood and Society.* New York: W. W. Norton.

———. 1959. *Young Man Luther.* New York: W. W. Norton.

Erikson, E.; Erikson, E.; and Kivnick, H. 1986. *Vital Involvement in Old Age: The Experience of Old Age in Our Time.* New York: W. W. Norton.

Essex, M., and Nam, S. 1987. "Marital Status and Loneliness among Older Women: The Differential Importance of Close Friends and Family." *Journal of Marriage and the Family* 49:93–106.

Ferraro, K. 1984. "Widowhood and Social Participation in Later Life: Isolation or Compensation." *Research on Aging* 6:451–68.

Fine, B.; Joseph, E.; and Waldhorn, H. 1959. *Recollection and Reconstruction/Reconstruction in Psychoanalysis* (Monograph 4 of the Kris Study Group). New York: International Universities Press.

Firth, R.; Hubert, J.; and Forge, A. 1970. *Families and Their Relatives: Kinship in a Middle-Class Sector of London.* London: Humanities Press.

Fiske, M. 1980. "Tasks and Crises of the Second-Half of Life: The Interrelationship of Commitment, Coping, and Adaptation." In *Handbook of Health and Aging,* ed. J. Birren and R. B. Sloan, pp. 337–73. Englewood Cliffs, N.J.: Prentice-Hall.

Fiske, M., and Chiriboga, D. 1985. "The Interweaving of Societal and Personal Change in Adulthood." In *Life-Span and Change in a Gerontological Perspective,* ed. J. Munnichs et al., pp. 178–210. New York: Academic Press.

Fisseni, H-J. 1985. "Perceived Unchangeability of Life and Some Biographical Correlates." In *Life-Span and Change in a Gerontological Perspective,* ed. J. Munnichs et al., pp. 103–132. New York: Academic Press.

Flarsheim, A. 1974. "The Therapist's Collusion with the Patient's Wish for Suicide." In *Tactics and Technique in Psychoanalytic Therapy, Vol. II,* ed. P. Giovacchini et al. New York: Science House.

Fleiss, R. 1942. "The Metapsychology of the Analyst." *Psychoanalytic Quarterly* 11:211–27.

Freeman, M. 1984. "History, Narrative, and Life-Span Developmental Knowledge." *Human Development* 27:1–19.

———. 1985. "Psychoanalytic Narration and the Problem of Historical Knowledge." *Psychoanalysis and Contemporary Thought* 8:133–82.

Friedländer, S. 1978. *When Memory Comes,* trans. H. Lane. New York: Farrar, Straus & Giroux.

Freud, A. 1965. *Normality and Psychopathology in Childhood.* New York: International Universities Press.

Freud, S. [1900] 1958. "The Interpretation of Dreams." In *Standard Edition,* ed. J. Strachey, vols. 4–5. London: Hogarth Press.

———. [1909] 1955. "Analysis of a Phobia in a Five-Year Old Boy." In *Standard Edition,* ed. J. Strachey, vol. 10, pp. 5–152. London: Hogarth Press.

———. [1910] 1957. "Five Lectures on Psychoanalysis." In *Standard Edition,* ed. J. Strachey, vol. 11, pp. 3–55. London: Hogarth Press.

———. [1913] 1958. "Recommendations to Physicians Practicing Psychoanalysis." In *Standard Edition,* ed. J. Strachey, vol. 12, pp. 109–120. London: Hogarth Press.

———. [1914] 1958. "Remembering, Repeating, and Working Through: II. Further Recommendations on the Technique of Psychoanalysis." In *Standard Edition,* ed. J. Strachey, vol. 12, pp. 145–56. London: Hogarth Press.

———. [1915] 1957. "The Unconscious." In *Standard Edition,* ed. J. Strachey, vol. 14, pp. 159–95. London: Hogarth Press.

———. [1915–1917] 1961–1963. "Introductory Lectures on Psychoanalysis." In *Standard Edition,* ed. J. Strachey, vols. 15–16. London: Hogarth Press.

———. [1930] 1961. "Civilization and Its Discontents." In *Standard Edition,* ed. J. Strachey, vol. 21, pp. 64–148. London: Hogarth Press.

Gademer, H. G. [1960] 1975. *Truth and Method.* New York: Crossroads.

Galatzer-Levy, R. M. 1976. "Psychic Energy: A Historical Perspective." *Annual of Psychoanalysis* 4:41–64.

———. 1978. "Qualitative Change from Quantitative Change: Mathematical Catastrophe and Psychoanalysis." *Journal of the American Psychoanalytic Association.* 26:921–35.

———. 1983. "The Regulatory Principles of Mental Functioning." *Psychoanalysis and Contemporary Science* 6:255–89.

Galatzer-Levy, R. M., and Cohler, B. 1988. *The Essential Other.* New York: Basic Books.

Garmezy, N. 1987. "Stress, Competence, and Development: Continuities in the Study of Schizophrenic Adults, Children Vulnerable to Psychopathology, and the Search for Stress-Resistant Children." *American Journal of Orthopsychiatry* 57:159–74.

Gedo, J. 1979. *Beyond Interpretation: Toward a Revised Theory for Psychoanalysis.* New York: International Universities Press.

———. 1984. *Psychoanalysis and Its Discontents.* New York: Guilford.

Geertz, C. 1973. "Thick Description: Toward an Interpretive Theory of Culture." In *The Interpretation of Cultures,* C. Geertz, pp. 3–32. New York: Basic Books.

———. [1966] 1973. "Person, Time, and Conduct in Bali." In *The Interpretation of Cultures,* C. Geertz, pp. 360–411. New York: Basic Books.

———. [1980] 1983. "Blurred Genres: The Reconfiguration of Social Thought." In

Local Knowledge: Further Essays in Interpretive Anthropology, C. Geertz, pp. 19–35. New York: Basic Books.

———. [1974] 1983. " 'From the Native's Point of View': On the Nature of Anthropological Understanding." In *Local Knowledge: Further Essays in Interpretive Anthropology,* C. Geertz, pp. 55–72. New York: Basic Books.

———. 1983. "Local Knowledge: Fact and Law in Comparative Perspective." In *Local Knowledge: Further Essays in Interpretive Anthropology,* C. Geertz, pp. 167–234. New York: Basic Books.

George, L. 1982. *Role Transitions In Later Life.* Monterey, Calif.: Brooks/Cole.

Gergen, K. 1977. "Stability, Change and Chance in Understanding Human Development." *Life-Span Developmental Psychology: Dialectical Perspectives on Experimental Research,* ed. N. Datan and H. Reese, pp. 32–65. New York: Academic Press.

———. 1980. "The Emerging Crisis in Life-Span Development Theory." In *Life-Span Development and Behavior,* ed. P. Baltes and O. G. Brim, Jr., vol. 3, pp. 32–65. New York: Academic Press.

———. 1982. "From Self to Science: What Is There to Know?" In *Psychological Perspectives on the Self,* ed. J. Suls, vol. 1, pp. 129–49. Hillsdale, N.J.: Lawrence Erlbaum.

Gergen, K., and Gergen, M. 1983. "Narratives of the Self." In *Studies in Social Identity,* ed. T. Sarbin and K.E. Scheibe, pp. 245–73. New York: Praeger.

———. 1986. "Narrative Form and the Construction of Psychological Science." In *Narrative Psychology: The Storied Nature of Human Conduct,* ed. T. Sarbin, pp. 22–44. New York: Praeger.

Gibson, D. 1986–87. "Interaction and Well-Being in Old Age: Is It Quantity or Quality that Counts?" *International Journal of Aging and Human Development* 24:29–40.

Gill, M. 1976. "Metapsychology Is not Psychology." In *Psychology Versus Metapsychology: Essays in Memory of George Klein,* ed. M. Gill and P. Holzman, pp. 71–105. New York: International Universities Press.

———. 1979. "The Analysis of the Transference." *Journal of the American Psychoanalytic Association* 27(suppl.):263–89.

———. 1983. *Analysis of the Transference. Vol. 1. Theory and Technique.* New York: International Universities Press.

Gilligan, C. 1982. *In a Different Voice: Psychological Theory and Womens' Lives.* Cambridge, Mass.: Harvard University Press.

Glick, P. 1979. "The Future Marital Status and Living Arrangements of the Elderly." *The Gerontologist* 19:301–9.

Green, A. [1975] 1986. "The Analyst, Symbolization and Absence in the Analytic Setting." In *On Private Madness,* A. Green, pp. 30–59. London: The Hogarth Press and Institute of Psychoanalysis.

———. [1978] 1986. "Potential Space in Psychoanalysis: The Object in the Setting." *On Private Madness,* A. Green, pp. 277–96. London: The Hogarth Press and Institute of Psychoanalysis.

Greenacre, P. [1966a] 1971. "Problems of Training Analysis." In *Emotional Growth,* ed. P. Greenacres, pp. 718–42. New York: International Universities Press.

———. [1966b] 1971. "Problems of Overidealization of the Analyst and of Analysis: Their Manifestations in the Transference and Countertransference Relationship." In *Emotional Growth,* ed. P. Greenacres, pp. 743–61. New York: International Universities Press.

Greenough, W.; Black, J.; and Wallace, C. 1987. "Experience and Brain Development." *Child Development* 58:539–59.

Guiteras-Holmes, C. 1961. *Perils of the Soul: The World View of a Tzotzil Indian.* New York: Free Press.

Greenblatt, M.; Becerra, R.; and Serafetinides, E. 1982. "Social Networks and Mental Health: An Overview." *The American Journal of Psychiatry* 139:977–84.

Greenson, R. 1971. "A Dream While Drowning." In *Separation-Individuation: Essays in Honor of Margaret S. Mahler,* ed. J. McDevitt and C. Settlage, pp. 377–84. New York: International Universities Press.

Grunbaum, A. 1984. *The Foundations of Psychoanalysis: A Philosophic Critique.* Berkeley, Calif.: The University of California Press.

Gutmann, D. 1977. "Parenthood: A Comparative Key to the Life-Cycle." In *Life-Span Developmental Psychology: Normative Life Crises,* ed. N. Datan and L. Ginsberg, pp. 167–84. New York: Academic Press.

———. 1987. *Reclaimed Powers: Towards a Psychology of Men and Women in Later Life.* New York: Basic Books.

Gutmann, D.; Griffin, B.; and Grunes, J. 1982. "Developmental Contributions to the Late-Onset Affective Disorders." In *Life-Span Development and Behavior,* ed. P. Baltes and O.G. Brim, Jr., pp. 244–263. New York: Academic Press.

Habermas, J. [1968] 1971. *Knowledge and Human Interests.* Boston: Beacon Press.

———. 1983. "Interpretive Social Science vs. Hermeneuticism." In *Social Science as Moral Inquiry,* ed. N. Haan et al., pp. 251–70. New York: Columbia University Press.

Hagestad, G., and Neugarten, B. 1985. "Age and the Life Course." In *Handbook of Society and Aging,* 2d ed., ed. R. Binstock and E. Shanas, pp. 35–61. New York: Van Nostrand & Reinhold.

Hannson, R.; Jones, W.; Carpenter, B.; and Remondet, J. 1986–87. "Loneliness and Adjustment to Old Age." *International Journal of Aging and Human Development* 24:42–53.

Hareven, T. 1986. Historical Changes in the Construction of the Life-Course." *Human Development* 29:171–80.

Hartmann, H. [1950] 1964. "Comments on the Psychoanalytic Theory of the Ego." In *Essays on Ego Psychology,* ed. H. Hartmann, pp. 113–41. New York: International Universities Press.

Hazan, H. 1980. *The Limbo People: A Study of the Constitution of the Time Universe among the Aged.* London: Routledge and Kegan Paul

Hess, E. 1959. "Imprinting." *Science* 130:133–44.

Hochschild, A. 1975. "Disengagement Theory: A Critique." *American Sociological Review* 40:553–69.

Hogan, D. 1981. *Transitions and Social Change: The Early Lives of American Men.* New York: Academic Press.

Holzman, P. 1985. "Psychoanalysis: Is the Therapy Destroying the Science?" *Journal of the American Psychoanalytic Association* 33:725–70.

Holmes, T., and Rahe, R. 1967. "The Social Readjustment Rating Scale." *Journal of Psychosomatic Research* 11:213–18.

Holt, R. R. 1972. "Freud's Mechanistic and Humanistic Image of Man." In *Psychoanalysis and Contemporary Thought,* ed. R.R. Holt and E. Peterfreund, vol. 1, pp. 3–24.

Holton, G. 1973. *Thematic Origins of Scientific Thought: Kepler to Einstein.* Cambridge, Mass.: Harvard University Press.

Horton, P. 1981. *Solace: The Missing Dimension in Psychiatry.* Chicago: The University of Chicago Press.

Huttenlocher, J., and Smiley, P. 1988. "Emerging Notions of Persons." In *Affect and Cognition,* ed. N. Stein et al. Hillsdale, N.J.: Lawrence Erlbaum.

Husserl, E. 1954. *The Crisis of European Sciences and Transcendental Phenomenonology.* Evanston, Ill.: Northwestern University Press.

Isaacs, B. 1971. "Geriatric Patients: Do Their Families Care?" *British Medical Journal* 4:282–86.

Jacobson, D. 1986. "Types and Timing of Social Support." *Journal of Health and Social Behavior* 27:250–64.

Jacobson, E. 1964. *The Self and the Object World.* New York: International Universities Press.

Jaques, E. 1965. "Death and the Mid-Life Crisis." *International Journal of Psycho-Analysis* 46:502–14.

———. 1980. "The Mid-Life Crisis." In *The Course of Life. Vol. III: Adulthood and the Aging Process,* ed. S. Greenspan and G. Pollock, pp. 1–23. Washington, D.C.: U.S. Government Printing Office.

Jung, C. C. 1933. *Modern Man in Search of a Soul.* New York: Harcourt, Brace, and World.

Kafka, J. 1973. "The Experience of Time." Panel Report. *Journal of the American Psychoanalytic Association* 21: 665–667.

Kagan, J. 1980. "Perspectives on Continuity." In *Constancy and Change in Human Development,* ed. O.G. Brim, Jr., and J. Kagan, pp. 26–74. Cambridge, Mass.: Harvard University Press.

———. 1981. *The Second Year of Life: The Emergence of Self Awareness.* Cambridge, Mass.: Harvard University Press.

Kagan, J., and Moss, H. 1962. *From Birth to Maturity.* New York: John Wiley & Sons.

Kagan, J.; Kearsley, R.; and Zelazo, P. 1978. *Infancy: Its Place in Human Development.* Cambridge, Mass.: Harvard University Press.

Kahn, R. 1979. "Aging and Social Support." In *Aging from Birth to Death,* ed. M. Riley, pp. 77–91. Boulder, Colo.: Westview Press.

Kahn, R., and Antonucci, T. 1980. "Convoys over the Life Course: Attachment, Roles, and Social Support." In *Life-Span Development and Behavior,* ed. P. Baltes and O.G. Brim, Jr., vol. 3, pp. 253–386. New York: Academic Press.

———. 1981. "Convoys of Social Support: A Life-Course Approach." In *Aging: Social Change,* ed. S. Kiesler et al., pp. 383–405. New York: Academic Press.

Kakar, S. 1978. *The Inner World: A Psychoanalytic Study of Childhood and Society in India.* New Delhi: Oxford University Press.

———. 1982. *Shamans, Mystics, and Doctors: A Psychological Inquiry into India and Its Healing Traditions.* New York: Knopf.

Kaminsky, M. 1984. "The Uses of Reminiscence: A Discussion of the Formative Literature." In *The Uses of Reminiscence: New Ways of Working with Older Adults,* ed. M. Kaminsky, pp. 137–56. New York: Haworth Press. *Journal of Gerontological Social Work* 7, nos. 1–2.

Kaufman, S. 1986. *The Ageless Self: Sources of Meaning in Late Life.* Madison, Wisconsin: The University of Wisconsin Press.

Keith, P. 1982. "Perceptions of Time Remaining and Distance from Death." *Omega* 12:269–80.

Kearl, M. 1980. Time, Identity, and the Spiritual Needs of the Elderly." *Sociological Analysis* 41:172–80.

Kernberg, O. 1980. "Normal Narcissism in Middle Age." In *Internal World and External Reality: Object Relations Theory Applied,* ed. O. Kernberg, pp. 121–53. New York: Jason Aronson.

———. 1982. "Self, Affects, Ego, and Drive." *Journal of the American Psychoanalytic Association* 30:893–917.

Kessler, R.; Price, R.; and Wortman, C. 1985. "Social Factors in Psychopathology: Stress, Social Support and Coping Processes." *Annual Review of Psychology* 36:531–72.

Killilea, M. 1982. "Interaction of Crisis Theory, Coping Strategies, and Social Support Systems." In *The Modern Practice of Community Mental Health,* ed. H.C. Schulberg and M. Killilea, pp. 163–214. San Francisco: Jossey-Bass.

Klein, G. 1976. *Psychoanalytic Theory: An Exploration of Essentials.* New York: International Universities Press.

Klein, M. [1928] 1976. *The Psychoanalysis of Children.* New York: Delacorte.

———. [1932] 1952. "Notes on Some Schizoid Mechanisms." *Developments in Psychoanalysis,* ed. M. Klein et al., pp. 292–320. London: Hogarth Press.

Kohli, M., and Meyer, J. 1986. "Social Structure and Social Construction of Life Stages." *Human Development* 29:145–80.

Kohut, H. [1959] 1978. "Introspection, Empathy and Psychoanalysis: An Examination of the Relationship between Mode of Observation and Theory." In *The Search for the Self: Selected Writings of Heinz Kohut, 1950–1978,* ed. P. Ornstein, vol. 1, pp. 205–32. New York: International Universities Press.

———. [1966] 1978. "Forms and Transformations of Narcissism." In *The Search for the Self: Selected Writings of Heinz Kohut, 1950–1978,* ed. P. Ornstein, vol. 1, pp. 427–60. New York: International Universities Press.

———. 1971. *The Analysis of the Self: A Systematic Approach to the Psychoanalytic Treatment of Narcissistic Personality Disorders* (Monograph 1 of the Psychoanalytic Study of the Child Series). New York: International Universities Press.

———. [1974a] 1978. "Remarks about the Formation of the Self: Letter to a Student Regarding some Principles of Psychoanalytic Research." In *The Search for the Self: Selected Writings of Heinz Kohut, 1950–1978,* ed. P. Ornstein, vol. 2, pp. 737–70. New York: International Universities Press.

———. [1975] 1978. "The Psychoanalyst in the Community of Scholars." In *The Search for the Self: Selected Writings of Heinz Kohut, 1950–1978.* ed. P. Ornstein, vol. 2, pp. 685–724. New York: International Universities Press.

———. 1977. *The Restoration of the Self.* New York: International Universities Press.

———. [1978] 1985. "Self Psychology and the Sciences of Man." In *Self Psychology and the Humanities: Reflections on a New Psychoanalytic Approach by Heinz Kohut,* ed. C. Strozier, pp. 73–94. New York: W. W. Norton.

———. 1982. "Introspection, Empathy, and the Semi-Circle of Mental Health." *International Journal of Psycho-Analysis* 63:395–407.

———. 1984. *How Does Psychoanalysis Cure.* Chicago: University of Chicago Press.

Kohut, H., and Seitz, P. [1963] 1978. "Concepts and Theories of Psychoanalysis." In *The Search for the Self: Selected Writings of Heinz Kohut, 1950–1978,* ed. P. Ornstein, vol. 1, pp. 337–74. New York: International Universities Press.

Kohut, H., and Wolf, E. 1978. "The Disorders of the Self and Their Treatment: An Outline." *International Journal of Psycho-Analysis* 59:413–25.

Komarovsky, M. 1950. "Functional Analysis of Sex Roles." *American Sociological Review* 15:508–16.

———. 1956. "Continuities in Family Research: A Case Study." *American Journal of Sociology* 62:466–69.

LaPlanche, J., and Pontalis, J. 1973. *The Language of Psychoanalysis.* New York: W. W. Norton.

Lecky, P. [1945] 1969. *Self-Consistency: A Theory of Personality.* New York: Doubleday, Anchor Books.

Lee, G. 1979. "Children and the Elderly: Interaction and Morale." *Research on Aging* 1:335–59.

Levinson, D. 1986. "A Conception of Adult Development." *American Psychologist* 41:3–13.

Levinson, D.; Darrow, G.; Klein, E.; Levinson, M.; and McKee, B. 1978. *The Seasons of a Man's Life.* New York: Knopf

Lichtenberg, J.; Bornstein, M.; and Silver, D. 1984. *Empathy.* 2 vols. Hillsdale, N.J.: The Analytic Press/Erlbaum.

Lieberman, M., and Falk, J. 1971. "The Remembered Past As a Source of Data for Research on the Life Cycle." *Human Development* 14:132–41.

Lieberman, M., and Tobin, S. 1983. *The Experience of Old Age: Stress, Coping, and Survival.* New York: Basic Books.

Livson, N., Peskin, H. 1980. "Perspectives on Adolescence from Longitudinal Research." In *Handbook of Adolescent Psychology,* ed. J. Adelson, pp. 47–98. New York: John Wiley & Sons.

Low, B. 1978. "The Relationship of Adult Daughters to Their Mothers." Paper presented at the Annual Meeting of the Massachusetts Psychological Association.

Loewald, H. 1960. "The Therapeutic Action of Psychoanalysis." *International Journal of Psycho-Analysis* 41:16–33.

———. 1962. "The Super-ego and the Ego-Ideal. II. Super-ego and Time." *International Journal of Psycho-Analysis* 43:264–68.

———. 1972. "The Experience of Time." *The Psychoanalytic Study of the Child* 27:401–10.

Lorenz, K. [1937] 1965. *Evolution and Modification of Behavior.* Chicago: The University of Chicago Press.

Lowenthal, M. F. 1964. "Social Isolation and Mental Illness in Old Age." *American Sociological Review* 29:54–70.

Lowenthal, M., and Haven, C. 1968. "Interaction and Adaptation: Intimacy As a Crucial Variable." *American Sociological Review* 33:20–30.

Lowenthal, M., and Robinson, B. 1976. "Social Networks and Isolation." In *Handbook of Aging and the Social Sciences,* ed. R. Binstock and E. Shanas, pp. 432–56. New York: Van Nostrand Reinhold.

Lutz, C. 1985. "Ethnopsychology Compared to What? Explaining Behavior and Consciousness among the Ifaluk." In *Person, Self, and Experience: Exploring Pacific Ethnopsychologies,* ed. G. M. White and J. Kirkpatrick, pp. 35–79. Berkeley: The University of California Press.

McMahon, A., and Rhudick, P. 1964. "Reminiscing: Adaptational Significance in the Aged." *Archives of General Psychiatry* 10:292–98.

McMahon, A., and Rhudick, P. 1967. "Reminiscing in the Aged: An Adaptational

Response." In *Psychodynamic Studies on Aging; Creativity, Reminiscing, and Dying,* ed. S. Levin and R. Kahana, pp. 64–78. New York: International Universities Press.

Mahler, M.; Pine, F.; and Bergman, A. 1975. *The Psychological Birth of the Human Infant.* New York: Basic Books.

Mancini, J. 1979. "Family Relationships and Morale among People Sixty-Five Years of Age and Older." *American Journal of Orthopsychiatry* 49:292–300.

Mancini, J.; Quinn, W.; Gavigan, M.; and Franklin, H. 1980. "Social Network Interaction among Older Adults: Implications for Life Satisfaction." *Human Relations* 33:543–54.

Marcus, M. 1973. "The Experience of Separation-Individuation in Infancy and Its Reverberations through the Course of Life. II: Adolescence and Maturity." Panel Report. *Journal of the American Psychoanalytic Association* 21:155–67.

Marriott, K. 1980. "The Open Hindu Person and Interpersonal Fluidity." Paper presented at the Annual Meeting of the Association for Asian Studies, Washington, D.C.

Marris, P. [1974] 1986. *Loss and Change.* rev. ed. London: Routledge and Kegan Paul.

———. 1982. "Attachment and Society." In *The Place of Attachment in Human Behavior,* ed. C. M. Parkes and J. Stevenson-Hinde, pp. 185–201. New York: Basic Books.

Marshall, V. 1975. "Age and Awareness of Finitude in Developmental Gerontology." *Omega* 6:113–29.

———. 1981. *Last Chapters: A Sociology of Death and Dying.* Belmont, Calif.: Wordsworth.

———. 1986. "A Sociological Perspective on Aging and Dying." In *Later Life: The Social Psychology of Aging,* ed. V. Marshall, pp. 125–46. Beverly Hills, Calif.: Sage.

Matthews, S. 1979. *The Social World of Old Women.* Beverly Hills, Calif.: Sage.

———. 1986. "Friendships in Old Age: Biography and Circumstance." In *Later Life: The Social Psychology of Aging,* ed. V. Marshall, pp. 233–70. Beverly Hills, Calif.: Sage.

Meissner, W. 1981a. *Internalization in Psychoanalysis* (Psychological Issues Monograph 50). New York: International Universities Press.

———. 1981b. "A Note on Narcissism." *Psychoanalytic Quarterly* 50:77–89.

———. 1981c. "Notes on the Psychoanalytic Psychology of the Self." *Psychoanalytic Inquiry* 1:233–48.

———. 1983. "Phenomenology of the Self." In *The Future of Psychoanalysis,* ed. A. Goldberg, pp. 65–96. New York: International Universities Press.

———. 1986a. "Some Notes on Hartmann's Ego Psychology and the Psychology of the Self." *Psychoanalytic Inquiry* 6:499–522.

———. 1986b. "Can Psychoanalysis Find Its Self?" *Journal of the American Psychoanalytic Association* 34:379–400.

Merton, R. 1973. *The Sociology of Science.* Chicago: The University of Chicago Press.

———. 1985. *On the Shoulders of Giants. The Vicennial Edition.* New York: Harcourt, Brace and World.

Miller, A., with Cohler, B. 1971. "Identification and Ego-Development." *Bulletin of the Chicago Society for Adolescent Psychiatry* 1:1–17.

Miller, N., and Dollard, J. 1941. *Social Learning Theory and Imitation.* New Haven: Yale University Press.

Moody, H. 1984a. "Reminiscence and the Recovery of the Public World." In *The*

Use of Reminiscence: New Ways of Working with Older Adults, ed. M. Kaminsky, pp. 157–66. New York: Haworth Press. *Journal of Gerontological Social Work* 7.

———. 1984b. "The Meaning of Life and the Meaning of Old Age." In *What Does It Mean to Grow Old: Reflections from the Humanities,* ed. T. Cole and S. Gadow, pp. 9–40. Durham, N.C.: Duke University Press.

Munnichs, J. 1964. "Loneliness, Isolation, and Social Relations in Old Age." *Vita Humana (Human Development)* 7:228–38.

———. 1966. *Old Age and Finitude: A Contribution to Psychogerontology.* New York: Karger.

Murphy, G. [1947] 1966. *Personality: A Biosocial Approach to Organization and Structure.* New York: Basic Books.

Myerhoff, B. 1978. "A Symbol Perfected in Death." In *Life's Career-Aging: Cultural Variations in Growing Old,* ed. B. Myerhoff and A. Simic, pp. 163–205. Beverly Hills, Calif.: Sage.

———. 1979. *Number Our Days.* New York: Dutton.

Nagera, H. 1966. "Early Childhood Disturbances, the Infantile Neurosis, and the Adulthood Disturbances." New York: International Universities Press (*The Psychoanalytic Study of the Child,* Monograph 2).

Nemiroff, R., and Colarusso, C. 1985a. "The Literature on Psychotherapy and Psychoanalysis in the Second Half of Life." In *The Race Against Time: Psychotherapy and Psychoanalysis in the Second Half of Life,* ed. R. A. Nemiroff and C. Colarusso, pp. 25–44. New York: Plenum.

———. 1985b. "Adult Development and Transference." In *The Race Against Time: Psychotherapy and Psychoanalysis in the Second Half of Life,* ed. R. A. Nemiroff and C. Colarusso, pp. 59–72. New York: Plenum.

———. 1985c. "Friendship in Mid-life: With Reference to the Therapist and His Work." In *The Race Against Time: Psychotherapy and Psychoanalysis in the Second Half of Life,* ed. R. A. Nemiroff and C. Colarusso, pp. 73–93. New York: Plenum.

———. 1985d. "Issues and Strategies for Psychotherapy and Psychoanalysis in the Second Half of Life." In *The Race Against Time: Psychotherapy and Psychoanalysis in the Second Half of Life,* ed. R. A. Nemiroff and C. Colarusso, pp. 303–329. New York: Plenum.

Neugarten, B. 1969. "Continuities and Discontinuities of Psychological Issues into Adult Life." *Human Development* 12:121–30.

———. 1973. "Personality Change in Late Life: A Developmental Perspective." In *The Psychology of Adult Development,* ed. C. Eisdorfer and M.P. Lawton, pp. 311–38. Washington, D.C.: The American Psychological Association.

———. 1979. "Time, Age, and the Life-Cycle." *American Journal of Psychiatry* 136:887–94.

———. 1985. "Interpretive Social Science and Research on Aging." In *Gender and the Life-Course,* ed. A. Rossi, pp. 291–300. New York: Aldine.

Neugarten, B., and Datan, N. 1974a. "Sociological Perspectives on the Life Cycle." In *Life-Span Developmental Psychology: Personality and Socialization,* ed. P. Baltes and K. W. Schaie, pp. 53–69. New York: Academic Press.

———. 1974b. "The Middle Years." In *American Handbook of Psychiatry. I: The Foundations of Psychiatry,* ed. S. Arieti, pp. 502–606. New York: Basic Books.

Neugarten, B., and Hagestad, G. 1976. "Age and the Life Course." In *Handbook of Aging and the Social Sciences,* ed. R. Binstock and E. Shanas, pp. 35–55. New York: Van Nostrand Reinhold.

Novey, S. [1968] 1985. *The Second Look: The Reconstruction of Personal History in Psychiatry and Psychoanalysis.* New York: International Universities Press.

Orgel, S. 1965. "On Time and Timelessness." *Psychoanalytic Quarterly* 13:102–21.

Pearlin, L.; Lieberman, M.; Meneghan, E.; and Mullen, J. 1981. "The Stress Process," *Journal of Health and Social Behavior* 22:237–56.

Peskin, H., and Livson, N. 1981. "Uses of the Past in Adult Psychological Health." In *Present and Past in Middle Life,* ed. D. Eichorn et al., pp. 154–83. New York: Academic Press.

Peterfreund, E. 1978. "Some Critical Comments on Psychoanalytic Conceptualizations of Infancy." *International Journal of Psycho-Analysis* 59:427–41.

Piaget, J. [1936] 1953. *The Origins of Intelligence in Children,* trans M. Cook. New York: International Universities Press.

———. [1975] 1977. *The Development of Thought: Equilibration of Cognitive Structures,* trans. A. Rosin. New York: Viking.

———. [1975] 1985. *The Equilibration of Cognitive Structures: The Central Problem of Cognitive Development,* trans. T. Brown and K. J. Thampy. Chicago: The University of Chicago Press.

Polanyi, M. 1958. *The Study of Man.* Chicago: The University of Chicago Press.

Polkinghorne, D. 1983. *Methodology for the Human Sciences: Systems of Inquiry.* Albany, N.Y.: Press of the State University of New York.

Pollock, G. 1961. "Mourning and Adaptation." *International Journal of Psycho-Analysis* 42:341–61.

———. 1971a. "On Time, Death and Immortality." *Psychoanalytic Quarterly* 40:435–46.

———. 1971b. "On Time and Anniversaries." In *The Unconscious Today: Essays in Honor of Max Schur,* ed. M. Kanzer, pp. 233–57. New York: International Universities Press.

———. 1980. "Aging or Aged: Development or Pathology." In *The Course of Life. Vol. III: Adulthood and the Aging Process,* ed. S. Greenspan and G. Pollock, pp. 549–85. Washington, D.C.: The U.S. Government Printing Office.

———. 1981. "Reminiscence and Insight." *Psychoanalytic Study of the Child* 36:278–87.

Polanyi, M. [1949] 1974. "The Nature of Scientific Convictions." In *Scientific Thought and Social Reality,* ed. F. Schwartz, pp. 49–66. New York: International Universities Press.

———. [1965] 1974. "On the Modern Mind." In *Scientific Thought and Social Reality,* ed. F. Schwartz, pp. 131–49. New York: International Universities Press.

Prado, G. 1984. "Aging and Narrative." *Journal of Applied Philosophy* 1:1–14.

Pruchno, R.; Blow, F.; and Smyer, M. 1984. "Life Events and Interdependent Lives." *The Gerontologist* 27:31–41.

Rabinow, P., and Sullivan, W. 1979. "The Interpretive Turn: Emergence of an Approach." In *Interpretive Social Science: A Reader,* ed. P. Rabinow and W. Sullivan. Berkeley: The University of California Press.

Rapaport, D., and Gill, M. 1959. "The Points of View and Assumptions of Metapsychology." *International Journal of Psycho-Analysis* 40:153–62.

Ricoeur, P. 1970. *Freud and Philosophy: An Essay on Interpretation.* New Haven: Yale University Press.

———. 1977. "The Question of Proof in Freud's Psychoanalytic Writings." *Journal of the American Psychoanalytic Association* 25:835–72.

———. 1983. "Can Fictional Narratives be True?" *Analecta Husserliana* 14:3–19.

————. 1984. *Time and Narrative: vol. 1,* trans. K. McLaughlin and D. Pellauer. Chicago: The University of Chicago Press.

Roberts, P., and Newton, P. 1987. "Levinsonian Studies of Women's Adult Development." *Psychology and Aging* 2:154–63.

Robertson, J. 1977. "Grandparenthood: A Study of Role Conceptions." *Journal of Marriage and the Family* 39:165–74.

Rook, K. 1984. "The Negative Side of Social Interaction: The Impact of Psychological Well-Being." *Journal of Personality and Social Psychology* 46:1097–1108.

Rosaldo, R. 1976. "The Story of Tukbaw." In *The Biographical Process: Studies in the History of Psychology and Religion,* ed. F.E. Reynolds and D. Capps, pp. 121–51. The Hague, Netherlands: Muton.

Rosenmayr, L. 1977. "The Family: A Source of Hope for the Elderly." In *Family, Bureaucracy, and the Elderly,* ed. E. Shanas and M. Sussman, pp. 132–57. Durham, N.C.: Duke University Press.

Rosenmayr, L., and Kockeis, E. 1963. "Predispositions for a Sociological Theory of the Family." *International Social Science Journal* 15:410–426.

Rossi, A. 1968. "Transition to Parenthood." *Journal of Marriage and the Family* 30:26–39.

Roth, J. 1963. *Timetables: Structuring the Passage of Time in Hospital Treatment and Other Careers.* Indianapolis, Ind.: Bobbs-Merrill.

Roustang, F. [1976] 1982. *Dire Mastery: Discipleship from Freud to Lacan,* trans. N. Lukacher. Baltimore: Johns Hopkins University Press.

Rowe, J., and Kahn, R. 1987. "Human Aging: Usual and Successful." *Science* 237(July):143–49.

Russell, J. 1987. "Art Born in the Fullness of Time." *New York Times,* 23 August.

Rutter, M. 1987. Psychosocial Resilience and Protective Mechanisms." *American Journal of Orthopsychiatry* 57:316–31.

Ryder, R. 1965. "The Cohort As a Concept in the Study of Social Change." *American Sociological Review* 30:843–61.

Ryff, C. 1984. "Personality Development from the Inside: The Subjective Experience of Change in Adulthood and Aging." In *Life Span Development and Behavior,* ed. P. B. Baltes and O. G. Brim, Jr., vol. 6, pp. 244–79. New York: Academic Press.

————. 1986. "The Subjective Construction of the Self and Society: An Agenda for Life-Span Research." In *Later Life: The Social Psychology of Aging,* ed. V. Marshall, pp. 33–74. Beverly Hills, Calif.: Sage.

Sander, L. 1962. "Issues in Early Mother-Child Interaction." *Journal of the American Academy of Child Psychiatry* 2:141–66.

Sander, L. 1964. "Adaptive Relationships in Early Mother-Child Interaction." *Journal of the American Academy of Child Psychiatry* 3:221–63.

————. 1975. "Infant and Caretaking Environment: Investigation and Conceptualization of Adaptive Behavior in a System of Increasing Complexity." In *Explorations in Child Psychiatry,* ed. E. J. Anthony, pp. 129–66. New York: Plenum.

————. 1983. "To Begin with—Reflections on Ontogeny." In *Reflections on Self Psychology,* ed. J. Lichtenberg and S. Kaplan, pp. 85–104. New York: International Universities Press.

Schachtel, E. 1947. "Memory and Childhood Amnesia." *Psychiatry* 10:1–26.

Schafer, R. 1959. "Generative Empathy in the Treatment Situation." *Psychoanalytic Quarterly* 28:347–73.

————. 1960. "The Loving and Beloved Superego in Freud's Structural Theory." *Psychoanalytic Study of the Child* 15:163–88.

————. 1968. *On Internalization.* New York: International Universities Press.

————. 1976. *A New Language for Psychoanalysis.* New Haven, Conn.: Yale University Press.

————. 1978. *Language and Insight.* New Haven, Conn.: Yale University Press.

————. 1980. "Narration in the Psychoanalytic Dialogue." *Critical Inquiry* 7:29–53.

————. 1981a. "Action Language and the Psychology of the Self." *The Annual for Psychoanalysis* 8:83–92.

————. 1981b. *Narrative Actions in Psychoanalysis.* (Volume 14 of the Heinz Werner Lecture Series.) Worcester, Mass.: Clark University Press.

————. 1982. "The Relevance of the 'Here and Now' Transference to the Reconstruction of Early Development." *International Journal of Psycho-Analysis* 63:77–82.

————. 1983. *The Analytic Attitude.* New York: Basic Books.

Schachter, S. 1959. *The Psychology of Affiliation.* Stanford, Calif.: Stanford University Press.

Seton, P. 1974. "The Psychotemporal Adaptation of Late Adolescence." *Journal of the American Psychoanalytic Association* 22:795–819.

Shanas, E. 1987. "Discussion of Family Caregiving and Alzheimer's Disease." Chicago Area Consortium on Aging.

Shapiro, T. 1977. "Oedipal Distortions in Severe Character Pathologies: Developmental and Theoretical Considerations." *Psychoanalytic Quarterly* 46:559–79.

————. 1981. "On the Quest for the Origins of Conflict." *Psychoanalytic Quarterly* 50:1–21.

Sinnott, J. 1982. "Correlates of Sex Roles of Older Adults." *Journal of Gerontology* 37:587–94.

Sill, J. 1980. "Disengagement Reconsidered: Awareness of Finitude." *The Gerontologist* 37:587–94.

Sirgy, M. J. 1986. *Self-Congruity: Toward a Theory of Personality and Cybernetics.* New York: Praeger.

Skolnick, A. 1986. "Early Attachment and Personal Relationships Across the Life Course." In *Life-Span Development and Behavior,* ed. P. B. Baltes et al., vol. 7, pp. 173–206. Hillsdale, N.J.: Lawrence Erlbaum.

Sontag, S. [1978] 1988. *Illness as Metaphor.* New York: Farrar, Straus & Giroux.

Sorokin, P., and Merton, R. 1937. "Social Time: A Methodological and Functional Analysis." *The American Journal of Sociology* 42:615–29.

Spence, D. 1982. *Narrative Truth and Historical Truth.* New York: W. W. Norton.

————. 1986. "Some Contributions of Symbolic Interaction to the Study of Growing Old." In *Later Life: the Social Psychology of Aging,* ed. V. Marshall, pp. 107–124. Beverly Hills, Calif.: Sage.

Stechler, G., and Kaplan, S. 1980. "The Development of Self." *Psychoanalytic Study of the Child* 35:85–105.

Stern, D. 1985. *The Interpersonal World of the Infant.* New York: Basic Books.

Sternschein, I. 1973. "The Experience of Separation-Individuation in Infancy and Its Reverberations through the Course of Life. III: Maturity, Senescence, and Sociological Implications." Panel Report. *Journal of the American Psychoanalytic Association* 21:633–45.

Strachey, J. 1934. "The Nature of Therapeutic Action in Psychoanalysis." *International Journal of Psycho-Analysis* 15:127–59.

Strachey, J., and eds. 1961a. "Editor's note: 'The Ego and the Id.' " In *Standard Edition*, vol. 19, pp. 3–13. London: Hogarth Press.

———. 1961b. "Editor's Annotation Remarks on the Theory and Practice of Dream Interpretation." In *Standard Edition*, vol. 19, p. 133. London: Hogarth Press.

———. 1961c. "Editor's Note: 'Civilization and Its Discontents.' " In *Standard Edition*, vol. 21, pp. 65–66. London: Hogarth Press.

Sulloway, F. 1979. *Freud: Biologist of the Mind.* New York: Basic Books.

Swanson, D. 1977. "The Psychic Energy Concept: A Critique." *Journal of the American Psychoanalytic Association* 25:603–44.

Taylor, C. [1971] 1985. "Interpretation and the Sciences of Man." In *Philosophy and the Human Sciences: Philosophical Papers,* ed. C. Taylor, vol. 2, pp. 15–57. Cambridge: Cambridge University Press.

Tinbergen, N. 1951. *The Study of Instinct.* Oxford: Clarendon Press.

Toulmin, S. 1977. "Self-Knowledge and Knowledge of the 'Self.' " In *The Self,* ed. T. Mischel, pp. 291–317. Oxford: Basil Blackwell.

———. 1979. "The Inwardness of Mental Life." *Critical Inquiry* 6:1–16.

———. 1981. "On Knowing Our Own Minds." *Annual for Psychoanalysis* 9:207–21.

———. 1986. "Self Psychology as Postmodern Science." In *Commentaries on Heinz Kohut's "How Does Analysis Cure,"* ed. M. Bornstein et al. Hillsdale, N.J.: The Analytic Press/Erlbaum (*Psychological Inquiry* no. 3).

Townsend, P. 1957. *The Family Life of Old People.* London: Routledge and Kegan Paul.

Troll, L., and Smith, J. 1976. "Attachment through the Life-Span: Some Questions about Dyadic Relations in Later Life." *Human Development* 9:156–70.

Turner, J. 1981. Social Support As a Contingency in Psychological Well-Being." *Journal of Health and Social Behavior* 22:357–67.

Uhlenberg, P. 1979. "Demographic Change and the Problems of the Aged." In *Aging from Birth to Death,* ed. M. Riley, pp. 153–66. Boulder, Colo.: Westview Press.

———. 1980. "Death and the Family." *Journal of Family History* 5:313–20.

Uhlenhuth, E., and Paykel, E. 1973a. "Symptom Intensity and Life Events." *Archives of General Psychiatry* 28:473–77.

———. 1973b. "Symptom Configuration and Life Events." *Archives of General Psychiatry* 28:744–48.

von Wright, G. H. 1971. *Explanation and Understanding.* Ithaca, N.Y.: Cornell University Press.

Wallace, E. IV. 1985. *Historiography and Causation in Psychoanalysis.* Hillsdale, N.J.: The Analytic Press/Erlbaum.

Wallerstein, R. 1977. "Psychic Energy Reconsidered—Introduction." *Journal of the American Psychoanalytic Association* 31:529–36.

———. 1986. "Psychoanalysis As a Science: A Response to the New Challenges." *Psychoanalytic Quarterly* 55:414–51.

Watson, L. 1976. "Understanding a Life History as a Subjective Document: Hermeneutical and Phenomenological Perspectives." *Ethos* 4:95–131.

Weber, M. [1905–06] 1955. *The Protestant Ethic and the Spirit of Capitalism,* trans. T. Parsons. New York: Scribners.

Weiss, R. 1974. *Loneliness: The Experience of Emotional and Social Isolation.* Cambridge, Mass.: MIT Press.

———. 1982. "Attachment in Adult Life." In *The Place of Attachment in Human Behavior,* ed. C. M. Parkes and J. Stevenson-Hinde, pp. 171–84. New York: Basic Books.

Weiss, S. 1988. Personal communication.

Werner, H. [1926] 1940. *The Comparative Psychology of Mental Development.* New York: Harper & Row.

Wertz, F. 1986. "Common Methodological Fundamentals of the Analytic Procedures in Phenomenological and Psychoanalytic Research." *Psychoanalysis and Contemporary Thought* 9:563–603.

Wessman, A., and Gorman, B. 1977. "The Emergence of Human Awareness and Concepts of Time." In *The Personal Experience of Time,* ed. B. Gorman and A. Wessman, pp. 4–56. New York: Plenum.

White, H. [1972–73] 1978. "Interpretation in History." In *Tropics of Discourse: Essays in Cultural Criticism,* H. White, pp. 51–80. Baltimore: Johns Hopkins University Press.

———. [1980] 1987. "The Value of Narrativity in the Representation of Reality." In *The Content of the Form: Narrative Discourse and Historical Representation,* H. White, pp. 1–25. Baltimore: The Johns Hopkins University Press.

———. [1984] 1987. "The Question of Narrative in Contemporary Historical Theory." In *The Content of the Form: Narrative Discourse and Historical Representation,* H. White, pp. 26–57. Baltimore: The Johns Hopkins University Press.

White, S. H. 1965. "Evidence for a Hierarchical Arrangement of Learning Processes." In *Advances in Child Development and Behavior,* ed. L. Lipsitt and C. Spiker, vol. 2. New York: Academic Press.

Winestine, M. C. 1973. "The Experience of Separation-Individuation in Infancy and Its Reverberations through the Course of Life. I: Infancy and Childhood." Panel Report. *Journal of the American Psychoanalytic Association* 21:135–54.

Winnicott, D. W. 1953. "Transitional Objects and Transitional Phenomena." In D.W. Winnicott, *Collected Papers: Through Paediatrics to Psycho-Analysis,* pp. 229–42. New York: Basic Books.

———. 1960. "The Theory of the Parent-Infant Relationship." *International Journal of Psycho-Analysis.* 41:585–95.

———. [1963] 1966. "Psychiatric Disorder in Terms of Infantile Maturational Processes." In *The Maturational Process and the Facilitating Environment,* ed. D. W. Winnicott, pp. 230–41. New York: Basic Books.

Wolf, K. 1953. "Observations of Individual Tendencies in the First Year of Life." In *Problems of Infancy and Childhood: Proceedings of the Sixth Conference,* ed. M. Senn, pp. 97–137. New York: Josiah Macy Foundation.

Wolff, P. 1987. *The Development of Behavioral States and the Expression of Emotions in Early Infancy.* Chicago: The University of Chicago Press.

Wood, V., and Robertson, J. 1978. "Friendship and Kinship Interaction: Differential Effect on the Morale of the Elderly." *Journal of Marriage and the Family* 40:367–75.

Woodward, K. 1984. "Reminiscence and the Life Review: Prospects and Retrospects." In *What Does It Mean to Grow Old: Reflections from the Humanities,* ed. T. Cole and S. Gadow, pp. 135–62. Durham, N.C.: Duke University Press.

Wyatt, F. 1962. "A Psychologist Looks at History." *Journal of Social Issues* 26:66–77.

———. 1963. "The Reconstruction of the Individual and the Collective Past." In *The Study of Lives: Essays in Honor of Henry A. Murray,* ed. R. W. White, pp. 305–20. New York: Atherton Press/Aldine.

Zaleznik, A. 1987. "Essays on leadership." (Review of C. Strozier and D. Offer, ed., *The Leader: Psychohistorical Essays.*) *Contemporary Psychology* 32:323–24.

Zweibel, N. 1987. "Study of Intergenerational Attitudes Regarding Prolongation of

Life." Preliminary Report. Center for Aging, Health and Society, University of Chicago.

DISCUSSION

Drs. Cohler and Galatzer-Levy have undertaken for us a scholarly integration of multidisciplinary studies ranging from social psychology to psychoanalysis, including original work of their own. They address nothing less than the significance of psychoanalytic perspectives, particularly those emphasizing the study of the self, of morale, and of adjustment across middle and later life. Initially they show how modern psychoanalytic self psychology can be applied to the study of lives and particularly how it enriches understanding of empirical and clinical findings about development in the second half of life.

Contemporary psychoanalytic theory views the self as an intrapsychological attribute, constructed through experience of and with others, and accessible to study through empathy. Cohler and Galatzer-Levy argue that the most effective empathic investigations focus on the construction of a story of the relationship between remembered past and anticipated future in the context of the present, the analytic situation. Further, the psychoanalytic psychology of the self emerging from the collaborative effort between analyst and analysand is more consistent with "postmodern" scientific thought than with the mechanistic, experience-distant ego psychology that was the intellectual legacy of Freud's metapsychology.

Cohler and Galatzer-Levy join a growing cadre of authors who are coming to the view that although early experience profoundly affects the formulation of the self, no single event (satisfying or traumatic) or even age range (critical period) assumes a primary position. They describe how "intersubjectivity" results from "living with" caregivers and family over long periods of time. They have observed that people have a continuing capacity to use others to foster self-regulation and maintain a sense of meaning. This capacity provides a sense of continuity between past and present, and the feeling that others may be supportive leads to increased optimism and facility in using others in the development of the self. Kohut's (1977) "selfobject," Stein's (1985) "evoked companion," and Galatzer-Levy and Cohler's (1988) "evoked or essential other" are described as consisting of attributes of another person that are initially experienced as actions undertaken by the self, and remain significant in providing solace, vitality, and integration over time. Via internalization theory, classical psychoanalysis has described the self as built up from attributes of others represented within oneself. On the other hand, self psychology places the emphasis on how the self evolves from variations in the *intrapsychological experience of others,* with functions experienced from the outset as being done by and for the self.

In accord with Cohler and Galatzer-Levy, we find the new concepts of self psychology very useful in defining the characteristics of the self in adulthood and describing the factors that shape it. We agree that it is essential to view the self in adulthood as dynamic and changing, and we have suggested the term "authentic" to characterize the mature adult self because it describes the capacity to accept what is genuine within the self and the outer world regardless of the narcissistic injury involved (Colarusso and Nemiroff 1981). The capacity for authenticity emerges from the developmental experiences of *both* childhood and adulthood. Among the most important influences in adulthood that we found were narcissistic issues related to (1) the aging body; (2) significant relationships, particularly with spouse, children, and parents; (3) middle-age time sense; and (4) the vicissitudes of work and creativity. We conceptualized a normal narcissistic regression precipitated by confrontation of the developmental tasks of midlife as leading to a reemergence of aspects of infantile narcissism, which we characterized by using Kohut's concept of the grandiose self. We see the reworking and eventual integration of aspects of the infantile grandiosity as an integral part of normal development in midlife.

Cohler and Galatzer-Levy make an important contribution when they trace the origins of the genetic point of view in psychoanalysis from writings of Freud, Abraham, and through Erikson. They rightly challenge any rigid causal connection between earlier and later states by citing studies showing that imprinting plays a minimal role in human learning and development and that ethological modes are largely irrelevant to the study of human infant development. Moreover, longitudinal studies of personality from childhood through middle and late life demonstrate that lives are *less* continuous and predictably ordered than is assumed in lockstep epigenetic models.

They model development as a series of *transformations* leading to dramatic reordering of the meaning of time and the use of memory in accounting for the present experiencing of prior experience. These transformations are precipitated by crises requiring resolution rather than by a series of well-ordered stages. Successful transformations provide a sense of disruption, requiring *narrative resolution* in order to preserve meaning and a sense of continuity of self. They assert that this view of development, as a series of drastically reorganizing crises producing distress over the loss of continuity and calling for reparation through reconstruction of the narrative of the self, is more consistent with clinical formulations about development. For decades this reparation is what psychoanalysts have been talking about when they address the need to resolve the nuclear neurosis emanating from ages five to seven. However, the adult development research presented by Cohler and Galatzer-Levy, as well as other contributors to this volume, demonstrates the existence and importance of later transformations, including those from early to middle childhood, childhood to adolescence, young adulthood to midlife, and the transformations involved in early old age and later old age—all of which share the characteristically dramatic alteration in the sense of time and the use of memory.

Cohler and Galatzer-Levy have deepened and enlarged on our hypothesis that development in adulthood is an ongoing, dynamic process. We have lamented that psychoanalytic recognition of the importance of adult experiences like pregnancy, marriage, aging, illness, and approaching death has usually been in relation to past experiences and conflicts, with little or no emphasis on these experiences as developmental issues in and of themselves, regardless of the past. Morton Shane's (1977) developmental view of adulthood was most helpful to us in formulating our own ideas. He wrote:

> The developmental *orientation* must be distinguished from the genetic (sometimes called "developmental" or "genetic developmental") *point of view.* Not only is the concept on a lower level of abstraction, closer to the clinical data, but it is also different in that "developmental" implies an on-going process, not only with a past, but also with a present and a future, while "genetic" is limited to the past, especially in terms of how the past is retrospectively perceived, related to and understood in the present, and is exclusively derived from the analytic situation. The use of the developmental approach implies that the analytic patient, regardless of age, is considered to be still in the process of ongoing development as opposed to merely being in possession of a past that influences his present conscious and unconscious life. (Pp. 95–96)

We further stated that the developmental processes in adulthood are influenced by the adult past as well as the childhood past and expanded the genetic approach (reference to the past) to place equal importance on adult experience. In the past the term *genetic* was used to refer only to the childhood past—for example, how the events of the oedipal phase determine the formation of a neurosis in our adult patients, or how the successful traversal of adolescence resulted in the uniqueness of adult character formation. But what of the young adult past or the middle-age past? In a more open-ended concept of development, "genetic" takes on a longitudinal dimension, incorporating new experiences that occur at each developmental phase throughout life. Adult experiences undoubtedly relate to, and are influenced by, the events of childhood, but cannot be fully explained by them.

Of Cohler and Galatzer-Levy's many provocative ideas, we shall mention only one more for the present. They describe the psychoanalytic psychology of the self as focusing on the *meaning* of social ties over time. The self psychology perspective is distinguished by the ways in which issues of meaning are examined and by what is construed as adequate explanation of psychological experience. They emphasize that social relationships change in meaning as one moves through life, and they discuss the uses of loneliness, solitude, and reminiscence by people at midlife and beyond as they reorder the memories of their experience to construct meaningful narratives for their lives, thus maintaining their psychological integrity and sense of continuity.

REFERENCES

Colarusso, C. A., and Nemiroff, R. A. 1981. *Adult Development: A New Dimension in Psychodynamic Theory and Practice.* New York: Plenum.

Galatzer-Levy, R. and Cohler, B. 1988. *The Essential Other.* New York: Basic Books.

Kohut, H. 1977. *The Restoration of the Self.* New York: International Universities Press.

Shane, M. 1977. "A Rationale for Teaching Analytic Technique Based on a Developmental Orientation and Approach." *International Journal of Psycho-Analysis.* 58:95–96.

Stern, D. 1985. *The Interpersonal World of the Infant.* New York: Basic Books.

PART III

CLINICAL PERSPECTIVES

10

A Developmental Approach to Psychoanalytic Psychotherapy with the Aged

BRIAN P. GRIFFIN AND JEROME M. GRUNES*

From a developmental perspective, psychoanalytic psychotherapy and psychoanalysis are procedures directed toward promoting individual growth and adaptation. The fundamental aspect of psychoanalytic therapy—insight through interpretation in the context of the psychoanalytic situation—fosters structural change by helping the individual relinquish pathological self-conceptions internalized during prior periods of development. To an important degree, relinquishing old self-conceptions is contingent upon internalizing a new relationship with the therapist in which transference distortions, based on past experiences, are resolved (Loewald 1960; Blatt and Behrends 1987). By helping the individual attain sufficient independence from the past, with its familiar but painful enactments, therapy encourages the individual to enter the future, with its unfamiliar but potentially rewarding possibilities. Thus, in our usual conceptions, the perpetuation of the past in the present—the continuity of self-conceptions developed in the past—is seen as both the enemy of present adaptation and the proper focus of psychoanalytic intervention.

To some degree, the emphasis in psychoanalytic theory on the negative aspects of continuity is understandable: psychoanalytic theory is a developmental theory, and our existing models of development and adaptation

*This chapter was supported by grants from the Retirement Research Foundation (grant #80–14) and the National Institute of Mental Health (grant #MH 17383–05).

emphasize, perhaps inordinately, processes of change over processes that foster continuity. That is, we are prone to think of development as involving only structural change in response to the adaptive demands of the environment; generally ignored is the view that change *requires* the presence of prior structures, and that change is adaptive only insofar as it can be integrated with prior structures (Langer 1969; Werner 1948). Without such integration, the organism risks fragmentation.

In addition, the emphasis on promoting change in psychotherapy has been based almost exclusively on work with young patients. When working with young adults, one is readily impressed by the extent to which the repetition of the past in the present, as reflected in the persistence of infantile conflicts or archaic modes of relating, interferes with subjective well-being and the ability to find satisfactory sources of intimacy and work. In effect, the past impedes the younger adult's ability to move into the future and act in harmony with the developmentally appropriate needs for expansion and creation (Buehler 1935; Kuhlen 1964).

However, we shall argue here that the emphasis on change as the guarantor of adaptation in general, and the focus of psychoanalytic therapy in particular, is misleading when one considers adaptive processes and strategies for psychotherapeutic intervention in later life. More specifically, the following tripartite thesis will be advanced: (1) Development in later adulthood is characterized by the adaptive construction of a highly stable sense of self; (2) Maladaptation can arise for the *first time* in later life when internal or external events attack crucial bases of self-continuity; and (3) One approach to psychoanalytic therapy with the aged is to focus on the reconstruction of self-continuity in order to cope with the myriad changes of later life.

Continuity, Change, and Adaptation in Adulthood

As an ideal construct, adaptation has generally been defined in developmental psychology as maintaining a balance or equilibrium between organismic processes that foster continuity and those that foster change. Certainly the cognitive-developmental theories of Jean Piaget (1954) and Heinz Werner (1948) are quite specific about the need for the organism to maintain a sense of coherence and continuity as new structures come on line in the course of development. For Piaget, the tension between continuity and change is expressed in his conception of development as a process of assimilation and accommodation resulting in higher levels of cognitive equilibria. For Werner, the dialectic between continuity and change is expressed in his orthogenetic principle, which holds that development is a process of differentiation (change) and hierarchical integration (continuity). In effect, this principle describes the forces at work in any living system:

> There is, on one hand, the tendency of organisms to *conserve* their integrity, whether biological or psychological: in the face of variable and often adverse internal and external conditions, the organism tends to maintain its existence as an integrated entity. There is, on the other hand, the tendency of organisms to undergo transformation from the status of relatively little differentiated entities to relatively differentiated and integrated adult forms. (Werner and Kaplan 1963, p. 5)

With the emergence of self psychology and object relations theory, there has been a progressive move toward integrating the perspectives of Piaget and Werner in psychoanalytic conceptions of development and adaptation. A prime example of this integrating trend is in the conceptualization of psychological adaptation as a balance between processes of continuity and change. As Robert Stolorow and George Atwood (1983) write:

> The healthy person has the ability to achieve an optimal balance between the maintenance of his psychological organization on the one hand and his openness to new forms of experience on the other. On the one hand, his self and object representations have become sufficiently consolidated that they can assimilate into their structure a wide range of experiences of self and other and still retain their integrity and stability. His subjective world, in other words, is not unduly vulnerable to disintegration or dissolution. On the other hand, his representational structures are sufficiently flexible to accommodate new configurations of experience of self and other, so that the organization of his subjective life can continue to expand in both complexity and scope. (P. 107)

Like most ideal constructs, this view of adaptation is somewhat at odds with empirical reality, as attested to by several studies of normative psychological changes across adulthood. Furthermore, an extensive body of psychological and ethnographic literature suggests that younger and older adults differ in the extent to which the quest for change, new experience, and expansion are normative features of their motivational, behavioral, and cognitive orientations. For example, Charlotte Buehler's (1935, 1968) investigations into changing patterns of goals and motivations over the life course indicate that adolescence and young adulthood are characterized by "creative-expansive" needs, whereas later life is marked by needs centering around "the upholding of the internal order." In a similar vein, Raymond Kuhlen's (1964) work clearly points to two broad motivational trends characteristic of adulthood: In young adulthood, "growth-expansion" motives predominate; in later life "constrictive" motives hold sway, manifesting the need to preserve oneself in the face of the threats of aging. In addition, numerous studies have consistently found age to be negatively related to the willingness to pioneer or adopt innovations in tribal customs (Simmons 1945; Barnett 1953), social movements (Sorokin 1947; Gutmann 1982), science (Lehman 1953), agriculture (Rogers 1962; Green, Rich, and Nesman 1985), and medicine (Belcher 1958). Investigations into the representational world of the young and old utilizing dream reports (e.g., Brenneis 1975; Krohn and Gutmann 1971), and projective techniques (Rosen and Neugarten 1964; Gutmann 1987; Shanan 1968) clearly point to an age-related tendency away from unfamiliar, less differentiated and complex depictions of self and others to more constricted, familiar ones. Finally, studies of cognitive functioning in later life (Botwinick 1977; Horn 1970) suggest that the aged, relative to the young, are either less able or less willing to deal with novel, complex problems that involve the manipulation of unfamiliar information.

An increasing body of evidence indicates that psychological adaptation in old age is related to the ability to maintain a highly stable and continuous self-representation in the face of a variety of life transitions. For example, Morton Lieberman and Sheldon Tobin (1983), in a study of adaptive processes in later life, assessed 870 elderly individuals before and after they underwent various changes in living conditions (operationalized as the stress variable). Some were people on the way to a home for the aged, others were state hospital patients moving to new therapeutic communities, and others were relatively robust elders facing relocation. Unlike prior work with younger adults, which indicated that coping was related to operationalized measures of ego strength, Lieberman and Tobin found that (1) the degree of change required of the subjects (across groups) determined whether the elderly considered the event "stressful"; and (2) while cognitive and physical resources may pattern the base of adaptative processes, the only indicator of current adequate functioning that predicted positive reaction to the stress was the ability to retain a constant self-conception in confronting the environmental change. Those individuals who could not find meaningful ways of maintaining selfsameness in the face of change showed significant deterioration.

Moreover, there is evidence that the link between maintaining a highly stable self-organization and positive adaptation is *specific* to later life. For example, Brian Griffin (1985) explicitly tested the hypotheses that normal, community-dwelling younger and older men would differ in their representations of self as an agent of continuity versus change and that the relationship between *perceived* self-continuity and adaptation would vary by age. Using autobiographical interviews conducted by a blind interviewer, Griffin derived a reliable and valid measure of the extent to which the subject portrayed his present psychosocial world as being consistent with his past ideals, ambitions, and characteristics. The major findings of this study were (1) the older men, relative to their younger counterparts, significantly depicted themselves as agents of continuity rather than change; and (2) the relationship between portrayed self-continuity and adaptation varied by age. For the older men, higher degrees of portrayed self-continuity were related to higher life satisfaction and fewer psychiatric symptoms. For the younger men, the pattern of correlations was reversed: the more they depicted their present psychosocial world as continuous with their past, the lower their life satisfaction and the greater their psychiatric symptoms. Thus, the study clearly implies that, at least at the level of self-conceptions, continuity and change may have differential adaptive correlates for the young and the old. For the old, the maintenance of a highly stable sense of self seems vital to psychological adaptation; for the young, too much persistence of the past in the present may have maladaptive consequences.

From a phenomenological point of view, the perception and maintenance of the self as an enduring and *reliable* entity may be adaptive because it provides a counterbalance to the physical, existential, and social dislocations characteristic of later life. Thus, Tobin and Lieberman (1976) argued:

The inability to maintain a rather high stability may be the ultimate sign of complete disorganization. The maintenance of a high degree of stability may be of greater importance for aged persons because of their need to cope with external crisis and internal degenerative change. Living until the late 70's or 80's may necessitate an ability to maintain the sense of self in the face of environmental and personal upheavals. (Pp. 141–42)

In addition, self-continuity may have special existential implications for the ability of the aged to validate or justify a life *as lived.* Robert Kastenbaum (1975) has remarked on this use of the past by the aged. Virginia Revere and Tobin (1980) have demonstrated the elderly's tendency to dramatize the past in the service of maintaining a personal "myth"—a story intended to be believed in order to justify a life. They argued that the older person needs to view the past in a dramatic, idealized way to achieve a degree of immortality, to "see onself as a hero of a life worth remembering" (p. 16).

Unfortunately, little is known regarding the psychological capacities or strategies that the aged employ to maintain a constant sense of self in later life. Presumably, this capacity is based on the integrity of several ego functions, like memory and conceptual processes (see Grunes 1981), which might set a minimum threshold on the ability to underwrite a sense of self-continuity. In addition, the work of Lieberman and Tobin (1983) vividly illustrates how the past takes on a special meaning for the elderly in maintaining self-identity. As part of their Home for Life Study, they assessed various mechanisms employed by institutional and community elderly, as well as adolescents, to validate their self-concepts. Unlike the adolescents, who validated their perceived self-identity through exclusive references to their *present* lives and interactions with people, the elderly respondents maintained self-continuity through a variety of mechanisms. In addition to the present (which was used less than half the time), the elderly employed the *past* to maintain self-continuity. The use of the past included references to specific past interactions to validate a perceived aspect of self-identity as well as references to the generalized past—"I am who I always have been." When both the present and the past failed as sources of validation, the elderly abandoned reality and used evidence based on wish and distortion.

In addition to "internal" capacities, the aged often rely on "external" objects to bolster self-continuity. The work of Graham Rowles (1980) illustrates the use of the external world in that manner. Employing the participant-observation method, he was interested in studying how an "attachment to place" facilitated the maintenance of a constant personal identity and linkage to the past among very old rural subjects in Appalachia. He noted that when he asked his subjects to tell their life stories, they would take him to significant landmarks, geographical structures, and places in order to relate episodes of their lives. He commented on how the aged's intense bonding to the physical and social dimensions of their habitat provided a major support for their sense of personal history and identity. For these oldsters, the habitat and its various niches were experienced as both a part and a representation of the self and its history. Rowles nicely captured his subjects commingling of their internal and external worlds when he wrote:

> Each of them has a heavy historical investment in this place. Each has created an environment . . . laden with personal meaning in relation to a life history. Over the years, each one of them has become more and more a part of the place to the point where it has become an autobiography—literally an extension of self. In the same way that each person is generally unaware of the movement of his limbs—the clasping of his fingers, the extending of his arm, the process of walking across a familiar room—so too does being a part of Colton on this level of intimacy come to be taken-for-granted by the existential insider. (1980, p. 162)

A similar reliance on the external world to support a stable sense of self was noted by Schmitt, Redondo, and Wapner (1977, cited in Wapner, Kaplan, and Ciottone 1981) in their study of the mechanisms older people adopted in adjusting to nursing home placement. They reported that those individuals who brought with them "transitional objects"—objects from their old arenas of action, like pictures, mementos, rocking chairs, and so forth—adapted better to the new scene than those who moved without them. The authors argued that such "transitional objects" provided a bridge between the old and the new worlds and allowed for an affirmation of selfsameness.

These observations suggest that the maintenance of self-continuity may be somewhat dependent upon a sustaining object world—a world that is experienced, to some extent, as part of the self. Just as we all rely, to some degree, on external objects to affirm and reinforce functions of the self (for example, self-esteem) and serve as id and superego protagonists, it is evident that the aged also use various external objects to affirm the historic self in later life. Theoretically, the type of object is variable: a spouse, job, geographical place, building, or even one's body. However, the function of the object would be invariant—to affirm constant, esteem-maintaining self-conceptions in facing the transitions of old age. Although people rely on the environment to underwrite the continuity of the self in varying degrees, that reliance is clearly a crucial adaptive strategy in later life.

In summary, adaptation has been generally defined as a balance between organismic tendencies toward continuity and change, but the theoretical and empirical work detailed in the preceding review suggests that adulthood may be characterized by developmental reorderings of psychological commitments in those two domains. Earlier adulthood appears to be characterized by a higher motivational, behavioral, and cognitive commitment toward discontinuity, expansion, and complexity; later adulthood appears to bring a normative reversal of these priorities. Furthermore, these contrasting orientations appear to be differentially related to psychological health. That is, if the elderly have difficulty adjusting to *change,* by the same token, the young may not be well equipped to deal with *constancy.* In addition to relying on external objects, the use of the past may support a sense of selfsameness in encountering later life transitions. The implications of these findings for understanding psychopathological and psychotherapeutic processes in old age will now be addressed.

Self-Continuity and Psychopathology in Old Age

If the preservation of self-continuity is integral to adaptation in old age, it patently suggests that psychoanalytic theory needs to accommodate this finding in its theories of pathology and therapy. To reiterate, the usual psychoanalytic conception views the persistence of the past in the present as an impediment to adaptation—something which, in therapy, needs to be "worked through" and undone. Although that concept is consistent with the developmental needs and capacities of the young, it may be invalid when indiscriminately applied to the aged. Far from needing and wishing to be freed from the past, the first-time aged patient may have to re-cathect the past and make it viable in the present.

That late-onset functional psychopathology among the aged can arise when internal or external events undermine core bases of self-continuity is part of a model of late-life pathogenesis that we are currently evaluating at Northwestern University Medical School's Older Adult Program.* The essential idea is that pathogenesis in the eighth and ninth decades of life often reflects the loss, or threatened loss, of the conviction that the self is a *constant, reliable,* and *trustworthy* object. The basic model holds that for certain predisposed individuals normative, age-related life events (physical illness, widowhood, retirement, etc.) assume pathological proportions because they attack supports of self-constancy and usher in profound crises of self-discontinuity—a frightening feeling of estrangement from the past, from all that one thought one was and from all one most needed to be—and these crises are manifest in symptom formation. For example, Mr. A., an eighty-three-year-old man, who, prior to the onset of crippling arthritis had been vigorously independent and had cared for his sick wife, became depressed and stated on admission, "I used to be independent, now I am a baby. This is not me."

While self-continuity may be important for the aged in general, a sophisticated model of pathogenesis should be able to account for the range of vulnerabilities in the maintenance of selfsameness. Our pilot observations of normal and clinical aged have alerted us to many factors that seem to constitute a vulnerable predisposition. In regard to external factors, some people have more supports for the historic sense of self and are therefore less vulnerable to any one normative loss; some have less need to use the environment to reflect the constancy of the self—they have an internalized sense of self-continuity and are more impervious to the changes of later life. In some individuals, a severe or sudden loss of an external support prevents a requisite degree of internalization of the function supplied by the support—as happens when an individual unexpectedly loses a spouse. Rather than being able to mourn the loss, the result is melancholia, along the lines Sigmund Freud (1917) first proposed. Similarly, the characteristics of the objects that support the self are sometimes overly concrete and particularistic in their phrasing, therefore less generalizable to new circumstances (e.g., not a job, but a particular job; not a house, but a particular house in a specific neighborhood, etc.). Thus the

*This work is being conducted in collaboration with David L. Gutmann, Ph. D., principal investigator.

concreteness of the object impedes the ability both to mourn its loss and to pioneer new versions of it to serve the old function.

From a more internal point of view, individuals vary in the breadth or extent of the historic self-conception *structure* itself—that is, less vulnerable aged are able to identify and value a multitude of enduring self-attributes, and can compensate for the loss of one of them by strengthening those that remain. Thus, those who develop psychiatric conditions are driven to maintain *one* base of self-continuity to protect self-esteem. When this need is attacked, symptoms result. Another observation is that individuals vulnerable to breaches of self-continuity are characterized by the *thematic content* of the self-conception structure—contents that are particularly difficult to maintain in old age. For example, since many changes of later life are not under personal control and involve increasing dependency (e.g., widowhood, illness, etc.), an individual whose sense of self-continuity is based on a conviction of total control or independence is vulnerable. Finally, in some individuals several internal and external factors interact to constitute a vulnerable predisposition.

In the course of our clinical work, we have often observed a particular pattern of cases that illustrate the interaction between the internal and external factors discussed earlier. The internal factors involve structural and substantive aspects of the hitherto sustaining self-conception; the external factors involve specific losses of hitherto constancy-affirming objects. Moreover, we have been impressed by the frequency with which the self-conception structure and its content was compensatory for earlier trauma. As David Gutmann and associates (1987) have observed, this compensatory structure is validated in a range of confirmatory habitats. Pathology comes about when the structure is undermined as a consequence of assaults on its confirmatory support. The eighty-three-year-old man cited earlier (Mr. A.) exemplified this pattern. He had developed a first-time depression after circulatory problems and arthritis made it impossible for him to walk and care for his invalid wife, who had recently moved into a nursing home. The wife had been sickly throughout their marriage, and he prided himself on his ability to care for her—"to fix her" in his mind, better than her doctors did. He had retired nearly twenty years prior to admission, as a mechanic.

In the course of his treatment he recalled his traumatic early history, but related it with pride.

Case 1

He lost his mother when he was three years old, and remembered his father as alcoholic and unreliable. The patient was placed in an orphanage by the father, where he recalled his years of scrapping for survival with tough pride. When the father remarried, the patient returned to the home at age five. His stepmother was described as cold and rejecting and repeatedly threw him out of the house. His earliest memory was of his father sending him to buy three cents worth of sour cream, and skimming some of it for himself as he walked home. His next earliest memory was a vivid image of him consoling his younger brother by holding him. Because of his situation at home, the patient reported that his aunt decided to put him back in an orphanage, where he recalled feeling happy to be back in his "element." He married at age eighteen, had three children, and worked as an auto mechanic. As mentioned, the wife had a series of illnesses, which the patient prided himself on being able to "fix," much as he did cars.

The constant theme during treatment was his valued ability to be totally independent, denying any needs of his own, and seeing others as needy and dependent. This valued basis of continuity that served him well during adulthood was undermined by (1) his own illness, which threatened him with his own disavowed dependency; and (2) the loss of the presence of his wife, who probably served to affirm and sponsor his self-conception by functioning as a projective ecology: *she* was the needy one (not him), and his job, as with his cars, was to "fix" her.

We see how this man, owing to earlier trauma around unreliable parenting, fashioned a *compensatory* self-conception of being totally self-sufficient, independent, and in control. This man used the world and the various developmental arenas in his life-space (his work, body, and marriage) to sustain a crucial self-conception, one that formed the only basis for his self-continuity in old age. Although he was able to retire without difficulty, he lost the sense of self-continuity when his body and his wife no longer could provide a support for his self-conception. His crisis of self-discontinuity was fashioned around a threatened eruption of a disavowed self-conception, one that was experienced as alien. That is, his body, which had been the guarantor of self-sufficiency and control, had become "damaged" and no longer could function as a provider of help and nurture to his wife. Even though his wife was still needy, he could no longer physically care for her. At that point, his sense of identity threatened to be revealed as fantasy, rather than personal reality; and he experienced this threat as a devastating loss of self-continuity. "I am not what I used to be (and maybe I never was.)"

Another example of how internal and external factors interact to produce a crisis of self-discontinuity in later life is exemplified by Mr. B., a seventy-two-year-old man who attempted suicide by jumping into a river.

Case 2

Mr. B.'s failing eyesight, a result of bilateral macular degeneration, forced him to retire from his job as a "security man" at a local gambling operation. In addition, one week prior to his suicide attempt, a friend stole his life savings, leaving Mr. B. without the ability to support himself. Upon admission to the hospital, Mr. B. stated, "I am in a deep depression. I used to be independent, but my eyesight took me down. I was living pretty good, then my eyes did me in."

In the course of his treatment, Mr. B.'s investment in his independence and autonomy were predominant themes. An only child, he recalled his mother as "always sick" and unavailable during his childhood and adolescence. He described his father as a "good" but "strict" man who was preoccupied with his job and his wife's health. Mr. B. stated that his parents unavailability allowed him to "take advantage of the situation" and he fondly recalled playing hooky from school to swim with his friends in the local canal. He obtained his working papers at age fourteen, and prided himself on his ability to bring home money to help his parents. He married at age twenty-seven and obtained steady employment with the railroad. Six months after his marriage, his mother died, and his father passed away five years later, "of a broken heart." Mr. B.'s marriage lasted sixteen years, and ended in divorce after his wife discovered his philandering. The couple was childless because of his wife's inability to conceive.

Although coronary artery disease necessitated his retirement from the railroad, Mr. B., through an "associate," was able find work at a bookmaking operation. He valued his work, reporting that he spent twelve hours a day at his job. His job afforded him some financial security, and he proudly stated that he never applied for Social Security because he "didn't want a handout."

Like Mr. A., Mr. B. had a history of unreliable parenting, which fostered the development of a counterdependent character structure. In Mr. B.'s case, his work and body supported his sense of self as being independent and autonomous, not needing anyone to survive. The loss of his body's capacity to underwrite his ability to work undermined his self-identity and threatened him with the emergence of a disavowed self-conception, based upon an unconscious identification with his sick and dependent mother. That loss of self-continuity was implicated in his suicide attempt can be illustrated by his response when asked what his thoughts were as he jumped into the river: "I remember my pants came off and I thought back to when I was a kid swimming in the canals. I surprised myself—I was swimming for thirty minutes and I thought that

I could still swim. Then I wanted to live." This memory enabled Mr. B. to have a profound sense of *linkage* to his past, and his fear that he was no longer any remnant of his past self was partially alleviated.

Mr. A. and Mr. B. are only two examples of how a breach of self-continuity can induce first-time psychiatric conditions among the elderly. While it is easy to discern the outlines of unconscious conflict and threatened character defenses in both men, we feel that these factors are secondary to the perceived loss of the *reliable* and *constant* self in stimulating their depressive episodes. In other words, the intrapsychic conflicts and associated defenses had long ago been incorporated into the fabric of a congenial and unique self-organization. In later life, it was this congenial self that had become the basis of a vital sense of continuity. In effect, the character structure had taken on an additional (and superordinate) functional meaning in old age—the provision of a reliable sense of selfsameness in the face of change; and it was the sense of selfsameness that needed to be preserved, independent of its origin in earlier trauma.

The Therapeutic Reconstruction of Self-Continuity

Based on our clinical experience, we have come to appreciate the importance of reconstructing self-continuity as a fundamental psychotherapeutic goal with first-time patients of advanced age. Rather than using therapy as a source of insights about the self, or using the therapeutic relationship as a context to explore new parameters of interpersonal relatedness, our experience suggests that the aged use therapy to reconstitute, as much as possible, core bases of selfsameness that have been undermined in later life. Our clinical work is beginning to provide some insights into the therapeutic mechanisms that make such an outcome possible.

In essence, the therapeutic goal of reconstruction is reflected in the patient's successful accommodation to the changing realities of his or her life while reconstituting the essential themes that had formed the basis of self-identity. The therapeutic relationship provides a context within which the patient can reconstruct aspects of his disconnected self. In effect, the therapeutic relationship serves as a temporary replacement for the functions that had hitherto been performed by constancy-sustaining objects in the patient's psychosocial world. In part, this involves the therapist's ability to understand the importance of the patient's memories as vehicles for reviving the viability of the "old" self in the present. In addition, the therapist must understand that transference in the aged often serves as a basis for reconstructing a sense of self-continuity.

Our clinical experience dovetails with empirical reports (e.g., Revere and Tobin 1980) documenting the aged's heightened investment in and dramatization of their past. In therapy, this is manifest in the patient's reviving memories that illustrate the central themes forming the basis of self-identity. For example, Mr. A. repeatedly recalled episodes from his life wherein he portrayed himself as caring for others—his younger brother in childhood, other children at the orphanage, his wife during adulthood, and so on. Similarly, Mr. B. relished relating memories to his therapist that depicted himself as an independent, strong man who never needed help from others in order to survive. It was as if both Mr. A. and Mr. B. were attempting to communicate to their therapists those aspects of self that needed to be revived in the present.

By paying careful attention to the content of the patient's memories, the therapist can gradually formulate a clear notion of the "old" self that had been undermined in later life. In the beginning stages of therapy, the patient's memories tend to have a *decathected* quality: that is, the patient regards them as reflecting an aspect of the self no longer alive in the present. The therapist must not become bound to the patient's current perception of "reality." Instead, the therapist must follow the patient into the past and experience the vitality contained in the patient's memories. If the therapist responds appropriately to the patient's memories (i.e., instead of interpreting them as defensive against the present, the therapist listens with interest and enjoyment), the patient can begin to re-experience the past in the presence of a benign person whose involvement in the memories can revivify them. In effect, the patient externalizes decathected memories onto the figure of the therapist; and the therapist's involvement in the memories provides for a re-cathexis of them by the patient. As the patient gradually reactivates his memories by this process of "working through," he can begin to reintroject them as his own, thereby bolstering self-continuity. It is as if the patient can say: "Here I can experience myself as I once was; and because I can experience myself in this manner, I must still be the same person."

The reintrojection of decathected memories represents one aspect of the reconstruction process; the other part of therapy involves the transference relationship. In our experience, we have been impressed by the extent to which the therapist comes to be viewed as a representation of the patient's disconnected self. As the therapist participates in eliciting memories, the patient begins to view the therapist as a repository for his "old" self. That is, the patient begins to attribute to the therapist characteristics of the undermined self. For example, Mr. A. began to see his therapist as a "fighter" who "probably had to scrap a lot" when he was young. Although this form of relating has obvious narcissistic elements, we do not understand it as a simple manifestation of an idealizing or mirroring transference (Kohut 1971) because we do not regard the content of the projections as archaic, childhood imagos. Instead, the projections contain those aspects of self that, at one time, had constituted the basis of self-continuity.

This "old self" transference is a phenomenon that develops concurrently with the revival of memories. In part, the transference represents the patient's adaptive attempt to use the therapist as a vessel to contain and protect the "old self." It is crucial that the therapist refrain from interpreting this transference as defensive against the present. For example, Mr. A.'s therapist would remark: "You have always prided yourself on the ability to rise to any challenge; your circumstances today constitute another in a long series of challenges. Though you are unable to walk, you are still the same man." This intervention clarifies and supports an aspect of Mr. A.'s identity in the present; at the same time, it addresses a reality basis for his fear that he is not the same man. Through such interventions, the therapist reflects to the patient a crucial aspect of identity while also working to split it from the *concrete* support (that is, his legs) that had hitherto affirmed an aspect of self-continuity. In addition, as the therapist gradually understands the nature of the projected identity elements, he can use this information to help the patient find evidence in the present for manifestations of the "old self." These therapeutic interventions constitute another form of "working through" in therapy and eventually sponsor the *reinternalization* of aspects of the "old" or disconnected self.

Reconstructing self-continuity does not necessarily depend upon reinternalizing identity elements *isomorphic* with the "old" self that the patient *initially* presented to the therapist. In part, those identity elements tend to contain *exaggerated* self-representations, which are a defensive response to their threatened dissolution. In addition, our clinical experience indicates that therapy results in some accommodation of the "old" self to present realities, although this accommodation is not registered in the patient's *conscious* experience. This unconscious alteration of self-identity is subtle and occurs as a result of processes active in the patient and the therapist. In regard to the former, our experience suggests that there is an unconscious process in the patient that works toward modifying the past to achieve a better fit with present reality. That is, we have observed how, in the course of treatment, subtle alterations occur in the content of the patients' recalled history and the nature of the projected image onto the therapist. For example, Mr. A. subtly altered his memories of childhood to de-emphasize his *total* self-reliance; he gradually incorporated a few memories where he portrayed himself as receiving some limited help from others. At the same time, he slightly altered his projections to his therapist: the therapist, too, was perceived as less of a "scrapper." These limited manifestations of accommodation to the present are also sponsored by the therapist's verbal reflection of the projected image to the patient, that is, by the therapist's ability to perceive the patient in the past and the present. Through this interactive process, some accommodation of the patient's identity structure occurs without a loss of continuity. Thus, Mr. B., who had always avoided doctors and never applied for his Social Security, was able to do both without shame or anxiety during the course of his therapy. Nevertheless, he never *consciously* experienced these "new" behaviors as reflecting an alteration in his conviction that he was an independent man.

An important theoretical issue arises concerning the management of the transference to reconstruct self-continuity. That is, in the absence of systematically interpreting the defensive and distorting elements of the transference, how can reinternalization occur? It could be argued that the avoidance of transference interpretations constitutes simply a form of "gratification" that undermines the patient's "motivation" to reinternalize the image projected onto the therapist. We would argue, however, that internalization is a characteristic of normal developmental processes. As Hans Loewald (1960) has pointed out, ego development is predicated on the child's ability to internalize aspects of the parent, including the parent's image of the child—an image that is mediated to the child in numerous experiences and contacts. We think that a similar process occurs in the course of treatment with the aged. The many "frustrations" of treatment—separations, empathic failures, and so on—constitute the "motive" for reinternalization, as in normal development.

Conclusion

Freud (1924) argued long ago that psychoanalysis, formulated at that time as the interpretation of resistance (including the transference), was not the ideal vehicle for treating patients of advanced age. In addition to the wealth of material, Freud maintained that the mental rigidity of the aged made such a procedure unwarranted. In this chapter, we have arrived at a similar conclusion, though for different reasons. Although we agree with Freud that traditional psychoanalytic approaches are not the intervention of choice with the aged, we do so in view of certain developmentally informed theoretical and empirical considerations that modify core psychoanalytic assumptions regarding pathology and treatment.

In essence, we argued that *development* in later life consists of the construction and perpetuation of a highly stable sense of self. The search for self-continuity constitutes a superordinate functional requisite of adaptation in later life; as such, it assumes a hierarchical relationship to other motives influencing a person's orientation toward the self and the object world. We do not imply that conflict resolution is unimportant in later life, yet we view this organismic need as hierarchically integrated with (and therefore subordinated to) the need to consolidate self-continuity. Thus, we have argued that it is most productive to view pathogenesis in the aged as reflecting derailments of self-continuity; and we have proposed that, in essence, psychoanalytic therapy should be oriented *primarily* toward structural reconstruction and restoration, as opposed to change.

REFERENCES

Barnett, H. G. 1953. *Innovation: The Basis of Cultural Change.* New York: McGraw-Hill.

Belcher, J. 1958. "Acceptance of the Salk Vaccine." *Rural Sociology* 23:158–70.

Blatt, S. J., and Behrends, R. S. 1987. "Internalization, Separation-Individuation, and the Nature of Therapeutic Action." *International Journal of Psycho-Analysis* 68:-279–97.

Botwinick, J. 1977. "Intellectual Abilities." In *Handbook of the Psychology of Aging,* ed. J. E. Birren and K. W. Schaie, pp. 580–605. New York: Van Nostrand Reinhold.

Brenneis, C. B. 1975. "Developmental Aspects of Aging in Women: A Comparative Study of Dreams." *Archives of General Psychiatry* 32:429–35.

Buehler, C. 1935. "The Curve of Life as Studied in Biographies." *Journal of Applied Psychology* 19:405–409.

———. 1968. "The Course of Human Life as a Psychological Problem." *Human Development* 11:184–200.

Freud, S. [1917] 1957. "Mourning and Melancholia." In *Standard Edition,* ed. J. Strachey, vol. 14, pp. 243–58. London: Hogarth Press.

———. [1924] 1940. "On Psychotherapy." In *Collected Papers,* vol. 1. London: Hogarth Press.

Green, S.; Rich, T.; and Nesman, E. 1985. "A Cross-Cultural Look at the Relationship Between Age and Innovative Behavior." *International Journal of Aging and Human Development* 21:255–66.

Griffin, B. P. 1985. *Age Differences in Psychosocial Orientations Towards Continuity and Discontinuity: Keys to Understanding the Adaptive Value of Psychological Change in Later Life.* Ph.D. Diss., Northwestern University, Evanston, Ill.

Grunes, J.M. 1981. "Reminiscences, Regression, and Empathy—a Psychotherapeutic Approach to the Impaired Elderly." In *The Course of Life: Psychoanalytic Contributions Towards Understanding Personality Development, Vol. III, Adulthood and the Aging Process,* ed. S. I. Greenspan and G. H. Pollock, pp. 545–48. Washington, D.C.: National Institute of Mental Health.

Gutmann, D. L. 1982. "Age and Leadership: Cross-Cultural Observations." *Psychoanalytic Inquiry* 2:109–120.

———. 1987. *Reclaimed Powers: Towards A New Psychology of Men and Women in Later Life.* New York: Basic Books.

Gutmann, D. L.; Grunes, J. M.; Griffin, B. P.; and Jacobowitz, J. 1987. "A Model of Late-Onset Psychopathology." Paper presented at the 40th Annual Scientific Meeting of the Gerontological Society of America, Washington, D.C.

Horn, J. L. 1970. "Organization of Data on Life-Span Development of Human Abilities." In *Life-Span Developmental Psychology: Research and Theory*, ed. L. R. Goulet and P.B. Baltes, pp. 424–67. New York: Academic Press.

Kastenbaum, R. 1975. "Time, Death, and Ritual in Old Age." In *The Study of Time*, ed. J. T. Fraser and N. Lawrence, pp. 99–113. New York: Springer-Verlag.

Kohut, H. 1971. *The Analysis of the Self.* New York: International Universities Press.

Krohn, A., and Gutmann, D. L. 1971. "Changes in Mastery Style with Age: A Study of Navaho Dreams." *Psychiatry* 34:289–300.

Kuhlen, R. G. 1964. "Developmental Changes in Motivation During the Adult Years." In *Relations of Development and Aging*, ed. J. E. Birren, pp. 209–46. Springfield, Ill.: Charles C. Thomas.

Langer, J. 1969. *Theories of Development.* New York: Holt, Rinehart & Winston.

Lehman, H. C. 1953. *Age and Achievement.* Princeton: Princeton University Press.

Lieberman, M. A., and Tobin, S. S. 1983. *The Experience of Old Age.* New York: Basic Books.

Loewald, H. W. 1960. "On the Therapeutic Action of Psychoanalysis." *International Journal of Psycho-Analysis* 41:16–33.

Piaget, J. 1954. *The Construction of Reality in the Child.* New York: Basic Books.

Revere, V., and Tobin, S.S. 1980. "Myth and Reality: The Older Person's Relationship to His Past." *International Journal of Aging and Human Development* 12(1):15–26.

Rogers, E.M. 1962. *Diffusion of Innovations.* New York: Free Press.

Rosen, J. L., and Neugarten, B. L. 1964. "Ego Functions in the Middle and Later Years: A Thematic Apperception Study." In *Personality in Middle and Later Life*, ed. B. L. Neugarten et al., pp. 90–101. New York: Atherton Press.

Rowles, G. D. 1980. "Growing Old 'Inside': Aging and Attachment to Place in an Appalachian Community." In *Transitions of Aging*, ed. N. Datan and N. Lohmann, pp. 153–70. New York: Academic Press.

Shanan, J. 1968. *Psychological Changes During the Middle Years*, vol. 1. Jerusalem: Gons and Grafica.

Simmons, L. W. 1945. *The Role of the Aged in Primitive Societies.* New Haven: Yale University Press.

Sorokin, P. A. 1947. *Society, Culture, and Personality.* New York: Random House.

Stolorow, R. D., and Atwood, G. E. 1983. "Psychoanalytic Phenomenology: Progress Toward a Theory of Personality." In *The Future of Psychoanalysis*, ed. A. Goldberg, pp. 97–110. New York: International Universities Press.

Tobin, S. S., and Lieberman, M. A. 1976. *Last Home for the Aged.* San Francisco: Jossey-Bass.

Wapner, S.; Kaplan, B.; and Ciottone, R. 1981. "Self-World Relationships in Critical Environmental Transitions: Childhood and Beyond." In *Spatial Representation and Behavior Across the Life Span*, ed. L. S. Liben et al., pp. 251–82. New York: Academic Press.

Werner, H. 1948. *The Comparative Psychology of Mental Development.* New York: International Universities Press.

Werner, H., and Kaplan, B. 1963. *Symbol Formation.* New York: John Wiley & Sons.

DISCUSSION

In "Clinical Implications of Adult Developmental Theory" (Colarusso and Nemiroff 1987), we wrote that if the study of adult development is a psychiatric frontier, the clinical application of adult developmental theory is surely a lonely outpost on that frontier. We also predicted at the time that "as our knowledge of developmental processes in the second half of life increases, we should see continuous enhancement in psychotherapeutic technique and the need to continuously revise existing theories of normal development and pathology" (p. 1269). Further, we suggested that "perhaps we have reached the point where a detailed understanding of the second half of life may put the first half of life into perspective, instead of always the other way around" (p. 1269).

Drs. Griffin and Grunes's chapter fulfills many aspects of our hopes for and predictions of an adult developmental approach. The material presented here both enhances psychotherapeutic technique with older patients and advances our understanding of the second half of life. Theoretically, they make an important contribution in discussing the relationship between continuity and change through the life cycle. Writing from the perspectives of self psychology and object relations theory, they have presented a conceptualization of psychological adaptation in developmental theory, as maintaining an equilibrium between organismic processes that foster *both* continuity and change.

Specifically, psychotherapy has emphasized promoting change, particularly in working with younger patients. Griffin and Grunes cogently state that changes as the major factor in adaptation in general, and the focus of psychoanalytic therapy in particular, are misleading when considering adaptive processes and strategies for psychotherapeutic intervention in later life. They make the following organizing points about working therapeutically with the older patient:

1. Development in later adulthood is characterized by the adaptive construction of a highly stable sense of self.

2. One way that maladaptation can arise *for the first time* in later life appears to be when internal or external events attack crucial bases of self-continuity.

3. One approach to psychoanalytic therapy with the aged is to focus on the reconstruction of self-continuity in order to cope with the myriad changes of later life.

The authors present data from many studies that indicate that psychological adaptation in old age is related to the ability to maintain a stable and continuous self-representation in the face of various life transitions.

Further, these investigations suggest that the maintenance of self-continuity may be dependent upon a sustaining object world and that this object world is experienced as an important part of the self. Griffin and Grunes write:

> Just as we all rely, to some degree, on external objects to affirm and reinforce functions of the self (for example, self-esteem) and serve as id and superego protagonists, it is evident that the aged also use various external objects to affirm the historic self in later life. Theoretically, the type of object is variable: a spouse, job, geographic place, building, or even one's body. However, the function of the object would be invariant—to affirm constant, esteem-maintaining self-conceptions in facing the transitions of old age. Although people rely on the *environment* [italics ours] to underwrite the continuity of the self in varying degrees, that reliance is clearly a crucial adaptive strategy in later life. (p. 273)

The stated emphasis on the importance of the older patient's environment extends our concepts based on Spitz's (1975) definition of *development* as the emergence of forms, function, and behavior that are the outcome of exchanges between the organism on the one hand and the inner and outer environment on the other; and Hartman's ([1939] 1989) concept of *adaptation,* which he describes as primarily a reciprocal relationship between an organism and its environment. The critical concept in both those definitions is that development is the result of the *interaction* between biological organisms and their environments. One or the other pole may exert more influence, but never to the exclusion of the other. We took issue with the commonly held psychoanalytic idea that the adult, compared with the child, is relatively free of environmental influences. In contradistinction, we (1981) suggested that "in the achievement of new and phase-specific developmental tasks of adulthood, the individual is as dependent as the child on the environment" (p. 62). We described the influence of the environment mainly in young and middle adulthood, including the parents being replaced by the spouse and children, and the play environment being supplanted by the work environment. Creativity and work—including the most introspective, as in music, art, and literature—are empty unless they interpret human experience in relation to the environment and with others in mind. Clearly, Griffin and Grunes have shown how *crucial* aspects of the environment are for successful adaptation in later life.

Returning to clinical issues, they demonstrate the importance of reconstructing self-continuity as a fundamental psychotherapeutic goal with patients of advanced age. They and their older patients use therapy less as a source of insights about the self or a context to explore new parameters of interpersonal relatedness; rather, they find that the aged use therapy primarily to reconstitute *core bases of selfsameness that have been undermined in later life.* One of their useful techniques includes paying careful attention to the context of the patient's memories, gradually formulating a clear notion of the "old" self that had been undermined in old age, and helping the individual return to aspects of that former self.

Other clinicians have had this experience as well. In *The Race Against Time* (Nemiroff and Colarusso 1985) we described the adaptive value of both reminiscence and conduct of a life review with older patients in psychotherapy. Pollock (1981) has described the many ways in which reminiscence is important in work with older, particularly elderly patients. These include adaptational attempts, relational communication attempts, and self-therapeutic attempts.

> The recollections or fantasies of the past expressed in reminiscences help the elderly maintain a sense of continuity between past and present and between inside and outside. The events, relationships, and feelings recalled also maintain a sense of "me-ness." The recollection-reminiscences bridge time and maintain the sense of individual personality, especially when there is an inner awareness of diminishing ego intactness and competency. . . . In some, the obsessive reiteration-and-recounting is similar to mourning work where recalling-and-expressing is part of the self-healing process. . . . The insight of the psychoanalytic observer allows for understanding the meaning of what is otherwise considered "the ramblings of old men and women." (Pp. 279–80)

Robert Butler (1963) first postulated the important concept of *life review,* which systematically uses reminiscence in insight-oriented psychotherapy. After years of research, M. L. Lewis and Butler (1974) were able to describe the life review as a prominent developmental process of late life. They devised a number of methods of evoking memory in older persons that are both useful and enjoyable, and which, we feel, promote the process of recovery of self that Griffin and Grunes find essential in working with the older patient. These methods and techniques include (1) written or taped autobiographies; (2) pilgrimages; (3) reunions; (4) genealogies; (5) scrapbooks, photo albums, old letters, and other memorabilia; (6) summation of life work; and (7) preserving ethnic identity. Lewis and Butler (1974) sum up their life review methods by saying

> The success of the life review depends on the outcome of the struggle to resolve old issues of resentment, guilt, bitterness, mistrust, dependence, and nihilism. All the really significant emotional options remain available until the moment of death—love, hate, reconciliation, self-assertion, and self-esteem. (P. 171)

REFERENCES

Butler, R. N. 1963. "The Life Review: An Interpretation of Reminiscence in the Aged." *Psychiatry* 26:65–75.

Colarusso, C. A., and Nemiroff, R. A. 1981. *Adult Development: A New Dimension in Psychodynamic Theory and Practice.* New York: Plenum.

———. 1987. "Clinical Implications of Adult Development Theory." *American Journal of Psychiatry* 144(10):1269.

Hartman, H. 1958. *Ego Psychology and the Problem of Adaptation.* New York: International Universities Press.

Lewis, M., and Butler, R. N. 1974. "Life Review Therapy." *Geriatrics* 29:165–73.

Nemiroff, R. A., and Colarusso, C. A. 1985. *The Race Against Time: Psychotherapy and Psychoanalysis in the Second Half of Life.* New York: Plenum.

Pollock, G. H. 1981. "Reminiscence and Insight." *Psychoanalytic Study of the Child* 36:278–87.

Spitz, R. 1965. *The First Year of Life.* New York: International Universities Press.

11

The Awareness of the Nearness of Death, Depletion, and the Senescent Cell Antigen:

A Reconsideration of Freud's Death Instinct on the New Frontier between Psychodynamic Theory and Biology

STANLEY H. CATH

Introduction

Tucked away at the end of a summary on recent studies of molecular changes and the immune system associated with normal aging and the "Sustenance of Life" (Kay 1985), I found an immensely significant paragraph related to the practice of psychotherapy and psychoanalysis. Long-buried embers of doubt about dismissing Freud's (1921) dualistic life and death instinct theory as unduly pessimistic or philosophical immediately burst into flame.

I remembered Freud's caution: "What follows is speculation . . . which the reader will consider or dismiss according to his individual predilection. It is further an attempt to follow out an idea consistently, out of curiosity to see where it will lead" (p. 24).

My heuristic synthesis of aging, immunology, and the psychophysiological awareness of the biological force that returns us to an organic state is offered in the same spirit. Freud's experience-distant theory will be anchored more in reality by a presentation of an experience-near clinical encounter in which a patient's anxiety about the workings of her inner being and the imminence of death was contradicted by both medical experts and members of her family.

New Data on "The Frontier"

Marguerite Kay reports:

Investigations into the primary mechanisms of aging at a cellular level have demonstrated that molecular changes occur within membranes as cells age. A terminal differentiating antigen, the senescent cell antigen (SCA) appears on the membrane of cells . . . the appearance of this antigen marks the cell for destruction. IgG auto-antibodies in human cell serum attach to cells carrying senescent cell antigen and initiate their removal by macrophages. SCA seems to be generated by age-related degradation of band 3, the major anion (chlorine and bicarbonate) transport protein, also responsible for structural integrity of the plasma membrane. *Changes in cell membrane molecules affect not only the ability of the cells to interact with other cells in its environment but also the ability of subcellular components to interact within the cell. Many of the membrane molecules are structural components of micro-tubules and micro-filaments.* *

Kay characterized her work as a discussion of the ways in which the efficacy of the immune system's policing activity is diminished by age-related changes in its component parts and thus are reflected in intracellular and intercellular communication.

A Synthesis of Cath's Depletion Theory and Kay's Senescent Cell Antigen

> There are so many misleading sensations, they change their locality and quality to such an extent that there remains sufficient ground for "vague apprehensiveness." And they are so taxing that only a fraction of my interest is left over for the impressions of daily life.
> —Freud, *The Dissolution of the Oedipus Complex*

Freud's statement has always resonated with my own theories of a normative age-related depletion-restitution process monitored by the aging ego as it occurs in various components of five basic anchorages (Cath 1965). These include the biological or intact physical body, the family system, the social network, the economic anchorage, and the meaningful purposes to life. In the first half of life most changes across this range of anchorages may be regarded as developmentally evanescent, but in the second half of life more become depleting or senescent. Throughout the life span these losses are compensated for and adapted to by whatever restitution environmental resources and ego strengths allow. Various senescent changes interfere not only with intracellular functioning but intra-

*The most consistent pathological features found in primary senile dementia.

psychic balance and interpersonal communications as well. If one lives long enough, the ego's monitoring of the inner and outer worlds shifts inwardly, albeit unconsciously and invisibly, and to be depressed intermittently is inevitable. Much evidence suggests these bio-psychosocial transitions begin in the mid-thirties and continue at an accelerating rate unto the end of life (Schock 1961). Each individual grieves in his own fashion, restituting as well as he can to these nomethetic changes. Still, due to enhanced conscious and unconscious awareness of the nearness of death, the ego becomes more absorbed in policing depleting intrapsychic (for example, memory), interpersonal, and physiological processes. And post-midlife depletion of all basic anchorages is set in the real world, in contrast to a fantasied background in which the disappearance of loved ones predominates, but contrasts with reality. This grieving awareness may initiate or accelerate the "Race Against Time" with its secondary depleting effects upon the immune system (S. H. Cath and C. Cath 1984).

Selective diminishment of extero- enteroceptive and adaptive faculties may be set in an individual whose sensitivity receptors remain intact and tuned-in to the body's messages of pain and dysfunction. Even though ever greater quantities of psychic energies are needed to deal with these age-specific psychophysiological harbingers of death, more often than not, less is available. Granted, the achievements of creative mourning and enhanced integrity in some, a condition posited as desired norms by Erik Erikson (1959) and G. Pollock (1982), is not what I encounter in most of my elder patients. Rather a "silent information overload" related to the insidious onset of not yet diagnosable diseases (such as arteriosclerosis) accompanies awareness of a general depletion of reserves (loss of endurance) and omniconverges with increasing familiarity with the dying and death of relatives and friends. These changes require new disavowals of the realities of aging and new levels of adaptive defenses. As it was with Freud, these compromises may be channeled into a morbid but adaptive somatic preoccupation linked to depressive or hypomanic proclivities of middle and later years. On the basis of clinical data I hypothesized that the nature and quality of the last days of our mid-years and our final years are likely to be the result of the coping capacities for the unique combination of the above traumas, depletions, and exhaustions plus *a still undeciphered genetic program*. This determines "the mean-time to failure" of specific, sometimes localized cells, tissues, organs, or systems. It may not all happen at the same time or at the same rate. With a limited "jugfull of immunity," given at birth, stressed by nutritional deficiencies or abuses, developmental failures or arrests, exposure to noxious agents, toxins, and undue stress (some avoidable, like tobacco, and some not), most elders struggle with an age-altered ego to intrapsychically and intraphysiologically balance and restitute for this crescendo of assault-losses. Kay's observation that age seems to promote the growth of invasive cells approximates my formulation (Cath 1984) that age and stress increase immunologic vulnerability to viruses and virions that we have lived with intimately all our lives.

Another impression of the later years, at least partly androgen-linked, involves increasing differences in the destinies of males and females. Women seem more resistant to disease than men and outlive the opposite sex by 7.4 years (Hazzard 1986). This discrepancy enhances the out-of-sync life-span trajectory, which creates in the long-married a dragged-out conflict about their differing perceptions of disease and death at the same age. Oftimes a man in his sixties is more like his wife in her seventies. Many women are secretly furious that their husband's decline so seriously hinders their ongoing relationships with peers.

With Kay's work I would suggest we must consider the elderly person's perception of loss of internal vitality as related, at least, in part, to the effects of SCA. This seems a basic truth and challenges the overused, oversimplistic diagnosis of neurotic depression in late life. The differences in male and female tolerance for the experiences of aging may be a reflection of the timing of SCA appearance or other sex-linked characteristics related to genetic differences in their life-span trajectory manifested by various hormonal levels. Decades of experience in psychotherapy and psychoanalysis with long-lived people reinforce the value of correlating significant gender bio-psychosocial differences in coping with (or disavowing) various forms of depletion, depression, and annihilation anxiety as it is stimulated from within the organic substrata of the total self. The differential diagnosis of depression, depletion, excessive antigen production, and dementia is becoming ever more complicated, requiring a team of interdisciplinary specialists to facilitate diagnosis and treatment.

Beyond and Beyond the Pleasure Principle

After my initial aha! reaction to Kay's observations, I promptly reread Freud's (1920) "Beyond the Pleasure Principle," attempting to understand even more his reasoning of a death instinct in terms of his mind set, his age, and his milieu.

At the end of the first World War, Freud, in his early sixties, had enjoyed many psychoanalytic successes but suffered many defeats as well. "Resistant" patients remained unaffected by his best efforts; and, as part of a defeated and humiliated Germany he was hungry, ill, and disillusioned. From his own letters, it seems safe to assume he was depleted by personal losses and the traumatic "defections" in his professional and sociopolitical life. In this frame of mind, he once again, as in 1896–97, turned his still resilient mind to the eternal problem of why his patients (and people in general) resisted "change," tending instead to repeat endlessly and compulsively the most painful and destructive patterns of behavior, including that of war. In this work, he reasoned that a strong tendency toward the pleasure principle exists, but it is opposed by certain other forces, which are not always in harmony with pleasure or survival. Noting that the exceptions to pleasure were the war neuroses and the traumatic neuroses of peace, he saw the common element as surprise without time to prepare.

At that time Freud postulated a dualism between life and death wishes. He considered traumatic dreams, theater audiences, or the child at play similarly repeating stories of great unpleasure because the repetition produced unpleasure of another sort, more primitive and more independent. He had found in transference and in life the compulsion to repeat not only frequently overrode the pleasure principle but also often recalled experiences marked by narcissistic scars, a sense of inferiority, and the impression of being pursued by a malignant fate. To the best of my knowledge, by "primitive" he did not mean, as I do, the predetermined biological aspects of selective repetition in neuronal networks due to cellular chemistry. But he did describe man as

> a living vesicle with its receptive cortical layer . . . a little fragment of living substance suspended in the middle of an external world . . . charged with the most powerful energies . . . his cells would be killed by the energies emanating from these were it not provided with a protective shield . . . by its outermost surface ceasing to have the structure proper to living matter . . . it becomes to some degree inorganic . . . by its death the outer layer has saved the deeper ones from a similar fate . . . protection against stimuli is an almost more important function than reception of them. (1920, p. 27, italics added)

It is my hypothesis that the protection just noted is also needed by the ego; protection against the bombardment of messages of organic cellular decline, fighting inner stimuli heralding the death of tissue, or even more ominously, the death of personhood (Cath and Herzog 1982). Freud's concept of an external shield protecting against a hostile extential environment and my theory—an omniconvergence of organic and psychological changes requiring protection against overwhelming and shattering inner messages—are concordant with Kay's current scientific findings on senescent processes. The need for a protective shield is underscored by appreciating the complexities involved in living long, including the inevitable loss of immunosurveillance and *loss of adaptive capacities for restitution.*

In hindsight Freud was both brilliant and of necessity, limited by his time, oversimplistic. But, his own aging would bring additional insight. For example, he wrote that the death instincts work unobtrusively (Shur 1972).

Not unconsciously, he may have been responding to SCA and probably a host of other unknown messengers. I believe it is "healthy narcissism" to be reluctant to accept the inevitability of the blows our genetic fate has in store. Jones (1957) entitled his chapter delineating Freud's losses and restitution "Progress and Misfortune," an apt description of the sixth and seventh decade of life for most of us. Do we not all shudder at the slow wasting process in any finely attuned and uniquely trained human being, or the aggressive ravages inherent in the passage of time, as observed first in grandparents or in others near and dear to us? In this light, nature seems quite random but probably is exquisitely designed and timed in its manufacture of SCA. The processes involved provide for the removal of dying and dead cells, thereby protecting the whole body from the toxic accumulation of waste materials. Thus aging cells will be (age-appropriate) marked for destruction no matter what we do, who we are, or how well we have lived. While beneficial, it still seems indiscriminate and sadistic, as we apply our own value systems to the death of an innocent child or a Sigmund Freud. But, since I am reassessing Freud's theory in light of new biological findings, let me return to his subsequent salient observations (1921–23) to illustrate why I think Freud changed his mind as he "cooly" experienced the forces of organic nature as "not so unobtrusive."

Jones (1957) reports "About this time Freud's constant complaints about being old took a sudden turn":

> On March 13 of this year I quite suddenly took a step into real old age. *Since then the thought of death has not left me. Sometimes I have the impression that seven of my internal organs are fighting to have the honor of bringing my life to an end.* There was no proper occasion for it, except that Oliver said goodbye on that day when leaving for Rumania. Still I have not succumbed to this hypochondria, *but view it quite cooly, rather as I do the speculations in* Beyond the Pleasure Principle. (Pp. 78–79)

As we will see, Freud's coolness was then replaced by a comprehensible indifference. In February 1923 the first signs of leukoplakia appeared. Freud did nothing about it for a couple of months, nor did he mention it to anyone. But later he wrote,

> Not an hour free of pain since the treatment ceased . . . a comprehensible indifference to most of the trivialities of life shows me that the working through the mourning (for a grandson) is going on in the depths. Among these trivialities I count science itself, I have no fresh ideas and have not written a line.* (P. 91)

*He seemed able to admit he was mourning, with comprehensible indifference not only for his grandson, but also for his intellectual life force, e.g., "no fresh ideas."

As if this were not enough depletion and tragedy, further trauma was waiting in the wings. It happened another grandchild, "Heinerle," of whom Freud was extremely fond (the one he called the most intelligent child he had ever encountered), had had a tonsillectomy and adenectomy at the same time as Freud's first surgery on his jaw. When they met postoperatively, Heinerle had especially cheered him by the question, "I can eat crusts, can you?" But, four months later (in June 1923) Heinerle was dead of military tuberculosis. It was said to be "the only occasion of his life when Freud was known to have shed tears" (Jones 1957, p. 92).

To summarize: Freud was remarkably accurate "in his enteroceptive perceptions" of his "so soon exhausted capacities" as reflecting the return to the inorganic. His progressive imagery is not only in accord with Kay's findings but with my concept of midlife ego monitoring and reflecting, in mood and behavior, both natural and pathological depletion-restitution processes, summating over time in all basic anchorages (Cath 1965). In sociology, this phenomenon has been described as "disengagement" (Cummings and Henry 1961), a theory almost as unpopular as my own or as Freud's (1966) "return to the inorganic," "the goal of all life is death" (p. 47), and "in the long run the pleasure principle actually serves the death instincts" (p. 63), for they all are severe blows to our pride.

In 1914, in "the project" Freud had hypothesized "all provisional ideas in psychology will presumably some day be based on an organic substructure" (p. 48). Recently many analysts (e.g., Reiser 1984; Cooper 1985; Cath 1987; Schwartz 1988) have addressed this interface between the dynamic and the organic, heralding a long-overdue rapprochement between neurology and psychodynamic theory. To me it seemed the SCA may be considered a factor far beyond Freud's "pleasure principle," beyond his "primary masochism," and even beyond his concept of a "death instinct." I believe he would have agreed that with this additional biological data we may indeed limp a little less.

A Clinical Application of this Synthesis

Let me now explicate the role of a psychoanalyst-psychiatrist interested in the complex interface between aging, stress, the awareness of the nearness of death, immunocompetency, and the family system. This will be a report on a brief (six-contact) intervention in a case that not only plied his

By not mentioning it to anyone he seemed to disavow that which he admitted consciously to others in the past, that he knew his smoking had led to this harbinger of a disease that might kill him (Jones 1957, p. 91).

taxonomy, but challenged old basic paradigms and therapeutic strategies. The richness of the history underscores Freud's reservations about the complexity of working with people in their later years.

A former patient telephoned to say, "You helped me when I felt lost and wanted to die . . . maybe you will do the same for my eighty-year-old sister. She has been discharged from the hospital and is at home with a nasogastric tube and on intravenous feedings. She is weak, seriously depressed, very demanding, and going downhill fast. When she says she wants to die, I just can't handle it. I become angry and rude and, like the rest of the family, try to force her to eat. She is ruining her husband's and son's life, not to mention mine. When I told my brother-in-law my sister seemed to have a death wish, he cried and said maybe the kindest thing would be to let her die. But then she asked me to get someone to talk to. I described you as a psychiatrist who was also a geriatric genius. She agreed to see you. I remembered you do home visits, won't you come?"

At the end of the day, with the family's permission, I spoke to the internist on the phone. Used to rather atypical syndromes of overlapping depressive-depletion and/or dementia in the elderly, I still found Dr. N's description of his patient unique. "She demands lots of time . . . holds my hand . . . won't let me go . . . even in the middle of the night. I tried everything . . . she just will not eat or swallow food, not even liquids. She says 'I can't' and at one point she even asked for the nasogastric tube herself. I can't tell if she's catatonic, just starving herself to death, or on a hunger strike, but she's down to eighty-six pounds. One day she was speaking a language no one could understand but seemed to have moments of clarity. Even though she will not comply with medical treatments, she seems to have a tremendous life force. She talks about wanting to speak to one of her children and the rest of the family before she dies. There is a history of psychiatric problems. She was psychotically depressed in the seventies. In the last month, she hallucinated a vivid sexual encounter and talked about the religions of the world, so I put her on some Haloperidol. With this history of mood swings, I hospitalized her. Our liaison psychiatrist prescribed antidepressants, but that only exacerbated things, constipation you know. She had so many phobias we tried Alprazolam, but that depressed her more and she developed some arrthymias. She always had gastrointestinal complaints. She's tried est, yoga, transcendental meditation, et cetera. In her early sixties it all led to abdominal surgery and several operations for adhesions after that. She has had cystic breasts, a myocardial infarction in 1971, and hospitalization for a severe virus infection the first of this year. Following this illness, she spent a recuperative period somewhere in the

South. There she saw a psychiatrist twice a week for a spell. But, she has still not recovered her strength and has not worked in the kitchen or at her art since. She cannot finish a meal and seems to have lost interest in everything. A GI series, chemistries, ultrasound, a CAT scan—all negative. I sure hope you can do something to help."

The next day the husband, a most intelligent, successful, and sensitive man described his despair to my social worker. "I love my wife very much. It wasn't all roses but I respect and admire her. How do you respond when your wife says 'help me, I want to go. If you don't I'll slash my wrists!' " Then in front of you she pulls out her nasogastric tube. I tell her she'll be fine and that I don't want to lose her, but I can't stand to be in the same room with her and see what she's doing to herself. She's still so beautiful and lovely. It breaks my heart. Some nights when we can't get a nurse I spend the 12 to 8 A.M. shift with her. We just get weepy together and I try to cheer her up but it doesn't work. There are two people in her, one who wants to go and is bent on self-destruction and one who wants to live. It's too much, I can't be a male nurse. One of my sons can tolerate his mother being this way, but I and the others find ourselves avoiding her. All except the chaplain, she's become very religious. None of the doctors seem to know what is happening."

My first contact at 9 P.M. on a weeknight with this bedridden, wan, and emaciated patient is not to be forgotten. The setting was her bedroom in which her art was intermingled with hospital equipment. Far from being withdrawn or typically depressed, she was warm, appealing, engaging, and quite rational. Because she could not swallow even liquids, she knew she was dying from some fatal disease. Like Tolstoy's Ivan Illyitch, she found no one either believed or could accept her version of her state or her sense of the imminence of death. Wanting to eat to please her family, she denied being on a hunger strike, the accusation initially made by one consulting psychiatrist. She asked if not eating was the reason her husband kept away from her? She had no explanation for not being able to swallow except that food would just not go down. The doctors could find nothing. It was all so hopeless. Her eyes were so dry, she could not read, "a terrible loss." She also kept repeating "it can't be all in my head." When I noted agreement and observed, "There are many possible reasons for such symptoms"; that she did not seem inappropriately disturbed or inordinately depressed to me; that indeed we doctors did not always know what was wrong; and that she may be more accurate than anyone else in her perceptions of herself or her body, she held my hand and began to tell me of her life, its highs and lows.

Remember, my patient had a built-in transference from her sister. In a short time my countertransference was colored by the impression of being in the cachectic presence of a remarkable, talented, beautiful, and insightful woman. She had come to this country as an adolescent. In this finely tuned first encounter, she shared intimate details of many things she felt she had missed in her life. These covered a wish for a more rewarding, affectionate, sexual life with her busy, ambitious husband; disappointments in the careers, marriages, and divorce of her children and in the lack of grandchildren; and finally in the suicide of one of her parents.

Despite her current fear of dying too soon—she felt she had still much to say in her art—she still longed to stop her pain and the emotional burden on her family. She had thought of suicide; her father had gone that way; but she especially wanted to know it was not "all in my head." When she realized I could understand and accept that she was attuned to something no one else could feel, she begged me to return anytime, any day, and every day if I could. She was obviously lucid, in excellent contact, and quite available for a therapeutic relationship—even if furious at psychiatrists who had told her she was noncompliant, suicidal, or on a hunger strike.

It was about 11 P.M. when the family convened in the kitchen to hear, in the husband's words, "what the expert had to say." For the purpose of this chapter, I will focus on the heuristic application of psychoanalytic understanding as enriched by new basics in immunocompetency to family dynamics.

I had learned from an intake interview by my social worker that this was a patriarchal family organized around an intense, well-put-together, successful, and verbal man. His children had trouble succeeding except in very protected, noncompetitive settings. Obviously, they were in awe of their father as well as of their strikingly beautiful, talented, but frail European-style mother. Strong ambivalent eddies about her living and dying were sensed under a concerned, superlogical surface. But they asked me to be frank and to explain what I thought was going on. In such contradictory circumstances, just what were they to believe?

After listening to their concerns, I told them that after only one meeting with her any statements I made should be taken tentatively, despite my experience with elderly patients and families. I would consider their modifications of my evaluation welcome since they knew much more about her life than I. While appreciating their immediate overload, I considered it possible to work out a less-conflicted and more humane approach to this very difficult situation. In my opinion we were confronted by a woman who was convinced she was dying even though no one could find out why. Our challenge would be how not to isolate her by our tendency to deny her perceptions in the face of ambiguity and the reality of our wishes to the contrary. Because it was difficult to see her this way, we wanted her to believe what we wished her to believe about the terrifying changes that she sensed going on inside herself. I proposed that we begin by considering it possible for people to sense their own depletion and final decline into death.

I expressed my respect for their mutual support of each other. Indeed, they had organized and ensured the best possible nuturance, protection, and medical care for their mother and wife at home. I suggested that in the face of conflicting medical evidence, they could not possibly determine the right approach. The family's anxiety about her suicidal impulses was especially high. For them, the issue became whom and what to believe.

The following, in somewhat less technical but expanded terms, is my best reconstruction of what I tried to convey about the aging process in this "kitchen consultation."

My cardinal premise is that with the passage of years every person's ego becomes increasingly preoccupied, both when awake and asleep, with changes related to aging by means of a sensing or monitoring apparatus working deep within. This includes all the bio-psychosocial-physiological changes inherent in living long. These changes not only alter the meaningful activities in life in general but also lead to reiterated inventories of the meaningful roles and interactions actualized within the family. In late life, the one certain, still growing part of the self may be this "ego sensor" (Cath and Berezin 1965). It converts and synthesizes potentially threatening information from cells, tissues, organs, and psychological systems into affectively charged imagery. Each unit of input from all tissues and systems reinforces the other and determines basic moods and relationships by influencing neural transmission. But these changes are interpreted and reinterpreted by the unique style of coping permitted by an often intermittently declining memory bank, thereby impacting differently upon functioning. As a result of the combination of this continuous feedback process and the person's characteristic responses to disease, the degree of aged-intactness may lead to either sensed well-being (eutonia) or a form of miserable depletion-depression. The sense of well-being, or the lack of it, emerges anew every day. It is reflected in the affectively charged energic supply played out in the interpersonal realm and recognized by others in a general way as mood or energy. It is reported to the family and to the doctor in emotionally charged self-evaluative reports on energy or lack thereof, as well as the degree of appetite for life, love, and food.

This ongoing synthesis of conscious and unconscious assessments from multiple sources is then interpreted under the aegis of and according to the characterological index of anxiety about body intactness held by the individual, the family, and the doctors involved. Awareness of depletion of reserves is amplified by the sensed nearness of death. But they can be multiplied by each person's intolerance for imperfection in the ideal, productive, loving, and active self. A feedback loop between intrapsychic, organic, and psychosocial factors is created that is difficult for family and professionals to evaluate. In my opinion such people have often been erroneously and oversimplistically labeled as depressed. To be sure, they are depressed secondarily, but the depression is only part of a highly complex and little-appreciated syndrome. The effects of the multitude of medications usually found in the medicine chest of those over sixty-five have to be considered as well.

This problem is compounded when someone close to us, like a mother or wife, seems to shrink before our eyes or exhibits symptoms for which no organic cause can be found. Often clinical and laboratory evidence is either obtuse or negative: especially in the presence of a positive psychiatric history, the tendency of most caregivers is to dump both patient and mysterious syndromes into the wastebasket of "functional" or "psychiatric," and the patient's interpretation of the referral is "they think it's all my imagination!" But "referral dumping" creates the residual suspicion that something is being overlooked. Furthermore, every elder worries about the most dreaded phobia of all time, namely, losing one's mind. In my experience the most helpful first step has been to listen to an elder's attempts to apprehend and acknowledge the multiple distressing realities in and under which he or she lives.

I instinctively felt that this patient knew more accurately than her physicians what might be going on inside of her. I had reassured her about the intactness of her mind. In essence, I believed her perception of her reality and would advise the family to do the same. Her depressions in the past may have misled them into discounting today's immediate perceptions and complaints. Anyone experiencing that degree of pain, apparent wasting (cachexia), and obvious discomfort has a right to feel despair, if not a wish to die. Indeed, she did not seem typically or atypically depressed to me, nor did her anxious concern seem inappropriate. Rather, she seemed to be listening to her body and her discomfort, learning when and what she could or could not swallow.

Like Illyitch she felt isolated and disbelieved—feelings that contributed to her despair. Admittedly, some emotionally predisposed people may sense disaster and disintegration at any age, either as a result of premonitions of or internal perceptions; and, with no objective findings, such a dilemma challenges the best differential diagnostic skills. When a skilled psychotherapist cannot be sure how much is fantasy or reality, it should not be a loved one's responsibility to decide. The first step for this family was to accept her premise, based upon self-scanning, that something serious was keeping her from swallowing, causing pain, anergia, and severe emaciation. Furthermore, under the circumstances, I believe that her wish to die had rational components.

I added there were two things I could now do. The first was to respond to her request for someone to talk to who believed her. The second, with their permission, was to reopen the possibility of further medical investigation—a procedure I suspected was strongly indicated. By adopting these approaches we could reduce, almost immediately, a terrible load upon her and them. At least for tonight, despite her complaints I felt her demeanor, affect, and associations all indicated she really wanted to live.

She had implied, if only she could be comfortable and not a burden while still lucid, that she wished "to set things right with her family." I doubted that she was really uncooperative, noncompliant, or seriously suicidal, but I also understood that such severe pain can make death appealing. Although she had been delirious and hallucinated in the past, I reassured them she was not now psychotic. I speculated it was possible that not eating might reflect microscopic damage to her appestat in the central nervous system; or it might be caused by some undefined difficulty in swallowing, just as she alleged. I was reasonably certain she was not on a "hunger strike." Her hallucinations might be explainable on some biochemical ground ranging from isolation to a hepato-cephalic toxicity. I told them that her history rendered the latter as the more likely potential generator of her delusions. They were visibly affected and moved by this new perspective, looking at each other with incredulity. I left at midnight to sneak quietly into bed beside my sleeping wife.

After a telephone consultation with the internist the next day, the patient was rehospitalized within the week. An ultrasound of the abdomen revealed secondary neoplastic masses in the liver, primary from the esophagus. They now extended up and around her esophagus, explicating all her symptoms. The husband reported the whole family had felt tremendous relief, especially from the guilt and the pressure to force her to act differently. Now despite the nearness of death, they were impressed by "the life force within." The patient called various members of the family together to say goodbye. The family and doctors agreed to medicate her to alleviate inordinate pain. Before she died, I had three more talks with her and three with the family. In their words, they were "brief but most meaningful."

Concluding Remarks

Undoubtedly, because death is evitable, the death instinct, in contrast to a life force, has made few friends. Most analysts have preferred to think of its roots in Freud's lifelong preoccupation with his own death and his persistent pessimism about man's blind pursuit of the art of destruction.

It is true that Freud's concept of a life and a death instinct arose in the context of his time and appeared in a terminology that was in vogue. Although his theories became a troublesome set of contradictory ideas, they reflected the best scientific knowledge available. His notions were not based primarily upon clinical psychoanalytical data and, accordingly, lacked the seductive intelligibility of most of his other writings.

Reiser (1984) has observed, appropriately, that such ideas, theories and constructs should be judged independently of the context in which they were written or of the limits of scientific knowledge at the time. Thus, we may well take exception to Freud's wording, but the essential elements now need to be reintegrated into the context of emerging current scientific data, such as the presence of a senescent cell antigen. The ideas presented here have been set in the author's accumulated body of clinical experience derived from working with elderly, who are keenly aware of the nearness of death.

Today the increasing potential for a silent return of the earth to lifelessness, to an inorganic state, may seem less instinctual and more related to another of Freud's overt concerns, namely, mankind's designed grasping for immediate comfort, power, and wealth; our capacity to spoil the world we live in—to pollute its atmosphere. We can be grateful to those who, following in Freud's footsteps, continue to explore the frontiers between biological and psychological forces. Our life forces can be enhanced only if we accept the responsibility to study and differentiate the reality of the necessary and unnecessary destructive forces generated from within as well as those that surround us—some of which seem, indirectly at least, to determine our destiny.

REFERENCES

Cath, S. H. 1987. "The Psychodynamic Implications of the Senescent Cell Antigen: A Hypothesis and Clinical Illustration." Paper presented at a scientific meeting of the Chicago Psychoanalytic Society, June 23.

Cath, S.H., and Berezin, M., 1965. *Grief, Loss and Emotional Disorders in the Aging Process.* New York: International Universities Press.

302 CLINICAL PERSPECTIVES

Cath, S.H., and Cath, C., 1984. "The Race Against Time." In *Psychotherapy and Psychoanalysis in the Second Half of Life,* ed. R. A. Nemiroff and C. A. Colarusso, pp. 241–62. New York: Plenum.

Cath, S.H., and Herzog, J. M. 1982. "The Dying and Death of a Father." In *Father and Child,* ed. S. H. Cath et al., pp. 339–53. Boston: Little, Brown.

Cooper, A. M. 1985. "Will Neurobiology Influence Psychoanalysis?" *American Journal of Psychiatry* 142:1395–1402.

Cummings, E., and Henry, W. E. 1961. *Growing Old. The Process of Disengagement.* New York: Basic Books.

Erikson, E. 1959. *Identity and The Life Cycle.* New York: International Universities Press.

Freud, S. [1921] 1966. "Beyond The Pleasure Principle." In *Standard Edition,* ed. J. Strachey, vol. 18, pp. 3–64. London: Hogarth Press.

———. [1924] 1966. "The Dissolution of the Oedipus Complex." In *Standard Edition,* ed. J. Strachey, vol. 19, pp. 173–79. London: Hogarth Press.

Hazzard, W.R., 1986. "Biological Basis of the Sex Differential in Longevity." *American Geriatric Society* 34:455–71.

Jones, E. 1957. *The Life and Work of Sigmund Freud,* vol. 3. New York: Basic Books.

Kay, M. 1985. "What is Normal Aging? Part IX: Immunological Changes Associated with Normal Aging." *Geriatric Medicine Today* 4 (1):30–39.

Pollock, G. 1982. "Mourning and Creativity." Presented at the Fiftieth Anniversary of the Institute for Psychoanalysis, Chicago, Illinois.

Reiser, M. 1984. *Mind, Brain, Body: Towards a Convergence of Psychoanalysis and Neurobiology.* New York: Basic Books.

Schock, N. W. 1961. "Symposium on Aging." *American Association for the Advancement of Science.*

Schwartz, A. 1988. "On Narcissism: An(other) Introduction—Neurobiologic, Experimental Psychologic, and Ethologic Looks at Pleasure, Pain, and a Needlessly Controversial Phenomenon." Presented at the American Psychoanalytic Association Convention, Montreal, Canada, May.

Shur, M. 1972. *Freud, Living and Dying.* New York: International Universities Press.

Wantanabe, H. 1981. "The Aging Changes of Apical Dendritic Spines in Human Pyramidal Cells." *Yokufukai Journal* no. 6, Tokoyo, Japan.

DISCUSSION

Dr. Cath begins his chapter with a discussion of Kay's theory of senescent cell antigen (SCA), a putative product of aging cells that is thought to mark them for destruction by macrophages. The presence of SCA in the cell membrane means that the cell cannot function normally internally or interact normally with others in its environment.

Dr. Cath goes on to relate Kay's theory of cellular destruction to his own notion of depletion and restitution, a psychological process in which the ego continually assesses the effects of aging and the approach of death. As the intact physical body, the family system, the social network, economic conditions, and meaningful purposes to life—five anchorages—shift from evanescence in response to developmental progression in the first half of life toward depletion and senescence in late adulthood, "various senescent changes interfere not only with intracellular but intrapsychic balance and interpersonal communications" (pp. 289–90). In other words, a parallel and interrelated process of depletion and senescence occurs at both organic and psychological levels. Dr. Cath's discussion is important precisely because he provides us with a plausible theory that increases our understanding of the interaction between biological and psychological forces in late adulthood.

If one is lucky enough to live a long life, intermittent depression is inevitable, Dr. Cath tells us, because of the conscious and unconscious monitoring of the processes of physical decline and the contemplation of loss of the self through death. A possible stimulus to the life review described by Butler (1963), this "healthy depression" is an affective indication that the depletion-restitution cycle is doing its job. As Dr. Cath reminds us, depression in older patients is an exceedingly complex phenomenon and requires intense diagnostic study if it is to be understood and treated correctly.

In a statement that may surprise some, but which is consistent with our own theory, Cath, along with Schock (1961) suggests that this bio-psycho-social transition begins in the mid-thirties. We feel their choice of the mid-thirties as a starting point for the process may be a bit late. In our scheme, psychological development from birth to death is intimately related to the body's maturational progression during childhood and its beginning decline from the mid-twenties on. Signs of aging such as premature balding and loss of a youthful appearance are present in a few by age twenty-five, in many by age thirty-five. By their mid-thirties, most individuals have begun to monitor actively the aging process in their bodies, particularly women, who are acutely aware of the impending loss of the ability to bear children.

Dr. Cath describes how the elderly devote more and more psychic energy to the containment of the "silent information overload." This is a critically important process because the quality of life in late adulthood is directly related to the individual's ability to erect defenses against the growing awareness of depletion and to continue to channel psychic energy and attention into meaningful activity in the present.

The value of the depletion-restitution cycle as a theoretical construct was enhanced for us when Dr. Cath related it to the organic substrata, to the "still undeciphered genetic program" which determines *when* specific cells, tissues, and organic systems will fail (p. 290). The considerable clinical usefulness of the concept was demonstrated when it served as the theoretical framework on which he built his understanding of his patient's symptoms and reconstruction of her physical and mental state for the family. In a similar manner, this skilled clinician brings to life the 7.4-year statistical difference between men and women. He suggests that a man in his sixties is more like his wife in her seventies. Many women are very angry because their husband's decline seriously hinders their ongoing relationships with peers (p. 291). In our experience, the fury is sometimes not so secret. The clinician who works with older patients should be keenly aware of the effect of a major illness on the *healthy* partner, be it husband or wife. The therapist may need to give permission, even active encouragement, to the healthy partner to maintain relationships and interests in the face of the spouse's illness and possible approaching demise.

Dr. Cath describes Freud's state of depletion in relation to his age, his clinical work, and his post–World War I experience. After describing Freud's ideas on the repetition compulsion and the death instinct, he brings together his own ideas, Kay's, and Freud's, finding in all three the need for the aging body/mind to protect itself from internal and external threats to its integrity. Dr. Cath suggests that in the light of our current knowledge of "the inevitable loss of immunosurveillance and loss of adaptive capacities for restitution" (p. 292) Freud's death instinct does not sound implausible.

Always the clinician, and using Freud as an example, he reminds us that the muting of empathy so essential to our work must to be included in this late-life inventory of diminished responses. If we are sensitive to our own inner processes, we will begin to recognize, as Freud did, when he felt that a crust of indifference was slowly creeping up around him, and end our clinical endeavors before we become a burden to our patients.

In the final section of his chapter, Dr. Cath allows us to see how a creative, experienced gerontologist thinks and works. Meeting his eighty-year-old patient and her family in their home—all meaningful diagnosis and therapy need not take place in an office or hospital—he begins his work. We are struck by the difference between his matter-of-fact description of his interaction with her internist and husband and the animated account of his first meeting with the patient herself. The point we wish to make is how completely he was able to *engage* his patient, to listen to her, empathize with her plight, and validate *her* perceptions that something was wrong with her body. She immediately recognized this accepting attitude, so different from that of her family, physicians, and previous psychiatrists, and quickly developed an intense therapeutic relationship with him.

Equally fascinating is the diagnostic seminar with the family, held at the kitchen table. How many clinicians would take the time to explain in such detail to these troubled and confused people what was going on in their loved one? The puncturing of their tension is palpable.

Dr. Cath does not describe his subsequent sessions with the patient and her family after the diagnosis of esophageal cancer, but we can assume that he helped those involved accept the nearness of death and the separation it would impose on all of them. This is an often-avoided form of psychotherapeutic intervention that can be extremely gratifying, not only for the dying patient and the family, but for the therapist as well, who is privileged to share and to facilitate one of life's most powerful and poignant moments.

In his concluding remarks, Dr. Cath makes a plea for a reexamination of Freud's death instinct and continued exploration of the frontiers between biological and psychological forces. He also reminds us that the study of dying is not popular, since we prefer to avoid the "responsibility to study and differentiate the reality of the necessary and unnecessary destructive forces generated from within as well as those that surround us—some of which seem, indirectly at least, to determine our destiny" (p. 301).

12

Time, Context, and Character:

A Life-Span View of Psychopathology during the Second Half of Life

JORDAN JACOBOWITZ AND NANCY NEWTON

The Complexities of Later Life Psychopathology

Paradoxically, the older adult psychiatric patient presents a mixed picture of frailty and strength. Frailty, an alleged hallmark of the aged, has been well attended to by the psychiatric literature. Depletion, depression, and dementia reign as the major three "Ds" in the aspiring psychogeriatrician's curriculum. Oddly, short shrift has been made of the strengths of the aging and aged with some notable exceptions (Gutmann et al. 1982). The mere fact of survival to later years bears testimony to at least past effectiveness in adaptive capacities.

This chapter addresses the question: whatever happened to the elder's strength? In particular, years of clinical work with older adult psychiatric patients has directed our attention to a large subgroup of patients whose symptoms first appeared or were greatly exacerbated after age fifty-five. Our interest centered on understanding both how these patients functioned for five or more decades without debilitating psychiatric symptoms, and why in later life their adaptation faltered. Noting the characteristics of their coping and defensive strategies during the adult years as well as their reported early childhood development, we began to focus on the dynamic interactions between changes in the situational context of adult development and character structure.

A descriptive study comparing the social and developmental characteristics of older adult psychiatric outpatients with a group of nonpsychiatric older adults (Jacobowitz and Markus-Kaplan 1986) highlighted an association among early childhood experience, lifestyles during young adulthood, and reactions to later life stressful changes, such as death of a spouse or retirement. The majority (76 percent) of the 116 outpatients examined suffered from late-onset disorders, that is, did not seek treatment before age forty-five. These outpatients, 80 percent of whom complained of depression and/or anxiety, were much more likely than persons in the nonpsychiatric group to report parental losses and/or traumatic disruptions in family functioning during childhood, difficulties in forming or maintaining marriages and in producing children during young adulthood, less success in vocational and social endeavors, and more current disengagement from society as reflected in work and marital status. Clinical examination and psychological tests of many of these and other older adult patients usually revealed inveterate deficits in personality functioning, in areas such as interpersonal relatedness, self-concept, and coping style. Although many of these patients initially attributed their current distress to external events, it was clinically evident that they harbored long-standing intrapsychic conflicts and vulnerable defensive structures, which were compromised *in some way* by the current external stress and attendant events.

We stressed "in some way" since conventional approaches to understanding psychopathology during the second half of life tend to emphasize either age-related external or internal determinants. Rarely considered are the interactions among those age-related stressors, the particular character structure involved, the specific social contexts within which the character structure emerged and to which it adapted, and changes over time in both the character structure and social context. Although it is easy, and perhaps convenient, to attribute later life pathology to external and/or internal losses such as loss of social resources or depletion of psychological energy, careful clinical analysis of older adult patients reveals a highly complex picture. Moreover, research on normal (i.e., nonpsychiatric) populations of older adults has not found consistent or significant relationships between external losses and the onset of psychiatric symptomatology (Palmore et al. 1979; Chiriboga and Cutler 1980; Newton et al. 1984) or any noticeable change in the capacity to adapt (Costa and McCrae 1980; Fiske 1980), although certain changes have been noted in the style and psychological structure of coping strategies (Shanan and Jacobowitz 1982; Shanan 1986).

Personality Theories, Later Life Development, and Psychopathology

The tendency to attribute later life pathology to specific losses or deficits without regard to the dynamics of character and social context is perhaps predicated on the divergent nature of psychological theory itself on one hand, and the vague, tenuous knowledge about biological and behavioral associations on the other. In a comprehensive, and perhaps singular, endeavor to derive from the compendium of extant personality theories a guiding theoretical foundation for investigating the psychology of adult development, Klaus Riegel (1959) concluded "no theory exists which takes full account of the aging personality" (p. 844). Two decades later, Bernice Neugarten (1977) concluded that research on personality development during the second half of life was in disarray. More recently Joel Shanan (1986) argued that diversity in adult personality development and adaptation is sufficient across different personality "types" and social or cultural contexts, that researchers should, at least temporarily, abandon normative or global theories of development and adopt differential and idiographic approaches. It appears that we are far from Riegel's goal of a theory of adult psychological development, which is "represented by a formal system and viewed as a network of the many structural and dynamic psychological variables, their interactions and their dependency on inner biological and outer sociological components" (p. 844).

Aside from a shaky theoretical and empirical background in normal personality development from which to base its understanding of pathological phenomena, psychogeriatrics traditionally has been exposed to the more frail segment of patients, living usually for want of choice in constrictive settings. Considerable attention, consequently, has been allotted to the symptomatology and limitations of the "depleted" aged residing in nursing homes and in long-term psychiatric facilities (Cath 1963; Lieberman 1975). Little is known about the psychological weaknesses and strengths of a wide range of community-dwelling older adults. The proportion of older adults treated at outpatient clinics is far below the 11 percent proportion of older adults in the population at large (Rednick et al. 1973, LaRue et al. 1985).

Theoretical speculation concerning the etiology and dynamics of psychopathology among older adults, particularly those suffering from functional as opposed to organic disorders, has been diverse and nonsystematic. Some authors have suggested that the dynamics of functional disorders are essentially the same in younger and older adults and can be traced to early childhood development (Roth 1976). The eruption of these disorders during late adulthood were viewed as consequences of natural losses in ego and social resources (Zinberg and Kaufman 1963). Why some individuals develop pathology and others do not, despite common "natural" losses, remains unanswered. Other authors have postulated that events during young or mid-adulthood can affect the onset or nature of psychopathology during the later years (Nemiroff and Colarusso 1985; Pollock 1981). Unarticulated were specific processes linking early, middle, and later years of development. Mentioned as possible determinants have been particular "developmental tasks" currently confronting the individual (Klerman and Weissman 1984), such as retirement, widowhood, and bodily changes. Yet, who is susceptible to react poorly to these "challenges" is unclear. A life-span view of late-onset psychopathology was presented by David Gutmann et al. (1982). Late-onset pathology was conceived of as a function of childhood experiences, early adult lifestyles, and age-related, *intrapsychic* developmental changes in motivation and mastery styles. These authors assumed a normative process of adult development for the two genders, and focused primarily on two kinds of character structure: "syntonic" and "dystonic" dependent types. The possibility of other patterns of development, other character structures, and variations in social circumstances remains an area for further exploration.

An Interactional Perspective

Our clinical experience has led to the proposition that psychopathology in later life is a function of the interactions among character structure, the social context of the character structure, and changes over time in both the character and social context. It is hypothesized that older people who evidence late-onset psychopathology are individuals with character deficits derived from childhood experiences. During adulthood they create constricted or deviant life patterns to promote security and/or to gratify needs that were aroused, frustrated, or threatened during childhood. Often these defensive life patterns are at least partially adaptive during the younger adult years. Nevertheless, these individuals enter the second half of life with impairments in psychological flexibility and find it difficult to establish a new equilibrium either through internal changes or through reestablishment of need-fulfilling lifestyles. Adding insult to injury is a common consequence of these defensive life patterns, namely, the failure to master certain adult skills that foster psychological growth, such as intimacy and generativity, which in turn diminishes the repertoire of psychological skills *and* the availability of social support resources. The following sections will explore the various aspects of this process.

Role of Character Structure in Adult Development

A core component of character structure is the means employed to mediate between internal needs and drives and the demands of the external world (Rapaport 1967; Shapiro 1965; Shanan 1973). In general, this adaptive function of character structure can be evaluated on a continuum of effective adaptational capacity, depending on the extent to which the internal world/external environment interface is successfully negotiated; that is, the degree to which intrapsychic needs are optimally gratified while meeting external demands without resorting to behaviors or intrapsychic defensive maneuvers that result in pathological cognitive, affective, or behavioral disorders.

Character structure with its mediating synthetic functions generally is considered consolidated by young adulthood. During adulthood it is thought to be a relatively constant force, shaping the course of behavior and strategies for adaptation and growth. Externally imposed constraints on the ability to choose and shape lifestyle are usually at a minimum during the earlier phases of adulthood. Reflecting sociocultural factors, these years offer unsurpassed accessibility to other people, activities, and work experiences, and the degree to which these opportunities are exploited is a matter of individual choice. To a large extent, choices made during these years in fashioning and modifying the adult life structure and in establishing an interface with the external world reflect the impact of character structure. The individual's inner needs, the conflicts surrounding their expression, and the intrapsychic skills organizing and integrating those needs with environmental contingencies, determine the choices made.

Nevertheless, the opportunities and challenges of adulthood necessitate a continual integration of past and present needs. New needs and opportunities arise as adulthood progresses. Intimacy with an adult partner, parenting, productive use of vocational and avocational skills, engagement in communal social, political, religious organizations—all to some extent depend upon prior training and experience; but they also require an openness to novelty, new learning, flexibility in attitude and behavior, and in general, a *relative autonomy* from earlier developmental conflicts, anxieties, and inhibitory or reality distorting defenses.

Clinical experience with outpatients suggests that individuals prone to develop late-onset pathology enter adulthood with a psychological "dependency" upon earlier unresolved interpersonal or intrapsychic conflicts and injuries. Consequently, adulthood experiences and choices are filtered through these unresolved issues to a greater degree than normal. The majority experienced major disruptions in childhood, including early loss of parents, parental abuse, alcoholism, and in general unreliable, disappointing, and often belligerent parenting. Consequently, the formation of character structure and the resultant creation of a lifestyle reflect the need to defend against the repetition of these experiences during adulthood and/or to gratify unmet infantile needs in a manner that attempts to avoid reexperiencing painful injuries to self-esteem. Individuals undergoing this process tend to create an adult lifestyle that either (1) avoids adult developmental tasks that reify childhood experiences; (2) repeats earlier developmental experiences in a rigid, infantile manner that attempts to undo earlier experience and gratify unmet needs; or (3) restricts adult functioning to those areas that were either relatively conflict free during childhood or to areas in which the individual has special talents to succeed.

In sum, it appears that individuals vulnerable to developing later adulthood pathology create during early adulthood a lifestyle that becomes inextricably linked to the defensive needs of their character structure. They limit adult functioning to areas that represent the means to gratify unmet childhood needs; they avoid areas that represent the painful failures of childhood development. Unlike normal adults who can use the opportunities of adulthood to expand their competencies and to experience new forms of interpersonal development, vulnerable adults remain, at least unconsciously, obsessed with unresolved childhood experiences.

The Role of Adult Development in Formation and Modification of Character Structure

The previous section addressed the way that character structure impacts on adulthood, and in turn the way that the lifestyle established in adulthood becomes an integral part of the character structure. Although this interaction may serve to stabilize personality functioning in adulthood, albeit rigidly and restrictively, it tends to leave the individual vulnerable when life changes undermine the girders necessary to maintain that stability.

There are, in addition, ways in which this interaction interferes with experiences during young/middle adulthood that potentially can serve to prepare the individual for later life; namely, these earlier adult years offer opportunities for development and expansion of personality and social resources.

Although the core personality structure is seen as established by early adulthood, the longitudinal research on normal adults of George Vaillant (1977), Dorothy Eichorn et al. (1981), and others indicates that further elaboration of and movement toward the use of more flexible and "mature" defense mechanisms continue throughout middle adulthood. In contrast, this growth in adaptive capacity is problematic for less healthy individuals, that is, those with defensive-oriented character structures. In fact, there is some evidence that for these people regression to the use of less adaptive, more primitive defenses is commonly indicated (Jacobowitz 1984). It is likely that in approaching old age those persons who were healthier during early adulthood will benefit more from the opportunities for psychological growth during adulthood than the less healthy.

Marjorie Fiske's (1980) research on adaptation to stress during adulthood also suggests ways in which lifestyle choices play an important role in enabling the individual to cope with stress. Her conception of areas of commitment suggests that individuals choose to invest their energy in areas (i.e., achievement-oriented activities, interpersonal interaction, social values, self) that provide sources of self-gratification. She found changes in commitment areas through middle age. In addition, individuals with more areas of commitment appeared to cope with stress more adequately than those with fewer commitments.

Thus, adulthood provides the opportunity, through continuing psychological development, to build up internal psychological strengths and external resources (relationships, sources of self-esteem, connectedness with sustaining values) that can serve to promote adaptation during the later phases of adulthood. The more psychologically vulnerable the individual is at the onset of adulthood, however, the less likely it is that he or she will take advantage of the opportunities. In this vulnerable individual, adulthood experiences serve, as described previously, to shore up defenses rather than expand functioning. As a result, this individual is doubly handicapped in later life.

The Role of Aging Processes

The individual who is vulnerable to later life pathology maintains adequate functioning in adulthood through a process in which aspects of the lifestyle serve to reinforce fragile defensive functions by alternately avoiding activities that represent early developmental failures and selecting and "overworking" areas that promise gratification with minimum risk of re-experiencing childhood conflicts and failures. With age, however, the individual-environment interface will likely be disrupted in some essential way. These disruptions either remove the restricted area of functioning or force the person to confront avoided areas. Age-related changes also make it increasingly difficult for the individual to replace losses, that is, to reestablish a compensating lifestyle. In contrast to earlier periods of adulthood, externally imposed constraints on the individual-environmental interface become greater, so that opportunities for replacing lost lifestyle components become more limited, whether those components are other people, work roles, health, or the like. Thus, for several reasons, *it becomes more difficult for the individual to repeat defensive and coping strategies that were effective during earlier adulthood.*

In addition, alleged normative age-related personality changes may render the maintenance of defensive lifestyles more difficult. Gutmann's (1975) research indicated that aging impacts upon character structure and the defense mechanisms available to the individual. For example, he reported that as men age, they become less oriented toward coping with stress by directly mastering the environment and more oriented toward accommodating themselves to it. As a result, adjustment is increasingly achieved through changes in perceptions of the self in relationship to the environment. Diminishing psychological energy as well as physical energy undermines the individual's capacity to maintain aspects of lifestyle that require unrelenting vigor and confidence (Jacobowitz 1984).

Case Illustrations

The following cases illustrate how changes associated with aging can disrupt earlier adult lifestyles. These lifestyles were consciously and/or unconsciously devised to defend against childhood anxieties and perceived failures by (1) avoiding, limiting, or sabotaging interpersonal or instrumental activities that were linked with conflict or distress during childhood; and (2) promoting in a compensatory manner personal strengths and competencies that either were left relatively conflict-free during childhood or that showed, at least unconsciously, the most promise to gratify needs. Changes associated with aging disrupt adaptation, that is, precipitate pathology by either (1) removing the opportunity to avoid areas linked with intrapsychic conflicts, or (2) debilitating or threatening the strength or competency to maintain the defensive lifestyle. In either case, the individual is confronted with long-defended psychological conflict, usually within the context of limited social and personal resources. This limitation generally resulted from the consequences of the characterologically driven tendencies to constrict engagement in the social sphere and thus forgo growth-promoting opportunities during early adulthood.

We present four cases, each representing a different decade of life but reflecting the dynamics described earlier.

Case 1: An Abused Woman at Midlife

When Ms. A. presented for treatment, she was fifty-four years old, divorced (for seventeen years), lived alone, and had been recently fired from her job as an executive secretary. She complained of a distraught emotional state including diffuse anxiety, anger, and depression. The immediate precipitant of this state was the reluctance of her thirty-five-year-old married son to financially support her idea of beginning an independent business. At this time she had infrequent and conflictual interchanges with her single, thirty-year-old daughter, her only other child. Ms. A. had no prior psychiatric treatment, although she reported chronic feelings of frustration and anxiety stemming back to childhood.

She grew up in a midwestern city in a family described as being comprised of an abusive father, a self-centered, hypercritical mother, and a pampered sister. The father abused her physically up to the age of eighteen. He also reportedly made sexual overtures toward her during late childhood and adolescence. The mother was narcissistically involved in her own physical appearance and pleasures, and continually blamed Ms. A. for being a "bad girl." The patient felt that she was like "Cinderella," forced to do housework without love, while her sister was idealized by the parents.

Ms. A. entered early adulthood with a "masochistic" character structure. She felt she was "bad," did not deserve love or success, and was incompetent. Later in therapy it became apparent that she repressed enormous rage toward her parents and sister. She blamed herself for not receiving love and decided that she must continually strive to please others in order to atone for her "bad" behavior, with the hope of attaining love and acceptance.

She married immediately after high school to escape the hostile atmosphere at home. Whether by "chance" or unconscious design, her husband turned out to be as abusive as her father. He demanded obedience, strict cleanliness, and toleration of his temper and whims. After the birth of her first child, Ms. A. remained "house-bound," devoting herself to taking care of the baby and household. Because her major source of gratification was eating, she eventually became obese. A family crisis occurred when she discovered that her husband was having an affair with her mother. She divorced her husband and supported her two children with secretarial jobs until they left home.

Her postparental lifestyle consisted primarily of work and a ten-year affair with an "abusive" married man. His abusive behavior manifested itself in frequent ridicule of her, failure to keep appointments, and physically aggressive outbursts toward her. Eventually, he was transferred to another city and the relationship ended. Ms. A. continued to work, but grew to feel unappreciated and exploited. She was fired "for lack of work" after the firm underwent a reorganization. At this point, living alone without mate or friends, she turned to her son to help finance a business venture. His unenthusiastic response precipitated her desperate emotional state.

Ms. A. perceived her son's "rejection" as an indication that love by a significant other would not be forthcoming. She felt that despite her subservient stance, particularly toward men, she was left with nothing but memories of abuse. The "empty nest," forced "retirement," and the absence of spouse or intimate relationship compelled her to face the prospects of living autonomously, alone but without abuse—a future that unconsciously meant without the prospect of attaining love. She became enraged and frightened simultaneously. The rage initially was directed at her son, whom she perceived as the last link in a chain of abusive men, beginning with her father; it was also directed at her daughter-in-law, whom she perceived as self-pampering and as representative of her mother and sister. Yet she also feared that expressing this rage would "cut her off" from the possibility of receiving love and protection. She also doubted her ability to live autonomously, since she perceived herself as "incompetent" and "worthless."

Case 2: An Adolescent Retiree

Mr. B. was referred for psychotherapy by his internist after a panic attack during which Mr. B felt he was having a heart attack. Mr. B., a college graduate, was sixty-four-years-old, divorced (for two years), lived alone, and was the father of six adult children, none of whom lived in the city in which he resided. Aside from two recent panic attacks, he complained of sleep disturbance and diffuse tension. The immediate precipitant of his generally anxious state was an offer at work to delay his impending retirement a few years and assume a new position in the company as an executive manager. Mr. B. was in good physical health, had no history of psychiatric or medical hospitalizations, although he had been in "counseling" many years back, regarding his tendency to quit jobs or be fired from them. He had been working at his present company for about fifteen years, primarily as a salesman and later as an actuarial consultant.

Being an only child, he was devoted on by his parents. However, this doting took the form of an anxious overprotection. He spent most of his early years in the secluded presence of his parents and was warned to keep away from potentially "nasty and rude" children. His father inherited a business, which initially promised to support a leisurely, cultured life. However, the business collapsed during the depression, and his father was forced to work as a salesman, albeit not a successful one. In fact, his father, who was described as having a penchant for poetry, seemed to lack the finesse or motivation to succeed at work. Mr. B.'s mother apparently had entered her marriage with great expectations for her husband's success. As the family's economic status deteriorated, the mother became disenchanted and critical of her husband. Mr. B. said that although he loved his gentle father, he was also ashamed of his father's passivity and inability to defend himself against the mother's constant ridicule. Both parents, however, conveyed to the son their expectation that one day he would be "successful," a man of prestige, wealth, and culture. Nevertheless, they vigorously "protected" him from the "harsh" reality outside his home and encouraged him to avoid all sports and any other aggressive interchanges with his peers.

Mr. B. entered adulthood with a passive-dependent personality, covered to some extent by an outward mien of a polished, articulate, and knowledgeable "gentlemen." On one hand, he carried great expectations of himself, and on the other he felt "passive," and "incompetent," and lacked the ability to be assertive and effective. (During his early adulthood years, for example, he had recurrent episodes of secondary impotence.) This major theme of needing to be "important," "powerful," and "successful" versus the sense of being ineffective and impotent, mimicked the internalized dynamics of his parents while serving as the prototype of the lifestyle he created.

His experiences during the war years exemplified his characteristic mode of behavior. He became an officer in the armed forces; but when given the opportunity to "take command," he faltered, reacted with panic, and was demoted to office work.

After the war and college he married an extroverted, zesty woman who he felt was "taken in" by his outward demeanor. He fathered six children, enjoyed being home, playing with the children, going to church, but he dreaded work. He repetitively was appointed to high-status positions at various companies but consistently failed to meet either his own expectations of himself or those of his employers. He moved from one job to the next, and from one city to another. In particular, he could not "assert" himself, but kept hoping that one day he would be successful.

His wife became disenchanted with him. After the youngest child left home, she refused to move to another city with him and eventually she divorced him. Interestingly, Mr. B. had obtained a "lower-status" job as a salesman and later was offered and accepted a relatively unstressful job as an actuarial consultant.

For a number of years, he worked, went to church, but for the most part led a solitary life. He wanted to date women, but "didn't know" how to approach them or what was proper. He resented being nothing more than a "clerk," but was afraid to request a promotion. In fact, when he was offered a promotion, he reacted with panic, which forced him to seek psychiatric help.

Mr. B. was confronted at age sixty-four with an issue that he had avoided all his adult years. Without the "protection" of a wife and children, with the realization that this was his "last chance" to "succeed" or suffer "humiliation," he was compelled to deal with his fear of being assertive and "manly" or face the prospects of a severe depression. In many respects, he began therapy as an "adolescent" entering the adult world: could he now handle life in an autonomous, self-directing manner, or was he doomed to "failure?"

Case 3: A Counterdependent Woman

In Ms. C. we see the first onset of psychosis in an elderly woman following a series of late-life events that undermined her narcissistic defenses and disrupted her lifelong independent, self-reliant stance. Ms. C., a divorced, childless woman, was admitted to an inpatient psychiatric facility at age seventy-five with paranoid delusions and auditory hallucinations. On admission, she was socially appropriate and cooperative, but guarded. She appeared frightened, and although willing to describe her delusions and hallucinations, she was not open about much else in her life. Ms. C. reported that she had begun to hear people having loud parties outside of her senior citizen apartment building about six months earlier. When her complaints were not taken seriously by the police or building manager, she stopped complaining, and gradually became more withdrawn and isolated. Over the following months, the voices became increasingly hostile, demanding, and frightening. The content was primarily sexual, and Ms. C. believed that people had come into her apartment at night and sexually molested her. She increasingly experienced sleep disturbances; her self-care and care of her apartment deteriorated.

Although she had functioned without disabling psychiatric symptoms prior to age seventy-five, her difficult and chaotic childhood experiences make it likely that she entered adulthood with specific psychological vulnerabilities and coping mechanisms. After her parent's divorce when she was an infant, she went to live with her grandmother, the only nurturant, idealized figure of her childhood. However, her grandmother died when Ms. C. was four, and she maintained a vivid memory of waking up next to the dead grandmother. She then went to live with her mother and stepfather. Their relationship with each other and with Ms. C. was conflictual, dominated by frequent fights and arguments. Ms. C. was also sexually abused by her stepfather throughout much of her childhood. She married briefly at age seventeen, primarily to get away from her parents. After her divorce, she left the small southern town in which she had been raised and came to a large midwestern city, at the invitation of a male friend.

Despite these early life experiences, Ms. C. entered adulthood with certain strengths: She was physically attractive and had good superficial social skills; she was also a feisty, self-reliant young woman, committed to taking care of herself. At the same time, her capacity to trust others was very limited. Instead, she seemed to see others primarily as a means of gratifying her own narcissistic needs. It is likely that she functioned throughout adulthood without psychiatric symptoms or treatment because she was able to create a lifestyle that built on these strengths while compensating for her vulnerabilities. Ms. C. saw her adulthood as satisfying and happy, in contrast to her unhappy childhood.

Throughout adulthood, Ms. C. did factory work and was successful in her work. She lived alone and never remarried. Her adult relationships with men provided her with the opportunity to master actively the feelings experienced as a child in reaction to her sexually abusive stepfather. She had many extended sexual relationships through adulthood. However, she always maintained her own independent lifestyle, viewing men as needing her much more than she needed them. She expected her lovers to express their admiration of her both physically and financially, through expensive gifts and money. Although these relationships served to verify that she was attractive and desirable, these men did not seem to be psychologically real to her. For example, she was unable to describe any of these men in a way that differentiated one from another. Instead, her most vivid memory was of an incident in which she not only physically defended herself against a jealous lover, but also seriously wounded him.

Although the lifestyle that evolved for Ms. C. during adulthood complemented her strengths and vulnerabilities, thus reinforcing her psychological defenses, she was left vulnerable to specific losses and assaults that tend to accompany aging. That is, when sources of narcissistic gratification were no longer readily available and when her capacity to maintain an independent, self-reliant stance was challenged, Ms. C.

became vulnerable to long-repressed dependency needs and associated fear and mistrust of others. This vulnerability occurred through a series of incidents over several years. First of these was a fire that destroyed her apartment and her possessions, including the most valued one: a photograph of herself when she was young and beautiful. Following the fire, she moved into a large senior citizen building where the constant interaction with nosey gossiping neighbors undermined her sense of privacy and ability to carry on secret sexual relationships. A year later, she gave up her child-care job, which left her more socially isolated and with little structure in her daily life. The final incident was a mugging that occurred outside her building. For the first time in her adult life, Ms. C. was confronted with inability to defend herself physically. The auditory hallucinations began shortly after this incident.

In the early stages of her psychotic experiences, efforts at restitution of her defenses could be seen, as she initially found the voices narcissistically gratifying. She felt attractive and desirable, as if she were reliving earlier experiences. However, with time, she felt increasingly assaulted and vulnerable. As the hallucinations and delusional material dissipated during hospitalization, Ms. C. became increasingly needy and dependent, looking to others to care for her and feeling frightened that there was no one to provide that care. This preoccupation overshadowed the objective evidence that Ms. C. continued to have the physical, cognitive, and financial resources to remain independent. Indeed, the life structure that functioned well for her in adulthood precluded the formation of relationships with peers or family that might have constituted a network of supportive, caregiving others in later life. In addition, her adult lifestyle merely strengthened her defenses against the remaining childhood vulnerabilities rather than leading to a more mature resolution of her fears and insecurities. Thus, when the effectiveness of the defensive components of her lifestyle was undermined, these vulnerabilities re-emerged with force, and Ms. C. lacked the resources to cope with them.

Case 4: A Soldier without an Army

Mr. D., an eighty-five-year-old childless, retired male, was referred for his first outpatient psychiatric treatment following the death of his wife after a lengthy illness. When initially seen, he was severely depressed, with marked sleep disturbance, loss of appetite (accompanied by a forty-pound weight loss over the preceding two years), frequent crying episodes, loss of interest in self-care and daily activities, social withdrawal, and active suicidal ideation. He was preoccupied with feelings of guilt about his wife's illness and death, and could see nothing to live for since her death. For him, his life had ended, and he was simply waiting to die. Despite the severity of his depression, Mr. D.'s strong, independent, self-reliant stance was very evident. He presented the facade of a stubborn, assertive man who was accustomed to being in command of any situation and of being respected by others. Weakness and vulnerability were intolerable to him. His suicide plan seemed a way of taking control of this intolerable situation in an aggressive, masculine way.

Mr. D.'s adult lifestyle was consistent with this self-image. He left home at age fourteen to join the army and remained in the military for the following twenty-seven years. The majority of his military career was spent in some type of combat or semicombat situation, in World War I, China, the Spanish Civil War, and World War II. He consistently served abroad, primarily in the Orient and South America. He obtained the rank of sergeant as a young man and then refused further promotions so that he could remain "where the action was."

The role of sergeant clearly suited his tough, in-command personality, and provided him with a socially and family-approved means of meeting his high needs for excitement and adventure. At the same time, underlying this facade, there was a warm, nurturant, caring side, which became evident as he described his relationship to the younger men who served under him. For example, he was proud of the fact that as the director of an Oriental prison of one thousand men, he was perceived as fair by the prisoners and maintained order while eliminating some of the harsh measures used by previous directors.

This dichotomy was also present in his relationship with women. As a young man he appears to have been a socially and sexually active bachelor, filling a masculine role in his relationship with women that was consistent with his tough-sergeant image. In his forties he returned home to marry his childhood sweetheart. Their marriage proved to be a stable, sustaining relationship until her death forty years later.

Mr. D. became unaccountably vague when discussing his early childhood. His father was a "good" man, but harsh and strict. He too was a career military man. One of the few times that Mr. D. returned home during his military career was to care for his father before his death. Mr. D. had three older brothers and one sister. He did not maintain contact with his brothers after his parents' deaths. Although reportedly very fond of his sister, he also discontinued contact with her for unexplained reasons. This marked estrangement from his siblings, his strong determination to live as far from his family as possible in young adulthood, and his leaving home at a young age, suggests that he had a strong and overdetermined need to separate and maintain distance from his family. The army and his friendships there, however, served as a replacement, and to some extent, a psychologically reparative family. It is possible that the army provided him with a much-needed means of establishing his own toughness and masculinity in the eyes of his father and of compensating for his role as the youngest son. The army also provided him with a means of living out his more nurturant, caregiving side in a masculine way. The death of his wife challenged his adequacy as a competent caregiver and removed his only social support.

Discussion: The Life Course and Psychopathology

In our experience the preceding four cases typically represent older adult patients with functional disorders seeking psychiatric intervention. Although each patient has unique characteristics in terms of character, development, and sociocultural milieu, common among them is their late-onset pathology as part of a life course, and not a discontinuous age-induced aberration. Changes over time "wear down" an *adult lifestyle* that is inextricably linked to an *intrapsychic defense system,* both of which were established to ward off psychological injuries stemming from childhood experiences. The psychological structure of these individuals is overinvested in defense and modes of infantile gratification, thus inhibiting growth toward maturity in the earlier adult years and disrupting the formation of sturdy relationships with significant others and/or with broader, more supportive social networks. Although age-related stressors and social isolation are said to induce pathology in the later years, it is more likely that character pathology creates that social isolation and induces or at least renders the individual vulnerable to certain stressful events. Furthermore, psychological "depletion" is more likely attributable to a regression to *pathological* childhood states rather than to a natural aging process. The following discussion illustrates these points, using the four cases presented to exemplify the life-course pathological process.

Age-related stressors

Each of the four cases reported an external stressor that precipitated the symptoms. Ms. A. lost a job and was rejected by her son; Mr. B. was given the choice of accepting a promotion or retiring; Ms. C. experienced a series of traumatic events, the last being a criminal assault upon her; and Mr. D. was widowed. Each of these stressors would tax the resources of any older adult; yet, the pathogenic impact of the stressor for the four patients resided in the psychosocial context within which each lived.

Disruptions in lifestyle

The consequence of each stressor was to threaten the continuation of a defensive lifestyle. Ms. A. was compelled to face her life autonomously without an "abusive other." Mr. B. was forced to be assertive and "successful" without a "protective other" or recourse to select another promising but unchallenging job. Ms. C. lost her independence, or more specifically, her protection against "abusive and rejecting others." Mr. D. lost his "protected other"; with no "war" to fight he was rendered helpless.

Character structure and lifestyle

For characterologically vulnerable individuals, disruptions in lifestyle are like the crumbling walls of an ill-defended fortress. Ms. A had a "masochistic" structure. Neediness for love was combined with aggression turned inwards. She possessed a capacity to tolerate abuse with self-soothing overeating and an ingrained belief that one day outer love would be forthcoming. Relinquishing that belief and adopting an assertive-autonomous stance was tantamount in her mind to unleashing pent-up rage, and perhaps more frightening, overwhelming retribution and ultimately total isolation. Her adult lifestyle was predicated on an attachment to some abusive figure whom she was compelled to please. Change and growth in mutual intimacy and security with an adult figure did not occur. Her children grew to perceive her as easily manipulated and submissive. House-bound and with a poor self-image, she made no friends. Thrust into a situation where she had to depend upon herself, she lost the outer circumstances to keep her rage and anxiety contained; and perhaps more important, she lost her belief in some ultimate outer-loving salvation.

Mr. B.'s character structure revolved around the need to be a "successful" man. He feared that lack of success would lead to a form of castration, total humiliation. The protection afforded by nurturing others soothed his fears and helped him to believe that one day he would be successful. As long as he clung to that protection and avoided having to "prove" himself an assertive, potent male, he kept his anxiety in check and his belief in eventual success intact. Earlier in life he used his intelligence, sensitivity, empathic qualities, and boyish charm to play the role of a nurturing father. Particularly, his charm and outer innocence seemed to rally significant others to protect him and tolerate his "incompetencies" at work. Finally, his being divorced, his children having grown, and especially his having to choose either a promotion or retirement, compelled him to meet the challenge of "manhood" without protective others. He had avoided this task throughout the adult years.

Ms. C.'s character structure was founded on an intrapsychic and lifestyle *reversal* of her childhood experiences. Whereas in earlier life she was abused and rendered helpless, in her adult life she felt in control and even domineering. In contrast to Ms. A., who tended to *repeat* her childhood experiences, Ms. C. maintained a superautonomous stance during her adult years: She used her natural beauty to attract men and admiration; she had a feisty courage to repel those who threatened to exploit her; and she used work as a means to promote her independence. Even though she successfully warded off external abuse, she also avoided establishing an intimate relationship based on mutual respect. She had no children or committed friendships. Committed resolutely to everlasting independence, she opted for psychotic fantasies rather than for acceptance of a dependent position when the constraints of reality threatened her independence.

Mr. D. led an unusual life, centered on the need to attack an enemy while simultaneously protecting those close to him. He was a compulsive war seeker. His reticence about his childhood leads one to speculate that it was far from ideal. He left home at age fourteen and later severed all ties to his large family. He didn't marry till his forties, and even then periodically left his spouse for war. His character was based on the need to protect others from his own aggression, which he projected onto an "enemy," while at the same time, he protected those whom the enemy sought to destroy. Only when wounded could he let others tend to him. This restriction suggested that he suffered intense unconscious guilt over his repressed hostile wishes. He perceived the death of his wife as his failure to protect her from his own rage. Ultimately his aggression was turned against himself.

Support systems

Each of the four patients had isolated themselves from potential significant others who could have helped support them during their psychological crises. Ms. A. had no one to turn to except abusive and derisive relatives. Mr. B. had lost his wife to divorce, and his children were scattered about the country. His other relationships were formal and distant, limited to co-workers and church members. Ms. C. had kept everyone away from her. Mr. D. continued to reject any help from his wife's relatives. He initially alienated what support there was.

Childhood and aging

All four patients' adult lifestyles appeared dominated by an unconscious need to deal with unresolved experiences emanating from childhood. All individuals are confronted to some extent with the same need. However, persons vulnerable to later life disorders overinvest their psychological resources in dealing with these issues. For one thing, their earlier experiences are likely to be more traumatic and difficult than those of normal older adults. Second, their particular means of defense, which incorporates most of their social functioning, decreases the opportunity for growth and change during the adult years and leaves the original childhood experiences unmodulated by adult development.

Nevertheless, the adult lifestyles that these individuals create succeed in preventing serious psychiatric crises in early adulthood, and even promote achievements in limited areas of functioning. In many of these individuals, however, aging is the nemesis of their defensive strategy. Many common age-related events—such as the empty nest (Ms. A.), retirement (Mr. B.), loss of physical strength (Ms. C.), and widowhood (Mr. D.)—unhinge the outer accouterments of intrapsychic defensive systems. Moreover, with age it becomes progressively more difficult to replace central components of the lifestyle, such as young children, occupation, health, and even spouses. The timing of the loss or event also seems to play a crucial role. Ms. A., for example, was relatively young when forced to be autonomous; there was a realistic possibility of achieving autonomy. Mr. B. perceived that he had "one last chance" in his life to attain "success" before "being put to pasture." Ms. C. ran out of options and opportunities to maintain her independence. And Mr. D. felt he was close to death and had run out of time.

Finally, the rigidity of these patients' defensive structures and lifestyles encumbered the use of potentially age- or stage-related developmental potentials, not only during the earlier but also the later years of adulthood. Ms. A. perceived her postparental years and increased "freedom" as a threat rather than challenge; Mr. B. viewed retirement as a decree of failure rather than as an opportunity to engage in religious and aesthetic experiences that he previously had valued; and neither Ms. C. nor Mr. D. could achieve a sense of integrity in their lives, both being entrapped by their childhood fears.

Sex differences

These four patients differed in their presenting complaints, late-life stressors, character structure, and life histories. However, the particular issues with which each patient struggled emerged from a common life-course pathological process. Congruent with our general clinical experience there were notable sex differences in both the context of the emergent issues and the ways in which these issues were expressed. For the women, lifelong problems revolved around the difficulty in establishing and managing an appropriate balance between autonomy and dependency needs regarding self-image and interpersonal relationships. Neither Ms. A. nor Ms. C. was able to establish such a balance. Ms. A.'s overdependent, masochistic stance and Ms. C.'s rigidly counterdependent or overautonomous stance represented polar strategies of character structure to gratify the need to obtain love while protecting the integrity of the self and self-esteem. Interestingly, the eventual outcome of their psychological crises saw the emergence of repressed character tendencies. Ms. A. grew to develop autonomous strivings as she gradually "let go" of abusive love objects. Ms. C. "deteriorated" into intolerable dependency.

In contrast, the difficulties for the men revolved around the need for self-assertion in instrumental roles. Mr. B. and Mr. D. evolved very different patterns for managing threatening, aggressive impulses. Mr. B. constructed a lifestyle in which he could comfortably express and experience his more nurturant, caring side, but one in which he could avoid self-assertion. In fact, he went to great lengths to repress and deny his aggression, even though such efforts failed in the workplace. Only when the dissolution of his family robbed him of the nurturant arena was he willing to confront his difficulty in expressing aggression. Mr. D., on the other hand, managed his anger and aggressive impulses through investing in a lifestyle that allowed their expression in a "safe," socially approved manner. He thus protected his family from his aggression by distancing himself from the home. His wife's death exemplified his lifelong fear that his aggression could destroy people he loved.

It is interesting to note that these sex differences are consistent with recent research and theory describing developmental differences between males and females. Carol Gilligan (1982) suggested that a lifelong issue for females is developing and maintaining a sense of autonomy while remaining sensitive to the needs of others. For men, adult development has been described as establishing mastery of the environment through instrumental and work roles (Levinson 1977). In the wake of contemporary changes in the socialization process and vocational opportunities for women and perhaps less so for men, core issues of character structure for women and men may change in currently developing cohorts. However, for older adults today those noted sex differences are likely to persist for the next few decades.

The extent to which normative age-related personality changes, such as the contrasexual shifts hypothesized by Gutmann (1964, 1980), played a role in the emergence and resolution of psychopathology in these patients is less clear. To some extent, Ms. A. and Mr. D. can be viewed as exemplifying internal struggle with and then incorporation of those shifts. Ms. A.

eventually moved toward a more autonomous, self-assertive stance; Mr. D. during the course of therapy became better able to express his nurturant qualities without fear that his aggression would intrude. On the other hand, both of these patients had experienced lifelong struggles in trying to reconcile these competing demands; and the late-life push toward integration reflected the undermining impact of external stressors as much as the new emergence of internal needs. In response to that stress, their ability to achieve new levels of integration may, however, reflect this internal shift.

Nevertheless, Mr. B. and Ms. C. exemplified different patterns of possibly sex-related aging changes. Ms. C. was assertive and autonomous throughout her life, defending against her nurturant needs, whereas Mr. B. always felt more comfortable with his nurturant side. Thus rather than having other sides of the self emerge in later life, these individuals exemplify nontypical sex-role patterns from an early age.

Implications for Therapy

Understanding the nature of the older patient's character structure, lifelong coping mechanisms, and the role of later life stressors in exposing underlying unresolved psychological issues, provides a useful framework for psychotherapeutic intervention. If it is to be effective, psychotherapy cannot simply facilitate "adjustment" to the precipitating losses. Instead, the importance of these stressors is that they evoke psychological conflicts and issues which have been long-defended against. The individual's distress, awareness that this may be a "last chance" to live a more satisfying life, and, ironically, loss of the external reinforcers of internal defensive systems, can at least open the door for change to take place. In addition, a long history of repeated patterns of defensive maneuvers can alert the therapist to the meaning of these behaviors as well as provide the patient with examples of the patterns being discussed. Obviously, the specific treatment interventions will not only reflect this understanding but also will depend upon the patient's capacity for insight, openness to self-awareness, motivation to change, and availability of ego and/or social resources. Paradoxically, it is the "breakdown" during the second half of life that offers the patient an opportunity to restructure characteristic modes of negotiating the interface between internal needs and outer opportunities and constraints. In other words, the patient can shift from a defensive character position, which had provided a kind of pseudoadaptation during the earlier phases of adulthood, to a more autonomously controlled and constructively energetic stance.

The patients presented can serve as examples of variations in uses of treatment and the nature of the therapeutic interventions.

For Ms. A. and Mr. B., psychotherapy involved developing increased awareness of their underlying issues and the self-defeating defensive maneuvers that had been employed throughout most of adulthood.

Ms. A. gained insight into how she "permitted" others to abuse her in the hope that they would ultimately gratify her needs for love and self-esteem. She came to see that beginning with her parents and down the line with her ex-husband, ex-lovers, and adult children, others "convinced" her that she was "incompetent" and "worthless" in order to continue to exploit her. Furthermore, she came in contact with her own rage and fantasies of retribution should she express it. Gradually, by recognizing her dynamics as well as changing her behavior toward others, she underwent a search for a new "identity" as an autonomous, self-respecting person.

In a similar fashion, Mr. B. began to recognize that his ultimate fear was to become like his "father," whom he perceived as a failure. He also came in contact with his own fantasies of unbridled aggression and licentious wishes, which were never modulated or incorporated into his adult lifestyle and self-image. Feeling accepted by his male therapist, he gradually integrated the more "masculine" side of himself into his self-image and also behaved more assertively at work and with women.

Although Mr. D. gained little understanding during therapy of his guilt, fears of his aggressive drives, and his need to protect others from those drives, the management of these issues in the transference relationship successfully freed Mr. D. to initiate new and sustaining relationships in his life.

During previous crises in his life, Mr. D. had relied on strong but nurturant women as sources of strength. For example, an often-repeated story was of a nurse who stayed at his side while he was delirious and near death following a severe war injury. The initial stages of treatment involved repeated testing of his female therapist's persistence and investment in him as well as her capacity to be as strong as he was, and thus not be overwhelmed by his aggression. Gradually, Mr. D.'s therapist was accepted as providing this function in his current life. A crisis then developed in treatment when Mr. D. became aware of sexual feelings toward the therapist. He was ashamed that he had become a "dirty old man" and feared that he could not control those impulses, thus threatening the therapist and his relationship to her. Labeling of these feelings for the patient as well as demonstrating that she was neither threatened nor put off by his impulses, the therapist alleviated Mr. D.'s fears that his sexual and aggressive impulses were both shameful and unmanageable. After these issues were addressed, Mr. D. was able, on his own initiative, to reestablish a social support system, first with a niece with whom he had not had contact for many years, and finally with several female neighbors. These relationships served as both a source of self-respect through his fatherly stance and a means for receiving nurturance. Thus, despite the severity of Mr. D.'s presenting symptoms, and the magnitude of the loss he had sustained, his response to treatment suggests that sustaining life structures can be recreated by even the elderly patient.

Conclusions

We have argued that between the range of normal older adults who manage to deal effectively with age-related stressors and severely impaired older adults with either a chronic psychiatric history or current organic or debilitating medical illnesses, there is a sector of patients where the dynamics of later life psychopathology are complex. The tendency to view these patients in simplistic terms of "loss"—whether internal "depletion" or external stress—appears highly misleading, both in understanding them and in planning intervention strategies. Understanding them involves identifying underlying motivational needs and conflicts that came into being during childhood; recognizing the defensive systems of character structure that became crystallized during early adulthood and became enmeshed with lifestyle; considering the particular psychosocial context of their current environment; and, finally, realizing that psychological strength, once bound in defense and pseudo- or partial adaptation, can, in many cases, be rechanneled to promote gratifying changes during the later years.

REFERENCES

Cath, S. H. 1963. "Some Dynamics of Middle and Later Years: A Study in Depletion and Restitution." In *Normal Psychology of the Aging Process*, ed. N. E. Zinberg and I. Kaufman, pp. 21–71. New York: International Universities Press.
Chiriboga, D. A., and Cutler, R. 1980. "Stress and Adaptation: Life-Span Perspective." In *Aging in the 1980's*, ed. L. W. Poon. Washington, D.C.: American Psychological Association.
Costa, P. T., Jr., and McCrae, R. R. 1980. "Still Stable After All These Years: Personality as a Key to Understanding Some Issues in Adulthood and Old Age."

In *Life-Span Development and Behavior,* ed. P. B. Baltes and O. G. Brim, Jr., vol. 3, pp. 65–102. New York: Academic Press.

Eichorn, D. H.; Clausen, J. A.; Haan, N.; Honzik, M. P.; and Mussen, P. H. 1981. *Present and Past in Middle Life.* New York: Academic Press.

Fiske, M. 1980. "Tasks and Crises of the Second Half of Life: The Interrelationships of Commitment, Coping and Adaptation." In *Handbook of Mental Health and Aging,* ed. J. E. Birrin and R. B. Sloane, pp. 337–73. Englewood Cliffs, N.J.: Prentice-Hall.

Gilligan, C. 1982. *In a Different Voice.* Cambridge, Mass.: Harvard University Press.

Gutmann, D. 1964. "An Exploration of Ego Configurations in Middle and Late Life." In *Personality in Middle and Late Life,* ed. B. Neugarten et al., pp. 114–48. New York: Atherton Press.

———. 1980. "The Post-Parental Years: Clinical Problems and Developmental Possibilities." In *Mid-Life: Developmental and Clinical Issues,* ed. W. H. Norman and T. J. Scarramella, pp. 38–52. New York: Bruner/Mazel.

Gutmann, D.; Griffin, B.; and Grunes, J. 1982. "Developmental Contributions to the Late-Onset Affective Disorders." In *Life-Span Development and Behavior,* ed. P. B. Baltes and O. G. Brim, Jr., vol. 4, pp. 243–61. New York: Academic Press.

Jacobowitz, J. 1984. *Stability and Change of Coping Patterns During the Middle Years as a Function of Personality Type.* Ph.D. diss., Hebrew University of Jerusalem.

Jacobowitz, J., and Markus-Kaplan, M. 1986. "Clinical, Social and Developmental Characteristics of Older Men and Women Seeking Outpatient Psychiatric Treatment." Paper presented at the Thirty-ninth Annual Scientific Meeting of the Gerontological Society of America, Chicago.

Klerman, G. L., and Weissman, M. M. 1984. "An Epidemiologic View of Mental Illness, Mental Health and Normality." In *Normality and the Life Cycle: A Critical Integration,* ed. D. Offer and M. Sabshin, pp. 315–44. New York: Basic Books.

LaRue, A.; Dessonville, C.; and Jarvick, L. F. 1985. "Aging and Mental Disorders." In *Handbook of the Psychology of Aging,* 2d ed., ed. J. E. Birren and K. W. Schaie, pp. 664–702. New York: Van Nostrand Reinhold.

Levinson, D. J. 1977. *The Seasons of a Man's Life.* New York: Ballantine Books.

Lieberman, M. A. 1975. "Adaptive Processes in Late Life." In *Life-Span Developmental Psychology: Normative Life Crises,* ed. N. Datan and L. H. Ginzberg, pp. 135–59. New York: Academic Press.

Nemiroff, R. A. and Colarusso, C. A. 1985. *The Race Against Time: Psychotherapy and Psychoanalysis in the Second Half of Life.* New York: Plenum.

Neugarten, B. L. 1977. "Personality in Middle and Late Life." In *Handbook of the Psychology of Aging,* ed. J. E. Birren and K. W. Schaie, pp. 626–49. New York: Van Nostrand Reinhold.

Newton, N. A.; Lazarus, L. W.; and Weinberg, J. 1984. "Aging: Biosocial perspectives." In *Normality and the Life Cycle: A Critical Integration,* ed. D. Offer and M. Sabshin, pp. 230–85. New York: Basic Books.

Palmore, E.; Cleveland, W. P.; Nowlin, J. B.; Ramm, D.; and Siegler, I. C. 1979. "Stress and Adaptation in Late Life." *Journal of Gerontology* 34:841–51.

Pollock, G. H. 1981. "Aging or Aged: Development or Pathology." In *The Course of Life: Psychoanalytic Contribution Towards Understanding Personality Development, Vol. III, Adulthood and the Aging Process,* ed. S. I. Greenspan and G. H. Pollock, pp. 549–85. Washington, D.C.: U.S. Government Printing Office.

Rapaport, D. 1967. "Some Metapsychological Considerations Concerning Activity and Passivity." *The Collected Works of David Rapaport,* ed. M. M. Gill. New York: Basic Books.

Rednick, K. R. W.; Kramer, M.; and Taube, C. A. 1973. "Epidemiology of Mental Illness and Utilization of Psychiatric Facilities Among Older Persons." In *Mental Health in Later Life,* ed. E. W. Busse and E. Pfeiffer. Washington, D.C.: American Psychiatric Association.

Riegel, K.F. 1959. "Personality Theory and Aging." In *Handbook of Aging and the Individual,* ed. J. E. Birren, pp. 797–851. Chicago: University of Chicago Press.

Roth, M. 1976. "The Psychiatric Disorders of Later Life." *Psychiatric Annals* 6:417–445.

Shanan, J. 1973. "Coping Behavior in Assessment for Complex Tasks." *Proceedings of the Seventeenth International Congress of Applied Psychology, Vol. 1.* Bruxelles: Editest.

———. 1986. *Personality Types and Culture in Later Adulthood.* Basel: Karger.

Shanan, J., and Jacobowitz, J. 1982. "Personality and Aging." *Annual Review of Gerontology and Geriatrics* 3:148–78.

Shapiro, D. 1965. *Neurotic Styles.* New York: Basic Books.

Vaillant, G. E. 1977. *Adaptation to Life.* Boston: Little, Brown.

Zinberg, N. E., and Kaufman, I. 1963. *Normal Psychology and the Aging Process.* New York: International Universities Press.

DISCUSSION

Drs. Jacobowitz and Newton help to dispell the tendency among clinicians to understand the psychopathology of late adulthood only in terms of "loss" and "depletion." They demonstrate through clinical examples that symptom formation in late adulthood results from complex, multidimensional dynamic conflict.

Most intriguing is their explanation of a phenomenon that has puzzled mental health professionals for a long time: the onset of demonstrable symptoms *for the first time* in late adulthood. Their conclusions are convincing because the data were gleaned from detailed study of the life courses of individual patients, a procedure we have described as the taking of an *adult developmental history* to complement and be integrated with the usual developmental history of childhood. The detailed study of the life course of an individual, regardless of age, provides both clinician and theoretician with profound insight into the nature of symptom formation at five or at eighty-five.

These authors conclude, correctly we believe, that the onset of symptoms for the first time in late adulthood is based on the same set of factors that apply earlier in life: the intrapsychic interaction between past and present issues and conflicts. What has been lacking up to now is a plausible explanation for how the phenomenon occurs. According to Jacobowitz and

Newton, their patients experienced parent loss or family disruption in childhood followed in adulthood by the creation of "constricted or deviant life patterns to promote security and/or gratify needs that were aroused, frustrated, or threatened during childhood" (p. 309). Because these defensive life patterns were partially adaptive during the younger adult years, they did not result in symptom formation *but did compromise the mastery of phase-specific developmental tasks of adulthood* such as marriage and parenthood. The individual thus became vulnerable to the developmental pressures of *late* adulthood, which were engaged without a support system composed of the multigenerational object ties necessary for intrapsychic stability and growth.

It seems to us that the major contribution here is the elucidation of the "deviant life patterns," that is, character pathology, present but unobserved in early and middle adulthood because it did not produce enough discomfort or stereotypical symptoms to bring the patient to the attention of mental health professionals. Deeply ingrained internal conflicts, bred in childhood, evolved and elaborated upon in adulthood, were tolerated and contained until late adulthood when the loss of important objects, illness, retirement, or other dramatic changes rendered the character defenses inadequate and led to symptom formation. Clearly, late adult symptoms do not spring mysteriously, *de novo,* to life. Within a life-cycle approach, which incorporates adult developmental concepts, they are readily understandable, the result of lifelong patterns of conflict, maladaptation, and destabilization.

Drs. Jacobowitz and Newton consider the questions that we have raised concerning the importance of adult experience. In the normal situation "adulthood provides the opportunity, through continuing psychological development, to build up internal psychological strengths and external resources (relationships, sources of self-esteem, connectedness with sustaining values) that can serve to promote adaptation during the later phases of adulthood" (p. 312). In other words, as in childhood, success in engaging and mastering the developmental tasks of any one phase of development determines, in part, the individual's ability to deal with the next. In the material presented by these authors, it is clear that for their patients, unresolved conflicts from childhood compromised young adult development in their patients, and adult inhibitions and restrictions similarly affected their ability to manage late life. The continuous interaction between past and present development can be followed throughout the life course.

Thus late adult psychopathology, in both its onset and its nature, is the result of complex, multiple factors from *all* preceding stages of development, each playing a role in its origin (mostly, but not exclusively in childhood) and elaboration (mostly in adulthood). The *form* of the psychopathology may shift even in late adulthood, from long-standing character pathology and inhibitions to florid symptoms. The late-adult ego can be quite flexible, initiating sudden changes in defensive activity to cope with changing internal and external circumstances.

If we are careful in drawing conclusions, we can construct a theory about normality from the study of pathology. Although the criteria are not necessarily new, the clinical material in this chapter demonstrates convincingly that the keys to healthy development in late adulthood are biological intactness, work, or other meaningful activity (one that contributes to family and society), and continuous engagement in multigenerational object relationships. The presence of these factors in late adulthood is directly determined by the degree to which early and middle adulthood developmental tasks—such as maintaining the aging body, marriage and parenthood, and work achievement—were engaged and mastered. Unfortunately, knowledge of the interrelationships among developmental stages is not enough to produce change; somehow we must convince young and middle-aged adults to consider and plan for their late adult future, a subject they would rather avoid.

13

Modifications in the Frequency of Altered Ego States throughout the Life Cycle

WAYNE A. MYERS

In this chapter I present clinical material and observations on the change in frequency of certain altered ego states during the life cycle, focusing particularly on modifications in old age. Following the clinical discussion, I review the literature to date on the ego states related to micropsia and the Isakower phenomenon. I have discovered no mention of fluctuations in the frequency of such phenomena across the life course such as I have observed clinically.

Clinical Material

Case 1

Mr. A. was a seventy-three-year-old retired business executive who entered treatment because of feelings of emptiness after his wife died. Although he readily acknowledged not having loved her very much, they had shared artistic interests, and he was certain that he would miss that aspect of their relationship. Life seemed barren without her, despite their dull sexual relationship.

As treatment progressed and he began to feel better, Mr. A. experienced a reawakening of sexual desire. He masturbated while watching pornographic films and was surprised that he did not feel guilty. Earlier in life, especially during the first years of his marriage, he had felt considerable guilt when he masturbated with fantasies of women other than his wife.

With the return of sexual feelings and enthusiasm for living, Mr. A. began to search for new interests. As a young man, he had seriously considered art as a career, but ultimately opted for business because it seemed "the more stable course of action." After painting in his spare time for many years, he had given up the hobby in his mid-thirties. His completed canvases were still in the attic of his country home.

After spending a weekend looking at some of those old paintings, Mr. A. told me of his surprise that he no longer experienced his earlier "distortions" while viewing them. In response to my inquiry about the "distortions," he said that he had been subject to upsetting perceptual disturbances during different periods of his life. Specifically, from his late oedipal or early latency years onward, he had experienced bouts of micropsia in which objects appeared small and distant, as if viewed through the wrong end of a telescope. These episodes first occurred in conjunction with repeated eye infections and happened most often when he was falling asleep, particularly when he disobeyed parental and medical injunctions not to rub his infected eyes.

The frequency of the micropsia diminished during preadolescence—only to increase again during early adolescence. In response to my query, Mr. A. related most of the episodes to masturbation before sleep, in other words, to times when he was disobeying a second parental injunction not to rub a part of his anatomy.

In young adulthood the episodes of micropsia became less frequent, but during this developmental phase they became associated with "frenzied bouts" of painting. In retrospect, it became clear that the episodes were an important reason for his abandoning painting and choosing a business career; Mr. A. experienced the micropsia as highly disruptive, a threat to his sanity.

During his twenties and thirties the episodes decreased as he gradually painted less. Significantly, during this period they rarely occurred at bedtime; those episodes were almost exclusively associated with artistic activity, particularly when he stared intently at the canvas.

In our work together, we came to recognize that artistic endeavor was associated with an upsurge of conflicted sexual desires and aggressive feelings. This became very clear after Mr. A. recalled a dream from the early years of marriage in which twin paintbrushes sprouted from his eyes, reached toward his wife's nude body, and penetrated deeply into her flesh. In his mind they traced out a brilliant canvas inside her body as she writhed suggestively before him in an inchoate combination of sexual ecstasy and premortem pain. On awakening, he looked at his wife sleeping beside him; her body appeared distant and tiny.

In his forties, after a marital argument resulting from an unsatisfactory sexual encounter, he felt himself "looking daggers" at her and experienced another episode of micropsia in which she suddenly appeared small and far away.

I came to understand this patient's micropsic distortions as the result of defensive modifications of the ego functions involved in maintaining perceptual object constancy, which he used to protect himself against the terrifying intensity of his sexual and aggressive wishes toward his wife. Moreover, it seems likely that the upward displacement from penis to eyes was based in part on a need to defend against derivatives of incestuous masturbatory fantasies emanating from the oedipal and adolescent periods. Superego injunctions against rubbing his eyes and penis and masturbatory fantasies led to the compromise formation, the micropsia.

As he returned to painting, tentatively at first, then with increasing fervor, Mr. A. experienced no further episodes of micropsia, even when working with explicitly sexual and aggressive themes. For instance, on one canvas he depicted the dream in which his wife's body was dismembered by the penetrating twin paintbrushes.

In the third year of treatment, Mr. A. became ill with Parkinson's disease. As the illness progressed, he found painting increasingly difficult, owing to his physical incapacity and a relapse of the micropsia. He decided to stop painting altogether: "I can't deal with strong things anymore. I thought I had gotten hold of my feelings as I got older, only the Parkinson's took the reins away from me again. It's as if there's only part of me left to control things. All my life I've struggled for control over my emotions. I never really had it as a child, an adolescent, or a man. Then I found the strength to deal with them in my old age, and now the Parkinson's done me in again. It's not exactly what I'd call fair."

Unfortunately, life was not fair to Mr. A. in other ways. In addition to the rapid progression of his Parkinson's disease, he began to suffer from malignant hypertension and died after a series of increasingly severe cerebrovascular accidents.

The changes in ego states precipitating Mr. A.'s recurring episodes of micropsia correlated roughly with fluctuations in the intensity of the drives and the strength of the defenses associated with them at different developmental stages. The period of late adulthood was notable for the rare occurence of episodes of micropsia because of the diminished intensity of the drives and the increased understanding and acceptance of his feelings gained in therapy. That equilibrium continued until Parkinson's disease intervened and once again changed the equation.

Case 2

Mrs. B. was seen in psychotherapy for almost a year before she died at the age of eighty. The death of her second husband, three months before she sought treatment, was only one in a series of major losses. As a preadolescent, she had lost her mother, and shortly before she turned twenty, her father died. Her first husband died in a train crash during her forties, and one of her two children died of breast cancer when the patient was in her fifties.

Aside from the sense of tragedy that seemed to pervade this woman's life, most germane to this discussion is that Mrs. B. suffered from episodes of Isakower-type phenomena throughout her life. The episodes were characterized by the sensation that a large round mass was moving toward her and pressing against her face and mouth, then decreasing in size as it moved away and receded from view. During these experiences her lower body felt "distant," "detached," or "dead."

The first episodes occurred in childhood, although Mrs. B. could not pinpoint the time of onset. She was certain that they began before the death of her mother when she was eleven years old. She clearly recalled several episodes after her mother's death. They occurred most often as she was falling asleep. She remembered feeling "peculiar" (her word for the experience) on many occasions after her father came into her room to talk with her, hold her close, and kiss her good night on the lips. He had not been given to such "indulgences" before her mother died, and despite the unpleasantness associated with the altered ego state, Mrs. B. still relished the memories of those periods of closeness with her father. Although we never uncovered any discrete memories to corroborate the hypothesis, we agreed that the father's visits most likely stirred oedipal masturbatory fantasies with which she dealt defensively by means of the altered ego state. (That conclusion is in keeping with my previous findings [see Myers 1977] and those of Isakower [1938] and Richards [1985].)

What is relevant here is that similar alterations in her ego state did *not* recur after the death of Mrs. B.'s second husband shortly before her eightieth birthday. When I asked her for more detail about the earlier episodes, she rather quickly connected them with her strong sexual desires and lifelong difficulty in controlling masturbation: "Guess I'm not the same lively woman anymore," she commented when I asked her why she thought she had not experienced any "peculiar" episodes after the death of her second husband. "Even though I still think of it [sex] off and on, I don't get the same feelings in my blood as I used to. Must be getting old. I used to feel guilty when I'd feel peculiar like that, but I think I'd welcome the chance to feel that way again. I'd know I was still alive. This way, it's hard to tell."

In the latter part of her treatment with me, Mrs. B. was diagnosed as having a rapidly progressing carcinoma of the lung. Generalized metastases, including some to the brain, led to a dramatic downturn in her health, and she sank into ever-lengthening periods of coma. These were temporarily aborted with chemotherapy, but the downhill course was inexorable. I visited her in the hospital during one of her lucid periods. Although recent memory difficulties and other signs of organicity were obvious, she recalled much of what we had reconstructed during the past year. She steered the conversation around to the Isakower phenomena and told me that they had returned on a few occasions in the hospital when she was either lapsing into or emerging from delirium. It struck her fancy that in one such instance she had imagined that her father or I was there in her hospital room, tucking her in bed and kissing her on the lips. The hallucination led to considerable sexual arousal and masturbation, which was interrupted by a nurse who seemed upset by Mrs. B.'s behavior. Shortly after that visit, Mrs. B. lapsed into an irreversible coma and died.

As was the case with Mr. A., the phenomena associated with altered ego state in childhood had disappeared as she aged and then recurred under organic stress, in her case cerebral metastases.

Review of the Literature

The earliest psychoanalytic reference to micropsia was by Sándor Ferenczi (1927). With regard to dreams about giants and dwarfs, he wrote:

> The sudden appearance of giants or magnified objects is always the residue of a childhood recollection dating from a time when, because we ourselves were so small, all other objects seemed gigantic. An unusual reduction in the size of objects and persons, on the other hand, is to be attributed to the compensatory, wish-fulfilling fantasies of the child who wants to reduce the proportions of the terrifying objects in his environment to the smallest possible size. (P. 44)

I would add that the micropsic diminution in the size of objects is also related to the child's wish to remove objects from the terrifying intensity of his or her own feelings and wishes.

In a brief paper based on interviews with the mothers of two latency-age children, W. Inman (1938) related the children's experiences of micropsia to the mother's presence and to the reactivation of early nursing experience. Unfortunately, his evidence did not confirm a preoedipal origin for the micropsia; one could as well have postulated that the arousal of oedipal wishes in the children precipitated perceptual regression that resulted in the micropsia.

In 1938, Otto Isakower described the phenomena that now bear his name: sensations of a large round object pressing on the mouth, skin, and hand, associated with falling asleep. On occasion the giant objects were described as shrinking in size and moving into the distance, a phenomenon akin to micropsia. In conceptualizing such states, Isakower attributed them to cathectic shifts in libidinal energy associated with falling asleep. Removal of libido from the external world to the body ego caused a reactivation of attitudes from infancy related to sucking at the breast and falling asleep satiated. Isakower further suggested that the revival of early ego states was a consequence of defense against oedipal masturbatory fantasies aroused when falling asleep.

Isakower's hypothesis fails to explain why libidinal cathectic shifts result in this *specific* phenomenon and not others. Dealing with the episodes primarily in libidinal terms, he gives short shrift to derivatives of the aggressive drive, which are readily apparent in such cases.

Leo Bartemeier (1941) related micropsia to a defense against oral sadistic wishes. His exclusion of oedipal wishes is at variance with my own clinical material. Ernst Lewy (1954) described periods of micropsia during psychotic episodes in a schizophrenic adolescent boy. He hypothesized that the micropsia might represent projection of the patient's internal sense of smallness and insignificance. He too used cathectic shifts in energy to explain the phenomenon and saw micropsia and the allied depersonalization as related to a reactivation of early oral experiences.

Otto Sperling (1957) described a number of patients with Isakower-like hypnagogic hallucinations. The analysis of related dream material confirmed for him the oral basis of such experiences, although he linked the phenomena to thumb sucking rather than nursing at the breast.

E. James Anthony (1960) wrote of naturally occurring and experimentally induced micropsia in children. He spoke of a phase during the middle years of childhood in which stability and constancy in the sizes and shapes of objects are present, but shaky. External or internal stresses may lead to regression to the earlier, inconstant state. He further noted that object stability suffers in adults during periods of psychological and physiological stress, as was the case in the latter days of the two patients I describe in this chapter.

In a series of papers on micropsia, Jerome Schneck (1961, 1969, 1971) postulated that his patient suffered episodes of this phenomenon in childhood as a means of coping with feelings of weakness and inferiority.

Ira Miller (1963) related micropsia and other body-image alterations to challenges to ego-syntonic character attitudes from reality or from confrontations in therapy. His clinical data highlight the central role of oedipal conflicts in the genesis of micropsia.

In 1966, Michael Woodbury related micropsia and the Isakower phenomenon to cathectic shifts in self and object representations. He viewed childhood inconstancy of object size and shape, which he called visual perceptual primacy, as intensified or fixated in such patients because of constitutional factors. The altered body ego experiences were understood to result from regression to an oral state in which visual perceptual primacy predominated. Unfortunately, he neglected the role of unconscious fantasies and concentrated instead on manifest thoughts.

In an earlier paper (Myers 1976), I described episodes of depersonalization in an individual who perceived herself as split into observing and participating selves. The participating self-representation was seen as tiny and distant compared with the observing aspect of the self because of an unconscious association with unacceptable actions and thoughts. These states were closely related to episodes of micropsia.

In a subsequent paper on micropsia per se (Myers 1977), I described a patient with pronounced testicular movements who also suffered from episodes of micropsia. Anxieties arising from concerns about testicular size and shape were displaced onto, and symbolically represented in, the symptom of visual perceptual inconstancy. Masturbatory fantasies from the oedipal and latency years connected the testicular and ocular areas (as in Mr. A.'s case they bridged the gap between the phallic and ocular areas) and were dynamically significant in the genesis of the micropsia and its reactivation in transference during adult psychoanalysis. Castration and separation anxieties aroused by the masturbatory fantasies were defended against by regressive modification of the ego functions involved in visual perception. Similar ego changes in the service of defense are seen in states of déjà vu and depersonalization.

Rene Spitz (1955) expressed the belief that the approaching mass in Isakower phenomena represented the mother's face as well as the maternal breast, a formulation with which Renato Almansi (1958) concurred. Spitz also included the presence of the mother's voice in his description, and Geraldine Fink's (1967) detailed survey of the phenomenology of such experiences elaborated on that idea.

A number of other authors (Little 1970; Pacella 1975; Stern 1961) have suggested that the psychoanalytic recovery of primal scene memories and the arousal of concomitant castration and separation anxieties are responsible for the defensive mobilization of Isakower-like phenomena in treatment sessions. Arnold Richards (1985) argued convincingly for an oedipal etiology in conflicts responsible for the genesis of such phenomena in analytic sessions.

Conclusions

Although it would be unreasonable to posit far-reaching conclusions from the limited clinical data presented here, I feel that the material allows the formulation of certain tentative hypotheses. Specifically, the material demonstrates an evolution in the frequency of altered ego states throughout the life cycle.

In both patients, the upsurge of the drives seen in the oedipal and latency years gave rise to prominent incestuous masturbatory fantasies. Those in turn led to intrapsychic conflict and to the mobilization of castration and separation anxieties that were defended against by an alteration of the ego functions involved in assessing the perceptual constancy of objects.

For both patients, the defensive alterations in ego function and resulting episodes of micropsia or Isakower phenomena increased in frequency as adolescent drives intensified. Relative diminution in the intensity of the drives and accompanying maturation of defenses led to a gradual decline in the frequency of such episodes during young and middle adult years.

In late adulthood both individuals experienced a phase of freedom from such altered ego states. It would seem that the disappearance of the perceptual distortions was related to a combination of factors: diminishing intensity of drives (as alluded to by Mrs. B. in comments about her decreased sexual desire); continuing maturation of defenses; and the greater degree of acceptance of less critically drive-derivative wishes seen in many older patients.

The return of the altered ego states in both these patients before death was related to organic factors that affected the central nervous system directly: the Parkinson's disease in Mr. A.'s case and the cerebral metastases in that of Mrs. B. In other words, an organically based weakening of the capacity to evaluate reality and deal with drive intensity led to a recrudescence of the phenomena. I hope that other investigators working with older individuals in dynamically oriented treatments will offer data to corroborate or refute these findings.

It seems to me that the evolution in the frequency of altered ego states as described here is another example of adult developmental phenomena which, as indicated by Colarusso and Nemiroff (1981, 1985) do not stop at the oedipal phase or during adolescence, but continue throughout the life cycle.

REFERENCES

Almansi, R. J. 1958. "A Hypnagogic Phenomenon." *Psychoanalytic Quarterly* 27:539–46.

Anthony, E. J. 1960. "An Experimental Approach to the Psychopathology of Childhood Micropsia." In *Psychiatric Research Reports (Child Development and Psychiatry), vol. 13,* ed. E. Shagass and B. Pasamanick, pp. 63–107. Washington, D.C.: American Psychiatric Association.

Bartemeier, L. H. 1941. "Micropsia." *Psychoanalytic Quarterly* 10:573–82.

Ferenczi, S. [1927] 1955. "Gulliver Fantasies." In *Final Contributions to the Problems and Methods of Psycho-Analysis,* ed. M. Balint, pp. 41–60. New York: Basic Books.

Fink, G. 1967. "Analysis of the Isakower Phenomenon." *Journal of the American Psychoanalytic Association* 15:281–93.

Inman, W. 1938. A Psycho-analytical Explanation of Micropsia." *International Journal of Psycho-Analysis* 19:226–28.

Isakower, O. 1938. "A Contribution to the Patho-psychology of Phenomena Associated with Falling Asleep." *International Journal of Psycho-Analysis* 19:331–45.

Lewin, B. D. 1946. "Sleep, the Mouth, and the Dream Screen." *Psychoanalytic Quarterly* 15:419–34.

———. 1948. "Inferences from the Dream Screen." *International Journal of Psycho-Analysis* 29:224–31.

———. 1953. "Reconsideration of the Dream Screen." *Psychoanalytic Quarterly* 22:174–99.

Lewy, E. 1954. "On Micropsia." *International Journal of Psycho-Analysis* 35:13–19.

Little, R. B. 1970. "Behind the Dream Screen." *Psychoanalytic Review* 57:137–42.

Miller, I. 1963. "Confrontation, Conflict and the Body Image." *Journal of the American Psychoanalytic Association* 11:66–83.

Myers, W. A. 1976. "Imaginary Companions, Fantasy Twins, Mirror Dreams and Depersonalization." *Psychoanalytic Quarterly* 45:503–24.

———. 1977. "Micropsia and Testicular Retractions." *Psychoanalytic Quarterly* 46:580–604.

Pacella, B. L. 1975. "Early Ego Development and the *Déjà vu.*" *Journal of the American Psychoanalytic Association* 23:300–318.

Richards, A. D. 1985. "Isakower-like Experience on the Couch: a Contribution to the Psychoanalytic Understanding of Regressive Ego Phenomena." *Psychoanalytic Quarterly* 54:415–34.

Rycroft, G. 1951. "A Contribution to the Study of the Dream Screen." *International Journal of Psycho-Analysis* 32:178–84.

Schneck, J. M. 1961. "Micropsia." *American Journal of Psychiatry* 118:232–34.

———. 1969. "Micropsia." *Psychosomatics* 10:249–51.

———. 1971. "Psychogenic Micropsia." *Psychiatric Quarterly* 45:542–44.

Sperling, O. 1957. "A Psychoanalytic Study of Hypnagogic Hallucinations." *Journal of the American Psychoanalytic Association* 5:115–23.

Spitz, R. A. 1955. "The Primal Cavity: A Contribution to the Genesis of Perceptions and its Role for Psychoanalytic Theory." *Psychoanalytic Study of the Child* 10:215–40.

Stern, M. M. 1961. "Blank Hallucinations: Remarks about Trauma and Perceptual Disturbances." *International Journal of Psycho-Analysis* 42:205–15.

Woodbury, M. A. 1966. "Altered Body-ego Experiences: A Contribution to the Study of Regression, Perception and Early Development." *Journal of the American Psychoanalytic Association* 14:273–303.

DISCUSSION

Dr. Myers uses his experience with elderly patients to shed new light on unusual clinical phenomena of altered ego states throughout the life cycle. We have known for many years that childhood experience can help us understand adulthood, but only recently have we begun to use our knowledge of the second half of life to understand the first.

In the case of Mr. A. we observe a reawakening of sexual desire at age seventy-three following the death of his wife. We speculate that this phenomenon may not be an unusual experience in the elderly. In structural terms, the reawakening is related to an alteration in the superego. According to adult developmental thinking, the superego continues to evolve throughout the life cycle; in childhood primarily because of interaction with the infantile objects and in adulthood, we suggest, because of the influence of significant, long-standing relationships, particularly one with a loved spouse. The death of a spouse is akin to the decathexis of the parents during adolescence. Both are based on loss, real and intrapsychic, and diminish the power of the introjects, which form the core nuclei of the superego. The developmental task is the same for both the adolescent and the bereaved elderly spouse: reintegration of the superego based on new and revised object ties, real and intrapsychic.

Dr. Myers gives a clear description of Mr. A.'s micropsia, relating its inception to an internal neurotic conflict between sexual and aggressive impulses and the superego. The symptom waxed and waned throughout his *entire* life cycle in response to constantly changing developmental pressures.

The changes in ego states precipitating Mr. A.'s episodes of micropsia correlated roughly with fluctuations in the intensity of the drives and the strength of the defenses associated with them at different developmental stages. The period of late adulthood was notable for the rare occurrence of episodes of micropsia because of the diminished intensity of the drives and the increased understanding and acceptance of his feelings gained in therapy. That equilibrium continued until Parkinson's disease intervened and once again changed the equation. (P. 335)

Until recently, late adulthood would have been excluded from such a developmental formulation by many authors, being seen only as a time of degeneration and decay. Dr. Myers's case material—in itself unusual because elderly individuals are rarely seen in dynamic psychotherapy—clearly demonstrates the developmental process operative in late adulthood, with increases and decreases in drive state and defensive activity caused by changes in the body and the environment, as in all earlier developmental stages. This clinical material adds to our growing conviction that the developmental process in late adulthood is qualitatively the same as at all earlier developmental stages.

The second patient, Mrs. B., seen at ages seventy-nine and eighty, suffered from Isakower-type phenomena, which were related to incestuous wishes toward her father, particularly after her mother's death.

Dr. Myers raised the intriguing question of why the Isakower phenomena did not recur after the death of Mrs. B.'s second husband, just before her eightieth birthday. The patient, who understood the relationship between the symptom and her sexual feelings, fell back on a deeply ingrained cultural stereotype that she "must be getting old." But this was clearly not the case. As she lay dying of cancer, the patient told Dr. Myers of the return of the Isakower phenomena as she lapsed into or emerged from coma. In addition, the symptom was related to transference phenomena, since the patient fantasized that both her father and Dr. Myers were in her hospital room kissing her. Soon after, she lapsed into an irreversible coma.

This remarkable clinical material demonstrates the extraordinary human and scientific rewards awaiting the therapist who follows elderly patients through terminal illnesses—a therapeutic principle we advanced earlier in *The Race Against Time* (1985). Dr. Myers was able to follow the powerful sexualized transference and the masturbatory activity and fantasy that continued almost to the moment of Mrs. B.'s death. This material adds to the growing body of clinical evidence demonstrating the intensity of a dynamic intrapsychic life replete with infantile and adult sexual themes, symptom formation, and transference until the moment of death, even in the face of organic illness that temporarily clouds consciousness.

In his review of the literature, Dr. Myers describes Ferenczi's 1927 reference to the infantile origin of micropsia. Those pioneering ideas continue to merit attention. But our understanding of micropsia and the Isakower phenomena has been greatly advanced by Dr. Myers and others who have described the contribution of oedipal conflict to the formation of these symptoms. In addition, Dr. Myers has given us a conceptual framework within which to understand the evolution of these phenomena across the life cycle: the presence or absence of these curious symptoms in relation to the intensity of the drives versus the integrity of the ego. The symptoms tend to increase during periods of great drive intensity such as the oedipal phase and adolescence, and to diminish in frequency when the ego has the upper hand, as it does in latency and certain intervals in adulthood.

But the chapter adds most to our understanding of these phenomena in late adulthood in relation to the greater degree of acceptance of less critically drive-derivative wishes seen in many older patients (p. 340). We have also found this to be true and relate its presence, in part, to the integration of another adult developmental task, the acceptance of the approach of personal death. When the universal experience of death is accepted, the drives are seen from a more benign, humane standpoint: in accepting their own end, the ego and superego become more tolerant of aggressive and sexual thoughts and actions. Another example of how the developmental themes of late adulthood interface with the drives, producing continual intrapsychic change, was clearly indicated in both of Dr. Myers's patients, until death brought their development to an end.

REFERENCES

Nemiroff, R. A., and Colarusso, C. A. 1985. *The Race Against Time: Psychotherapy and Psychoanalysis in the Second Half of Life.* New York: Plenum.

14

Clinical Lessons from Adult Development Theory

ROGER L. GOULD

Introduction

"Thank God for the developmental process!" That summary remark by Max Gitelson, a well-known Chicago analyst, in response to the question of how psychoanalysis works has stuck with me for fifteen years. Until I heard it, I had been confusing my conduct of the analysis and observation of the transference with the more fundamental developmental process going on within my patients, a process which I neither initiated nor sustained. I came subsequently to see my role as that of privileged observer, who occasionally makes interventions that may alter the pace or direction of the process, but not as the prime mover of the therapeutic enterprise. It was not long before my interest in the developmental process led to the study of how development takes place in the life course without formal therapeutic mediation.

A decade later, the question that took hold of me (and which is the focus of this chapter) was, "What would a therapeutic intervention look like if it were specifically designed to acknowledge, facilitate, and amplify the ongoing adult development processes?" Such an intervention would be based on the relationship between current reality and developmental conflict, a notion in sharp contrast to Freud's focus.

Freud began by observing what he thought was a natural curative process and adopted the "chimney sweep" method. He did not start with

345

developmental processes in mind. Current reality, already covered by the psychology of his day, was uninteresting to him. He started with symptoms and focused on the mental processes of repression and the conflicts of memory. That starting point is represented still in the core of both psychodynamic theory and the theory of transference neurosis. It is "depth" psychology, where depth means unconscious, primary process, and distant past events.

Since Freud, psychoanalytic theory has evolved steadily and now embraces ego psychology and adaptation (the general theory), the psychosocial stages of Erik Erikson (1980), adult development as an extension of ego psychology (Rappaport 1959), and as witnessed by this book and other works during the last decade, a not yet fully integrated theory of adult development as independent and driven by a person's consciousness of time and death. Concepts of time, aging, and death represent the "entities" of the life-cycle developmental process. Therapeutic attention can no longer focus entirely on the conflicts of memory; it must include current reality and the struggle to adapt to ever-changing time. I propose here a model of treatment based on adult development that shifts focus toward these entities of the life cycle without sacrificing the insights of depth psychology. I believe therapy constructed to facilitate the natural process of change, as seen in the struggle to adapt, will be more effective.

The model is based on four overlapping but distinct frames of reference that constitute the critical reality space of therapeutic activity.

1. Patients are asking important questions about how to live their lives. There is always some decision to be made that will affect their futures in an unknown way. This is the *existential* frame of reference, which is more important in adulthood than in childhood for obvious reasons and is profoundly influenced by the sense of time and position in the life cycle.

2. Patients are experiencing conflict with the facts of their immediate life situations. The conflict is usually driven by complex factors that call for new behavior(s) to effect successful adaptation. The conflict among the agencies of the self about adopting new behavior is a developmental conflict in a specific context. This is the *contextual/developmental* frame of reference.

3. The new behavior called for represents the recovery of some function sacrificed to previous adaptation. Earlier influences explain the origin of the inhibition of function while structures (construals) emanating from those earlier influences maintain the inhibition through unexamined, fear-producing assumptions or conclusions about self and others. This is the *developmental/psychodynamic* frame of reference.

4. Recovery of function and successful adaptation to an adult situation

take place in a framework where childhood deterministic influences are contrasted and questioned. This is the framework of the *volitional conflict*, where past memories and present perceptions compete to determine what action will occur. In this framework an abiding transformation of perspective can unfold.

I believe that in a successful natural developmental process, all four of these frameworks are muddled through. The four frameworks of therapeutic reality cover the domain between the patient's conscious reality preoccupation and the unconscious blocking in a way that allows for a systematic exploration from surface to depth and back to the will, yet does not confuse depth with past and memory.

The Natural Change Process

As an adult develops, he or she responds to the changing context of life as mediated by time, situation, and internal shifts. The end product is behavior newly integrated into the repertoire of behaviors characteristic of that individual. The conflict-free sphere of the ego is enlarged, and the new behavior is contained in an enhanced definition of self. This kind of development takes years to complete and usually is accomplished in a series of small steps. Situational variables are extremely important to the success of the process.

I have in mind a man who was earlier cold and withdrawn in his relationships and eventually was able to develop nurturing behaviors. He was self-critical in the earlier stages of the process, when he failed to demonstrate the capacity to care in situations that called for it. He also received ample criticism from his wife. His self-criticism was compounded by and confused with that external criticism. Being dissatisfied with oneself in this way is a painful state of mind and results in instability, which can lead to added defensiveness to avoid the conflict or to further development to resolve it. Unhealthy defensive responses may be frequently chosen. Progression takes place only when the developmental response takes place more often than the defensive response.

Usually, the mental effort to forget about the conflict—that is, to stop being dissatisfied with oneself—is accompanied by defensive behavior such as being distant and preoccupied; finding justification for an aloof or above-it-all posture; or becoming too busy to care. The man to whom I refer used all three maneuvers. Defensive behavior is directly competitive and incompatible with caring behavior. Defensive behavior creates problems: it is not responsive to reality but serves to deny a painful state of mind. Although such behavior is inevitably problematic, it is not extinguishable by ordinary contingencies of reward and punishment specific to a context, because it is driven by the more powerful motive to relieve pain through temporary unawareness.

Therefore, like any developmental conflict, a conflict about becoming caring has two inappropriate sets of behavior. In this man's case, the primary behavior was the inability to respond to his own intent. The secondary patterns were the defenses expressed as behavior, namely, always being too busy.

During this man's first marriage, his inability to develop the caring function was an ingredient *and* a consequence of the failed relationship. However, when he remarried at age forty-three, he was able to be a different kind of husband—busy still, but not too busy to care about his wife. Five years later, his eighteen-year-old son from the first marriage almost died in his arms from an overdose of drugs. Up to that point, the man had been a critical, cold father who could only fight with his son. He was tough and competitive with colleagues at work and with his son at home. His caring was limited to his wife.

In the four months after his son's close call, he gained forty pounds, his diastolic blood pressure went up to 120, and he slept and concentrated poorly. Dissatisfied with his inability to express a nurturing side of himself to his son who was in great distress, he experienced intense conflict whenever he found himself compounding his son's problem by his uncontrolled tough approach. The unfinished developmental conflict about caring was transformed into a poignant *existential* conflict ("My actions can determine his life or death struggle") and an unremitting *volitional* conflict ("How can I control myself?") under the influence of a highly specific *contextual/developmental* situation.

The confluence of these three frames of reference set the stage for an apparent "accidental" insight representing the remaining frame of reference, the *developmental/psychodynamic* frame. While having dinner with a friend from his high school years and sharing his woes, his friend reminded him of how hurt he had been as a teenager by his father's rough and rigid approach. He began to question why he had become so much like his father. He realized that he did not have to be a tough disciplinarian as his own father had been with him. He thought, "At work you take charge, compete, and show your employees how tough you are. At home it is not a win-lose situation. You aren't going to be destroyed by being soft and loving and cooperative." In a flash of insight he saw that the dangers of experimenting with being caring were bogus and based on false conclusions formed by a child's mind and enmeshed in an overdetermined identification with his own father.

Over the next few months, with the encouragement and support of his wife, the man became more nearly the caring and nurturing father he had always intended to be. Development occurred without formal treatment but progressed in a way that can be understood in formal theory.

Adult development can be defined as becoming attuned to the changing context of reality by healing the split that inhibits integration of important functions and simultaneously giving up inappropriate defensive maneuvers. The driver of development is the painful state of dissatisfaction with oneself. The final decision about change is made in the action center of the volitional conflict.

Short-term Therapy

The frameworks I have delineated can be used to understand a case and shape the therapeutic intervention. For clinical purposes the first two frames of reference, existential and contextual/developmental, can be condensed into one simple probing question: "What is the patient's conflict with his current reality?" The pursuit of this question keeps both the patient and the therapist focused on the patient's pain. To pursue the question effectively, the clinician needs wisdom gained from living and an understanding of life-cycle developmental processes.

In a similar way, the developmental/psychodynamic and volitional frames of reference can be condensed into the complex clinical question: "What intrapsychic realities interfere with the solution of the patient's conflict with the current reality situation?" The answer to this question requires a thorough working knowledge of psychodynamics.

Frequently, the second, complex question is pursued without the continuous balancing orientation of the first, the simpler question. It is easy to get lost in the fascination of the psychodynamic puzzle, but that foray is unacceptable when the therapeutic goal is dictated by short-term treatment. The interplay of the two questions representing the four frames of reference is critical, as the following case discussion will illustrate.

A twenty-two-year-old, recent college graduate has come to treatment because of an existential question: he is about to decide in favor of a gay lifestyle. He is a virgin to both sexes. He dates women and gets an erection while petting, but he is also a "pretty boy" who allows himself to be fondled by wealthy older men. Since graduating from college five months ago, he has had four jobs. He has been asked to be the lover of a powerful and persistent older gay man and is tempted to agree. What is the conflict with reality?

The conflict was obvious in the contextual/developmental frame, even though it was not initially declared by the patient: "Steven, your biggest conflict is that you can't do what you need to do to earn a living. College is over. Your parents' support is withdrawn. You're broke and you're on your fourth job. What is it that you need to do for yourself that you're not able to do?"

In other words, reality (as represented by commonly accepted social values and expectations, and mediated by friends and relatives) is making an age-appropriate demand that Steven take full responsibility for his food, shelter, entertainment, and transportation. Steven is failing. Becoming responsible for himself must be the guiding light of treatment. His failure to become self-sufficient is the source of painful dissatisfaction with himself. That is where he is developmentally stuck. That simple truth contains the most "reality power." All other psychodynamic considerations should be seen as partial answers to this dominating question. The short-term treatment episode will be successful when Steven understands enough to act adaptively to this demand inherent in his age-related context. At that time treatment might terminate, or other reality-driven issues might be addressed, such as his inability to have a healthier connection with either men or women. But at the moment, those issues are decoys. The psychodynamic issues explored in this case were organized around the simple truth that Steven could not earn a living.

In the first two sessions we discovered that Steven was the father surrogate for two younger sisters. His family was poor. His father was a "failure," and his mother left to find herself and establish a career and make money for the family. Steven was smart, very good looking, and pleasant to be with. He parlayed this into success at a rich kids' college where nobody knew about his past. During college he met and became part of the international set and was invited all over the world. After college, his rich friends left while he became a trainee at a local department store. Two weeks after that he was fired because he did not fit in.

The facts of his college life supported the fabricated identity that he, too, was a rich and privileged person, that he had never really been poor and never would be poor and, above all, was not a failure like his father. His looks, charm, and connections were all integrated into this fabricated reality. He adapted well to it. His postcollege situation required new qualities, including the acceptance of the new reality and the ability to persist—to learn and master the mystery of how to make a living. But Steven did not want to know about this reality, much less adapt to it. To continue his successful identity of the college years, he was required to make a quick fortune. If he did not, he would be a failure like his

father. The truth would be revealed: he had been poor and would probably always be poor; and furthermore, he had been a fraud at college, not
a success. He would be failing the dream of manhood—to be rich in
order to take care of his younger sisters and to rescue his mother from
her new husband who had money but who, in Steven's eyes, kept his
mother subjugated and unhappy. The wish to become rich, with no
business experience, connections, or specialized knowledge conflicted
with the reality of the business world.

By the second session, Steven had taken the bleach out of his hair,
looked straight instead of gay, and had ended his relationship with the
older gay man. The existential question of whether he was gay or
straight collapsed into the contextual/developmental question. Being
gay and taken care of would have been the quick and easy way to make
a killing with his looks and to soar once again with the rich. He saw that
it was wrong for him. But he had not entirely given up the idea that there
was an easy way to become rich. He was not sure he had the capacity
to stick to something and make it work. He was seriously thinking about
plastic surgery to make his face less boyish and more ruggedly masculine. "People in business trust those kinds of faces, and it's an important
edge when making big deals."

"How will it help you now when you have to learn how to be an
apprentice in some line of work?" was my question that brought him
back to his current conflict with reality. When the simple question is
pursued—"Why can't you develop the skill and capacity to learn as a
novice and build your work life from a solid foundation?"—the complex
developmental/psychodynamics are loaded into the volitional framework where the information can be ordered and applied to the task at
hand.

His debilitating fear of the future is partially based on projections
from the past. Will he become a man (rich) or a helpless little boy (poor,
impulsive, grandiose) like his castrated father? He wants to get rich
quick to offset the conviction that he is destined to repeat his father's
life, but of course without a substantive skill, the attempt becomes the
mechanism that might doom him to "failure" and threatens to fulfill his
worst fear of compulsory identification with his father. This imperative
attempt to counteridentify and ward off the anxiety through a grandiose
mechanism explains his conviction that he lacks the capacity to build
slowly and solidly as his current life demands. This self-doubt is central
to the current developmental task.

Given the presenting sexual identity diffusion and the romantic imagery of himself as the hero-father, it would have been tempting to pursue
oedipal interpretations directly. But within the confines of short-term

treatment based on adult development, the *derivatives* of the Oedipus complex involving inhibitions about work and love are center stage. The remaining treatment hours focused on helping Steven understand the dynamics that would enable him to start to work. When Steven works through his inhibition about work and builds on his talents, he may gather enough self-esteem to resolve his inhibitions about love without added treatment. If in his eyes he becomes a man different from his father, he may be free enough to proceed from petting to intercourse. If development can continue without formal treatment, a short-term intervention that returns the patient to a stream of experience with one more set of conflict-free functions may be all that is needed, or indeed possible. Steven might not be ready to integrate more than one unit of developmental work.

The Unit of Developmental Work

In the two preceding examples, new behavior patterns were indicative of the adaptational response and the partial resolution of a corresponding developmental conflict. Now, the task is to anchor those clinical observations to the general adaptational theory (and the theory of ego functions) while preserving the vantage point of adult development. To accomplish this, I propose the term *unit of adult development.* The following comments are meant to define a unit of psychological work in common-sense observations closely associated with the clinical (not metapsychological) theory of ego functioning. The work is essentially an adaptational response that is required to meet some demand implicit in a situation. That context is frequently categorized as a transition, a crisis, a stress situation, or a challenge.

All people change with age because new priorities in the life cycle require new attitudes and new behavior. Change is a conflict-free adaptational response to the reality of the present and can only be straightforward when there is no internal conflict among the agencies of the self. Sometimes people simply cannot respond to the facts of current reality with the appropriate adaptational response because that response is mired in internal conflict (inhibitions, defenses, character patterns). The adaptational demand challenges them to free that response from underlying conflicts in order to be flexible enough to respond appropriately and effectively to the perceived present reality. If they succeed in resolving the conflict that had caused them to be rigid, they recover a necessary function that is defined by the action they take.

Most patients come to treatment with symptoms that are consequences of a developmental struggle triggered by an adaptational demand. Since any demand inherent in the situation calls for psychological work, we should call *developmental* only those responses that represent a significant effort involving the *resolution of a conflict,* and *having structural change as an outcome.* The critic who says there is no adult development, but merely change in behavior responsive to changing circumstances is observing a simple nondevelopmental pattern change in a person who has little conflict about making that specific change. On the other end of the spectrum, therapists frequently observe struggles like Steven's in patients responding to normal demands in the environment. The resistance to change is tied to either a nuclear neurotic belief system or a powerful defense strategy. The attempts at change activate increasing negative affect, the content of which is catastrophic predictions about potential adverse consequences. Patients present themselves as either anxiously confused or depressed that their efforts have failed.

When a patient is having difficulty in changing a simple behavior pattern, the patient is often observed to be confused between the inherent demand of the *current* situation (which calls for a relatively easy change of behavior) and some earlier adaptational demand that required him to install or maintain the pattern he or she is now trying to change. The patient's conflict is between two different time frames of reference, where holdovers from the past have more behavior-determining power than the current situation.

Given these considerations, a unit of adult developmental progression would contain the following three elements.

1. There is a specific demand inherent in the situation calling for a new behavior pattern.

2. The patient accomplishes this behavior pattern change only after engaging in significant psychological work and sorting out the difference between current reality and past realities confounded with the current situation.

3. The patient arrives at a clearer and grounded understanding of current reality, and from that strengthened position is more able to manage the easier tasks of psychological work that do not require him or her to sort out past and present in the midst of a confounding negative affect experience.

This definition of a unit of adult developmental progression permits a meeting of the minds for the divergent schools of thought about adult development. The recent works of Erikson (1980), Levinson (1978), Vaillant (1977), Gould (1978), Pollock (1981), Colarusso and Nemiroff (1987), and others can be viewed from this perspective.

Ambiguity attends the terms used to conceptualize psychological change. The nuclear neurotic conflict (including the residual states of self) is hard to pin down or agree upon and varies with each school of thought in the depth-psychology camp. Defenses are easy to define, but in actuality distinguishing between defenses that are either counterproductive or productive is often difficult because of the complexities of any situation and the profound importance of dialectical swings in the solution of psychological conflicts.

One solution for these ambiguities is to define the outcome of the psychological work that constitutes a developmental unit of work in structural terms that are more easily observable and better fit the adult situation. The outcome is the *disinhibition of a blocked function* or the recovery of an inhibited function so that the function becomes a legitimate part of the patient's positive self-definition and part of the patient's proactive stance in life. Some common examples of this kind of change ordinarily observed in the course of successful psychotherapy or psychoanalysis are the recovery of the abilities to stand up for oneself, to become more playful or fun-loving, to interact with others with deeper connectedness, to be more honest with oneself, to work, and to love.

Throughout the history of psychoanalysis, recovery of function has been the goal of treatment. Freud helped patients recover function by ridding them of the symptoms that interfered with function. Heinz Hartman (1958) described the process as a dichotomy between conflictual and conflict-free zones of ego function. The goal of development and therapy is to move as many functions as possible into the conflict-free zone. Heinz Kohut (1977) describes the same process with more color, as "transmuting internalization of self object functions." Others have labeled the same process as integrating or destroying those identifications and internalizations that serve as splits in the self. Recovery of function (healing the split in the self) also leads to rehabilitation of the negative self-image.

Calvin Settlage and others (1988) have accurately captured the essence of the underlying developmental process to which I refer and have framed it within the more familiar language of ego-psychology:

The disturbance of the previously satisfactory functioning creates an unsettled state or disequilibrium with varying degrees of mental and emotional stress. The state can be ego-syntonic, as in the case of the self-initiated desire to develop, or it can be ego-dystonic, as in the case of the thrust-upon, intrusive, traumatic experience.

A sequence of developmental process

A developmental response to the dissatisfaction of the unsettled state activates a sequence of developmental process. This sequence includes the following elements:

1. *Developmental Challenge* Either consciously or unconsciously, the individual perceives and accepts a developmental challenge. Examples of developmental challenges are the need for new skills, new modes of regulating feelings and impulses, and new attitudes and values. Acceptance of a specific developmental challenge engages developmental process and transforms the unsettled state into an organized, goal-directed state.

2. *Developmental Tension* Within this goal-directed state, the gap between where the individual is and where the individual now wants or needs to be creates a developmental tension. This positive tension, which replaces the negatively experienced disequilibrium of the unsettled state, serves as a motivating and development sustaining force.

3. *Developmental Conflict* The engagement of developmental process also generates developmental conflict. The acceptance of a developmental challenge transforms the internally generated or environmentally presented expectations and demands, and the resulting unsettled state, into an internal developmental conflict. The desire to change, as it includes the wish for approval and fear of disapproval, commonly evokes fear of loss of the security experienced in the status quo, fear of failure and discouragement at seeming lack of progress, and anxieties about imagined negative consequences of success. Optimally, developmental conflict causes only transient or no symptomatic behavior and is resolved through development.

4. *Resolution of Developmental Conflict* Resolution of developmental conflict leads to self-regulatory or adaptive structure formation. It proceeds hand-in-hand with the mastery, internalization, and integration of the new function.

5. *Change in the Self-Representation* Finally, the development and integration of a new function or structure is marked by a change in the self-representation and in the individual's overall sense of identity.

A sequence of developmental process results in one or more of the following accomplishments: (a) the formation of a new function; (b) the elaboration of refinement of an existing function; (c) the further integration of an existing function toward greater autonomy and structural stability; (d) the reorganization of psychic structure to a higher level of function. (Pp. 356–57)

Settlage sees the developmental process as part of a lifelong separation-individuation struggle involving autonomous self-regulation, as the following quotation demonstrates:

> The attainment of a new function by the child requires a corresponding relinquishment by the child of the mother's no longer needed participation as an external auxiliary ego, and the relinquishment by the mother of the new function to the child. Such relinquishment is essential to the full internalization of functions in the progression toward integration and relative autonomy. Self-regulation means that a function, although still related to its source, is operative without immediate external support. Successful developmental process thus leads to a diminishing developmental need for the human subject. (1988, p. 353)

Settlage quotes Margaret Mahler to reinforce his statement and to drive home the point that each step of independent functioning (self-regulation) involves the threat of object loss:

> Mahler (1972), in her conceptualization of the separation-individuation process, observed that a minimal threat of object loss is inherent in every new step of independent functioning. Separation is obligatory in normal development and the threat of object loss is an indispensable developmental catalyst (p. 333). Thus, loss in the course of development is associated with advances in ego and superego development resulting from internalization and identification. The full structuring of an identification-derived function entails the attenuation and eventual relinquishment of the function-associated involvement with and tie to the love object. (1988, pp 354–55)

As the clinician focuses on the developmental process, he is intimately and immediately involved with the separation-individuation themes expressed in the transference. The recurring themes are related to discrete conflicted functions that are at different points on the developmental continuum. During the course of an analysis, the "relinquishment of function-associated object involvement" takes place over different functions. This aspect of the transference is familiar clinical and theoretical ground. The underlying struggle to resolve developmental conflicts in order to increase functionality is the prerequisite for being able to separate, but that ground is not familiar. Settlage (1988) mentions the developmental conflict as a step toward integration, but the critical process of the conflict resolution has not yet been described.

Toward a More Detailed Theory of
Transference Interpretation

We have now introduced two concepts derived from the field of adult development:

1. Four distinct but overlapping frames of reference are necessary to understand the natural developmental processes: existential; contextual/developmental; developmental/psychodynamic; volitional/conflictual.

2. The unit of adult developmental work can be used as a guide to the process as well as a measuring device.

These concepts have implications for psychoanalytic treatment in general and for the use of transference interpretations in particular. In contrast to the goal of short-term treatment, which is to move a patient forward one unit of adult developmental work, the goal of psychoanalysis might be seen as either to create a more thorough and quicker recovery of one major function (such as the caring function in my first clinical example, which took twenty-three years to complete without formal intervention) or to work on and integrate many interrelated functions, centering attention on one at a time. This approach departs markedly from the traditional study of transference.

Although the obvious goal of the psychoanalytic treatment process is to help the patient resolve conflicts and regain health, the methodological goal is usually stated as the resolution of the transference neurosis, a notion that resides exclusively within a psychodynamic frame of reference. In the psychoanalytic literature, transference is essentially divorced from the other three frameworks introduced in this chapter. Transference phenomena are not tied to the patient's adult life cycle, inasmuch as the emphasis is almost invariably on isolating and describing memories, object relationships, projections, and displacements as they are played out with the analyst. Colarusso and Nemiroff (1987) have corrected the earlier limitation of parental transference with their introduction of three forms of multigenerational transferences. Notwithstanding that important addition, the transference is not tied directly to a unit of work. If the distortions collected in the transference could be played against the processes of achieving a unit of work, a connection would be achieved with the patient's immediate life-cycle dilemma as expressed in the four frames of reference.

If psychoanalytic treatment were seen as a procedure that dealt with multiple units of adult development work in serial fashion, the amorphousness of the concept of "working through" might be diminished.

Repetitive transference images would be seen as distortions of reality representing the generic resistance to any significant developmental change. Each person would have his or her own set of internal images representing superego-like figures that warn and stand against recovery of function. Therefore, the same transference interpretations may be made several times over the course of analysis—a process that may look like repetition and working through but is in fact work being done on other units as the analysis proceeds. Presumably the more difficult units of work would be done nearer the end of the analysis.

For example, if Steven, in the example of short-term therapy, were in analysis, the recovery of his ability to love and trust women would undoubtedly be a subsequent unit of work following the immediate developmental need to recover the ability to work as an apprentice in a context that is not "special."

Coltrera (1979) spoke directly about transference:

The transference neurosis is very much developmentally determined, its character and focus changing throughout the life cycle according to phase-specific developmental and conflict resolutions and their subsequent internalizations (Pp. 304–305).

More precisely, the transference neurosis can be broken down into a series of transference phenomena related to specific units of developmental work. If others find this structuring useful in their clinical work, we will have moved toward specifying the work that is accomplished in psychoanalysis and also gained another termination criterion.

The following case vignette illustrates some of these points. This analysis was completed after a thirteen-year interruption. I believe two factors are particularly instructive. The first is related to the patient's age at the time of resumption; the second is related to the focused use of transference during the last phase when the transference phenomena were translated into information about a key unit of development and its specific volitional conflict.

The patient first sought treatment at age thirty-one because of work problems related to his grandiose expectations, extreme sensitivity to disappointments or slights, and uncontrollable temper with his co-worker and clients. As an afterthought, he includes some questions about whether his preference for heterosexual bondage was normal. Analysis proceeded on course for three-and-a-half years with excellent results in the domains of work and friendships, but no progress whatever on the bondage activities. There was a complete inability to be a nurturing, caring, vulnerable heterosexual man. The patient could not spend a second day with any woman, especially after sexual contact. The transference was a lively combination of oedipal, preoedipal, and narcissistic material with supporting dreams. The patient worked hard, generated material, understood pathodynamics, and was quite good at making his own interpretations and converting them into appropriate behavior outside the analysis, except in the area of heterosexual relationships. In the domain of intimacy, he carried out all the analytic activities except for converting insights into actions.

At thirty-four he was good-looking, successful, had a date or sexual encounter almost every day, and had bachelor locker-room buddies to regale with his stories of hunt and conquest. He saw no good reason to become vulnerable, intimate, or "get tied down." As far as he was concerned, everyone, including the analyst, was envious of his good fortune and wanted to talk him out of paradise in this world's capital of available beauties. When he left the analysis by mutual agreement, he said he would be back when he was ready to go further.

When he returned at age forty-seven he was calm, successful, and reported having been relatively happy, but he was becoming more lonely and wanted to marry and have children. He felt left out of a rich portion of life. The women he dated were the same age as women he dated when he was thirty-four, in their early to mid twenties. But now he was older, did not enjoy their company, and was tired of going through a dinner just to go to bed with one. His old buddies were married, and he felt others viewed him as odd because he had never married. The bondage was still somewhat exciting but no longer gave him the same sense of mastery and had begun to make him feel perverted and abnormal. This patient was ready to deal with the love domain of his life. The existential and contextual developmental frameworks of the reality space were aligned and pointed toward the unquestioned need to accomplish this all-important unit of work.

The negative transference material in the latter part of the analysis was *almost* identical to that encountered and worked through in the first part. The analyst was seen as an oedipal father trying to rob him of his rights for exclusivity and control and to tame his passions in order to trick him into ordinary reality so that ultimately he might be laughed at and humiliated by everyone, but by women in particular. He anticipated a particular kind of torture, which was to be bound up, captured, and abused by women who taunted him first with total devotion and then capriciously swung to cold withdrawal of affection and concern. Their mood swings caused him acute pain. This was worked through repeatedly in the first part of the analysis with many variations and subthemes.

That exact transference was repeated with full intensity as the analysis resumed, but with a difference. The patient had accomplished the units of adult development having to do with friendships with both males and females and with work. Those were well-integrated, conflict-free autonomous activities, which did not regress during the second part of the analysis. But along with his strong desire to succeed in achieving intimacy with a woman, certain elements in the transference shifted. Since he was no longer defending his blocked growth by asserting his special status as a woman's man, he no longer saw the analyst as an oedipal father who envied him. The analyst's motives were believed to be malicious, not merely envious of the patient's one-night stands with playmates. The analyst was perceived as having the love-life success that the patient wanted. The analyst wanted him to strive for that intimacy, but at the last moment the analyst would magically and sadistically prevent him from accomplishing his goal.

In the first phase of analysis, the transference had been interpreted in the psychodynamic framework as a transference neurosis to be resolved in order to understand in detail the situation of childhood. In contrast, during the second phase of the analysis, the transference distortions were compared with an alternative world view within the framework of the volitional conflict about experimenting with the new action steps required to enter the domain of intimacy. The psychodynamic framework had been exhausted in the first phase and had become a defense that the patient used to avoid dealing with the volitional conflict in the second part of the analysis.

When the patient saw clearly that his fears of experimenting with the new behavior were displaced and projected onto the transference, he was able to investigate those fears and to conclude that they were patently irrational. He moved on to action. After taking a step, he attained a more reality-bound view, making new adult options available to him. Each new step led to a strengthening of his adult perspective but also required him to move to a more dangerous step, which in turn triggered the inhibitory anxiety. The latent fears were unavailable until each succeeding step had been accomplished, and the intent to take the next step was strengthened by the success and perspective gained from the previous step. This dialectic of steps is the rhythm of the work within the volitional frame of reference: experiment, success, and new fear attached to the next intended step. At each step the transference distortion was critically important information about the irrational fear of necessary realistic action.

Since interpretation of the transference is the most powerful tool in psychoanalysis, it ought to be used with exactness. At some points in the analysis the transference is indispensable to understanding the developmental psychodynamics. At other points, the psychodynamic understanding must yield to the work of the volitional frame. Then the transference must be aimed directly at the volitional conflict.

Volitional Framework and Transference Interpretations

The argument presented thus far is that the analyst ought to listen to the transference in light of his knowledge of a developmental perspective and should, at selected points in the analysis, interpret the transference accordingly.

On a practical level, the analyst has a choice about how to listen. Is the reporting about the struggle to integrate a conflicted function selectively ordered to prominence by the contextual developmental demand? Or is it only a message or clue about the history of object relations repeating itself? If the answer is *both,* then it is possible to hear the repetition of the past as current information about the current struggle to complete a particular unit of adult developmental work. If that kind of listening occurs, the interpretation of the transference can at times be disciplined to help the patient complete a unit of work taking place within the volitional framework. When a patient is convinced that acting in a new way would represent recovery of function and that not acting accordingly are not valid contemporary reasons but old fears based in the past, the patient has a volitional conflict. As long as the act is not carried out, the past reality is more credible than the current reality.

The moment of "truth" occurs when the intent to act is as intensely experienced as the fear. This subtle state is only momentarily achieved because usually there is a split between the intent and the fear, and a confusion about what is "real." Such moments appear when the patient is unsure whether the analyst is the concerned helper or the sadist waiting for him to make a mistake. The transference is used to capture those moments of change, but can also be used as a deflecting mirror to prepare the stage for those kinds of moments to occur outside the analytic hour.

For example, the patient in the preceding case history experienced a moment of truth outside the analytic hour when he finally experimented with breaking his pattern regarding intimacy. Because he intended to develop a serious relationship with a woman, he was constrained to subjugate his sexual desires to the overall relationship rather than to use his sexual prowess to conquer and flee. A mundane step to initiate that process was simply to stay and talk with the woman after intercourse. He intended to do this because he was convinced that this particular woman was a good and decent woman and *just a woman.* He understood that his fear was based on a distorted image of her as a devilish trap promoted by the analyst.

The transference interpretations revealed to him that his fear of her was rooted in early memories of his experience with his mother. Prior to the action, his confusion and intense anxiety compelled him to believe the woman was a trap. Only after acting and experiencing the reality of the relationship did that image of the woman recede.

The transference interpretation was aimed at a point in the contemporary developmental process. It was not only a piece of the puzzle that informed about the past but an instrument that stripped away a defense and forced appositional confrontation between two contrasting views of reality controlling the action center of the volitional conflict. At such moments, conclusions about reality determined by childhood experiences are understood in the perspective of contradictory adult conclusions that have been carefully processed by the adult mind. In this sense the other three frames of reference must collapse into the volitional framework if recovery of function is to be effected. Only in the volitional framework can intellectual understanding be transformed into a new view of reality where old "truths" are familiar ghosts but no longer credible as bases for action.

Summary

When Max Gitelson said, "Thank God for the developmental process," I think he meant that adults are driven to recover as many functions as possible in order to be free and flexible enough to respond to the age-related demands of the life cycle and to the contingencies of situation. Each time a function is recovered, the person becomes more separate and whole, and less dependent on other people to carry out self-object functions. The person learns that it is safe to be more whole.

The theme of ownership of the self is as important in adulthood as it is during the parent-child authority conflicts of youth. The youthful identity crisis of ownership is just a point in a lifelong continuum; it is not the point of final resolution. Self versus self-object control of self-function is a critical aspect of adult consciousness that is in the background of other conflicts at all times and frequently becomes a foreground issue presenting itself as a developmental dilemma to be resolved. In that sense the developmental process is fundamental to psychoanalytic and psychotherapeutic processes. This definition of the adult developmental process strongly implies a critical role for current reality as a factory in the therapeutic enterprise.

When Erikson opened the era of theory building for adult development, he extended the useful concept of childhood stages into the adult part of the life cycle. Others have continued the stage concept or modified it to avoid the lockstep implication with such words as "phases of adult life." Both stages and phases point toward changes over time in response to new realities in the life cycle. Clinically, the concepts of phases, stages, and tasks can be better understood as two pressing reality processes. Having to respond to the demands of external idiosyncratic situations triggers a developmental conflict. Specific situations that evoke the push for growth may include geographical moves, a divorce, a promotion, a sudden illness, or the loss of a child or spouse.

There is another, less obvious stimulus to the internal imperative to recover functions. A slow cumulative process tied to age and time subtly challenges illusions of safety over decades and stimulates the self to produce more realistic strategies of safety based on present-day knowledge, clear thinking, and flexible action emanating from an autonomous self. The process is tied to age-related expectations and marker events signifying the passage of time, but essentially it is an inner imperative to liberate the self from being controlled by internal objects or external pressures. Leaving college, starting a marriage, parenthood, and retirement are some marker events generally related to a person's time in life.

The two processes involve similar phenomena: One process, emanating from a critical situation, we can call a situational demand process; the other, emanating from an imperative linked to time in life, we might call the life-cycle demand process. Both processes represent demands to undertake structural psychological work, that is, to recover or add functions.

The situational and life-cycle demands can be positively adapted to but still not be developmental in the sense employed here. If the demands are easily accommodated by using new combinations of conflict-free functions, we attribute change to the health and flexibility of existing mental structures and regulatory functions. When, however, the demands of age or task point toward a conflicted function, a unit of developmental work must occur.

Information about the task, phase, or stage of life needs to be translated into the four therapeutic reality frames of reference to achieve maximal clinical leverage. For example, the midlife developmental tasks relating to time, aging, loss, and shifting relationships with adult children and parents are properly interpreted as part of the existential framework inasmuch as they lead to both small and large life-course decisions. The immediate contextual factors bear on and point to the specific contextual/developmental issue largely through the instrumentality of life-course decisions.

The focus for the therapist must be on the idiosyncratic function that is required to meet the demand of the task as translated through the first two frames of reference. For Steven, the age-appropriate tasks—namely, to be able to work productively as an apprentice—involved several conflicted functions. Other patients will have to respond to the same task, but the functions in conflict may be different, and therefore the unit of work to be accomplished will be different.

Once the specific unit of development is identified, a new set of considerations comes into play. Where is the patient in the developmental process relative to this unit of work? The question leads to the psychodynamic and volitional frames of reference. The point reached in the developmental process is a major consideration for the clinician. The work to be done can be more readily identified if we break the process into four steps that expand our understanding of the psychodynamic and volitional frameworks.

1. Recognition of the Underdeveloped Function. The demand of the situation unbalances the ambivalence about recovering a specific inhibited function. Defenses maintain and rationalize the underdeveloped function while a low-intensity, enduring internal imperative pushes against the defenses. The demand of the situation makes the person challenge the ambivalence.

2. Articulating the Intentional Action. The conscious conflict that mobilizes the internal conflict is represented by the decision whether to act in a way that represents the right to recover the conflicted function. A positive answer represents an attempt to recover the function (at least temporarily) and master the pertinent confusion among past, present, and future of self-doubt and of other memories mobilized in the catastrophic prediction. In order to act, one must differentiate the present conflict from the unconscious resistance to action based on past conclusions about a past reality. When the intended action is carried out, the person is opting for probable safety on the basis of reality testing and is giving up a cherished *illusion* of safety.

3. Resolving the Internal Conflict. This centers our attention on the self-definition boundary as a critical clinical concept, since the threatened transgression of the boundary-controlling rule that organizes past adaptational experience triggers the boundary-maintaining superego-like forces. These boundary-maintaining phenomena include predicting catastrophe (exaggerating the possible consequences of the intended act), confusing memories of painful experiences with future reality, and fearing exposure of a deeply hidden sense of a damaged or helpless self-state.

4. The Resolution of an Interpersonal Conflict. Recovery of function takes place in a social context. A change in self-definition invokes a system change in that context. The current self-definition is confirmed and supported by family and fellow workers and the meaning attached to various work and social roles. An enlarged self-definition may pose a threat to others or trigger developmental envy. In order to create or find a niche that is confirming of the enlarged self-definition, the individual may have to resolve several interpersonal conflicts. The failure to resolve those conflicts threatens the viability of an expanding self-definition.

With these four steps, the clinician can locate, describe, study, and facilitate an adult developmental unit of work within the frameworks of current reality and still be intimately connected to the observations and concepts about nuclear neurotic conflicts and defenses (functions are inhibited originally because of adaptations to nuclear conflicts, which result in rigidification of immature defenses). Inasmuch as the recovery of a function represents a partial solution, or an unraveling of a nuclear conflict and a remodeling of the defense system toward responsiveness to current reality, the clinician can work in the depths while remaining in touch with the driving developmental processes that give immediacy and impact to each therapeutic hour.

Conclusion

Why should clinicians be interested in the subject of adult development? How will it affect their daily work?

Understanding the concepts outlined in this chapter and applying them to clinical practice will allow clinicians to be more precise in their understanding of the patient and in their transference interpretation. I use these concepts in psychoanalytic as well as short-term treatment and have used them to develop a computer-assisted short-term psychotherapy whose goal is to accomplish one unit of adult development. The steps exactly follow the developmental process described here. Some artificial intelligence theorists have argued that one measure of a good theory is that it is precise enough to be implemented as a useful computer program. That criterion would not prove that the theory is correct but would demonstrate that it is a coherent operational theory. If treatment is successful, it is "useful."

Since the computer-assisted short-term therapy program has been used, two thousand patients have indicated that it was a powerful learning experience that helped them experiment with new action representing the critical function in conflict. These positive results suggest that the program is based on a theory that is meaningful to patients' lives and indicates that the theory is a useful guide for designers of remedial interventions.

Although the language used in the computer-assisted short-term therapy program differs from the technical language used in psychoanalytic theory, the patient using the program comes to understand that the process starts with a state of dissatisfaction and ends with a different self-representation and that the work of the program is to help him or her recover an inhibited function.

The efficacy of the computerized program illustrates that a structured, detailed, step-by-step therapeutic program can be built on the understanding of a naturally occurring developmental process. In that radical departure from traditional methods, I have reached my goal of building a therapeutic model and intervention that facilitate the natural growth process. I have also indicated in this chapter how current therapeutic methods can be modified to the same end.

REFERENCES

Colarusso, C. A., and Nemoriff, R. A. 1987. "Clinical Implications of Adult Developmental Theory." *American Journal of Psychiatry* 144:1263–1270.

Coltrera, J. 1979. "Truth from Genetic Illusion: The Transference and the Fate of the Infantile Neurosis." *Journal of the American Psychoanalytic Association* (suppl.) 27:289–313.

Erikson, E. H. 1980. *Identity and the Life Cycle.* New York: W. W. Norton.

Gould, R. L. 1978. *Transformations: Growth and Change in Adult Life.* New York: Simon & Schuster.

———. 1981. "Transformational Tasks in Adulthood." In *The Course of Life, vol. III. Adulthood and the Aging Process,* ed. S. I. Greenspan and G. H. Pollock, pp. 55–90. Washington, D.C.: U.S. Department of Health and Human Services.

———. 1989. "Adulthood." In *Comprehensive Textbook of Psychiatry V.* 5th ed., ed. H. I. Kaplan and B. J. Sadock, pp. 1998–2012. Baltimore: Williams and Wilkins.

Hartman, H. 1958. "Ego Psychology and the Problem of Adaptation." *Journal of the American Analytic Association,* monograph no. 1. New York: National University Press.

Kohut, H. 1977. *The Restoration of the Self.* New York: International Universities Press.

Levinson, D. J. et al. 1978. *The Seasons of a Man's Life.* New York: Knopf.

Mahler, M. 1972. "The Rapprochement Subphase of the Separation-Individuation Process." *Psychoanalytic Quarterly,* 41:487-506.

Mahler, M.; Pine, F.; and Berman, A. 1975. *The Psychological Birth of the Human Infant.* New York: Basic Books.

Pollock, G. H. 1981 "Aging or Aged." In *The Course of Life: Psychoanalytic Contributions toward Understanding Personality Development,* vol. 3., pp. 549–85. Washington, D.C.: U. S. Department of Health and Human Services, Public Health Service, National Institute of Mental Health.

Rappaport, D. 1959. "Historical Introduction." In "Identity and the Life Cycle:

Selected Papers." *Psychological Issues,* vol. 1, no. 1. New York: International Universities Press.

Settlage, C. F. 1980. "The Psychoanalytic Theory and Understanding of Psychic Development During Second and Third Years of Life." In *The Course of Life: Psychoanalytic Contributions Toward Understanding Personality Development, vol. 1, Infancy and Early Childhood,* ed. S. I. Greenspan and G. H. Pollock, pp. 523–39. Washington, D.C.: U.S. Department of Health and Human Services, Publication No. (ADM) 80–786.

Settlage, C. F., Curtis, J., Lozoff, M., Lozoff, M., Silbershatz, G., and Simberg, E. J. 1988. "Conceptualizing Adult Development." *Journal of the American Psychoanalytic Association* 36(2):347–69.

Vaillant, G. E. 1977. *Adaptation to Life.* Boston: Little Brown.

DISCUSSION

Roger Gould was one of the first psychiatrists to recognize a predictable sequence of changing patterns and preoccupations during the adult years. In a ground-breaking study, "The Phases of Adult Life: A Study in Developmental Psychology" (Gould 1972), he and his colleagues first studied group-psychotherapy patients in the University of California in Los Angeles outpatient department. After factoring out problems common to all age groups (for example, anxiety and depression), patterns specific to the age groups emerged. Next, using a questionnaire incorporating salient statements about the age-related feelings of the treatment group, Gould asked 524 nonpatients from ages sixteen to fifty to rank the statements in relation to themselves. He found that patients and nonpatients of the same age had roughly the same general concerns about living and those were quite specific to their ages.

His book, *Transformations: Growth and Change in Adult Life* (1978) was a landmark contribution to adult developmental theory. There he outlined the developmental steps in which adult consciousness is gradually achieved by understanding and overcoming the childhood consciousness that invades adult lives and interferes with developmental progression. He specifically described an infantile remnant, which he called the angry demons of childhood consciousness, that is, an overstimulation of hostility in ourselves and others. These angry demons of childhood are released as we strive for a fuller, more independent adult consciousness. As we grow and reform our selves, *transformation* becomes a dangerous act. Adult consciousness progresses by mastering childhood fears and by learning to understand and modulate the anger released by change in the course of confronting new developmental tasks.

Gould demonstrated that underlying every new self-defining issue in adult life is an unconscious, restrictive set of protective devices that form a boundary of safety. He described how in the process of self-definition we must traverse a "moat of terror" and abandon the childhood illusion of absolute safety. The protective devices include irrational acts, rigid childhood rules, fantasy, and a number of false assumptions contained in the illusion. The basic false assumptions are

1. We'll always live with our parents and be their child.

2. They'll always be there to help when we can't do something on our own.

3. Their simplified version of our complicated inner reality is correct, as when they turn the light on in our bedroom to prove there are no ghosts.

4. There is no real death or evil in the world.

Gould explained that by the time one enters young adulthood (years eighteen to twenty), these assumptions are abandoned intellectually, but unconsciously they continue to play an important role in experience. The gradual shedding of these immature beliefs makes possible the shift from childhood to adult consciousness and is the cornerstone of Gould's thinking about adult development in *Transformations.*

In the present chapter, Gould focuses his approach more directly on the clinical psychotherapeutic and psychoanalytic situation. After many years of clinical work he has come to see the developmental process as fundamental in psychotherapeutic work.

I had been confusing my conduct of the analysis and observation of the transference with the more fundamental *developmental process* going on within my patients, a process which I neither initiated nor sustained. I came subsequently to see my role as that of privileged observer, who occasionally makes interventions that may alter the pace or direction of the process, but not as the prime mover of the therapeutic enterprise (p. 345, italics added)

He has cast a new light on the role of the therapist who, when he focuses on his patient's developmental issues, is likely to function in a more accurate and useful way.

Gould addresses how development takes place in the life course without formal therapeutic mediation. He formulates the question: "What would a therapeutic intervention look like if it were specifically designed to acknowledge, facilitate, and amplify the ongoing adult developmental processes?"

In response, he proposes an intervention based on the relationship between the current reality of the patient and his ongoing developmental conflict. In contrast to Freud's original focus on memory and its conflicts,

Gould proposes a model of treatment based on naturally occurring adult development, which shifts the focus toward the entities of the life cycle, including the existential issues of time, aging, and death. The past and difficult memories must be integrated with a focus on current reality and the ever-present struggle to adapt to changing time. Such an approach need not sacrifice the insights of depth psychology.

Gould believes that therapy, which is constructed to facilitate developmental adaptation, will be more effective. He uses his model in both psychoanalysis and short-term dynamic psychotherapy, and has adapted the model for an effective computer-assisted short-term psychotherapy program. The model is based on four overlapping but distinct frames of reference, which he characterizes as the critical "reality space" of therapeutic activity:

1. *The existential framework:* Focuses on questions and decisions that will affect the patient's future life course.

2. *The contextual/developmental framework:* Focuses on the patient's conflicts with his or her immediate life situation, which may call for a new behavior to achieve successful adaptation.

3. *The developmental/psychodynamic framework:* Focuses on inhibitions from the past, frequently encountered as unexamined, fear-producing assumptions or conclusions about self or others, which block the emergence of the new behavior. This may represent the recovery of some functions sacrificed to earlier adaptation.

4. *The framework of the volitional conflict:* Focuses on developing a perspective that aids in acting to recover or initiate the behavior representing successful developmental adaptation.

We are in complete agreement with this effort to construct a model of therapy that asks the important adult developmental question and preserves at the same time the richness and depth achieved by exploring childhood fears, inhibition, and conflicts. In our essay in this volume, we also describe an approach to clinical work that includes use of the developmental dimension to complement established frameworks of psychoanalytic formulation (e.g., genetic, dynamic, structural). Such integration can be organized around four key concepts: (1) the adult developmental diagnosis, which can serve as a constant reference point during the evolution of transference, interpretation, working through, and interpretation; (2) adult developmental lines, an expansion of the concept of childhood developmental lines; (3) adult developmental arrest, another elaboration of a concept from child psychoanalysis, to demonstrate the importance and salience of events from the adult past; and (4) developmental resonance, the awareness of developmental issues affecting *both* analyst and analysand.

Gould reminds us that it is relatively easy to get lost in the psychodynamic puzzle and to swim endlessly in the unconscious without finding a welcoming shore of resolution. Only by continually asking the adult developmental questions while exploring the childhood past can therapist and patient achieve a balanced understanding of past, present, and future.

REFERENCES

Colarusso, C. A., Nemiroff, R. A. 1981. *Adult Development: A New Dimension in Psychodynamic Theory and Practice.* New York: Plenum.

Gould, R. L. 1972. "The Phases of Adult Life: A Study in Developmental Psychology." *American Journal of Psychiatry* 129:521.

———. 1978. *Transformations: Growth and Change in Adult Life.* New York: Simon & Schuster.

Nemiroff, R. A., and Colarusso, C. A. 1989. "New Dimensions in Adult Development." In *New Dimensions in Adult Development,* ed. R. A. Nemiroff and C. A. Colarusso. New York: Plenum.

15

The Catastrophic Reaction:

Developmental Aspects of a Severe Reaction to Loss in Later Life

BERNARD CHODORKOFF

The catastrophic reactions described in this chapter occurred in older women after the loss of their husbands.* These widows experienced prolonged mourning states followed by depression, somatic complaints, acute distress, and disorganization, which sometimes had the features of a continuously flowing panic state. They were unable to resume their lives despite material and psychological support from family and social resources. Their sons and daughters, in particular, experienced extreme helplessness because they could not find ways to relieve their mothers' demanding, irrational, and regressive behavior.

Such patients fall into two groups. Members of one group are younger and show milder responses and intermittent, transient reactions. Although the catastrophic quality of their psychic states fluctuated from session to session, depending upon ongoing life experiences and issues arising in the treatment process, they did respond positively to intensive interpretive psychotherapy. Their more intense reactions appeared in the context of associations to earlier unresolved conflicts and/or continuing developmental deficits. The second group, usually older, suffered more severe and prolonged reactions. They were not as receptive to interpretive psycho-

*My describing this reaction in women does not mean that I believe men do not experience similar psychic states, precipitated by similar life events, resulting in similar intrapsychic and developmental consequences, but that my clinical experience with this specific reaction to loss has been primarily with women.

therapy, but rather sought a supportive relationship with the therapist, and often requested medication. Most individuals in both groups entered treatment two or three years after their husbands' deaths following long marriages.

To understand these patients and the intense reactions they experienced, I have identified developmental and adaptational processes that undergo disruption after object loss, thus limiting functional capacity. They are:

1. Loss of the "mirror."
2. Disruption of the self-caregiving function.
3. Loss of the opportunity for "identification progression" and the reemerging search for a transitional object.
4. Loss of shared fantasy.

Understanding these processes was helpful to both patient and therapist when insight was the therapeutic goal and guided my interventions when supportive and chemotherapeutic measures were primary. Three clinical examples will illustrate these reactions.

Patient A.

Mrs. A., age seventy-three, had lost her husband two years previously after fifty years of marriage. She had two daughters and one son, all married and with families, who were desperate about their mother's psychological state and could no longer tolerate her behavior. Having exhausted their psychic resources, they sought psychiatric help.

The patient complained about multiple cardiac-like symptoms and intense anxiety and despair. Her behavior was very disorganized, and every action was filled with uncertainty and terror. She had stopped seeing her friends and had become increasingly dependent on her daughters, even for food and sleep. This childish, regressive behavior occurred even though she was financially secure and had every advantage that a woman in her circumstances might wish. Although cognitive, intellectual, and memory functions were intact, and physical findings were minimal or absent, Mrs. A. was unable to define feelings and mental states except for describing her anxieties and disorganization.

In my initial work with this patient it became evident that she was primarily motivated for relief of pain, was not psychologically minded, and at that time was too distressed and limited in her psychic functions to participate in an intensive experience. Even a supportive approach with the use of medication proved to be difficult. Often she complained that she was not being helped and became terrified if I responded, interpreting my comments to mean that I would stop seeing her.

She experienced some minimal relief following four months of therapy and was able to spend the better part of the winter in her Florida condominium. I had arranged for her to work with a psychiatrist in that area while she was away. I later learned that she had seen several psychiatrists in Florida and another upon return home who hospitalized her and proceeded with a vigorous psychopharmacological treatment plan. When she improved, she called to let me know that although she no longer was my patient, she felt that I had started her on the way to recovery.

This patient illustrates the catastrophic reaction in its most severe form; it appeared in an individual who managed to function reasonably well through the years as long as she had available to her the sustaining support and apparent strength of her husband. When she could no longer identify with his strength and confidence, the regression that followed included first the reemerging search for a transitional object, and later the wish to return to a symbiotic union with the mother.

In her case, the losses of mirroring and of the opportunity for shared fantasies were not prominent clinical features, although we may infer their participation in her extreme response to loss.

Patient B.

Mrs. B. was a woman in her seventies who had been married for twenty-eight years to her second husband, a successful businessman. Her first husband's death had left her alone to raise two sons, both of whom were currently trying to help her. Her relationships to both husbands had been close and intimate. During both marriages, Mrs. B. and her husband preferred a small but active group of friends. She had occupied herself with volunteer activities while her husbands engaged in business.

Over the past several years her husband's physical condition had progressively deteriorated, and he was now sometimes confined to a wheelchair. At his insistence he was driven to his office several times each week. Mrs. B. explained that although he was too disabled to work, going to the office helped keep his spirits up.

One year previously, Mrs. B. had suffered what was described as a breakdown in response to her husband's progressive decline. After a brief hospitalization, the psychiatrist had continued to see her for "medication review." Her sons were concerned about this approach, especially when it appeared that she "needed someone to talk to."

Although Mrs. B. was in good physical health and continued to drive, she had limited her activities to looking after her husband even though he was provided with round-the-clock care. It was important, she said, to be with him as much as possible in the time remaining. She enjoyed doing things for him, but suffered deep despair watching his valiant efforts to go on. Mrs. B. experienced her husband's progressive decline as a growing sense of loss within herself for which there was no possible accommodation or adjustment.

In discussing her marriage, Mrs. B. emphasized how wonderful life had been with her husband. His present state clashed with her memories of him as vigorous and highly successful. Their lives had become so intertwined that these changes were experienced as "losing a part of (her)self." She repeatedly stated in one way or another, "I don't know who I am anymore . . . I'm alone, empty . . . I can't share my personal feelings with him anymore and there's no one else to do this with . . . I can't make him better, so I wonder if I can take care of myself." She actively complained of a loss of the personal strength that had enabled her to endure life's hardships and compensate for a childhood feeling of inadequacy. Her marriages had stabilized her self-esteem and made her feel complete.

Mrs. B. was an intelligent, articulate woman, who effectively conveyed her feelings and inner psychic experiences. She readily described the consequences of the loss of her husband as an object source for progressive identification and her diminished capacity for self-caregiving. I believe loss of the mirroring function and shared fantasies also played important roles, as in the preceding quotations.

These changes were not precipitous but rather, paralleled Mr. B.'s progressive decline. They were increasingly difficult to endure, producing profound suffering and eventual breakdown.

Both Mrs. A. and Mrs. B. were of a generation that had not conceptualized the value of psychotherapy or fully accepted a need for it. Mrs. B. did accept the form of our work and was able to do some exploring, but not on a continuing basis. Her terror of the impending separation from her husband was a formidable source of resistance, and as a result our efforts were only partially successful.

Patient C.

Mrs. C., who was approaching her sixty-fifth birthday, had been widowed three years before entering treatment for depression, guilt over her husband's death, and confusion about her life. The intensity of her distress fluctuated, but at times her anxiety reached extreme levels. Mrs. C. resented her "identity crisis" and doubted her ability to survive because she was "too old to deal with this." She felt like "half a woman," a "nobody," and asked, "Who do you bounce thoughts off, who do you share reading the newspaper with?"

Living alone in the home that she and her husband had built, Mrs. C. developed a fear of vandalism. That fear, among others, served to externalize anxieties about her ability to maintain personal integration. She felt "bad" because she had not prevented her husband's death or recognized its inevitability. Perceiving herself as "nothing without a husband," she excluded herself from interpersonal involvement. Mrs. C. could not decide on priorities and wished for magical solutions to problems; she became angry when she had to acknowledge that there would be no magical solutions.

Mrs. C. had been professionally trained and had returned to part-time work prior to her husband's death; she continued to work at the time she consulted me. She was intelligent, introspective, psychologically minded, and knowledgeable about psychotherapy. Her personal strengths and energies provided her with reasonable coping resources. She was well suited and well motivated to undertake an intensive psychotherapy experience.

Many of the patient's early transference reactions expressed the wish that I replace her lost spouse and help her become complete again. She had effectively used him to help sustain her self-esteem—he was like a "crutch"—and now saw me as a suitable replacement. Without me, Mrs. C. had to confront the difficult task of consolidating her sense of self and self-esteem. Later she expressed the wish that I serve as an impulse-regulator, moderator, much as her husband had done. He had become an idealized parent, allowing her to feel free to enjoy being "expansive," particularly in her interactions with others, but she could not be certain of my willingness to do the same. Together we had to recognize that certain aspects of her superego and self-sustaining, self-supporting narcissistic functions had not been firmly and completely internalized—deficiencies that did not permit her to enjoy greater spontaneity in social relationships and that did not provide a more secure internal sense of self.

In an early dream Mrs. C. saw "animals . . . one running with its head cut off." The dream reflected her state of mind, singled out from others because of feelings of anger and disorganization.

In a later session, she began by noting that she had come to her hour early and walked downtown to buy an ice cream cone; it was enjoyable on a hot summer day. Although her husband had been particularly fond of ice cream, he had remarkable control and never overate. Then she related the following dream:

A small figure of a person, no penis, a woman, or girl, but spread out . . . white. Looked more like a double breast of chicken . . . empty inside, cleaned out. I thought somehow I was looking at myself. I heard, or said, "Why don't you sew it up?"

Her first reaction to the dream was to dismiss it as "strange." Gradually she overcame her fear and began to associate the figure as a little girl because it was small and had no breasts. She went on to talk about the emptiness of her childhood and early family life. Mrs. C. could only recall one pleasant occasion, when a visiting uncle prepared especially delicious sour cream pancakes. Referring to her dream, she recalled dissecting a fish head in a biology class. What a mess that was, all cartilage; she couldn't do anything with it.

At one point, following a silence, I inquired about her statement that there was no penis. At first she thought it referred to Freud's theory that women feel incomplete unless they are married and can possess their husband's penis. Then she remembered another animal in biology class, the fetal pig. During that dissection she had destroyed the possibility of recognizing the sexual parts of the animal. This remarkable dream work highlighted Mrs. C.'s feelings of being incomplete without a man. In effect she viewed me as tearing her asunder in therapy. In our work, and in the dream, she assigned to me the task of fixing her feelings of incompleteness and wished that I could fill up her emptiness by feeding her. Much more work was necessary before this patient could deal with her own aggressive and destructive wishes.

With time and therapy the impact of the loss of her husband and the symptoms of this milder form of "catastrophic" response diminished. The patient began to deal with unrelated conflicts over sex and aggression. We focused increasingly on childhood and adolescent experiences that had contributed to her faulty self-esteem and uncertainty about the effectiveness of her self-caregiving capacity. It was most interesting to observe that when resistances became particularly intense the earlier manifestations of the catastrophic reaction returned; these were then interpreted as resistance, in contrast to our earlier recognition of them as complex responses to major object loss.

Mrs. C. is now in her second year of treatment. As her wishes for magical solutions and fusion with a love object have faded, she has begun to live with her loneliness and to seek a new relationship with a man who no longer needs to be a "clone" of her dead husband. Sadly, as her desire for such a relationship grows, so does the realization that such a man may be unavailable to her.

Loss of the Mirror

Joseph D. Lichtenberg (1985) has explored the relationship between look-ing into a mirror and the "mirroring" experiences that provide emotional sustenance throughout life, pointing out that the capacity for imaging may be observed in the child between fifteen and eighteen months of age. As physical exposure to the mirror fills the gap between the infant's budding sense of self and his inability to directly observe his face, a primary compo-nent of selfhood, "mirroring" similarly provides a lifelong mechanism for "reading the unconscious" of others and learning about the self—espe-cially in regard to emotional content and psychological reflection.

Mothers use the responsiveness of their babies, derived from their ca-pacity to imitate, to teach them to follow instructions. For example, when mother opens her mouth, baby does the same, thus facilitating the feeding process. Lichtenberg believes that affect comes closest to communicating the unconscious. Crucial exchanges occur not only through imitation but also through "affect attunement" as described by Daniel Stern (1984). He described behavior patterns that express the quality of a shared affect state; these go beyond imitation since they do not remain in the same mode of perception and expression. For example, instead of going from face to face, voice to voice, or gesture to gesture, the sequence moves readily from gesture to vocalization.

Gradually an interactive repertoire develops between parent and child, which stimulates the child's development and produces a sense of connect-edness in an ongoing process. A similar mirroring occurs between analyst and analysand, friend and friend, and husband and wife. This continuous process provides each member with recognition and emotional resonance, and establishes the humanity of the two partners in the exchange. Every relationship is partially dependent upon this unconscious process to main-tain adaptation and provide direction. Only when a member of the pair is missing, and the availability of mirroring is removed, does the remaining individual recognize how important this process was to his or her personal integration and functioning.

The Self-Caregiving Function

In an article titled, "The Search for Confirmation: Technical Aspects of Mirroring"(1985), Ernest S. Wolf provides us with a bridge from mirroring to the self-caregiving function. Following the work of Heinz Kohut (1971), he clarifies the concept of "selfobject." Selfobjects, a class of objects, symbols, or ideas, represent objects that perform the specific functions of providing a self-evoking and self-sustaining experience to the potential and emerging self. It is, therefore, a subjective intrapsychic response to a relationship, which does not describe its interpersonal aspects; rather it denotes the experiences of imagos that are needed for the sustenance of self. The function of the selfobject is to provide experiences for the self that evoke and maintain cohesion; these experiences include mirroring (the others are idealizing and alter-ego aspects). The absence of such experiences, because of absent or faulty selfobjects, is followed by impaired self-structure. These self-sustaining, self-caregiving functions are important from earliest infancy onward; at issue is the child's capacity to internalize this function or related set of functions and the parents' ability to stimulate that process.

Henry Parens (1970) has pointed out that inner sustainment occurs when an individual feels loved and supported from within. At all ages this state depends on internal representations, the actions of the assimilative processes, and the affects related to ego and superego functioning, self concepts, and identity formation. The core affects are basic trust and confidence. Parens makes it apparent that inner sustainment changes through the life cycle: "Changes in internal representations by the action of assimilative processes effect changes in psychic structure not only in childhood and adolescence but even in adulthood; and this fact is important for treatment" (p. 237).

In a long-term relationship, especially in marriage, modification takes place in self-caregiving, self-sustaining functions. Each relinquishes at least a portion of the self-caregiving function to the other. With the death of a spouse, the surviving partner may experience a diminished capacity to care for the self. In the three women described here, this inability to sustain the self was manifested over various lengths of time. The response, normal versus pathologic, depends on the presence of a well-developed sense of self-caregiving prior to marriage versus the use of the spouse as compensation for the lack of a firmly internalized function, that is, a developmental deficit.

Taken together, the loss of access to the mirroring function and the disruption in self (or inner)-sustainment and self-caregiving functions produce:

1. Loss of emotional sustenance and source of well being.

2. Inability to read unconscious and derivative mental states.

3. Loss of opportunity for emotional resonance, the affective exchange between individual and spouse.

4. Increasing sense of isolation, aloneness, despondency, futility, and loss of self-esteem and drive or impetus.

5. Disruption in developmental progression and loss of the impetus for growth

6. Loss of self-object and its responses supportive of self-cohesion.

7. Impairment in self-structure and functional capability of the self, that is, impairment in expressing interests, ambitions, talents, and purposes.

8. Loss of a productive mourning process sequence (inasmuch as mourning for others is easier in the presence of the primary self-object.)

9. Regression, disorganization, and narcissistic insult.

10. Inevitable disruption of the meaningfulness of life.

Identification Progression

All identification has as its basis the emotional ties existing between two individuals. Sigmund Freud (1905, 1921) called the earliest form of identification "narcissistic." This primary form of identification, which allows the child to build inner feelings of strength and power, derives from the illusion of oneness with the parental source of relief from pain and discomfort. Freud (1905, 1921) also described "hysterical" identification, which allows the child not only to defend against the anxieties and defeats that are inevitable in developmental experiences, but also to unite with parents in ways that permit the borrowing or acquisition of selected strengths and internalized feelings, attitudes, and approaches to life's demands (Silverman 1986). Between the ages of three and six, oedipal identifications appear. These are partial and selective and differ between boys and girls because of the need to select aspects and attributes of their male and female parents.

The partial identifications acquired during early development are subject to ongoing, active transformation during later periods of life. What was earlier internalized may later be discarded or revamped and may eventually become unrecognizable in its content, form, and source. Such progressive structuralization within the ego provides for considerable developmental advance (Jacobson 1954, 1964).

In effect, what takes place is an intrinsic developmental thrust toward active, assertive, self-expressive autonomous functioning, more or less supported and facilitated by parents and the world at large. The child transforms earlier yearnings for the blissful, enveloping union with an all-giving, all-powerful mother into the pursuit of separate, external love objects. However, within relationships with external love objects, the individual may recapture the illusion of mingled union with the primary object by means of hugging, kissing, and sexual relations (Silverman 1986).

Here we are particularly interested in the ongoing process of revising, reorganizing, and integrating earlier and partial identifications, a process of *identification progression.* It takes place not only following the oedipal period, but throughout the life cycle, especially during critical or changing times such as marriage. Under stress and anxiety the identifications that enable the individual to make his or her way in adaptational efforts may be disrupted, producing a regressive pull toward recapturing the illusory narcissistic union with the all-giving and powerful mother.

With the death of a spouse, two major events take place. First, the identifications based on the marital relationship are loosened and the continuing reinforcement received from the spouse is lost. Second, the mourning process temporarily disrupts ongoing identification progression. The individual experiences a kind of stalemate because past identifications related to the spouse are tenuous but reorganization has not yet taken place.

Furthermore, loss of the spouse means that an individual has lost intermittent opportunities to recapture the illusion of union or merged identities. In some situations the surviving spouse searches for a transitional object; in others, more severe regression produces a quest for a primitive, narcissistic union. The latter is expressed in infantile, demanding behavior and appears in those patients who suffer considerable functional disorganization.

Shared Fantasies

The concept of shared fantasies was reintroduced by Harold Blum (1986), who recognized that they were ubiquitous and clinically important but neglected in the clinical and developmental literature. Freud (1908) recognized shared fantasies as an aspect of aesthetic communication in the works of artists and poets. The fantasies expressed in their works serve to awaken similar fantasies in the observer or reader and invite identification with the character and content of the artistic or poetic creation. He (1917) also demonstrated that myth, legend, and folklore converge with the fantasies disguised in literature and art. Universal fantasies such as those of incest, parricide, birth and death, castration, and omnipotence are shared between writer and reader, artist and observer.

In a similar way, shared fantasies play a role in the psychoanalytic situation, especially as a component of the transference-countertransference experience. For example, an analysand's erotic transference may trigger a reciprocal countertransference in the analyst, mediated by a shared fantasy.

Blum (1986) furthered our understanding of the importance of shared fantasies by pointing out that they form a distinct group with special features because of their ego and object-related dimensions. Communication of a fantasy to another individual provides an opportunity for identification and enhancement of the content of the fantasy. When shared with a child, a parent's fantasy becomes part of the child's reality and takes on developmental influence. It may determine the direction of the evolving superego, lend authority to the parent's directives and injunctions, and contribute to the formation and structure of adaptations and sublimations. The influence of these fantasies on the child's development ultimately depends on the investment and exclusive attachment of the parent, the developmental phase, and the sensitivity and proclivities of the child. Every adult biography contains within it the essence of shared fantasies acquired over a lifetime.

In summation, in normal development the sharing of fantasy begins in early childhood, emerging from the intimacy of parent-child exchanges. Every child takes from those interactions certain attitudes, values, and fantasies, which he adopts as his own. Every meaningful relationship from childhood onward includes a repertoire of shared fantasies established over stretches of time. Such sharing contributes a special character to the marital relationship. With loss of the spouse, the unity that shared fantasies helped to create is lost, the bonds are loosened, and the surviving partner is left in a state of disorganization. Other relationships and behavior patterns that depend upon shared fantasies are also disrupted.

Clinical Implications

The three patients described illustrate many of the characteristics seen in catastrophic reactions. Mrs. C. is an example of the group of younger patients who show milder, intermittent, and transient reactions and have good prognosis and suitability for intensive psychotherapy. Mrs. A. and Mrs. B. are examples of an older group who experience more intense and prolonged reactions and are either not receptive to interpretive psychotherapy (Mrs. A.) or only minimally so (Mrs. B.). Although Mrs. A. and Mrs. B. are classed together, there were nevertheless considerable differences between them. Mrs. A. could be treated only supportively. On the other hand, Mrs. B. could express precisely what she was experiencing and, on occasion, could explore the genesis of her experiences and understand what produced her disorganization; she had difficulty accepting treatment because in her mind it interfered with the remaining time with her husband and required her to face her strong ambivalence toward him.

Mrs. C. continues to be involved in intensive psychotherapy, which explores the origins of her reactions to the loss of her husband. In her treatment, we carefully try to relate behavior, affective responses, and self-concepts to one or another of the developmental processes described earlier. For the most part, the earlier phases of her treatment focused on symptom relief and current relationships and functioning; subsequent work explored the underlying conflict. In such patients the work of intensive psychotherapy can be undertaken only after attention has been paid to the reestablishment of ego- and self-integration.

Summary

In this chapter I have described a severe, specific type of psychic reaction to object loss late in life and explored the importance of viewing aging and the vicissitudes encountered during the process from a developmental perspective. In emphasizing development deficit, past and current, and the interplay that produces severe psychic distress and personal disorganization, I do not mean to imply that conflict and derivative symptoms played no part in the psychopathology observed. Developmental aspects have been stressed because many clinicians have not fully recognized them, yet they often require immediate attention by patients suffering severe reactions to loss. Furthermore, in many patients the neurotic conflicts could not be managed effectively without prior attention to the reestablishment of ego- and self-integration.

REFERENCES

Blum, H. 1986. "Shared Fantasy." Colloquium, American College of Psychoanalysis, Washington, D.C.
Freud, S. [1905] 1953. "Three Essays on the Theory of Sexuality." In *Standard Edition*, ed. J. Strachey, vol. 7, pp. 125–244. London: Hogarth Press.
———. [1908] 1959. "Creative Writers and Daydreaming." In *Standard Edition*, ed. J. Strachey, vol. 9, pp. 141–54. London: Hogarth Press.

------. [1917] 1963. "Introductory Lectures." In *Standard Edition,* ed. J. Strachey, vol. 15, pp. 3–228. London: Hogarth Press.

------. [1921] 1955. "Group Psychology and the Analysis of the Ego." In *Standard Edition,* ed. J. Strachey, vol. 18, pp. 67–134. London: Hogarth Press.

Jacobson, E. 1954. "Contribution to the Metapsychology of Psychotic Identifications." *Journal of the American Psychoanalytic Association* 2:239–62.

------. 1964. *The Self and Object World.* New York: International Universities Press.

Kohut, H. 1971. *The Analysis of the Self.* New York: International Universities Press.

Lichtenberg, J. D. 1985. "Mirrors and Mirroring: Developmental Experiences." *Psychoanalytic Inquiry* 5(2):199–210.

Parens, H. 1970. "Inner Sustainment: Metapsychological Considerations." *Psychoanalytic Quarterly* 39:223–39.

Silverman, M. A. 1986. "Identification in Healthy and Pathological Character Formation." *International Journal of Psycho-Analysis* 67:181–92.

Stern, D. 1984. "Affect Attunement." In *Frontiers of Infant Psychiatry,* vol. 2, ed. J. Call et al., pp. 3–14. New York: Basic Books.

Wolf, E. 1985. "The Search for Confirmation: Technical Aspects of Mirroring." *Psychoanalytic Inquiry* 5(2):271–82.

DISCUSSION

Dr. Chodorkoff's careful clinical work with these grieving widows is further evidence that analytically oriented psychotherapy is the treatment of choice for some elderly patients. The prejudice against dynamic intervention with individuals in this age group is slowly diminishing. Careful diagnostic evaluation, as exemplified by Dr. Chodorkoff's work with the widows in this chapter is the key to proper therapeutic intervention.

Mrs. B.'s sense of "losing a part of (her)self" as she watched her husband deteriorate leads us to consider a distinguishing characteristic of object relationships in late adulthood. In some intact individuals in long-standing marriages (not necessarily represented by these patients), we have observed an intrapsychic fusion with the spouse to a degree that it resembles the symbiotic state of the early mother-child dyad. However, this late-life "symbiosis" occurs in a setting of object constancy, clear self-object differentiation, and sophisticated psychic structure.

The intensity and depth of this intrapsychic connectedness is the result of many years of physical and psychological union, and shared experience over time, which constitutes the basis of mature love in long-lasting marriages. The intensity and degree of normative late-life "symbiosis" may explain why late-life mourning takes so long in healthy individuals and is so traumatic in more fragile persons such as Dr. Chodorkoff's patients. It may also clarify why some widows and widowers remain in a state of gratifying fusion with dead spouses, manifesting no need to begin new object relationships of a similar nature.

Mrs. C. demonstrated aspects of the transference relationship between an elderly patient and her therapist. Her transference to Dr. Chodorkoff contained elements from the infantile and adult past, involving dependency issues as they were elaborated across the life cycle. Again, similarities between dependency on the infantile objects in childhood and the spouse in adulthood are readily seen in the transference. Dr. Chodorkoff's ability to recognize and address both the infantile and the adult themes is clearly demonstrated in the fascinating analysis of Mrs. C.'s dream.

Mirroring is a concept that originated in the study of infants and young children, as have many current concepts in psychiatry. In this chapter Dr. Chodorkoff has fleshed out the ways in which this phenomenon from childhood continues to express itself in the second half of life. It seems clear to us that the mirroring function plays a vital role in maintaining and elaborating all important relationships throughout the life cycle, including those between husbands and wives. Contributing greatly to the evolution of normal development in late adulthood, mirroring "provides each member with recognition and emotional resonance, and establishes the humanity of the two partners in the exchange. Every relationship is partially dependent upon this unconscious process to maintain adaptation and provide direction. Only when a member of the pair is missing, and the availability of mirroring is removed, does the remaining individual recognize how important the process was to his or her personal integration and functioning" (p. 377).

Of course, a close relationship exists between mirroring and self-caregiving. As Dr. Chodorkoff points out, in a long-term relationship such as marriage, aspects of the self-caregiving function are relinquished to the spouse. It is our impression that this process takes place in *every* marriage. To Dr. Chodorkoff's suggestion that whether the process is normal or pathological depends on the presence of a well-developed sense of self-caregiving prior to marriage versus the use of the spouse as compensation for the lack of a firmly internalized function, we would add the influence of the continued growth of the personality in adulthood along other related lines of development. In other words, the capacity of individuals to care for themselves has its roots in childhood, but is added to in each subsequent developmental phase by all-important adult object ties.

This idea is also exemplified in Dr. Chodorkoff's "identification progression," a framework from which to explore the adult developmental line of identity. He describes the process as an "ongoing process of revising, reorganizing, and integrating earlier and partial identifications" (p. 380). In many ways this adult process is similar to another in adolescence. Both deal with the loss of vital object representations and prepare the individual for the next stage of development. Both are associated with a mourning process and lead to a new integration. Although the adolescent has an abundant future in front of him and the person in late adulthood does not, it is clear from Dr. Chodorkoff's clinical examples that even the impaired older adult can be helped to live a fuller, enriched life.

16

The Oppositional Couple:

A Developmental Object Relations Approach to Diagnosis and Treatment

SHEILA A. SHARPE

Introduction

"Opposites attract" and "like marries like" are epigrams often applied to love and marriage. One may say "opposites attract" to explain why so many couples disagree about everything or why vivacious, life-of-the-party Miss A. married the drab, introverted Mr. B. On the other hand, for those couples who share multiple common interests, agree on almost everything, and may even look alike, the principle of "like marries like" is often invoked. Although these popular solutions to the mystery of mate attraction and selection seem incompatible for any coherent theory, the kind of couple I call oppositional would appear to reconcile these two plausible yet apparently contradictory notions. Superficially, the oppositional couple looks like a marriage of opposite personalities, relentlessly engaged in a specific form of painful combat. However, a closer look reveals that the partners share approximately the same level of identity formation and object relations development, as well as the same "internal object" (Dicks 1967).

This chapter identifies and describes the characteristics of the oppositional couple in the context of a developmental approach to the assessment

NOTE: The author wishes to thank Drs. Allan D. Rosenblatt, Robert A. Nemiroff, and Allan E. Mallinger for their valuable comments and criticisms of earlier versions of the manuscript.

and treatment of dysfunctional marital relationships. In my experience, the oppositional couple frequently seeks therapeutic help and poses predictable and difficult problems for treatment. The delineation of their diagnostic profile is part of my general effort to develop a classification of dysfunctional love relationships, based on the idea of regression to, or recapitulation of, phases in the child's development of object relations as described by Margaret Mahler and her colleagues (1975). Such a theoretically coherent way of understanding marital relationships allows for a more rational treatment plan and therefore more effective intervention. In a previous paper (Sharpe 1981), I presented a diagnostic profile of the symbiotic marriage—a type of relationship characterized by the most primitive developmental level of object relating. The oppositional couple represents a more mature, differentiated level of object relations development.

Although prominent aspects of the oppositional couple have been identified in the literature (e.g., the "power struggle," the "anal power struggle," the "symmetrical relationship," "sadomasochistic interaction"), I have found neither an elaborated diagnostic profile of this relationship type nor an attempt to classify dysfunctional love relationships based theoretically on the development of self and object relations. However, a couple of related efforts underscore the importance of psychosexual phases as an origin of specific patterns of relating in couples. Both Herbert Strean (1980, 1985) and Jürg Willi (1982) describe collusive patterns of interaction derived from unresolved conflicts of the oral, anal, and phallic-oedipal phases. Willi's description of the marital "anal power struggle" and Strean's (1980) description of "the sadomasochistic marriage" represent important facets of this comprehensive profile of the oppositional couple. (A brief summary of other classification attempts will be presented in a later section.)

The term *oppositional* has been chosen to suggest the two-year-old developmental level of this relationship syndrome, and to capture the most obvious, predominant interactional theme, namely, to oppose, defy, thwart, or in some way openly combat or covertly resist whatever the partner says, does, wants, feels, or values. In extreme instances of this interaction, the oppositional stance invades almost all aspects of the couple's life, including modes of affective expression, interpersonal style, and defense.

For example, if the husband is an archconservative, the wife is a flaming liberal. If he's a physical fitness nut, she revels in junk food and vegetating. If she wants sex in the evening, preceded by a long romantic build-up, he has to have it in the morning—preferably a quickie. If she's an extroverted optimist, he's a dedicated introvert and pessimist. If she is flamboyantly temperamental, then he specializes in emotional blandness, or low-grade depression, and superrationality. One bright young man summed it up this way: "She's the butterfly and I'm a moth."

The preceding scenarios come across (in the telling and observing) as almost farcical—dramatized caricatures that hardly ring true—true, that is, in the sense of reflecting real differences between two fully formed identities. In taking the marital history one finds, however, that the polarities have been created by the couple for important reasons. The overriding purpose of the exaggerated positions (usually accompanied by passionately contentious battling and one-upmanship), would seem to be the partner's need to preserve, bolster, or redefine a shaky sense of self and autonomy by acting and feeling in opposition to the other. The adversarial other is most often perceived as a critical, controlling parent who must be defied overtly or covertly to sustain the illusion of an independent, grown-up self.

In this light, the interaction can be viewed as a positive attempt to master the childhood and adolescent tasks of separation-individuation and identity formation. These tasks have not been mastered in the past and have come to the foreground once again, in part because of the regressive pull of an intimate relationship and in part because of the normative reworking of separation-individuation processes occurring whenever a new developmental step in object relations is attempted (Blos 1979; Sharpe 1984).

Separation-Individuation

The oppositional interaction of such couples is particularly reminiscent of the rapprochement subphase of separation-individuation, as described by Mahler and colleagues (1975)—the feisty two-year-old saying "No! No!" to an exasperated mother, in order to express a sense of autonomy and power. However, as soon as that heady sense of power is won, the toddler runs back to cling and be comforted in Mother's arms, suddenly acutely aware of being small, helpless, and needy.

On another level, the marital interaction also resembles the "snotty" teenager in a defiant, push-pull interaction with devalued, exasperated, but still-needed parents, indicative of the middle phase of adolescence. Peter Blos (1979) has most usefully described the adolescent period in terms of the second round of separation-individuation. Marriage provides the third major arena for reworking this process. And for those individuals who have had great trouble in negotiating the first two rounds, the marriage relationship becomes a highly charged, painful battleground for the replay.

The attempt to resolve the issues of dependency versus autonomy, intimacy versus distance, and establishment of identity are normal aspects of all marriages or intimate relationships. But the kind of relationship I am defining as oppositional is characterized by a chronic form of this developmental conflict that is acted out in certain specific, highly dysfunctional ways. The partners are developmentally stuck at that painful, ambivalent point where dependent feelings threaten to stimulate regressive wishes to merge (opening up feelings of insatiable neediness) and where truly autonomous actions and strivings threaten to arouse fears of failure and abandonment.

For these partners, there is no comfort to be found with either closeness or distance, dependence or independence. Hence, what we see in their interaction are transactions and communications that *look like* power struggles, but are really a vying for dominance in which no one is allowed to win. If one partner succeeds in winning a point or determining a course of action, he or she rather quickly tosses the power back, just like the teenager who is still afraid of the responsibility that truly independent behavior entails. The following example of an oppositional couple in conjoint marital therapy illustrates this typical kind of interaction.

Mrs. T. had spent the last year trying to decide whether to change from full-time to part-time work, in order to explore other career or educational possibilities. She had come to hate her job and wanted to find a career with more challenge and status. Frequently she expressed the feeling that her husband was denying her the chance to "find herself" because he would resent the loss of her income. Mr. T. vociferously denied this accusation and insisted she would have his full support for whatever she decided. With much unacknowledged anxiety about failure to achieve her goals, Mrs. T. made the decision to cut back her work time. Within the first week of this course of action and following Mr. T.'s discussion of a new financial plan, Mrs. T. accused her husband of not stopping her from the "foolish" decision to cut back her work time and income. Now they were going to be financially strapped, and it was all his fault!

The activity of arguing in such a way that nobody can really win or lose can be seen as a dysfunctional "solution" to the couple's needs to be close (dependent) and distant (independent) at the same time.

Theoretical Framework

At this point, it is important to discuss briefly the theoretical framework on which this relationship typology is based. The idea of basing this profile on a phase of child development (separation-individuation) evolves from the belief that the most significant factors influencing the origin and quality of interaction in a marriage are the *kind* of object relations and the *extent* of self-object differentiation the partners have attained. Hence, the most crucial distinction in assessing and treating a relationship is the developmental level of object relations at which the partners primarily function. Three basic assumptions underlie the creation of this typology derived from psychoanalytic marital-family theory and family systems theory. The validity of these assumptions has been argued extensively in the literature (Framo 1965; Dicks 1967; Blanck and Blanck 1968; Bowen 1978; Sharpe 1981; Willi 1982; Strean 1985; Scarf 1987; Scharff and Scharff 1987).

1. Mate selection is no accident, and mates often tend to choose each other unconsciously in order to reenact developmental issues (usually in connection with parents) that have not been completely mastered in the past.

2. Partners in an enduring intimate relationship are functioning at nearly the same level of object relations development, despite the appearance of different defensive styles.

3. Interaction between partners in a marriage produces a dynamic, stabilized system, wherein the whole is greater than the sum of its parts. (Haley 1963; Lederer and Jackson 1968).

A marriage relationship viewed from the last assumption has certain definable and stable characteristics. Although every relationship is unique, just as every individual is, there appear to be enough similarities among relationship systems (including modes of internal relatedness, modes of external relatedness, relationship history, defense mechanisms, transactional styles, therapeutic resistances, and use of therapist) to warrant the delineation of diagnostic profiles.

Previous efforts to characterize or classify love relationships have used the following approaches: (1) descriptions of various dovetailing patterns representing need complementarity between spouses (Mittelmann 1956; Winch 1958); (2) the highlighting of basic relationship dynamics (Ackerman 1965; Pittman and Flomenhaft 1972; Ravich 1974); (3) descriptions of personality style combinations (Sager 1977); (4) defining degrees of stability and need satisfaction between spouses (Lederer and Jackson 1968); (5) personality or psychiatric disorders of one or both spouses (Willi 1976;

following is a schematic summary of the marital assessment model based on Mahler's phases.

The symbiotic mode. I have previously described a kind of couple demonstrating the most primitive level of relating (Sharpe 1981). These couples, conceptualized as recapitulating the symbiotic mode, exhibit an extreme form of mutual dependency—a desperate need to sustain the fantasy of fusion through starkly polarized (either idealized or devalued) perceptions of self, spouse, and parents. The partner's sense of self or identity is preserved only through annexing the other in a sort of psychological cannibalism. In these cases, the use of primitive defenses such as collusive splitting and projective identification are usually paramount and acted out in ferocious blaming exchanges, sadomasochistic interactions involving physical battering, or the wholesale scapegoating of a child.

This level of object relating would appear to have its roots in the symbiotic phase, wherein the infant perceives and relates to the mother as an extension of self and the establishment of basic trust in the self and the human world is the major developmental task—a task that has not been mastered by couples operating in the symbiotic mode.

The oppositional mode. The oppositional couple functions at a more differentiated level of object relating. As mentioned previously, a major component of this relationship level is the partners' striving for independent identities within the marriage, a striving that conflicts with the regressive pull of strong symbiotic wishes (wishes to be totally taken care of, to merge with an idealized parent figure who becomes represented by the spouse). To combat those wishes, the partners try to deny or project them, aiming to bolster shaky identities and wishes for independence by oppositional stances in relation to one another. In these cases the interaction looks less like pure blaming and more like push-pull power struggles or courtroom battles about who is right or superior. Distorted perceptions of partner and self and the use of splitting, projection, and projective identification are still evident, but not to such rigid extremes.

This level of object relating is reflective of Mahler's separation-individuation phase of object relations development, particularly the rapprochement subphase, wherein the toddler alternates between clinging and defiant behavior in relation to mother. In oppositional couples the dependent side of the conflict is often expressed more by one partner or is consciously denied by both and expressed covertly, usually by behaviors designed to elicit caregiving, such as getting sick or becoming depressed, overworking to the point of exhaustion, running out of money, being irresponsible about chores or self-care, and so on.

Strean 1985; Lansky 1986); and (6) interactional patterns based on psy
sexual developmental phases (Strean 1980, 1985; Willi 1982).

Many of these efforts are limited in their diagnostic utility by b
unidimensional, purely phenomenological, or connected to only one
cumscribed aspect of theory. In part because of those limitations,
profiles often do not result in clear or comprehensive implications
therapeutic intervention. This criticism, however, does not apply to
conceptualizations of Willi, Strean, and particularly Lansky, which
grounded in a developmental point of view and embody theoretical
sound strategies for therapeutic intervention.

Alan Gurman and Neil Jacobson's (1986) recent critical overview of th
literature points up the rapid progress made in theory development under
lying the clinical practice of marital therapy since this lack was under
scored over a decade ago by other reviewers (Olson 1975; Berman and Lief
1975). As the recent volume demonstrates, although we now have coherent
theoretical formulations of the psychoanalytic approach, the behavioral-
social learning-cognitive approach, the structural-strategic approach, and
Bowen's family-of-origin approach, we are still left with the diagnostic
question of which approach is best applied to a given couple at a given
time. This chapter presents an object relations framework for making this
kind of diagnostic judgment and provides a theoretically coherent means
of integrating techniques from a variety of theoretical approaches.

Classifying and assessing dysfunctional marriage relationships on the
basis of the maturity or immaturity of the partners' object relations functioning is not the only possible or potentially useful classification system.
Other developmental lines may also be pertinent in classifying marital
interactions. As mentioned, phases in psychosexual development (oral,
anal, phallic-oedipal) have already been used in this manner. Of other
established lines, gender identity and superego development would seem
particularly relevant. However, for the most comprehensive and clinically
useful understanding of a marriage relationship, the partners' development
of object relations is considered here to be central to the developmental
lines.

The developmental assessment model

Mahler's well-known developmental line, on which this classification is
based, involves the infant's progression from a fused, undifferentiated mode of relating (symbiotic phase), through increasingly differentiated modes of perceiving and relating (the subphases of separation-
individuation), to the attainment of a more securely differentiated sense of
self and mother in the final subphase of libidinal object constancy. The

The collaborative mode. Developmentally beyond the oppositional mode of relating is the relatively mature level of object relations wherein perceptions of self and spouse are more realistic and differentiated. Imperfections in self and mate have become accepted to some degree. Ambivalent love-hate feelings are tolerated, because loving feelings can be sustained in spite of periods of frustration and deprivation. Independent action and intimacy are not usually experienced as a threat to either spouse's personal or marital security. Thus the compulsive need to prove individuality or separateness through opposition and defiance is less or not at all necessary. This description marks Mahler's last phase of object relations development, during which libidinal object constancy is attained by the three-year-old child in relation to mother. Couples operating at this level can usually collaborate, negotiate, and compromise in many if not all areas of their lives.

Existing at the lower end of this broad and loosely defined category are the couples who contend with issues related to the phallic-narcissistic and phallic-oedipal phases of psychosexual and object relations development. Comprehensive profiles of couples operating at those levels are yet to be formulated, though Willi (1982) and Strean (1980, 1985) have made an auspicious beginning.

It is important to note that this conceptualization does not imply that Mahler's phases are replayed in dysfunctional adult marriage relationships in a form identical to their original occurrence in early childhood. The notion put forth here is that earlier developmental themes are *recapitulated* in more advanced forms later in development (Sharpe 1984). This point of view would apply to both pathological and normal development. Even if the pathology in the partners of an oppositional marriage involves either a developmental arrest in the rapprochement subphase of separation-individuation or a regression to that mode of relating, the current form of expression cannot be a pure replica of the original scene, though it sometimes seems as if a pair of two-year-olds have come to squabble in the therapist's office.

In the case of normal development, Mahler's original conception has been expanded by many (Kaplan 1972; Blos 1979; Colarusso and Nemiroff 1981; Sharpe 1984; Stern 1985) toward viewing the early phases as developmental themes that are reworked or recapitulated throughout life, rather than as fixed and final in childhood. In my view, the early sequence of phases is recapitulated (in more advanced forms) every time we enter a new, significant relationship—that is, a relationship that involves a significant degree of dependency (e.g., familial, close friendships, student-mentor, therapist-patient, love or marital relationships). Thus, in the normative course of any love relationship, the original sequence is recapitulated as follows: (1) an initial idealizing period and a fused mode of perceiving and relating to the partner (normative symbiotic); (2) a subsequent disillusion- ment in the ideal and a thrust toward separation-individuation (normative oppositional); (3) the eventual acceptance of reality—of ambivalent feel- ings (love and hate) and imperfections in the self and mate (i.e., the re- attainment of object constancy), which results in a more secure, realistic sense of self and other (normative collaborative).

This recapitulatory model can be used to differentiate three distinct developmental processes that the identified oppositional mode of operat- ing could represent. The first two possibilities reflect the milder kinds of disturbances and include (1) the couple that has, under stress, regressed from a higher level of relating (collaborative) to an oppositional level; or (2) the couple that is experiencing trouble in moving through the norma- tive separation-individuation phase of the marriage. Often a couple becomes frightened about the state of the marriage when normative moves toward greater individuation expose unacknowledged differences between the partners, leading to more and more disagreements. In both of these situations the treatment task can be relatively brief, involving identifica- tion of the stressor causing regression in the earlier circumstance and clarifying the normative nature of separation-individuation processes in the later situation.

In the case of regression, I have found that certain events in the marital life cycle are the most likely to trigger a regression to an oppositional mode of relating. Often the first stressor to emerge is a conflict between the spouses over whether to have a child. The mere contemplation of moving from a dyadic mode to a triadic mode with the attendant revival of oedipal and preoedipal conflicts and disappointments can set a regres- sion in motion. When the couple's child or children enter the separation phase of early childhood and later, in adolescence, a regression to an oppositional mode is potentiated for obvious reasons. The unavoidable situation of greater dependency brought about by the retirement of both spouses (or of the man when the woman is a housewife) is another com- mon life-cycle change that is likely to cause regression to the opposi- tional mode of relating.

Although the cases involving regression can require long-term treat- ment, by far the most difficult therapeutic task involves the couple that represents the third diagnostic possibility, namely, a developmental arrest at the oppositional level of object relating. The assessment of an arrested condition can be determined by the marital and personal relationship histories of both partners, which reveal the prolonged, rigidified nature of these dysfunctional interactions. If the partners have never operated beyond the oppositional mode in any close relationship, then a developmental arrest is the most likely assessment.

Subtypes and Presenting Complaints

In considering the common characteristics and patterns associated with oppositional couples, it is useful to begin with typical presenting complaints within the context of three identified subtypes. These subtypes are conceptualized according to the ways couples characteristically handle the intimacy-distance, dependence-independence conflicts, and are roughly classified according to degree of dysfunction. However, all oppositional couples are motivated to seek treatment because of the problems caused by a disruption in the precarious intimacy-distance balance.

The fight-flight-fuse couple

On the most severe level of dysfunction are the couples who appear to be desperately trying to break out of a symbiotic mode of relating. These couples are so riddled by ambivalence, fear of commitment, and identity loss that they are not able to marry, nor are they often able to sustain living together. The "fight-flight-fuse" designation reflects the predominant interactional pattern. Fighting is usually precipitated by a fear of overbearing closeness—one partner begins to feel more acutely the threat of losing self-boundaries, whereas the other is usually pushing for greater commitment to counter feeling insecure, unloved, and bedeviled by the omnipresent threat of abandonment. A heated outbreak of this pervasive struggle typically results in the flight of one partner, resulting in a physical separation of varying duration. Sooner or later, the separation is abruptly terminated by the couple's impulsive reconciliation in a state of mutual neediness and fusion, because the increased distance has mobilized intolerable fears of loss and abandonment. The pattern then repeats itself in a never-ending cycle.

These couples usually come for therapy because the one pressing for more commitment becomes unable to tolerate the other's ambivalence any longer and is threatening to terminate the relationship, or because the sexual acting out of one or both has come to light. The case of Lisa and Jack is illustrative of this version of the oppositional couple.

Lisa and Jack came for evaluation at the point of their most recent separation, which had been precipitated by Lisa's announcement that she was about to pursue an affair and wanted to terminate the relationship. This attractive, highly intelligent, professional couple in their mid-thirties had lived on and off together for nine years, withstanding three previous separations, which had occurred for the same ostensible reason, Lisa's affairs.

The repetitive pattern that emerged involved Lisa's accurate perception that Jack made love with her very infrequently and also avoided her attempts to improve their sex life. The additional unsupportable injury was that he ignored her various proposals of marriage. Feelings of being deprived and rejected led her to press Jack for more—a pressure he resisted with copious rationalizations and intellectualizations. Ultimately, Lisa would involve herself with another man whose fantastic sexual prowess would then be flaunted under Jack's nose. Intense fighting would ensue, followed by one or the other leaving their apartment. (It is pertinent to note that Jack had kept his own apartment for the nine years of their relationship.)

Separations would last from three to nine months, during which time Lisa would "go through" a number of men, while Jack would beg for her return, promising to meet all of her sexual needs in the future. Since Lisa invariably chose men with equally severe commitment problems, her affairs always fizzled, leaving her feeling unloved, lost, and longing for stable, parental Jack. A passionate reunion would then occur, followed by a brief blissful "honeymoon." Gradually, the old distancing pattern would reassert itself, fueled by Jack's unexpressed rage over being rejected, Lisa's insatiable demands for more, and the fear of both about sustaining a dependent, intimate relationship.

Although Jack appears to have the major commitment problem, Lisa has a more disguised version of the same problem. Lisa represents the characteristic pattern of the partner who is only *ostensibly* more committed and more capable of intimacy, in her dedicated selection of men who assiduously avoid commitment and in her use of a specialized repertoire of behaviors designed to drive the partner away lest he get too close. The interaction of this couple also reflects a kind of mutual torturing, suggestive of the sadomasochistic subtype of the symbiotic marriage. However, this form of sadomasochism is not pervasive or virulent and seldom involves physical battering. These kinds of couples are very difficult to treat, particularly in a conjoint modality, in part because the commitment difficulty extends to the therapeutic relationship, impeding the development of a workable transference and enduring alliance.

The pseudo-independent couple

A notch further up the scale of diminishing dysfunction and severity of conflict is the pseudo-independent couple. This couple has been able to marry and sustain a relationship but manages the intimacy-distance, dependency-independence conflict by opting for the solution of great distance. An overt or covert pact is made to glamorize pseudoindependence, the passionate pursuit of self-fulfillment, and "doing one's own thing," even though deep resentment underlies this solution. This couple basically leads parallel lives, although they may come together to discuss the children or to snipe at each other briefly on their way to different meetings, different activities, different friends, between their respective extramarital affairs.

The pseudo-independent couple tends to come for therapy when one partner begins wanting and requesting more intimacy, threatening to leave, or when the marital boundaries become so diffuse that the relationship is in total ruin and separation has already occurred. When couples of this kind actually break up, the supposedly glorified states of self-fulfillment and self-expression ostensibly achieved by outside activities usually go totally flat without the safety of a family structure and the foil of a disapproving, controlling parent-spouse to defy or act out against.

The push-pull couple

The most advanced and functional form of the oppositional syndrome (and the one with the best prognosis) is the couple I identify as the push-pull subtype. This style represents a contained version of rapprochement: the spouses carry on the push-pull, intimacy-distance oscillation within an intact marital relationship. They do not run as far from each other as do pseudo-independent couples, nor allow themselves to regress to states of symbiotic merger as do the fight-flight-fuse couples. The oscillation between intimacy and distance is therefore more balanced and less extreme, although it is still acutely and painfully present.

Escalated arguing, alternating with periods of strained, hostile alienation during which each goes his or her separate way, are the most common presenting complaints. Threats of separation or divorce are rampant, and the sex life has dramatically declined or ceased. As with the other subtypes, too wide a swing in the intimacy-distance balance has usually precipitated the increased arguing and estrangement.

One partner may step up the pressure for greater closeness (e.g., more sex, affection, time together) for several reasons, and the other partner, feeling the threat of engulfment and concomitant identity loss, responds with overt and covert forms of stubborn refusal to oblige. The reverse situation involves the traditionally more dependent partner making a developmental step toward greater individuation (for example, getting a job,

becoming more involved in the outside world), and the other partner
becoming threatened by the increased distance.

These kinds of threats do not lead to a physical rupture in the relationship (as they do with the fight-flight-fuse couples). However, they do lead
to the handling of the resultant hurt, anger, and resentment by creating
greater and greater emotional distance and to increased diffusion of the
marital boundaries, thus endangering the couple's sense of being a defined
unit. A common adjunct to this process is the "third-party syndrome,"
wherein one or both become more attached to a third party (i.e., friend,
relative, child, lover) or to an activity such as work, at the expense of their
attachment to each other. In more recent years, the intrusive third party
is often represented by an inanimate object—that is, in one partner's
passionate devotion to his or her personal computer.

In contrast to the symbiotic marriage, in which the marital boundaries
are almost impermeable to the outside world, the opposite condition,
wherein there is too much inclusion of the outside world, is a typical
condition of the oppositional couple. A repetitive phrase used by these
couples to describe their distancing, counterdependent defense is, "We
never seem to get together; we are like ships passing in the night."

Sexual Life

In all these subtypes of the oppositional relationship, the partners' affectionate expression and sexual interaction are characterized by the same
theme of missing each other, of ships passing in the night. The sexual and
affectionate desires of one are typically out of sync with those of the other.
And when they finally do get together sexually, the oppositional combat
goes on: if he wants oral sex, she thinks it's disgusting; she is turned off
or becomes gigglish over his clumsy attempts to arouse her; he seems to
do deliberately everything that she has told him time and time again not
to do, and so forth.

Mild to severe sexual dysfunctions often appear as side effects of the
erosion of self-esteem and threats to masculinity and femininity engendered by this kind of demoralizing, rejecting interaction. Frequently, by
the time the couple seeks therapy, one partner has frequently lost sexual
interest in the other and is contemplating, if not already engaged in, an
affair.

Although a major cause of the oppositional couple's avoidant sexual
sparring is the need to defend against fears of being engulfed, of giving-in,
and of feeling helplessly vulnerable in relation to a more powerful parent-

spouse, unresolved gender identity conflicts are also significantly involved. Since the partners' sense of identity in general has not been securely achieved, it is not surprising that sexual identity is usually quite conflicted and unstable. Bisexual conflicts have typically not been resolved, aggravating each partner's sense of inadequacy as an attractive, sexual male or female, attended by feelings of hostility toward, and envy of, the opposite sex. Overt or covert attacks on the partner's sexual attractiveness and competency are often the defensive expression of these conflicts, which are acted out with painfully destructive results both in and out of the bedroom. The following interaction of Kenny and Jane on the subject of their unsatisfying sexual encounters is a particularly blatant example of these difficulties:

KENNY: *You know it's not that easy to get something going sexually with you. First, the bed is always littered with all your books that I have to crawl over or clear out of the way, and then when I start something you wriggle and squirm like some sort of slippery fish.*

JANE: *Well, you're always going for my left breast, it's always the left one, and then you just diddle with it, diddle and diddle. This is not exciting; it's just irritating, so I try to move away from that.*

KENNY: *Well, so I'm a breast man, so what's wrong with that? (To Therapist) Jane has small breasts. They're not that easy to get a hold of (ha! ha!). Of course she can't help that. I mean they're nice, small breasts.*

JANE: *(Angrily) You and your fetish about big breasts. (To Therapist) You should see him drool over some woman with big, sagging mammary glands. We all know what that means. You want a woman with big breasts so you can be sure you're the man!*

Family of Origin, Marital Transference, and Transactional Roles

The dysfunctional expressions and methods of coping with gender identity conflicts, fears of intimacy and commitment, along with unmet (and denied) needs for nurturance, reflect the partners' lack of intrapsychic separation from their families of origin. Unlike the symbiotic couple, oppositional partners have managed to effect an actual separation from parents—that is, the parents are not usually living next door or physically inside the marriage habitat. In fact, the problem of separating from parents has usually been fraught with excessive conflict such that great physical distancing and emotional cut-off from the family of origin is a common solution.

However, parents cannot be gotten rid of so easily. As object relations theory has spelled out, they continue to live inside of us as introjects. The particular focus of the internal, though unconscious, relationship with parental introjects that emerges and becomes reenacted in the oppositional marriage is that of the little child struggling for validation and approval of his or her uniqueness and individuality, in interaction with a highly critical, perfectionistic, controlling parent. In accord with Henry Dick's (1969) theory of "the shared internal object," I have found that partners engaged in an oppositional mode of relating tend to share the internal object of a critical, controlling, omnipotent parent, and have likely selected each other, in part, for this reason. One motivation for selecting a close representative of an internal object as soul mate is the implicit hope of changing the disappointing outcome of this relationship and resolving the original ambivalent love-hate, push-pull tie.

The negative side of the marital transference, then, takes the form of each partner perceiving the other (via projection) as the reembodiment of a critical, controlling, demanding parent and experiencing the self as a small, ineffective, unheard cry against the other's omnipotent power. Concurrently, each partner's identification with the controlling, critical, manipulative aspects of his or her own parents (along with the more hidden preservation of his or her grandiose self) tends to justify and reinforce this perception of the other as controlling, critical, and manipulative.

The oppositional behavior of the spouses and their verbalized accusations of each other clearly identify the marital transference: "You're trying to control me"; "You're trying to manipulate me"; "You want me to act like a puppet on your string"; "You're taking too much of my space"; "You make me feel trapped"; "You want everything your own way"; "You won't accept me for who I am." Even though these accusations represent projections of the internal parent, they also represent disavowed aspects of the self. Hence there is considerable accuracy in the partner's overall distortion of each other.

This characteristic marital transference is played out transactionally in certain typical dovetailing roles. One spouse most commonly plays the dominating parent role and the other the defiant two-year-old or teenager. Another common set-up is that one plays the dependent, needy role, and demands more time, affection, sex, closeness, and commitment via pursuing the more indifferent, independent-acting one. However, these roles are not fixed and usually flip-flop over time, sometimes even in the course of a therapy session.

Communication: Style of Argument

Oppositional argument, to a greater or lesser degree, replaces the direct expression of feelings, particularly those pertaining to dependency needs and the suffering resulting from experiences of rejection, criticism, and disapproval. In other words, the oppositional style of argument is used by the couple as a joint defense against revealing dependent longings and feelings of being inadequate and unlovable. The arguing these couples engage in is distinctive and can be distinguished from other kinds of fighting, more indicative of lower or higher developmental levels.

For example, the courtroom style of battling in which no one can win is quite different from the constant bickering and blaming of the lower-level symbiotic couple. The bickering of these symbiotic couples has a reproachful, clinging, hostile-dependent, clutching quality. This fretful whining seems to represent (developmentally speaking) the wish to attach oneself symbiotically, like a sticky barnacle, to some undifferentiated, all-nurturing spouse-mother figure.

In contrast, the power-struggle battling of oppositional couples is a crisp, highly defined and coherent interaction. The nagging, picking, blaming style is not as prevalent as are bolder, more certain, differentiated statements that generally carry the following kind of message: "We should do it my way, because my way is the right way and yours is wrong, sick, stupid for all of these obvious and/or logical reasons."

The tendency to blow one's horn loudly enough so that the other is drowned out represents the wish to differentiate more firmly and to hold on to the temporary illusion of a strong, certain, whole self. Even listening to the partner's point of view is difficult, for the risk of being influenced by the other is experienced as tantamount to losing the precariously held sense of self. When Jane, the wife from the preceding vignette, was confronted with her constant interruption of Kenny, she replied, "I just don't want to listen to what he has to say, because if I start to listen, I can feel myself losing or even forgetting what I am trying to say."

That neither partner can sustain the winning for long or with any comfort must also be distinguished from superficially similar behavior occasioned by guilt over oedipal victory or triumph over a sibling—issues reflective of more advanced development. The discomfort of an oppositional partner with winning and following through on a victory results from the fear of independence, which revives the dread of abandonment, of being alone and helpless.

Personality Traits: Narcissistic Vulnerability

A personality assessment of the partners in an oppositional relationship reveals a variety of different pairings. Among the most common is the passive-aggressive, withholding, obsessional man and the demanding, rather castrating, hysterical woman (as in the case of Lisa and Jack). However, underlying all possible personality style combinations, one usually finds a cluster of traits in both partners indicative of considerable narcissistic pathology. The narcissistic vulnerability of these partners is apparent: their inability to tolerate criticism and their need to project unacceptable traits; their extreme dependence on external support, praise, and admiration for maintenance of self-esteem; their perfectionistic and grandiose expectations of self and other; their wish for the other to be a mirroring twin; and their variably disguised feelings of entitlement. These traits and vulnerabilities do not appear as severe or rigidified in oppositional couples as they do in symbiotic couples.*

Because of these narcissistic vulnerabilities, behaviors geared toward soothing narcissistic injury, such as drug abuse (more often mild than severe) and sexual acting out, are not uncommonly found in at least one of the partners. From a developmental point of view, the presence of narcissistic pathology in these couples is not surprising, since these disorders of the self have their roots in the earliest separation-individuation phase of object relations development (Kohut 1971; Kernberg 1975).

Case Example

The case of Frank and Betsy is illustrative of the arrested push-pull subtype of the oppositional couple, rapidly regressing down the scale to a pseudo-independent mode of functioning. To use a last name or initial to identify this couple would not be an accurate reflection of their situation, because they had different last names. Regarding the younger generation, one of the possible clues to an oppositional couple is the wife's insistence upon keeping her maiden name, though obviously this preference does not always signify an oppositional mode of relating.

Frank and Betsy, a couple in their mid-thirties and married two years, came for marital therapy because they had become alienated over their

---

*Lansky (1986), in his profile of couples with narcissistic disorders, is describing a more severe pathology than is displayed in the oppositional couple. In this framework, Lansky's profile represents a form of the symbiotic mode of object relating.

differences and were seriously considering divorce. The couple traced an increase in explosive arguments and long periods of estranged angry silences to a six-week visit of Frank's parents, who had since moved to their town. Although this couple disagreed about everything, the central deadlock issues involved the management of Frank's rather intrusive parents (who were beginning to drop by on a daily basis) and Frank's overinvolvement with his former wife, who had custody of his son.

The oppositional stance invaded all aspects of their lives. They had separate bank accounts; they had separate friends (with whom they felt closer than to each other). They had constructed their work schedules so that they had minimal contact. He was an optimist; she was a pessimist. He was always angry, given to explosive outbursts; she was usually withdrawn and depressed. He was a compulsively tidy physical fitness nut; she was a slob who abhorred physical exercise, preferring to sit and read. He liked quick, action-packed sex in the middle of the night; she liked a slow, romantic build-up in the late afternoon (and so on and so forth). The parallel nature of their lives and the triangling of third parties were reflected in a parallel communication style, in which each would conduct a monologue to me without listening to the other.

The marital history, history of previous love relations, and families of origin revealed that neither partner had progressed beyond an oppositional mode of relating. Both had been "good," overresponsible children in relation to their parents, with minimal displays of rebelliousness in adolescence. In both families one parent had dominated (the father in his case, the mother in her case). Strong ambivalent ties to parents were expressed in split, alternating idealized and devalued perceptions. They were both perfectionistic, exhibited thinly disguised grandiosity, and were allergic to criticism. Both shared the internal object of a critical, controlling, demanding, unattuned parent, with whom each unconsciously identified, but these traits were disowned and projected onto the other. Dependency needs were consciously denied but covertly expressed in his insatiable angry demandingness and her withdrawn depressions. Underlying the oppositional power struggle aspects of their interaction was the more poignant struggle for nurturing, the need for the tender, attuned, maternal caregiving and mirroring that neither had adequately received in their families of origin.

Treatment Intervention

Obstacles to successful treatment

Oppositional couples of the arrested type represented by the preceding case example present formidable obstacles to successful treatment intervention. First, the dependence-independence conflict is often immediately transferred to the therapist in the same oscillating fashion characteristic of the couple's interaction. The fears of being dominated, of being taken over or engulfed, or being told what to do, or criticized are expressed in initial and ongoing challenges to the therapist's authority. It is easy to be lured into a power struggle with these couples, and the bait often appears in the initial evaluative interviews as resistance over meeting time or one partner's move to take over the treatment plan. The dependent side of the conflict (the feelings of helplessness, powerlessness, and inadequacy) are expressed in strong bids for the therapist to take sides as a parent-judge who will decide who is right or wrong. Frequent requests are, "Tell us what to do!" or "Give us homework!" However, if the therapist does make suggestions or give advice or homework, the couple typically overtly or covertly rebels.

Second, the overtly rebellious or covertly resistant response to directiveness makes a highly programmatic, behavioristic, or authoritarian approach to treatment doomed to failure. On the other hand, an unstructured, nondirective approach leads to escalating anxiety, runaway arguments during the sessions, takeover of the therapy by the couple, and anger over abandonment. Premature termination is the most likely outcome in both cases.

Third, the couple's narcissistic vulnerabilities (particularly the hypersensitivity to criticism) and tendency to project unacceptable traits make early confrontation or interpretation of noxious behaviors and personality traits almost impossible. Increased defensiveness is the usual response. Communication and negotiation training are difficult because even mild interventions are interpreted as criticisms or as the therapist's taking sides or as the therapist's exacting submission from one or the other. The idea of negotiating differences is usually resisted because the couple does not want to negotiate, are not developmentally advanced enough to negotiate, and view negotiation and compromise as meaning submission, or domination, or surrender of one's individuality. The grandiose fantasy of entitlement is another obstruction to negotiation—the concealed belief that "I should always have my way and that not having my way means that I am unloved."

The strong countertransference reactions of the therapist engendered by these couples constitute a fourth obstacle to successful treatment. The difficulty in establishing a position of authority, of being heard by the couple and validated, often provokes frustration and anger in the therapist and a regression to feeling and responding in the same oppositional mode. Hence the therapist becomes like a third adultified two-year-old in the room, competing to be heard, insistently arguing for his or her point of view, stubbornly refusing to collaborate or compromise. The feeling inside the therapist, usually cloaked by rationalizations about the need to establish authority, is something like, "I must show who is boss by stamping my therapeutic foot and having my way." Other common reactions include wanting to respond as a benevolent, all-knowing parent who will fix the problem with copious suggestions and advice, or as a punitive parent who must scold the couple for their bad behavior. The urge to side with the more rational, receptive, or compliant partner against the more "impossible" one can also be compelling.

Treatment strategy

Given these obstacles, what is the therapist to do? From this point of view, the overall therapeutic goal entails the unblocking of the stuck or stalled individuation process, so that the couple can allow the intimacy, dependency, and full expression of individuality necessary to real marriage. Interventions, particularly in the initial phase, can most successfully be focused on two interlocking aspects of the dysfunction: (1) an individualized supportive focus in order to build more secure and fully formed identities; and (2) a focus on exploring the meaning of collusive-defensive oppositional interactions as attempts to master fears of intimacy and distance, and of dependence and independence in relation to each other and then in relation to family-of-origin experience.

In treating oppositional couples of the arrested type, the therapist should make clear that long-term therapy is indicated for an in-depth working through of the developmental conflicts and deficits. In my experience, a successful outcome usually takes from one to three years. Although the length of treatment is greatly affected by the couple's motivation, their willingness, and their financial ability to engage in intensive therapy involving more than one session per week—preferably a combined-individual and conjoint modality of treatment or adjunctive individual psychoanalytic psychotherapy or psychoanalysis—are also crucial factors.

Modality

In working with oppositional couples, I have found a combined individual and conjoint modality to be the treatment of choice, given an ideal set of circumstances. Individual interviews can more easily and effectively be geared to addressing identity issues and to building a therapeutic alliance more rapidly with each partner. Conjoint interviews are necessary for management of the dysfunctional interaction patterns, and most important, they provide a safer place for the couple to get together.

It is important to underscore that I do not recommend the combining of individual and conjoint interviews for all couples, even all oppositional couples. A central purpose in creating a system of developmental diagnosis of relationships is to provide a sound theoretical framework for designing more effective and tailor-made treatment plans. In regard to choice of modality, the point is to tailor the modality to the couples' developmental needs, conflicts, and capabilities rather than fit every couple into one format (such as only treating couples in a conjoint modality or always combining modalities).

For example, an awareness of the developmental conflicts and deficits of symbiotic couples should alert the therapist to proceed cautiously in the use of individual sessions with the partners early in therapy because these couples are easily overwhelmed with profound separation anxiety and are grossly impaired in their ability to trust. Separating the couple with individual sessions before a trusting alliance with each is established tends to exacerbate profoundly both partners' fears of betrayal and abandonment (by the therapist and the other partner). These fears usually cannot be dispelled or utilized therapeutically in the earlier phases of treatment.

On the other hand, individuals in an oppositional relationship usually have the capacity to tolerate a greater degree of separation and the ability to work therapeutically with, and therefore contain, fears of being left out and of a two-against-one alliance forming between the therapist and one partner. Additionally, these individuals have a tremendous developmental need for individualized support and can more freely allow the vulnerability of self-exploration without the presence of the partner, who tends to provoke a more guarded stance of vigilant defensiveness. However, for a combined modality to be effective, it is necessary for the therapist to verbalize to the couple the potential fears that may be more strongly generated by individual sessions, encourage their discussion when experienced by either partner, and be alert to behaviors reflecting feelings of betrayal or distrust. Rules regarding confidentiality, that is, what information will or will not be available for the therapist's use in conjoint sessions, must also be made explicit.

Contraindications to combining regular individual sessions with conjoint treatment of oppositional couples include the following: (1) the couple has a strong resistance to the idea; (2) one or both partners is already engaged in individual therapy; (3) the couple's budget allows for only one session per week; (4) paranoid personality traits are present in one or both partners; (5) the therapist is inexperienced in managing the potential problems implicit in effectively using a combined modality; and (6) the therapist feels uncomfortable with hearing and handling secrets.

In managing conjoint sessions, I usually do not initially work using a communication model with oppositional couples; I allow and often encourage them to interact with me instead of each other. This approach is experienced as more supportive and avoids destructive experiences of escalating arguments, which generate defensiveness and anger and render interventions ineffective.

Therapist's role

While a parental, authoritarian, highly directive, confrontational, limit-setting approach is usually indicated for the lower-level symbiotic couple (who initially requires a contained, highly structured, predictable holding environment), the oppositional couple initially requires the therapist to act and react in a flexible, nonauthoritarian, and consistently collaborative way. Before defenses can be interpreted successfully and underlying fears exposed, the therapist needs to demonstrate *in action* that a respect of the partner's needs for autonomy and control (to be fully heard and in some way validated and supported) is consistently guaranteed. The acknowledgment, acceptance, and support of each partner's view is far more important than getting the couple to agree, compromise, or negotiate. The modeling of listening and negotiation skills with each partner is more effective than taking an overt "teaching" role in relation to their interaction.

The therapist does not look particularly flashy in this early phase of treatment, which is geared mostly to building an alliance with the couple through carefully, seriously, and empathically focusing on each partner's point of view individually. During this process, it is helpful to encourage an historical perspective on the problem presented and to clarify why each may feel different, based on particular experiences in his or her respective family of origin. Questions about how their parents handled the same kind of problem and how each partner may have interacted around similar issues with parents, siblings, or other important people, are useful in fostering individualized exploration.

It is equally important to cull from each partner's story on a given issue the developmental struggles held in common that the different styles of reacting and coping may conceal. The beginning recognition by the couple of their shared developmental conflict (or "shared internal object") softens defensiveness, promotes empathy toward the self and other, and introduces the major therapeutic theme to be reworked throughout therapy. This method of handling a heated issue presented in the opening phase of treatment can be demonstrated by the following clinical vignette taken from an early conjoint interview with Frank and Betsy.

The session began with a heated interchange initiated by Betsy's accusation that Frank's parents, who had recently moved to town, were "dropping by" too often. She complained that her house no longer felt like her house, and she was particularly upset about the day they "hung around" for three hours when she was sick. She demanded that Frank do something about this intolerable situation. Frank responded defensively, arguing that he had said something to them about calling first, and he resented having the problem dumped on him. Why should he be the one "to hurt their feelings?" It was Betsy's problem, "right?" he looked to me for support. Why didn't she get off her "lazy ass and do something about something for a change?" Betsy retaliated by insinuating that Frank was a coward, emphasizing that it was his place to deal with his parents, not hers. "Wasn't that right?" she posed the question to me.

This interaction, typical of the opening phase behavior of the oppositional couple in the accusative-defensive, self-righteous, rapidly escalating style of argument, occurs in the context of a marital boundary problem and involves the invasion of a third party who exposes each partner's inability to set appropriate limits. Moreover, each partner's wish that the other act as the responsible parent is reflected in strong bids for the therapist to take sides. The pitfalls for the therapist in responding to this kind of interaction, often engendered by strong countertransference reactions, include temptations (1) to respond as the "critical parent" and exacerbate narcissistic vulnerabilities by "therapeutically" scolding the couple for their destructive communication and by giving instructions for improvement (for example, lecturing about the importance of "I" statements, refraining from name calling, and so forth); (2) to take sides on the content by saying, in effect, that limits should be set on the parents' intrusion, an intervention that would close the door to exploring both partners' conflicts about handling this problem; (3) to withhold support from both partners and prematurely force them to work out the problem as adults ("What I think isn't important. You need to resolve this with him or her."); (4) to take an equally premature "adult" problem-solving approach ("How can you each compromise on this issue to solve the problem?"); (5) to respond to the couple's inducement to act as the parent by giving advice on how the

problem should be solved ("Why don't you both decide what the limits should be and speak to Frank's parents together?").

Although some of these possible responses may be of use later on in treatment and might be appropriate with higher- or lower-functioning couples, none of them address the initial basic need of each partner to be heard, validated, and understood first by the therapist and then, it is hoped, by each other. Hence, it is crucial for the therapist to respond to the pleas for support, but not to take sides.

In this situation, I responded by stating that each obviously had strong views and feelings on this issue for probably very good reasons that we should try and understand better. Probing for what was behind Betsy's reactions revealed that she treasured privacy, and the intrusion of Frank's parents (or anyone else's) left her feeling put-upon and obliged to "take care" of them when she needed time to herself. She felt unable to put her own needs first when confronted by their needs to visit, for fear of offending them and being viewed as the "bad daughter." Encouraged to relate those feeling to past feelings in her own family, Betsy revealed that she was always obliged to take care of her depressed, ailing mother, especially as a teenager, when she wanted to be with her friends or do other things. Torn with guilt and anger, she felt she must comply with what her mother wanted or would experience unbearable, silent, reproachful disapproval. She also wished her weak, henpecked father would intervene and protect her from having to cope with her mother's constant demands for compliance and caregiving. Anger at Frank for not helping her enough with this current problem and her own inability to assert herself were connected with the resurgence of the powerful feelings about her past familial situation.

In exploring Frank's anger and conflict over the intrusive parent issue, we discovered that he, too, had always felt the need to comply with his parents' wishes. It was automatic for him to feel that his parents' wishes must come first. His parents had been dominated by his grandmother (father's mother) who had lived with them. Additionally, open disagreement with his mother caused her to withdraw and become morose for days; open disagreement from anyone triggered violent rages in his father. It also became evident that Frank had lifelong problems controlling his own temper (which had mostly been directed at his younger brother), and felt he had to live down his "black sheep" reputation in this respect by being an excessively good, responsible, and compliant son.

I underscored the dynamically similar developmental theme—the experience of feeling obliged to subjugate their own views, wants, and needs and to overcomply with parental demands to ensure love and acceptance—

and linked it with their conflict in handling the current problem. The shared wishes to have unconditional support of their feelings, and to have the other confront the frightening task of self-assertion in relation to the intruding parents, became clear to them.

When the therapist has established a degree of trust and safety through these methods, the therapist will also have proved that he or she is not an embodiment of the feared "internal parent." At that time, it then becomes possible to confront more directly the communication problems, such as not listening, interrupting, blaming, disparaging or insulting the partner, making global accusations, speaking for the partner, shifting subjects, cross-complaining, and so on. Directives about changing communication behaviors can now be given without provoking either defensiveness or dismissal of the directive. However, it is usually more effective to begin by eliciting from the couple what the communication problems are, so that an observing ego can be fostered and the changes can be experienced as collaborative. Some couples are good at identifying communication problems when asked to review an interaction; others need to be trained to observe in this fashion.

Interpretation of defensive transactions

When defensiveness subsides, the couple becomes able to to listen and respond to each other with some understanding and without constantly resorting to escalating accusations and anger. The therapist can then address more fully the meaning behind the collusive distancing defenses—the diffuse marital boundaries, the triangling of third parties, synchronized avoidance, the polarization of affects, traits, positions, and courtroom combat. Eventually, the couple begins to deal more pointedly with those issues on their own volition (e.g., spending more time together, limiting individual pursuits or "workaholism," ending affairs). Anxiety comes to the foreground with those kinds of efforts and can be effectively interpreted.

For example, I pointed out to one couple that their experience of greater closeness seemed to result in fear that led one or the other to sabotage their progress (with a fight, a pointed rejection, a flurry of separate activities, or the desire to terminate therapy). The wife responded, "Yes, I start to feel very scared when we get close, scared that I'll lose myself—who I am and what I want—and scared of a bottomless pit feeling that I'll just want more and more and more and never have enough. That's the worst!"

At this juncture, when the need for defensive projection fades and the partners can look at their own feelings, actions, and reactions, a deeper phase of treatment can begin. The genetic roots—the painful, disappointing relationship with parents replayed in the marital transference—can

now be fully explored and bit by bit laid to rest, so that the couple can move on developmentally and become truly married.

REFERENCES

Ackerman, N. W. 1965. "The Family Approach to Marital Disorders." In *The Psychotherapies of Marital Disharmony,* ed. B. L. Green, pp. 153–67. New York: Free Press.

Berman, E. M., and Lief, H. I. 1975. "Marital Therapy from a Psychiatric Perspective: An Overview." *American Journal of Psychiatry* 132 (6):583–92.

Blanck, R., and Blanck, G. 1968. *Marriage and Personal Development.* New York: Columbia University Press.

Blos, P. 1979. *The Adolescent Passage.* New York: International Universities Press.

Bowen, M. 1978. *Family Therapy in Clinical Practice.* New York: Jason Aronson.

Colarusso, C. A. and Nemiroff, R. A. 1981. *Adult Development.* New York: Plenum.

Dicks, H. V. 1967. *Marital Tensions.* New York: Basic Books.

Framo, J. L. 1965. "Rationale and Techniques of Intensive Family Therapy." In *Intensive Family Therapy,* ed. I. Boszormenyi-Nagy and J. L. Framo, pp. 143–212. New York: Harper & Row.

Gurman, A. S., and Jacobson, N. S. 1986. "Marital Therapy: From Technique to Theory, Back Again, and Beyond." In *Clinical Handbook of Marital Therapy,* ed. N. S. Jacobson and A. S. Gurman, pp. 1–13. New York: Guilford.

Haley, J. 1963. "Marriage Therapy." *Archives of General Psychiatry* 8:213–34.

Kaplan, L. J. 1972. "Object Constancy in Light of Piaget's Vertical Decalage." *Bulletin of the Menninger Clinic* 36:322–27.

Kernberg, O. F. 1975. *Borderline Conditions and Pathological Narcissism.* New York: Jason Aronson.

Kohut, H. 1971. *The Analysis of the Self: A Systemantic Approach to the Psychoanalytic Treatment of Narcissistic Personality Disorders.* New York: International Universities Press.

Lansky, M. R. 1986. "Marital Therapy for Narcissistic Disorders." In *Clinical Handbook of Marital Therapy,* ed. N. S. Jacobson and A. S. Gurman, pp. 557–75. New York: Guilford.

Lederer, W. J., and Jackson, D. D. 1968. *The Mirages of Marriage.* New York: W. W. Norton.

Mahler, M. S.; Pine, F.; and Bergman, A. 1975. *The Psychological Birth of the Human Infant.* New York: Basic Books.

Mittelmann, B. 1944. "Complementary Neurotic Reactions in Intimate Relationships." *Psychoanalytic Quarterly* 13:479–91.

———. 1956. "Analysis of Reciprocal Neurotic Patterns in Family Relationships." In *Neurotic Interaction in Marriage,* ed. V. W. Eisenstein, pp. 81–100. New York: Basic Books.

Olson, D. H. 1975. "A Critical Overview." In *Couples in Conflict,* ed. A. S. Gurman and D. G. Rice, pp. 7–63. New York: Jason Aronson.

Pittman, F. S., and Flomenhaft, K. 1972. "Treating the Doll's House Marriage." In

Progress in Group and Family Therapy, ed. C. J. Sager and H. S. Kaplan, pp. 509–20. New York: Brunner/Mazel.

Ravich, R. A., and Wyden, B. 1974. *Predicatable Pairing: The Structures of Human Atoms.* New York: Peter H. Wyden.

Sager, C. J. 1976. *Marriage Contracts and Couple Therapy.* New York: Brunner/Mazel.

Scarf, M. 1987. *Intimate Partners.* New York: Random House.

Scharff, D. E., and Scharff, J. S. 1987. *Object Relations Family Therapy.* Northvale, N.J.: Jason Aronson.

Sharpe, S. A. 1981. "The Symbiotic Marriage: A Diagnostic Profile." *Bulletin of the Menninger Clinic* 45 (2):89–114.

————. 1984. Self and Object Representations: An Integration of Psychoanalytic and Piagetian Developmental Theories. Ph.D. diss., The Fielding Institute, Santa Barbara, Calif.

Stern, D. N. 1985. *The Interpersonal World of the Infant.* New York: Basic Books.

Strean, H. S. 1980. *The Extramarital Affair.* New York: Free Press.

————. 1985. *Resolving Marital Conflicts: A Psychodynamic Perspective.* New York: John Wiley & Sons.

Willi, J. 1976. "The Hysterical Marriage." In *Contemporary Marriage, Dynamics and Therapy,* ed. H. Grunebaum and J. Christ, pp. 435–56. Boston: Little, Brown.

————. 1982. *Couples in Collusion.* New York: Jason Aronson.

Winch, R. F. 1958. *Mate Selection: A Study of Complementary Needs.* New York: Harper & Row.

DISCUSSION

Organized psychoanalysis has largely ignored marital process and therapy as a field of inquiry or practice. If we look at the major journals, *Journal of the American Psychoanalytic Association, International Journal of Psycho-Analysis,* or *Psychoanalytic Quarterly,* we find scarcely any articles discussing this central and vital aspect of life. Similarly, in looking back over the scientific programs of the American Psychoanalytic Association, we can recall no panel or section devoted to marriage or to the treatment of its ills. Why is this so? As a partial explanation, we think it is related to a not-infrequent reaction of psychoanalysts, identified by Ralph Greenson (1969) in his article, "The Origin and Fate of New Ideas in Psychoanalysis." He wrote about the tendency for psychoanalysts to dismiss new ideas, innovations, or challenges as very interesting, but "not psychoanalysis." Thus they need not deal with different realms of data or information from related fields. In part we think this is what has happened to psychoanalytic study and facilitation of such areas as family therapy, group therapy, and the subject under discussion here—psychoanalytic marital therapy. We feel the consequences of this neglect have been detrimental to the clinical and scientific growth of psychoanalysis and its training programs and curricula, which should prepare trainees for the diversification required by modern clinical challenges.

Sharpe's valuable contribution in this discussion spans both theory and technique. Marital therapy was said to be "a technique in search of a theory." Sharpe here provides us with a coherent model of marital interaction, dysfunction, and intervention based on developmental object relations theory, particularly the work of Mahler and colleagues (1975). Sharpe bases her profiles of the "symbiotic" couple and the "oppositional" couple on phases of child development. This emphasis evolves from her observation and belief that most significant factors influencing the quality of interaction in a marriage—and how the relationship/system develops—are the kind of object relations and the extent of self-object differentiation attained by the individual partners. Thus sustained dysfunctional interaction in a marriage most often represents a reenactment of the kinds of relatedness to a parent (or parents) that the partners experienced in connection with developmental tasks that were not truly mastered.

With the oppositional couple highlighted here, the major component of the relationship is the partners' striving for independent identity within the marriage. This is reminiscent of Mahler's (1975) rapprochement subphase during the early separation-individuation process, wherein the toddler alternates between clinging and defiant behavior in relation to the mother. Sharpe describes how both partners of the adult oppositional couple strive for independent identities, but the striving conflicts with the regressive pull of strong symbiotic wishes, that is, the wish to be totally taken care of, to merge with an idealized parent figure, who comes to be represented by the spouse. Fearing those regressive wishes, the partners try to deny or project their longings. Aiming to bolster their shaky identities and independent wishes, they take the oppositional stance toward each other. It is as if they were saying, "I *have* to take a position different from yours, in order to exist as a person. If we agree, I'm lost in you—I'm not a separate person." We feel this formulation has great validity and clinical usefulness in helping couples recognize the problem and move toward more collaborative adult functioning.

However, Sharpe's conceptualization does not imply that Mahler's phases from early childhood are simply replayed in dysfunctional adult marital relationships. It is clear that those earlier developmental themes are recapitulated in a more advanced form later in development. Looking at development as being potentially lifelong, she asserts, and we agree, that the early sequence of phases may be recapitulated in more advanced form *every time* we enter a new significant relationship, that is, any relationship that involves a significant degree of dependency. Sharpe describes the normative adult developmental process that leads to a collaborative relationship: First (1) there is an initial idealizing period and a fused mode of perceiving and relating to the partner, the normative symbiotic phase; second (2) there is subsequent disillusionment in the ideal and a thrust toward separation-individuation, the normative oppositional phase; and third (3) there is the eventual acceptance of reality—ambivalent feelings of love and hate for the partner, including imperfections in self and mate, leading to a more secure, realistic sense of self and other, the normative collaborative phase.

We (1981) have described a similar process in normal marital growth, calling it the "grinding" process, and we stressed the eventual acceptance of self and partner as separate, different, and valued individuals. However, we emphasized that, at least in long-standing marriages, this process seemed to be a bi-modal experience. That is, in the first twenty years a couple is working on

1. separation from parental psychic representations;

2. narcissistic transfer and construction of an idealized spouse representation in the psyche;

3. conflict between the idealized spouse and real spouse representations (the "grinding");

4. gradual abandonment of the idealized spouse representation and more acceptance of the real spouse representation.

The bi-modal aspect comes into play with the need to engage a second process starting in midlife when the normative issue is to process and accept inevitable aging in both self and spouse. In the middle years, the aging of the spouse and the self becomes the major narcissistic issue in the marriage. The narcissistic injury felt in the aging process, particularly in relation to sexual activity, is compensated by the now long-standing gratification of intimacy in the marital relationship. Normative conflict is experienced between the pull toward youthful bodies and sexual reassurance and the realistic acceptance of the adult body and the internal body image. The second development or reworking of the real spouse representation enhances the achievement of deep intimacy and diminishes the narcissistic sting of aging.

Sharpe makes a particularly valuable contribution in her description of the *marital transferences* observed in the oppositional couple. It is crucial to understand and help couples in marital therapy to identify and resolve the transferences that occur in their relationship. Sharpe puts it concisely when she says that parents "cannot be gotten rid of so easily"; they continue to live inside us as introjects. In the oppositional couple, the unconscious relationship reenacted with parental objects is that of the little child struggling for validation and approval of his or her uniqueness and individuality, interacting with a highly critical, perfectionistic, and controlling parent. For marital therapy to be successful, the therapist must help the couples see how they repeatedly project and provoke these images and transferences.

An excellent description and integration of psychodynamic and behavioral approaches to marital therapy can be found in R. Taylor Segraves's (1982) book, *Marital Therapy*. He sets out three useful hypotheses about transference:

1. Faulty interpersonal schemas (or transferences) for the perception of intimate members of the opposite sex are of primary importance in both the genesis and maintenance of chronic marital discord.

2. Individuals have inner representation models for significant others and tend to behave toward other people in ways that invite behaviors congruent with that inner representational world.

3. In marital therapy, contrasted to individual psychotherapy or psychoanalysis, most patients are highly effective in eliciting reciprocal behavior from their spouses. Each spouse arrives in therapy with a full-blown transference reaction involving the spouse. In some ways, marital therapy can be more complex than individual psychotherapy because the transference relations are often bilateral, and the therapist often encounters a highly evolved complex interactional system.

REFERENCES

Colarusso, C. A., and Nemiroff, R. A. 1981. *Adult Development: A New Dimension in Psychodynamic Theory and Practice.* New York: Plenum.

Greenson, R. 1969. "The Origin and Fate of New Ideas in Psychoanalysis." *International Journal of Psycho-Analysis* 50:503–15.

Mahler, M.; Pine, F.; and Bergman, A. 1975. *The Psychological Birth of the Human Infant.* New York: Basic Books.

Segraves, R. 1982. *Marital Therapy: A Combined Psychodynamic-Behavioral Approach.* New York: Plenum.

PART IV

APPLICATIONS
OF
ADULT DEVELOPMENTAL
THEORY

17

Adult Dreaming:

Frontiers of Form

ROBERT JAY LIFTON

If we do not dream, then the day is not very good.
—Zinacantec Indian saying
Of Wonders Wild and New—Dreams from Zinacantan

I am dreaming and I would
act well, for good deeds
are not lost, even in dreams.
—Pedro Calderón
Life is a Dream

This essay was originally given at a large symposium on dreams sponsored by the department of human development and health sciences of the University of California, Los Angeles, and the Southern California Psychoanalytic Society and Institute. I had long been making use of dreams of research subjects in all of my studies, while also recording dreams of my own. I had begun (in both *The Life of the Self* and *The Broken Connection*) to outline a theoretical perspective I wished to develop, and wanted to go about the matter more systematically.

Freud's discovery of ways in which dreams served as what he called a *"via regna* to the unconscious" made it necessary, I believe, for any new psychological thought to reassess the twists and turns of that *via regna.* In connection with my work, dreams are crucial to an understanding of what

419

I call "formative process," and to the overall life-continuity paradigm. This essay has at least one particularly hopeful message: dreams of individual people in extreme circumstances can contribute to a process of forward-looking integration and moral questioning.

Some years ago, when embarking on a study of Nazi doctors, I had a talk with a friend who was both an authority on the Holocaust and himself an Auschwitz survivor. I complained to him about the horrors of the material I was uncovering, that it was affecting me a great deal, especially in my dreams—that I was having horrible dreams about concentration camps, dreams that involved not only me but also my wife and children. My friend looked at me with a combination of sympathy and toughness. "Good!" he said. "Now you can do the study." We smiled at each other in recognition. He was telling me that my dreaming about this terrible subject meant that it was entering my mind in some important way, that I was not remaining distant from it but permitting it, however involuntarily, to connect with my own internal images. He could confirm and approve, as a survivor, my coming from the outside, so to speak, and experiencing a survivor's dreams. And still further, he was implying that dreaming about these events was also necessary to my *intellectual*—broadly speaking, *creative*—function in the work.

Those dreams have by no means disappeared. But the dreaming function is never simple. In doing the work and getting even closer to the material (through interviews with both Nazi perpetrators and Auschwitz survivors), I not only have dreamed of camp and other expressions of Nazi cruelty but have also had much more pleasant dreams, as if to counteract the fearful ones, some of them highly erotic.

The principle revealed here—and the central theme of this chapter—may be expressed in an anthropologist's comment on the dream patterns of the Zinacantec Indians of southern Mexico: "Dogs dream and cats dream. Horses dream, and even pigs, say the Zinacantecs.* No one knows why; but there is no question in the mind of a Zinacantec why *men* dream. They dream to lead a full *life*. They dream to *save* their lives" (Laughlin 1976, p. 3).

Or to put the matter another way: dreams have a more central role in the human imagination than we have realized. They are formative events and ingenious renditions of "the state of the mind"—its conflicts and prospects. In many ways an advanced psychic domain, they are notably prospective: that is, in their symbolizations, they can bring qualities of ingenuity that suggest, more than other forms of waking thought, directions in which the self is seeking to move and often will move.

---

*Mesoamerican Indian group of southern Mexico and Guatemala.

Most of these veterans had come to oppose the war and were struggling with emotions they experienced both in Vietnam and upon their return. Any dream reported was responded to by other members of the small group and would become a fulcrum for collective insight—and for connecting their immediate situation with their Vietnam experience.

For instance, the men often discussed their images of dying in Vietnam—and, indeed, their rejection of that fate was in many cases the beginning not only of opposition to the war, but of additional personal transformation as well. In one such discussion in a rap group, a veteran recalled his feelings while in combat: "I wanted to die clean. It didn't matter if I died—but I just didn't want to die with mud on my boots, all filthy. Death wasn't so bad if you were clean." Another man strongly agreed, and told of a repetitive dream he used to have in Vietnam, always with the same terrifying conclusion: "I would end up shot, lying along the side of the road, dying in the mud."

There was intense response in the group, as one veteran after another told of similar fears. And in their associations it became clear that "dying in the mud" meant dying in filth or evil, without reason or purpose—without nobility or dignity of any kind.

Then the man who had said virtually nothing in the group for several weeks suddenly spoke up, and everyone listened with close attention as he blurted out a story:

I heard of one helicopter pilot in Nam who was carrying a shit-house [portable toilet] on his helicopter. He crashed and was killed, and was buried under the whole shit-house and all the shit. I thought that if I was going to die in Vietnam, that's the way I would like to die. I didn't want to die a heroic death. That was the way to die in Vietnam. (Lifton 1973, pp. 222–23)

The group again responded with comments and associations having to do with filth and excrement alone providing the appropriate burial ground in Vietnam. I, in fact, heard no more telling evocation of what they had come to view as the war's absurdity and evil.

And from there they went on to contrast that filth, and the bleeding and bodily mutilations of men in Vietnam, with the "clean" deaths portrayed in various expressions of the American mass media. "In Flash Gordon no one ever bleeds" was the way one man put it. Here we may trace a sequence in a dream's prospective potential: the original dream in Vietnam provides a beginning, but still largely inchoate, insight about the futility and ugliness of dying in Vietnam. That dream is recalled a couple of years later in connection with the group's effort to deepen more general understanding of ways of dying and the nature of the Vietnam enterprise. The dream in turn evokes an image of ultimate filth—the helicopter pilot being killed and buried "under the whole shit-house and all the shit"—through which they can confront some of the most painful aspects of their Vietnam experience. That image, in turn, leads to a critique of a more general false American mass media romanticism, in which "no one ever bleeds." The dream was clearly the key event in the sequence—and the associations of others in the group maximized its prospective potential.

And a Vietnam veteran, Michael Casey, echoes this sentiment in a poem entitled "On Death," from a prize-winning collection appropriately entitled *Obscenities:*

> Flies all over
> It like made of wax
> No jaw
> Intestines poured
> Out of the stomach
> The penis in the air
> It won't matter then to me but now
> I don't want in death to be a
> Public obscenity like this

And the veterans brought to the group other related dreams, such as a fragment of one by a former marine: "I was alone in a garbage dump. There was nothing but garbage all around me. I made a fire by burning *Life* magazines and things like that" (Lifton 1973, pp. 180–81). The dreamer and the rest of the group associated not only to actual garbage piles in Vietnam but to the accumulation of dead and the ultimate "garbage" there—not just because they were dead but because of their grotesque, premature, and unacceptable deaths. Again, the group was groping toward the insight that, for Vietnam, "garbage was truth," as opposed to any more romantic claim to nobility or "victory." And that sentiment was again expressed by a stanza of poetry written by a Vietnam veteran:

> The Holy Army trampled
> In the sun of Christmas Day,
> But when they passed, the garbagemen
> Took all the dead away.
>   (Harrison Kohler, *Winning Hearts and*
>   *Minds: War Poems by Vietnam Veterans*)

Dreams, that is, can propel individuals and groups toward the most painful kinds of insight—and in that very function and in the ingenious imagery with which it is carried out, they can also resemble illuminating imagery of poetry.

Among these veterans, I encountered what I came to describe as an "animating relationship to guilt." Feelings of guilt, of self-condemnation, could be experienced and then converted into anxiety of responsibility—so that the initial guilt became a source of reflection, commitment to humane principles, and constructive personal change. During some of the group sessions, men would try to make inner contact with a sense of guilt they thought they should but could not feel. One such veteran kept insisting, "I just can't *feel* any guilt"—despite an incident in which he saw a grenade he had placed blow a Vietnamese person apart so that pieces of the corpse flew fifty yards into the air—and that at the time he remembered "just laughing out loud."* When others suggested that his laughter might have been a way of covering up his feelings, especially ones of guilt, he merely shrugged his shoulders inconclusively. But just a few minutes later, he reported a rapid series of disturbing recent dreams, including the following three:

> I was riding on some kind of vehicle—a bus, I think—down Fifth Avenue. Somehow it turned into a military truck—and the truck got bigger and bigger, until it reached an enormous size. I was a soldier on the truck—and . . . I fell off . . . and was killed.

> I was riding on a subway—underground—and somehow [along the course of the ride] I seemed to turn into a soldier in uniform. . . . There was a lot of confusion and then there was a battle with the police . . . in which I was killed.

> I was in Vietnam and off in the distance there was a firefight. One of the guys near me panicked and kept telling me he thought he heard something, . . . acting very scared. . . . I was so disgusted with him that I said, "Why don't you light a flare?" Anyone who's been in Vietnam knows that that was ridiculous, and that I was only kidding him— because it would be crazy to light a flare since that would locate where you were for the VC. But this guy didn't know any better, being new in Vietnam, so he actually lit the flare. . . . There was firing and he was killed. [The veteran explained that this last dream re-created an actual incident in Vietnam, in which he had actually advised a GI to light a flare as a kind of joke, which the GI did, but no harm had actually resulted.]

The group responded actively to these three dreams, emphasizing the dreamer's fear of the military and especially the sense of guilt: the idea that he had done something wrong and had to be punished or killed—that he was not finished with the military or the war and still had important

*All quotations from Vietnam veterans in this section are from Lifton 1973, pp. 110–21.

psychological work to do in connection with both; and also the idea of the dream being a message from the underground (suggested concretely by the subway) which had to do with the question of guilt, contradicting his surface (conscious) insistence that he was not experiencing any. (These last two interpretations were essentially my own.) The dreamer responded by saying, "Maybe I don't *want* to feel guilty—maybe I'm afraid to"—perhaps because, as he explained, he was already burdened with violent impulses and feared that feeling guilty would make things much worse and some-how undermine his control over his violence. I had the clear impression that he was moving closer to a recognition of a sense of guilt, but not to the point, he insisted, of *feeling* guilt.

But then something else happened. His sequence of dreams triggered another struggle with guilt in a former Marine sergeant. The latter, a forceful man with an aura of masculine strength, expressed antagonism to the idea of guilt, insisting that "guilt is just plain useless"; that he had no reason to feel guilty; that he had no malice toward the nineteen people he killed and had killed them because "I saw my buddies dead." But as he went on, he spoke, in a tone of extraordinary pain and bitterness, of "one very big mistake" he had made in Vietnam, that of trusting someone unworthy of his trust to lead a patrol and of not having given sufficiently precise orders to this man, with the result that twelve of his best men were ambushed and killed in the most grotesque fashion—so that some could not even be found. And this former Marine added:

> You know, when you see dead men—whether they're round-eyes or gooks, they're all the same. Their faces are screwed up—they're all fucked up. . . . I don't know why it all happened—there was the damned fool war—and maybe I just wasn't old enough to have responsibility for so many men.

At that point this man got up and ran out of the room, explaining that he just wanted to be alone for a while; but it was clear to everyone that he was beginning to confront guilt feelings of the most disturbing kind. At just that point, the other veteran who had dreamed those three dreams spoke up, now in tremulous tones:

> You know, I'm shuddering. . . . I'm shaking all over . . . because what he said hit me hard. . . . Before . . . we talked about guilt . . . but I didn't feel too much. But now I really feel remorse. I feel very badly about what I did in Vietnam—and it's a terrible feeling.

This sequence had much to do with the group's continuing struggle with guilt and with the effort to form an animating—that is, a morally energiz-ing—relationship to it. But what I want to stress here, once more, is the role of dreams as the pivotal psychic force in this shared effort. Dreams seemed to possess something on the order of mythic power, of special illumination, that in turn enabled the veterans—as individuals and as a group—to make their special psychic leaps into the most painful mental terrain.

Sometimes the sequence can move, so to speak, from dream to dream: A veteran appearing at a rap group for the first time told of a frightening recurrent dream, in which an NLF soldier would shoot and kill him. The figure in his dream was the same NLF soldier he had actually confronted in what was, literally, face-to-face combat: as each of them shot they could see one another clearly. The veteran was wounded in the leg, and, without quite making things clear, gave us the impression that the NVA soldier had been killed. The combat incident had occurred a year earlier, but the recurrent dream together with diffuse anxiety had been intensified by two kinds of experience—the veteran's increasing involvement in antiwar protest, and his having been surprised by a mugger near his home in Manhattan a short time before.

In the midst of these associations to his dream one of the other men suddenly asked him, "Do you feel guilty about being alive?" He answered without hesitation: "Yes. You're supposed to be dead."

Right afterward, another veteran reported a brief but pointed dream of his own: "I was arguing with myself. Then there were two separate selves, and one of them finally shot the other, so that I shot myself." The dream, and a few associations to it, epitomized the survivor conflict: an inner split that is both guilty and deadly; a simultaneous transgression and retribution—the self murdering the self. It also suggests the classic literary and mythological theme of the double, in which one self can represent life (sometimes immortal life) and its replica death (or mortality). Above all, it is the starkest of images—at the same time concrete and metaphorical—of one as both victim and executioner.

Here the two dreams in tandem brought the veterans to the very heart of their overwhelmingly painful, war-linked existential dilemma. It was after such a discussion that one man told of killing a Viet Cong soldier with a knife, and then added softly, "I felt sorry. I don't know why I felt sorry. John Wayne never felt sorry."

The dreams in these sequences are clearly formative and prospective, in their early illumination of evolving insight and action. At the same time they are historical dreams, in their intertwining of personal and social change having to do with the shifting currents of their historical era.

Dreams and Moral Conflict: A Nazi Doctor

In my final exploration of a particular dream sequence, I must move to a still more painful realm, that of the Nazi death camp, the source of three dreams of a particular Nazi doctor (Lifton 1986). In this case, the dreams, in their formative and historical characteristics, suggest a moral struggle and a direction of partial resolution.

I had interviewed one doctor, a man in his late sixties, for a total of about thirty hours—five full-day meetings over a little more than two years. Dr. Ernst B.—not his real name—came from an academic family of some standing, was as a child and adolescent in considerable rebellion against his father and the latter's wish for his son to enter medicine, and succumbed to that wish only after his brief effort at becoming an artist ended in dismal failure. He developed a *modus vivendi* of being liked and being very adaptable in a variety of environments. Thus Ernst B. got along well with fellow students and with the Nazis who quickly came to dominate the faculty and student structures—his standing greatly enhanced when he became one of the winners of a contest sponsored by a Nazi science group to discover a local product to replace imported ones in bacterial culture media. Though not a strong ideologue, he was impressed with some aspects of the Nazis, and certainly did not hesitate to join the party when advised to do so for the benefit of his personal and professional future. There were many aspects to his being called into the Waffen SS and assigned to Auschwitz—he had himself experienced some patriotic fervor and requested a military appointment; but one reason was undoubtedly the regime's perception of his ideological reliability. In Auschwitz he continued his pattern of getting on with everyone—with his Nazi medical colleagues, and also with inmates, especially prisoner physicians with whom he came to have close contact. This latter I confirmed through interviews with survivor physicians in different parts of the world—and through his having been acquitted in an Auschwitz trial on the basis of testimony of former prisoner doctors, to whom he had been particularly kind in Auschwitz and, in a number of cases, whose lives he had saved. He got on, then, with his captors when he became a prisoner; and then with his patients when he returned to medical practice in southern Bavaria; and, for the most part, with me, during our interviews. But the whole process was not quite as smooth as it may sound.

Upon arriving in Auschwitz, which he claims to have previously known nothing about, Ernst B. was appalled and overwhelmed and had a strong impulse to leave (which would probably have been possible). But he was taken aside by his immediate superior, who turned out to be an old friend who had helped him in the past. This friend told Dr. B., in effect: "Yes,

Auschwitz represents the 'Final Solution' of the Jewish people; what happens here is not pretty but there is nothing we can do about it; and I need you here for my unit [the Hygienic Institute, which was outside the ordinary hierarchy of camp medical officers], and if you stay it will strengthen us greatly and we will be able to keep our hands completely clean." Dr. B. stayed.

A few days after his arrival in Auschwitz he looked out a window early in the evening and saw prisoners returning from their work outside the camp, marching double-time six abreast, and thought he saw among them a former classmate from his old *Gymnasium* (secondary school), named Simon Cohen. Ernst B. ran outside to find him, but the prisoners had already disappeared into their blocks. For the next couple of days he went desperately about the camp trying to locate Simon Cohen—and in the process learned at first hand about the killing and working arrangements at Auschwitz and about the status of Jews as nonpeople. At one point he went running into the office area he was assigned to and asked the prisoner physician working there whether he knew a Simon Cohen in the camp. The answer came back cautiously that "tens, thousands of Jews . . . come through," that "many of them were named Cohen," and that it would be impossible to find any such person. The prisoner physician answered that way, as I confirmed in a later interview with him, because he believed that the attempt to find such a person was hopeless and could be harmful both to him and to Dr. B. himself. And even though the Nazi doctor seemed compassionate, the prisoner doctor might have been worried about the intention of a man in an SS uniform inquiring about a Jewish prisoner. In the course of his fruitless inquiries, Dr. B. saw more clearly the labyrinthine, murderous nature of Auschwitz.

Later he came to wonder whether he had really seen Cohen—or whether it had been an illusion or perhaps even a dream. In any case, he immediately began to have a series of dreams about the incident that were really one basic repetitive dream with many variations. In every dream Simon Cohen's face would appear:

> He was always a very attractive young man. And now [in the dream] he had really deteriorated. . . . And he looked at me with a reproachful, beseeching expression . . . sort of [saying], "It can't be possible that you stand there and I am . . . [like this] . . ." or more like a disappointed expression: "How can you belong to those people? That can't be you." (Lifton 1986, p. 306)

In telling me about these dreams, Ernst B. further explained that he and Cohen had been special friends during the early 1930s (the dream had occurred in about May 1943), having in common their mutual lack of interest in schoolwork and enjoyment of drinking alcohol. They took long bicycle trips together during vacations and remained personally close despite living quite far from one another and despite the already extensive general anti-Semitism.

Dr. B. had the dream most frequently after drinking and associated it at the time with what he called the "especially bad situation" in which he found himself in Auschwitz and with "my problem: Is it right to stay, or would it be better to leave?" On the side of staying was his feeling that "I could do something good here, . . . something humane."

And, indeed, the dream could be understood as a call to residual inner humanity—just as he recalled feeling, at the time he thought he saw Simon Cohen among the prisoners, that "if I can find him, I can make some kind of human contact."

These specific dream images are important: the identification with the "beaten down" or macerated face of the victim, who as a close school friend and a central character in the dream represented an important part of Ernst B.'s own self-process. And the pleading, reproachful look, together with disbelief—in effect, "That can't be *you* standing among *them*"—this representing B.'s own sense of unreality in, and partial removal from, the overall Auschwitz situation. And perhaps the formative aspect in the dream lies exactly there—in its consistency with his subsequent capacity to divide himself to the extent that he was, so to speak, both: one of *them* (them being the Nazi victimizers) and *not* one of them (in the sense of standing apart from them sufficiently to be a consistent source of help to prisoners—so much so that a later historian of Auschwitz described him as "a human being in an SS uniform"). The dream is also, of course, replete with historical imagery—concerning Germans and Jews, and the historical transformations that turn friends into enemies.

One could argue, of course, that Ernst B.'s decision to remain in Auschwitz instead of leaving violated that prospective dream message of calling forth residual humanity. And one could support this argument by Dr. B.'s own insistence to me that, despite the extent to which he was appreciated and even admired by the inmates, he belonged, after all, to the group of Nazi doctors—to the Auschwitz camp structure. Toward the end of our interviews, he expressed for the first time a certain nostalgia for what he considered a few positive features of the Nazi era. He did not cease, that is, being one of "them."

But it is also true that, during his time in Auschwitz, he was unique in his consideration for inmates, especially those prisoner doctors who worked in his unit—taking personal risks to help them in such small (but, in Auschwitz, very big indeed) matters as enabling husbands and wives among prisoners to meet and carrying letters and messages from inmates to people on the outside. So, at least in that sense, the dream's prospective call to personal humanity was by no means totally ignored. And that call had its greatest effect when it was most needed—during his nineteen months at Auschwitz—after which it did not entirely disappear but became much more infrequent.

A second dream Ernst B. described to me also emerged from the Auschwitz situation—though he insisted he never had the actual dream in Auschwitz, but only years later upon returning to his home in Germany. It concerned a young Jewish laboratory assistant who had worked at the Hygienic Institute. In the dream he fled with her from Auschwitz to nearby mountains, where they joined a group of Polish Partisans (anti-Nazi underground fighters). That was the central theme of a recurrent dream that he had in a number of different versions. Dr. B. gave me the impression that he had a special relationship to this dream, a kind of proprietary affection. He introduced it to me, in response to my asking about dreams other than the one about Cohen, by saying, "Perhaps there is one other dream, . . . a purely, deeply psychological question perhaps. Maybe it is a key. I can't exactly explain it."

And when describing the dream's few details, he quickly added, "That is the only other Auschwitz dream that has remained. I'm sure that there was no erotic background to this. In fact, . . . to the contrary."

An erotic component is of course very much present, but in a particular way. In discussing the dream, Dr. B. explained that this Jewish laboratory assistant had a certain artistic talent, which SS men took advantage of by having her make drawings from photographs, which they (the SS men) would then try to sell or make some other use of. All that, he explained, was part of the prevailing corruption in Auschwitz: everyone there was likely to be corrupted in some way: everyone, as Ernst B. put it in the German idiom, had "dirt on his walking stick" *(Dreck am Stecken)*. And everyone knew about everyone else's "dirt."

Although to Ernst B. the girl "seemed so young and so primitive," she had an uncanny ability to vary the style of each drawing according to what she perceived the taste of individual SS men: drawing "simple red-checked" pictures for simple SS men and more delicate, aesthetically sophisticated pictures for more sensitive SS officers like himself—and, in fact, she did draw for him what he considered a "beautiful picture" of his wife and young children from a photograph he provided. He became preoccupied with this seeming dichotomy in her, suspecting that "she just fooled around during the day and then took the whole thing to an artist in her block every evening": "I just couldn't believe that this girl would be able to do these kinds of things by herself"—adding that precisely that kind of suspicion was "in Auschwitz the normal reaction." Eventually he became convinced that she did indeed do all the drawings herself; though

434   APPLICATIONS OF ADULT DEVELOPMENTAL THEORY

when he further observed her and spoke to her, he was "again and again surprised at how primitive she actually was," and concluded that "she was a primitive, naturally talented person." The mountains to which they flee in the dream were near the area from which she had come; and in one conversation they had when he spoke of his possibly taking a drive into that area, she warned him not to because there were likely to be too many partisans there.

He managed to take the picture with him from Auschwitz and to retain it despite his subsequent years of custody and trial. Upon returning to medical practice, he first hung it in his office and later in his bedroom. But he eventually, as he explained, "took it out of the room to get rid of the dream"—though the dream persisted after he had removed the picture. As we talked about all this, he had his wife bring in the picture, which he looked at affectionately; and when I asked whether he still valued it very much, he answered, "Yes, of course—I had it in Auschwitz the whole time, you understand. And later I kept it here." He added that now, with more detachment, he could say that it was "really a very nice picture but close to being *kitsch*"—a word that usually means "shoddy, pretentious, and without artistic merit." But Dr. B. qualified that judgment, and somewhat defended the picture, by adding, "Many good artistic things, including Goethe's *Faust,* always move close to kitsch."

And he went on to associate the picture further with "this emotion I had in Auschwitz . . . my bad feelings to my family"—what he had described as a "bad conscience" toward his wife for his having initiated the steps (asking for military duty) that led him to be assigned to Auschwitz—so that when he managed to get away from Auschwitz briefly to visit his wife, "I had a good feeling and a bad feeling. . . . I was of course very happy to be there but I . . . hoped to make things good again."

Ernst B. was right in seeing the dream as a special psychological key, as it contains virtually every conflict and contradiction he experienced in Auschwitz. At the heart of the dream, I believe, is a doubling, rather than a splitting, of the self: that is, Dr. B. had two virtually autonomous selves: the one, the older, relatively humane self of healer and family man; the other, the Auschwitz self (with its numbered adaptation and capacity to witness or participate in mass murder* and continuous brutality). Characteristically, the older, more humane self was reinforced by visits to his wife and family, but his guilt toward his wife suggests that he was less able than many former Nazi doctors to carry through successfully this doubling process. Indeed, the image of affectionate and compassionate flight with the young Jewish inmate is a way of reconnecting erotic feelings with

*Dr. B was able to avoid direct participation in Auschwitz murder and brutality.

human acts, all within the context of Auschwitz itself—and, in that sense, is a rejection of the doubling process and an assertion of at least prospective wholeness. But the dream also contains his profound doubts about himself, while in Auschwitz and before, concerning authenticity (his discussions of kitsch and of the "primitive"—the latter with a strong element of German and Nazi worship of what is ostensibly primitive and natural) and his concern about corruption and corruptibility (his own "dirt on his walking stick") in Auschwitz particularly. I believe one reason he values this picture so much is its association for him—via the dream and his perception of the Jewish girl—with a struggle toward authenticity and humanity. And that struggle is the dream's prospective thrust: his message is to "go over to the other side"—to the side of those who would kill the killers, to the side of love and life enhancement. And that prospective message has to do once more with extreme historical currents engulfing Germans, Jews, Poles, and in important ways all others.

I cannot say that Ernst B. has, in his postwar existence, fully embraced this prospective message—but he has gone much further than most former Nazi doctors in that direction.

Ernst B. told me of a third dream—really a merest fragment of a dream, not even a clear image. But it is nonetheless important to us.

When held for trial after the war, he learned that the authorities had in their possession what he called "a room full of files dealing with the routine work of the [Hygienic] Institute"—his own working place in Auschwitz. At the judge's request, he agreed to study the materials and from them make a scientific projection of the relationship between caloric intake permitted the prisoners, the work they did, and the length of average survival of those not subjected to the gas chambers. The impact of the experience was profound—so much so that he stuttered somewhat in conveying it and mentioning his dreams:

> That room with all those files and the computations that occupied me and all that, . . . I still dream of it sometimes, somehow. . . . Whenever I have a dream that is related somehow to Auschwitz, those papers will appear too.*

He worked methodically, over months, with the files, which were remarkably detailed, and eventually demonstrated that the Auschwitz near-starvation diet created a general life expectancy of three months. He knew that these findings were not in themselves of the greatest importance, but rather that something else was:

> What is important is that for months I was alone in a room [a cell] with these files. . . . And through dealing with these papers I established a

---

*The extracted quotations in this section are from the author's transcripts.

special contact with Auschwitz. . . . It was an absolute reflection [of what went on in Auschwitz]. All of a sudden I was in this room confronting the problem and the memory in a different way and not under pressure to suppress things in the face of these confrontations—so one could deal with these thoughts without constraint. And that was very good. . . . You are dealing with the experience all the time with these files, so you couldn't waste energy in trying to forget.

He contrasted his approach to Auschwitz with my own:

It is a completely different route to the camp itself. You are starting out now by identifying these things (or approaching this subject) on a theoretical basis—and you have no practical experience. And I started out on the practical side and later came to the theoretical point of view.

We may say that he, like most other former Nazis, has never been able to confront fully the directly human consequences of the Nazi project. But in undertaking this study, he could abstract those consequences—the deaths and the suffering—in ways that nonetheless brought them closer to his awareness. Of great importance was that he conducted the study as a physician and prepared from it what was essentially a medical-scientific paper. He could at least touch some of the Auschwitz cruelty and in the process reclaim more of his pre-Auschwitz self.

Significantly, he bracketed this overall experience with his earlier adaptation to Auschwitz—the transition into Auschwitz, during which he consciously sought to integrate himself with his colleagues and the overall camp structure. This was, so to speak, his transition out of Auschwitz, during which he was now reintegrating himself—under the reversed circumstances of being himself a prisoner—with the non-Auschwitz, the anti-Auschwitz world. The dream fragment of the papers and files represents the burden of having been part of Auschwitz—the prospective message here that of confronting the experience, evaluating it, putting it in terms of human beings, applying to it humane medical standards.

An Evolutionary Achievement

A few conclusions—or rather, visions or dreams of conclusions. Let me state three principles:

First, the dream is prospective; it prefigures psychological and frequently behavioral functions. More than that, it is propulsive—it helps propel one toward certain kinds of experience.

Second, the dream has an immediate or proximate psychological level, where it records and contributes to the self's struggles toward vitality—toward connection, integrity, and movement.

Third, the dream operates also at an ultimate level: it suggests conflicts and directions in the self's larger historical relationships, and in efforts to maintain or recast forms of symbolic immortality.

Thus, the dreams of Japanese youths propel them toward new ways of looking at the world, combining confusing elements in the direction of integration and vitality and ordering their larger relationships to a partly desired past and a projected historical future. The dreams of Vietnam veterans help propel them toward painful insights and hard-won individual change, toward a new vitality based on experiencing and moving beyond guilt, and an equally new worldview with shifting relations to American historical currents. And the dreams of the Nazi doctor prodded him toward earlier standards of compassion and integrity amid murder and corruption (the dreams also, it must be added, had the more dubious function of helping him to adapt to those Auschwitz conditions), and ultimately toward confronting what Auschwitz actually had been.

If a dream can do all this—encompassing a trinity of propulsive psychic power, renewed vitality, and questions about ultimate concerns—then it must have even greater power and significance than we had imagined. Indeed, my claim here is that the dream has a central, life-enhancing, evolutionary function.

Precisely such a function is suggested not only by the somewhat unusual array of dreams I have been discussing, but also by laboratory studies, by the recent work on sleep and dreaming. The so-called REM state—named for its most dramatic feature, the rapid eyeball movement—is the time during which most dreaming occurs and is sufficiently distinct from both wakefulness and other sleep as to have been called a "third state" of the mind. In addition to rapid eyeball movements, the REM state includes increased muscle movements (sometimes with sucking activity), disappearance of postural tone, various forms of irregularity of the cardiac and respiratory systems, increased brain activity as recorded by the electroencephalogram, and, in men, penile erections.

Can a newborn infant, in whom the REM state is certainly identifiable (or for that matter the guinea pig in utero), be said to dream? Here one is reminded of Samuel Beckett's question, "Who knows what the ostrich sees in the sand?" The most reasonable interpretation of REM data, I believe, is that the dreaming function follows pretty much the same sequence I have described in connection with other imagery: at first, an "inchoate image" or mere neurophysiological directions of the organism; then, the formation of pictorial and other sensory images; and, finally, more elaborate symbolization. This interpretation stresses the importance of that state for general nervous-system function—for the daily or nightly processing and reordering of information and emotional experience—and for the regular restoration of the nervous system. The human newborn, then, does not dream in the sense of experiencing the images and symbols we associate with dreams—but enters the world with actively functioning neurophysiology specific to the later psychic elaboration of the dream. As Howard Roffwarg and his associates (1966) have put it, "whether or not 'dreaming' understood as subjective sensation exists in the newborn, 'dreaming' understood as physiological process certainly does" (p. 612).

This same body of research suggests that the inborn REM state could well be a central step to the overall capacity for image formation—that process taking place, as the same research states in their more technical language, as a "neurophysiological setting for hallucinatory repetition of accumulated experience" (p. 612). The penile erection, whatever its relationship to specific imagery, would seem to reassert the centrality of sexual elements in dreams. And when sexual imagery is prominent, dreams reveal their special biological power in their capacity to produce orgasm quite readily by means of that sexual imagery alone—in contrast, say, to pornographic films, which are very unlikely to result in anything more than sexual arousal.

Here one can raise an interesting evolutionary question: Why should a species be provided with such an everyday—or every night—means of discharging its reproductive fluids in a nonreproductive setting? How can such an arrangement be squared with encouraging the productive act as means of preserving the species? The answer to that question, I believe, begins to get at fundamental functions of the dream, and of the human symbolizing process in general.

We must first assume that sex in humans, as Freud's discoveries make clear, had hallucinatory evolutionary functions far beyond that of direct reproduction. In our sex lives, we epitomize much of our immediate struggle for vitality—and much of our ultimate quest for transcendence. Indeed, I believe that sexual experience is our everyday path to transcendence—to the state of mind usually equated with "ecstasy" or with what Freud called the "oceanic feeling." More generally, that experience of transcendence reaffirms the self's sense of larger connectedness through other modes of symbolic immortality. My argument here is that the sexual element in dreams is central to their relationship to immediate vitality and to ultimate concerns. Sexual elements can also relate directly to the prospective or formative aspects of dreams—as we saw so well in the case of the Nazi doctor's dream of running off with the young Jewish woman prisoner. As with other elements of the dream, we have so emphasized the pastness of sexual imagery that we have greatly neglected its formative or prospective significance.

To further answer that evolutionary question, we need to return to the dream's special relationship to symbolization. Freud was surely right (and Erikson strongly concurred) in stressing that "the dream is fundamentally nothing more than a special *form* of our thinking, which is made possible by the conditions of the sleeping state"—and that "the dream work . . . is the only explanation of its singularity" (Erikson 1954, 17n). But exactly what that dream work—really dream "process"—consists of is much less certain. Here again, even the pastness in a dream—its old memory elements—can contribute to its experiential and prospective push toward new combinations and even resolutions. That very pastness, in fact, can, as a reservoir of formative possibilities, provide much of the energy for precisely those new combinations and resolutions. Nor can we be satisfied with the two central functions of Freud's dream work—condensation and displacement—but must see these functions as aspects of the dream's overall symbolizing power.

I am suggesting that the dream's indisputable biological rootedness is inseparable from its advanced symbolizing function. We can thus begin to view the dream less as a "cover-up" and more as an "opening-out" of the psychic domain that is both close to organicity and unique in imaginative reach. For dreams permit ephemeral experimentation with the freest play of images and the most radically absurd and innovative symbolizations. Dream work or dream process would seem to be nothing less than the anxious edge of the mind's explorations. And the dream's ingenious symbolizations are highly subversive to the psychological status quo. This is so because of the sensitivity of the dream process to the contradictions and vulnerabilities of existing psychic forms, which is what we mean when we say that dreams reveal inner conflicts. It is the reason dreams are so disturbing.

Just why the symbolizing function of dreams is freer and more innovative than that of adult waking life is difficult to say. There are probably neuropsychological reasons we do not fully understand, and which are not adequately explained by the traditional concept of repression. The relaxation of censorship in dreams may be related to in-built psychobiological elements of the symbolizing process bound up with REM sleep.

So that, to return once more to our evolutionary question, we may say that symbolization provided by dreams is no less biological—no less central to species preservation—than is the reproductive function itself. Or to put the matter another way, to carry out our reproductive function we need to have our symbolizing capacity in working order: we need the capacity to *feel* alive, and the sense of larger human connectedness. Sex in dreams is in the service of those capacities and is therefore, in an evolutionary sense, far from wasted.

It should be clear by now that symbolization here is by no means the same as the more "primitive" function to which Freud relegated it—namely, the form of one-to-one symbolism Freud thought "characteristic of unconscious ideation": the idea that a particular dream symbol stands for a particular person or thing—emperor and empress for parents, an elongated object for the male organ, a room for a woman, and so on. Rather, we are talking about the *process* of symbolization—of construction, combination, and re-creation of images and forms—which is the essence of dreaming no less than of other expressions of human mentation. Even when we encounter relatively consistent meanings for certain symbols, there is an ever-present possibility that those meanings will be joined or replaced by others in the continuous play of the formative process.

We can thus view dreams as providing a perpetual dialectic between the most "primitive" psychic fragments and the most "enlightened" frontier of the formative imagination. Within this dialogue the dream flashes its powerful and yet fluid symbolizations before us, ours for the using according to the mind's readiness and capacity.

The dream, then, is central to our evolutionary heritage. In it we find, most profoundly, both clue to and expression of the human capacity for good and evil—for holding visions, for prospective imagination. More than ever, we must dream well if we are to confront forces threatening to annihilate us, and if we are to further the wonderful, dangerous, and always visionary human adventure.

REFERENCES

Casey, M. 1972. "On Death." In *Obscenities*. New Haven: Yale University Press.

Erikson, E. 1954. "The Dream Specimen in Psychoanalysis." *Journal of the American Psychoanalytic Association* 2: 17n.

Kohler, H. 1972. "Victory." In *Winning Hearts and Minds: War Poems by Vietnam Veterans*, ed. L. Rottman et al. Brooklyn, N.Y.: First Casualty Press.

Laughlin, R. M. 1976. *Of Wonders Wild and New—Dreams from Zinacantán*, p. 3. Washington, D.C.: Smithsonian Institution Press.

Lifton, R. J. 1970. "Youth and History: Individual Change in Postwar Japan." In *History and Human Survival*, pp. 30–32. New York: Random House.

———. 1973. *Home from the War—Vietnam Veterans: Neither Victims nor Executioners*. New York: Simon & Schuster.

――――. [1979] 1983. *The Broken Connection: On Death and the Continuity of Life.* New York: Basic Books.

――――. 1986. *The Nazi Doctors: Medical Killing and the Psychology of Genocide,* pp. 301–336. New York: Basic Books.

Roffwarg, H. P., Munzio, J. N., and Dement, W. C. 1966. "Ontogenetic Development of the Human Sleep-Dream Cycle." *Science* 152:604–16.

DISCUSSION

Dr. Lifton elevates our understanding of dreams to new heights. His claim that dreams have a "central, life-enhancing, evolutionary function" (p. 439) and an "indisputable biological rootedness" that is "inseparable from its advanced symbolizing function" (p. 439) provides a framework within which to consider the relationship between dreams and adult development. In harmony with our definition of development, dreams tap the deepest layers of the biological substrata and are closely involved with the inner and outer environment. In short, they are a reflection of the constantly changing developmental process, not only in adulthood, but throughout life. Consequently, there is much to be learned about development through the profoundly human experience of dreaming, particularly when drawing on Dr. Lifton's magnification of the dream work through his study of individuals in extreme circumstances. Even in the most bizarre human situations dreams "can contribute to a process of forward-looking integration and moral questioning" (p. 420). It would appear that little short of death stops the developmental momentum.

His own concentration camp dreams, which indicated his immersion in the study of the Nazi doctors, were a necessity for, and a reflection of, his creativity. Clearly, the dream continues to use, in adulthood as in childhood, the highest level ego functions available to it at each developmental stage.

In healthy adults such as Dr. Lifton, despite the universal preoccupation with time limitation and personal death (Colarusso and Nemiroff 1981), dreams are, he suggests, a psychology of life, not a thanatology. There is a continuous struggle to preserve the sense of the self as alive, not dead. Again his words eloquently express the manner in which dreams reflect the progressive developmental thrust for "they are notably prospective: that is, in their symbolizations, they can bring qualities of ingenuity that suggest, more than other forms of waking thought, directions in which the self is seeking to move and often will move" (p. 420). In addition, dreams reflect the interaction between past and present, and phase-specific developmental concerns. By facilitating a new relationship between past and present, dreams point the way to future integrations.

However, some life experiences, such as combat in Vietnam, can be singularly noxious, so that the progress of development is arrested in adulthood. The repetition compulsion forces reexamination after reexamination, but without mastery.

The dreams of Dr. B., the Nazi camp doctor, demonstrate the power of adult experience (as opposed to that of the child). Although not an innately evil man, he was unable to free himself from Auschwitz. His involvement in its horrors became the dominant influence of his psychic life—apparently to his dying day.

REFERENCES

Colarusso, C. A., and Nemiroff, R. A. 1981. *Adult Development: A New Dimension in Psychodynamic Theory and Practice.* New York: Plenum.

18

Becoming a Medicine Man:

A Means to Successful Midlife Transition among Traditional Navajo Men

MARTIN D. TOPPER AND G. MARK SCHOEPFLE

Introduction

Anthropological studies of human development have generally focused on childhood and adolescence. Margaret Mead's (1928) classic study in Samoa is an early example. The Six Cultures Project* undertaken by John and Beatrice Whiting and their colleagues in the 1950s also represents this tendency of anthropologists to focus on early life. More recently, the work of Paul Bohannan and Kevin Eckert (Eckert 1980) has reflected an emerging interest in the elderly. However, except for the work of Stanley Brandes (1985) and Judith Brown (1982) there are few anthropological studies of midlife. This neglect is not entirely unexpected, since interest in adult development in Western cultures is relatively recent (Colarusso and Nemiroff 1981). Now that a theoretical perspective is evolving, a broader opportunity exists to examine adult development cross-culturally. This chapter examines the achievement of medicine-man status among the Navajo as an example of male midlife transition in a traditional Native American culture.

---

*The Six Cultures Project represented an attempt to study child development in cross-cultural perspective.

The Navajo

The Navajo are the largest Indian tribe in the United States. They number approximately 200,000 and live on a 15 million acre reservation in the Four Corners region of Arizona, Utah, and New Mexico. Because they are such a large and dispersed population, there is considerable subcultural diversity among them. An earlier article (Topper 1985) described five Navajo subcultures that manifest various degrees of acculturation. Here we are concerned with only two of them, the semiacculturated rural and the rural elderly Navajo. They represent the conservative end of the acculturation spectrum and are rapidly becoming a cultural minority in contemporary Navajo society. Because they observe many of the traditional practices, these two subcultures will be used to contrast development among Western peoples for the purposes of our cross-cultural examination of the midlife transition.

In many ways, the contemporary traditional Navajo live as their ancestors did in the mid-1800s. Although the pressures of acculturation are creating ever-increasing changes in their lifestyle, today's traditional Navajos, like their forebearers, still earn a significant portion of their income raising sheep, goats, cattle, and horses; live all or part of the year in one-room structures called hogans; and practice their ancestors' religion. They eat a diet of mutton, homemade bread, and homegrown fruits and vegetables (mostly corn, beans, squash, and melons); speak their native Athabascan language; and retain many old social and political customs.

Navajo Socioeconomics

The traditional Navajo reside in extended family camps. These usually contain from two to four households related through women who belong to the same clan. Clans are matrilineal and trace their descent through the female line. A typical extended family unit is composed of a woman, her husband and unmarried children, and the households of from one to three of her married daughters. Because the Navajo are matrilocal, a man goes to live in the home of his wife's family immediately after marriage. If the marriage is successful, he builds his wife a house in her mother's camp. There they raise their children and participate in the economic life of the extended family. As their children grow, each daughter and her husband will eventually move to other grazing areas. Because the subsistence economy of the Navajo is unable to support even moderate concentrations of people, extended families of more than a dozen individuals are unusual (Witherspoon 1975).

The economy and environment of the reservation are important elements in Navajo social life. While the reservation contains about half a million acres of ponderosa pine forest, most of it is arid or semiarid grassland. Rainfall averages between six and twelve inches per year over most of the reservation, and there are few permanently flowing rivers. Most of the water is obtained from springs, shallow wells, and small earthen dams that catch the runoff in creek beds and washes. Ground cover consists of a variety of brushes and grasses. Given the sparse rainfall, the land is generally unproductive, requiring an average of five acres to support a sheep or goat and twenty-five acres to support a cow or a horse year-round. Because good agricultural land is scarce, farming is generally restricted to the bottoms of washes and canyons. Approximately ten sheep (Downs 1964; Witherspoon 1975) are kept to meet the subsistence needs of each member of a Navajo household for a year. An extended family of twelve would need at least 120 sheep, a number that would require almost one square mile of grazing area. Add a few horses and cattle, and a traditional extended family could easily require two square miles of grazing area.

The extended family (which Witherspoon refers to as the "subsistence residence unit") is the largest continuously operating social and economic unit of traditional Navajo culture. It is also the largest unit of continuous religious and political activity. However, an important difference exists between these two areas of Navajo life. Descent, residence, ownership of herds, and rights to grazing and agricultural property are passed on primarily through women. Men, on the other hand, control politics and religion. A Navajo leader is *nat' áanii* (chief); a religious leader or medicine man is *hataalii* (singer). In actuality, the two are frequently the same person. Witherspoon (1975) found that 20 percent of the extended family households in his study were headed by medicine men. "Outfits," which are clusters of extended family households related through women, are frequently headed by medicine men.

The Traditional Navajo Medicine Man

The traditional Navajo medicine man plays a multifaceted role within his culture. He is a social, economic, and political leader; a counselor and therapist; and a religious leader and repository of cultural knowledge. In extended families that have medicine men, he is frequently the eldest married male. In an outfit, usually the oldest practicing medicine man is the leader.

The most widely recognized role of the medicine man is as a practitioner of the traditional religious healing arts. His complex ceremonial interventions combine elements of native chemotherapy, behavior modification, psychodrama, somatic therapy, and supportive psychotherapy. (See Martin Topper [1982, 1987] and Donald Sandner [1979] for detailed discussions of these modalities.) Treatment takes the form of healing ceremonies. They may last from one to nine days and follow a highly prescribed pattern of daytime and nighttime activities, the best known of which is sand painting.

Ceremonies are a central part of Navajo culture. Donald Sandner (1979) lists thirty-two major rituals. Each is an elaborate complex of mythology and practice. The ceremonies are based on myths about a tribal ancestor who is said to have become afflicted after breaking a taboo. Assisted in learning a curative ritual by a supernatural being, the ancestor applied the procedures to himself and was cured. Then he returned briefly to the Navajo to teach them the procedures to be used to cure others who become afflicted after breaking the same taboo (Spencer 1957). After teaching the cure, the ancestor finds he can no longer live in the company of normal humans because of his increased spirituality. He goes to live with the Holy People who helped create the present-day world, leaving the knowledge of his ceremony behind him.

When a Navajo becomes ill, the first person to be consulted is a diviner specializing in one of three major forms of divination: star gazing, wind listening, or hand trembling (Reichard 1952). In performing the divination he describes the nature of the taboo that was broken or other evil that has afflicted the patient and the ritual needed to cure the condition; often he names the medicine man who can perform the ceremony.

The family of the afflicted person then speaks to the medicine man and negotiates a payment and a date for the performance of the ceremony. Ceremonies can last one night and cost less than one hundred dollars, as in *hoch' ooji jint' éésh* (evil blackening), or take nine days and cost several thousand dollars, as with *'ana'iji* (enemy way) or *tl' ééji* (night chant). See Sandner (1979). Many medicine men practice more than one ceremony. Generally the more ceremonies a medicine man knows, the greater his status in the community.

The Navajo believe that all illness and misfortune is the result of a supernatural imbalance in the forces that control the universe, usually precipitated by the breaking of a taboo or the intrusion of "evil" into the body through witchcraft or the action of a ghost (Kluckhohn and Leighton 1963). The medicine man, having learned the relevant ceremony, is believed to have the power to restore the universal balance, thus placing his patient back in harmony with those forces controlling the universe and curing the underlying problem that produced the patient's symptoms. The possession of such powers makes the medicine man an object of awe among his people.

This respect and authority allow the medicine man to occupy a generalized leadership role within his extended family and the community at large. Economically he is important in at least two ways. Because he receives considerable payment for his services, wealth can become concentrated in his hands. As the head of an extended family or outfit, he is often a source of economic assistance for less-well-to-do relations and others who have meager economic resources. Due to his considerable influence over the local economy, he can influence community projects, like the building of dams and roads, and create local employment by hiring people to work with his stock and in his fields.

It is obvious that in a subsistence economy a person with such economic power would have considerable social and political influence. Jerrold Levy and Steven Kunitz (1974) have referred to economic leaders among the Navajo as *ricos.* Medicine men who have livestock are ricos whose opinions are sought on many subjects. Socially they are asked to settle family disputes, counsel individuals whose behavior is objectionable, consult on the arrangement of marriages, and instruct young people in the Navajo way of living, *yá' át' ééhgo iina'* (good life). Such men exercise authority when they speak at community chapter meetings (the local unit of government on the reservation) and may also control blocks of votes in tribal council elections. Their opinions are frequently sought on local political issues, and candidates for both local and tribal offices solicit their opinions and support. This generalized leadership role of the medicine man in Navajo culture is a product of the limited productivity of the Navajo subsistence economy and the restrictions placed on the size of economic and social systems by the semiarid conditions of the Colorado plateau.

Becoming a medicine man is not only a solution to problems that exist in Navajo socioeconomic life, it is also a solution, perhaps one of the better ones, to the individual problems that face Navajo males during the transition between young and middle adulthood. To understand this more fully, we need to consider the achievement of medicine man status in relation to the social and psychological development of the traditional Navajo male.

Navajo Male Development

The psychological and social development of the Navajo male is viewed by contemporary traditional Navajos to have five discrete periods (table 18.1). In addition, Schoepfle and colleagues (1979) have elicited nine stages of culturally recognized mental development from their Navajo informants (table 18.2). It is interesting that the first stage begins at age two and the last ends at the beginning of midlife when, according to Navajo tradition, the mature mind is fully formed. These data and the major change in status from "boy" to "elder" between the ages of thirty and thirty-five demonstrate the importance of the midlife period in Navajo psychological development.

Period 1 (awéé)

From birth to age two a child is seen as passive and very dependent upon his mother. In marked contrast to Western developmental theory, which views infancy as a time of great developmental importance, traditional Navajo do not believe that any significant mental development occurs during this stage.

Period 2 (ashkii yázhi)

According to Western developmental theory, between weaning and puberty a boy traverses the anal, oedipal, and latency stages of development. The Navajo see this basically as a single period in which there are four stages of mental development. The first two, *háni' hazlíí* (one becomes aware) and *ádaa' ákozhniidzíí* (one becomes self-aware), focus on the boy's first awareness of things around him, then on his growing understanding of himself in relation to other people and the land. During these stages the child begins to acquire memory, and his parents begin to teach him practical knowledge about his culture. From oral instruction and demonstration he learns how to perform various household tasks (Schoepfle et al. 1979),

TABLE 18.1

Periods in Navajo Male Development

1	*awee'*	Baby
2	*askkii yázhiĭ*	Small boy
3	*ashkii*	Boy
4	*hastiin*	Elder male
5	*hastiin sáni̇*	Aged elder male

TABLE 18.2

Male Development from Two Perspectives

Navajo Tradition

Period/Stage	Characterization	Age (*years*)	Features
1	Baby	0–2	Undefined
2	Small boy	2–puberty	Four stages:
2/1	Becomes aware	2–4	Becomes aware of self; first memories
2/2	Becomes self-aware	4–6	Sex-role identification; learns male work, taboos, obedience
2/3	Begins to think	6–9	Competes in male activities; is integrated into male daily routine; receives first lambs
2/4	Thought begins existing	10–puberty	Starts herding; expected to remember myths, prayers, religious teachings
3	Boy	15–30	Three stages:
3/1	Begins to think for self	15–18	Thinks, acts more independently; prepares for marriage
3/2	Begins to think about all things	18–22	Masters kin relationships, adult work skills; marries
3/3	Begins to think ahead for self	22–30+	Establishes herd and residence with wife; develops own economic strategy; becomes a parent; acquires initial ritual knowledge

TABLE 18.2 *(Continued)*

Navajo Tradition

Period/Stage	Characterization	Age (*years*)	Features
4	Elder male	30–60	"Thinks ahead for all things"; acquires ritual knowledge; may become medicine man; increases community leadership; increases economic independence; assumes mentor role; assumes father-in-law role; becomes a grandparent; prepares for old age
5	Aged elder male	60+	Continues as medicine man; continues as mentor when possible; experiences declining physical capacities and increasing dependency; experiences decline in health

Male Development
Psychoanalytic Perspective

Stage	Characterization	Age (*years*)	Features
Oral	Infant	1–18 mo.	Mother-child dyad
Early anal	Toddler	18–24 mo.	Object constancy; early separation-individuation; walking; sphincter control
Late anal	Toddler	2–3	Separation-individuation
Early phallic	Little boy	3–4	Engagement in oedipal triangle; expanding speech capacity

TABLE 18.2 *(Continued)*

Male Development
Psychoanalytic Perspective

Stage	Characterization	Age (*years*)	Features
Late phallic	Young boy	4–6	Resolution of oedipal conflict; identification with father
Latency	Boy	6–12	Sublimation of sexual energy; focus on learning, cognition
Early adolescence	Adolescent	12–15	Emergence of sexual feelings; growth of peer influence and independence from parents
Late adolescence	Teenager	15–18	Formation of adult ego defenses and ego ideal; maturation of superego; waning of peer influence; interest in sex and marriage
Early young adulthood	Young man	18–22	Refining of ego ideal; increase in capacity for work; choice of vocation; longer term sexual attachments; initial definition of place in society
Later young adulthood	Man	22–35	Increased capacity for sexual intimacy; marriage; parenthood; refinement of work goals; definition of place in society

TABLE 18.2 *(Continued)*

Male Development
Psychoanalytic Perspective

Stage	Characterization	Age (*years*)	Features
Midlife	Middle-aged man	30–60	Acceptance of bodily changes; sense of time running out; acceptance of eventuality of death; acquisition of mentor role; increase in creativity; marriage of children; grandparenthood; community involvement
Late adulthood	Old man	60+	Continuation of community involvement and mentor roles; decline in physical prowess; retirement; increasing dependency, acceptance of object losses; decline in health; acceptance of mortality; concern with place in history

particularly those designated as masculine, for example, carrying firewood.

The next two stages of mental development, *nitsídzíkees dzizlíí* (one begins to think) and *hanitsékees niliínii hazlíí* (one's thought begins existing), are understood to be the time when the young male begins to think for himself and to do things on his own, applying the lessons he has been taught. He is expected to perform the morning fitness run on his own, offer help with certain household chores, and begin to care for the livestock. In addition, he should begin to learn more about the religious beliefs that form the basis of Navajo social and economic activities.

This traditional Navajo view of development is, of course, quite different from the observations that might be made by a Western psychologist or psychoanalyst. The Navajo view focuses on gaining the capacity for adult functioning and acculturation; the Navajo concern is to mold an individual who conforms to the Navajo concept of *yá' át' ééhgo iina'* (good life) and who contributes to the support of his family. A psychologist or analyst would be more concerned with the development of intrapsychic structure. If one looks at a Navajo boy's development from birth to puberty from the Western perspective, several interesting distinctions arise in early object relationships, particularly the mother-child dyad. Among the Navajo any woman of one's mother's clan is considered to be a viable surrogate mother. A Navajo boy can call any such woman *shimá* (my mother) and expect that she will provide him with the same basic support that his own mother would. In practice, the biological mother provides much of the basic care, but since maternal aunts, maternal grandmothers, and older sisters are also involved in childcare, a boy develops significant object relationships with a number of mother surrogates.

For example, a fifteen-year-old Navajo boy maintained partial membership in two households other than that of his parents. He frequently took meals, slept, and performed chores at the homes of his maternal grandmother and mother's younger sister, spending approximately 30 percent of his nights in the households of his *shíma' sání* (maternal grandmother, literally "my mother, the old one") and *shíma' yázhí* (mother's younger sister, literally "my mother, the small one"). Although he recognized that he was primarily a member of his parents' household, he also recognized strong reciprocal relationships with the households of the other two women and would not hesitate to ask them for help or to offer them his labor to accomplish necessary tasks in their households. This reciprocity has continued into adulthood.

As a result, boys like the one in this example learn to seek satisfaction of their dependency needs from the women of their matrilinear clan instead of from their mothers. Among the Navajo this sharing of maternal responsibility among clanswomen is a highly valued attribute, important for survival in hard times. Social and economic circumstances in traditional Navajo life mandate sharing resources within the extended family and the outfit as well. For the young male this sharing requires that he learn early in life to depend on and to care for many women. This dispersed network of reciprocal obligations to one's clan and later to one's in-laws cements Navajo social structure.

The practice of sharing the responsibilities of motherhood tends to create in the child a personality in which basic dependency issues are not resolved to the degree that they are among people of Western cultures. This less complete resolution, of course, alters the process of separation-individuation. It is interesting that the Navajo terms for the third and fourth stages of mental development within the *ashkii yázhí* period are "one begins to think" (and do things) on one's own and "one's thought begins existing." Until this time, age six to puberty, a boy's mind is not thought to have the capacity for significant degrees of independent decision making. While in practice Navajo boys between two and six have a great deal of freedom in determining their play activities, among adults that behavior is not seen as purposeful; accordingly, the boys are considered dependent upon the women who are caring for them. Such developmental landmarks as weaning and toilet training are achieved without pressure and over a longer time than in Western cultures. The Navajo rationale for such child-rearing practices is that the boys' minds are still forming and should be gradually developed. In addition, some Navajos state that boys are allowed a great deal of freedom when they are young because after marriage they will move in with their wives' families and work very hard for their fathers-in-law.

Although this raises many issues about oedipal and latency stage development, it is not within the scope of this chapter to explore either one fully. Nevertheless, we should note that the matrilineal and matrilocal kinship system of the Navajo, along with the isolation of residence, presents a situation in which the oedipal triangle is not well balanced. The position of the father in that system is less central than that of the mother. Gary Witherspoon (1975) stated that in some ways a Navajo father is in the position of being an in-law to his children; indeed they sometimes refer to him in jest as *shaadaani* (my in-law). Thus the father is not as much of a threat to a son as he is in Western cultures; as a result, there is considerably less pressure to resolve oedipal issues during early development. Because of the prolonged early dependency and a lack of emphasis, separation-individuation and oedipal issues remain largely unresolved during childhood among traditional Navajo boys.

Period 3 (ashkii)

The third period of male development recognized by the traditional Navajo is the *ashkii* (boy) period, which extends from age fifteen to thirty. During this time the young male undergoes puberty and usually marries and becomes a parent. He is, however, still considered to be a boy because his mental development is unfinished. The Navajo divide this period of life into three substages (Schoepfle et al. 1979): *ádá nitsídzíkees dzizlíí* (one begins to think for himself); *t' áá altsoní baanitsídzíkees dzizlíí* (one begins to think about all things); and *ádá náá nitsídzíkees dzizlíí* (one begins to think ahead for himself).

During the first stage (from fifteen to about eighteen) traditional Navajo boys behave much as they did during the previous period. They still have considerable freedom but are increasingly involved in the work of adults, particularly with animals and in the fields. By that age a boy will probably have acquired a few animals of his own to herd along with the animals of his parents, and may have been given part of a field to cultivate. His parents and others in the extended family will encourage him to think on his own and to take responsibility for his work, in preparation for marriage.

The second and third stages occur at the time of separation from the extended family of origin and the establishment of a new household. Usually a traditional Navajo man will enter into an arranged marriage between the ages of eighteen and twenty-two, although some do not marry until their late twenties. Marriage brings dramatic change. Because Navajos practice clan exogamy, a young man must marry outside his clan. This means leaving the supportive group of women who raised him and moving as far as fifty miles away to live with the family of his wife. There he will depend upon a strange group of women and work under the direction of an unfamiliar father-in-law.

Men who agree to arranged marriages into distant clans often describe themselves as frightened by the prospect of living with strangers. If possible, a man might try to marry into an extended family that contains a brother, or he might try to convince a younger brother to marry his prospective wife's younger sister. Even so, it is common for young men to resist such arranged marriages. Parents commonly tell their sons to try the marriage for a year; if it does not go well, there will be no objection to the young man's returning to his mother's home, an event that occurs with some frequency. The divorce rate during the first year of traditional Navajo marriages is as high as 30 percent.

For example, a young traditional Navajo man in his early twenties returned home from combat service in the army. His readjustment was difficult. He was not making progress toward becoming more independent and getting married as everyone had expected. One day a relative came to his house and told him that his blind maternal uncle desperately needed to see him "right away!" The young man rushed to his uncle's hogan. When the uncle shook his nephew's hand, he held it tightly with both his hands, an act which is not the Navajo custom. After he held the young man's hand for some time, the young man asked why this was so. The uncle explained that the family was concerned for the young man's lack of progress in his life. He stated that the family had located a promising young woman from a good family and that a wedding was planned for two days hence. He urged the young man to get his affairs in order and marry the girl.

At first the young man refused, saying that he was making progress and might marry in the future. The uncle said that he was not asking for a permanent commitment from the young man, but an agreement to try the arranged marriage for a year or so. The young man still refused. The uncle stated that he would not let go until the young man agreed. The uncle held his nephew's hand tightly for more than an hour; the young man, fearing for the loss of his hand from decreased circulation, finally agreed.

Marriage is doubly traumatic for the young traditional Navajo male. First, there are the dependency issues. During the *ashkii yázhí* period, dependency was promoted through a strong attachment to the women of his mother's clan. When he marries, the young man is asked to give up these relationships abruptly and form new ones with the women in his wife's clan. Because traditional Navajo marriages are often arranged at distances of forty to fifty miles, the young man may have met his prospective wife and her family only one or two days before the marriage ceremony, providing no opportunity for him to form any relationships with his in-laws or to develop any sense of security about their ability, or desire, to meet his needs.

The second major reason that traditional marriage provokes anxiety involves the new husband's subservience to his father-in-law. During childhood his own father was in all probability not an authoritative figure, and oedipal issues were not fully engaged because of the strength of the mother-child bond. Now he enters a situation in which he is neither a dominant male nor a pampered child. The women in his new family have a long-established relationship with his father-in-law, who has been working for their support for many years and who, with the consent of those women, is in charge of many day-to-day tasks in which the new husband will have to participate in order to fulfill his marriage contract and gain acceptance.

It is not surprising that the relationship between a newly married traditional man and his father-in-law is often very tense. Having been under the direction of his own father-in-law for many years, the older man sees his daughter's marriage as an opportunity to establish himself in a position of authority over another male. At the same time, the younger man represents his eventual replacement as the head of an extended family when his future daughters grow up, marry, and bear children. Having a son-in-law is, in many respects, a mixed blessing. The difficulties in the relationship between these two men is well recognized among the Navajo and encoded in the myth of the witch father-in-law (Spencer 1957), who allegedly wanted to kill his son-in-law so that he could possess his daughter himself. The stress of this relationship is also apparent in the custom of avoiding the mother-in-law; a young man is forbidden to speak to or look directly at his mother-in-law. The oedipal equivalents of this conflicted situation are readily apparent.

The potential for conflict is highest during the first year or two of a marriage. Often by the second year a child will have been born, and the young man will have proved to be a good worker and provider. If the young man settles down, the older man will become more accepting and will begin to share some of his knowledge. At first he will teach practical things such as improving the tasks of agriculture, of animal husbandry, and of craft production. As time goes by, if the younger man shows interest and is willing to pay for training, the older man will impart some of his ritual knowledge, gradually assuming a mentor role: conflict is resolved through identification.

For example, a traditional Navajo man of about thirty was married to the daughter of a powerful and well-respected medicine man. He had been unable either to challenge successfully the medicine man's position or to form a close bond with him through identification. Although several children had been born to the couple, the young man was becoming increasingly isolated within the extended family. He was showing the strain of this isolation behaviorally and was becoming careless with valuable family property. The marriage was deteriorating as the young man's transition between the *ashkii* and *hastiin* periods was foundering.

One day, the medicine man's house began to burn. The young man distinguished himself in fighting the intense fire. At one point several relatives held him by the legs while he leaned into a burning room through a broken window to save his father-in-law's medicine bundle from the fire. The young man's in-laws immediately acknowledged the bravery of his act. A few days later he participated with the rest of the family in a traditional Navajo healing ceremony to mitigate the spiritual imbalance which, according to traditional Navajo belief, had caused the fire. After the ceremony, the young man's relationships with his wife and her family improved. As time went by, he occasionally assisted his father-in-law in performing the ceremonies. Although the man did not become a medicine man, this episode, the resulting improvement in relations with his father-in-law and other in-laws, and his increase in status within the extended family, facilitated a smoother transition from *ashkii* to *hastiin* status. His adjustment improved markedly, and his marriage has been stable for nearly twenty years since the incident.

As the traditional young man's relationships become more firmly established within his wife's extended family, he "begins to think ahead for himself." During this period he will build his spouse a hogan and establish a separate household. As he approaches the age of thirty, he and his wife may build another home at some distance from her parents where they will graze their sheep as a separate herd and clear a small agricultural plot of their own. He and his wife will have established a separate economic unit, and he will have gained respect from local individuals as "one who has and knows how to plan for his possessions" (Schoepfle et al. 1979).

Period 4 (hastiin)

Usually between the ages of thirty and thirty-five a traditional Navajo man undergoes a marked change in status. People stop calling him *ashkii* and begin calling him *hastiin* (elder male). He is ready for the final stage of mental development, *t' aa altsoníbá nááś nitsidzíkees dzizlíí* (one begins to think ahead for all things). He is ready to become a teacher and leader of others, expressing his opinion at chapter meetings and teaching his children and the children of others the lessons that his parents taught him. He seeks and acquires additional ritual knowledge, which he uses to protect his family and their economic enterprises. As time passes, if his economic ventures are productive, if he has sons-in-law who can work for him, and if he has the inclination, he may apprentice himself to a medicine man and begin the five to seven years of expensive and rigorous training required to learn a ceremony.

This period includes what Western psychologists and analysts would refer to as middle adulthood, during which individuals grow more aware of their own limitations and the finality of death (Colarusso and Nemiroff 1981). People from Western cultures become concerned about the contributions they have made to society and begin to reorganize priorities. In the midst of continuing creativity and productiveness, it is time to consider the end of life and the succession of the next generation.

The Navajo experience of this period of life is both similar to and different from that of people in Western cultures. Certainly midlife represents a major transition for the Navajo. The acquisition of the status of *hastiin* represents a clear break from the earlier periods. However, for the Navajo man this transition is not an acceptance of the approach and the finality of death as much as it is a long-awaited entry into full adult status. It is only in middle adulthood that he achieves less dependence on his wife's extended family and is freer to reorder his priorities. As in Western cultures, the change involves turning outward from family to community concerns. However, for the Navajo it represents an opportunity for and concern with personal growth more than an interest in how one's contributions will be remembered. Teaching is important at this time among the Navajo as it is among Westerners, but the cultural rationale is based on the need to instruct children and care for their needs so that they will provide for one in old age. Traditional Navajos recognize eventual decline, but thoughts about death are taboo.

A Navajo medicine man in his mid-seventies stated the following when asked about how Navajos raise their children: He said that children should not be forced into doing their chores, nor should they be struck. At most they should be lightly switched on the back of the legs. The reason for this was that childhood should be a time when a young person is allowed to develop on his or her own. There will be time enough later on for the children to experience the hard work of adulthood. He stated that parents should pamper their children and give them everything they could because there would be a time when the parents would become old and would be as dependent upon their children as their children had been upon them. As the parents had been tolerant of the children, the children would reciprocate. He stated this firmly in front of his children and grandchildren. A decade later, as his health failed, his children and grandchildren shared the responsibility of caring for him and his wife.

There are two reasons for these differences in interpretation of midlife. First, it would be destructive psychologically and culturally to become concerned with the finality of death just as the first major possibilities for individual development are realized. Allowing such conflicting thoughts into consciousness would be depressing and would rob the individual of a great deal of his motivation to achieve. The midlife response of the traditional Navajo to the slowing of his physical capabilities and the increasing evidence of his finiteness is to concentrate on the growth of his economic, social, political, and ritual capacities. He does this in planning for his and his wife's security in old age, not in anticipation of death.

A second reason for the difference in interpretation of middle adulthood can be found in the traditional Navajo belief in the compulsive word (Reichard 1944). They believe that words, thought, and breath are all closely connected and originate in the spirit wind that stands inside one's chest. The formation of thought and the release of words have spiritual force. Thinking, and especially talking, about death may indeed cause it to arrive prematurely. The only acceptable death is one from extreme age. Therefore as one plans for old age those thoughts and words assure that old age will come and that it will be comfortable. Only when he is terminally ill does a traditional Navajo accept the finiteness of life and plan for its end.

Although the changes in priorities and biological processes of midlife among the Navajo are similar to those of Western cultures, there is a major socioeconomic difference. A Western man has been independent for many years prior to midlife, but a traditional Navajo man finds himself for the first time mostly free of dependence upon his wife's kinsmen for support and able to support himself and others. As his daughters marry, he gains the opportunity to direct the work of his sons-in-law and increasingly becomes absorbed in issues of growth and generativity, casting midlife in a positive, optimistic light.

Period 5 (hastiin sáni)

The fifth and final period in the life of a Navajo male is one in which he is referred to as *hastiin sáni* (aged elder male) The phrase is rarely used to describe individuals younger than sixty; it is often not applied to a man until he is well into his seventies. Its application depends on the rate of decline and the degree to which the individual is still able to perform the routine tasks of Navajo daily life.

Because there are no additional stages of mental development defined for this period, the key to understanding *hastiin sáni* is the concept of decline. It is a time of gradual loss of mental functioning and physical prowess. The old man's sons-in-law are establishing their own extended families and assuming roles of increasing leadership in the community. Their social and political power is on the increase. As the Navajo recognize, it is a time of increasing dependency on one's children and grandchildren.

One might think that this is a bleak and depressing period for a Navajo man. However, if he has ritual knowledge and retains his memory, he can still play an important role. He may no longer be strong enough to herd sheep or build a hogan, but if he is a medicine man and well enough to travel (and can tolerate staying up at night), with the help of his apprentice he can provide an important service in the community and generate income for his family.

Obviously the possession of ritual knowledge and especially the achievement of medicine-man status provide an important buffer against the emotional stress resulting from losses experienced through aging. Given the nature of Navajo religion, the ability to perform ceremonies implies the power to influence the forces that control the universe. To have such power and to use it to heal the sick and to earn a living at a time when one's physical capacities and social and political influence are beginning to decline is a powerful reinforcement for the Navajo man's ego defenses, allowing him to avoid thoughts of dying until he is severely debilitated and death is imminent.

Becoming a Medicine Man

Although not every traditional Navajo man becomes a medicine man, the acquisition of ritual knowledge is an important part of Navajo male development. Every traditional boy begins learning about ritual when he is instructed by his parents to avoid taboo thoughts and actions and is taught how to live *yá' át' ééhgo iiná* (good life). At those times a boy is exposed to Navajo religious mythology and the reasons some things must be done and others must not. He also becomes acquainted with ceremonies that protect him from illnesses caused by transgression against Navajo tradition and by the malevolent acts of witches and ghosts. He learns to view his religion as a guidepost for living and protection against the vicissitudes of fate and evil acts by others. He learns to revere the medicine man, who has the power to use religious formulas to heal the sick and provide continued good fortune.

It is not surprising that he would want to gain ritual power at midlife when he is coming into his full adult capacities. At that time, all traditional Navajo men seek to learn some protective rituals and prayers to ensure health and social and economic well-being. The more ritual knowledge a man has, the better off he will be. Unfortunately, not everyone has the resources or the time to become a medicine man. To do so requires good health to undertake the training, the wealth to pay for lessons, sons-in-law who will work for you while you learn, and access to a medicine man who will agree to teach you. For those who possess these advantages, apprenticeship provides an extremely smooth midlife transition.

Becoming a medicine man has other advantages that facilitate midlife social, economic, and political development. Medicine men receive payment for their services that, at times, can be high by Navajo standards. In addition, they have the authority to cause a redistribution of wealth during ceremonies because extended families, and occasionally outfits, pool their resources to support the performance of ceremonies. During a major ceremony like *ana' íjí* (enemy way), as much as two thousand dollars can be collected by the relatives of the patient and redistributed for the support of the ceremony. Both the income that they accumulate and the ability to redistribute during ceremonies gives medicine men considerable influence and authority in the local community. Frequently medicine men, especially those who are the heads of outfits, develop clients who depend upon them for a portion of their income. Because the traditional Navajo economy is not highly productive and is communal, sharing of wealth is expected. Those who share the fruits of their labor with the less fortunate are greatly respected, develop social and political authority, and are honored as examples of *yá' át' ééhgo iiná* (good life). Achieving this condition is a major goal in traditional Navajo society and signifies full adult status in the community.

Before clinical medicine came to the reservation, the skills of medicine men in treating fractures were well known. Their poultices are effective in healing minor skin infections. They prescribe various herbal medications that have antianxiety, muscle relaxant, and/or decongestive properties. They are also quite effective in performing psychological treatment, which helps Navajos reconstitute their ego defenses in the face of emotional stress or trauma.

Becoming a medicine man allows the best available resolution of issues of dependency, separation-individuation, and oedipal conflict, which make young adulthood such a difficult time, and provides a smooth transition between the two halves of life. Moreover, it opens the door to the period of greatest personal growth that a traditional Navajo man can experience and provides him with economic security, social support, and political authority. If he performs his duties faithfully, he will be known as *hataalii yá' ééhi* (the good singer) and respected as a living example of *yá' át' ééhgo iiná* (good life). His position in middle adulthood and even late adulthood will be secure, and he will have the ego strength to defend against the unconscious realization that the declining abilities and losses of middle and late adulthood foreshadow the finiteness of his existence.

Conclusions

In this chapter we have viewed the achievement of medicine-man status as one form of culturally appropriate midlife transition for traditional Navajo men by taking a dual perspective and examining male development from both the traditional Navajo and the psychoanalytic viewpoints. This approach demonstrates clearly that Navajo men undergo midlife transitions and that the transition is both similar to and different from the midlife transitions experienced by men in industrialized Western cultures.

Midlife brings with it a significant expansion of social, economic, and political opportunities for the traditional Navajo man. It offers him a chance to achieve full adult status and to achieve more complete resolution of what we call oedipal, dependency, and separation-individuation issues that may have been partially unresolved since childhood and may have been exacerbated by his culture's traditions regarding marriage and young adult development.

For the Navajo male, midlife is similar to the comparable period for men in our industrialized cultures: in either setting, community leadership and mentor roles become important adaptations. However, for the Navajo man, midlife is not a time to take stock of one's self in light of an increasing realization that life is finite. It is instead a time to concentrate on personal growth and deny the increasing evidence of age and impending death.

We find Judith Brown's (1982) study interesting in this context. Examining the middle years of women in a number of nonindustrialized societies, she demonstrates that, especially in patrilineal societies, midlife can also be a time of increasing social and economic opportunity for women, a time when they begin to assume teaching roles as well as to attend more fully to their own psychological development. She argues that among such women the midlife transition and the onset of menopause "suggest a new developmental phase rather than forebodings of death and a retreat into fantasy." Brown's findings tend to corroborate some of our observations about the Navajo.

For both men and women in nonindustrialized cultures there are similarities to and differences from their counterparts in industrialized societies. The biological processes of the life cycle are, of course, the same. There is also social progression in which the parenting and grandparenting can often combine with increasing economic success and life experience to create opportunities for community involvement and, in some cases, leadership and the assumption of the mentor role.

It is apparent, however, from Brown's (1982) observations and our own that cultural and psychological *interpretations* of midlife and middle adulthood can differ markedly among people in industrialized cultures versus those who live in cultures that have subsistence economies. These interpretations appear to be grounded in the respective overall patterns of development and enculturation that are required to produce an individual who can function effectively in the socioeconomic setting in which he or she must live.

As individuals at a common point of biological, psychological, and social development are confronted by sets of problems unique to their cultures, they are afforded different, culture-specific opportunities to resolve those problems. Some solutions, like increased community involvement and assumption of a mentor role, do seem to be common across a spectrum of cultures. Others, like our Western acknowledgment of approaching death and compulsion to complete an individual agenda before the end, do not.

We can conclude at least that midlife transition and individual development at midlife are not solely artifacts of the developmental patterns exhibited within specific cultures, nor are they solely the products of the demands of genetic, species-wide facts of biological, psychological, and social development. They are, rather, the products of interaction between culture and the genetic capacities of man. It is cultural interpretations of this interaction during development and aging that lead to the contrasting midlife behaviors observed among peoples.

REFERENCES

Brandes, S. 1985. *Forty: The Age and Symbol.* Knoxville: University of Tennessee Press.

Brown, J. 1982. "Cross-cultural Perspectives on Middle-aged Women." *Current Anthropology* 23:143–56.

Colarusso, C. A., and Nemiroff, R. A. 1981. *Adult Development: A New Dimension in Psychodynamic Theory and Practice.* New York: Plenum.

Downs, J. F. 1964. *Animal Husbandry in Navajo Society and Culture.* Berkeley and Los Angeles: University of California Press.

Eckert, J. K. 1980. *The Unseen Elderly: A Study of Marginally Subsistent Hotel Dwellers.* San Diego: Campanile Press.

Kluckhohn, C., and Leighton, D. 1963. *The Navajo,* rev. ed. New York: Doubleday.

Levy, J. E., and Kunitz, S. J. 1974. *Indian Drinking: Anglo-American Theories and Navajo Practices.* New York: Wiley-Interscience.

Mead, M. 1928. *Coming of Age in Samoa.* New York: Morrow.

Reichard, G.A. 1944. *Prayer: The Compulsive Word.* Monograph 7, American Ethnology Society, Washington, D.C.

———. 1952. *Navajo Religion: A Study of Symbolism.* New York: Bollingen Foundation, Pantheon.

Sandner, D. 1979. *Navajo Symbols of Healing.* New York: Harcourt Brace Jovanovitch.

Schoepfle, M.; Begishe, K.; Morgan, R. T.; and Johnson, A. 1979. "The Human Impact of the Navajo-Hopi Land Dispute: the Navajo View." Manuscript at Navajo Community College, Shiprock, N.M.

Spencer, K. 1957. *Mythology and Values: An Analysis of Navajo Chantway Myths.* Philadelphia: American Folklore Society.

Topper, M. D. 1982. "The Traditional Navajo Medicine Man as a Psychotherapist." *Listening Post: Journal of Mental Health Program,* U.S. Indian Health Service, Albuquerque, N.M.

———. 1985. "Navajo 'Alcoholism': Drinking, Alcohol Abuse, and Treatment in a Changing Cultural Environment." In: *The American Experience with Alcohol, Contrasting Cultural Perspectives,* ed. L. A. Bennett and G. A. Ames. New York: Plenum.

———. 1987. "The Traditional Navajo Medicine Man: Therapist, Counselor, and Community Leader." *Journal of Psychoanalytic Anthropology* 10(3):217–49.

Witherspoon, G. 1975. *Navajo Kinship and Marriage.* Chicago: University of Chicago Press.

DISCUSSION

Drs. Topper and Schoepfle present a truly new dimension in adult development because they were among the first to examine in detail cross-cultural phenomena from an *adult* developmental theoretical framework. The focus on adult development grows naturally out of a developmental conceptualization, which recognizes the constant interaction among biological, intrapsychic, and environmental factors, and delineates those characteristics that shape the Navajo heart and soul. Take, for example, the vivid description of the relationship between climatic and topographical conditions and social patterns. The typical extended family of twelve needs two square miles of grazing area to support themselves. Thinly spread over vast distances, the Navajo have adapted to their environment and evolved patterns of child rearing, marriage, and intrafamilial relationships that mold the Navajo character.

In addition to using a definition of development similar to most dynamic psychiatrists and psychoanalysts, the authors are fully aware of the relationship between child and adult experience. Their fascinating description of Navajo male development differs from most Western models, yet it is conceptualized in familiar terms. Infancy and childhood are seen very differently by the Navajo. They solve the problem of child care and child rearing in a manner consonant with their clan society: the young are raised by several "mothers." Preoedipal developmental tasks such as weaning and toilet training are achieved "without pressure," and oedipal issues are minimized. This achievement is possible because "The Navajo view focuses on gaining the capacity for *adult* functioning and acculturation" (pp. 452–53, italics added). Their focus on adulthood rather than childhood contrasts sharply with the Western emphasis on child development and raises many intriguing issues for us to consider.

One of these issues is oedipal development in the Navajo male. In phase three, ages fifteen to thirty, the young man is "still considered to be a boy because his mental development is unfinished" (p. 454). What is demanded of him during this phase—work, marriage, and most significantly, moving away from his clan to live with his wife's family—is considerable. In breaking his dependency ties to his "mothers" and becoming subservient to his father-in-law, the young Navajo man "enters a situation in which he is neither a dominant male nor a pampered child" (p. 456).

It appears that the Navajo culture has created a circumstance *in young adulthood,* not childhood, when major oedipal and preoedipal themes must be reengaged and, it is hoped, mastered. The occurance of oedipal and preoedipal themes in young adulthood underscores our contention that the oedipus is not a character limited to the oedipal phase; it is, instead, a codified lifelong theme, crystallized between ages three and six because a level of mental and psychological sophistication sufficient to create it occurs then for the first time. Drs. Topper and Schoepfle have provided us with a remarkable insight into the life course of the oedipus in which young adult experience may be the most important for oedipal engagement and resolution. These data encourage us to broaden our notions of oedipal development and diminish our tendency to reduce the oedipal complex to the brief period in childhood when it begins to exert its influence on human development.

In Navajo culture full recognition as an elder male who "is ready for the final stage of mental development" when "one begins to think ahead for all things" (p. 458) is reserved for those young men who successfully make the transition from the family of origin to the family of procreation, mastering basic preoedipal and oedipal developmental themes in the process. Then they are ready for midlife, having traversed childhood and young adulthood in a manner very different from the American culture that surrounds them.

Whereas Western man begins to consciously address his own death in midlife, the Navajo man denies it—"thoughts about death are taboo" (p. 459)—and concentrates instead on his newly won power, prestige, and wealth; only recently wrested from his oedipal father-in-law. ". . . it would be destructive psychologically and culturally to become concerned with the finality of death just as the first major possibilities for individual development are realized" (p. 459).

Becoming a medicine man is a challenging but rewarding way to accomplish a smooth midlife transition in the Navajo culture. In Western culture becoming a professional can often smooth the transition to young adulthood. Consider this comparison: "Unfortunately, not everyone has the resources or the time to become a medicine man. To do so requires good health to undertake the training, the wealth to pay for lessons, sons-in-law who will work for you while you learn, and access to a medicine man who will agree to teach you" (p. 461).

19

The Other Side of the Wall:

A Psychoanalytic Study of Creativity in Later Life

H. PETER HILDEBRAND

I wish to address myself here to the notion of creativity in later life. I do not intend to do more than briefly summarize the classical view of creativity as put forward originally by Sigmund Freud and developed by other psychoanalysts over the last eighty years. I wish instead to bring together several strands of thought arising from consideration of object relations theory and the application of structuralist ideas to psychoanalytic thinking together with recent interest in the developmental stages of later life. I will combine this approach with a critique of certain notions put forward by René Major (1985) in his work on *Hamlet* and apply the amended theory to an outstanding creative work of later life, namely William Shakespeare's last complete play *The Tempest.*

The Tempest, although the last complete play written by Shakespeare, is accorded pride of place in the Folio of 1623. Subsequent to its presentation at Court in 1612 on the occasion of the marriage of the Winter Queen, Elizabeth of Bohemia, Shakespeare seems to have retired to Stratford, where he lived with his married daughter and her husband at New Place, until his death some four years later.

The play is in the form of a romantic comedy and contains a masque, or a play within a play. It recounts the events of a few hours when the galleon carrying Alonso, King of Naples and his retinue sails near the island where Prospero, once Duke of Milan and his daughter Miranda are living in exile. Using magic arts, Prospero conjures up a storm and creates

467

the illusion that the ship has been cast ashore. With the aid of his familiar spirit Ariel, he achieves a situation that enables him to regain his Dukedom, to marry his daughter to the King's son, and redress the wrongs he has suffered at the hands of his usurping brother. This bald summary gives no indication of the subtlety and beauty of the play and the intricacy of much of the verse, which has made it one of the best loved and perhaps most misunderstood of Shakespeare's plays.

I take it as a given that any psychoanalytic theory of creativity needs to account for such mature work in creative artists as well as relating them to their early productions. Freud said, "In the exercising of an art, it [psychoanalysis] sees once again an activity intended to allay ungratified wishes—in the first place in the creative artist himself and subsequently in his audience or spectators" (Freud 1913, p. 187). In Elizabeth Wright's view, Freud suggested that the writer produces a surrogate neurosis, which incited both a public (cathartic) transferential relationship as well as a private one (Wright 1984). This is a view that has been developed by a number of writers, notably Janine Chasseguet-Smirgel (1984), who has developed her own version of classical psychoanalytic theory concerning creativity. While acknowledging the importance and fruitfulness of the classical psychoanalytic tradition and its roots in biological theory, I am always struck by the parallel between this type of approach to psychological phenomena and the economic theories of the modern Tory Party in Great Britain. Just as everything in Mrs. Thatcher's views seems to be reduced to the notions of financial probity and good management typified by her family's corner shop in Grantham, I sometimes feel that everything in classical theory must be reduced to drive derivatives. Thus Chasseguet-Smirgel says "Creation has a function that goes further than that of sublimation. In fact, it is a matter of using the sublimated creative act to gain access to one's integrity by passing through a spectrum of sublimated impulse discharges. . . . The creative act is an attempt to achieve integrity, to overcome castration at every level" (1984, p. 399). While I have no wish to minimize the importance of psychosexual factors in our understanding of creative work in human beings, one has to recall that Freud himself laid down his arms before the problem of creativity at a time when psychosexual factors were central to his thinking and that he maintained, wrongly as we now know, that after the age of forty people became too fixed and rigid in their cognitive patterns to be amenable to analysis or psychic change and development. Plainly we need an extended theory to account for certain creative productions in later life. Moreover, I suspect that I am not alone in finding the classical approach unsatisfying whatever its attractions in terms of simplicity and heuristic value. Personally, I prefer complexity and subtlety and feel that of all human attributes, the capacity to create works of art fashioned through symbolic representation is perhaps the most human and the most complicated.

In this chapter, therefore, I shall present a series of rather disjunctive thoughts as a way of approaching the problem of later life creativity and throwing a different, personal, though in no way more profound light on the topic. Thus, object relations theorists in Great Britain have refused to assume that the unconscious is merely a cauldron of seething excitement and have underlined a basic unconscious human need to maintain meaningful contact with others. Charles Rycroft (1985) states that "man is innately a symbolizing animal who generates meanings whenever he acts."

Rycroft continues:

By assuming, as Freud did in his theoretical writings but not always in his clinical papers, that the unconscious, the id, was "a chaos, a cauldron of seething excitement . . . which was a slave to the pleasure principle and neglected the reality of the external world" and had therefore to be repressed, modified and organized before an integrated, rational and realistic ego could develop, Freud was, it seemed and still seems—to me, taking an intellectualist, anti-emotional stance. By describing unconscious mental processes as primitive, archaic, irrational and unrealistic and attributing to the healthy ego a rational, objective state of mind which is in fact that of a scientist or professional man while at work and that of an ordinary, healthy human being at home, at play or in love, he ensnared his theory in a paradox, to which most of his followers have loyally accommodated themselves: the effect of psychoanalytical treatment is to create personalities which embrace just those emotional, imaginative elements that its theoretical conception of a rational ego excludes. (P. 122)

Rycroft resolves the paradox in the following way:

This is that human behaviour is actuated not only by the need to satisfy instinctual impulses but also by the need to maintain meaningful contact with others—that, as Susanne Langer herself put it, "human behaviour is not only a food-getting strategy, but is also a language . . . every move is at the same time a gesture." Another way of putting this is to say that man is innately a symbolizing animal who generates meanings whenever he acts.

According to Susanne Langer there are two types of symbolism available for expressing and communicating meanings: discursive symbolism, which is language as the term is ordinarily understood, i.e. words with fixed meanings arranged in series according to agreed rules, and non-discursive symbolism, in which images are presented simultaneously and derive their meaning from their context in the total pattern. In *The Innocence of Dreams* I have argued that dreaming is an intra-psychic communicative activity using non-discursive symbolism and that the "primary" processes—condensation, displacement and symbolization—which Freud discovered to be characteristic of dreaming, are the figures of speech of a non-discursive language which uses images, particularly bodily images, as its vocabulary and sources of metaphor. Such a view of the matter implies, of course, an agent, a self who is more than our usual waking state, who generates meanings, sends messages and constructs dreams and symptoms, and it regards dreams not as "mental phenomena" that we sometimes observe but as expressive activities to which we sometimes listen. (P. 124)

Clearly this argument can also be related to the creative act as well.

I wish to add to this object relations hypothesis of a fundamental world of unconscious meanings, which is as fundamental an unconscious structure as the id, a structural hypothesis (Kuper 1986). Adam Kuper considers that an understanding of the work of Claude Lévi-Strauss and his "logic of the concrete" (Lévi-Strauss 1962), is crucial to the understanding of dreams and creativity. This was a mode of thought that constituted symbolic objects in terms of a set of binary oppositions, and combined these constructs for messages. Lévi-Strauss assumes that a mental structure, typically a myth, formulates its message along two dimensions. One—the metaphoric dimension—involves selection of items from a series of binary oppositions (such as male/female, up/down, hot/cold, young/old). The other, the combinatory dimension, has to do with the organization of these items in series, syntagmatic chains. The combinatory sequences are less strictly limited than the selective choices, but they are also constrained by transformation rules. Once a particular situation has been specified in a myth, the movement forward is achieved through formal transformations, in which the items are inverted, reversed, negated, and so on.

Consider the opening sequences of four North American myths about bird-nesters, discussed in the final volume of his *Mythologiques* (1981). Each of these "overtures" (as Lévi-Strauss calls them, exploiting his own favorite analogy between primitive myth and classical European music) features a hero and one of three female relatives. The first hero has a sister, who is protective; the second a grandmother, who tries to commit incest with him; and the third, a cannibalistic mother. In the fourth myth the hero is confronted with all three female relatives, but their attributes are juggled. In this myth, the sister is incestuous, the grandmother cannibalistic, and the mother protective. In other words, the three female relatives are defined in terms of three contrasting feminine attributes, which are systematically rotated. Each female character appears twice in this set of four myths. On each appearance she has a different label (incestuous, protective, or cannibalistic). Moreover, in no myth are two of these women given the same label. This set of three defining attributes may itself be reduced to two sets of oppositions—tabooed versus permitted behavior, and sexual versus culinary regulations.

The women are also further contrasted in terms of another cluster of symbols which oppose menstruating women, pregnant women, and post-menopausal women. These attributes are more obviously mutually exclusive. Menstruating women cannot be pregnant, pregnant women cannot menstruate, and postmenopausal women can neither menstruate nor fall pregnant. These qualities in turn refer to culturally more fundamental oppositions, between youth and age, fertility and sterility, birth and death. They also tie in with ideas about the phases of the moon.

By specifying these basic oppositions, the myths arm themselves with the means by which they are able to communicate culturally resonant messages.

Kuper then suggests that while the binary oppositions are rather rigid and mechanical, the transformations of mythical constructions are comparatively free. "Theoretically, at least, there is no limit to the possible number of transformations . . . from the purely theoretical point of view, there is no way of deriving . . . any principle from which it would follow that the states of the group are necessarily finite in number" (p. 7). And yet, transformations seem to follow certain rules. Lévi-Strauss believes that this points to the existence of further mental universals:

If, between one variant and another of the same myth, there always appears differences expressible, not in the form of small positive or negative increments, but of clear-cut relationships such as contrariness, contradiction, inversion of symmetry, this is because the "transformational" aspect is not the whole story: some other principle must come into play to determine that only some of the possible states of the myth are actualized, and that only certain apertures, not all, are opened up in the grid which, theroetically, could accommodate any number. This additional constraint results from the fact that the mind, which is working unconsciously on the mythic substance, has at its disposal only mental procedures of a certain type. (1981, pp. 675–76)

The next step in my argument is to suggest that psychoanalysis needs to acknowledge that we organize our creative and imaginative life through both psychosexual and nondiscursive meanings: and moreover, that we all have individual grids of meanings which can be thought of as having the same structures as myths. In this sense we constantly create and re-create our personal and unique myths from the raw stuff of our existence through the medium of our dreams, neuroses, and creative work. Moreover, creativity is a lifelong process, which may find differing expression at different developmental phases in the life of any given individual. I think it likely that *mature* creativity in later life may well transmute and express earlier infantile and adolescent themes in a more ego-syntonic and satisfactory way than earlier theorists have suggested. The form that this may take may well be more fragmentary and allusive than earlier works, and yet carry a greater charge of meaning than the more structured works that the individual has produced earlier in his or her life. An excellent example would be the late watercolors of Cezanne.

I would like to bring together, at this point, the notions of Elliot Jaques (1965), with whose basic tenet concerning the universality of a midlife crisis at the age of thirty-seven I cannot agree, but whose notion of different types of creativity at different times of life, that is, hot-from-the-fire creativity in youth versus sculptured creativity in later life, I find sympathetic; and George Pollock (1982), who in his various papers on creativity in later life has made very convincingly the point that later life work has to do with mourning for one's own losses and the transmutation of these through creative processes as one ages. I hold that there are grounds for suggesting that as well as there being primal fantasies concerning birth and the primal scene, there are also primal fantasies concerning one's own death and that these often become central to and are expressed in many ways in the creative work of artists, particularly as they age (Hildebrand 1985, 1987).

The Importance of Names

I would like to turn now to the work of a French colleague, which it seems to me, is of importance to this area of creativity, namely René Major's paper entitled "Names: Proper and Improper" (1985). In this paper, Major analyzes *Hamlet* in terms of a psychoanalytic theory of proper names, and says,

> Proper names distinguish one person from another. The proper name is thus a mark without meaning (an unmeaning mark) . . . insignificant and yet remarkable, in both senses of the word. It allows us to recognize someone, but the mark can be used more than once and even endlessly. The mark is valid at the time for one person and for all those who have the same name. This produces homonymy; names which have no relationship (in terms of what they designate) may coincide. As far as proper names are concerned coincidence may just as well make them homonymous.

Using terms derived from Antonin Artaud, Major designates the theater as a place "where transference makes itself felt through excess." Major's notion is that the proper name is the medium through which—in classical theater—transference effects itself. As he says, "The nomination and exchange of names assures the reproduction of representation, but the necessary split in representation introduced by repression takes place between desire and death. With *Hamlet* (which Freud considers to be the first modern play) it becomes *exemplary.*" He claims that in *Hamlet* the use of proper names carries a challenge of signification, which enables us, the audience, to understand the psychological transferences that are going on on the stage. He points out that Hamlet has to believe the ghost who may at the beginning of the play be no more than a projection of his own fantasies. In order to convince himself and to convince one important other—Horatio—Hamlet has to stage a play within a play.

Hamlet has the actors perform The Dumb-Show, the mime, and then the play which reproduces the scene in which a character pours poison into the ear of the sleeping King. But the pantomime only tells the "argument" of the piece. It doesn't reveal its secret. The latter must be uttered. "The players cannot keep counsel; they'll tell all." Nonetheless, producing the play within the play is not enough. From being an actor, the tragedy's King (Claudius) has become a spectator. And in so far as he is a spectator, he knows that the player-king doesn't die. He can remain impassive. Claudius might have shown no particular distress if what I call a *practicable* in French—a linking dialogue—had not taken place between Hamlet and himself, interrupting the unfolding of the play. Their dialogue bears essentially on the title of the piece and the name of the characters. The title: *The Mousetrap.* The subject: a murder committed in Vienna. Claudius does not know that Hamlet knows that he is the murderer of his father. The court in attendance for the performance know nothing, nor does the Queen. These are all things the audience know. For Hamlet, the nub is to make it known that he knows through making manifest in Claudius the uneasiness which will prove to him that what he knows is accurate and will assure him that from that moment on Claudius will be certain that he knows. To get to that point, there is only one means available: to get the names of the one play to pass over into the other. Hamlet replies to Claudius' questions: "Gonzago is the duke's name; his wife, Baptista." Lucianus is the character who pours poison into Gonzago's ear; "the story is extant, and writ in choice Italian." "You shall see anon," Hamlet announces, "how the murderer gets the love of Gonzago's wife." With these words, whereby Claudius and Lucianus become equivalent, the king rises and leaves the show. An unusual situation: a spectator, who has come to the theatre to live an imaginary life, there finds a representation of his real life.

Please keep these words in mind when we consider *The Tempest.*

Major goes on to say:

Through the play of proper names which the Italian play introduces, the scenes become interchangeable. To the extent that Gonzago represents the old King Hamlet, Claudius, occupying Lucianus' place, may end up in Gonzago's place if Prince Hamlet, the nephew of Claudius, becomes the homonym of Lucianus, Gonzago's nephew. All the dramatic force of the piece consists in the fact that names that have no relationship come to coincide with one another. If one adds to the chessboard the death of Shakespeare's father around the time of the writing of *Hamlet* and the name of Shakespeare's son, Hamnet, dead at an early age, the circle is closed, running from Shakespeare's son to the play's spectator, identified with the Prince who dies by the poisoned sword. Across the centuries, Shakespeare continues to bring his son to life, in each of us.

The name of Hamlet renders those of Gonzago, of King Hamlet, and of Claudius homonymic. Even though they have no relationship with each other, it makes them coincide. With the name Hamlet—this is also true for Oedipus—there is an end to a dynasty, which gives these names an exceptional significance.

Let me try and summarize my argument up to this point. I suggest that in the theater the proper names chosen for the characters will convey not only something about them, but also reflect significations that are part of the dramatist's own personal myth as well as reverberating through both the spectator's external world and his inner personal nexus of meanings. I would add that *Hamlet,* in particular, because it so clearly and yet so densely treats the themes of oedipal rivalry between sons and fathers, the desire for the mother, guilt, and the whole question of denomination and identity in a doubly theatrical way, that is, the play, the play within the play, the play within the spectator, has always been paradigmatic for the psychoanalyst to consider and understand.

The Central Reflector

Bearing these very different strands of my argument in mind in considering *The Tempest,* I will assume a reasonable knowledge of the plot and characters and treat specifically some hitherto unaddressed aspects of the work. Jan Kott (1964) says "Shakespeare's dramas are constructed not on the principle of unity of action, but on the principle of analogy, comprising a double, treble or quadruple plot, which repeats the same basic theme; they are a system of mirrors both concave and convex which reflect, magnify and parody the same situation" (p.172). I am suggesting that the same notion can be applied across the Shakespearian canon. After all, Henry James, no mean authority when it comes to ghost stories, called *Hamlet* the *central reflector!* My thesis is that indeed *Hamlet* represented certain oedipal themes that Shakespeare worked and reworked throughout his life, and that in this, his last major work, *The Tempest,* he returns to the themes of succession, usurpation, identity, and retribution in order to work them through once again. Because it is a romance, the play is not ostensibly about the tragic aspects of these themes, but to my mind they are linked as closely to the themes of *Hamlet* as is manifest content to latent content.

The Tempest is a play deeply concerned with magic. It centers around the arrival near the Island of exile of Prospero, former Duke of Milan, of a galleon carrying *inter alia* Alonso, King of Naples, his son Fernando, his brother Sebastian, Antonio the usurping Duke of Milan and brother to Prospero, and Gonzalo, honest old counselor to the King. Prospero, rightful Duke of Milan, has been cast adrift to die with his infant daughter Miranda but they and his magic books are saved thanks to the care and mercy of Gonzalo. He has since lived in isolation on the island with his spirit Ariel, whom he had freed from imprisonment by the now dead witch Sycorax and also with her son Caliban, a monster who wishes to ravish Miranda and has rejected Prospero's attempts to civilize him. Nevertheless, Caliban can understand and respond to beauty although he is overtly sexual and aggressive—like the rest of mankind.

The play opens when the ship carrying the King of Naples and his retinue is apparently wrecked by a magical storm conjured up by Prospero. When Miranda pities those drowned, Prospero's first words are, "Be collected. No more amazement. Tell your piteous heart there's no harm done":

> MIRANDA—O, woe the day!
> PROSPERO—No harm.
> (I.2.15)

I think these words are significant beyond their immediate meaning. Prospero's signature in the play is immediately set. There is to be no harm done. This is not to be a tragedy of blood and revenge and despite the supernatural elements which will shortly appear there is to be no parricide or ghostly paternal apparition on this stage. Prospero's speech continues:

> I have done nothing but in care of thee,
> Of thee, my dear one, thee my daughter, who
> Art ignorant of what thou art, naught knowing

> Of whence I am, nor that I am more better
> Than Prospero, master of a full poor cell.
> And thy no greater father.   (I.2.16–21)

Prospero now asks Miranda to pluck his magic garment from him, "So, lie there, my art" and proceeds to tell her a nonillusory truth about their joint identities. His concern is with daughters and the succession—a theme hardly surprising for a writer who has one daughter married to a successful and well-trusted physician and another daughter still to be married. Shakespeare's father and son are both long dead—but daughters do not need to be deceived.

> Wipe thou thine eyes. Have comfort.
> The direful spectacle of the wrack, which touched
> The very virtue of compassion in thee.
> I have with such provision in mine art
> So safely ordered, that there is no soul—
> No, not so much perdition as an hair
> Betid to any creature in the vessel
> Which thou heard'st cry, which thou saw'st sink.
>   (I.2.24–32)

The Tempest is a romance. Prospero's care for his daughter and his deliberate lack of malice are at once established. The audience are shown that they have been the objects of a nonmalicious theatrical illusion and that the ship and its passengers have survived. Yet no one can be sure what is illusion and what is truth in this magical matter—rather like the quest for truth at the opening of Hamlet. The meanings slide over one another. Prospero now suggests finding the roots of these events in the past, "What seest thou else in the dark backward and abysm of time?" and uses Miranda's childhood memories to demonstrate that he is the true Duke of Milan (writ in choice Italian). Her natural question is "What foul play had we, that we came from there?" Prospero tells her that his brother has seized the city while they slept (O my prophetic soul, my Uncle!) "I pray thee mark me that a brother should be so perfidious" (I.2.49–67). He has usurped the throne while Prospero has been absorbed in the study of his magic arts. But thanks to the old nobleman Gonzalo who has secretly preserved them, they have landed on the island and Prospero has developed his magic powers.

The Practicable

The name Gonzalo is absolutely crucial to my argument here. I consider that the homonym Gonzalo/Gonzago provides the *practicable*—the unconscious link between the two plays of *Hamlet* and *The Tempest* and signifies for us that the later piece represents a different age-specific treatment of some of the major themes of the earlier play. For example, it is now revealed to us that Prospero, as well as being a magician, can employ a familiar spirit called Ariel who has separated the King's son, Ferdinand, from the other members of the crew whom he has cast into an enchanted sleep. After a brief entry to establish Caliban and his fury and hatred of Prospero, and his wish to rape Miranda, Ferdinand enters, together with Ariel, who is invisible to Ferdinand, and says,

> Sitting on a bank,
> Weeping again the King my father's wrack,
> This music crept by me upon the waters,
> Allaying both their fury and my passion
> With its sweet air. Thence I have followed it,
> Or it hath drawn me, rather. But t'is gone
> No, it begins again.   (I.2.390–96)

This is followed by Ariel's beautiful song "Full fathom five thy father lies." In a most extraordinary and haunting echo of Hamlet's scene upon the battlements, Ferdinand says "The ditty does remember my drowned father. This is no mortal business, nor no sound that the earth owes." But it is not the comrades of the watch on the battlements who are the spectators, but Prospero and Miranda, who falls in love immediately with Ferdinand, the first young man whom she has ever seen. Prospero watches the scene with pleasure, confirms their mutual infatuation, and then says to Ferdinand, who now believes that he has succeeded his father as King and wishes to offer this newfound kingdom to Miranda: "One word more I charge that thee that thou attend me. Thou do'st here *usurp the name* thou own'st not"; that is, challenging his claim that he has now become the King.

Prospero gives Ferdinand menial tasks to do in order to confirm the love of the two young people, while the scene changes. And what is fascinating here is that Gonzalo, whom I have nominated as the "practicable," acts as the animator of the next and most significant scene in which Alonso, Sebastian, Antonio, and he take part. After Alonso has expressed grief for the supposed loss of his son, Gonzalo presents us with his picture of a Golden Age—an idealized fantasy which may make up for what is the insupportable loss of an adult child (Hildebrand 1985), until under the spell of Ariel, all fall asleep except for Sebastian and Antonio, who discuss the possibility of Sebastian usurping the Kingdom of Naples. Antonio works Sebastian up saying,

There be that can rule Naples as well as he that sleeps: lords that can prate as amply and unnecessarily as this Gonzalo. I myself could make a chough of as deep chat. O, that you bore the mind that I do! What a sleep were this for your advancement! Do you understand me?

> *SEBASTIAN*—Methinks I do.
> *ANTONIO*—And how does your content tender your own good fortune?
> *SEBASTIAN*—You did supplant your brother Prospero.
> *ANTONIO*—True. And look how well my garments sit upon me. Much feater than before. My brother's servants were then my fellows. Now they are my men.
> *SEBASTIAN*—But, for your conscience?
> *ANTONIO*—Ay, sir, where lies that? If 'twere a kibe,
> 'Twould put me to my slipper; but I feel not
> This deity in my bosom. Twenty consciences
> That stand 'twixt me and Milan, candied be they,
> And melt ere they molest. Here lies your brother,
> No better than the earth he likes upon,
> If he were that which now he's like—that's dead—
> Whom I with this obedient steel, three inches of it,
> Can lay to bed for ever; whiles you, doing thus.   (II.1.267–89)

They are just about to kill the King and his companions *as they sleep* when Ariel enters and awakens the sleepers. The whole scene has been orchestrated by Prospero, so that we, like Claudius in *Hamlet,* think we are going to see an innocent play, until we are forced to realize our own complicity in the piece. The parallel with *The Mousetrap*—the play within the play—where we are shown Hamlet the Dane, who is sleeping in his orchard when he is murdered by his brother, who then takes his Kingdom and his wife and usurps the throne, is phenomenal. But unlike Claudius, we cannot leap to our feet and cry for torches—we needs must watch, and watch again while the tragedy of usurpation is played again as tragicomedy by Caliban, and the drunkards. Prospero on his island is showing the world to Miranda, and of course, us to ourselves—our follies, our sexual infatuations, and our illusions. While Hamlet poses the question "Who am I?" we are asked "Who are you?"

Let us leave *The Tempest* for a moment while Shakespeare works out his plot, and look further at some elements of myth which seem common to *Hamlet* and *The Tempest.* We find the rivalry between the good and wicked brothers; the murder of the king while sleeping contrasted with the preservation of the king while sleeping; the supernatural appearance of the dead king versus the supernatural appearance of the supposedly dead king; the ruler is murdered and demands revenge versus the ruler is threatened with murder but forgoes revenge. The themes here are greed, envy, desire, contrasted with loving kindness, trust, and generativity both within and between generations. I suggest that without the addition of these basic meaningful relationships analyzed in structuralist terms, any psychoanalytic interpretation must remain incomplete. With them the work of art carries more effect for the reader or spectator, in the sense that the meanings are multilayered and convey multiple resonances of this particular myth.

So we can identify with and enjoy the irony of Miranda's comment when she exclaims on meeting the King and his retinue of villains and would-be murderers for the first time.

> Oh, wonder,
> How many goodly creatures are there here!
> How beauteous mankind is! Oh brave new world
> That has such people in't!

To which Prospero replies, "Tis new to thee" (V.1.181–84).

While we are aware of the writer's irony and our own skepticism, since we think we know who they are—despite the fact that Miranda, as spectator, may be observing us who think that we are spectators but are of course as much embedded in the drama through our own transferences as are the actors themselves—it nevertheless seems plausible to suggest here that Shakespeare may be using the piece to work out his problem of generativity and renunciation by and through each of us.

Such an approach would speak against Major's notion that the doomed dynasty of the Hamlets *denominates* itself in death. Moreover, in the companion case of Oedipus this is certainly not true, since by the manner of his death Oedipus donates his generativity to the Athenian state. If *The Tempest* does indeed represent a reworking of the same themes, then the message is that power can be handed on if it is relinquished voluntarily and accepted neither enviously or greedily but worked and sacrificed for.

I must also discuss the two magic appearances in acts III and IV, where first we have the mime of presenting and then removing the spectral banquet to the King and Court, in the course of which Ariel accuses Alonso of complicity in Prospero's exile and the King acknowledges his guilt and states what he considers to be the appropriate punishment.

> Therefore my son ith ooze is bedded, and
> I'll sink deeper than ever plummet sounded,
> and with him there lie mudded.
>
> (III.3.102–4)

This is an extraordinary evocation of Hamnet Shakespeare whose death and burial in the churchyard of Stratford church are recorded in the parish register for 1596. To this day the churchyard lies hard by the water meadows of the Avon and the reference is surely to the loss of an adult child (Hamnet was nearly twelve) which, as I have shown elsewhere, it is never really possible to accept and work through (Hildebrand 1985).

This episode is followed by the Ceres masque presented to Ferdinand and Miranda, which leads Ferdinand to say,

> Let me live here for ever!
> So rare a wondered father and a wise
> makes this place Paradise.
>
> (IV.1.122–24)

But the villains now break in.

Most commentators on the *The Tempest* have suggested that Shakespeare has used Prospero as his voice in the marvellous speech in act IV in which he says to Ferdinand:

> Be cheerful, Sir
> Our revels now are ended. These our actors,
> As I foretold you, were all spirits, and
> Are melted into air, into thin air;
> And, like the baseless fabric of this vision,
> The cloud capped towers, the gorgeous palaces,
> The solemn temples, the great globe itself,
> Yea, all which it inherit, shall dissolve,
> And, like this insubstantial pageant faded,
> Leave not a wrack behind. We are such stuff
> As dreams are made on; and our little life
> Is rounded with a sleep.   (IV.1.147–58)

Usually they suggest that the speech marks his farewell to the stage. Apart from the fact that he contributed considerable chunks of *Henry VIII* some years later, I don't see either Shakespeare or Prospero in such a sentimental way. Prospero is a realist, and is saying that you cannot cope with evil, with drunkenness, with sexuality without tenderness and compassion by means of *illusion*. While illusion has been enormously powerful in his exile, it is in the end theater. Something else needs to be done in reality and he will do it by bringing the villains under control. They have spoiled the illusion and must be punished—this is the penalty that you pay for ignoring them.

Prospero is under no illusion himself about the situation that he is handing over. If the exile on the island has been his withdrawal into study and magic arts, he must now return to reality, "my every third thought shall be of death," and he now finally releases Ariel—the Imaginary is transformed at last into the Symbolic—reluctantly but for good. He returns to Milan and to the humdrum daily round. That this may be a disaster is of course a danger which he cannot ignore, but if he wants to hand on the succession to Miranda and Ferdinand this in reality is the only choice that he can make. Acceptance of one's own mortality is the life-giving choice which will secure the dynasty. Nothing could be harder headed than Prospero's choice—nothing further from the holocaust at the end of *Hamlet*. Where Major speaks of the "denomination of Hamlet," perhaps we should speak of the "nomination" of the children who are to succeed and who are to make their way at whatever cost to themselves.

Shakespeare, of course, has one more trick up his sleeve—we are not to get off lightly. In the Epilogue, Prospero says,

> Now my charms are all o'erthrown,
> And what strength I have's mine own,
> Which is most faint. Now 'tis true
> I must here be confined by you,
> Or sent to Naples. Let me not
> Since I have my dukedom got
> And pardoned the deceiver, dwell
> In this bare island by your spell;
> But release me from my bands
> With the help of your good hands
> Gentle breath of yours my sails
> must fill, or else my project fails,
> Which was to please. Now I want
> Spirits to enforce, art to enchant;
> And my ending is despair,
> Unless I be relieved by prayer,
> Which pierces so, that it assaults
> mercy itself, and frees all faults.
> As you from crimes would pardoned be,
> Let your indulgence set me free.

Conclusions

The editor of the Penguin *Tempest* says, "The superior knowledge possessed by the theatrical audience does not pluck the heart of mystery out of Prospero's masque. It merely leads into an appearance-reality dilemma more profound and much more complex than the one actually perceived by the characters on the stage" (p. 47). When Prospero addresses himself to the audience, he may well be said to be anticipating those French analysts and literary historians who "deconstruct" by some four hundred years. The question being asked is "Who has constructed the play?" Are Prospero, Caliban, Alonso and the rest illusions of the audience or only of Shakespeare? Whose life is ending and who is facing death? Is it the play which comes to an end or is it the life which each member of the audience will have to create for himself outside the revels which have created a temporary island of refuge from reality? Prospero has been created by the response of the audience to the play—now he and they must return home. The audience's prayers are now the source of magical power—like Ariel, Prospero must pray them to release him. If they refuse, he must live in an illusion, but they cannot be free. So to be free they have to give the magic and the illusion up. Hamlet the Dane dies, and we are purged with pity and sorrow. Horatio says "Good night, Sweet Prince." Prospero asks us, where shall we all lay our heads tomorrow?

I will conclude by saying that I have felt most inadequate to the task which I have set myself. I have tried to comment on the phenomenon of late life creativity through a work of art, and I fear that the complexity and subtlety of the task have been beyond me. Fortunately, a great modern English poet was fascinated by *The Tempest,* and it is good that I can give him the last word. This is to be found in the opening poem from W. H. Auden's poetic response to *The Tempest* entitled "The Sea and the Mirror" (1944).

> The aged catch their breath,
> For the nonchalant couple go
> Waltzing across the tightrope
> As if there were no death
> Or hope of falling down;
> The wounded cry as the clown
> doubles his meaning, and O
> How the dear little children laugh
> When the drums roll and the lovely
> Lady is sawn in half.
>
> O what authority gives
> Existence its surprise

Science is happy to answer
That the ghosts who haunt our lives
Are handy with mirrors and wire,
That song and sugar and fire,
Courage and come-hither eyes
Have a genius for taking pains.
But how does one think up a habit?
Our wonder, our terror remains.

Art opens the fishiest eye
To the flesh and the Devil who heat
The Chamber of Temptation
Where heroes roar and die.
We are wet with sympathy now;
Thanks for the evening: but how
Shall we satisfy when we meet,
Between Shall-I and I-Will,
The lions mouth whose hunger
No metaphors can fill?

Well, who in his own backyard
Has not opened his heart to the smiling
Secret he cannot quote?
Which goes to show that the Bard
Was sober when he wrote
That this world of fact we love
Is unsubstantial stuff:
All the rest is silence
On the other side of the wall;
And the silence ripeness,
And the ripeness all.

I am pleased that I discovered Auden's poetic cycle in the course of the reading that I have done for this chapter. His poem suggests a different kind of "practicable"—the link between the understanding of two great poets about the eventual impossibility of illusion to hold back and deny the reality of death. Creativity is not just about life, it is about death as well. His near contemporary, Rowe, reports of Shakespeare that the latter years of his life were spent, as all men of good sense wish theirs may be, in ease, retirement, and conversation with his friends. He has the good fortune to gather a considerable estate, and, in that, to his wish; and is said to have spent the years before his death at his native Stratford. Perhaps Shakespeare's greatest achievement late in life was to be able to give up the need to deal with his inner world through illusion. May we all have such good fortune before we too discover what is on "The Other Side Of The Wall."

Summary

I present a theory of creativity in later life that draws not only on classical psychoanalytic thinking but also the work of the object relations theorists in Great Britain and structuralist accounts of myth. I then critically consider the application of psycholinguistic hypotheses to the understanding of *Hamlet,* particularly the views of Major on the significance and symbolism of proper names.

I then apply this theory to *The Tempest,* the last complete play of Shakespeare, to try to demonstrate that the play represents the reworking and reintegration of such themes as sibling rivalry, usurpation, murderous impulse, and acceptance of mortality in ways that link the work to themes which have already been treated dramatically in earlier plays. I lay particular importance on Shakespeare's acceptance of his own mortality and his renunciation of illusion as a defense against the fear of death. Links between the plays are demonstrated and the essay ends with a reference to the work of Auden, whose poetic style on the theme of the play complements the ideas presented.

REFERENCES

Auden, W. H. 1944. *Collected Poems,* ed. E. Mendelson. New York: Random House.

Chasseguet-Smirgel, J. 1984. "Thoughts on the Concept of Reparation and the Hierarchy of Creative Acts." *International Review of Psychoanalysis* 11:399–406.

Freud, S. [1913] 1955. "The Claims of Psychoanalysis to Scientific Interest." In *Standard Edition,* ed. J. Strachey, vol. 13, pp. 165–89. London: Hogarth Press.

Hildebrand, H. P. 1985. "Object Loss and Development in the Second Half of Life." In *The Race Against Time,* ed. C. Colarusso and R. Nemiroff. New York: Plenum.

———. 1987. "Psychoanalysis and Aging." *Annual of Psychoanalysis* 15.

Jaques, E. 1965. "Death and the Mid-life Crisis." *International Journal of Psycho-Analysis* 46:502–14.

Kott, J. 1964. *Shakespeare, Our Contemporary.* London: Methuen.

Kuper, A. 1986. "Structural Anthropology and the Psychology of Dreams." *Journal of Mind Behaviour* 7 (2–3).

Lévi-Strauss, C. 1962. *Structural Anthropology.* New York: Basic Books.

———. 1981. *The Naked Man: Introduction to a Science of Mythology* 4. London: Cape.

Major, R. 1985. "Names: Proper and Improper." Invited Address, I.C.A. London.

Pollock, G. 1982. The Mourning-Liberation Process and Creativity." *Annual of Psychoanalysis* 10:333–353.

Rycroft, C. 1985. *Psychoanalysis and Beyond.* London: Hogarth Press.

Wright, E. 1984. *Psychoanalytic Criticism: Theory in Practice.* London: Methuen.

DISCUSSION

Dr. Hildebrand asks us to work with him to develop a theory that accounts for the uniqueness of creativity in late life. After rejecting Freud's static notion that after the age of forty or fifty, most individuals are too rigid to be amenable to the demands of psychoanalysis. He calls for an extended theory that accounts for creative productions in later life. The adult developmental framework provides such a theory because it suggests that development is lifelong and that each stage of life, including late adulthood, confronts the individual with new developmental tasks and issues as well as the necessity to relate them to the past.

When understood within this context, late-life creativity is unique; it combines talent with wisdom and the normative developmental conflicts of late adulthood. Wisdom may be defined developmentally as the realistic, empathic understanding of the human condition and is the result of having engaged the major developmental tasks of childhood, adolescence, young and middle adulthood, tempered by the acceptance of the finiteness of time and personal death.

Shakespeare's genius was enhanced by his wisdom. He accepted the basic sexual and aggressive nature of man, illustrated by his consideration of Hamlet's aggression and Miranda's sexuality, and could relate these drives to thought and behavior at any point in the life cycle. He was able to use his own experience, such as the death of his son, to illuminate his understanding of the human condition, and from the vantage point of late life, to speak eloquently to us of the centrality of death, his and ours, in the psychology of life.

In *The Tempest,* a wondrous expression of late-life creativity and wisdom, Shakespeare poignantly and searingly reminds us that the storm of life is temporary and will eventually, inevitably be replaced by whatever is on "the other side of the wall."

Dr. Hildebrand convincingly addresses the unique contribution of late adulthood to creativity through his own work on loss in adulthood and the efforts of George Pollock on mourning. Life is full of losses, some small, some large, which must be mourned in order to be mastered. The ultimate loss, of the self through death, is inevitably anticipated and mourned before it happens. This preoccupation with retrospective and prospective loss and the need to attempt to answer the unanswerable permeate late adulthood and must be expressed in all aspects of mental life, including creativity. It is facilitated, suggests Dr. Hildebrand, by primal fantasies about one's death. We think this preoccupation with loss is a crucial concept, which may be as important to psychic development in the second half of life as primal scene fantasies are to the first. Both grow out of phase-specific developmental preoccupations and have a profound influence on mental life, stimulating healthy and pathological development, and creativity.

Thoughts of personal death, particularly in old age, force one to consider the transmission of power and possessions to the next generation. Parents and children may shrink from the issue or tear themselves apart, King Lear for example, or as Prospero and Shakespeare, deal with the matter more generatively. Prospero's hardheaded realization that his every third thought would be of death allows him to accept his own mortality and work to secure the dynasty, the next generation. If wisdom grows out of the *resolution* of developmental conflict then Shakespeare is indeed wise for recognizing that power should be passed on voluntarily.

It is our belief that some aspects of creativity are possible only in late adulthood, growing as they do out of the fabric of late-life development, out of the inevitable fascination with "the other side of the wall."

20

The Struggle for Otherhood:

Implications for Development in Adulthood of the Capacity to Be a Good-enough Object for Another

MORTON SHANE AND ESTELLE SHANE

Some time ago a patient who had been ill said he was irritated by a friend's calling and waking him up three times in one day to ask about his health. The patient was grumbling that people's concerns about others are not as great as their concerns about themselves and that only their problems lead them to be solicitous of others. He was, of course, commenting on the familiar psychoanalytic defense of altruism as a disguise for other feelings or for expressing unconscious needs. Further, he denied the existence of concern for others and could affirm only self-interest. When I inquired about caring in relationships within his family, he could think of no instances that would demonstrate his conviction, but he remained convinced all the same. Of course as psychoanalysts we can easily make a case for the patient's position, and obviously it is the psychoanalytic view to look for what is hidden or disguised; yet to conclude that only the concealed is significant excludes an important aspect of human behavior. Although ultimately everything is done for selfish reasons, since all action is generated from within the self, nevertheless feigned altruism, which intends to manipulate, intrude, or restrict another (Sandler and Freud 1985) differs from authentic altruism, which aims to expand the other's self and to foster the other's sense of freedom. This discourse with the patient soon converged on transference issues: what kind of self-interest masked the analyst's ostensible concern for him? But the discussion led us to speculate about the differences between neurotic altruism and mature altruism, and the connection of mature altruism to Erikson's stage in adult development, which he termed *generativity.*

In this chapter we address an issue that we believe is a product of adult development: How does an individual attain the status of serving as an "other" for another person's self? What capacities are required to assume this heroic yet ordinary life task? But before addressing this question, we want to introduce it with a much abbreviated history of the concept of adult development.

The contention that psychological development does not end with childhood, but proceeds throughout life, became a distinct and acceptable aspect of psychoanalytic theory only with the work of Erik Erikson in the 1950s. Almost concomitant with Erikson's contribution in both time and significance is Teresa Benedek's (1958; Parens 1975) insight that parenthood is in itself a developmental process. Loewald (1960) advanced the idea that the analytic process includes a developmental valance: The patient's improvement is a result not only of his or her attaining insight but also of the patient's being lifted to a higher level of organization through interaction and identification with the analyst—a process similar to the way in which the child is facilitated to grow through interaction and identification with the parent. Then Margaret Mahler (1968, 1975) conceptualized the process of *separation-individuation* as being recapitulated during all developmental phases through adolescence, to be reexperienced in parenthood. In the early seventies the Commission of the American Psychoanalytic Association (COPER) (Goodman 1977) caused a ferment in the analytic community when it emphasized in its report on the future of psychoanalysis that infant and toddler observational studies of development would create a revolutionary change in both child and adult analytic theory and practice. The COPER prediction was borne out, for example, by the work of Joseph Lichtenberg (1983) and Daniel Stern (1985). Further contributions to the concept of adult development have been made by Roger Gould (1978), whose research suggests specific phases of adult development; D. J. Levinson and colleagues (1978), whose research delineates a male midlife crisis; Calvin Colarusso and Robert Nemiroff (1981, 1985), who focus clinically on transference implications of adult development; and Morton Shane's studies (1977, 1979), which correlate the analytic techniques of the adult and of the child and delineate how the concept of adult development informs both the working-through process and countertransference.

Influential from another vantage point has been self psychology's developmental conceptions. Although the contributions already mentioned were organized in terms of object relations, which included narcissistic as well as libidinal aspects, the full range of narcissistic experience in adult life awaited Kohut's formulations. Beginning with what Kohut had first designated (1971) as "transference-like" experiences, what came to be termed the *self-selfobject relationship* in the analytic situation was later perceived (1977) to lead to self-enhancing transmuting internalizations, which had developmental impact. In time, this self-enhancement was conceptualized as the resumption of normal development in the narcissistic sphere. The line of development of narcissism implies that the mature forms of narcissism, humor, wisdom, and the appreciation of life's transience, are adult attainments. These characteristics are not static but, rather, mature over time. This perspective is consistent with Erikson's view of wisdom as a late developmental achievement. Self psychological elaborations of adult development were contributed to by M. Elson (1984), H. Muslin (1984), and D. M. Terman (1984)

Altruism, the topic with which our discussion began, is another aspect of adult development. The range of experiences in adult life where one serves the needs of another, where that other's emotional requirements are perceived to have priority over one's own comprises a state of being we call *otherhood.* It is a general term that defines the many adult relationships wherein mature empathy and healthy altruism are seen as prerequisite to performing functions on behalf of another person. To illustrate, we can cite being a parent or grandparent, a mentor, a teacher, a physician or attorney, an analyst or therapist, and yes, a friend and lover. For while these last two examples are between two people who share the same gradient, who presumably exist on the same emotional developmental level, and the other examples describe a relationship between two people who are unequal in respect to the function that identifies the relationship between them, there are important respects in which a friend and lover, to function adequately, must become an other dedicated to serving his or her partner's needs and desires. Otherhood requires what Buie (1981) refers to as *full adult empathy.* He says, "It is object centered, not self centered. Adult (object centered) empathy, (as opposed to self centered empathy), is concerned with much more than the other person's giving, non-giving or threatening attitudes towards oneself" (pp. 281–307). Buie adds that in adult empathy there is the capacity to learn about one's objects in their own right. Borrowing from Stern, we can identify three overarching functions in the domain of otherhood: the selfobject function of the self-regulating other; the function of the intersubjective attention-intention- and affect-sharing other where the other is perceived sometimes as selfobject and sometimes as object in itself; and the libidinal-love object function of the sensual-sexual (hedonic) intimacy-sharing other. Whenever we fulfill an other's need to shore up or maintain the other's self or to satisfy the other's libidinal desires—that is, to perceive the other as an object in its own right—we are concomitantly experiencing the other as serving to satisfy our own needs, namely, as selfobject. Moreover, this simultaneity, while always present, can be a source of profound difficulty and can contribute to the derailment of the other's development.

Before I illustrate the domain of otherhood with clinical material from adult analysis, I think it is important to demonstrate the validity and origin of these universal motivational states; that is, the ever-present, lifelong need for both selfobject support and sustenance, and libidinal object gratification and sharing. As predicted in the COPER Report, we can turn to studies on infant development, specifically to Daniel Stern who has summarized extensive current research on infants. Stern offers data from replicated experimental studies organized from the subjective viewpoint of the infant through the achievement of symbolic capacity and language. He delineates four different senses of self, which arise sequentially beginning at birth and persist throughout life. At the age of two months, Stern postulates an emerging sense of the *core self*. The core self depends upon an *essential other*, which Stern calls a self-regulating other: one who regulates, modulates, and controls the infant's self-experience, including such feeling states as security, comfort, excitement, joy, rage, and, later, hatred and destructive aggression. Stern maintains that his concept of the core self in relation to the self-regulating other, based on observations of normal infants, is similar to the selfobject concept of self psychology. As with the selfobject concept, the self-regulating other is necessary for the stability and cohesiveness of the self throughout the life cycle. Thus, we have strong inference based on infant observation that the individual begins life psychologically attached to others and remains attached to others. Hence our contention that the capacity to serve as a self-regulating other (selfobject) becomes an essential attribute of good-enough otherhood.

Stern's next evolving domain of the self, emerging at seven months, is the subjective self in relation to the state-sharing other. Stern emphasizes that this domain of subjectivity does not replace the domain of core relatedness, but emerges alongside it and persists throughout life. And like the self-regulating other, the state-sharing other is vital to the maintenance of the self, creating the difference for the developing individual between psychic human membership and psychic isolation. Thus, in the adult, the capacity to serve as a state-sharing other becomes another essential attribute for good-enough otherhood. Finally, in this same subjective realm of the self, hedonic libidinal state-sharing—the preeminent function in psychoanalytic theory—also emerges, providing the third of the three essential experiences for the developing self. Thus, the capacity to serve as a hedonic libidinal object completes the requirements we are establishing for the good-enough other of otherhood.

Although we have separated these aspects of otherhood for heuristic purposes, just as Stern separated the domains of the self in relation to the corresponding other, we are, of course, talking about dimensions of a single relationship between two people.

In the the clinical material that follows, we will demonstrate how this capacity for good-enough otherhood is developed in the course of adult life, in this instance through psychoanalytic treatment. Because our goal is to illustrate the attainment of mature object-centered altruism and mature empathy with others, as a consequence of empathy with oneself, our focus will stress the patient's relationship with significant others rather than the relationship with the analyst. This, of course, does not accurately reflect the primary focus on the transference as it was experienced by these patients in their treatments. Another feature in this presentation is the emphasis on the experience of these patients as they assume a role in the psychological lives of those important to them. Once again this was not the principal focus of the analysis. Because the inner lives of those who surround our patients can never be directly known by us, the role of our patients in their lives can only be inferred secondhand, through the patients' experiences of it. Therefore, we cannot say with any certainty what kind of parent, lover, friend, our patients actually are in the experience of that significant person; we can only note the changes our patients note, and only from their points of view. With these caveats we will proceed.

Case 1*

Jeffrey E., a young man now in his seventh year of analysis, began working with me in his late twenties. At that time his main problems centered around difficulties in making decisions in his work as an architect and conflicts about marrying his girlfriend Elizabeth.

The patient especially suffered from discomfort over his successful career, yet felt, in relation to his father, as if he were a little boy. The little-boy feeling also emerged after experiencing orgasm during lovemaking. Mr. E. resented the restraints placed upon him by his mother who both controlled and clung to him during his childhood; he remembers especially fighting with her over bedtime during latency, and less clearly, earlier struggles over toilet training. In this context, he recalls quite vividly the shame of making a bowel movement on his potty in the middle of the living room while his older sister and mother looked on. He also felt controlled and ashamed about his burgeoning sexual

*Case material is presented in the first-person singular form for greater immediacy. Patients' names have been changed to preserve their anonymity.

curiosity, associating in particular to the doctor games he had played with a neighborhood girl at age five, and his fascination with that girl's mother. He was certain that his mother and father tried to contain and curtail his sexual interest, primarily through shaming. As one might imagine, a strong transference theme in analysis was the struggle with me for control, especially connected to revealing details of his inner life and adhering to the analytic schedule.

It turned out that the struggle for control was impeding his making a decision to marry Elizabeth. Mr. E. managed to elicit an ultimatum from her so that he could feel bullied into marriage. This typical opposition continued in the marriage as well—with Elizabeth's complaining about his sloppiness and his complaining about her personal cleanliness. During this period of the analysis, working through of his relationship to his mother was substantially accomplished both in the transference and in connection with his wife. A major breakthrough occurred when he discovered his ability not only to provoke an argument with Elizabeth, but, more important, to calm her down and disarm her with a simple expression of his felt love—his understanding of her real pain and neurotic defensiveness, and his sharing with her his own hurt feelings, rage, and sense of vulnerability. That is, by expressing his understanding of her, by finding ways to accept her anger *and* calm her down, and by acknowledging to her that he, too, felt overwhelmed, he was functioning as a mature self-regulating other and state-sharing other. Although he had to learn this capacity for himself, he could attain this ability only when his neurotic tendencies and narcissistic vulnerabilities were attenuated. He had to feel strengthened, more confident, and less ashamed of being a person in his own right—and less guilty for being one—before he was able to give up the need to protect and assert himself by endlessly fighting with his mother via his wife. That is, he had to learn to see his wife as an object in her own right.

One could speculate that life experience with his wife might have gotten him to that point. She might have had to repeat many more times than she did in actuality, "I am not your mother," for this to be accomplished. If this life interaction were in itself effective, it would serve as an example of what, in the spirit of Benedek, could be called marriage as a developmental process. In this case, however, Mr. E. needed to work through that developmental struggle to a significant degree in the transference before he could shift his emotional concern enough to understand his wife's complex inner world: what made her so easy for him to provoke, and what contributed to her reluctance to end arguments once started.

An additional impediment to Mr. E.'s capacity for state-sharing with another involved the mutuality of sensual-sexual experience. His little-boy feelings had steered him toward a sexual partner who would take the initiative in lovemaking so that he might avoid the criticism of forceful domination of the other. Morover he was imbued with a particular cultural ideal familiar to all of us, the *Playboy* girl in interaction with the James Bond man. He could and did describe to me in lyric detail the attributes of his ideal woman. The form and face are by now a cliché, but what my patient came to focus on in particular was what he termed the *Playboy* look. From the pages of that magazine the girl looks unflinchingly at the man, open, direct, and unashamed in her sexual desire. She is without conflict or vulnerability; she is, in his words, "tough." She can take his brute force as well as his neurotic hesitation. She has, of course, no difficulty whatsoever in attaining orgasm in any mode. Unfortunately, this idealized girl, whom my patient believed in fervently, was attainable to him only through masturbation while looking at photographs of her. Yet, as I say, he was utterly convinced of the reality of her being, although he would admit he had never, up to the present, encountered such a woman. The women he had met, including his wife, tended to be rather more complicated, less forthright, and more hesitant. These women experienced varying degrees of difficulty with orgasm, especially as he got to know them better. It was a mystery to him that women who seemed absolutely without sexual problems at the beginning of the relationship would become less spontaneous in their open desire and less sexually responsive as he got to know them better; and he, in turn, would begin to feel more caring and responsible, and as he said, "more like they were family."

If these reactions were not difficult enough to bear, Mr. E. realized that he fell far short of the James Bond model he had established for himself after a humiliating adolescence. James Bond was always ready for sex, no matter what danger surrounded him; and once having seduced the woman, or being seduced by her, he was capable of repeated performance throughout the night or day, impervious to inner doubts, fears, or longings for little-boy passivity.

As one might imagine, it took considerable work over many years to understand why it was necessary for Mr. E. to hold on to this fantasy, undeterred by any brushes with actual people or actual situations. The problem was that he loved Elizabeth, but she was a painful disappointment in this area. He wanted her to wear alluring and revealing nightwear; she preferred flannel jammies. He wished for exotic perfumes; she would barely concede to wash her genitals. During a romantic evening preceding sex he wanted her to wear tight jeans, high heels, and contact lenses. She chose comfortable clothes, sensible shoes, and glasses. Yet, as I said, he loved her faithfully and found her sexually attractive despite what he saw as her efforts to the contrary. The best sexual sharing for both of them were encounters in the middle of the night after both had been sleeping. In those moments they would embrace without much thought, expectation, and feelings of vulnerability, and then return to sleep, keeping the experiences isolated from their mutual neurotic complications. In particular, his tendency after he had an orgasm to feel like a little boy who had soiled himself would be buried in the middle-of-the-night experience.

Mr. E. had to work through his oedipal conflicts and guilt over desiring someone who was like family, as the *Playboy* girl clearly never was. He needed to be reassured that his frustrated destructive aggressiveness toward an intractable and difficult woman would not destroy her, that the actual woman could prove as tough as the tough girl in fantasy. At times he had to accept his feeling like a vulnerable little boy without the fear of being shamed for it by his wife. Through insight and through empathy with himself, Mr. E. was then able to appreciate his wife's doubts about her desirability as a woman and to understand her defenses against sexual openness, which protected her from feeling shame and humiliation not unlike his own. Gradually, he became able at times to accept her as more than a selfobject, an object in her own right whose emotional requirements had priority over his own. I say "at times" because, of course, another's needs can never have absolute priority, nor should they.

Mr. E.'s insight into and understanding of women as persons in their own right were consolidated and enhanced when he and his wife had their first child, a daughter. The following excerpts from Mr. E.'s analyses expand on that consolidation of otherhood toward his daughter.

This patient, then in his fourth year of analysis, had been married for three years. His daughter Kelly was four months old. Mr. E. began the hour with a dream of making love to a desirable forty-year-old woman whom he is attracted to in real life and with whom he fantasizes about having an affair. In the dream they are standing very close to each other in a greenhouse. He gives her a kiss as though she were just waiting for it. The dream stops there. He awakens sexually aroused, thinking of masturbating, but feels conflicted because his wife is next to him and available. He describes the dream as his shameful secret. The next day he reports yet another dream about the same forty-year-old woman, perhaps a continuation of the dream from the night before. He is sitting on a bed with her, kissing her, and feeling her genitals. "I don't remember feeling her breasts," he tells me, "and that isn't the way sex usually goes for me. And while she seemed sexually excited, her genitals are not wet. I was afraid she would smell, but she didn't. She's the kind of person who would put on powder and perfume. I start to have oral sex with her, but she had no pubic hair and her genitals seem kind of different. Most women have a little hump at the front of their genitals, but she didn't seem to have that. I thought I was being too aggressive. When I had oral sex, her genitals didn't smell at all, no odor. I woke up excited from the dream. I thought of getting the *Playboy* magazine, but I didn't feel like masturbating. I felt like I wanted a real woman, not some recollection of a dream."

In talking about these two dreams together, Mr. E. thought about the hairless genital, and associated to changing his daughter's diapers, feeling curious about and attracted to her genitals, so familiar to him and yet so different. He realized suddenly and fully that she was the forbidden woman he was excited by and making love to. The greenhouse stood for the sunlit, airy window by the changing table, and her waiting to be kissed reminded him of Kelly's own excited expectation of love and attention at such moments. It was Kelly, then, with the infantile genital, no breasts, no womanly smell, and the forty years standing for four months. The thought of his wanting to make love to his daughter, whom in his waking life he adored and wished to do everything in his power to protect, appalled him. Yet the two dreams initiated a deeper appraisal of his view of the opposite sex, and a renewed appreciation of their status as unique and precious individuals. More specifically, it was Mr. E.'s first glimpse of the desirable woman Kelly was to become, and the momentous, restrained, and complex role he was destined to serve as her father.

With these dreams and new insight as background, it is possible to appreciate the depth of his concern and his sensitivity when Kelly, at age two-and-a-half, surprised him in the bathroom and asked if she might see his penis. Trying to do what would be best for Kelly, he fumbled at first, and then spontaneously responded, "I don't have time this morning, I have to get to work," leaving her with the impression that it was something to discuss further, maybe in the evening when he returned home. In his hour with me that day, he questioned whether his reply was the right thing to say to her. He thought that what he wanted for her when she became a teenager was to feel free about boys but able to wait to be sexual until someone she really liked was interested in her. He was surprised by my comment that he seemed to be preparing her for this by asking her to wait, rather than just responding to her impulse. On the other hand, he could not endure provoking shame in her for her sexual curiosity and interest (behavior, I know, he wanted to avoid owing to his own experiences of being shamed for his curiosity).

In this illustration we can see the operation of fatherhood potentiating the development of a mature capacity for empathy with another, as well as healthy other-directed altruism. His own sexual impulses emerging in a dream shocked and upset him because they threatened to interfere with his capacity to be an appropriate other for his daughter. However, by the time she turned two-and-a-half, he became more confident of himself as a protector, who could both appreciate her inner world and keep her well-being at the forefront of his interest.

Mr. E. has successfully traversed a developmental path in his adult life, which has facilitated his attaining the mature functions of otherhood. He can serve, when it is appropriate, as a self-regulating, state-sharing other for both his wife and his child. We don't mean to suggest that such capacities constitute legitimate goals in analysis in and of themselves, unless the patient himself perceives them as such, or that they indicate the analysis can be terminated. Analysis is, after all, for the patient and his perceived needs, not for the well-being of those around him. But setting aside this complex issue, we would suggest that the capacity for good-enough otherhood is one measure of successful adult development inside or outside of the analytic sphere.

We will conclude by referring briefly to several clinical instances in which the adult attainment of the capacity to be a good-enough object for another is still in question.

Case 2

Nancy R., three years into analysis, complained bitterly about a good friend's slighting her by canceling a small dinner she had been planning in honor of Ms. R.'s birthday. This would have been the third consecutive year that her friend had celebrated with her in this way. Ms. R. had been looking forward to the dinner, and now was faced with the prospect of being alone on a day significant to her. The depth of her pain, genuine and understandable, was the center of her focus. It was only in passing that she noted the reason for the cancellation: her friend, who had struggled for years to become pregnant, was now bleeding and was terrified that she would have a miscarriage which, in fact, occurred the next week. Ms. R. herself was able to tell me about this event and to notice her own reluctance to commiserate with her friend's grief, which she could not understand. She said, "I always expect her to feel for me, but I cannot, and am not interested in, feeling for her."

The patient is a very intelligent woman who has an unusual capacity to introspect. She was perfectly able to see the irony in the situation, that she who expects so much from others is unable to reciprocate or even to empathize with them. This patient illustrates an underdeveloped capacity for mature altruism and object-centered empathy. Whether she will develop this in the course of analysis I cannot say, and of course, it is not the focus of our work together. But the patient senses the disparity between what a good friend is able to give her and how much less she can do for her friend. She is concerned that when a good friend does not provide for her, that friend is no longer of interest to her. Needless to say, this struggle goes on in the transference; and for this patient, I am certain the capacity for otherhood, should it develop, will do so only through a transference resolution.

Case 3

Another patient, a highly successful professional who prides himself on his intellectual ability and attainment, has two children: one, like himself, academically accomplished for her young age, and the other, while very likable, outgoing, and engaging, a reluctant student more concerned with sports and friendships. The father struggles to like the second daughter as much as the first, but is confronted with his own narcissistic pleasure in the child more like himself. His conclusion that the second child is not smart enough to be a professional, though she is only in the second grade, leads him to choose a less expensive, less high-powered private school for her. This choice means that she will lose her place in the social and sports world she has established and will suffer by comparison with her sister. It is clear that this man wants to punish his daughter for disappointing him and for subjecting him to narcissistic injury. This unconscious intention overrides his preconscious intellectual understanding that there are several ways of being intelligent. In fact, as he told me, an outgoing, charming professional makes her way much better in this world than a bookish, intellectual, constricted one. Because my patient is helpless in his own need to use his daughters to serve selfobject functions for him, he is unable, as yet, to assume a good-enough other role for them. In an attempt to strengthen his own self-esteem, this patient may be in danger of contributing to the derailment of his younger daughter's development.

We have presented in this chapter an analytic example illustrating the attainment in adult life of the capacity to serve as a good-enough object, that is, a good-enough other for a self. We have also shown, more briefly, instances in which this capacity is not yet available. Data from observational studies as synthesized by Stern substantially support our contention that the need for an other to perform functions for the self is necessary throughout life, and they delineate the nature of these functions.

REFERENCES

Anthony, E. J., and Benedek, T. 1970. *Parenthood: Its Psychology and Psychopathology.* Boston: Little, Brown.

Benedek, T. 1959. "Parenthood As a Developmental Phase: A Contribution to Libido Theory." *Journal of the American Psychoanalytic Association* 7:389–417.

Buie, D. H. 1981. "Empathy: Its Nature and Limitations." *Journal of the American Psychoanalytic Association* 29:281–307.

Cohen, R. S.; Cohler, J.B.; and Weissman, S.H. 1984. *Parenthood: A Psychodynamic Perspective.* New York: Guilford.

Colarusso, C.A., and Nemiroff, R.A. 1981. *Adult Development: A New Dimension in Psychoanalytic Theory and Practice.* New York: Plenum.

Elson, M. 1984. "Parenthood and the Transformations of Narcissism." In *Parenthood: A Psychodynamic Perspective,* ed. R.S. Cohen et al., pp.297–314. New York: Guilford.

Erikson, E. [1950] 1962. *Childhood and Society.* New York: W. W. Norton.

Freud, A. 1965. *Normality and Pathology in Childhood.* New York: International Universities Press.

Gould, R. 1978. *Transformation, Growth and Change in Adult Life.* New York: Simon & Schuster.

Goodman, S., ed. 1977. *Psychoanalytic Education and Research: The Current Situation and Future Possibilities.* New York: International Universities Press.

Kohut, H. 1971. *Analysis of the Self.* New York: International Universities Press.

———. 1977. *The Restoration of the Self.* New York: International Universities Press.

Levinson, D.J.; Darrow, C.N.; Klein, E.S.; Levinson, M.H.; and McKee, B. 1978. *The Seasons of a Man's Life.* New York: Knopf.

Lichtenberg, J. 1983. *Psychoanalysis and Infant Research.* Hillsdale, N. J.: Laurence Erlbaum.

Loewald, H., 1960. "On the Therapeutic Action of Psychoanalysis." *International Journal of Psycho-Analysis* 41:16–33.

Mahler, M. 1968. *On Human Symbiosis and the Viscissitudes of Individuation.* New York: International Universities Press.

Mahler, M.; Pine, F.; and Bergman, A. 1975. *The Psychological Birth of the Human Infant.* New York: Basic Books.

Muslin, H. 1984. "On the Resistance to Parenthood: Consideration on the Self of the Father." In *Parenthood: a Psychodynamic Perspective,* ed. R.S. Cohen et al., pp. 315–25. New York.: Guilford.

Nemiroff, R. A., and Colarusso, C.A. 1985. *The Race Against Time.* New York: Plenum.

Parens, H. 1975. Panel Report, "Parenthood as a Developmental Phase." *Journal of the American Psychoanalytic Association* 23:154–65.

Sandler J., and Freud, A. 1985. *The Analysis of Defense: The Ego and the Mechanisms of Defense Revisited.* New York: International Universities Press.

Shane, M. 1977. "A Rationale for Teaching Analytic Technique Based on a Developmental Orientation and Approach." *International Journal of Psycho-Analysis* 58:95–110.

———. 1979. "The Developmental Approach to 'Working Through' in the Analytic Process." *International Journal of Psycho-Analysis* 60:375–82.

Stern, D. 1985. *The Interpersonal World of the Infant.* New York: Basic Books.

Terman, D.M. 1984. "Affect and Parenthood: The Impact of the Past on the Pre-

sent." In *Parenthood: a Psychodynamic Perspective,* ed. R.S. Cohen et al., pp. 326–37. New York: Guilford.
Vaillant, G.E. 1977. *Adaptation to Life.* Boston: Little, Brown.

DISCUSSION
Doryann Lebe

This chapter stimulated many ideas, but because of space limitations I shall focus on just two. The first concerns the difference between the normal age ranges for the development of "otherhood" in men and women. In general, women develop their capacity for empathy, for "otherhood," earlier than men do—how much earlier I am not sure. I suspect that on average there is about a ten-year difference, with women's adult capacity for otherhood established by their twenties and men's by their thirties. Of course, as with many psychosocial behaviors, there is more variation *within* the sexes than *between* them, and one can easily find men who develop their empathic or nurturing capacities very early.

One reason for the general difference between the sexes is that the selfobject functions of otherhood are usually encouraged in and taught to little girls but rarely to little boys. Sisters are expected to care for younger siblings, and daughters are expected to be concerned about whether their father's or mother's needs are being met. Even these days, females remain the more active caregivers in the family. In a cross-cultural study by B. Whiting and C. P. Edwards (1973), boys who had to care for younger siblings and do household chores were, as adults, much more attuned to the needs of others than counterparts who had not borne such responsibilities. The obvious conclusion is that differential emphases in early socialization do affect the development of the capacity for "otherhood."

The difference between the ages at which women and men develop skills of empathy and nurturing can become a major factor in intimate male-female relationships, particularly when partners are in their thirties and forties. A disparity in the acquisition of these capacities, whether it is the female or the male whose "otherhood" is late to bloom, can cause difficulties in the relationship. Someone who expects more mutuality from a mate than that person is capable of will be left feeling deprived. Women in particular experience a high incidence of depression in their late twenties and early thirties. At a time when they may be holding an outside job, caring for young children, and shouldering most of the household tasks, being "good-enough" for everyone in the environment becomes overwhelming if there is no one to "be there" for oneself.

The second idea I wish to explore here is how the development of otherhood is encouraged or achieved in the process of psychoanalysis. I agree with the Shanes that if the neurotic proclivities and narcissistic vulnerabilities of our patients can be attenuated, the patients will learn for themselves. If we, as therapists, become good-enough others for them, they feel regulated, more zestful, because of our sharing of affect, and they experience pleasure from the intimacy of psychoanalysis. If this is internalized, the consequent structural changes can rapidly increase their capacities for otherhood.

For example, a married woman in her late thirties with two young children entered analysis desiring to control her anger toward her children and husband. If the children spilled milk, did not do their homework, or fought with their friends, she felt God was punishing her for being a bad person, a bad mother. Anything less than perfection in them was seen as evidence that she was defective and was being punished. The patient felt victimized by her children and envied other adults whom she saw as having more success, better children, et cetera. She would lose control, fly into rages, screaming, swearing, and at times hitting the children. These episodes were followed by terrible remorse. In the seventh month of analysis the patient described how her daughter had dropped a Slurpy in the car, and at first she had laughed and helped her daughter wipe it up. However, when some stain got on her own shirt, she began yelling, "You idiot, never again, you ruin everything!"

In the account, she said, "I saw it was inappropriate. That evening I was angry with myself, feeling terrible. Things changed when I took your voice in, you will still accept me. It is OK. I thought, I could do it for myself too. There is hope. It is not the end of the world. I am scared to grow up. I will have to put up with more shit. If I am little, God will not give me as much. Change can occur by finding soothing acceptance that I internalize."

The next day the patient came in tearful, saying that she felt analysis was at a different level. "I can take in your caring for me. I don't have to be always right." Then she reminded me of her first dream. In the dream, I said I was interested in her, but I was being phony, like her mother. I was more interested in my needs than hers. Now she feels that was her transference and not really me. She knew it before, but did not feel it. Now she felt it.

The next two sessions were again different. She cried when thinking about her aging father. He was immobilized, alone. How sad it was for him. Previously she felt victimized because after her parents separated, her father chose to live near her. She considered him a fool and a burden. This day she said, "I'm the only one who can make him feel a whole lot better. I can do that. It has been so childish of me."

We can observe at close range the effects of the analytic relationship on this woman. Since she has begun to attenuate her neurotic struggles, internalize me as a soothing selfobject, and decrease her narcissistic vulnerabilities, she can now serve as a self-soothing object for herself. This change has led to greater object-centered empathy and a healthy altruism toward the members of her family. The patient has noted her own unempathic behavior and fear of growing up. We can readily observe in her the adult developmental push toward a healthy altruism and object-centered empathy, or "otherhood."

REFERENCES

Whiting, B., and Edwards, C. P. 1973. "A Cross-cultural Analysis of Sex Differences in the Behavior of Children Aged Three through Eleven." *The Journal of Social Psychology* 91:171–188.

21

Women Leaders:

Achievement and Power

CAROL C. NADELSON

When the nineteenth-century author George Sand wrote "Work is not man's punishment. It is his reward and his strength, his glory and his pleasure," the link she made between work and pleasure was a relatively new idea. Sigmund Freud (1930), somewhat later, proposed a duality of love and work, stating that human life had "a two-fold foundation: the compulsion to work, which was created by external necessity, and the power of love" (p. 79). His contemporary, the actress Eleanora Duse, emphasized the integration more forcefully when she said, "work also means freedom. Without it, even the miracle of love is only a cruel deception" (Nardi 1942, p. 107).

Work has come to be seen as a means to consolidate identity and self-image. In achievement there is gratification, an expression of creativity and ambition, and an assertion of values and beliefs. As Freud (1930) noted, "One gains the most if one can sufficiently heighten the yield of pleasure from the sources of physical and intellectual work" (p. 79). He spoke of "an artist's joy in creating . . . or a scientist's in solving problems or discovering truths" (p. 79).

Obviously, work can also be dull and exhausting, stressful and disappointing. It expresses inner needs and offers rewards even when it serves defensive purposes, yielding relief from guilt, escape from other life stresses, and a means for channeling energy and ameliorating pain. Work

502

has been called a sublimation, and its component urge to mastery a sublimation of aggressive impulses.

What is most striking is that formulations about work and achievement have rarely depicted women as deriving the gratification or rewards from it that men do. Despite the realities of today's world, work continues to be conceptualized as masculine activity, with relatively little attention paid to its importance or its patterns and styles for women.

Definitions of gender role with regard to work and achievement are not seen as components of "femininity," and woman's personal goals are still considered secondary to serving the needs of others, particularly the family. Women's investment in interpersonal relationships rather than in work-related activity has become the means by which power, effectiveness, and reinforcement of self-esteem are experienced (Gilligan 1982).

In adolescence, as young women become socialized into adult feminine roles, competitiveness and ambition are often perceived as threats to an evolving sense of femininity and as impediments to relationships with men. As gender roles become consolidated, there continue to be differences in expectations and pressures about work and career. Throughout adolescence and early adulthood men are reinforced in more focused occupational directions and link their identity with work roles. Although women increasingly incorporate career goals into their internalized self-expectation, they are aware of their ticking biological clock during those years, and focus on reproductive goals as well (Nadelson, Notman, and Bennett 1978).

Many young women in careers demanding autonomy and assertiveness also experience conflict because early internalized prohibitions do not support these traits. Internal conflict between past identifications, past expectations, and the demands of the contemporary situation are often generated. In fact, self-esteem in women frequently diminishes as they learn to recognize and express aggression or its derivatives—assertion, achievement, competence, success (Nadelson et al. 1982). The manifestations of this lowered self-esteem can include a sense of failure or worthlessness and even depression and anxiety. It is still difficult for a woman to say "I want to be chief justice," or "I want to be president of the company."

Although changes in career opportunities have led to higher female school enrollments for many traditionally male-dominated professions such as medicine, architecture, engineering, the sciences, and law, there continues to be a wide gap between the proportion of women in professional training and those who have attained positions of leadership in their fields (Suter and Miller 1973; Epstein 1975; Kilson 1976). In this chapter I will explore the role of work, achievement, and power in women's lives,

considering the experiences and conflicts of women leaders and our attitudes toward them, as well as the cumulative data documenting the resistances and influences that have affected women as they moved into leadership roles.

Women in Power: A Historical Persepctive

Just over a century ago, Benjamin Disraeli ([1844], 1933) stated that "the
only useless life is woman's." That opinion was notable, and odd, for a
man who was twice prime minister for Victoria, one of the world's most
influential monarchs. But how far have we actually advanced from his
stated view? How do we understand society's ambivalence toward woman
leaders? Will his opinion perpetuate the perception and actuality of
women's experience as leaders?

To formulate answers to these questions one can explore the experiences
and contributions of notable women leaders: Joan of Arc, Elizabeth I,
Catherine the Great, Victoria and, more recently, Indira Gandhi, Golda
Meir, and Margaret Thatcher, to name a few. Throughout history there
have also been other notable and influential women in government, the
arts and sciences, and literature. That many of these women are not well
known to us may say more about those who write history than those who
make it. What accounts for this neglect? Although a thorough exploration
of this issue would encompass more than is possible in this chapter, we
must keep in focus that women's contributions have generally been
viewed through their child-bearing functions, not through their place in
cultural, political, or economic history. This distortion has occurred despite
women's documented achievements in all of those areas. Recent historians
have rediscovered and reminded us of the proud legacy of women's contributions.

If we begin in ancient Egypt, we note that the woman pharaoh, Hatshep-
sut, is often left off pharaonic lists, and her enormous influence on the art
and culture of her times has not been fully appreciated until recently. In
biblical times, some women do appear as heroic and significant figures;
they were acknowledged in the ancient world, although history has often
dimmed the extent of their influence. During the Crusades and in the
Middle Ages, women contributed to the founding of hospitals and the
establishment of public health systems. By the tenth and eleventh centuries, women studied medicine, wrote textbooks, and taught at universities.
In 1405 Christine de Pisan wrote an eloquent discourse critical of traditional views of femininity and feminine roles, challenging male authority

on that subject. (It is ironic that almost six hundred years later the discourse is so similar to that of today!)

Although the beginning of the fifteenth century can be considered the beginning of "modern" feminism, by the end of that century the Inquisition and the cultural acceptance of a view of women that presumed their "spiritual and mental" inferiority prevailed (Malleus Maleficarum 1486). What allowed that view to take hold, yet shortly afterward enabled one of the world's most powerful rulers, Elizabeth I, to rule Britain and an extensive empire?

Even Elizabeth directly addressed the debate about men's and women's nature and her own ambivalence about her gender, stating, "I have the heart of a man, not a woman" (Sitwell 1962, p. 72). Sitwell, her biographer, notes, "And the Houses of Parliament, to their astonishment, were soon to know what lay in that heart of fire, that temper of the finest steel, that man's brain in a woman's body. She ruled Parliament as her father had done, spoke to them as a king, not as a woman" (p. 71).

In the eighteenth century, Catherine of Russia was called the Great. She ruled after ascending to the throne by her own stealth and determination. A powerful sovereign, she extended her empire and wielded enormous influence, despite many personal peccadillos and a lifestyle that would have been easier for the populace to tolerate in a man. It is interesting that she took the throne after the death of her husband and did not remarry during her rule. As did Elizabeth I of England and Christina of Sweden, she safeguarded her political power by remaining unmarried, thereby eliminating a husband who would assume the power of the monarchy.

These women rulers were the objects of respect, awe, fear, and ridicule. They were not unlike the male leaders of their times but were visibly at odds with prevailing views of femininity. The historian Amaury de Riencourt (1974) has stated, "Few women have been granted the opportunity to rule large states or empires, but most of those who did outperformed most male rulers, save for a few exceptional, and not always beneficent, geniuses. From Cleopatra to Russia's Catherine the Great and India's Indira Gandhi, they have proved that they were matches for their male rivals; and this for an obvious reason: an effective ruler governs by suggestion rather than coercion, and that rule by suggestion presupposes a social sensitivity and a consideration for others which men often lack" (p. 338). He also notes that women with power who are at the top of the social strata often compensate for the usual inferior position of women in the patriarchal structure and "prove to be more ruthless and deadly than the male in their own game of power politics" (p. 237). He cites as examples Salome, Cleopatra, and Eleanor of Aquitaine.

In this century, Indira Gandhi, Golda Meir, and Margaret Thatcher have been most often cited as women who command respect and awe as well as fear, anger, and ambivalence. In their personal accounts many women leaders tell us of the impact of isolation and lack of support, the constant questioning of their femininity, the perception of their deviance as women, and the expectation that they cannot be women and lead.

Jeane Kirkpatrick (1984), former ambassador to the United Nations, noted, "I've come to see here a double bind. If a woman seems strong, she is called 'tough,' and if she doesn't seem strong, she's found not strong enough to occupy a high level job in a crunch." She added, "terms like tough and confrontational express a certain very general surprise and disapproval at the presence of woman in arenas in which it is necessary to be—what for males would be considered—normally assertive."

Women in Power: Contemporary Views

While we applaud the contemporary picture of progress regarding the status and condition of women, there has not been substantial or permanent change in the attitudes and values that shape our behaviors. This resistance is true in academia as well as in business, politics, medicine, and other fields. One need only look at recent emphasis on the "feminization of poverty" to understand that most women continue to remain an underclass.

Theodore (1986) in her book on women in academia, noted that academic women's status remained virtually the same between 1970 and 1983 and in certain areas their position worsened. She reported that women constitute less than one-fourth of college and university faculties across all disciplines and professional areas and that they were concentrated in the lower ranks in nonladdered, untenured positions, working primarily in traditional women's fields, with predominantly female students. In all types of academic institutions, women progressed more slowly toward promotion than did men and they were disproportionately involved in activities that would not reap rewards or tenure. They were conspicuously absent in leadership positions. Academic women, like other working women, also received less compensation and other benefits than their male counterparts, even for comparable positions.

Women continue to be sparsely represented on granting agencies and private foundations sponsoring research, as well as in policy-making positions. They are not well represented in publishing or on the editorial boards of scholarly journals. Likewise, women are absent from the power structure in administration and are barely represented as deans, presidents, and chancellors. A small minority serve as department heads, and in those fields in which the students are substantially female, men tend to be the administrators responsible for policy decisions (Theodore 1986).

Since criteria for promotion, tenure, and appointments can never be entirely objective, how one defines good scholarship or "future promise" is not as specifically defined as many have assumed it to be. In fact, since we know that choosing a specialized area or inquiry may be considered lower status or even trivial, contributions in so-called minor areas, such as Women's Studies, can be demeaned.

The picture is not very different in other fields. Less than 10 percent of judges, 12 percent of local elected officials, 5 percent of the United States House of Representatives, and 2 percent of the Senate are women. In 1984 there were sixteen thousand men on major corporate boards, while there were only four hundred women. Despite the dramatic influx of women into the corporate world, barely 5 percent of middle and 1 percent of top management are women, and few women are full partners in law firms or hold major banking positions (American Association of University Women 1988).

Among the reasons given for the discrepancy is that younger women have not yet accumulated the experience necessary for leadership positions, or that they are not interested because of family responsibilities. That these reasons are questionable is attested to by data indicating that women continue to rise more slowly in organizational structures than comparably qualified men, despite their commitment and hard work. Moreover, while family issues are of concern and present more conflict for women than for men, women do pursue their goals, these pressures notwithstanding. One study of women physicians reported that family size and achievement were not correlated (Westling-Wilkstrand et al. 1970).

Women's Experience as Achievers

Women are generally aware from early in life that unanticipated and even surprising responses occur by virtue of gender-related expectations, even in those who are manifestly egalitarian. This bias is often attributed to early socialization and to the differences in life experiences. Those with power can rarely understand the experience of those whose commitment, qualifications, and capabilities are questioned and doubted at every juncture.

Many have described the socialization of males as more akin to management training than that of females. Adults, including parents, respond differently to male and female children, contributing to their different developmental experiences; this socialization has implications for future behavior. For example, boys until recently were far more likely to participate in team sports, often with those they disliked, and compete with those they liked, but girls have generally felt more conflicted about competition with friends (Block 1982). The implications of these different experiences may be important for later achievement.

J. Kagan and H. A. Moss (1962) found that childhood passivity and dependence predicted passivity and dependence in adulthood for women, but not for men. They suggested that a passive, dependent boy would experience great social pressure to suppress those behaviors, but a girl would not. Furthermore, behavior that deviated markedly from sex-role standards would be inhibited because of a child's desire to model himself or herself after positively valued role models and to avoid social rejection.

Since life choices are substantially influenced by parents, as well as peers, teachers, and others in their environment, it is important to explore these communications, especially regarding gender role expectations. One study reported that students who saw their parents as emphasizing and favoring careers were more likely to share that view (Hauser and Garvey 1985). Both traditional and nontraditional women selected careers consistent with what they believed significant men in their lives favored. Women's career choices were also influenced by the perception of their mothers as role models.

Another investigator noted that college seniors who were nontraditional pioneers had better-educated mothers than those who were traditional (Crawford 1978). Women who were raised by working mothers tended to be more career-oriented than those who were not, particularly if their mothers had positive attitudes about employment.

Margaret Hennig and Anne Jardim (1977) studied a group of women managers and found that most often they were only children or had no male siblings. In childhood, these women enjoyed a close relationship with a father who did not emphasize sex roles. They reported that both parents allowed them to develop their own interests and strengths without feeling denigrated or controlled. Although they perceived themselves to be "social deviants," they were successfully able to adapt to this sense of being different. Early in their lives autonomous functioning became important to them.

Although some studies provide us with contradictory data on specific parental interactions, the influence of family on future career direction and achievement is clear. For example, one study of women physicians (Rushing 1964) reported that academically achieving women had poorer early family relationships than less achieving women and tended to give the worst ratings to the quality of the father-daughter relationship.

The disparities in the data invite a number of interpretations. On the one hand, women who perceive their fathers as distant may interpret this distance as a reaction to their imagined inadequacy. For such women successful professional achievement would compensate for this inadequacy and would help them gain paternal acceptance. On the other hand, high-achieving women may enter careers that are traditionally male as part of a wish to establish closeness with their fathers.

The experiences of women in corporate life have been studied by Rosabeth Moss-Kanter (1977), who described what psychotherapists would call *transferential aspects* of the roles of women. She speaks of these roles as mother, seductress, maiden aunt, or kid sister rather than colleague and peer. M. E. Milwid (1982), also citing the good-daughter role, reported that these women disclosed their need to be deferential, to be nonthreatening, and to see the men they worked with in family roles. They acknowledged that they must learn to be more assertive, firm, and self-confident. She noted that "the psychological baggage women bring to masculine culture is packed with the need to be nice and to be liked." These transference-countertransference responses tend to persist and are present in individuals growing up in every culture and every generation. They may require generations to change.

The so-called "feminine" characteristics of responsiveness, accommodation, and nurturance make it difficult for many women to assume and project authority. They may feel uncomfortable about relinquishing these traits or allowing the emergence of others that have been characterized as masculine. Conflict is generated between their needs for competence and success and the comfort of a socially sanctioned role and style, despite its lack of fit or reward. There is a risk to self-esteem and a loss of more traditional manifestations of affirmation when familiar postures are relinquished.

As Moulton (1977) has indicated, women are accustomed to assuming a "good-girl" role, often achieving success by maintaining a self-effacing facade, avoiding situations of possible disapproval, relying on authoritative directives, and not saying no. They are unaccustomed to open rivalry or hard negotiation. Some research suggests that women become anxious after asserting themselves, whereas men experience relief (Dunbar et al. 1979).

Cultural expectations also have a substantial impact on women's performance. Women's opinions have been observed to spark negative and resistant responses, and their credibility in positions of leadership has often been questioned (Nadelson 1987). Many women leaders confirm these findings and perceive them as substantial problems in their careers despite apparent success.

A recent National Women's Political Caucus survey (*New York Times*, 17 August 1987), repeating what other surveys have noted regarding the qualities associated with women, included compassion, honesty, the ability to compromise, and being "moral and upright." The qualities most often associated with men included toughness, decisiveness, emotional stability, and being able to handle a crisis. "The rub comes when one considers that the public does not seem to associate traditionally 'female' character traits with leadership."

In another survey, college students were asked to list the qualities they sought in an ideal presidential candidate. They listed dominance, aggressiveness, and the ability to take risks (*Boston Globe*, 21 September 1987). Again, these are qualities that have been traditionally associated with men. Thus, "in order to broaden her appeal, any woman candidate needs to remind voters of her unique qualifications—some of which are at odds with deeply held notions of leadership" (*Boston Globe*, 1 November 1987).

Because women are socialized to achieve vicariously and to measure their success by the success of individuals to whom they are related, with whom they identify, and to whose success they have contributed, they are often inexperienced in acting on their own behalf (Lipmen-Blumen 1983). Men in positions of authority lead men they predominantly consider peers and competitors; women lead men to whom they are socialized to be less assertive. These factors inevitably influence the expectations and success of women in leadership roles.

The assumption of leadership roles by women is further complicated by the lack of peer support and of mentors or models functioning in similar roles or assuming equivalent responsibilities. Women leaders must cope with their own and others' resistance to their adopting attitudes and behaviors necessary for effective leadership and must face the internal conflict generated by contradictory self-perceptions and expectations.

The power of gender-role expectations is illustrated by a description of the analysis of a series of Tavistock-type group experiences held at a university undergoing turmoil as the result of an initiative by women to gain greater access to positions of power and authority. Mayes (1979) found significant and pervasive behavioral differences depending on the gender of the group leader. In female-led groups, men described feelings of loss of control because their ability to function "as males" was hampered, and they expressed relief and a "return to normalcy" when they were able to join male-led groups. Initially the women in female-led groups were assertive, instrumental, and task-oriented. However, over time their assertiveness and identification with their leader dwindled, and they began to vie for male attention in traditional ways. Women who refused to relinquish their assertive roles received the majority of male and female anger. Groups with male leaders reported traditional sex-role patterns of behavior in both men and women.

Different attitudes toward male and female leaders have important implications for perceptions of leadership as well as for performance. One study noted that in order to have power a mentor should fill the "masculine" role of team player and possess needed information and expertise (Yoder et al. 1985). Since women are perceived to have fewer sources of power than do men (Johnson 1976), potential female mentors may consider themselves inadequate for the role, and novices may avoid female mentors in favor of males whom they perceive to have more power. Thus, although there are few women who could be mentors, those few might be disregarded as mentors by other women.

A recent study of women leaders, including vice presidents and managers, in male-dominated fields such as banking, law, and architecture, reported that even these "successful" women felt excluded from office networks, and resistance to them in higher echelons (Milwid 1982). They experienced the intractability of male orientation and culture in their fields. Earlier in their lives, they believed that the revolution had been won and that gender was no longer a limitation to advancement. Few anticipated that sexism would continue to affect profoundly their professional development and lives.

It is sobering to note that a report issued by the National Research Council indicates that sex segregation in employment has not changed much since 1900 (Reskin and Hartmann 1986). The report suggests that to restore the imbalance, 30 percent of workers would have to move into job categories dominated by the opposite sex. It concludes that women's occupational choices and preferences cannot account for occupational segregation by sex and indicates that the barriers are the result of persistent effects of discriminatory laws, personnel practices, and beliefs about women's proper roles and traits. Fear of sexual distraction and concern about women in supervisory and leadership positions are contributing factors. The report states that the discrepancy in men's and women's career paths is reinforced by early rearing patterns, training programs, and even by the tax structure. Thus a more realistic and less enthusiastic view of the future suggests that change is likely to be slow.

Reinforcing this note of pessimism, Moss-Kanter (1987) pointed to another hurdle: the rules for promotion in industry seem to be changing, setting back many women who have achieved management positions. A "glass ceiling" phenomenon, although not visible from below, presents itself as an impenetrable barrier as one comes crashing into it while ascending the career escalator (Jones 1987).

Men and women view those concerns differently, a contrast undoubtedly related to their disparate life experiences and their perceptions of problems. A recent survey at a medical school searching for a dean revealed that 0.1 percent of the women students and faculty and 50 percent of the men rejected the idea that *more* women leaders are needed in medicine (Scadron et al. 1982). This revelation has important implications for affirmative action policies and for the future of women should those policies be discarded.

Differences in perception and life experience cannot be ignored. They engender the double standards and insensitivity that can be seen most blatantly when one listens to some of the questions put to women. "When Golda [Meir] was asked by a journalist how it felt to be a woman minister she told him tartly, 'I wouldn't know. I've never been a man minister' " (Mann 1971, p. 182). Representative Patricia Schroeder, announcing her interest in being a candidate for the United States presidency, was asked, "Why are you running as a woman?" She stated, "I never knew I had an option" (*New York Times,* 16 August 1987). These queries would sound quite odd if "man" were substituted for "woman"!

The polarization of masculine and feminine traits and the assumption of male values affects us at every level. How does it feel for a woman to be complimented for so-called masculine traits? Or to be complimented by attending to an assumed polarization? Golda Meir's political advisor, Simcha Dinitz, "summed up her most unique combinations of leadership attributes in these words: 'She has the best qualities of a woman—intuition, insight, sensitivity, compassion—plus the best qualities of a man—strength, determination, practicality, purposefulness. So we're lucky. We have double qualities—in one person' " (Mann 1971, p. 231).

Probably the most flagrant recent example of the double standard related to Representative Schroeder's crying when she announced that she would not run for president. The response of the public and the media was profoundly ambivalent. She noted, "Many people said that when I cried—and I will never apologize for that—I drowned the prospects for women for the rest of the decade" (*Boston Globe,* 2 February 1989). She has also pointed out that men at emotionally charged events in recent years were either praised or not remarked upon when they behaved similarly (*New York Times,* 30 September 1987).

Golda Meir's poignant comment when she was elected is perhaps what we can hope for in our leaders. "I have often been asked how I felt at that moment, and I wish that I had a poetic answer to the question. I know that tears rolled down my cheeks and that I held my head in my hands when the voting was over, but all that I recall about my feelings is that I was dazed. I had never planned to be Prime Minister; I had never planned any position, in fact . . . I only knew that now I would have to make decisions every day that would affect the lives of millions of people, and I think perhaps that is why I cried" (Meir 1975, pp. 378–79).

That emotional awareness expressed by tears can be viewed as a sign of weakness reflects an important gender-related bias due to its prevalence among women. A surgical colleague once asked me whether a woman resident was emotionally stable because she sometimes cried in the operating room when the situation was tense or the outcome poor. He was not aware that her emotional expression was in response to the same tension that he and other male residents experienced; but they found losing their temper or hurling an instrument across the room more acceptable. The response was different, but no better or worse. Women continue to live with conflicting expectations, especially when they achieve in nontraditional or "masculine" arenas, but feel compromised by those conflicts.

Such dissonance can undermine women's self-esteem and affect performance. E. S. Person (1982) commented on the impact of labeling professional aspirations wrongly as masculine aspirations as another manifestation of a gender bias often not appreciated fully in its significance. Many authors have pointed to the problem of fear of deviance in women, especially Person (1982), who noted "fear of engaging in behavior that contradicts female gender-role behavior (a concept internalized from the culture) and thereby threatens feminine identity." The consequences of perceived deviance, such as success in a masculine area, may be the loss of love, isolation, and abandonment. Thus, successful women who attribute their success to external events rather than to their own efforts often collude with the male view. The result is that the achievement of success costs far more for women than is generally acknowledged.

REFERENCES

American Association of University Women. 1988. Telephone communication to author.

Block, J. H. 1982. "Psychological Development of Female Children and Adolescents." In *Women: A Developmental Perspective,* ed. P. Berman and E. Rainey (NIH Publ. #82-2298). Bethesda, Md.: Department of Health and Human Services, Public Health Service, National Institute of Health.

Carroll, L. [1872] 1977. *Through the Looking Glass.* New York: St. Martin's Press.

Crawford, J. D. 1978. "Career Development and Career Choice in Pioneer and Traditional Women." *Journal of Vocational Behavior* 12:129–39.

de Pisan, C. [1405] 1982. *The Book of the City of Ladies.* Reprint. New York: Persea Books.

de Riencourt, A. 1974. *Sex and Power in History.* New York: David McKay.

Disraeli, B. [1844] 1933. *Coningsby, Book IV.* New York: Scholarly Reprints.

Dunbar, C., Edwards, V., Gede, E., Hamilton, J., Sniderman, M. S., Smith, V., and Whitfield, M. 1979. "Successful Coping Styles in Professional Women." *Canadian Journal of Psychiatry* 24:43–46.

Epstein, C. 1975. "Encountering the Male Establishment: Sex-Status Limits on Women's Careers in the Professions." *American Journal of Sociology* 15:6–9.

Freud, S. [1930] 1961. "Civilization and Its Discontents." In *Standard Edition,* ed. J. Strachey, vol. 21, p. 79. London: Hogarth Press.

Gilligan, C. 1982. *In a Different Voice.* Cambridge, Mass.: Harvard University Press.

Graves, P., and Thomas, C. 1985. "Correlates of Mid-Life Career Achievement Among Women Physicians." *Journal of the American Medical Association* 254:781–87.

Hauser, B., and Garvey, C. 1985. "Factors That Affect Non-Traditional Vocational Enrollment Among Women." *Psychology of Women Quarterly* 9:105–17.

Henning, M., and Jardim, A. 1977. *The Managerial Woman.* New York: Doubleday, Anchor Press.

Johnson, P. 1976. "Women and Power: Toward a Theory of Effectiveness." *Journal of Social Issues* 32:99–110.

Jones, L. (President of Women in Management): cited in Brophy, B., with Linnon, N. "Why Women Executives Stop Before the Top." *U.S. News and World Report* 29 December 1986, 5 January 1987.

Kagan, J., and Moss, H. A. 1962. *Birth to Maturity.* New York: John Wiley.

Kilson, M. 1976. "The Status of Women in Higher Education." *Journal of Women in Culture and Society* 1:935–942.

Kirkpatrick, J. 1984. Remarks delivered to the Women's Forum, New York City, 19 December.

Lipman-Blumen, J. 1983. "Emerging Patterns of Female Leadership in Formal Organizations: Must the Female Leader Go Formal?" In *The Challenge of Change,* ed. M. Horner, C. Nadelson, and M. Notman. New York: Plenum.

Mann, P. 1971. *Golda: The Life of Israel's Prime Minister.* New York: Coward, McCann & Geoghan.

Mayes, S. 1979. "Women in Positions of Authority: A Case Study of Changing Sex Roles." *Signs: Journals of Women in Culture and Society* 4:556–68.

Meir, G. 1975. *My Life.* New York: G. P. Putnam's Sons.

Milwid, M. E. 1982. "Women in Male Dominated Professions: A Study of Bankers, Architects, and Lawyers." Ph.D. diss., Wright Institute, Berkeley, Calif.

Moss-Kanter, R. 1977. *Men and Women of the Corporation.* New York: Basic Books.

———. 1987. "Men and Women of the Corporation Revisited." *Management Review* 76:14–16.

Moulton, R. 1977. "Some Effects of the New Feminism." *American Journal of Psychiatry,* 134:1–6.

Nadelson, C. 1987. "Women in Leadership Roles: Development and Challenges." In *Adolescent Psychiatry,* ed. S. Feinstein, vol. 14, pp. 28–41. Chicago: University of Chicago Press.

Nadelson, C.; Notman, M.; Baker-Miller, J.; and Zilbach, J. 1982. "Aggression in

Women: Conceptual Issues and Clinical Impressions." In *The Woman Patient,* ed. M. Notman and C. Nadelson, vol. 3, pp. 17–28. New York: Plenum.

Nadelson, C.; Notman, M.; and Bennett, M. 1978. "Success or Failure: Psychotherapeutic Considerations for Women in Conflict." *American Journal of Psychiatry* 135:1092–1096.

Nardi, P. [1942] 1978. *Vita de Arrigo Boito.* Quoted in *The Quotable Woman,* ed. E. Partnow. Garden City, N.Y.: Doubleday, Anchor Press.

Person, E. S. 1982. "Women Working: Fears of Failure, Deviance, and Success." *Journal of the American Academy of Psychoanalysis* 10:67–84.

Reskin, B., and Hartmann, H. 1986. *Women's Work, Men's Work: Sex Segregation on the Job.* A report from the Committee on Women's Employment and Related Issues, A. Ilchman, Chair. National Research Council, Washington, D.C.

Restak, R. 1986. "We Need More Cheap, Docile Women Doctors." *Washington Post,* 27 April.

Rushing, W. A. 1964. "Adolescent-Parent Relationship and Mobility Aspirations." *Social Forces* 43:157–66.

Scadron, A.; Witte, M.; Axelrod, M.; Greenberg, E. A.; Arem, C.; June, E.G.; and Meitz, J. 1982. "Attitudes Toward Women Physicians in Medical Academia." *Journal of The American Medical Association* 247:2803–2807.

Sitwell, E. 1962. *The Queens and The Hive.* Boston: Little, Brown.

Summers, M., ed. and trans. [1928] 1969. *Malleus Maleficarum* (1486). Reprint. New York: Arno Press.

Suter, L. E., and Miller, H. P. 1973. *Income Differences between Men and Career Women: Changing Women in a Changing Society,* ed. J. Huber. Chicago: University of Chicago Press.

Theodore, A. 1986. *The Campus Troublemakers: Academic Women in Protest.* Houston: Cap and Gown Press.

Westling-Wilkstrand, H.; Monk, M.; and Thomas, C. B. 1970. "Some Characteristics Related to the Career Status of Women Physicians." *Johns Hopkins Medical Journal* 1217:273–86.

Yoder, J.; Adams, J.; Grove, S.; and Priest, R. 1985. "To Teach Is to Learn: Overcoming Tokenism with Mentors." *Psychology of Women Quarterly* 9:119–31.

DISCUSSION

Dr. Nadelson begins her chapter by pointing out that power and achievement have rarely been related to women, although there have always been the notable, rare exceptions. Until recently, society broadly viewed the role of women as caregivers to husband, children, and home; in other words, their "work" was limited to providing an atmosphere in which the next generation could be created and thrive. Few occupations were available beyond the home, and those that were resembled the work of the home, for example, nursing or teaching. These traditional attitudes toward women still predominate in many parts of the world and have some social value since, in our opinion, they insure the healthy development of the next generation.

Even when women do achieve positions of power, they must be careful not to project their femininity into their power roles. Congresswoman Patricia Schroeder was greeted by peers and the public alike with "profound ambivalence" when she tearfully announced that she would not, after all, run for the presidency of the United States. No such ambivalence greeted Senator Edmund Muskie when he shed a tear during the presidential primaries; his presidential hopes were instantly dashed by this "unmanly" show of emotion. We will not tolerate certain "feminine" characteristics in our female leaders, let alone in our male ones. British Prime Minister Margaret Thatcher aside, there is still widespread suspicion of weakness in women and a cave-man mentality, shared by the sexes, that society is no doubt safer with the reins of power gripped firmly by masculine hands.

The challenge and the developmental opportunity for women today is to expand the horizons of their work options, both intrapsychically and in society. Our era is a true nodal point in the development of women because for the first time in history, through the birth control pill, women have the capacity to control pregnancy. Birth control has affected all areas of female development, but particularly the arena of work. Formerly male-dominated career paths are now open to women because they can confidently choose when, or whether, to become pregnant and have those years formerly preoccupied with pregnancy and child care available for training, further education, and career advancement. As more and more women command executive positions in business, in professions, and in politics—and as described by Dr. Nadelson, there are still strong prejudices against them—the attitudes of both women and men in the workplace and society at large will gradually change, accepting more readily the combination of female achievement and power in the workplace and motherhood in the home. In fifty years or so many of the prejudices against women in power described by Dr. Nadelson will seem quite outdated as the *absolute* relationship between pregnancy and motherhood is further diminished by science, for example, by *in-vitro* fertilization, surrogate motherhood, and at some point in the future, the prospect of pregnancy sustained outside the female body.

Addressing the historical perspective, Dr. Nadelson asks the pivotal question: Why, despite the accomplishments of Joan of Arc, Catherine the Great, Golda Meier, and others have "women's contributions . . . generally been viewed through their child-bearing functions, not through their place in cultural, political, or economic history?" (p. 504). As striking as Dr. Nadelson's examples are, they are rare exceptions to the life course of the majority of women over the centuries. What these exemplary women do demonstrate is the *capacity* of the female to function as capably as the male of the species. But we still live in a world in which no woman has been pope or president of the United States, a world in which women in many regions must cover their faces and shroud their bodies in public. Whatever factors have been operating for centuries in both women and men to keep women subservient are still in place.

We feel the answer may be in the fascination of both men and women with the *power* of women to procreate. The ability to bear children is, in some respects, a power far greater than that achieved by men in the workplace. Men are intrigued by and fearful of that power. After all, every man was given life by a woman and began his extrauterine life nurtured and controlled by her; later he became dependent on other women for his emotional and sexual needs—to insure his masculinity and quest for immortality by producing his child.

In her remarks on "Women in Power: Contemporary Views," Dr. Nadelson bemoans that "while we applaud the contemporary picture of progress regarding the status and condition of women, there has not been substantial or permanent change in the attitudes and values that shape our behaviors" (p. 506). Certainly education alone has not changed the plight of women in business and the professions. Moreover, the feminist movement has not made a major dent in the prejudice against women, which has remained, according to the National Research Council, essentially unchanged since 1900. It is evident, and not surprising, that a basic change in society's attitudes toward women and power will be evolutionary, not revolutionary: the long-established societal roles of the woman and the man are rooted in the basic themes of human survival and propagation of the species. As the survival of the species becomes less dependent on the labor of women, both at home and during birth, attitudes will slowly change, and women will continue to expand their achievement and power into other areas.

22

Emotional Survival and the Aging Body

MARCIA KRAFT GOIN

The Link between Psychiatry and the Psychology of Body Change

Early in my career as a psychiatrist I was thrown into the company of plastic surgeons as the result of my marriage to one of them. I attended their scientific meetings and grew to know many of them socially. Over the years I became increasingly aware of the plastic surgeon's concerns about why some patients were satisfied with the outcomes of their operations and others were not and about the reasons for occasional bizarre postoperative psychological reactions. From time to time they came to me for clarification of complex psychological issues concerning the body and surgical changes wrought upon it. More often than not, I had no ready answers. The scientific literature was occasionally helpful. Some of the early psychological studies of plastic surgery patients were well done. Most others reflected the authors' psychoanalytic biases about the appropriateness of plastic surgery as a solution to dissatisfactions with the body, rather than an analysis of the dissatisfactions themselves; moreover, data were not obtained in an orderly, scientific way. Some of the less-biased studies showed highly individualistic and sometimes surprising reactions to changes in appearance after surgery.

An informal poll taken at a representative plastic surgery meeting showed that a majority of plastic surgeons believed the postoperative

depression was more common after face-lift surgery than after any other aesthetic operation. This result was one of several stimuli that led us (Goin et al. 1980) to undertake a prospective psychological study of fifty female face-lift patients. As a psychiatrist I was interested in probing the details of the depression, whereas the plastic surgeons hoped I could devise a tool to predict who would become depressed. This indicator would allow them to avoid accepting patients unlikely to be pleased with the results of their surgery.

I speculated that midlife concerns about aging and death would be at the core of the depression. My psychiatric colleague thought that the depression was more likely related to issues of narcissism. The plastic surgeons believed that the postoperative depression was related to a discrepancy between the patients' hopes and expectations and the reality of the physical outcome. As it turned out, we learned much about people, their feelings about their bodies, aging, widowhood, and magical hopes and expectations; but all of us had difficulty predicting who would get depressed and why.

Our original premise had been wrong. Statistically, there was no greater incidence of depression after face-lift operations than after any other major general surgery. But there was a difference in the attitudes of general versus plastic surgeons: general surgeons seemed relatively less concerned if a patient was transiently depressed after a gall-bladder operation; plastic surgeons faced with a depressed postoperative patient feared that they had operated on an inappropriate patient.

This study of face-lift patients and another study of fifty women having breast reconstruction following mastectomy for cancer (Goin, unpublished data) serendipitously provided a great deal of information about adult development and reactions to aging and body mutilation in midlife. For the most part the women in the two studies were between forty and seventy years old. While the face-lift patients requested surgery because of their feelings about aging, the cancer patients were concerned not only about the threat of the disease, but about the loss of a psychologically important body part. Pre- and postoperative interviews provided a setting in which to explore feelings about aging, body change, loss, ambition, life change, family, friends, and death and dying.

"The Ego Is First and Foremost a Bodily Ego":
The Psychological Importance of the Body and Body Image

The importance of the body in maintaining psychological integrity is not surprising considering its significance in psychological development. As Freud (1927) wrote, "The ego is first and foremost a bodily ego" (p. 26). Infants do not understand their environment intellectually; they experience and judge it through their bodies. When they are hungry, cold, or colicky, the world is cruel and ungiving. When they are well fed, warm, and at ease, the world is comforting and soothing.

As an infant reaches out, touches himself and others, and in turn is touched by them, he begins to form a picture of where he begins and ends. Students of early child development speculate that the infant has a fragmented and incomplete schema. At first he perceives only parts of himself and others: mouth, eyes, a breast. In fact, initially the infant seems unaware that he is a separate person; he experiences himself as an extension of his mother.* As body boundaries begin to coalesce, and the body image starts to conform more closely to reality, an awareness grows within the infant that he and his mother are separate individuals. Normally this occurs between six and ten months of age and is the source of what is sometimes called eighth-month anxiety. With awareness of separation comes the inescapable correlate: if two entities are separate, then one can leave the other. An infant at this age will commonly look anxious and cry when its mother leaves the room and can be reassured only by her return. Separation, individuation, and separation anxiety are useful in understanding the deep-seated origins of the anxiety triggered by loss or alterations of an important body part. Early anxiety about and vulnerability to the possibility of abandonment remain dormant in the brain. Changes in a body part decades later can evoke anxiety unconsciously related to those early fears of separation and abandonment.

Margaret Mahler and John McDevitt (1982) have reported some telling observations of infants' reactions to their mirrored images. At six or seven months of age infants are quite excited by seeing their mirrored reflections. In the ensuing months they become less interested in their own reflections and more interested in the reflections of others. Exceptions to this transition were noted in infants who had poor nurturing. They continued to be absorbed by their own reflections. Did this mean that they could look only to themselves for nurturing, or had they not developed enough of a sense of self to look away without fear of disappearing? What the study does

---

*Today some developmental researchers question the concepts of primary fusion and later differentiation (Stern 1985). This uncertainty does not affect the thesis regarding the importance of the formation of body image and its vicissitudes.

tell us is that the importance of one's mirrored reflection begins at a very early age.

It is important to keep in mind that one's body—where one begins and ends—is strongly linked to early developmental concepts of basic trust, separation and individuation, and an integrated sense of self. In their book on mood disorders, Peter Whybrow and colleagues (1984) state, "Intrapsychic formulations of depression have given increasing weight to the importance of actual and symbolic loss and injury to the ego during the individual's complex interaction with conjugal, familial, societal and cultural forces" (p. 34). Damage to the integrity of the body has a natural symbolic link to damage to the integrity of the ego. Michael Shaara (1975) sensitively describes this in *Killer Angels,* a novel that takes place during the Civil War. In one instance, General Lee speaks of one of his generals, a fearless leader, who displayed uncharacteristic hesitancy in battle after a war injury resulted in amputation of a leg. "A man loses part of himself, an arm, a leg, and though he has been a fine soldier he is never quite the same again; he has lost nothing else visible, but there is a certain softness in the man thereafter, a slowness, a caution. . . . Very little of a man is in a hand or a leg. A man is in his spirit and he has that in full no matter what part of his body dies, or all of it . . . you may not understand. It had not happened to you, so you don't understand" (p. 148).

Beauty: Is It in the Eye of the Beholder or the Beheld?

The thoughts and feelings associated with the body image are complex and varied. Such diverse factors as culture, society, family heritage, and interpersonal experience determine pleasure or displeasure with one's body. Beauty resides both in the eyes of the beholder and the eye of the beheld.

Studies have shown that there are cultural norms for what is considered to be an attractive body part. Paul Jourard and Sidney Secord (1955) had subjects describe ideal sizes of various body parts and attitudes on a seven-point scale ranging from extremely negative to extremely positive. In addition, they measured the subjects' body parts. Among the conclusions drawn from this study were that shared group norms exist for the ideal shape and size of body parts and that each individual's dissatisfaction or satisfaction with a given body part was directly related to the degree of deviation of that part from the group norm. There were no differences between the reactions of men and women in this regard.

Body Image Distortion

Body image is defined in the *Glossary of Psychoanalytic Terms and Concepts* (Moore and Fine 1968) as the "mental representation of one's body at any moment." This useful definition goes on to state that depending on the person's instinctual defensive needs, "the body image at any given time may be realistic or unrealistic." When the perception is unrealistic, a body image distortion is said to exist. These two concepts, body image and body image distortion, are important keys to the understanding of patients' motivations for and reactions to body change.

Some body image distortion is universal. Our minds rarely record the shapes and sizes of our body parts the way a camera does. Looking at vacation photographs, each family member may express personal distress over the incongruity of fact and perception. This body image distortion may reflect difficulty in adjusting to the passage of time and can function as a defensive mechanism that allows us to avoid acknowledging unwanted changes.

Other moment-to-moment, transient body image distortions occur because of physical or emotional changes. The body image may go from lean to fat during a holiday dinner, although no change is perceptible to fellow revelers. Behavior, like overeating, is only one of many factors that can alter body image. Compliments, disparaging remarks, obvious admiration, or disdain from others have variable impacts, depending on the individual's psychological state. Consider, for example, a day in the office seeing a series of patients who are depressed, suicidal, and angry or unhappy with therapy and the therapist. The psychiatrist may feel years older, gray, haggard, and burned-out. But if the last patient of the day reports a relief in symptoms and a major breakthrough in solving life's problems, self-esteem and vigor flow back to the therapist.

Life Cycle and the Body

Although the formation of body image plays an important part in an infant's psychological development, body appearance does not. It is parents who glow with pride when friends talk about the "beautiful baby." Similarly, it is parents, friends, or other observers who are concerned by a cleft lip, hemangioma, or other congenital defect. Infants are affected secondarily by their parents' contentment and joy or overprotection, rejection, and guilt about a deformity.

Children's reactions to another's appearance begin at an early age. Studies have shown that even in preschool, attractive appearance as defined by society plays a part in relationships (Bercleid and Walster 1972). The attractive children on the playground are sought out first as playmates or picked first in whatever game is being played. Children with deformities can usually be protected from abuse while in the confines of their families, but this safety changes when they step outside. Children, insensitive to the effects of their reactions on others, can be cruel mirrors. They may stare in fright at the severely deformed or may mock anything that looks different from the ordinary. Children whose ears stick out are called "Dumbo"; overweight children are called "Fatty." Some such children may defend against humiliation by taking pride in being class clowns.

Everyone experiences adolescence as a powerfully charged period affecting the body and body image. Adolescents must contend with an onslaught of hormonal, physical, and social changes. Josselyn (1960), an experienced adolescent psychiatrist, writes, "Marked social, psychological, and physical changes are characteristic of this age span and they do not occur unrelated to each other. The physical changes have definite effects on the social and psychological adjustments of the individual; social factors influence the psychological and physical changes; the psychological factors have repercussions both socially and physiologically" (p. 19).

Adolescence is also the time of life when noses and breasts reach their final states of development. Rhinoplasty is perhaps the plastic surgery operation most studied from the psychological standpoint. In a controlled study, Wright and Wright (1975) found a higher incidence of emotional instability and lower self-esteem, a poorer self-concept, and more acting-out in a group of patients who had rhinoplasty for cosmetic reasons as compared with a similar group who had noncosmetic head and neck operations. Their findings support the results of other studies about the psychological vulnerability of patients requesting rhinoplasty operations. This vulnerability is possibly linked to negative reinforcement created by the simultaneous occurrence of the psychosocial vulnerabilities of adolescence and self-consciousness about facial appearance. Wright and Wright also found that after rhinoplasty operations the patients' Minnesota Multiphasic Personality Inventory (MMPI) test profiles improved. They did not reach the normal levels of control tests, but they showed statistically significant improvement. The removal of self-consciousness about appearance seemed to cause a ripple effect leading to more self-confidence, less anxiety in social situations, and more positive experiences.

Similarly, studies of women having augmentation mammoplasties indicate that a majority are less self-conscious, less inhibited, and feel more feminine after that surgery (Baker et al. 1974). In a study of women undergoing breast reductions (Goin et al. 1977), we learned that many had felt traumatized during adolescence because of self-consciousness about their large breasts. In most cases breast development had begun early, around age ten or eleven. When other girls had small breast buds, these girls had been wearing brassieres with cups size D or larger. Their girl-friends were jealous, and boys, in their sexual uneasiness, leered and made lewd remarks. The assumption that girls with large breasts were sexually promiscuous resulted in even more embarrassing experiences.

The reactions of patients having rhinoplasty, augmentation mammo-plasty, or breast reduction provide a few examples of how looking "differ-ent" relates to the other psychological traumas of adolescence. These reac-tions are integral to the formation of a sense of identity, the process of separation-individuation, and the development of trust in peer relation-ships.

The appearance of one's body in midlife takes on a different significance. Efforts to remain trim and fit are not made to develop a sense of identity or to separate and individuate, but to maintain health and youthfulness and to deter the effects of aging. The struggle is to retain body integrity in the face of anxieties about aging, the vulnerabilities of failing health, and the potential loss of independence. At this time of life, plastic surgery is usually restorative or reconstructive, not designed to achieve a new size or shape.

In our study of the psychological courses of fifty women following face-lift operations, we interviewed at length several middle-aged, non-psychiatric patients and learned, among other things, their concerns about appearance, health, and death and dying. The women ranged in age from forty to seventy-nine. Sixty-four percent were self-employed, and except for one woman in the film industry, they worked as teachers, real estate agents, administrators, and the like. Each subject filled out an MMPI; except for one woman who showed paranoid trends, the results were within normal limits. The exception was of clinical interest because she associated her preoperative "haggard" appearance with the physical and emotional strain of caring for an extremely ill husband. Obviously, she harbored considerable resentment about him and his illness, and projected this criticism onto colleagues, believing that they saw her haggard, ex-hausted appearance as an indication of her diminished ability to perform. Her postoperative "refreshed" appearance appeared to mask her projec-tions. She no longer saw colleagues as critical and threatening. Instead she interpreted their attention as sympathetic and understanding.

Motivations for the operation were part of the preoperative discussions (Goin et al. 1976). Initially, the reasons stated were usually pragmatic, such as disliking the appearance of wrinkled, baggy, sagging skin. Later more personal reasons emerged, related to intolerable feelings of decreased self-confidence and self-esteem associated with an aging appearance. The pre- and postoperative comments of three women are examples:

I'm a teacher and no one wants to listen to an old woman. Because of my age they don't value anything I say.

My boss of twenty-five years retired, and the new manager is quite young. I know he's looking for a way to fire me and get in someone younger.

I'm competing at work with a lot of aggressive young women. I used to think I could rise to the top executive position, but I've given up that dream.

After their face-lift operations, these same women said:

I don't know why I thought the students weren't listening to me because of my age—they're at a stage when they don't listen to anyone.

My boss thinks I'm the most valuable secretary he's ever had. He doesn't seem to think about my age, but just talks about my extensive experience.

Suddenly I feel more confident at work. I've become more aggressive and have asked to be put on committees that could lead to the type of promotion I want. I may not make it to the top, but that will be all right. I'll know I tried.

The women's preoperative statements reflect conscious and unconscious fears of middle age: fears that they no longer *do* have anything of value to say, that young people really are more capable, that they may not have the ability to work at the top. Although often critical of parents, professors, and bosses, the young also invest them with omnipotency. Upon reaching seniority themselves and lacking that omnipotency, people feel a need to reconcile the fantasies of expected power and strength with the realities of life. These three women had been projecting their fears, anxieties, *and* expectations onto the world and responding to them as realities. Those projections were clearly debilitating.

The focus of their midlife anxieties was their aging appearance. There was no sense of pride that each wrinkle was hard-won and represented years of valuable experience. Instead the wrinkles represented ever-increasing decay. Fortunately, the operation not only provided a refreshed appearance, but freed them from what they perceived as a stigma and allowed a more realistic appraisal of their self-worth. As one women said, she did not have to win the battle; pride in knowing she had fought well was enough.

Not every woman in our series had this type of emotional reaction. Some had the operation and were pleased with the result and had no particular psychological response. A few had hoped the operation would alter the behavior of others (change a husband's impotence, revive a dying marriage) and were disappointed when their objectives dissolved, but did not blame the surgeon.

Another middle-age change, explored through the five widows in the study, was the part appearance plays in the reactions of others. Webb and colleagues (1965) had reported that widows often request a face-lift operation in order to mask grief. Friends associated their refreshed appearance with renewed physical and emotional well-being. The widows saw this response from others as less intrusive and more liberating than being seen as sad and depressed. In our study, some of the widows also discussed their giving little thought to appearance while they were growing old together with a loving companion. Widowhood meant entry into new situations where initial impressions and appearance took on more significance.

Two women with opposite reactions showed the different ways in which attention to appearance can affect adaptation to loss.

Mrs. A. was fifty-four. She and her husband had been a devoted couple. During the last twenty of their thirty-five years of marriage they had not only lived together, but worked together as business partners. Following her husband's unexpected death from a heart attack, Mrs. A.'s grief was intense. A year and a half after his death, she consulted the plastic surgeon about a face-lift. During her interview with the psychiatrist (MKG), which was part of the study, she revealed that her main concern about the operation was that the postoperative period would require her to take things easy for a few days. Since her husband's death she had been extremely agitated and prescribed for herself extreme activity—business, housework, in other words, constant motion. She would drop into bed exhausted so that she could sleep for a few hours. After the operation, she was surprised and relieved that she had no trouble slowing her pace. As she and the psychiatrist reflected about her behavioral change, she realized that the decision to have the face-lift was unconsciously motivated by her need to resolve her grief. It symbolized an acceptance of her husband's loss and an entry into a new phase of her life, which might include forming new relationships.

Mrs. B., a sixty-three-year-old widow looking much younger than her age, had a very different story to tell. She and her husband had a miserable marriage and she was glad to be free of his nagging and complaining. Mrs. B., who did not want any deep commitments, had been dating a great deal since her husband's death six months before and was enjoying it. Her expressed motivation for the face-lift was to look as young as she felt. Three months after the operation, the patient felt very different. She surprised herself by telling people how old she was and that she was tired of trying to act younger than she felt. Mrs. B. gradually realized that she missed her husband and was hoping to find someone with whom to share her old age. We had a glimpse of her struggle with aging, loss, and appearance. Giving up the idea of presenting herself to the world as a younger person was, for her, a major resolution of those struggles.

Middle Age and Body Loss

In middle age, any operation that necessitates loss of a body part will activate concerns and conflicts associated with physical retrogression. Loss of a limb in adolescence due to an osteogenic sarcoma, an orchiectomy in a young newlywed, or a mastectomy at midlife, carries with it the fears associated with cancer and the phase-specific struggle of the respective stage of life. The middle-aged woman with breast cancer is usually at a time of life when children are grown; she may be planning to return to work and in search of a new identity other than that of mother and housewife. She has fears about fading attractiveness and its effect on her relationships, and, most significantly, she is dealing with the midlife anxieties associated with failing health and fears of dependence (Goin and Goin 1981).

Fifty women seeking breast reconstruction following mastectomy described, in several unstructured interviews, their feelings about and reactions to their surgery. Following their psychological course after surgery, we could see how the reconstruction altered many of their feelings. The psychological effects of mastectomy have been well described (Renneker and Cutler 1952; Torrie 1971; Asken 1975): depression, despair, rage, decreased feelings of femininity, diminished self-esteem and self-confidence, and a sense of mutilation are common. In the aggregate, the fifty women in our study showed all of those symptoms. Frequently, however, they masked their depression and despair from others; spouses and friends were often surprised at their wish to have breast reconstruction. It was not uncommon for close friends to say, "But you seemed to cope so well!"

Some of these women felt obliged to cope with equanimity. They were often startled by how generally uneasy the mastectomy made them feel: less assertive in their interactions, fearful and cautious when driving on the freeway, for example. After breast reconstruction those feelings disappeared, and they felt capable of functioning at their preoperative level. Self-esteem, self-confidence, and sexuality were as they had been before the mastectomy. With their bodies once more intact, the anxieties associated with body loss and damage were dissolved.

Conclusion

In summary, it is not surprising that people focus on their appearance as they grow old. Signs of aging are the most prominent evidence of the passage of time. A strong investment in physical appearance is typical of the middle-aged of both sexes (Freedman et al. 1976). Many of the women in our face-lift study were dealing with emotional conflicts about their value as aging adults. These conflicts caused them to feel stigmatized by their aging appearance. For many, the operation not only freed them from their projections but seemed to provide an atmosphere suitable for a productive resolution of the struggle between growth and stagnation (Erikson 1950). They were able to achieve a productive outcome for this climacteric development period as described by Benedek (1950).

The women with mastectomies represent a middle-aged population dealing with fear of a potentially fatal illness and also anxieties associated with damage to and loss of a body part. The most frequent reaction to breast reconstruction is the feeling, "I'm whole again" (Zalon 1978). To reiterate, "The ego is first and foremost a bodily ego." Damage to the integrity of the body rekindles developmental anxieties related to loss, separation, individuation, and basic trust. The particular task for this age group is coping with these old fears while facing a new complex of midlife stresses.

REFERENCES

Asken, M. J. 1975. "Psychoemotional Aspects of Mastectomy: A Review of Recent Literature." *American Journal of Psychiatry* 132:56–59.

Baker, J. L., Jr.; Kolin, I. S.; and Bartlett, E. S. 1974. "Dynamics of Patients Undergoing Mammary Augmentation." *Plastic Reconstructive Surgery* 53:652–59.

Benedek, T. 1950. "Climacterium: a Developmental Phase." *Psychoanalytic Quarterly* 19:1–27.

Bercleid, E., and Walster, E. 1972. "Beauty and the Best." *Psychology Today* 5:10.

Erikson, E. 1950. "Eight Stages of Man." In *Childhood and Society,* pp. 219–234. New York: W.W. Norton.

Freedman, A. M.; Kaplan, H. I.; Sadock, B. J., eds., 1976. "The Middle-aged." In *Modern Synopsis, Comprehensive Textbook of Psychiatry II.* Baltimore: Williams and Wilkins.

Freud, S. 1927. "The Ego and the Id." In *Standard Edition,* ed. J. Strachey, vol. 19, p. 26. London: Hogarth Press.

Goin, M. K., and Goin, J. M. 1981. "Midlife Reactions to Mastectomy and Subsequent Breast Reconstruction." *Archives of General Psychiatry* 38(2):225–27.

Goin, M. K.; Burgoyne, R. W.; and Goin, J. M. 1976. "Face-lift Operation: the Patient's Secret Motivations and Reactions to 'Informed Consent.' " *Plastic Reconstructive Surgery* 58:273–79.

Goin, M. K.; Burgoyne, R. W.; Goin, J. M.; and Staples, F. R. 1980. "A Prospective Study of 50 Female Face-lift Patients." *Plastic Reconstructive Surgery* 62:436–42.

Goin, M. K., Goin, J. M., and Gianini, M. H. 1977. "The Psychic Consequences of a Reduction Mammoplasty." *Plastic Reconstructive Surgery* 59:530–34.

Josselyn, I. M. 1960. *The Adolescent and His World.* Family Service Association of America.

Jourard, S. M., and Secord, P.F. 1955. "Body Cathexis and the Ideal Female Figure." *Journal of Abnormal Social Psychiatry* 50:243–46.

Mahler, M., and McDevitt, J. 1982. "Thoughts on the Emergence of the Sense of Self with Particular Emphasis on the Body Self." *Journal of the American Psychoanalytic Association* 30:827–48.

Moore, B. S., and Fine, B. O., eds. 1968. *A Glossary of Psychoanalytic Terms and Concepts,* 2d ed. New York: American Psychoanalytic Association.

Renneker, R., and Cutler, M. 1952. "Psychological Problems of Adjustment to Cancer of the Breast." *Journal of the American Medical Association* 148:833–39.

Shaara, M. 1975. *The Killer Angels.* New York: Ballentine Books.

Stern, D. N. 1985. *The Interpersonal World of the Infant: A View from Psychoanalysis and Developmental Psychology.* New York: Basic Books.

Torrie, A. 1971. "Like a Bird With a Broken Wing." *World Medicine,* 7 April.

Webb, W. L., Jr.; Slaughter, R.; Meyer, E.; and Edgerton, M. 1965. "Mechanism of Psychosocial Adjustment in Patients Seeking 'Face-lift' Operations." *Psychosomatic Medicine* 27:183–92.

Whybrow, P. C.; Akiskal, H.S.; and McKinney, W. T. 1984. *Mood Disorders: Toward a New Psychobiology.* New York: Plenum.

Wright, M. R., and Wright, W. K. 1975. "A Psychological Study of Patients Undergoing Cosmetic Surgery." *Archives of Otolaryngology* 101:145–51.

Zalon, J. with Block, J. L. 1978. *I Am Whole Again.* New York: Random House.

DISCUSSION

One of our purposes in this book is to demonstrate the usefulness of developmental theory in different contexts. In this chapter Dr. Goin applies adult developmental ideas to both clinical examples and conceptual issues in plastic surgery.

She begins by reminding us of Freud's thought that in infancy the ego is first and foremost a body ego. Because his comment has stimulated enormous research over the years, the relationship between the maturation of the body and the psyche is childhood is well defined in psychodynamic theory. The concepts of erogenous zones, circumscribed areas of heightened sensation that emerge in the genetically determined sequence of oral, anal, and phallic stages; and the complex biological events surrounding puberty are recognized as powerful psychic organizers. After adolescence, the effect of the body on the mind is minimized until the climacteric.

In our own work we have attempted to fill this theoretical gap by suggesting that physical retrogression and aging have as powerful an influence on psychic development in adulthood as do physical growth and progression in childhood. Further, this effect begins in young adulthood and continues throughout life. Signs in the twenties, in some, are balding, graying of hair, slowing of reflexes, and loss of a "hard" body. In the thirties these signs are more evident, as is the imminent loss of the procreative function in women. In middle adulthood (ages forty to sixty) signs of physical retrogression and aging are inescapable, producing a continuous effect on mental life.

As Dr. Goin notes, the sense of where the body begins and ends is intimately linked with the *emergence* in early childhood of basic trust, separation-individuation, and an integrated sense of self. We would add to this emergence of basic trust the notion that the *maintenance, elaboration,* and *evolution* of those capacities in adulthood continue to be closely linked to the body and its functioning in health and illness. That notion expresses our belief that the basic developmental themes of childhood are not limited to the phase of development in which they first emerge but rather continue to influence psychic development for the remainder of life. Clearly, the unremitting importance of the body as an organizer of development in adulthood has been underestimated.

In the section "Beauty: Is It in the Eye of the Beholder or the Beheld?" Dr. Goin raises many interesting issues about the body image in adulthood. Her presentation clearly indicates that the body image changes and evolves in adulthood almost moment-to-moment. Further, the environment, particularly the attitudes of significant loved ones, continues to exert a significant influence; for example, the attitude of friends and family members following breast removal. They must alter their images of the person's body after surgery as well as their attitudes about the person, the latter depending substantially on the reasons for the surgery, the changes in appearance, and the presence or absence of pathology such as cancer.

The basic idea here is that plastic surgery, whether elective or required, has a profound effect on the internal representations of everyone involved and can significantly alter relationships. In midlife, feelings and attitudes are heightened by the already intense, normative preoccupation with the aging process in the body and the growing awareness of time limitation and personal death.

In her section on "Life Cycle and the Body" Dr. Goin beautifully describes the relationship between phase-specific developmental tasks and the motivations for surgery. After discussing the adolescent's fear of looking "different" from peers—a concern that generates the desire for rhinoplasty, augmentation mammoplasty, and breast reduction—she turns her attention to midlife. "At this time in life," she tells us, "plastic surgery is usually restorative or reconstructive, not designed to achieve a new size or shape" (p. 524).

Her use of the developmental framework clearly indicates that a detailed knowledge of normal development should be integrated into the psychological armamentarium of every plastic surgeon. Deciding whether to operate on questionable individuals is a difficult issue to resolve. A developmental history, which traces the person's lifelong experience with and attitudes about his or her body and correlates it with general psychological and physical health, will be manifestly helpful.

Among the most poignant parts of Dr. Goin's presentation was her description of those widows who felt the need for plastic surgery. Most striking was the powerful effect that a long-standing loving relationship can have on protecting mid- and late-life individuals against the narcissistic injury involved in physical aging. As long as one is loved by a partner, who is also aging, the process of physical retrogression is tolerable. Upon the death of the partner concerns about the body, which were managed within the relationship, may surface and lead to requests for appearance-altering surgery. As illustrated by the vignettes of the two widows, the surgery may act as a vehicle for the resolution of mourning or may promote a restructuring of attitudes, both of which facilitate the mourning process.

LIST OF PERMISSIONS

Index

LIFE AT DEATH

A Scientific Investigation
of the Near-Death Experience

KENNETH RING, PH.D.

Coward, McCann & Geoghegan   *New York*

Acknowledgment is made to the following for permission to quote copyrighted material:

Mind/Brain Bulletin for the selection from *Re-Vision:* "A New Perspective on Reality," by Marilyn Ferguson. *Re-Vision,* 1978, Volume 1, Numbers 3/4.

Confucian Press, Inc., for the selection from *At the Hour of Death* by Karlis Osis and Erlendur Haraldsson.

Doubleday & Company, Inc., for the excerpt from *The Astral Journey* by Herbert B. Greenhouse. Copyright © 1974 by Herbert B. Greenhouse.

Institute of Psychophysical Research for selections from *Out-of-the-Body Experiences* by Celia Green, Institute of Psychophysical Research, Oxford.

The Julian Press, Inc., for selections from *The Center of the Cyclone* by John C. Lilly, M.D. Copyright 1972 by John C. Lilly, M.D.

Lyle Stuart, Inc., for selections from *Out of the Body Experiences* by Robert Crookall.

Mockingbird Books, Inc., for selections from *Life After Life* and *Reflections on Life After Life* by Raymond A. Moody, Jr., M.D.

Pantheon Books, a Division of Random House, Inc., for selections from *Memories, Dreams, Reflections* by C. G. Jung, translated by Richard and Clara Winston, recorded and edited by Aniela Jaffe. Copyright © 1961, 1962, 1963 by Random House, Inc.

G. P. Putnam's Sons for selections from *Psychic Explorations* by Edgar Mitchell. Copyright © 1974 by Edgar D. Mitchell & Associates, Inc.

J. P. Tarcher, Inc., Los Angeles, California, for a selection from *The Probability of the Impossible* by Dr. Thelma Moss. Copyright © 1974, published by New American Library.

The Theosophical Publishing House, Wheaton, Illinois, for selections from *The Transition Called Death* by Charles Hampton, 1979 Quest Edition.

Ziff-Davis Publishing Company for selections from *Psychology Today:* "Holographic Memory," by Daniel Goleman, February 1979. Copyright © 1979 Ziff-Davis Publishing Company.

Library of Congress Cataloging in Publication Data

Ring, Kenneth.
    Life at death.

    Bibliography: p.
    1. Death—Psychological aspects. 2. Death,
Apparent. I. Title.
BF789.D4R56   155.9'37   79-27546
ISBN 0-698-11032-3

PRINTED IN THE UNITED STATES OF AMERICA

To Susan Palmer and Theresa Carilli,
who did the real work
to make this project possible.

CONTENTS

7

Appendixes

ACKNOWLEDGMENTS

For their support—of various kinds—of the research reported in this book I am indebted to many individuals and a number of institutions.

First of all, I wish to thank the University of Connecticut Research Foundation for its financial support throughout the two years this research was conducted. I am particularly grateful to Dr. Hugh Clark, Acting Vice-President of the Graduate School, who responded promptly and positively to every request I made in connection with this project: for an extension of time in which to complete it; for supplementary funds for additional personnel and analyses; and for travel funds in order to attend several conferences where my work was to be presented.

Second, my deep appreciation goes to the physicians and administrators of the various hospitals involved in our study for their help in enabling my research staff and me to obtain the names of potentially interviewable patients and former patients. It was through their assistance and the cooperation of their hospital staffs that this book was possible, and my debt to them is immense. So many hospital personnel provided help to us that it would be impossible to acknowledge them all, but I need to make special mention of these individuals: at Hartford Hospital, Dr. Cornelis Boelhouwer, Dr. Arthur Wolfe, Dorothy Riley, and Sue Thompson; at St. Francis Hospital, Francis J. Greaney, Dr. Robert M. Jeresaty, Martha Johnson, and Ann Gibbons; at Mount Sinai Hospital, Dr. Jacob J. Haksteen and Dr. Alfred Aronson; at Elmcrest Psychiatric Institute, Julie Minear.

Third, to the members of my own research staff who helped me to collect the data for this study no words of thanks are sufficient. Theresa Carilli and Susan Palmer undertook the mammoth job of arranging for the interviews and rating the tapes afterward, and the dedication of this book to them speaks for their indispensable role. I also owe a profound debt to Charlene Alling for conducting most of the interviews I was not able to arrange to do myself, as well as for securing for us a small sample of near-death survivors from Maine; she also helped in the laborious task of rating tapes. Deborah Stack-O'Sullivan and Jane Van Dusen each contributed significantly to the research by carrying out several interviews and by rating some tapes, and to them, in addition, my warmest thanks. Finally, to my friend and colleague Joyce Duffy, my appreciation for referring to us several near-death survivors who would not otherwise have come to our attention.

Fourth, there are many people who took the time to discuss the ideas in this book with me and to encourage me in various ways throughout the period I was working on it. For their contributions here I wish to thank: John Audette, Boyce Batey, the late Itzhak (Ben) Bentov, Dr.

Don McLaughlin, Nancy Miller, Dr. Karlis Osis, Bob and Thelma Peck, Dr. Michael Sabom, and Alexandra Teguis. I owe a special debt here to two exceptional men: to John White, whose expert editorial hand on this manuscript improved it immeasurably and whose general guidance was instrumental in the publishing of this work; and to Dr. Raymond A. Moody, Jr., who was kind enough to write the introduction to this book and to have otherwise laid the foundation for the research I have reported here. To Sherry Slate, who patiently typed and retyped all drafts of this manuscript, a thousand thanks for her labors. Finally, I am indebted to Patricia B. Soliman, my editor, not only for her professional work on the manuscript, but, even more, for her understanding of what I intended to convey through this book and for giving me the editorial freedom to attempt it.

Fifth, no list of acknowledgments could omit the members of my family, whose support, understanding, and love made the writing of this book truly a joyful experience. To my daughter, Kathryn, I owe the suggestion for the title I would have liked to use for this book (*The Death Experience*), but finally had to reject on the grounds that it was misleading. And to Norma, hugger to the world and helpmate to me, I give my thanks for her criticisms designed to keep my writing honest and restrained and for her willingness to put up with my obstinacy when I chose to disregard her strictures.

Finally, to all those whose story I try to tell in these pages—our near-death survivors themselves—I offer this book as an expression of my gratitude to them for being willing to share their experiences with me and, by so doing, teaching me more than they ever knew. And to three in particular—Helen, Virginia, and Iris—my teachers and my friends, much love.

Storrs, Connecticut
May 1979

Moving, yet holding still,
seeing yourself entering a new way.

Your essence feels the questioning
doubt. Must I? Where is this? Why?

It enfolds you, becomes you,
cradles you.

You look and you behold
yourself moving—yet holding
still, through time, into eternity,
into the source.

Dark, yet light, moving,
yet holding still, oblivion or
eternity.

Softly—silence—clear sound,
brilliant awareness—all these and
then—the deep abiding sadness
that comes—when you must stay.

How do you live with the
knowledge of what isn't yet to be?

By the remembrance of that
timelessness beyond—and the reassurance
that you will return to the light,
    the source and the way.

Fran Sherwood
A near-death survivor

INTRODUCTION

When, much to my surprise, my book, *Life After Life,* began to attract attention not only all over the United States but also throughout much of the world, I must confess that I was extremely uncomfortable. One of my concerns was that some of the sensational claims that were made for my work by other persons might have the effect of frightening off legitimate investigators from an area that I continue to believe has profound significance for clinical medicine and human psychology. Hence, it was profoundly gratifying (and also a great relief!) to me when, within a year or so of the publication of *Life After Life,* I learned of several studies that were underway to attempt systematically to confirm or to disconfirm the very preliminary observations made in that work. In consequence, at the present time, Dr. Kenneth Ring, author of this volume, Dr. Michael Sabom, a cardiologist, and other physicians who are yet publicly to announce their findings, have, in independent studies, verified that in a surprisingly large percentage of patients who undergo a close call with death there occurs a transcendent, clear, and spiritually life-changing experience, which, overall, is remarkably similar from individual to individual.

One thing must be emphasized about the work done by Dr. Ring, Dr. Sabom, and others, however. Their studies are at a much higher level of systematization than is the one reported in *Life After Life.* Therefore, when Dr. Ring honored me by asking me to write the introduction to his book, I expressed to him my own amusement at the idea, for it seems to me that his work is more sophisticated than my own. (Besides, at my age, I refuse to be regarded as the grandfather of research into near-death experiences!)

There are only three things I might add here. First, it is very important that many different points of view about near-death experiences be publicly aired and discussed. For, with the growing use of modern techniques of resuscitation, I suspect that near-death experiences are here to stay, and we need to be able to discuss them with patients who have them, to reassure them that they are not alone. We must keep an open mind about what these experiences mean. The finding of a common pattern of experiences occurring at or near death is unusual enough in itself; we can only guess at its significance.

Second, let us hope that the attempt everyone who learns about near-death experiences makes to "explain" them does not cause us to forget that they have a great *clinical* significance, too. Regardless of what one thinks of their explanation, the fact remains that doctors simply must deal sympathetically with patients who have them. Near-death experiences happen most often, after all, in *hospitals,* during the course of medical treatment.

Finally, it might be helpful for me to introduce Dr. Ring briefly to his readers. He is a warm, refreshing, careful, and thoughtful human being, and, in addition, has a fantastic sense of humor. His readers can be assured that, as incredible as what he reports may sound, it is not the work of a person who has any interest in sensationalizing what he has found. Indeed, these same observations have now been made by a number of qualified independent investigators. If I may take the liberty of speaking for all of us, I am sure that we all agree in one thing: The facts about near-death experiences are in themselves fantastic enough. Any exaggerations on our part could only succeed in making the case for their importance *less* plausible than it in fact is.

Dr. Raymond Moody
July 1979

PREFACE

Beginning in May 1977, I spent thirteen months tracking down and interviewing scores of people who had come close to death. I do not mean people who "merely" risk their lives by engaging in a hazardous occupation or avocation. Rather, I was interested to find people who had *actually* nearly died. In some cases, my research subjects had suffered "clinical" death, that is, they had lost all vital signs, such as heartbeat and respiration. In most cases, however, the men and women I talked to had found themselves on the brink of medical death but had not, biologically speaking, quite slipped over.

My aim in conducting these interviews was to find out what people experience when they are on the verge of apparent imminent death. What they told me is, in a word, fascinating—as I think the material presented here will amply demonstrate—and for two quite distinct reasons. One has to do with the intrinsic content of these experiences themselves: No one who reads of them can come away without having been profoundly stirred—emotionally, intellectually and spiritually—by the features they contain. The other is, if anything, even more significant: Most near-death experiences seem to unfold according to a *single pattern*, almost as though the prospect of death serves to release a stored, *common* "program" of feelings, perceptions, and experiences.

What to make of this common set of elements associated with the onset of death is the central challenge of this book. Whether this experience—what I have called the core near-death experience—can be interpreted in naturalistic terms is the overriding *scientific* issue raised by the findings presented here. The *meaning* of the core experience, which obviously depends on its interpretatin, is the major *metaphysical* question which must ultimately be addressed. Toward the end of the book, therefore, I will give my own views on these matters.

Because this study was undertaken in a scientific spirit of inquiry and was conducted using scientific procedures, I have made a deliberate effort to present my material as objectively as possible, letting my interviewees do most of the talking. In my descriptions of various aspects of the core experience, I have tried not to filter the data through the lenses of my own biases, and where I felt it appropriate to express a personal opinion or interpretation, I have always tried to label it as such. I am certain that I have not altogether succeeded in these efforts at impartiality, but it has at least been my ideal. Although my reasons for approaching my material in this manner may be obvious, I should perhaps be a little more explicit concerning my aims in writing *Life at Death*.

My interest from the start has been to examine near-death experiences from a scientific point of view. We already have a plethora of anecdotal books on the topic and, while they have done much to stimulate interest in near-death experiences, they have f..iled to answer many basic questions about these phenomena, as I will make clear in a moment. To make real headway in our understanding of near-death phenomena, we need, I believe, more scientific research.[1] If members of the scientific and medical community are to take these experiences seriously, they need sound research on which to base their evaluations. Accordingly, this book has been written with such professionals—as well as the public—in mind. That is why I have laced my chapters not only with illustrative quotations but with graphs and statistical tables as well. Readers not interested in these fine points may certainly skim this material, but professionals may wish to linger here. In writing *Life at Death*, I have consistently tried to strike a balance between the needs of the general reader and those of the interested professional. My hope is that I have written a book about near-death experiences that meets the criteria of scientific inquiry without sacrificing its appeal for anyone who is simply intrigued by these phenomena.

When I discuss my research publicly, however, audiences are rarely content to allow me to maintain my role of the "impartial scientist" or a "mere teller of other people's tales." They want to known such things as how I got into this unusual line of research, or whether I have had a near-death experience myself, or how *I* was affected by interviewing so many near-death survivors. I imagine some readers may also come to wonder about these questions and, since they will not be dealt with directly in the book itself, perhaps I had best try to answer them candidly here.

Concerning my reasons for embarking on this work, I am aware that both professional and personal motives had an influence on me. As a psychologist interested in altered states of consciousness, I have been familiar with near-death experiences for some years. My curiosity was further kindled by reading Raymond Moody's book *Life After Life*, shortly after it was published in 1975. I found that although I didn't really question the basic model Moody describes—it fit too well with other findings with which I was already familiar—I was left with many questions after finishing the book. How frequent were these experiences? Did it make any difference *how* one (almost) died? For example, do suicide attempts, which bring one close to death, engender the typical near-death experience? What role, if any, does prior religiousness play in shaping these experiences? Can the changes that allegedly follow from these experiences be systematically and quantitatively documented?

I doubt, however, that these "academic" questions in themselves would have been sufficient for me to undertake the research reported here. Were it not for certain personal considerations that were present in my life at the time of reading *Life After Life,* I would probably have only speculated on what the answers to these questions might be.

Although I myself have never had a near-death experience, I had for some time been highly intrigued by reports of their existence. This interest was to remain latent, however, until, for a variety of personal reasons, I entered a time of sorrow and inward emptiness in my life. I remember feeling spiritually adrift, as if I had somehow lost my way. Suddenly, I found that I simply did not know what to *do.* Concealing my barrenness and distress, I took myself that summer to a nearby convalescent home and offered my services as a "volunteer." I was, I guess, secretly hoping that some old, wise person, contemplating his own imminent death, would give me some clue as to what I might do to escape the pervasive feeling of "spiritual death" which was continuing to paralyze me. Instead, I spent most of my time playing cards with people in desperate physical straits and saw suffering all around. And our conversations were mostly about how adroitly someone had played a hand of bridge or when the refreshment cart would arrive. Philosophical reflections on life were not the vogue.

It was while I was vainly seeking "the answer" at the convalescent home that I "happened" to read Moody's book.

During the thirteen months of interviewing near-death survivors, I received my answer. These were mostly ordinary people, who described, in a consistent way, an extraordinary patterning of experiences that occurs at the point of death. The effect, combined with a certain quality of luminous serenity which many near-death survivors display, made me feel that I myself was undergoing an extended spiritual awakening. In any event, as my interviews continued, I found that I was no longer oppressed by the spiritual deadness that had, ironically, provided the initial impetus to my research. In fact, my feeling was becoming just the opposite.

Although my experience in conducting this study must of course remain private and nontransferrable, it is my personal hope that many readers, on finishing it, will find that they, too, have been moved and inspired by having had the opportunity to listen to the accounts of those who have returned from the brink of death to tell the rest of us what it is like to die.

ONE

The Near-Death Experience

During the 1970s, a wave of interest in the near-death experience swept over the public and professionals alike. The ground swell for this development was created by two remarkable physicians, first by the distinguished psychiatrist Elisabeth Kübler-Ross, who has become, over the last decade, this country's most renowned, if controversial, thanatologist. Celebrated for years for her pioneering work with dying patients, Kübler-Ross now claims to have spoken to more than one thousand men, women and children about their near-death experiences, and on this basis she declares that she "knows for a fact there is life after death." Although she has not published her findings in any systematic way, Kübler-Ross has been very energetic in disseminating the results of her investigations through her many public lectures, workshops, and interviews. As a direct result of her industry, eminence, and charisma, she has almost single-handedly brought about a high degree of public and professional awareness of near-death phenomena and their implications. Undoubtedly the climate of awareness generated by Kübler-Ross's work enabled an engaging small book on near-death experiences, written by another physician, to achieve bestseller status within a short time in this country, leading to its translation into at least twenty languages and enormous popularity abroad. *Life After Life* by Dr. Raymond A. Moody described the results of more than eleven years of inquiry into near-death experiences and was based on a sample of about 150 cases. Moody's findings largely dovetailed with those of Kübler-Ross, a fact acknowledged by her in a generous foreword she contributed to Moody's book. In a subsequent publication, *Reflections on Life After Life,* Moody indicates that he, like Kübler-Ross, has come to conclude that his data are indicative of a life after death.

The fact that these mutually supporting sets of findings were reported by two highly credible physicians, one eminent to begin with and the other compellingly persuasive in print, lent a certain "scientific aura" to these accounts, which previously had been, in the eyes of many, merely the kind of unauthenticated testimony that appears regularly in such periodicals as *The National Enquirer* and *Reader's Digest.*

Nevertheless, the impression of scientific validity is not really justified—and for two quite distinct reasons.

First of all, neither Kübler-Ross's nor Moody's data have yet been presented in a form that renders them susceptible to scientific analysis and evaluation. As I remarked earlier, although Kübler-Ross has spoken extensively about her findings, she has nowhere published them, and thus what the public record consists of are her summary descriptions and illustrative case histories—hardly a solid base for a scientific judgment of her material. As for Moody's published work, he is at pains to be explicit that his investigation should not be regarded as a scientific study. The case history material he presents appears to be highly selective, his "sampling procedures" were essentially haphazard, and his data were not subjected to any statistical analysis. Thus, though the findings they described were highly suggestive, and even credible to many who learned of them (including me), they cannot, by any rigorous standard of evaluation, be considered *in themselves* as constituting *scientific* evidence even for the experience of dying, much less the question of what Moody calls "life after life."

The second reason is this: The wave of interest in near-death phenomena, occasioned by the publicity given the work of Kübler-Ross and Moody, has obscured the fact that the scientific study of such phenomena dates back nearly a century.

Historically, the pioneers of what was then called "psychical research"—today, parapsychology—were among the first to tackle "the problem of survival," as it tends to be called in this field. Although by the 1930s, the evidential value of much of this work came to be questioned by parapsychologists themselves,[1] the contributions of such early researchers as Edmund Gurney, F.W.H. Myers, and Sir William Barrett need to be acknowledged as paving the way for more sophisticated parapsychological investigations.

Perhaps the best known of such modern studies have been conducted by Karlis Osis and Erlendur Haraldsson. These parapsychologists, building on a methodology first used more than half a century ago by Barrett, have examined both the phenomenological features of and mood changes associated with deathbed visions, as reported by physicians, nurses, and, occasionally, directly by the survivors. Osis and Haraldsson have undertaken these studies in both the United States and India, and have found impressive cross-cultural similarities in those experiential aspects of dying that their research is designed to examine. Despite severe problems in representative sampling and other methodological flaws, their results, presented in detailed statistical fashion, show a remarkable internal consistency and closely resemble those reported by Kübler-Ross and Moody.

The early psychical researchers were not the only investigators who made pioneering studies of near-death phenomena. Professor Albert Heim was a Swiss geologist fond of mountain climbing, who more than once nearly lost his life in mountain climbing accidents. Because of these experiences, he spent the last twenty-five years of his life systematically gathering accounts from others involved in a variety of life-threatening accidents. This material was originally published in the last century and, as with other studies to follow, disclosed a clear similarity among reported near-death experiences triggered by accidents.

Heim's work lay forgotten until interest in it was revived in the early 1970s by the psychiatrist Russell Noyes, Jr. and a colleague, Ray Kletti, who published a translation of it.[2] Noyes and Kletti have gone on to conduct some important descriptive and statistical studies in the Heimian tradition, which have supported and extended the data in Heim's original collection.[3] Their work, which emphasizes the experience of (apparently) impending accidental death, also reveals many of the transcendent features described by Kübler-Ross, Moody, and others, but it is worth observing that Noyes and Kletti use a very different explanatory framework from most investigators' in interpreting their findings. Specifically, they propose "depersonalization" as a response to the stress of (apparent) imminent death. Depersonalization is seen as an ego-defensive reaction to protect the individual against the unbearable prospect of his death. The result is a pervasive feeling of detachment and transcendence, which cushions the expected impact of the near-death crisis. This psychodynamic explanation of near-death phenomena provides a clear contrast with the Kübler-Ross–Moody "survival" view.

The original work of Heim and of his "methodological descendents," Noyes and Kletti, have in turn influenced other professional investigators interested in near-death phenomena. For example, Stanislav Grof, a Czech psychoanalyst and one of the foremost authorities on the effects of LSD on human consciousness, and Joan Halifax, an American anthropologist who is a student of visionary experience, have recently co-authored a volume, *The Human Encounter with Death,* in which they are concerned to compare the prototypic near-death experience (to be delineated shortly) with the psychedelically-induced experience. In making the case for the similarity between these differently engendered experiences, they draw heavily on the work of Heim and Noyes and Kletti and seem to adopt the latter's interpretative outlook.

These brief allusions to the work of other researchers[4] should be sufficient to show that while the spotlight of attention in recent years may have been focused on Kübler-Ross and Moody, other investigators with solid credentials have also been enlarging our knowledge of death-related experiences.

Despite these recent studies, however, it is evident that we are still very much in need of well-designed and thorough investigations of near-death experiences. When examined critically, the existing studies all suffer from such methodological failings as unsatisfactory sampling procedures, inadequate quantification of variables, and lack of proper comparison groups. These shortcomings, when coupled with the unscientific status of the Kübler-Ross and Moody studies, dictate that more rigorous research programs be undertaken in an effort to shore up the methodological weaknesses of already published research. The implications of near-death experiences are far too momentous to be allowed to rest on such an inadequate foundation.

Accordingly, early in 1977, I set out to conduct my own scientific investigation of near-death phenomena. Beginning in May 1977, my research staff and I interviewed more than one hundred people who had come close to death. In some cases, these were men and women who appeared to undergo "clinical" death, where there is no heartbeat or respiration; in most cases, however, the individuals we talked with had "merely" edged toward the brink of death but did not, so far as we could determine, actually "die." In this book, I will present the results of our research. With the exception of a study carried out concurrently and independently by a Florida cardiologist, Dr. Michael Sabom, I believe that our investigation represents the most systematic and exhaustive scientific study of near-death experiences thus far reported. As the next chapter will make clear, however, this study, too, is not without its methodological problems. Nevertheless, I believe that even the most critical reader, on assessing the evidence to be presented in the chapters to come, will be persuaded that we now have sufficient scientific grounds for asserting that there is a consistent and remarkable experiental pattern that often unfolds when an individual is seemingly about to die. I will call this reliable near-death pattern the *core experience.*

Now, to lay the groundwork for this study, it is necessary to return to Moody's account from *Life After Life* of the core experience. We need to know, *specifically,* of what elements it consists.

In presenting his account, Moody stresses that it is idealized and represents a composite experience, not an actual one. He observes that different people in his sample approximated this composite, but no one reported every feature he describes. Let me first quote Moody's idealized version of the core experience. Following it, I will list the major elements that Moody has abstracted from it.

A man is dying and, as he reaches the point of greatest physical distress, he hears himself pronounced dead by his doctor. He begins to hear an uncomfortable noise, a loud ringing or buzzing, and at the same time feels himself moving very rapidly through a long tunnel. After this, he suddenly finds himself outside his own physical body, but still in the same immediate physical environment, and sees his own body from a distance, as though he is a spectator. He watches the resuscitation attempt from this vantage point and is in a state of emotional upheaval.

After a while, he collects himself and becomes more accustomed to his odd condition. He notices that he still has a "body," but one of a very different nature and with very different powers from the physical body he has left behind. Soon other things begin to happen. Others come to meet him and help him. He glimpses the spirits of relatives and friends who have already died, and a loving, warm spirit of a kind he has never encountered before—a being of light—appears before him. This being asks him a question, nonverbally, to make him evaluate his life and helps him along by showing him a panoramic, instantaneous playback of the major events of his life. At some point, he finds himself approaching some sort of a barrier or border, apparently representing the limit between earthly life and the next life. Yet, he finds that he must go back to the earth, that the time for his death has not yet come. At this point he resists, for by now he is taken up with his experiences in the afterlife and does not want to return. He is overwhelmed by intense feelings of joy, love, and peace. Despite his attitude, though, he somehow reunites with his physical body and lives.

Later he tries to tell others, but he has trouble doing so. In the first place, he can find no human words to describe these unearthly episodes. He also finds that others scoff, so he stops telling other people. Still, the experience affects his life profoundly, especially his views about death and its relationship to life.[5]

The components of this experience that Moody designates as its recurrent motifs do not all occur in any actual instance, nor do they appear in an invariant sequence.[6] They are:

1. Ineffability
2. Hearing the news (of one's own death)
3. Feelings of peace and quiet
4. The noise
5. The dark tunnel
6. Out of the body
7. Meeting others
8. The being of light
9. The review

10. The border
11. Coming back

If we use Moody's account and componential analysis as a provisional basis for grasping the core experience, we are obviously left with a number of intriguing research questions—questions this book will attempt to answer.

I will begin with the fundamental one: How common is this experience in near-death episodes? Moody's publication gives the reader only the positive instances—only the "hits," as it were. But it would seem to be important to determine how frequently this experience occurs and whether this figure varies substantially with the population studied or with the condition associated with apparent imminent death. If, for example, the core experience is reported only 10% of the time, the interpretation of the effect is likely to be very different than if the figure is 50% or 90%. Indeed, if the overall figure turns out to be quite low, it could certainly be argued that Moody's book and Kübler-Ross's pronouncements may have deceived many people by implying that a transcendent experience of dying is the rule, whereas it might be the exception.

In *Reflections on Life After Life,* Moody reports that he has talked with many people who remember nothing in connection with a near-death episode, but he refuses, for cogent reasons, to speculate on how large this category of nonrecallers (or nonexperiencers) might be. Moody leaves the impression that any diligent and sympathetic investigator will find abundant evidence in support of the core experience he describes, but his discussion leaves the issue unresolved. In this book, I will undertake to provide at least a crude estimate of this important parameter.

A corollary question raised but not answered by Moody's research (or anyone else's for that matter) is whether the core experience, however common, is independent of the condition that brings it about. In other words, we may ask: Does it make a difference how one (almost) dies? For example, is the experience of nearly dying after a serious automobile accident different in certain characteristic ways from a near-death experience triggered by a heart attack? And what of suicide? There are certain dark hints in the literature, including Moody's books, that nearly dying as a result of a suicide attempt is *unlikely* to provide a transcendent near-death experience. Yet though such *opinions* are common, reliable empirical data on this point are remarkably rare and what data do exist tend to contradict this opinion.[7] The question of what is experienced during a serious suicide attempt is obviously one of both urgent theoretical and practical significance. If the experience tends *not* to be transcendent or is unpleasant, this will not only sharply reduce the limits of the core experience but should act as a deterrent to people who might be tempted to take their own lives after hearing about (and misconstruing) the findings of Kübler-Ross, Moody, and others.

A second purpose of this book, therefore, is to compare the experiences associated with three different modes of near-death onset: illness, accident, and suicide attempt.

A third issue left unexamined by Moody's work is the relationship between religiousness and the core experience. A frequent objection to the apparent religious quality of many near-death experiences is based on the assumption that the death crisis tends merely to trigger visual images based on a person's religious belief system. According to this argument, since most people are at least nominally religious and are known from various national polls to subscribe to some idea of life after death, it is to be expected that when death approaches, religious and otherworldly imagery will be found to predominate. In short, believing is seeing.

If this interpretation is correct, we ought to anticipate a positive correlation between religiousness, on the one hand, and the likelihood or the depth of a core experience, on the other. In short, religious individuals would be expected to have more or deeper core experiences.

The other view, for which some fragmentary support exists in the literature, holds that religiousness *per se* is not a determinant of core experiences but may affect their interpretation. Such a finding would tend to undercut the glib assumption that core experiences are fantasied or hallucinatory wish-fulfillments. We shall, accordingly, also explore what, if any, relationship exists between religiousness and near-death experiences.

Finally, a fourth focus of my investigation will be the subsequent life changes experienced by near-death survivors. Most existing studies have either stated or implied (as does Moody) that profound personal changes tend to occur following a near-death episode. For the most part, however, these changes have been illustrated only by selected cases, making it difficult to determine how representative they are. We have had many anecdotes (which have their place, of course) but little systematic reportage concerning these aftereffects. Another problem with interpreting what little data we do have is distinguishing the effects that can be attributed to the circumstance of nearly dying from those that are dependent on having a *core experience* at the time of one's near-death crisis. *Life at Death* will examine these matters in systematic and quantitative detail.

Life at Death

In sum, my objective in making this investigation has been to scientifically gather evidence bearing on the following unresolved issues of near-death research: first, the incidence of the core experience; second, the invariance of the core experience; third, prior religiousness as it relates to the core experience; and, finally, the nature of changes following near-death episodes.

T w o

The Connecticut Study

To carry out our investigation, arrangements were made with several large hospitals in central Connecticut and with a few smaller hospitals elsewhere in Connecticut and, finally, with one hospital in Maine, to secure the names of patients or former patients who met the criteria for inclusion. These criteria were: (1) the survivor had to have come close to death or been resuscitated from clinical death, as a result of a serious illness, accident, or suicide attempt; (2) the survivor had to be sufficiently recovered from his near-death incident to be able to discuss it coherently; (3) the survivor had to speak English well enough for an interview to be conducted in that language; and (4) the survivor had to be at least eighteen years old.

In the larger hospitals, we were able to use various contacts, including physicians, nurses, clergymen, and administrative personnel, in key locations (for example, cardiology, internal medicine, the emergency room, the chaplain's office, and so on) to serve as sources of referral. In smaller hospitals, usually a single contact was used. Members of my research staff would call our contacts on a regular basis to obtain the names of potential subjects. Once a name had been suggested, that individual's physician would be called and, if necessary, the purpose of our study would be explained and permission sought to interview the candidate. If the physician consented, the next step would be to get in touch with the candidate—who, in the meantime, may have been approached by a hospital staff member—and explain our interest in talking to him. If the candidate agreed to be interviewed, he was asked to sign an informal consent sheet and a time was set for the interview. If a candidate was no longer hospitalized or under the direct care of a physician, the person was called directly and the consent form was omitted.

Several months into our investigation, I realized that our hospital referrals were not likely to lead to a sufficient number of cases in our accident and suicide attempt categories to permit meaningful statistical comparisons to be made. At that point, we tried to increase our sample sizes in these categories by writing letters to many psychiatrists and by advertising in local newspapers. The letters and advertisements were always phrased in terms of our interest in speaking to persons who had come close to death as a result of either accident or suicide attempt. No mention was ever made of any special interest in near-death experiences *per se*, nor was any remuneration offered or given to individuals for their participation.

27

Life at Death

As word of our work spread, we found that we were also the recipients of word-of-mouth referrals. Several people referred themselves as a result of this kind of publicity, while others referred friends who had come close to death. Since we were still in need of respondents in certain categories, these persons were also interviewed.

As a result of these different recruitment procedures, it is necessary to present a breakdown of interviewees by source of referral. This information is given in Table 1.

Table 1
_____

Number of Referrals by Source

Source	Number
Hospital	54
Physician	5
Nonmedical	16
Self	6
Advertisement	21
Total	102

Interview Schedule

Our method of data collection involved the use of a structured interview schedule. The interview itself was composed of five distinct information-gathering segments:

1. Demographic information
2. A free narrative of the near-death episode
3. A series of probing questions designed to determine the presence or absence of the various components of the core experience as described by Moody
4. Aftereffects
5. Pre- and post-incident comparison of religious beliefs and attitudes

(A copy of the entire interview schedule can be found in Appendix I.)

Prior to the interview, each respondent was assured of both anonymity and confidentiality. Since the interview was to be tape-recorded, appropriate justification was given for this procedure. In order not to bias the respondent's comments, most questions about the study and its underlying purposes were deferred until the end, at which time all were answered. Before the interviewer left, he gave each respondent a card indicating where he could be reached. All those interested were also promised a report of our findings.[1]

Most of the interviews took between one-half and one hour to complete; a few required more or less time, but never longer than one and a half hours. Most of the interviews were conducted in the respondent's home. Some took place in hospitals, where usually a private room was available, and a few were held in my office or home. Of the 102 interviews obtained, I conducted 74. An additional 20, including all 10 Maine interviews, were the responsibility of a graduate student working closely with me;[2] the remainder were done by several graduate students affiliated with the project. All interviews were carried out between May 1977 and May 1978.

Respondents

A total of 102 persons recounting 104 near-death incidents were interviewed. Of these, 52 nearly died as a result of a serious illness; 26 from a serious accident; and 24 as a result of a suicide attempt. Some basic demographic information on all of the respondents is presented in Table 2.

Table 2

Demographic Data on Interviewees

Total interviewed	102
Sex	
Male	45
Female	57
Race	
White	97
Black	5
Marital status	
Married	47
Single	32
Divorced/separated	16
Widowed	7

Religious denomination
    Catholic   37
    Protestant   34
    None   21
    Other   3
    Agnostic/atheist   7

Education
    College graduate   11
    Some college/college student   34
    High school graduate   39
    Some high school   10
    Grade school only   8

Age range   18–84

Mean age at interview   43.01

Mean age of near-death incident   37.81

Although, for the most part, frequency data are given in Table 2, the frequencies are nearly equal to percentages, since the total number of interviewees was 102. For legal reasons, no one under eighteen was interviewed in this study. A perusal of Table 2 shows that, with the exception of youngsters and race, our sample of near-death survivors represents a considerable range of demographic diversity. Before turning to issues related to the selectiveness of our sample, the last entries listed in Table 2 call for some comment.

In this study, we made an attempt to interview respondents as soon after their near-death incident as was medically and ethically feasible. Our intention was to minimize both the tendency to embellish and the danger of forgetting. Despite our efforts, only slightly more than one-third of our respondents could be interviewed within a year of their incident. The average time gap between incident and interview, as can be seen from Table 2, is slightly more than five years, but this figure is misleading because a few people had their episode more than twenty years previously.[3] Table 3 presents these data in more precise detail.

Table 3

Interview-Incident Interval Data*

I-I Interval	No. of Respondents
<1 year	37
1–2 years	23
2–5 years	17
5–10 years	11
>10 years	16

*For purposes of this breakdown, all 104 near-death incidents were included.

Thus, about 60% of our respondents were interviewed within two years of their near-death episode; the proportion of respondents having had their episode in the distant past was quite small.

As can be inferred from what has already been said, the 102 persons who were interviewed for our study were drawn from a larger group, of which many members were either unable or unwilling to participate for a variety of reasons. These sampling problems are discussed in detail in Appendix II for the benefit of the interested professional reader, but they can be briefly summarized here in nontechnical language.

We found that participation in our study was strongly affected by the condition that had brought an individual close to death. Accident victims, while difficult to locate, were almost always willing to consent to an interview when contacted. On the other hand, only about half of the illness victims—who were by far the most numerous of near-death survivors—eventually took part in our investigation. Suicide attempters had, as expected, the lowest rate of participation, with only one of every five such individuals agreeing to be interviewed.

Moreover, there were differences between these categories in *source* of referral. Illness victims, for example, were generally referred to us by medical sources, whereas suicide attempters were recruited mainly by advertisements. Accident victims came to our attention by a variety of means, with slightly less than half being referred by medical personnel.

How much of a difference these differences in availability and source of referral *actually* make is not possible to state precisely. From my own examination of the data, I would hazard a guess that these differences are more likely to affect our estimate of the incidence of the near-death experience within each of these categories than they are to distort the

Life at Death

kind of experience that is described. As will be seen, however, our findings regarding the incidence of these near-death experiences *are* comparable to what other researchers have recently reported, despite these differences. In any case, these sampling factors should be borne in mind when interpreting our data, and the reader will be reminded of them in appropriate contexts.

Measuring the Near-Death Experience

In *Reflections on Life After Life,* Moody, in discussing what I have called the core experience, predicts that "any investigator who enters into this type of study sympathetically and diligently will find that there is ample case material."

In our investigation, Moody's prediction was completely upheld. Our evidence on this question is in total accord with the findings earlier reported by him and other near-death researchers.

Altogether, forty-nine of our cases, or 48% of our entire sample, recounted experiences that conform in an obvious way, at least in part, to the core experience pattern as delineated by Moody.

Nevertheless, in interpreting this data the reader should bear in mind all the qualifications concerning the estimate of the incidence of the core experience that were raised in the preceding section.

Moreover, it is important at this point to specify our criteria for deciding who did and who did not have a Moody-type experience.

On the basis mainly of Moody's analysis of the principal features of the core experience, as modified slightly by the form of our interview questions, I constructed a near-death experience index, which is essentially a weighted measure of the depth of the experience. The ten components of this index, together with their respective weights, are presented in Table 4. Although the weighting factors are slightly arbitrary, they were arrived at before the formal analysis of the data was undertaken.

Table 4
_____

Components and Weights for the Core Experience Index

Component	Weight
Subjective sense of being dead	1
Feeling of peace, painlessness, pleasantness, etc. (core affective cluster)	2*
Sense of bodily separation	2*
Sense of entering a dark region	2*

Encountering a presence/hearing a voice	3
Taking stock of one's life	3
Seeing, or being enveloped in, light	2
Seeing beautiful colors	1
Entering into the light	4
Encountering visible "spirits"	3

*Individuals could be assigned a score of either 1 or 2 on these components, if present. The rules for scoring were as follows: (1) for the affective cluster, assign 2 if the feelings were very strong, otherwise 1; (2) for the sense of bodily separation, assign 2 if a clear out-of-body experience was described, otherwise 1; (3) for entering into a dark region, assign 2 if perception was accompanied by a sense of movement, otherwise 1. A given score would then be multiplied by the appropriate *weight* for that component, resulting in a weighted score of *either* 2 or 4 for that component. All nonasterisked components were scored either present (1) or absent (0).

It can be determined that scores on this weighted index, abbreviated WCEI (for weighted core experience index), can range from a theoretical low of 0, indicating the absence of any kind of Moody-type experience, to 29, representing the deepest Moody-type experience. Thus the higher the index, the deeper, or richer, the experience. In fact, WCEI scores varied from 0 to 24.

How were these scores obtained?

Each interview was tape-recorded and each tape was rated by three people associated with the research, including myself, using a detailed rating schedule (see Appendix III). Determining the presence or absence or the strength of a given component for a given individual required taking into account three sets of ratings. Only if at least two of the three judges agreed on the presence of a given characteristic was it scored. Thus, if anything, the WCEI may err on the conservative side.

In using the WCEI for the purpose of classification, certain arbitrary but, in my judgement, reasonable cutoff points were assigned. If a person's score was less than 6, he was adjudged not to have had "enough" of an experience to qualify as a "core experiencer." This undoubtedly eliminates some people who might have been counted as positive instances by Moody (indeed, it was my impression that this index failed to include some interviewees who probably *did* experience some aspects of the Moody pattern), but again it seems better to err on the side of underinclusion than the reverse. Respondents scoring between 6 and 9 on the WCEI will be designated *moderate experiencers* and those with scores in excess of 10 will be referred to as *deep experiencers*.

In terms of this tripartite classification scheme, 27 persons (26%) were deep experiencers, 22 (22%) were moderate experiencers, while the remainder, 53 (52%) were nonexperiencers. This division is of course based on the entire sample and ignores the factor of *how* a person came close to death, a matter we shall consider later.

If we take into account the source of referral, we find that 39% of those who were referred by medical sources were found to have had a core experience, whereas for those who were referred either by nonmedical sources or were self-referred the corresponding figure is 58%. The difference here, though suggestive, is not statistically significant.[4] Since it seems likely that the 58% figure may be *more* inflated than the first, we may regard the figure of 39% as probably being closer to an accurate incidence estimate for a population of (relatively!) unselected near-death cases (in a ratio of approximately 2:1:1 for illness-accident- and suicide-attempt victims, respectively). Of course, because even these (59) cases were not selected randomly, this last assertion is not really warranted on statistical grounds. Nevertheless, used as a ballpark figure, it is not likely to be too misleading, especially in the light of Sabom and Kreutziger's own revised estimate of 43% (see Chapter Ten).

Incidentally, there were virtually no sex differences in either frequency or depth of the core experience. The percentages are as follows:

	Men	Women
Deep experiencers	27	26
Moderate experiencers	20	23
Nonexperiencers	53	51

Before examining the different facets of the core experience more closely in an effort to be quantitatively precise where Moody is vague, it will be relevant to provide some illustrative protocols for the different degrees of depth I have distinguished. Indeed, throughout this book I shall attempt to blend the statistical treatment of the data with the descriptive, in order to provide a comprehensive overview of the core experience.

I will begin with an account of a fairly minimal experience (at least in terms of our index). The man in question had been suffering from a malarialike disease and while hospitalized had the following experience:

> At that time, I was in a coma. I could hear everything that went on and I could see everything that went on, but I could not move, I could not talk. To all appearances, I was dead. I even heard the doctor tell the nurse to let me alone, that I was as good as

dead. . . . I could hear, I could hear very well. To me, it seemed as though I was standing alongside of myself and seeing everything that was going on. *(Could you actually see your physical body?)* Yes. I was strapped to the bed. I had no pain whatsoever at this time. Like I say, it almost seemed as though I was standing in the room watching the doctors come and look at me and the nurse come in and look at me, and I could hear them talking, and, as a matter of fact, the doctor was even playing grab-ass with the nurse. This is true, so help me. *(51)*[5]

This respondent received the lowest possible core experience score on the WCEI, 6. Four points were awarded for his description of his out-of-body state and an additional 2 were assigned for his description of his feelings at the time, amplified somewhat in another segment of his interview not quoted here.

The next case, that of a woman with a fairly deep experience, was occasioned by the onset of a very rapid loss of blood pressure while giving birth to her second child. She recounted her experience in these words:

All of a sudden, everything went absolutely black. I was not aware of any kind of time. What it was like, I was up in the left-hand corner of the room, looking down at what was going on. *(Could you see clearly?)* I could see very clearly, yeh, yeh. I recognized it as being me. I had absolutely no fear whatsoever. That is one thing that is *very* definite, that there was no fear. It was as if I was supposed to be watching it. It was part of what you were supposed to do. . . . I was aware that I felt good and felt increasingly more at peace very rapidly. . . . I would have been perfectly content to stay there forever and ever. I mean, I had no desire to do anything but stay right there. . . . I became aware of not a voice, but of thoughts that began to come very rapidly, to stop it. To say, "No, O.K., fine, you've had a taste of what this is all about, but you can't stay here. This isn't allowed. You've got to go back, you've got too much to do. You've got to go back, the child is in danger, there is something wrong with him. It is a boy" and the name Peter—now, we had thought about other names, in fact at that point it was going to be Harold—this was a name that came. [About her son's physical condition, she was told] that it was going to be a heart problem. Which did come out later after I came back and I was in labor when the doctor said to me, "We've got to hurry this thing up because this little thing is starting to do strange things." I told him that I knew there was a problem, that it was a heart problem, and I assured him that he was going to be all right,

that he was going to have the problem, but he wasn't going to die.
(25)

In this case, the woman scored 13 on our index—4 points for both the core affective cluster and her out-of-body experience, 2 points for entering a dark region, and 3 points for encountering a "presence" (later in the interview she asserts that these thoughts were not her own). I might mention in passing, that according to my interviewee, her son did have a heart problem, which cleared up spontaneously to the surprise of her physician. The presence also informed the mother that her son would be an unusual child, gifted with rare talents, and that her relationship with him would be especially close and different from that with her other children (she now has three). She has since informed me that all these things have come about, but I have not had time to investigate this myself. Even if independently confirmed, these developments are susceptible to a variety of interpretations. This "hint" of paranormal knowledge occuring at the time of a near-death experience, however, is by no means limited to this case in my collection, and has been reported by other investigators.

For an example of a very rich experience, I have selected the case of a woman in her mid-thirties, who, at the time of her near-death incident, was undergoing surgery for a chronic intestinal disorder. Her WCEI score of 18 was exceeded by only two others in our sample, though nine others achieved scores of 15 or higher, so it is presented strictly as illustrative of the deepest experiences I encountered, not as typical of core experiences.[6]

[She remembers hearing someone say that they were going to do a "cut down" on her and then] I remember being *above* the bed—I was not *in* the bed anymore—looking down on *me* lying in the bed and I remember saying to myself, "I don't want you to do a cut down on me." . . . I know [from what she was told afterward] that the doctors worked on me for many hours. And I remember being first above my body and then I remember being in, like a valley. And this valley reminded me of what I think of as the valley of the shadow of death. I also remember it being a very *pretty* valley. Very pleasant. And I felt very *calm* at that point. I met a person in this valley. And this person—I realized it later on—was my [deceased] grandfather, who I had never met. [She then describes how she was able to identify him after talking to her grandmother about it.] I remember my grandfather saying to me, "Helen, don't give up. You're still needed. I'm not ready for you yet." It was that kind of a thing. And then I remember *music. (Can you describe it for me?)* It was kind of like church music, in a sense. Spiritual music. *(Was*

there singing? Were there musical instruments that you could identify?)
No. No . . . it had . . . somehow a *sad* quality about it. A very
awesome quality to it. *(7)*

In this instance, the WCEI score of 18 was the result of the following
component values: one point was assigned for her subjective sense of
being dead, 4 points for both the affective cluster and her out-of-body
experience, 2 points for taking stock of her life, and 3 points for her
encounter with the (apparent) spirit of her deceased grandfather.
(Some of these values were also based on interview material not quoted
in the foregoing excerpt.)

Sometime after my interview with her, she sent me a poem that she
felt moved to write in order to capture something of her experience
and its effect on her. It is a simply written poem, but it expresses
eloquently, I think, the feeling, tone, and imagery encountered by
many near-death survivors who have deep experiences to relate.
Accordingly, I shall pause here long enough to quote it.

THE VALLEY OF PEACE

One summer's night,
I was totally free.
High up in the room,
Looking down at me.

I went through a tunnel,
at a very fast speed.
I knew not what was happening,
But knew I'd soon be freed.

Then thru a door-like entity,
Into a valley of peace,
Where music played God's tune to me,
and made my fear release.

Colors bright, dancing lights,
Such a sight to see.
A figure is coming into view,
Oh, God, it's my grandfather talking to me.

Your time has not come yet,
Your family needs you still,
Enjoy your life to the fullest
I love you and always will.

I've had the chance to see a man
I did not even know.
I had the chance to stay with him
But decided I had to go.

It was so good to be free of pain,
It felt good to be so free.
The Land I saw so beautiful.
Death no longer frightens me.

I have presented these three narratives, and the poem, mainly to illustrate the different levels of depth I found in the many near-death accounts my staff and I encountered in the course of our interviews. Any careful reader can see how each successive example in this small series appears to present a richer, more profound experience than its immediate predecessor. Nevertheless, if we are to progress in our understanding of these core experiences, beyond the descriptive and anecdotal level already available in Moody's and Kübler-Ross's writings, it will be necessary to bring some conceptual order and statistical comparisons to bear.

THREE

Stages of the Near-Death Experience

In my investigation of near-death experiences, I found that the core experience itself tends to unfold in a characteristic way. In general, the earlier stages of the experience are more common, and the later stages manifest themselves with systematically decreasing frequency. Thus, it seems that not only are some of Moody's categories more common than others, but also that they are meaningfully ordered in frequency.

In Figure 1, I have indicated five distinct stages of the core experience, as suggested by our data, along with their corresponding frequency. In the sections to follow, these five categories will be described fully and amply illustrated by reference to specific interviews. As this discussion proceeds, it will be apparent that when these five categories are considered in sequence, they form a coherent pattern. What we will have, then, is the *basic thanatomimetic narrative*—the experience of (apparent) death in its developmental form.

The Affective Component: Peace and the Sense of Well-Being

The first stage, and one that is emphasized in many of our accounts, relates to the affective accompaniment of the core experience. The conscious experience of dying is heralded by a feeling of such peace and contentment that many respondents claim there is simply no way they can describe it. Nevertheless, some of the attempts to do so—which I will shortly quote—are themselves deeply moving and compelling even when the words do ultimately fail. As can be seen from Figure 1, about 60% of our sample report this kind of experience, including many who never get beyond this stage and a few who do not really conform to other aspects of the Moody pattern. If we confine ourselves just to these respondents who are "core experiencers," thirty-five of forty-nine, or 71%, explicitly use the words *peaceful* or *calm* to characterize the feeling-tone of their experience.[1] Most of the others in this category, as might be inferred, use various synonyms to describe how they felt.

Before presenting a full statistical breakdown of the different aspects of the affective component accompanying the core experience, it seems

Life at Death

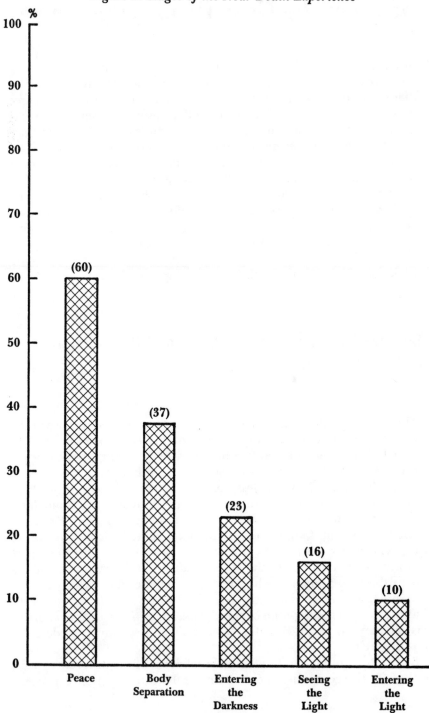

Figure 1. Stages of the Near Death Experience

necessary to provide some qualitative descriptive accounts. The illustrations given below are meant to convey something of the range of the affective response to apparent imminent death. Enough excerpts will be cited here to give, as well, a sense of "the central tendency" of these statements.

A woman who nearly died of a ruptured appendix observed:

I had a feeling of total peace. A feeling of total, total peace . . . it was just such a total peaceful sensation—I wasn't frightened anymore. *(30)*

Another woman who had a cardiac arrest said:

[There was] nothing painful. There was nothing frightening about it. It was just something that I felt I gave myself into completely. And it felt *good*. . . . One *very*, very strong feeling was that if I could *only* make them [her doctors] understand how comfortable and how *painless* it is . . . how natural it is . . . I felt *no* sadness. No longing. No fear. *(20)*

A woman who had attempted suicide by hurling herself into the ocean and was badly smashed by the waves against the rocks of a nearby cliff recalled:

This *incredible* feeling of peace [came] over me. . . . All of a sudden there was no pain, just peace. [Later in the interview she reflected on the sheer difficulty of describing how she felt.] I suppose it's because it's so completely *unlike* anything else that I've ever experienced in my life. So that I've got nothing to compare it to. A perfectly *beautiful*, beautiful feeling . . . to me, there's a definite feeling of sunlight and warmth associated with this peaceful feeling. [It should be noted that on the day this woman tried to drown herself the water temperature was 48°; she remembers feeling very cold in the ocean and was told that she shivered a great deal in the hospital afterward.] But when this feeling of peace came over me, I was warm. I felt warm, safe, happy, relaxed, just every wonderful adjective you could use. . . . This was perfection, this is everything anyone could possibly want and everything I could possibly want—is this, is this feeling. *(82)*

In case the reader may feel that these extravagant descriptions reflect a kind of feminine hyperbole, the following accounts from some of the

men in my sample should prove sufficient to dispel that impression.
A racing-car driver commented:

I guess the best description would be visualizing someone in a very
strenuous, active sport, and when they got through with it, they
take a sauna and have a massage. And if you can experience that
feeling of relaxation, then multiply it times one thousand, that's
how you would feel. It was just super, super-great. *(73)*

A young man who nearly died when a fever reached a temperature
of 106.9° said:

The mellowness and the passiveness that I felt in this state was just
so intense . . . like I said before, it was a very, very strong—I can
only use the words *mellow feeling, passive feeling.* There wasn't one
bit of discontentment that I felt. I felt [pause] I can probably say
the highest I've ever felt in my life. *(45)*

A man who tried to hang himself recalled:

I felt really good. It felt, like when you wake up in the morning
and you feel real good, you have a good feeling. *(100)*

A man who nearly died in a boating accident testified:

It's tough. Use *euphoric.* Use *orgasmic.* Or use *high.* It was very
tangible, very real. But it was doing magnificent things to me. You
know, afterward I looked at that lake and I said, "That lake made
love to me." It really did, it felt like that. *(66)*

A few more excerpts will perhaps add nothing except redundancy,
but somehow I feel that repetition here is not wasted space, if it serves
to convey just how frequently these powerful feelings are associated
with the onset of (apparent) death.
A sixty-year-old woman who had suffered a heart attack observed:

I think that probably the next thing I remember is total, peaceful,
wonderful blackness. Very peaceful blackness . . . the only other
word I might add would be *softness.* Just an indescribable peacefulness, absolutely indescribable. [This was] a total peacefulness, an
ABSOLUTE [said very slowly and with great emphasis] peacefulness. *(4)*

A man who nearly died as a result of a motorcycle crash said that as he lay (apparently) dying in the hospital:

> I felt *peaceful.* I felt *calm.* No pain . . . extremely peaceful. *(68)*

And finally, a woman who clearly struggled to find the words to describe the ineffable. Her comments were perhaps the most passionate of any of my respondents, but that may be because she was one of the few who at least attempted to articulate for me a sense that most others despaired of ever being able to communicate to another with the power of speech. She had suffered a cardiac arrest in connection with a tonsillectomy.

> . . . the thing I could never—absolutely *never* forget is that absolute feeling of [pause] peace [pause] joy, or something. . . . I remember the *feeling.* I just remember this *absolute beautiful feeling.* Of peace . . . and happy! Oh! So happy! . . . The *peace* . . . the *release* [pause] the fear was all gone. There was no pain. There was nothing. It was just *absolutely beautiful!* [said with the strongest emphasis] I could *never* explain it in a million years. It was a feeling that I think everybody *dreams* of someday having. Reaching a point of ABSOLUTE [said slowly and with great emphasis] peace. To me *peace* is the greatest word that I can express. *(24)*

These passages should be sufficient to convey the feeling tone which seems to serve both as an initial cue for the core experience and as an affective background during its unfolding. A more detailed statistical picture of the range of affective reactions accompanying the core experience is offered in Table 5. For purposes of comparison, I have given the percentages for both experiencers and nonexperiencers.

Table 5

Comparison of Core Experiencers and Nonexperiencers on the Ten Most Common Affective Reactions (ranking based on core experiencers only)

Characteristics	Core experiencers (49)	Nonexperiencers (53)
Peace	59%	15%
Painless	49%	13%
No fear	47%	9%
Relaxed	29%	4%

Characteristics	Core experiencers (49)	Nonexperiencers (53)
Pleasant	27%	0%
Calm	20%	6%
Happy	20%	2%
Joy	20%	0%
Quiet	16%	2%
Warm	16%	0%

Even a casual inspection of Table 5 reveals several interesting facets. First, the general affective response of experiencers was *extremely positive*. In fact, of the total of 170 feelings and emotions named by the experiencers, only 8 (or 4.7%) were negative. Most of the 8 were some form of fear. And even of these, most were transient, occurring at the beginning of the experience or after its termination, upon recovering. Second, there is no clear pattern of affective responses for the nonexperiencers, even though in their case also the qualities of peacefulness, painlessness, and the absence of fear maintain the same relative rankings. Nevertheless, despite the identical ranking of the first three characteristics, it is obvious that the percentage values are drastically lower. Even then, because of the conservative nature of our core experience index (the WCEI), we may very well have included a few experiencers among our nonexperiencers category—a state of affairs which, if true, would mean the modest percentages for peaceful-ness, painlessness, and the absence of fear in the latter category are somewhat inflated. In fact, most of the statements of peace from the nonexperiencer category (namely, six of eight) come from one sub-group—female suicide attempt cases—and appear to reflect more a sense of *relief* that their lives were (apparently) over than the feeling of transcendent peace expressed in the quotes from experiencers. Finally, implicit in this table but not clearly shown is that where only one experiencer failed to report any feelings or emotions, fully thirty-five (or 66%) of the nonexperiencers disclosed or implied that they felt none. Thus, the modal feeling or emotion for the nonexperiencers was—nothing.

Summing up the results of this analysis of feeling, there is a consistent and dramatically positive emotional response to apparent near-death by experiencers, whereas an absence of any emotional response is typical for the nonexperiencers. The experiencers often report overwhelming feelings of peace as well as a transcendent sense of well-being. The nonexperiencers, for the most part, are not con-scious of having had any emotions during their near-death episode.

Significantly, *no* person in our sample—including, of course, all our suicide attempt cases—recounted an experience that could be regarded as "a journey to hell." This is consistent with the findings of other large-scale studies.[2] Although some death experiences did include frightening aspects or moments of confusion and uncertainty, none was characterized by predominantly unpleasant feelings or imagery.

Body Separation: Leaving the Body Behind

The second stage of the core experience involves a sense of detachment from one's physical body. As can be seen from Figure 1, about three-eighths (37%) of our sample reached this stage. Most of these people reported a sense of being completely detached from their bodies, though they usually claim that they weren't actually able to see themselves or, at least in retrospect, they weren't sure. In addition, however, sixteen people did state that they had visually clear out-of-body experiences. (This figure represents approximately one-third of all those reporting a near-death experience.) Although these accounts do vary, it is typical at this stage in the experience for the individual to find himself in the room looking down on his physical body. Most of those reporting this commented that somehow they found it all very natural (at the time) and were aware of acute hearing and sharp but detached mental processes. Visually, they often describe the environment as very brightly illuminated.

At the most minimal level, respondents reported either no sense of bodily connection or no awareness of a body.

A suicide attempt victim commented:

Mostly it was like a real floating sensation. I don't remember seeing anything. It's real weird. It's like I was detached from everything that was happening. . . . But I didn't see me. *(90)*

A man who had suffered a heart attack observed:

It seemed like I was up there in space and just my mind was active. No body feeling, just like my brain was up in space. I had nothing but my mind. Weightless, I had nothing. *(33)*

The woman who had a cardiac arrest while undergoing a tonsillectomy found:

I was *above*. I don't know above *what*. But I was [pause] up . . . it was like [pause] like I didn't have a body! I was [pause] but it was *me*. Not a body, but me! You know what I mean? . . . It was a *me inside*. The real me was up there; not this here [pointing to her physical body]. *(24)*

At another level were several reports that indicated the respondent was aware of his "body" moving in some nonphysical dimension. Usually, the respondent stated that he had no bodily sense nor did he remember viewing his physical body from an external vantage point. "He" was just somewhere else. One individual (of the four cases in this subcategory), however, reported a kind of dual body perception—he not only saw "himself" moving through nonphysical space, but his physical body as well! One such report comes from the account of the man who tried to hang himself.

I also remember that I could see myself walking away. I was maybe twenty feet away. Everything was completely black and I could see me walking away. I was wearing this gray suit that I bought last year [he was actually attired differently] and I was walking away from myself hanging there. I could also see that from where I was in the suit I could see myself hanging there. I could see both people at the same time, more or less. *(100)*

Most commonly, an individual having an out-of-body experience would simply state that he was aware of seeing his body as though viewing it from outside and above its physical locus—often from an elevated corner of the room or from the ceiling. The following are typical accounts of this experience:
The young man who nearly died of a high fever said:

I experienced this type of feeling where I felt I had left my body and I had viewed it from the other side of the room. I can sort of remember looking back at myself—it was scary of course. . . . I can remember seeing myself lying there with a sheet and a hypothermia blanket on me. My eyes were closed, my face was very cold-looking. . . . It was like I was perched right up on a little level over near the side of the room. . . . I would be at the foot of the bed, but kind of more up onto the wall, closer to the ceiling, almost in the corner of the room. *(45)*

The woman whose case I cited earlier to illustrate a fairly deep core experience described her out-of-body experience this way:

I was up in the left-hand corner of the room, looking down at what was going on. *(Could you see clearly?)* I could see very clearly, yeh, yeh. I recognized it as being me. I had absolutely no fear whatsoever. That is one thing that is *very* definite, that there was no fear. *(25)*

A woman who had a very serious automobile accident told me that while in a coma:

I had what *I* term a *weird* experience. It's where my husband was in the [hospital] room, it was very late at night and I remember looking at the clock—out of my body. It was 11:10 P.M. and it was where I was looking *down* at my body; I was actually *out* of it! *(Did you have any difficulty recognizing yourself?)* Nope. *(How did you look?)* Very pale. Just lying there, arms outstretched, the IV in. I can remember a nurse coming in and tucking in the blankets and everything and making sure I was all right and everything. And my hair was all over the pillow. *(Where were "you" in relation to your physical body?)* I was, like, over in the corner, and being able to watch people walk in the door and being able to see my husband sitting here [she later implies that she felt that she was "up" as well as to one side of her bed]. *(64)*

A man, also badly injured in an automobile crash, remembered a point when:

At that time I viewed *myself* from the *corner* of my hospital room, looking down at my body which was very dark and gray. All the life looked like it was out of it. And my mother was sitting in a chair next to my bed looking very determined and strong in her faith. And my Italian girl friend at the time was crying at the foot of my bed. *(71)*

Lest the reader think that these apparently clearly perceived out-of-body episodes always occur within a hospital setting—hardly a surprising fact considering the source of most of our interviews—I will point out here that this same individual also reported an *earlier* out-of-body experience, occurring at the time of his accident:

[I was] *outside* of my body. Because my body was damaged. I was down. I was looking at my body. I was trying to move it, like it was walking, trying to walk—I had a broken leg—and I kept trying to get up and going, "*No,* I'm all right," and all this weirdness. It seems . . . that I actually was outside of my body. *(71)*

Finally, a woman who nearly died while giving birth said:

> I felt like I was up near the light, up on the ceiling, or something,
> looking down. . . . I seemed to be above. I could see myself lying
> on the table. *(29)*

These representative out-of-body experiences will be sufficient, I
think, to portray the observer's subjective sense of self relative to his
body. This sense of elevation was a typical feature in the out-of-body
descriptions of our respondents. There were, however, certain other
features that occurred often enough to warrant illustration here. One
had to do with the quality of illumination.

The fever victim:

> I can remember it being very, very bright, very bright, and also a
> very, very peaceful, mellow feeling that I had. *(Was the brightness
> from the illumination in the room?)* No, I don't think so, because, like
> I said, it was a private room and it had only one window that had a
> building next to it, so there wasn't much light coming in and I
> don't think the lighting in the room at that time was that bright. I
> remember it being very bright. And, like I said, that in combina-
> tion with a very peaceful, mellow feeling. *(95)*

During an operation to remove a part of his stomach, another man
suffered a heart stoppage. In connection with this event:

> I remember being up in the air looking down . . . and seeing
> myself on the operating table with all the people around working
> on me. I can remember, what sticks out in my mind mostly, were
> the colors. Everything in that operating room was a very brilliant,
> bright color. *(48)*

One of the women who nearly died in childbirth said:

> As I recall, everything seemed to be brighter. Everything seemed
> to be lighter and brighter. *(29)*

Thus, unusual brightness of the environment was one dramatic
aspect of the out-of-body experience for several respondents. Another,
commented on by at least three respondents, was the sense of viewing
oneself as though from a great height.

> I seemed to be very high in the air. The people I was looking at
> were rather small. I couldn't tell you how high I was, but I was up,

and I seemed to be looking through a hole in a cloud. It was like rainbows, it was bright rays shining down. *(48)*

It seemed like my body was further away. I seemed to be *higher* than the ceiling. *(29)*

Another woman who nearly lost her life in an automobile accident recalled:

Even though I was very close, physically, to the doctors, they seemed to be very far away while I was watching them operate on me. *(62)*

A final feature of these out-of-body experiences has to do with what may be called the "mind state" which accompanies them. The examples already cited have mentioned several *emotional* reactions, ranging from initial fear to the total absence of fear; we have also seen in them indications of a delicious sense of peacefulness. Nevertheless, from a reading of all the relevant interviews, the feature that clearly stands out as typical of the mind state of our out-of-body experiencers is the sense of *observerlike detachment*, often associated with a feeling that "all this is perfectly natural." One respondent said:

Mostly, I think I was just observing. . . . It didn't feel as though it was happening to me at all. I was just the observer. *(29)*

A young woman who nearly died of complications resulting from a faulty exploratory surgery procedure observed:

I was totally objective. I was just an onlooker. I was just viewing things and taking it in. But I was making no judgments—just waiting, I guess. Just waiting to die and realizing that all these things were going on. . . . I was the classic "fly on the wall." I was just there. *(22)*

It was as if I was supposed to be watching it. It was part of what you were supposed to do. . . . It seemed very natural. *(25)*

It seemed perfectly right. Everything about it seemed right. Perfectly natural. *(45)*

It seemed very [pause] it seemed like it was the thing to do. . . . It wasn't a problem to me. *(64)*

In order to avoid possible confusion, let me emphasize that all of the people whose remarks I've just cited *also* reported the core affective response of peace and a sense of well-being. The emotional response itself usually pervades the entire experience. The *psychological* mind state of detached observation or reflection is typical chiefly of the out-of-body stage of the experience. Later I will return to the quality of thought processes (as distinct from the emotional responses) associated with the core experience.

Occasionally, I was to discover a feature that suggested a more elaborate out-of-body experience than any described so far.[3]

Various studies have provided examples of individuals who can later accurately report visual and conversational events that took place while they were unconscious and close to death.[4] Here is one such instance from our investigation—the account of a young woman who appeared to have "died" (that is, suffered cardiac arrest) three times while in a hospital following a severe automobile accident.

[During this time] I heard Jack [the surgeon] saying to—the doctor's name was Cliff—"This is really too bad, the damage is severe. That liver's just about gone. But let's try to patch it up anyway, but the way it's been lacerated, I don't think it's going to function. Look at the pancreas, that's pretty well wrecked, too." I heard the conversation.

About two weeks later, I said to Jack, "What went on in the OR?" He said, "Hon, you died on us there. You just went out. And we had to rush to get you back." And I said, "Well, when?" And he said, "Well, halfway through the operation, your pressure just gave out on us again and we cut you open and starting working on your liver and (you) just went." And I said, "Was that the part when you said, 'Look at that liver and it's just about gone?'" And he said, "How do you know, how do you know that? You were out totally." And I said, "I could *see* you operating on me. I was awake." And he said, "You weren't awake, you were sleeping, you were totally out." I said, "I *was* awake, I saw what you were doing, I saw you lean over to Cliff to get some instruments and I saw how you were pointing around and I could see you standing here and Cliff was standing on this side of the table. . . . Cliff was giving you this instrument and you were doing this to me and, all of a sudden, all these people rushed over to me and they started sticking needles in me and doing all these things." "That's when you died [said the doctor]. Come on, how do you know that? Did Cliff tell you that?" And I said, "No, that's the only thing I can remember." And he said, "That's really freaky." *(62)*

Since I have not been able to check the authenticity of this conversation with the woman's physician, I cannot vouch for its accuracy. Nevertheless, it is consistent with other accounts reported elsewhere, and I have no reason, given the remainder of this woman's case history, to suspect that it was either fabricated or unduly embellished.

In one case, not only did the respondent minutely describe the operating procedures while she was out of her body, but could also, apparently, visualize scenes taking place *outside* the room itself. This kind of account has also been reported elsewhere,[5] and I furnish this material here mainly for its suggestion that in near-death states of consciousness, apparent spatial limitations may be transcended. Again, however, I am not in a position to authenticate the claim of this respondent:

> As my pressure dropped, it felt like an out-of-body experience. As I went out they kept calling my name. . . . I could see them with my eyes closed. I could see them vividly. . . . I could also see my sister, who was a nurse at ——— hospital [where the respondent was]—we're very, very close and if anybody should be close at the time, I'd want her—I could see her coming into the hospital to work. It was her time to be coming in. And I could follow her movements. . . . She walked in shortly after the alert was sounded and got to the emergency room where she worked and someone told her what was going on and she came ripping upstairs. I could see her doing it, I could see her coming up the elevator, telling people that they couldn't—and she told me all this afterward and I shared that with her—get off the floor, that she used the emergency elevator and she went straight up to the floor. *(So you were able to confirm the details of what you were aware of during the time you were unconscious with her afterward?)* Right. *(And you essentially confirmed what you had witnessed?)* Yes, yes. Many of the things she came out with first, but there were things that I told her that she didn't tell me that I could not have known. *(Could you give me an example?)* The elevator was one of them. *(22)*

She also told me that she could plainly see someone operating a defibrillator. She was aware that it was not functioning properly, she could hear the medical team shouting. She described all this as if she were a spectator. In addition, she said she was able to see her mother waiting outside her room and could experience her mounting anxiety. In short, this respondent, during the time she perceived herself to be out of her body, claimed to be able to see the actions and to experience the mental states of two people in remote locations outside the room, with whom she had strong emotional ties. As such, this case was unique in my files—though it is not rare in the literature on parapsychology.

Before turning to the next stage of the core experience, we need briefly consider two issues that concern researchers into out-of-body experiences. The first is: When individuals claim to be out of their body, are they typically aware of having "another body?" The answer is: No. Most persons are simply aware of the scene before (or below) them. When asked about "another body," they usually respond that they were unaware of having one or that they felt they existed, in effect, as "mind only." Only two people suggested some vague perception of a "second body." That "body" was sensed as incomplete. The most detailed description of this alleged "second body" was:

Interviewer: Were you aware of or did you feel you had *another* body? Or did you just feel that you had a kind of awareness of what was going on, without a body?

Respondent (64): I felt I had another body.

Interviewer: Could you see it?

Respondent: It's like I didn't even have to see it; I didn't have any real feeling in it. All I felt—I had a piece of clothing on; it was very, very loose. And I remember [having bare feet].

Interviewer: And did this body *seem* like your physical body, only somehow it wasn't your physical body? I mean, like the same shape and so on?

Respondent: No, it was very different. It was very thin, very delicate. Very light. Very, very light.

Interviewer: Could you see anything that was connecting your physical body on the bed with the body you felt yourself to be over in the corner of the room? Was there any kind of connection between the two that you can recall?

Respondent: [Misunderstanding the intent of the question] Just that I felt that my face and hand were the same. Because I remember trying to touch my face to make sure that everything was okay.

Interviewer: And could you feel it?

Respondent: I could feel it.

The second issue is the nature of the connection, if any, between the two "bodies"—a point that was raised with, but not answered by, the respondent just quoted. As is well known in occult literature[6] and in the literature on out-of-body experiences,[7] mention is often made of a "silver cord" (or tube, thread, rope, and so forth), which is said to unite the two "bodies." Did any of our interviewees report this phenomenon?

Unfortunately, the question was not systematically asked of all who reported an out-of-body experience, but *none* of those who were queried about it gave a positive response. One person, who was familiar with the notion from his reading, thought that he "might have" seen such a connecting cord, but even he was very unsure of it. The fragmentary data we have that bear on this question, then, must be regarded as negative.[8]

Entering the Darkness

The next stage of the experience seems to be a transitional one between this world and whatever may be said to lie beyond. I call it entering the darkness. This space is usually characterized as completely black or dark, very peaceful, and, at least in the majority of such accounts, without dimension. Most people have the sense of floating or drifting through it, though a few respondents reported that they felt they were moving very rapidly through this space.

Figure 1 demonstrates that slightly less than one-quarter (23%) of our sample encountered this feature of the core experience.

Moody's work implied that many individuals experience this phenomenon as traveling through a dark tunnel. We found some evidence for this interpretation, but only among a minority of our respondents who "entered the darkness." Specifically, nine people described their experience here in ways consistent with the Moody tunnel concept. These did, in fact, choose the word *tunnel* most frequently to designate the space they found themselves in, although occasionally other similar terms were used (for example, *funnel, pipe, culvert,* and *drum*).

A few brief excerpts will suggest the qualities of this kind of experience of the "darkness."

A woman who suffered a cerebral hemorrhage and temporary blindness told me:

> I remember going through a tunnel, a very, very dark tunnel. . . . *(Did you feel the tunnel was vast?)* Yes, *very,* very. It started at a narrow point and became wider and wider. But I remember it being very, very black. But even though it was black, I wasn't afraid because I knew that there was something at the other end waiting for me that was good. . . . I found it very pleasant. I wasn't afraid or anything. There was no fear attached to it. I felt very light. I felt like I was floating. *(17)*

Another woman who almost died during open-heart surgery remembered:

I was—it was—a great big drum and this drum was black. In my mind I says, "The Bible says we walk through a dark tunnel until we reach light." And I says, "When am I going to reach the light? *(You felt you were in the tunnel?)* I was in the tunnel, yeh. I was in this great big tunnel and I walked and I walked and I walked and I says, "When am I going to see the light? I'm dead, but when am I going to see the light." *(You felt you were dead?)* I was dead, yeh. . . . It seemed like [pause] there was no light. I never saw the light. *(21)*

A young woman who experienced a near-fatal asthma attack observed:

I do remember thinking to myself that I was dying. And I felt I was floating through a tunnel. . . . When I say *tunnel,* the only thing I can think of is—you know, those sewer pipes, those big pipes they put in? It was round like that, but it was enormous. I couldn't really see the edges of it; I got the feeling that it was round. It was like a whitish color.[9] I was just smack in the middle. My whole body, you know. I was lying on my back. I was just floating. And smoke or white lines or something were coming this way [toward her] and I was going the opposite way. *(What kind of feeling did you have as you were floating through this tunnel?)* Very peaceful, almost as if I were on a raft in the ocean, you know? *(2)*

A cardiac arrest victim's description:

Well, it seemed at that particular time, when my heart died, I seemed to go up into a spiral in a deep black, pitch black tunnel. . . . I saw nothing. It was just *pitch* black. I mean, you never saw anything so dark in your life. *(33)*[10]

More commonly, the experience of "entering the darkness" was phrased in terms of a journey into a black vastness without shape or dimension. An account that is seemingly a combination of the tunnel and the black dimensionless domain comes from a woman who experienced an immediate postdelivery embolism:

It's just like a void, a nothing and it's such a *peaceful*—it's so pleasant that you can keep going. It's a complete blackness, there is no sensation at all, there was no feeling. *(Did it have any kind of form to it?)* No—sort of like a dark tunnel. Just a floating. It's like [being] in midair. *(5)*

More typical expressions of this dark dimensionless space are given next. From a young man, badly injured in a motorcycle crash:

I felt as though I was—well, that's the hard part to explain—like you're floating. Like you're *there* and, believe it or not, the color is—there *is* no color [pause] it's like a darkness. *(Did the darkness have a shape of any kind?)* It was empty. Yeh, that's it. Space. Just nothing. Nothing but something. It's like trying to describe the end of the universe. *(68)*

An eighteen-year-old man, intent on committing suicide by jumping from a cliff in midwinter, lost his footing and sustained a head injury resulting in unconsciousness. While in this state, he found himself in

. . . a darkness, it was a very darkness . . . it was a total nothing. *(79)*

The woman who suffered a cardiac arrest while undergoing a tonsillectomy recalled:

Well, it was like night. It was dark. It was dark. But it was like, like [pause] like in the dark sky. Space. Dark. And it was—there weren't any *things* around. No stars or objects around. *(24)*

The woman whose remarks I cited earlier to illustrate the affective tone of the core experience provides a useful quote here also:

I think that the next thing I remember is total, peaceful, wonderful blackness. Very peaceful blackness. [She then heard her name called as though from a great distance.] I remember distinctly thinking to myself how easy it would be to slip back into that nice peaceful blackness. [Afterward, while still in the hospital, she was intensely happy, so much so that people commented on it.] My happiness had no connection with the fact that I was alive again; my happiness seemed at that time to be connected with that total peaceful blackness. *(4)*

Finally, let me quote a woman whose case is most unusual in our sample for two reasons. First, she had *recurrent* near-death episodes— she estimates twelve to fourteen of them—as a child between the ages of nine and sixteen as a result of heart stoppages resulting from rheumatic fever. Second, since at the time of her interview, she was a woman in her mid-fifties, she was describing experiences that, in some cases, took place nearly a half century before! Needless to say, reasonable questions can be raised concerning the accuracy of her recall of these childhood memories. She herself emphatically stated that the *form* of her experience was *identical* on the occasion of each such near-fatal episode. However that may be, her observations here are of some interest, if only because they seem to square with other, much more recent, accounts:

> [During these attacks she would reach a point where she would] go over is the only—descend into this feeling of soft velvet blackness. It wasn't like going into a tunnel [She had recently read Moody's first book]; I had no feeling of going into a tunnel. I just seemed to be surrounded by a velvet blackness and a softness and I would have absolutely no fear and the pain would disappear when I entered into this other state. *(16)*

Whether the experience is described as floating through a dark tunnel or as entering into a black spaceless void, it is clear that those who have reached this stage of the core experience have begun to encounter very nonordinary realms of consciousness. In the next stage, these realms reveal a distinctly transcendental quality, leading to the culminating phases of the core experience.

Seeing the Light

The passage from the third to the fourth stage of the core experience is marked by one singular feature: the appearance of light. It is usually described as a brilliant golden light. This light, however, almost never hurts one's eyes[11] but is, on the contrary, very restful, comforting and, apparently, of ineffable beauty. Some of our respondents told me they felt enveloped by this light, and virtually all who experienced it felt drawn to it. Figure 1 shows that sixteen people—or about one-third of our experiencers—reported seeing this kind of light.[12]

For many respondents, though not all, the golden light brings to an end the "time of darkness" and thus seems to signal an entirely new stage of the experience. In the minds of at least some of our respondents, the transition from darkness to light is packed with symbolic meaning: phenomenologically, if not ontologically, it is taken to signify the termination of the experience of dying and the beginning of new life.[13] Of course, for religiously minded individuals the golden light is sometimes interpreted as the visual manifestation of God, and two of our respondents appear to have had a vision of Jesus, in connection with their near-death incident, in which he was surrounded by this light.

Sometimes the transition from darkness to light is stated very simply, as it was by the woman who had recurrent near-death episodes as a child:

> I just seemed to be surrounded by a velvet blackness. . . . And then, sort of at the periphery of the velvet blackness, there was a brilliant golden light. And I don't remember feeling frightened at all, just perfectly at peace and perfectly comfortable, as if this is where I should be. *(16)*

In some cases, the transition from darkness to light is associated with a "presence" as it was in the following example when a voice told the respondent that she was being sent back:

> It was dark and it was like—hard to believe—like you were going from dark to light. I can't explain it . . . all of a sudden there was light. . . . And then when the voice was coming to me . . . it was just like light. *(Was the light bright?)* Not piercingly. *(Did it hurt your eyes?)* No. *(28)*

In other cases, the experience of the light is described in a more detailed way and in a definite "tunnel" context. The following is taken from an account from a seventy-year-old woman who was in ill health at the time I interviewed her. She had had a near-death episode stemming from a respiratory failure two years earlier:

> [After having had an out-of-body experience, she said, mentally, to herself] "I'm going to go over to the other side. There's a culvert over there. I want to go through [to] see what's in that culvert." I can see the culvert now. It was just like one of these big water culverts. Great big one. But when I went over there and walked into it, I could stand up. And I says, "Geez, that's funny, I never could when I was a kid." We'd crawl through them. Here I could stand up and walk. And as I started to walk, I saw this beautiful, golden light, way, way small, down the tunnel. I said, "That's a funny light. It doesn't even look like gold and yet it is gold and it isn't yellow. I'll go see what's on the other side. Maybe it—it must be pretty over there." And I kept thinking, "Well, yeah, I'll go, I'll go see." *(18)*

Another illustration of the magnetic pull of the light is taken from the testimony of a woman who had a cardiac arrest:

> [She found herself walking on a path] and as I was walking down . . . there was a wee bit of a light down at the extreme end of it and as I kept walking down, that light kept getting brighter and brighter all the time. Really, it was *beautiful* while it lasted, but it was such a short time, because then they gave me a shot . . . and I was out. *(10)*

In other instances, as I have already indicated, the light does not merely beckon from a distance, but appears to enfold the individual in what can only be described as a loving way. The following examples will serve to justify this subjective-sounding characterization.

> *Interviewer:* Were you ever aware at any point of a light or glow or any kind of illumination?
> *Respondent:* A light glow. There was a glow.
> *Interviewer:* Was it in the room itself, or was it somewhere else?
> *Respondent:* In the room.
> *Interviewer:* Different from the illumination that was provided naturally?
> *Respondent:* Oh, yes. Different, very different. It was like [pause] a tawny gold. It was just like on the outer ridges of where I was at. It was just like me looking through—and being apart from everything and just looking. And it was really, really [pause] I felt warm from that.
> *Interviewer:* So that was a positive aspect?
> *Respondent:* It was peaceful. *(64)*

I can remember it being very, very bright, very bright, and also a very, very peaceful, mellow feeling that I had. *(Was the brightness from the illumination in the room?)* No, I don't think so, because, as I said, it was a private room and it had only one window that had a building next to it, so there wasn't much light coming in and I don't think the lighting in the room at that time was that bright. I remember it being very bright. And, like I said, that in combination with a very peaceful mellow feeling . . . *(Tell me more about the light.)* Very, very bright, like the sun was right in my room shining down. And it seemed like, if there was any color, all the colors were their brightest. You know, everything just magnified a lot of light, it seems like. *(Did the brightness of the colors hurt your eyes?)* No, I could just see the colors so perfectly. *(What did you make of this?)* Well, I look at the whole thing as being like a kind of utopia. Like this is the way the colors are in Utopia, perfect. Perfect to their natural color. *(45)*

I had the sensation of a warm, a very warm sensation, of a very [pause] it was like a light. You know, I can't explain it, what the light looks like, but it has a very—and I can see it, just like I'm going through it right now—like a very warm, comforting light that I had. And it wasn't centered on anything; it was, like, all around me. It was all around me. *(It enveloped you?)* Right! It was all around me. And the colors, the colors, were very vivid—very vivid colors. I had a feeling of total peace. A feeling of total, total peace. . . . *Tremendous* peace. Tremendous peace. In fact, I just lay there—my bed was right near the window—and I remembered I stared out the window—and the light, and everything, was even outside! *(Did that light hurt your eyes?)* No. *(Was it bright?)* No. Not bright, it was not bright. It was like a shaded lamp or something. But it wasn't that kind of light that you get from a lamp. You know what it was? Like someone had put a shade over the sun. It made me feel very, very peaceful. I was no longer afraid. Everything was going to be all right. *(30)*

Although quite a few of our respondents felt they talked directly with God (see Chapter Four), *visions* of religious figures were actually reported very rarely.[14] When they were, however, the figures were usually described as though light radiated from them. One respondent specifically implied that the light she saw in connection with a vision of Jesus was similar to the golden light seen earlier while "in the tunnel." The number of these instances is entirely too small, of course, to justify any conclusions about the possible similarity or identity of the light associated with near-death religious visions and that which occurs without any particular form. Nevertheless if only for the sake of its intrinsic interest, I shall conclude this section with the clearest instance of a vision of Jesus reported by our respondents. It comes from the interview with the seventy-year-old woman whose record I cited at the beginning of this section.

This particular incident occurred *after* the respondent had survived her near-death episode, brought on by respiratory failure, but while she was still hospitalized for it. At this time, because of a medical implant in her throat, the doctors had told her that she would be unable to receive Communion that week.

I told [a friend] that I wanted to receive Communion. I [laughing a little with embarrassment] saw Jesus Christ. . . . I was crying. . . . All of a sudden, I was crying so, I felt something funny and I looked up and there I saw this light again. And it was almost the same light as it was at the end of the tunnel. It was this vivid gold, yellow. And then I saw a form there. And I can see that form now: It had blond-gold hair and it had a beard, a very light beard and a moustache. It had a white garment on. And from this white garment there was all this gold shining. There was a red spot here [she points to her chest], on his gown, there was a chalice in his hand, and it said to me, "You will receive my body within the week." And he went. And I thought to myself, "Well, that's funny, that can't be. Did I see something that I shouldn't see? Am I going crazy?" And I told my husband I saw Jesus. He said, "Don't tell anybody; they'll think you're losing your mind." And I never did. And then, that Friday [within a week of her vision—the doctors removed the implant after all], Good Friday, I received Communion."

[Later she commented on her vision] I'll never forget it. I can still see it so plain. *(18)*

The various manifestations of the light bring us to the threshold of the last stage of the core experience. From this point, the light no longer serves as a beacon or a warm, enveloping effulgence. Instead, it becomes the preternatural illumination of what to our respondents is perceived to be the world beyond death.

Entering the Light

The difference between the preceding stage and this one is the difference between seeing the light and entering into a "world" in which the light appears to have its origin. For, according to the reports indicative of having reached this stage, one does indeed have the sense of being in another world—and it is a world of preternatural beauty. The colors are said to be unforgettable. The individual may find himself in a meadow or see unusual physical-like structures, which, however, do not seem to correspond exactly to anything in *our* world. This is the stage where respondents report being greeted by deceased relatives. Five people claimed to see beautiful flowers here and four were aware of lovely music. Although resentment for being brought back from imminent death was not frequently expressed by our respondents, that sentiment was particularly evident for several people who were "returned to life" after experiencing this stage.

Figure 1 reveals that only ten people—or about one-fifth of our experiencer sample—gave evidence of penetrating into this final stage. Indeed, it is typically the case—at least among our respondents—that only a glimpse, rather than a protracted visit, is vouchsafed those who come this far. One person whose experience and reaction were representative of this group said that she was afforded "just a peek" into what she felt was "the hereafter." Accordingly, with only a few exceptions, the descriptions we have of this domain tend to be decidedly, perhaps disappointingly, pithy.

I will begin with a sampling of typical statements and conclude this section with excerpts from the interview that provides the most extensive impressions of this stage.

From a cardiac arrest victim:

> I happened to go down this path and it was *beautiful.* Beautiful flowers and the birds were singing, and I was walking down. . . . [After she was resuscitated] I did reprimand my surgeon and my cardiologist. I said, "Why, in heaven's name, did you bring me back? It was so beautiful." *(10)*

From a woman who suffered a respiratory failure:

> I was in a field, a large empty field, and it had high, golden grass that was very soft, so bright. And my pain was gone and it was quiet, but it wasn't a morbid quiet, it was a peaceful quiet. [Afterward] I said to Dr. _____, "Why did you bring me back?" I didn't want to come back. So I was really very happy in that place, wherever it was. [She later further described the field she found herself in.] Soft, silky, very brilliant gold. *(What was the quality of the light?)* Just bright, but restful. The grass swayed. It was very peaceful, very quiet. The grass was so outstandingly beautiful that I will never forget it. *(3)*

A man who appears to have come close to dying as a result of being ill during a tooth extraction [15] gave the following statement:

> I took a trip to heaven. I saw the most beautiful lakes. Angels— they were floating around like you see seagulls. Everything was white. The most beautiful flowers. Nobody on this earth ever saw the beautiful flowers that I saw there . . . I don't believe there is a color on this earth that wasn't included in that color situation that I saw. Everything, everything. Of course, I was so impressed with the beauty of everything there that I couldn't pinpoint any one thing. . . . Everything was bright. The lakes were blue, light blue. Everything about the angels was pure white. *(Tell me what the angels*

looked like.) I can't. *(Did the colors hurt your eyes?)* No. *(Was it restful?)*
It was. Everything about the whole thing was restful. *(53)*

A woman who nearly died as a result of a cerebral hemorrhage
described a part of her experience:

> There was music, very, very pleasant music. . . . The music was
> beautiful. . . . [Later] And then there was another part to it where
> two aunts of mine—they're dead—and they were sitting on a rail
> and it was a beautiful meadow and they started calling me. They
> said, "Come on, Giselle, come on." . . . And I was very happy to
> see them—it was a meadow lane. Beautiful grass, and they were
> sitting on this railing and calling me . . . and I went halfway and
> then stopped. And that's probably when I came to. *(17)*

The woman whose near-death episode was used to illustrate a deep
core experience (see pages 36–38) also reached this last stage. The
excerpts from her interview, already cited, disclose that she, too, heard
music she characterized as "spiritual" during an episode in "a very *pretty*
valley." At this time, she encountered her deceased grandfather, who
instructed her to return to life, saying that she was "still needed." I will
quote further from her interview in order to amplify her description
and interpretation of her surroundings:

> *Interviewer:* Could you describe the valley for me a little bit more?
>   You said it was like the valley of the shadow of death.[16] Are
>   there more things that come to mind in terms of what you can
>   recall about it? How you felt? What you were aware of? What
>   you saw?
> *Respondent:* I think I should say that the psalm happens to be my
>   favorite psalm. And while I've never seen the valley of the
>   shadow of death before, it was just a very beautiful, crystallike
>   place, and it just gave me a very good feeling once I realized
>   where I was.
> *Interviewer:* And you did have this realization at the time? It wasn't
>   something that you had come to *after* the experience, but at the
>   time it occurred you said, "This is where I am." Was it like—was
>   it comparable to any place that you've been to? Was it earthly?
>   Was it—
> *Respondent:* No. It wasn't earthly. I can't say if it was heavenly
>   because I really don't know what heaven is like, but it didn't
>   seem earthly at all.
> *Interviewer:* Can you say anything about the illumination of the
>   valley? Could you see it clearly?

Respondent: It was very bright. Very bright.
Interviewer: Did the bright light hurt your eyes?
Respondent: No. Not at all. *(7)*

The last passage is taken from the interview with a woman, who, on the basis of both my own judgment and her score on the WCEI (24), had the deepest experience of any respondent. In her case, she not only had a glimpse of the world that appears to individuals in stage V, but, in addition, received some quite detailed visual impressions. For the purpose of coherent exposition, I have had to rearrange some segments of this interview, but the order of the excerpts in no way distorts the substance of her account. She came to this experience as a result, apparently, of suffering cardiac failure at home, where, owing to some unusual circumstances, she lay comatose and undiscovered for three days. Finally, she was brought to a hospital, where she had a cardiac arrest before eventually recovering.

The first thing I remember was a tremendous rushing sound, a tremendous [searching for words]. . . . It's very hard to find the right words to describe. The closest thing that I could *possibly* associate it with is, possibly, the sound of a tornado—a tremendous, gushing wind, but almost pulling me. And I was being pulled into a narrow point from a wide area. *(Sort of going into a funnel?)* Yes! Yes. And it was [pause] nothing painful. There was nothing frightening about it. It was just something that I felt I gave myself into completely. And it felt *good*.

Then, suddenly, I saw my mother, who had died about nine years ago. And she was sitting—she always used to sit in her rocker, you know—she was smiling and she just sat there looking at me and she said to me in Hungarian [the language her mother had used while alive], "Well, we've been waiting for you. We've been expecting you. Your father's here and we're going to help you." And all I felt was a tremendous kind of happiness, of pleasure, of comfort. And then somehow she took me by the hand and she took me somewhere [pause] and all I could see was marble all around me; it was marble. It *looked* like marble, but it was *very beautiful*. And I could hear beautiful music; I can't tell you what kind, because I never heard anything like it before. . . . It sounds—I could describe it as a combination of vibrations, many vibrations. *(How did that music make you feel?)* Oooh, so *good*! The whole thing was just very *good*, very happy, very warm, very peaceful, very comforted, very—I've never known that feeling in my whole life.

[Yet] somehow, I was never right there with her [her mother].

She was always at a distance. And she seemed to be just smiling and saying or implying, "Wait." She was saying this in Hungarian, and smiling. And then I would see my father. There were many people or beings or whatever they were [pause] I never *saw* and yet I *knew* that I knew them.

Interviewer: They were familiar to you?

Respondent: Yes.

Interviewer: But the only persons that you specifically recognized were your mother and father?

Respondent: Yes.

Interviewer: What did they look like?

Respondent: The way I always remembered them looking; somehow they always looked the same. . . . I always remember [my mother] as being very dignified and very tender and quiet, and my father was just the opposite—very jovial, poetic, and artistic; and they were just that way. They were the way I always remember them.

Interviewer: Were you able to see them clearly?

Respondent: Oh, very clearly. Very, very clearly.

Interviewer: Did your father communicate anything to you?

Respondent: [Laughs] It's a funny thing because I've thought about it after and I remember when I was thinking about it later, as I was regaining consciousness, I kept saying, "Now why did he ask me that?" He asked me, "Did you bring your violin?" And I thought that was so funny. And I don't know if he really said that or if I imagined it, you know; it's really hard to tell.

Interviewer: Did that question make any sense to you afterward?

Respondent: Yes, it did. My father loved music and he played the violin, beautifully. I've always wanted to play the violin, but never could. I have a violin, but—

Interviewer: The other people there did not communicate anything to you?

Respondent: Yes, they did. They were all talking to me but I don't remember what they were saying. It was all, it was as though they were all—when I saw the groups of people, it was in sort of a *marble* [pause] something I've never seen in my whole life. I've never seen it in a movie, a picture—

Interviewer: Was it a building of any kind, a structure?

Respondent: Yes, it was and yet it seemed to have no walls. And yet there was a lot of marble and music and people were walking by and working and doing things, and just smiling. They weren't talking. They were not speaking to me and yet they were. I was hearing; they were communicating with me.

Interviewer: What were the people doing?

Respondent: [Pause] It seems that I saw one person carrying what looked like a *saw;* another was carrying a hammer, woodworking tools, but everyone was smiling. There was a great feeling of happiness around me. And everyone was [pause] not really walking. They seemed to be, you know, kind of floating.

Interviewer: Were they dressed in ordinary attire?

Respondent: [Pause] I wasn't aware of it.

Interviewer: I'd like you to describe as much of the scene as you can now recall.

Respondent: You know, I've tried to sketch this, but it's too difficult. I know I've never seen anything like it. The closest thing I could compare it to is possibly a mausoleum. But somehow there was a lot of marble. . . . It was *immensely* filled with light, with light. . . . I felt it surrounding, totally surrounding me and it surrounded everything—my mother, when I saw her, and my father—

Interviewer: You mean it was there sort of as a permanent but shifting background to your experience? You were just aware of this light?

Respondent: Yes, and it was especially powerful when I describe this building or whatever it was. . . . It was just so *illuminating!*

Interviewer: Did it hurt your eyes?

Respondent: No!

Interviewer: Could you see anything else besides this marble—whatever it was without walls? Were there any other features of the surroundings?

Respondent: Yes. There was one thing. It seemed like, like—and this was what puzzled me—it seemed like it was a big [pause] crypt. It was very beautiful and very ornate and somehow I was talking to someone—I don't know who it was. And I had the feeling that, well, this is where my mother and father were and I was to meet them right there. They weren't there at the moment, but I was to meet them right there. And I was waiting for them.

Interviewer: Was this after you had seen them or—?

Respondent: Yes, after I had seen them. And I was waiting for them. Suddenly, it was all gone.

Interviewer: Did that scene just end all of a sudden? Or did it fade out? Did it dissolve like they do in the movies?

Respondent: It ended very abruptly. It seemed, in my trying to understand it and comprehend it because I felt it was *so* important, to end just like that. But it was at the moment I felt . . . *tremendous* pain and that feeling of being torn away from something. . . . I think that I *really* made a decision, I can't tell you how or when or what, but I reached a point where [pause] I *knew* that I *had* to come back. . . . I cannot tell you exactly *what* happened—whether I heard *my* daughter or my children speak to me [at this time, several of her children were with her in the hospital room] and when they said, "We *need* you!"—suddenly, the immensity of what I had experienced made me realize I *had* to. I *have* to make them realize that death is not a frightening or a horrible end. *It is not. I know* it is not! It's just an extension or another beginning. *(20)*

A casual perusal of all the accounts presented in this section—even the very brief ones—will be sufficient to reveal that each of them, *without exception,* uses the adjective *beautiful* to describe the sensed features of the "surroundings" where these respondents found themselves. If, for the time being, I may take the liberty of speaking about this realm as a "world" of its own, then, plainly and without equivocation, it is experienced as a surpassingly beautiful one. Reading these accounts, it is understandable why a person entering such a world would be reluctant, even unwilling, to return to the world of ordinary experience.

Nevertheless, all those in my sample who reached the threshold of this world were obliged to return and no one reported venturing into any further realms that might be construed as transcending this one. With the description of this stage of the core experience, then, we have followed the phenomenological path of the dying as far as these accounts will take us. As Moody has implied, it seems to be the *same* journey, with different people encountering different segments of what appears to be a *single, common path.*

At this point, however, I must admit that I have deliberately omitted from this account one singular and extraordinary phenomenon which *crosscuts* the stages of the core experience and brings it to a resolution. Indeed, this aspect of the core experience appears decisive in determining whether an individual is to return from the journey upon which his near-death episode has launched him. Because of the crucial and unusual nature of this phenomenon, it is best discussed with all the stages of the unfolding core experience clearly in mind.

FOUR

The Decision to Return to Life

For the majority of the core experiencers, there is a point in their passage toward (apparent) death when they become aware that a decision has to be made concerning their future: Are they to return to life or continue toward death? Awareness of reaching this point of choice is usually signaled by one of several remarkable phenomenological features. Because of their similarity from case to case, these features, taken in their totality, are unquestionably among the most provocative of any of the elements regularly associated with the core experience.

The life review. A person may experience the whole or selected aspects of his life in the form of vivid and nearly instantaneous visual images. These images usually appear in no definite sequence (though they sometimes do), but rather as a simultaneous matrix of impressions, like a hologram. In some instances, they appear to include *flash-forwards* as well as flashbacks. They are usually overwhelmingly positive in emotional tone, even though the individual viewing them ordinarily (but not always) experiences them with a sense of detachment. Twelve people—or about one-quarter of our experiencer sample—reported this phenomenon.

The encounter with a "presence." Sometimes in association with the life review, sometimes independent of it, the individual may become aware of a "presence."[1] Among our respondents reporting this experience, the presence is never actually seen, but is always sensed, inferred or intuited. On occasion, however, it is *heard* to speak—though sometimes this is described as a "mental understanding"—and then it speaks with a voice both clearly audible to the experiencer and identifiable as to gender.[2] The respondent usually feels as though there is mutual direct communication between the presence and himself. Although there is some variation here, the presence usually states or implies that the individual is at a choice-point in his life and that it is up to him to elect whether to return to it (that is, physical life). At this point the individual seems led either to reflect on his life or to reexperience it in the form of the panoramic life review just described, as he attempts to make up his mind. In some cases, the individual seems to be given information about his future physical existence, should he decide to live. Altogether, twenty people in our sample—or slightly more than two-fifths of our experiencers—indicated that they were aware of what I have called a presence.[3]

The encounter with deceased loved ones. In a few cases—there were eight clear instances of this—the respondent becomes aware of the "spirits" of dead loved ones, usually relatives. In contrast to the phenomenon of the presence, these spirits are usually seen *and* recognized.[4] Typically, they greet the individual in a friendly fashion, while the respondent himself usually experiences a combination of surprise and great happiness at this apparent reunion. Nevertheless, these spirits usually inform the respondent that, in effect, "it isn't your time" and that "you must go back." Thus, while the presence usually appears to give the respondent a choice whether "to stay," the spirits usually urge the individual "to return."[5] This difference between the encounter with a presence and an encounter with spirits, especially when one bears in mind the (near) mutually exclusive relationship between them, suggests that they represent two quite distinct and independent phases of the core experience decisional process.

Making the decision. The result of the events just described is a decision, made either by or for the individual, whether to return to life or to continue further into the journey beyond this life. Not surprisingly, virtually all experiencers feel that either they themselves decided to "come back" or that they were "sent back" (in a few instances, apparently, against their own preferences). Sixteen people— about one-third of our experiencers—testified that they either chose, bargained, or willed themselves to return. Five stated that they felt they were sent back. For the remaining respondents—seven in number— who appear to have experienced at least one aspect of the decisional process, how the decision was made is not clear. In a few cases, however, a decision is apparently arrived at without any of the three features occurring in a clear-cut fashion.

Whether the individual feels he chose to return or was sent back, the reasons given usually have to do with one or the other of two nonindependent considerations: (1) the "pull" of loved ones—usually children or spouses—who are felt to have need of the respondent or (2) a sense that one's life's tasks and purposes are not yet accomplished—a feeling of "unfinished business."

In any case, reaching a decision is usually the last event of which an experiencer has any recollection. The decision appears to reverse the dying process and returns the individual to the world of ordinary reality.

The components of the decision-making process reveal themselves during various stages of the core experience. They may, in fact, appear in conjunction with *any* of the stages of the core experience (since they crosscut these stages), but they *tend* to occur in association with the intermediate stages, namely II, III, or IV. Altogether, by a conservative count, twenty-eight experiencers (or 57%) appear to have passed through a decisional phase, nineteen in a very marked way, the remainder to various lesser degrees.

In order to recreate the sense of these decisional episodes, it will be necessary here to reproduce some long passages from the interviews. This phenomenon is as complex as it is unusual, and the effort to grasp its meaning requires that these episodes be presented, as much as possible, in their full context.

The first involves a man who nearly died in a motorcycle accident at the age of eighteen:

During the time I was supposedly dead—according to *them* [the doctors], supposedly I was dead—during this time it was like I was talking to someone that—I never knew who they were; that was strange. I asked, but I never got an answer. The only thing I can remember is like a voice say, "Well, you've made it. You've finally made it." I say, "No, this is too early. What are you talking about?" He says, "Well, you've finally left; you don't have to suffer anymore." I had been sick as a kid and it hurt. And he says, "You don't have to suffer anymore. You made it." I say, "What do you mean? I want to go *back*. I can't [pause] I can't—I haven't *done* anything. I'm still trying to go to school. And work. I've got people that *need* me. And things I've *got* to do. And I'd like to go back—if that's possible." And then the voice says, "Well, it's up to you. If you go back, you're going to suffer. And you're going to have to endure some *real* pain." [Indeed, the respondent reports having suffered intense pain for the next year during his recuperation.] And I say, "Well, it doesn't matter to me. *That* I can handle. Just let me go back." And he said, "Well, okay." And at that instant, I felt a drop of water hit my—and then the doctor screamed, "He's alive, he's alive!"

Interviewer: Do you remember being aware of any unusual noises or sounds?

Respondent: The *only* sound I was aware of was the voice. And it sounded—it seemed to be a *man's* voice. It seemed to be soft, yet harsh. . . .

Interviewer: Were you aware of any other persons, voices, presences?

Respondent: Just one. Just the one voice and it was like an entrance.

Interviewer: Like an entrance?

Respondent: Yeah, it was like a walk-in person. Like a voice that says—like a *greeting* voice. Or like, "Well, here you are. You finally made it."

Interviewer: Now, this wasn't a voice of anyone you recognize—anyone in your family?

Respondent: No. This is why I tried to describe it as being a harsh voice yet soft—but sure.

Interviewer: You said before [referring to a portion of the interview not quoted here] that you kind of felt reassured when you heard this voice.

Respondent: Comforting. It was a comforting voice.

Interviewer: It essentially said, "You've made it now. You're not going to have any more pain." And then you kind of bargained to get back.

Respondent: Right. It gave me a *choice*. I had a choice of staying or going back. *(68)*

The next case is that of the woman who suffered a cardiac arrest during a tonsillectomy. According to her own account, she was told afterward that she was "clinically dead" for nearly three minutes.[6]

[At this point in the interview, the respondent is describing her sense of "being up," that is, elevated in space.]

Respondent: And I was *above*. And there was—a *presence*. It's the only way I can explain it—because I didn't see anything. But there was [pause] a *presence* and it may not have been talking to me, but it was, it was like [pause] like I *knew* what was going on between our minds.

Interviewer: Sort of like telepathy?

Respondent: Well, I *guess* so. It wasn't that I remember him *telling* me that I had to go down, but it was as if I *knew* I had to go down. And I didn't *want* to. Yet I *wanted* to. And it was like being *pulled* without being pulled. My feelings, I guess, were [pause] pulled apart. *I wasn't afraid to go that way.* This is the only way I can explain it. I wasn't *afraid* to go that way. I *wanted* to go that way. I *really did*.

Interviewer: In this upward direction?

Respondent: That way there [pointing upward, on a diagonal]. I wanted to go there. *Something* was there. . . . I remember that there was *something* there—a presence there. And I had no fear of it. And the *peace* . . . the *release* [pause] the fear was all gone. There was no pain. There was nothing. It was just *absolutely beautiful!* I could *never* explain it in a million years. It was a feeling that I think everybody *dreams* of someday having. Reaching a point of ABSOLUTE peace. To me peace is the greatest word that I can express. . . . That's all I can *really* remember—that I was being *drawn* back. It was a choice, evidently, that I made.

Interviewer: Do you feel that *you* made the choice?

Respondent: Yes, I *think* so. I wasn't afraid to go that way. And yet I'm sure it was my choice to come back.

Interviewer: Why do you feel you came back? Why did you choose to come back?

Respondent: I don't know. I think it's because I had two little children. And I felt they needed me more than—up there. And I think going up there meant *my* peace and joy, but it meant misery for my children. And I think *even then* I was *thinking* of these things—*weighing* things. I wasn't feeling any *pain* or *sorrow* or anything, but I was thinking *calmly* and *rationally*, making a decision—a rational decision, a logical decision—*without emotions involved.* Do you know what I mean? . . . I didn't make that decision *emotionally.* I made it *logically.* And the choice, both choices were—I mean, I wasn't afraid to die so *that* choice would have been just as easy for me. But the choice was made *logically.* And I'm sure it was *mine. (24)*

In the following instance, the respondent is unusual in that he reports that his experience came back to him bit by bit, like fragments of a forgotten dream, only after several years had passed since his near-death episode, brought about by an automobile accident:

Respondent: It was like I got to view my whole life as a movie, and *see* it and get to view different things that happened, different things that took place. [Pause] I think I got to see some things in the future; I might even have gotten to see how my whole life *might* have turned out or *will* turn out—I don't know—as far as the future destiny of it. It's hard to say. Sometimes I recognize things when I get there and go, "Wow!" . . . So anyway, I got to see, basically, what was a whole view of my life. Now, after I was shown a lot of things, which somehow it's very hard on words on describing . . . basically, it was like watching a movie. But this movie, although it is speeded up, probably to show you it all—it only seems to take a second—and the next thing was a voice coming to me after all this and saying, very compassionately—it was like an *all-knowing* voice, something that at the time I took to be the voice of Jesus, but I can take it to be the voice of any one God as far as the whole universe is concerned. I don't *know* who that person was. It was like a voice that I *knew* and it said to me, "You really blew it this time, Frank."

Interviewer: Did it actually use those words?

Respondent: Yes. Actual words, "You really blew it this time, Frank" . . . Right there it was like I was shown this movie and then the voice said that to me—and at that time I *viewed* myself from the *corner* of my hospital room, looking down at my body, which was very dark and gray. All the life looked like it was out of it. And my mother was sitting in a chair next to my bed, looking very determined and strong in her faith. And my Italian girl friend at the time was crying at the foot of my bed—in beautiful form—it was beautiful. But, anyway, at this time the voice said, "You really blew it this time, Frank." And I looked down at this scene and that scene compared with the fact that I had seen this view of my life and I said, "No! I want to live." And at that saying, it was almost like, it seems like, it was a snap [he snaps his fingers] and I was sort of inside my body. And the next thing . . . I was waking up and looking down at my girl friend and saying, "Jesus Christ, it's bad enough that I'm dying and you got to sit there and cry!" [He laughs.]

Interviewer: Those were the first words out of your mouth? You actually said that?

Respondent: Yup. First words.

Later, this respondent talked about the sense of choice he had and his feelings at the time:

Respondent: . . . looking at [my body] from the end of the bed, it looked dead to me. It was a choice of right at that split second— was the choice of, okay, do you want to go back to your body or not?

Interviewer: Did somebody give you that choice or did you feel that you had to make it yourself? Who gave you that choice?

Respondent: The voice that said, "You blew it." Like I said, I got to see a movie of basically my life, of what *had* happened and what *was* happening. It was like, I have a *mission* here to do, let's say, and I had a choice of what basically I call going on with the physical body or starting over again with a new one.

Interviewer: Can you remember what it *felt* like to be in that state? At the choice point?

Respondent: . . . how I felt—was I worried? Scared? It's good you asked that question. . . . In the beginning, it *is* scary for a little while. But then, all of a sudden, there's *such* love and great warmth and [pause] and security and strength in that . . . that . . . that All-Being, that All-Presence that is *there*. Whatever it is that's out there, that's the presence. There's great *comfort*.

Finally, I asked him to tell me more about the "movie" of his life he had viewed and what kind of response he had to it:

Respondent: I don't know if I actually did see *all* of my life—that's too hard to say—but I can remember it was like going to certain little things. Some of them seemed very insignificant . . . you wouldn't think that they had any significance in your life. . . . It was like I got to see some good things I had done and some mistakes I had made, you know, and try to understand them. It was like: "Okay, here's why you had the accident. Here's why this happened. Because so and so and so." . . . it all had meaning. Definitely.

Interviewer: Were most of [the things you viewed] positive? Negative?

Respondent: The interesting thing about that: They were *both*. But there was *no feeling* of guilt. It was all *all right*.

Interviewer: You weren't involved? I mean, it wasn't like you were *watching* them.

Respondent: That's why I say it was like a movie.

Interviewer: But you were watching like a spectator. But somehow you were understanding your life in a way that you've never been able to understand it before.

Respondent: Yeh, in a new context. A whole new context. *(71)*

In the next case, a woman recounts her decisional crisis, which appeared to take place while she was out of her body, in her hospital room, following an automobile accident. At the time of her experience, she had been in a coma for four days.

[While she was out of her body] I was trying to make up my mind whether I was going to live or die. So I went back through my childhood and I came back. It was like I could recall instances out of my childhood and I was trying to decide whether I wanted to live or die, because I had just gotten married. . . .

Interviewer: Can you reconstruct that [how she went about making up her mind] for me as best you can?

Respondent: Well . . . I had a very tough childhood. And I had been afraid even of getting married. And it was where I had to make a decision. I was going to trust my husband enough to go on to be here [i.e., to remain alive]. And it was where I was visiting all the painful places in my childhood and saying, "Well, am I going to experience this with a husband?" It was really *vivid* to me—all the different places that I had to go to. But yet I went to visit two places where I remember that I had a good time. One was on a playground when I was a child about eight years old, and one was on a Halloween night and it was where all my brothers and sisters were with me. And it was a really *good* time. What made the decision for me was, I said, "I have all the time, the rest of my life to find out if I really love this man. And

I really do love him so I think everything will be different." . . .
and I saw him so worried and it was just like he was—I don't
know—he was patting my hand and saying, "Come on, come on.
You've got to come out of this." And the next thing I remember
is, it was about two A.M. and I decided that I was going to live
and the next thing, I was sleeping. I woke up about eight-thirty
that morning. And I was out of the coma.

Interviewer: You said you felt the choice was yours as to whether to
live or die at this point, and because you felt that your feelings
for your husband were trustworthy, you could trust him—was
that what decided you that you were going to live?

Respondent: Right. There was no religion or anything connected
with it. It was just like [pause] *I* had that decision to make and
that it was *totally* up to me. And I never gave a thought about
God or anything else. It was totally up to me. And it was *my*
decision to make. And I felt *really good* about this.

Later she spoke about how she viewed the scenes of her childhood
and of how (possibly) images of her future manifested themselves to
her.

Respondent: Some [images] I watched in a very detached way.
Because I could see the stuff going on was like opening up a
door and just watching everything going on, and me stepping
back away from it and leaving it there. But some of the things I
got emotionally caught up in. Then I stopped and I said, "I
don't want to be here anymore; I don't like that situation."

Interviewer: The things that you saw—can you describe the quality?
Were they vivid, indistinct, fast, slow, and so forth?

Respondent: I would say most of them were not vivid, but not
indistinct. They were there, like they were all going on and they
were at a pace where they happened, but, like, all the garbage
got left behind. If that experience happened to me, I skipped
some of the things, and I just went on from the beginning until
I came to the end.

Interviewer: More or less in a chronological sequence? But you
could delete a lot of the stuff?

Respondent: Right.

Interviewer: Was it like, in a sense, that a tape of your life was
playing and when you got to a boring part you could just skip it?

Respondent: Right, and go on to another part.

Interviewer: Was it like your whole life was being laid out before
you; that you could look at it selectively in terms of what parts

seemed to be particularly relevant in the decision you had to make?

Respondent: Yeh. I would say yes. . . .

Respondent: [Speaking of other imagery she had] It was like . . . I saw my husband there and I had an image of us five years later. I had an image of us with our children. And it was like I had images and like [pause] I had knowledge [pause] of what children I was going to have.

Interviewer: Did you in fact have children?

Respondent: Yeh. And I had two boys.

Interviewer: What was contained in the image that you saw? Was it two boys?

Respondent: I saw two children, with their backs. That was all I saw.

Interviewer: So there was a sense in which you could not only review your past but also [see] scenes from the future?

Respondent: Right, and it was very close; it wasn't foggy. *(64)*

In this case, of course, there is only the suggestion of paranormal knowledge of the future, not any convincing evidence of it. The respondent's image of the children (assuming it was faithfully described) was not specific enough for any definite conclusion to be drawn. Nevertheless, the reader may recall case *(25)* mentioned on pages 35–36, which presents rather more striking data consistent with the assumption that near-death experiences can sometimes disclose precognitive information. In that instance, the respondent also reported an awareness of an external source of her thoughts that she must return to her body, though she did not actually term this source a "presence."

In the next case, we shall find another hint of paranormal knowledge of the future—again concerning an unborn child—but this time the source of this datum is very clearly linked in the mind of the respondent to an unmistakable "other." This material is drawn from the interview with the young man who tripped and accidentally knocked himself unconscious as he was about to commit suicide.

The first thing was, when I was out, I had a really weird feeling like [pause] I was *going* somewhere. I don't know *where* I was going but [trails off] . . . I don't know where I was going but I was moving to an emptiness. And then, all of a sudden, I heard this *voice*. And it was a really, a really [pause] calm; and it was just a great—it was a male voice. It was just really great. It was just a really—like someone talking to me as a *real close friend* or something like that. It was a really nice tone of voice, you know what I mean?

Interviewer: Compassionate?

Respondent: Yeh. It was *great.* Yeh. And, and, the first thing he said was, "Do you really want to die?" And I said, "Yes. Nothing has been going right all my life and at this point I really don't care if I live or die." And he says, "What about your mother? She cares about you. What about your girl friend?" And then it got kind of hazy and he said something about a *daughter* but—I don't *have* a daughter! So I think it's sort of like, like, you know, sometime in the near future I'm going to have a daughter and she's going to be something *important,* because if God wants me to live, there must be some *purpose* in my life. And my daughter is going to be something *important*—maybe she'll find a cure for cancer or maybe she'll [pause]—something like that. Or make something very important like—maybe she'll solve ecological problems or maybe the population or something very important that will help prolong the existence of mankind, which is coming very short, you know? And so, anyhow, then he said, "Do you want to go back?" And I says, "What do you mean, go back?" And he goes, "Finish your life on earth." And I go, "No. I want to die." And he goes, "You are breaking my *laws* to commit suicide. You'll not be with me in *heaven*—if you die." And I says, "What will happen?" And then after this I started coming to. So I don't know what happened after this. So I think that God was trying to tell me that if I commit suicide I'm going to hell, you know? So, I'm not going to think about suicide anymore [nervous laughter].

Further into the interview, he offered some illuminating observations concerning how the voice of the presence is experienced. His comments here are, to the best of my knowledge, very indicative of the *form* that this kind of "communication" takes in most cases.

Interviewer: Okay, let's focus on the voice then. You never saw anything?

Respondent: No, it was still. The whole time it was in complete darkness.

Interviewer: Even during the time that the voice was speaking to you?

Respondent: Yeh.

Interviewer: When you heard the voice, you heard it as a male voice. Did you actually hear the *words,* or—

Respondent: It was like it was *coming into my mind.* It was like I didn't have any hearing or any sight or anything. It was like it was *projected into my mind.*

Interviewer: What you told me before—is that the gist of what the voice said? Or is it pretty much the actual words?

Respondent: It was mostly *thoughts*, you know? It was mostly thoughts. It wasn't like somebody—you know, like you and I are communicating with words. It was mostly thoughts—like, I would picture in my mind my mother crying and my girl friend crying and then when there was the thought about a daughter, she [his girl friend] was holding a baby. It was like—the more I think over it, the more it comes out as words, but when it happened it was more like symbols—symbolic, you know?

Interviewer: So what you're doing now is trying to translate it into words?

Respondent: I'm trying to change it into English, yeh. It was very specific.

Interviewer: But the message to you was very clear?

Respondent: Yes. It was *very* clear. That my life isn't ended yet and that I shouldn't be trying to fool around with my life because it isn't under my control, you know?

Later, I asked him to describe to me his sense of choice in returning and to tell me how he interpreted his experience.

Interviewer: Was it your understanding that it was up to *you* to choose, or did you feel you were *sent* back?

Respondent: Whether I wanted to live or die? I feel that I was more or less *forced* back. Because, still in my mind, I *wanted* to die. I had some *doubts* about it but I still wanted [trails off]. Everything had been going so bad to this point in my life that it didn't seem worth it—that my earthly existence was no longer any good.

Interviewer: Do you think that you *could* have chosen to die if you were prepared to pay the consequences—of not going to heaven?

Respondent: Like, see, I didn't want to go to hell. When I saw the picture of—well, probably in my upbringing about hell being fire and all this and suffering and whatnot, I've gone through enough suffering in my life. I thought, maybe it's time for a change. So that's what probably changed my mind about dying. So I guess I *did* have a choice in a way.

Interviewer: You interpret this voice as God? You think God was speaking to you?

Respondent: I really do think it was, yeh.

Interviewer: What do you make of the image of your girl friend . . . and being told about your daughter—that she'd miss you or need you or something like that?

Respondent: It's a weird feeling, like, like [pause] knowing the future. I had already had thoughts of marrying this girl at this point and I had just a couple of months earlier given her a preengagement ring. And, you know, it was just like, like [pause] a *prediction* of the *future*. Like, I'm really going to marry this girl—because I saw her with the baby. It'll be *my* daughter. I mean, wow, I'm really going to marry this girl. And I didn't know if this was the real thing or not. I'm so young [18] still, I didn't know if I had found the right girl or not. But I guess God wants me to marry her! I mean, I guess she's the one. *(79)*

As I mentioned earlier (see footnote 2) several people, in addition to the young man just quoted, identify the presence with God and believe when they hear a voice speaking to them, that it is His voice. Although in most cases in which a presence is felt or heard the respondent believes that the choice to live or die is ultimately up to him, in those instances where the individual feels he is in direct communication with God the entire range of decisional possibilities seems to be represented: One may either choose to go back, bargain to get back, or find oneself sent back.

A woman who suddenly incurred a very high fever (106°) found herself "talking with God."

During this time, a feeling of complete calmness—the only way I can describe it is like a blanket being pulled up from my feet, gradually coming up. And a voice—and I believe the voice was God—telling me, "If you want, I'll take you now." And I recall thinking about it at this time. And I said, "No, I want to stay with my children." And I felt the same cool blanket being slowly removed.

Interviewer: How did you feel at the time?

Respondent: Total relaxation. Complete calm. It was more like a logical decision. I wanted to remain because my children were very small. And there was no anxiety. Cool, calm.

Interviewer: And logical?

Respondent: Logical. Yes, this was very definite.

Interviewer: You feel that you made this choice?

Respondent: Yes. Definitely. I feel that I was given the choice.

Interviewer: Can you tell me more about the voice?

Respondent: I would say it was very definitely God.

Interviewer: When you heard the voice, did you hear it mentally or actually?

Respondent: I heard the voice. It was a masculine voice. The voice was [pause] almost like over a megaphone. Amplified, but not echoing. Very clear. *(26)*

A person who felt she bargained her way back to life is the woman who nearly died of a ruptured appendix:

It was during that time that I came to, first with a lot of fright—I was scared to death—then, I got a very, very funny sensation. And the feeling was, like, almost like rebirth. Almost like rebirth. I lay there and I thought about things that I had planned to do, that I had better start making moves towards. For about two days—I didn't sleep—I had the sensation of warm, a very warm sensation, of a very [pause] it was like a light . . . I had a feeling of total peace. A feeling of total, total peace. [She felt she was conscious during this time.][7] . . . [And then] I was thinking to myself, my children—I've got these four children I've got to raise—and I remember thinking, "What's going to happen to my kids?" I definitely didn't want my mother-in-law to have 'em, you know? And my mother couldn't handle 'em.

Interviewer: It sounds as though you had to live.
Respondent: I had to. I had to! My kids were young, you know? And I said, "I can't leave 'em. I can't leave 'em. They're not ready for me to leave 'em yet."
Interviewer: When you were thinking about your kids, did you have any images of your kids?
Respondent: Yeh, mm-hmm. I had a very clear picture of them. Some of the things we had experienced together. Some of the things that my husband and I had experienced together. I felt a tremendous, *tremendous* love for my mother. Like if I'd been able to, I could have just hugged her, you know? Held on tight to her.
Interviewer: What were these images like?
Respondent: They were vivid. They were vivid. Lots of scenes.
Interviewer: Were they like flashbacks?
Respondent: Right, it was. It was. It was. It was.

Later, I asked whether she had been aware of "the presence of anything" during her decisional crisis:

I felt very close to God. I felt very, very [pause] like I was having a personal conversation with Him. Even though I wasn't saying it verbally, He knew what I was saying. He heard me.

Then I asked her to describe for me who made the choice:

Respondent: When I came to in the evening, it was like I was
holding on. And that was what the whole, *whole* mental
conversation was. "Cause I can't go now."
Interviewer: Who decided that you would live?
Respondent: I think I bargained. I think it was just a bargain that I
had struck.[8] [She promised to accomplish certain things she felt
she had a talent for, to raise her kids to be decent and loving
human beings, and so forth] [And] I was no longer afraid.
Everything was going to be all right. *(30)*

Finally, to take an example of a person who felt she was "sent back"
by God, we have this testimony from a woman who suffered massive
internal hemorrhaging two weeks after giving birth to her first child:

I could feel myself just slipping away. I could feel myself in a
chamber [apparently like an echo chamber]; I could hear them
[the medical team] say that I was in shock. I could hear the nurse
say, "I can't get a pulse. No respiration. She's gone." [She says she
was told later that she was "gone" for more than a minute.] . . . It
was all echoey. Meanwhile . . . I felt very detached and very at
ease. I was completely panic-stricken before when I was going in, I
was terrified, but when I was in there, it was the most *peaceful,*
happy time. I never saw God. No one ever came walking up to me.
But I did hear somebody say, "You're needed, Patricia, I'm
sending you back now." *(Was it a male or a female voice?)* It was a
man's voice, a male voice. And I opened my eyes. *(28)*

This respondent later observed, "I guess I know that there really is a
God."
Feeling ushered back to physical life by God is not, of course, the only
means by which a person can find himself again in the world of
ordinary reality. Sometimes, an individual is enjoined to return to life
by the exhortations of a "visible spirit" rather than an "audible
presence." An example of this kind of "forced re-entry" can be found in
the case history given to illustrate a deep core experience near the
beginning of the book (pages 22–24).
To round out my exploration of the decisional process, I will give just
one additional and detailed account of this effect. In this case, a woman,
while hospitalized, was experiencing severe respiratory problems,
owing to a chronic asthmatic condition:

[She had been feeling extremely uncomfortable, unable to

breathe, move or talk, but then became aware that she was feeling comfortable. Apparently without moving, she saw a room monitor go flat.] I thought, Gee, I feel so comfortable. And then I heard, I heard Mrs. Friedrich [a wealthy woman for whom the respondent had once worked. The respondent described Mrs. Friedrich as a very loving and much respected woman. She, herself, loved her and felt loved by her]. She had been dead for nine years at that time. I heard, in her very distinct voice—she spoke slowly and every word was brought out strong—and she had a low voice, and she said, "Miss Harper . . . *Miss Harper* . . . MISS HARPER [with gradually increasing volume and emphasis], I want you to live." And she appeared, not distinctly, but . . . it's hard to explain. . . . I don't think I saw her face; it was there but it was more of a [pause] . . . she was dressed in black. I don't think I could see her feet, but I could see the middle part of her, and it was almost as if you would look at the side of a tree, a straight tree. And I saw this simple black dress and it just sort of faded out, top and bottom. But she was there and she said, "Miss Harper. Miss Harper! I want you to live!" [This was repeated many times.] And she said, "I didn't build this hospital for my family to die in; I built this hospital so that my family could live!" She said it many times and distinctly. It was the wing of the hospital she had built. And finally I answered in my mind, "I'll try, Mrs. Friedrich, I'll try [said weakly]." And she said [forcibly], "Miss Harper. Miss Harper! I want you to live!" *(6)*

It is tempting to quote from additional interviews to illustrate further nuances of the decision-making process,[9] but perhaps enough men and women have already been seen to convey something of the sense of awe, wonder, comfort, and peace that usually accompanies the decision to return to life. Clearly, the decision whether to return to life is usually made in an atmosphere that has a very definite otherworldly ambiance. A specifically religious interpretation is given to it by many, though not all, of the experiencers. Although the phenomena described in this section do indeed cry out for interpretative commentary, this must be postponed until after we have completed the presentation of all our findings on the core experience. Despite the patterned coherence and consistencies among our accounts, there remain many aspects of these experiences that require clarification before any conclusions, however tentative, may legitimately be drawn.

FIVE

Qualitative Aspects of the Near-Death Experience

I have so far tried to delineate certain sequential features of the core experience in order to show something of its uniformity of content in different men and women. Now, I want to move to some characteristic features of the experience that will serve to deepen the reader's understanding of its feeling-tone, sensory qualities, and cognitive processes. Several of the factors I will be discussing here refer to qualities originally identified by Moody as constituting part of the core experience pattern.

Is It Like a Dream?

One of the first questions usually raised about the core experience is whether it has a dreamlike quality. Or whether it could, in fact, have actually been a dream. Quite apart from the improbability that at the moment of (apparent) death everyone should dream fragments of a common dream, the subjective reports of near-death survivors provide almost no support for the "dream interpretation."

Unfortunately, we did not incorporate a question relevant to this interpretation until our study was already underway. Nevertheless, we did raise the issue with twenty-two of our core experiencers. Of the nineteen who responded unequivocally to this point, only one claimed that her experience was like a dream; the rest denied it—usually, as the reader will see, emphatically. Three people gave equivocal or irrelevant responses to the question. Thus, of those who addressed this issue, 94.7% stated that their experience was *not* like a dream. Instead, you will see, they typically claimed, it was very *real:*

(Was it like a dream?) No. It was too real. Dreams are always fictitious. *This* was *me,* happening at *that* time and there was no doubt that it was reality. It was a very real feeling. *(25)*

Now, this *could* have been a dream. Or it could have been for real. I more or less feel it was real. *(It wasn't like your ordinary dreams?)* It was *not* an ordinary dream. No way . . . it was *real. (68)*

(Did this experience seem a dream to you? Or did it seem different?) Very, very *different* from a dream. In fact, it felt like actual reality happening. *(So that when it was happening . . . it did seem real to you?)* *Very,* very real. *(Was it more vivid than a dream?) Much* more. It was where I could recall colors, places, things [referring to a flashback phenomenon], just everything altogether. And it was very, very vivid. *(64)*

(Was it like a dream?) Yes [pause] it was. It was, in a way, but, then, in a way, it wasn't. It was very *real. (20)*

(Was this experience like a dream? Or was it different from a dream?) I wasn't sure at first. But to think back—recently, I've been dreaming a lot and there's a different quality to it. It was *more realistic* It was very *real* to me . . . The more I thought about it, the more I felt it was real; it really happened to me. *(79)*

(Was it like a dream?) No. I thought to myself for a while [afterward], it didn't really happen. But then I thought to myself, Boy, you were there and it really did happen. *(28)*

(Was this experience like a dream in any way?) No. It was very real. It's as real as you and I are. *(26)*

A related question is: Is the experience an hallucination? The preceding testimony, of course, offers no support for this supposition. Nevertheless, I did find some evidence for the occurrence of hallucinatory-like images among a small number of our respondents—there were perhaps a half dozen such cases—including both core experiencers and nonexperiencers. In every case, however, the hallucinatory images were completely *idiosyncratic* and were regarded afterward by the respondents as having been hallucinations, that is, not real. In the few instances where a core experiencer also reported having had hallucinations, these could be *distinguished* from the core experience itself as having had a distinctly different quality. Perhaps the most definitive comment was delivered by one of our core experiencers, who was herself a psychiatrist and who, accordingly, should know something both about dreams and hallucinations. She told me, without qualification, that, in her judgment, her own experience was neither the one nor the other.

The data here, then, are quite unambiguous: In the opinion of the respondents themselves, their core experience was not a dream nor an hallucination—it was real.

The Question of Ineffability

According to Moody, many near-death survivors find that their experience is, at bottom, ineffable—it cannot really be communicated in words. What do our respondents have to say on this point?

Table 6 presents the relevant data.

Table 6

Core Experiencers' Responses to the Question:
Is Your Experience Difficult to put into Words?

	No.	%
Yes	24	49
No	15	31
Equivocal/irrelevant	7	14
Not asked	3	6
Total	49	100

Percentages of unequivocal responders only

Yes	61.5%
No	38.5%

Inspection of the table discloses that there is considerable support for Moody's claim from the data furnished by our respondents. The bulk of those who answered the question directly admitted that they have difficulty in conveying their experience to others because of their inability to find the right words. Still, it should be noted, nearly 40% of those who responded unequivocally reported no particular problems on this score. This group, incidentally, includes a number of people who had "deep" experiences, so the apparent ineffability of the experience does not seem to be a simple function of its complexity or richness. Thus, on the question of ineffability, the data are by and large consistent with Moody's contention, but not overwhelmingly so.

When the experience *is* said to be ineffable, however, one can ask why is it so? On this point, our respondents are sometimes quite emphatic about the reasons for their frustrating inability to translate their experience into ordinary speech:

(Do you find it hard to convey this experience in words?) There are not

words. There are not words. . . . It can't [be conveyed]. And it cannot be fully understood. *(20)*

Yeah, it was like—it was *such*—I've *never* had an *experience like this.* I mean, like, there's, like, *no,* no words—to convey it. Like when I was trying to tell you how the voice was and how the *feeling* [pause] of just *drifting,* you know, it was [pause] it was *really weird.* It's hard to explain in words. *(79)*

It's very hard because there's nothing like it. There's nothing on earth, I think, that can compare to this feeling of total peace. *(5)*

Yeah, because I can't explain to you the feeling, the sensation. You know, I can't tell you what the sensation was. *(30)*

I'm not coming across at all as I want to. Maybe just the feelings that were felt at the time, being totally brand new, unable to put a label on them . . . *(32)*

It was just *absolutely beautiful!* I could never explain it in a million years. . . . I can *never* tell you what the feeling was like. *(34)*

I remember at the time, when I was in the hospital, trying to explain to one of the technicians how I felt. And I just couldn't get it across; I always felt like the words were *lacking.* You just couldn't describe it. *(99)*

This was different from a dream. And different than being on this physical planet. So it was something *other* than [pause] than what words can express on this planet for sure. *(77)*

The answer is repetitively clear: Over and over, the respondents state that there simply *are* no words that *can* be used to describe their experience adequately. Not only do their perceptions, while in this state, defy linguistic expression, but so do their feelings. Usually, the respondent's very *struggle* to communicate his experience to me was dramatic evidence. This was no mere matter of verbal fluency. When the woman said, "I'm not coming across at all as I want to," she was, in fact, voicing a common frustration.

There is still another and very different reason why the experience sometimes tends to remain private. This has nothing to do with the problem of ineffability, but rather with the fear of ridicule. Recall that Moody's account of the prototypic near-death experience includes an observation that survivors find that people often scoff when near-death experiences are related. This ridicule gradually leads to the experiencers suppressing their accounts. Although I did not systematically inquire into the reactions of others on hearing these accounts, enough respondents unburdened themselves on this point to make it clear that *fear* of ridicule was a powerful deterrent. In some cases, I was the first person to be told about these experiences. In most cases, respondents did not want to be regarded as "weird" or "nuts." As one young man put it:

> . . . If you go talk to people about this, they look at you like you're *weird*. Because they can't [pause]. How can you explain something to somebody that they can't believe? or visualize? or whatever it is? A lot of people have trouble with that. [He goes on to say that he believes this is changing somewhat as a result of the publication of *Life After Life*.] (71)

Another woman, who had had her experience seven and a half years before my interview with her, told me that only recently had she told anyone about her experience and that was her therapist. When I asked her why she had waited so long, she replied, ". . . I thought I was weird. . . . I thought I was off-the-wall." (64) Her reticence stemmed from her fear that others would confirm her own suspicions.

And in fact, such fears are not altogether insubstantial.

> I don't find it difficult [pause] to communicate this in words. But I find that people are very standoffish when you start talking about it. You know, they'll say, *"Oh, really?"* And they'll kind of hesitate away from you. I mean, it happened with the doctors at ——— hospital after the incident *did* happen to me. *(You described that to them?)* I *tried*, and they wouldn't listen. . . . For a while, I really felt that I was a little *crazy*, because every time I did broach the subject, somebody would *change* the subject, so I felt the topic probably shouldn't be discussed. (7)

Afterward, this woman tried to discuss her experience with her rabbi and again felt she received a response that indicated neither understanding nor acceptance. It was not until she came across *Life After Life* that she realized her experience was *not* unusual, given her closeness to death. She has since been emboldened to discuss it with many others and has even agreed to be interviewed by journalists and radio reporters.

In summary, Moody's assertion that the disclosure of near-death experiences tends to be inhibited because of anticipated ridicule or scoffing does receive some support from the spontaneous comments of a number of my respondents.[1] His claim that many near-death survivors believe that their experience is essentially ineffable receives even stronger and more systematic support. Together, these two factors operate to keep these near-death episodes in the domain of private events.

Perception of Death or Dying

When a person is apparently on the brink of death or has gone temporarily over that brink into "clinical" death, is he aware of his condition? I have already mentioned (see footnote 7, page 288) that with only two exceptions all our core experiencers were apparently or clearly unconscious or comatose at the time of their episode. It is during these periods, then, that the question of perceived death or dying is applicable.

A preliminary answer to this question can be obtained by comparing the perceptions of core experiencers with nonexperiencers:

Table 7

Perceptions of Dying and Death by
Core Experiencers and Nonexperiencers

	Did not perceive themselves to be dying	Perceived themselves to be dying	Perceived themselves to be dead	
Core experiencers	11	19	10	40
Nonexperiencers	21	17	0	38
	32	36	10	78

$$x^2 = 13.28 \; (p < .01)*$$

Data on this question were available for 87 of our 102 respondents. Nine respondents—6 core experiencers and 3 nonexperiencers—whose responses were either indeterminant or uncertain were dropped from this analysis.

*x^2 is the statistic used for evaluating the significance of the differences between rows; in this case, between core experiencers and nonexperiencers.

Core experiencers are significantly more likely to perceive themselves as dying or as already dead compared to nonexperiencers.
Indeed, all ten cases where an unequivocal perception of death is
reported come from core experiencers.

It is difficult to judge whether the impression that one is either
dying or dead should be regarded as an inference or as a datum.
How, after all, does one "know" that he is dying when he has had no
comparable prior experience? Does one merely infer that he is dying
or dead from the apparently overheard remarks of members of the
medical team who often observe that the patient is dying or has died?
Are experiencers more likely to form these impressions precisely
because they have otherworldly experiences on which to base such
an opinion? Is it the qualitatively discontinuous feeling of peace and
the sense of well-being that accompanies it which leads a person to
conclude that he has died? These questions do not lend themselves
to facile answers, and the exact determinants of the inference or
knowledge of one's own dying or death cannot be stated with
certainty.

Nevertheless, we can still examine this aspect of the core experience in the hope of arriving at some tentative conclusions. The fact
is, the overwhelming proportion of experiencers claim they knew
that they were dying or had died. Perhaps if we listen again to their
own comments, we shall gain a valuable insight into this feature of
the experience.

The woman who nearly died of massive internal bleeding two
weeks after giving birth to her first child recalled:

[In the emergency room she said inwardly] I'm leaving. Good-
bye. I felt myself just slipping away. I could feel myself in a
chamber [like an echo chamber]; I could hear them say that I
was in shock. I could hear the nurses say, "I can't get a pulse."
"No respiration." "She's gone." And I could hear a nurse
saying, "Get a line through her," but it was all [echoey]. . . .
Meanwhile . . . I felt very detached and at ease . . . it was a, the
most *peaceful*, happy time. [Soon thereafter she heard a voice
saying she was being sent back.] *(28)*

It was her sense that she was definitely dying, although she wasn't
sure that she was actually "dead" (even though she was told that she
was "gone" for over a minute).

The man who suffered a cardiac arrest and found himself
spinning up into a "deep black, pitch black tunnel" was soon

confronted with a "mental question": Did he want to live or die? He said that during that time:

> I just thought I was dying at that particular time. It didn't even affect me as far as being scared. Of course, being up there and knowing your mind was alive, but my mind was very much alive. I could think very clearly, even though I was considered dead [laughs]. *(33)*

The young man who fell on a rock while contemplating suicide also found himself drifting in a dark space:

> *Interviewer:* Did you actually think at any point that you *were* dying?
>
> *Respondent:* Yes, I did. I did at first. When I first started feeling that drifting, I thought to myself, Maybe I'm on my way to heaven.
>
> *Interviewer:* Did you actually think that you *were* dead?
>
> *Respondent:* I wasn't sure. I wasn't sure. *(79)*

A man, badly injured in a motorcycle accident, was taken to a nearby hospital, where he was declared "dead on arrival":

> *Respondent:* [I felt] no pain. Extremely peaceful. No sense of actual touch or anything of that sort. . . .
>
> *Interviewer:* You actually had this sense, then, that . . . you were actually dead?
>
> *Respondent:* Absolutely. To tell people this, they think I'm nuts. Okay, let them think so.
>
> *Interviewer:* The next thing that you were aware of was the doctor saying, "This man is alive." Did you hear anybody say, "This man is dead," or anything like that?
>
> *Respondent:* No. No. *(68)*

A woman involved in a severe automobile crash was in intense pain when she was brought to a hospital emergency room. Like the previous respondent, she also claims that she was and felt dead.

> Then the blood pressure started to drop really fast and they were losing me rapidly. At this point there was no pain. I felt *very*

comfortable, very euphoric, just *really* like it was okay and everything was still and calm. At that point they said I died, right there. . . . It was funny, at the point when I really died, it just felt so good. I don't know why the pain stopped. It was just such a peacefulness, it was just really strange. *(62)*

Finally, I will again cite the case of the woman who had the deepest core experience. She had been comatose for three days at home after an apparent heart failure. She was then taken to a hospital.

Respondent: I *know* that I had died. I know that I had died.

Interviewer: Do you know that according to your medical records if you were declared clinically dead?

Respondent: I've talked with Dr. —— about it. He said, "Margaret, I wouldn't have given two cents for your life. We were ready to give up so many times. . . ."

Interviewer: You felt at this time that you *were* dead, would you say? That you *had* died? This was your subjective feeling?

Respondent: Yes. Yes. I did. I did.

Interviewer: Did you hear anybody say, at the time, that—

Respondent: Yes, I did. . . . [She then recounts several such comments exemplified by the following remark, made, she says, by one of her physicians: "No *way* are we going to keep this woman alive."] *(20)*

From these brief excerpts, it may seem impossible to draw any firm conclusions about the factors associated with the perception of dying and death, but my examination of all of the relevant cases in their entirety does enable me to offer a provisional hypothesis. While it is probable that many cues combine to suggest to the person that he is dying or has died, in my judgment, the most *significant* are the sudden termination of bodily sensations (including, most importantly, the cessation of pain) and the onset of feelings of peace and well-being. When the individual realizes as well that his mind is "still alive," these features collectively tend to trigger the thoughts: I am dying, or, This is death. In my opinion, the external cues, such as seeing one's apparently "lifeless" body or hearing a physician's doubtful pronouncement, are not necessarily as potent or compelling as is that concatenation of internal indicators I have described.

Needless to say, further research is needed to clarify this issue, but it already seems established that the perception of dying or death is still another characteristic feature of the core experience.

Cognitive Processes

In conjunction with the out-of-body stage of the core experience, I mentioned that a number of people reported a sense of detachment characterized their state of mind while close to death. It is possible, however, to be more precise in describing the quality of the cognitive processes which operate during the time of decision. Respondents who commented on this matter (the issue was not raised systematically in our interviews) tended to claim that their thinking processes were clear and sharp—and governed by rational, rather than emotional, considerations. This generalization seems to hold both for people who found themselves out-of-body and for those who had no such impression:

I could think very clearly, even though I was considered dead [laughs]. *(33)*

(What were your feelings and sensations?) Total relaxation. Complete calm. It was more like a logical decision. I wanted to remain because my children were very small. And there was no anxiety. Cool, calm. *(And logical?)* Logical, yes. This was very definite. *(26)*

(How would you describe how your mind was working while in this state?) Very cognitive. Really, very rational. Very determined. *(62)*

(So the thing that is very hard to describe is the fact that you were very alert mentally?) *Extremely* alert [with feeling]. *(68)*

(Why do you feel you came back? Why did you choose to come back?) I don't know. I think it's because I had two little children. And I felt that they needed me—more than "up there?" And I think that going up there meant *my* peace and joy, but it meant misery for my children. And I think *even then* I was *thinking* of these things, weighing things. I wasn't feeling any *pain* or *sorrow* or anything, but I was thinking *calmly* and *rationally*—making a decision, a rational decision, a logical decision—*without emotions involved.* Do you know what I mean? Being a mother, she's ruled mostly by emotions. Being *human*, you're ruled mostly by emotions. I didn't make that decision *emotionally.* I made it *logically.* And the choice, both choices were—I mean, I wasn't afraid to die so *that* choice

would have been just as easy for me. But the choice was made *logically*. And I'm sure it was *mine*. Because I was *thinking* logically. Do you understand what I mean? *(24)*

The gist of these and similar observations implies that during the decision-making phase, not only is there no impairment of one's thinking processes, but, if anything, they appear to be enhanced. The decision to return to life seems typically to be made during a state of heightened mental clarity dominated by a (subjective) sense of logic, detachment, and rationality.

Sensory Processes

Sensory processes reported during the core experience seem to parallel the quality of the thinking processes. Although there are certainly exceptions to this generalization, sensory processes when an individual comes close to death seem best described by the word *clarity*. Just as the mind is lucid, one's sensory acuity tends to be sharp and precise. This is especially so when the individual finds himself out of his body.

There are, of course, limits. For example, with only one doubtful exception, olfactory and gustatory sensations are entirely absent. Bodily sensations, as we have already seen, are also lacking. What remain, obviously, are vision and hearing. These are the senses that appear to continue functioning, at least for a time, during the core experience, though even these, as we shall see, may drop out entirely. Finally, a number of people said that when they were subjectively close to death or dead, they existed, in effect, as "mind only."

When visual and auditory processes appear to be operative, however, they tend to have certain definite qualities:

I could see very clearly, yeh, yeh. I recognized it [her body] as being me. *(25)*

I heard the voice. It was a masculine voice. The voice was [pause] almost like over a megaphone. Amplified but not echoing. Very clear. *(26)*

My ears were very sensitive at that point. . . . Vision also. *(7)*

I heard everything clearly and distinctly. *(29)*

Seems like everything was clear. Everything was clear. My hearing was clear because everything was quiet; I felt like I could have heard a pin drop. My sight—everything was clear. I could specifically see myself or anything that I was looking at, although I was mostly looking at myself. *(45)*

Sometimes this heightened sensory awareness was not attributed to any particular sense organ per se:

It was as if my whole body had eyes and ears. I was just so aware of everything. *(23)*

In a few cases, as the last quote implied, there was no impression of sensory-mediated perception. Instead, the mind alone existed. This state of mind awareness was usually associated with the decision-making phase of the experience:

It seemed like I was up there in space and just my mind was active. No body feeling, just like my brain was up in space. I had nothing but my mind. Weightless, I had nothing. And it seemed like I was being asked a question, mentally, whether I wanted to live or wanted to die. . . . The thought was being given to me to decide on my own whether I wanted to die or to live. It didn't seem like it was a question from anybody. It was just like it was in my own mind and I took it for granted that someone was giving me my own powers to decide for myself. . . . I saw nothing. *(33)*

(When you heard the voice, you heard it as a male voice. Did you actually hear the words, or—) It was like it was *coming into my mind.* It was like I didn't have any hearing or sight or anything. It was like it was being *projected into my mind. (79)*

At the time I was talking to the person, I felt *peaceful* . . . I had a perfectly clear understanding of *what* was going on, except to *who* I was talking with. . . . It's like trying to explain [pause] oh, God. Can you imagine floating, suspended in midair, touching nothing, yet you're aware of things, but there's nothing there to be aware of. You've got no sense of feel or touch, but you've got *thought.* The mind's working, but there's no body. No vision. No vision, but the mind is working. And capable of thought. *(68)*

The common theme running through these passages is one of heightened sensory awareness and mental clarity. When present, the senses are sharpened; when absent, it is the mind itself that remains sharp. Sensory and thinking processes seem to work together to make the near-death experience vivid, distinct and subjectively real.

The Noise—and the Silence

According to Moody, many near-death survivors report that their experience was heralded by an unpleasant sound—whistling wind or a ringing or buzzing in the ears. Our own data, however, offer only a few corroborative instances of this auditory phenomenon. *Most* of our respondents report that either they can recall no such feature or that they simply cannot comment definitively on this point. Altogether only fourteen people reported remembering any unusual noises or sounds and this feature was more commonly reported by core experiencers than nonexperiencers (ten to four), the variety of the auditory stimuli mentioned and the uncertainty of many of these recollections make their reports of doubtful significance and validity. My tentative conclusion, then, is that this phenomenon is not likely to be so frequent as Moody's remarks suggest.

Nonetheless, this is *not* to say that it *never* occurs. There are a *few* instances in which a respondent did describe an effect that seems to correspond to Moody's specifications:

The first thing I remember was a tremendous rushing sound, a tremendous [pause] it's very hard to find the right words to describe [it]. The closest thing that I could *possibly* associate it with is, possibly, the sound of a tornado, a tremendously gushing wind, but almost pulling me, and I was being pulled into a narrow point from a wide area ... it was very high-pitched; it was almost piercing. *(20)*

It was, like, dull, like, I don't know. It was like I was in a mist. It was like a swish ... like mist going by. *(90)*

I felt like I might have had a buzzing in my ears. It was just a "zzzz." *(29)*

I think I went through a tunnel. I think I went through a tunnel and it *seems* to me that I heard something like a siren. A siren and something that might have been like a high rustle of trees. High wind of trees. *(71)*

Recall of these auditory impressions was not only rare but also, as these passages demonstrate, sometimes tentative. More often, respondents did not merely claim to remember no unusual sounds; instead, they would say something like, "Quite the contrary; it was very quiet."

Everything was perfectly quiet, the quietest I've ever heard anything. There wasn't a sound. *(48)*

. . . everything was quiet; I felt like I could have heard a pin drop. *(45)*

Silence. Clear silence. It was brilliant . . . but there wasn't any sound. It's brilliant, it's clear and it's sharp. *(23)*

. . . my pain was gone and it was quiet, but it wasn't a morbid quiet, it was a peaceful quiet. *(3)*

Although few people were perfectly explicit on this point, the implication of many of their accounts seems more consistent with this sense of peaceful silence than with auditory discomfort. Still, the fact is that the replies to the question on unusual noises, when specific, tend to fall into these apparently opposite categories. Why should this be so?

A review of our own data and the relevant literature[2] suggests a possible answer. Out-of-body experiences sometimes seem to be signaled by a ringing or buzzing sound. All the above cases come from respondents who also reported having had an out-of-body episode. Thus, the auditory effect, when it does occur, may be primarily a cue that an out-of-body state is about to occur. Once the out-of-body state, or a further stage of the core experience, is *established* in consciousness, however, sensory cues fall away and a profound inner silence is experienced. According to this hypothesis, it is the *total absence* of bodily-based cues that gives rise to the silence (as well as to the sense of extraordinary peace initiating stage I.) Presumably, those who reported awareness only of the silence were recalling this *later*, body-absent, period of their experience. The data here are far from clearcut, however, and this hypothesis needs to be evaluated through further research.

Sense of Body, Time, and Space

During the core experience, one's awareness of his body and of time and space undergo characteristic alterations. For most respondents, body, time, and space simply disappear—or, to put it another way, they are no longer meaningful constructs. In this respect, what we all take for granted in our ordinary state of consciousness may be nonexistent in the state of consciousness associated with (apparent) imminent death.

This generalization, too, has its limits. Sometimes the constructs of body, time, and space do not so much vanish as become radically transformed. In either event, coming close to death almost always drastically affects one's awareness of these constructs, as Table 8 makes clear.

Table 8

Perceptions of Body, Time, and Space
(Core experiencers only)

Body Sense	*No.*	*%*
Heavy	1	2
Normal	0	0
Light	13	27
None	25	51
(Not asked or indeterminate)	(10)	(20)

Time Sense	*No.*	*%*
Speeded up	1	2
Normal	1	2
Extended	3	6
None	32	65
(Not asked or indeterminate)	(12)	(24)

Space Sense	*No.*	*%*
Distorted	1	2
Normal	3	6
Extended	1	2
Infinite	6	12
None	11	22
(Not asked or indeterminate)	(27)	(55)

If, in interpreting this table, we restrict ourselves to the respondents who gave definite replies, we find that 97.4% of core experiencers felt that their bodies were light or absent; 94.6% found their sense of time either expanded or absent; and 81.8% experienced space as either extended, infinite, or absent. The *modal* response for all three constructs is overwhelmingly "absent."

The individual answers to these questions tend mainly to be terse and uninformative. Since they are usually nothing more than a denial of the meaningfulness of body, time, and space as experiential concepts, there appears to be no particular need to cite representative responses. Nevertheless, if only for the sake of thoroughness and consistency, consider these responses:

Well, it was like [pause] like I didn't have a body! I was [pause] but it was *me*. Not a body, but *me*. You know what I mean? *(24)*

(What about your sense of bodily weight. Bodily feeling?) Nothing. *(Absent?)* There was nothing there. *(68)*

I couldn't really see anything. I couldn't see myself there either. It was just like my *mind* was there. And no body. . . . *(You said you felt like you had no body, but did you feel that you were* [separate] *from your body in any way? or separated from it?)* Yeah, I think so. I felt more like just a mind moving. I left my body back on the bed. *(99)*

(What was your sense of time like?) My sense of time was way off. Time didn't mean anything. It seemed like time had no meaning. It was just [pause] well, I don't know how to explain it, even. *(Was your sense of space affected?)* Well, yes, due to the fact that it seemed like I was weightless, you know, and I could project myself wherever I wanted. *(51)*

(What was your perception of [time] *like when you were in this state?)* Very bad. I really have no idea of how long this went on. Sometimes, when I think about it, it seems like it was forever. . . . *(How about your sense of space?)* Oh, it was a very open space I was in. Very open. *(No limits to it?)* Not really. *(7)*

It was like I lost time. . . . I was like—I could go *anywhere*. *(You weren't bounded the way you normally are?)* No. I was very free. I could go anywhere, do anything. *(64)*

This is the interesting part . . . it *has* to be out of time and space. It *must* be, because the context of it is that it is just [pause] it can't be put *into* a time thing. . . . Okay, I can't explain the actual words, "You really blew it this time, Frank"—I couldn't tell you if this was said *before* that whole movie thing or after it. Because, somehow, even though I feel it was at the end, it could have just as well as been at the beginning. In other words, that statement related to the whole thing, before and after. I can't explain it. *(What was your sense of time during this whole experience?)* You couldn't relate to time. *(71)*

. . . I found myself in a space, in a period of time, I would say, where all space and time was negated. *(49)*

The difficulty most people had in dealing with the concepts of body, time, and space from the perspective of their near-death experience strongly reinforces the impression suggested by other data that the near-death experience represents a *distinctive state of consciousness,* in which many ordinary features of perception and cognition are completely transformed or altogether absent. From the standpoint of transpersonal psychology, this state of consciousness could legitimately be called *transpersonal* since it meets the three criteria required for it: transcendence of one's usual ego boundaries and the concepts of time and space. From the standpoint of recent formulations of brain functioning, the near-death experience seems to represent a "frequency domain" where time and space collapse and everything merely "coexists." These are matters to which we shall return when we consider the interpretative problems raised by near-death experiences.

Feelings of Loneliness

In *Life After Life,* Moody comments that many people described to him transient feelings of loneliness as part of their out-of-body experience near death. Although this matter was raised with only about half of our respondents, only about half a dozen indicated that they experienced any such feelings of loneliness. When such feelings were reported, however, they tended to occur in conjunction with either a sense of "drifting through space" without a body or as part of an out-of-body episode, which is consistent with Moody's observations. Moody does go on to state, though, that these feelings of loneliness are brief and are dispelled when an individual gets farther into the experience and encounters a reassuring presence of some kind. Though our number of relevant instances is obviously very small, we again did find some evidence to support Moody's contention:

> *(Did you feel lonely?)* For a while. *(When did that end?)* When I met my grandfather. *(7)*
> *(When you were in that state where it was a total nothing, you said you were drifting through an emptiness. Can you tell me more about what that was like?)* Okay, that was like, like, [pause] like wandering around and not knowing where you're going. Like, like going to a strange city or a strange area and you're trying to *find* something but you don't know where it's at and you just go up and down the street and [pause] and you're looking around and you can't find anyone to ask directions or something like that. *(So you felt you were sort of psychologically lost?)* Yeh. . . . *(Did you feel lonely, by yourself, at first?)* Yeh, I did. Until the voice came in. *(79)*

On the question of loneliness, then, our findings are consistent with Moody's when such instances are reported, but the incidence of such feelings seems to be considerably less than among Moody's informants. In our sample, at least, most tended to deny that they felt lonely, even at the outset of their experience.

Approaching the Threshold

Moody has stated that a few of his respondents indicated that they felt they approached some kind of a limit or border, such as a body of water, a door, a fence, and so forth, which presumably represents a threshold between life and death. When we asked our respondents, we found that the answers distributed themselves as follows:

Table 9

Responses to Question: Did You Ever Feel You Were Approaching Some Kind of Boundary or Threshold—a Point of No Return?
(Core experiencers only)

	No.	%
Yes	13	27
No	21	43
Not sure	6	12
Not asked	9	18

Although about a third responded affirmatively, no one said or implied that this experience was accompanied by an appropriate *visual image* corresponding to those reported by Moody.[3] Instead, as the chapter on the decision-making process makes clear, this threshold phenomenon was usually a cognitive affair—an encounter with a presence, a stock-taking of one's life—rather than an imagistic one.[4] Some people did report a gray or hazy mist, which Moody mentions, but this was quite rare and not necessarily associated with a feeling of transition. Thus, the *visual symbols* demarcating a barrier between life and death were not found here, but the *sense* of approaching that threshold was very much in evidence.

Coming Back

The event that terminates the core experience is the return to one's body and (eventually) to ordinary waking consciousness. In agreement with Moody, we found that most people were not able to recall just how they returned to their bodies. Often, as Chapter Four makes clear, the last feature remembered is the decision or the command to return; the return itself is usually a "blank."

In those few cases in which the man or woman was able to recall something of this process, the descriptions tally perfectly with those of Moody's respondents.

For example, one of the features mentioned by Moody is the return with a "jolt." In this connection, when I asked one of our suicide attempters how he felt when he found himself back in his body, he told me:

> The thing I remember most is a *falling* feeling. Like I was coming down really fast and then *hit*. And then I woke up with a *jolt*. (99)

This was not the only case where a jolting sensation was experienced. In some instances, however, a person would feel more than a jolt:

> I wanted to stay where I was. And then suddenly . . . I could hear my daughter and children and I realized I have to [pause], I *have* to, [pause], I have to come back. . . . [She felt a "horrendous pain"] And the strongest thing was that pain—no words can describe it. It was as though I was seeing many, many lightning and thunder storms all at once. . . . It was as if I were being pulled out of a *tremendous vacuum* and, and just being torn to pieces. (20)

Whether one is jolted or wrenched back, one somehow, as Moody says, "reunites with his physical body." But how exactly does one accomplish that return? Since most of our respondents blank out at this point—possibly because reentry into one's body is typically associated with the onset of pain—the details of the reunion are almost always lacking. *Almost* always. Here, Moody provides an intriguing clue. He states that in a few instances his respondents maintained that they returned "through the head." One of our core experiencers—but just one—also hinted, almost in passing, at this same perception:

> *(What were you next aware of?)* Oh. It was being—going back to my body. It was . . . I said, "No, I want to live," but that was looking at my body, yeah, and the next thing was just a [snaps fingers] flash; it *seems* like a flash. And I was back in my body. I wouldn't hesitate to say that I think I [pause] I [pause] I entered my body through my head [questioning intonation]. But I don't know *why* that is. *(71)*

To comment further on this point would entail a digression into the parapsychological literature on out-of-body experiences, which will not be undertaken here. Instead the intent is to call attention to an aspect of the reentry phenomenon that may be worth examining more systematically in future research on near-death experiences.

In any event, once the individual has returned, painfully or otherwise, to his physical body, the core experience is over.

Summary of the Principal Stages and Qualitative Aspects of the Core Experience

In view of the massive amount of data, both quantitative and qualitative, which has been presented in this and preceding chapters, it seems best at this point to sum up the major features of the core near-death experience. In doing so, I will write as though I am dealing with one individual case in which all the major stages and aspects of the experience are encountered. It is important to bear in mind that I am delineating a *composite* near-death experience—one suggested by the totality of my cases but which is only approximated even by my richest ones. This prototypical summary creates the risk of some distortion and idealization of the experience, but it has the advantage of enabling the reader to appreciate how all the facets of the core experience might cohere in a single, complete case. (The experience itself was found represented to a variable degree in 48% of our sample.)

The experience begins with a feeling of easeful peace and a sense of well-being, which soon culminates in a sense of overwhelming joy and happiness. This ecstatic tone, although fluctuating in intensity from case to case, tends to persist as a constant emotional ground as other features of the experience begin to unfold. At this point, the person is aware that he feels no pain nor does he have any other bodily sensations. Everything is quiet. These cues may suggest to him that he is either in the process of dying or has already "died."

He may then be aware of a transitory buzzing or a windlike sound, but, in any event, he finds himself looking down on his physical body, as though he were viewing it from some external vantage point. At this time, he finds that he can see and hear perfectly; indeed, his vision and hearing tend to be more acute than usual. He is aware of the actions and conversations taking place in the physical environment, in relation to which he finds himself in the role of a passive, detached spectator. All this seems very real—even quite natural—to him; it does not seem at all like a dream or an hallucination. His mental state is one of clarity and alertness.

At some point, he may find himself in a state of *dual awareness*. While he continues to be able to perceive the physical scene around him, he may also become aware of "another reality" and feel himself being drawn into it. He drifts or is ushered into a dark void or tunnel and feels as though he is floating through it. Although he may feel lonely for a time, the experience here is predominantly peaceful and serene. All is extremely quiet and the individual is aware only of his mind and of the feeling of floating.

All at once, he becomes sensitive to, but does not see, a presence. The presence, who may be heard to speak or who may instead "merely" induce thoughts into the individual's mind, stimulates him to review his life and asks him to decide whether he wants to live or die. This stock-taking may be facilitated by a rapid and vivid visual playback of episodes from the person's life. At this stage, he has no awareness of time or space, and the concepts themselves are meaningless. Neither is he any longer identified with his body. Only the mind is present and it is weighing—logically and rationally—the alternatives that confront him at this threshold separating life from death: to go further into this experience or to return to earthly life. Usually the individual decides to return on the basis, not of his own preference, but on the perceived needs of his loved ones, whom his death would necessarily leave behind. Once the decision is made, the experience tends to be abruptly terminated.

Sometimes, however, the decisional crisis occurs later or is altogether absent, and the individual undergoes further experiences. He may, for example, continue to float through the dark void toward a magnetic and brilliant golden light, from which emanates feelings of love, warmth, and total acceptance. Or he may enter into a "world of light" and preternatural beauty, to be (temporarily) reunited with deceased loved ones before being told, in effect, that it is not yet his time and that he has to return to life.

In any event, whether the individual chooses or is commanded to return to his earthly body and worldly commitments, he does return. Typically, however, he has no recollection *how* he has effected his "reentry," for at this point he tends to lose all awareness. Very occasionally, however, the individual may remember "returning to his body" with a jolt or an agonizing wrenching sensation. He may even suspect that he reenters "through the head."

Afterward, when he is able to recount his experience, he finds that there are simply no words adequate to convey the feelings and quality of awareness he remembers. He may also be or become reticent to discuss it with others, either because he feels no one will really be able to understand it or because he fears he will be disbelieved or ridiculed.

After reading this prototypic account, the reader may find it instructive to review the version originally given by Moody (see page 22). The parallels, and even the similar phrasings, are striking. I want to emphasize that this similarity in prototypic descriptions does not at all stem from any conscious desire on my part to parrot Moody; *it stems chiefly from the (apparent) extraordinary similarity between his findings and mine.* There are, to be sure, some points of difference, having to do with such facts as what Moody calls the "being of light" and the threshold phenomenon. These differences, and others, will be discussed in the appropriate place. But no one reading this who is already familiar with Moody's work can fail to be impressed with the similarities between the findings of these two studies. Insofar as Moody's overall characterization of the core experience is concerned, our own independent data are almost totally congruent with it.

There remain some further parameters which Moody himself was not in a position to examine systematically, one of which is the relationship between certain preconditions and the core experience.

S I X

Does It Matter How One (Nearly) Dies?

Does it make a difference *how* one (nearly) dies? One of the chief reasons for undertaking this investigation was to determine if the core experience was independent of the circumstances and motives that brought about a near-death episode. Obviously, if the core experience is invariant over a range of near-death conditions, one would be led to conclude that it is a very robust phenomenon indeed. If, on the other hand, manner of near-death onset is a significant factor in affecting either the likelihood or the form of the experience, it would help us to specify more precisely the conditions under which the basic phenomenon is likely to occur.

Accordingly, our investigation was designed to compare three distinct modes of near-death onset: illness, accident, and suicide attempt. Altogether, in our sample we had fifty-two illness victims, twenty-six accident victims, and twenty-four people who attempted suicide.

Since this section will deal with various comparisons across these groups, it is necessary at the outset to point out that there were several antecedent factors on which these groups differed. Whether any of these factors can be said to undermine the validity of the coming comparisons is an open question, but the evaluation of the data must certainly take them into account.

Before going further, however, I think it best to warn the reader that this chapter will be rather technical. It is necessary to be so because this is, after all, a scientific investigation. In keeping with my narrative stance—which is to present our work in a way that is accessible to the general public—I have tried to keep jargon and statistics to a minimum here, as elsewhere. However, I owe it to my colleagues to present what follows, and so I advise those who may not care to immerse themselves in analyses and statistics simply to skip to page 115, where I deal with my material in qualitative terms.

To continue, some of the differences referred to above have already been indicated. I have, for example, commented on the differences among these groups in respect to the source of referral and incidence of interview refusal (see pages 27–31). In general, illness victims were secured mostly through medical referrals, while suicide cases were drawn largely through self-referrals. Accident victims tended to fall in between. Accident victims were almost always willing to be interviewed, while suicide-attempt victims tended to refuse to be interviewed or else access to them was denied. Illness cases fell between these extremes. There were also significant differences in the average age at which the near-death episode took place. Table 10 presents these data.

Table 10
_____

Mean Age at Time of Incident
by Sex and Condition

	Illness	*Accident*	*Suicide*	
Females	52.14	38.20	34.61	44.16
	(29)	(10)	(18)	(57)
Males	54.21	28.06	29.00	41.55
	(23)	(16)	(6)	(45)
	53.06	31.96	33.21	43.01
	(52)	(26)	(24)	(102)

Respondents whose near-death episode resulted from illness were significantly older at the time than both accident victims and suicide attempters who do not differ from one another. The difference between the illness victims and the others is, on average, about twenty years. There are still other, and possibly more critical, differences among these groups which make unqualified comparisons hazardous, but these factors are best discussed in conjunction with the specific comparisons themselves.

We can begin, however, simply by examining the incidence of core experiences as a function of near-death condition. Table 11A gives the breakdown.

Table 11A

Incidence of Core Experience as a
Function of Mode of Near-Death Onset

	Illness	Accident	Suicide	
Core experiencers	29	11	8	48*
Nonexperiencers	23	15	16	54
	52	26	24	102

$$x^2 = 3.64 \ p \cong .06$$

*For analyses in this section, one person who had two near-death episodes—one involving an illness-related near-death *experience,* the other, a suicide attempt not associated with any experience—has been placed in the suicide category. This reduces the number of core experiencers available for these analyses from forty-nine to forty-eight.

This table discloses a trend suggesting that the indicence of core experiences is greatest in connection with illnesses, followed by accidents and suicide attempts, in that order. The respective percentages are 56% for illnesses, 42% for accidents, and 33% for suicide attempts. Nevertheless, this trend is only marginally significant (p ≅.06).

The data presented in Table 11A, however, conceal a complication that must now be dealt with. Table 11B will reveal that the incidence of core experiences across categories is significantly influenced by the sex of the respondent.

Table 11B

Incidence of Core Experiences as a Function of Mode
of Near-Death Onset and Sex of Respondent

	Illness		Accident		Suicide	
	♀	♂	♀	♂	♀	♂
Core Experiencers	21	8	2	9	4	4
Nonexperiencers	8	15	8	7	14	2

Illness versus Accident/Suicide
(Core experiencers only)

	Illness	Accident/Suicide	
Females	21	6	27
Males	8	13	21
	29	19	

$x^2 = 6.21$, p <02

Examination of the upper table demonstrates that women are most likely to have core experiences in conjunction with illness, whereas men's tend to occur in cases of accident or suicide. Thus, 72% of all female illness victims have a near-death experience, but the percentage drops to 21% for the accident and suicide-attempt categories combined. Only 35% of the men, on the other hand, have core experiences in conjunction with illness, but 59% have them when they come close to death through accident and suicide attempt. Various considerations enable a chi-square statistical test of this difference to be performed using the figures shown in the table at the bottom of Table 11B.[1] It is apparent that a significant interaction is obtained: 78% of all core experiences among women occur in connection with illness whereas among men, only 38% of core experiences are illness-induced (p <.02).

Thus, it seems clear that although mode of near-death onset is marginally related to the incidence of the experience, sex of respondent is even more strongly related. Among women, illnesses are likely to be associated with a core experience; accidents and suicide attempts, however, seldom lead to one. Among men, the pattern is just the reverse. This gender-related interaction then, needs very much to be borne in mind when considering the frequency data relating core experiences to manner of near-death onset.

The previous analyses were based on a simple dichotomous measure of the core experience, that is, whether it was present (WCEI $\geq$6) or absent (WCEI <6). A finer analysis is available, however, when the depth of the experience, as measured by the WCEI, is used as a basis for comparing the three types of near-death onset. It will be of interest to see whether the gender-related interaction holds up with this measure. The data are shown in Table 12.

Life at Death

Table 12

Weighted Core Experience Index Means
by Condition and Sex

	Illness	*Accident*	*Suicide*	
Women	8.83	3.00	3.22	6.04
	(29)	(10)	(18)	(57)
Men	3.83	6.75	8.67	5.51
	(23)	(16)	(6)	(45)
	6.62	5.31	4.58	
	(52)	(26)	(24)	

Inspection of the column means suggests the same rank order as before (illness >accident >suicide), but the difference here is not significant ($F = 1.13$, one way ANOVA).[2] The individual cell means again seem to point to the sex X condition interaction and this time the analysis (an unweighted means ANOVA) supports this impression ($F = 6.98$, with $2/96$ df, $p < .005$). The interaction term is, in fact, the only significant effect disclosed by this analysis. Thus, we see that the deepest core experiences for women tend to be associated with illness, whereas for men the deepest experiences tend to occur in connection with accidents and suicide attempts.

The results of this analysis, then, are broadly consistent with those of the cruder, dichotomous one presented earlier. Whether one is discussing incidence or depth of the core experience, both analyses suggest (but do not give strong evidence for) the same rank order of conditions: illness >accident >suicide. In both instances, however, the only statistically impressive effect is linked to the gender-related interaction, which shows the same pattern for both incidence and depth.

On the basis of these two analyses alone, what answer can we legitimately give to the question: does it make a difference how we almost die? So far, it would seem that although core experiences occur in connection with all three types of near-death onset, their *likelihood* and *depth* vary depending on a *combination* of one's sex and the manner of nearly dying. If one is a woman, for example, near-death through illness seems to have a high probability of inducing a core experience, but near-death through accident or suicide attempt offers a much lower chance. Exactly the reverse seems to be true for men, of course. Somehow, esthetically speaking, this doesn't seem a very satisfactory outcome, and it certainly wasn't one I had expected. Obviously, merely because an outcome is either "unesthetic" or puzzling is no reason to dismiss it as a fluke, but it does tend to make one look for other factors. I have already commented that respondents in the three categories differed from one another in a number of respects, but none of the previously cited differences bore any marked similarity to the pattern observed here. There was, however, another factor, so far unmentioned, that could, in principle, possibly account for the interaction effect. This is the *near-death rating*—an estimate of how close each respondent actually came to death. Could it be that the perplexing pattern of differences in near-death *experiences* is, in actuality, a function of differences in near-death *ratings*?

Near-Death Ratings as a Possible Factor

The tape recording of each interviewee in our sample was listened to and rated by at least three, and sometimes five, judges, including myself. At the end of each interview, each judge made an estimate of how close that respondent actually came to death, using the rating scale shown in Table 13. These ratings were based mainly on the statements provided by the respondents themselves, but whenever it was available, information from physicians or other medical personnel, or from spouses or friends, or from that person's medical records was also used in arriving at a final estimate. The arithmetical average of these ratings for any one person was taken to constitute that person's near-death rating.

Life at Death

Table 13

Near-Death Rating Scale

The following scale is used to judge how close the respondent came to dying.

Name of respondent _____

Name of rater _____

0	1	2	3	4
In no real danger of dying.	Serious illness, accident, etc., but *not clear* if individual would have died if condition persisted.	Serious illness, accident, etc.; *probably* would have died if condition persisted.	Obviously close to death; *would* have died if condition persisted.	Resuscitated; probably was clinically dead.

The reliabilities among raters on this estimate ranged from .69 to .86, with both a mean and median correlation of .78. These correlations were highest for accident victims (r = .89), lowest for suicide attempters (r = .65) and intermediate for illness victims (r = .71). Overall, then, the reliabilities among raters proved high enough to provide presumptively dependable estimates of respondents' closeness to death. The weakest category in this respect—the suicide attempters—afforded the lowest interrater reliabilities because many of our respondents never received any medical attention, a state of affairs that obviously would tend to increase the variability of our estimates.

The mean near-death ratings by condition and sex are presented in Table 14.

Table 14

Mean Near-Death Ratings
by Condition and Sex

	Illness	*Accident*	*Suicide*	
Women	3.13 (29)	2.52 (10)	2.18 (18)	2.72
Men	2.94 (23)	2.66 (16)	2.08 (6)	2.73
	3.05	2.61	2.15	

If one compares the pattern of data in this table with that in Table 12 (the core experience data), one observes a distinctly imperfect correspondence. The most striking consistency is that the "condition near-death" rating means follow the same rank order as do the core experience scores (that is, illness >accident >suicide) and the effect here is statistically significant (p <.001). It is also true that the individual cell showing the highest average core experience index, namely women/illness, also receives the highest near-death ratings. At this point, however, the correspondences cease. The *critical* pattern, reflecting a possible gender-related interaction, is obviously altogether absent here, a fact confirmed by the obligatory analysis of variance (F <1). From this analysis, it appears as if the near-death rating factor hypothesis does not stand up. Yet there may be *something* to it after all as shown by the parallelisms in condition means.

At this point, it becomes important to know whether there is any overall correlation between depth of near-death experience (that is, WCEI), on the one hand, and closeness to death (that is, near-death ratings), on the other. This information is furnished by Table 15.

Life at Death

Table 15
_____

Correlations between WCEI and Near-Death
Ratings by Sex and Condition

	Illness	*Accident*	*Suicide*	
Women	.48* (29)	.36 (10)	.07 (18)	.48**
Men	.24 (23)	.23 (16)	.33 (6)	.13
	.38*	.28	.11	

*p <.01
**p <.001

Table 15 shows that while the overall correlation is positive and statistically significant, its magnitude is distinctly modest. Similarly, while all the individual cell correlations are positive, only one is impressively significant, namely, that based on female illness victims. That cell, containing the largest number of cases, obviously has a disproportionate impact on the significant marginal correlations to which it contributes. This analysis suggests, then, that with the *exception* of female illlness victims, near-death ratings are neither highly nor significantly correlated with depth of near-death experiences.

As a final check on this possible factor, an analysis of covariance[3] was performed using near-death ratings as the covariant. If this factor were responsible for the original gender-related interaction, this effect should be substantially reduced by the covariance analysis. The outcome, however, was that the interaction remained significant at the same level as before (that is, p <.005).

This last result reinforces the conclusions drawn from the previous analysis presented in this section: Although near-death ratings appear to have a modest relationship to core experiences, they cannot in themselves be said to account for the gender-related interaction in these experiences. Whatever the explanation for this curious effect may be, it is not a simple function of a near-death rating factor. Since it appears to be a genuine finding rather than a statistical dependency, we must leave the matter noted but unresolved for now. We shall, however, be forced to reexamine it when we discuss and interpret our findings later in this book.

Mode of Near-Death Onset by Stages of the Core Experience

Another way to appreciate the quantitative differences in the core experience among the three conditions is to compare the conditions in terms of the five-stage model presented earlier. A graph that enables this comparison to be made is shown in Figure 2. (See p. 114.)

It is evident that the form of the three curves is generally similar across the first three stages of the core experience. After that point, however, there is a sharp divergence, with the illness curve continuing substantially higher through the remaining stages, while the accident and suicide curves decline sharply. In fact, it should be noted that *none* of the suicide attempters is found beyond stage III, a fact to which I will return in the next section. Though the graphical representation of these comparative data may suggest that this intercondition difference in the terminal stages of the core experience is of small magnitude, statistical analysis shows that this is not so. Altogether 36.5% of the illness victims reach either stage IV or V in contrast to only 6% of the accident and suicide groups (combined). This is a highly significant effect ($X^2 = 12.30$ with 1 degree of freedom, p <.0005).

This finding, of course, is largely consistent with the data presented earlier in suggesting that the core experience is more pronounced for illness victims than it is for accident victims or suicide attempters, with the latter seemingly having, on the average, the least pronounced experiences. This analysis by stages, however, has the advantage of revealing just where the intercondition differences are greatest, namely, in the latter stages of the experience. And here, unlike the earlier analyses where these differences were at best only marginally significant, illness victims are found to be clearly and highly significantly more in evidence. Indeed, their dominance of these stages approaches exclusivity. Since females are disproportionately represented among illness victims, it might be thought that this effect is due largely to them. Although there is a trend in this direction (45% of the female illness victims reach stage IV or V, compared to only 26% of the men), in this case, it is not significant. Thus the intercondition differences in the later stages of the core experience appear to be—possibly because of the relatively small sample size involved—independent of the sex of the respondent.

Figure 2. Percentage of Respondents Reaching Each Stage of the Core Experience, According to Category of Classification

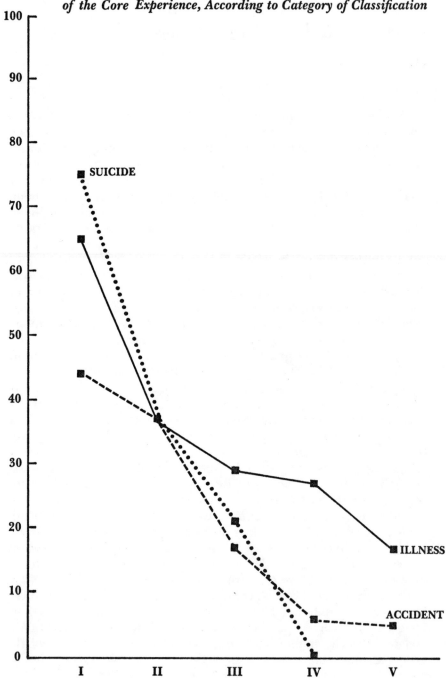

Qualitative Differences Among Conditions

So far I have presented evidence for some important quantitative differences in the incidence and depth of the core experience as a function of how one nearly dies. I have also shown, the last analysis notwithstanding, that the sex of the respondent may interact with the manner of near-death onset to affect the core experience. The graph presented in conjunction with the last analysis, however, suggests as well that there may be noteworthy *qualitative* differences among the conditions—and indeed there are. In this section, I will treat each mode separately in order to bring out these differences more clearly and to set the stage for a final comparison among the three modes of near-death onset.

Illness. All of the features delineated in the prototypical summary of the core experience (see pages 101–103) are to be found in the cases of near-death episodes brought about by illness. As Figure 2 reveals, illness cases represent, on the average, the most complete core experiences, and for this reason I propose to use them as a baseline against which to compare near-death experiences induced by accident or suicide attempt. For the purpose of these comparisons, the prototypical summary may itself be taken as indicative of the qualitative features of the core experience associated with illness. We need to ask, then, in what qualitative ways do experiences triggered by accident or suicide attempt deviate from this standard account?

Accident. Figure 2 has already furnished evidence that the later stages of the core experience tend to be rare (but not absent!) among accident victims. What Figure 2 does not disclose, however, is the *presence* of one feature which appears to be more frequent and more detailed in the experiences of accident victims than it is for either of the other categories. This feature is the *panoramic life review*, already discussed (see page 67). This phenomenon was reported by 55% of the accident victims, compared to only 16% of respondents in the two other categories combined. The small sample sizes involved and the ad hoc nature of the comparison suggests that we interpret this difference ($X^2 = 4.76$, p <.05) with considerable tentativeness. Nevertheless, the fact that it is consistent with the little systematic research we have on this point,[4] and the fact that the life review features seemed to be more vivid and extensive when they were triggered by an accidental near-death, incline me to regard it as a facet of the core experience that is *accentuated* by this way of nearly dying. Furthermore, although our sample size here is so small that one cannot legitimately make anything of it, my impression is that near-fatal falls or near-drowning episodes may be even more likely to induce a panoramic life review than are auto accidents. Further research with larger sample sizes in these categories is necessary before this hypothesis can be evaluated.

Something of the detail and vividness of this phenomenon is suggested by several accounts. One of my respondents miraculously survived a fall from an airplane when, at 3,500 feet, his parachute failed to open. In the course of his fall, he had the following experience:

> It's like a picture runs in front of your eyes, like from the time you can remember up to the time, you know, what was happening [that is, the present] . . . it seems like pictures of your life just flow in front of your eyes, the things you used to do when you were small and stuff: stupid things. Like, you see your parents' faces—it was everything. And things that I didn't remember that I did. Things that I couldn't remember now, but I remember two years ago or something. It all came back to me, like it refreshed my mind of everything I used to do when I was little. Like, I used to ask my friends, "Remember this, remember that?" And I say, "Wow, that was a long time ago, I don't even remember that." Everything refreshed my mind of everything. *(Was it a positive feeling?)* It was a nice feeling, it was a real nice feeling. [He then talks about very early childhood memories, when he was four or five years old]. I'll tell you, it was like the bad parts were almost cut out. It was good memories. It was like a picture, it was like a movie camera running across your eyes. In a matter of a second or two. Just boom, boom [snaps his fingers]! It was clear as day, clear as day. Very fast and you can see everything. It was, like, wow, like someone was feeding a computer or something, like putting a computer in your head and programming you, that's what it was like. *(Any sense of sequence?)* It was like starting in the beginning and working its way up to the end, what was happening. Like clockwise, just going clockwise. One right after another. *(70)*

A victim of an automobile accident also experienced this playback phenomenon, but in her case it occurred *after* her accident. Specifically, it took place while she was being operated on, when she thought she was "dead."

> I had a very—it seems as though it was fast—I had a span of my life, just, just everything that happened. Highlights of various very happy points in my life coming up and going backwards [she

mentions various memories] all fanned in front of me. Very rapidly. Just kind of went past me like a million and one thoughts. [She mentions some: the first time she visited a certain location, her first sports car, and so on] *(Was it like seeing a movie in some way?)* Very fast movie. Just highlights, just certain things. *(Were they mostly positive things?)* Very—everything was positive there. *(How did you relate to these images? Were you involved in them emotionally or were you just a spectator?)* I was a spectator, I was just watching them. *(62)*

Finally, the words of a young man who nearly drowned in a boating accident speak to the same experience:

. . . it was amazing, I could see in the back of my head an array, just innumerable array of thoughts, memories, things I had dreamt, just in general, thoughts and recollections of the past, just raced in front of me, in less than thirty seconds. All these things about my mother and grandmother and my brothers and these dreams I've had. It felt like this frame, millions of frames, just flashed through. *(What was this like?)* It was thoughts and images of people. And a lot of thoughts just raced [snaps his fingers several times] in split seconds. I had my eyes closed under water, but I could still see these images. *(Was it when you were feeling euphoric that these images and thoughts came to you?)* Exactly, exactly. *(Could you describe these memories in terms of their emotional quality?)* A lot of them were very emotional. [He describes his memory of his mother's death two years before and his recollection of various things that involved them both. He also thought that he might be reunited with his mother. He also thought of his grandmother, to whom he is very close and who was still alive.] I saw her [his grandmother] as not wanting me to die. I saw what my drowning would do to her and I think that was what drove me to always try to resurface. There were thoughts of my brother. Just [pause] silly things—just nitpicking things I thought I'd forgotten. Just [snaps his fingers] kept on racing through. It was like I was going through this memory and, ah, ah, like my whole memory was retaping. I was in reverse. And everything was just backtracking so I could go over it again like a tape recorder. But it wasn't in sequence. *(Like a jumble?)* Yes, yes. *(66)*

Still other accident victims, whose remarks were quoted earlier in other contexts, observed that this phenomenon was "like watching a movie" of one's life which "only seems to take a second" or that it was like a tape that one could selectively edit. There is variation in response to the question of sequence: Some people feel their life is (rapidly) playing in reverse, others say it is roughtly chronological, and still others imply that there was no clear sense of sequence. If we remember that the core experience tends to take place in an atemporal context, it is possible to understand these apparent nonuniformities as stemming from the attempt to place a "holographic experience" into a time frame typical of ordinary waking consciousness. What stands out in these accounts is the *tremendous rate* at which these images seem to be processed—experienced as millions of "frames" within seconds. Even allowing for exaggeration, such rates must utterly confound one's sense of time.

These panoramic life reviews represent the one qualitative feature that appears to distinguish accident victims from other near-death survivors, but only in that they may be more common and more vivid in such cases. Just why this phenomenon should be so pronounced among accident victims is a question we shall return to in Chapter Eleven. In all other qualitative respects, the patterning of the core experience in accident victims conforms to the prototypical summary.

Suicide attempt. The most striking feature of suicide-related near-death experiences that sets them apart from the prototypical episode is the total absence of stages IV and V. Among our suicide attempters, no one reported the tunnel phenomenon as such, or saw a brilliant but comforting light, or encountered a presence, or was temporarily reunited with loved ones who had died, or entered into a transcendent world of preternatural beauty. Instead, as Figure 2 makes clear, the suicide-related core experience tends to be truncated, aborted, damped down. It does begin with a feeling of relief or peace and continues with a sense of bodily detachment to the same degree as other categories. But it tends to end, if it gets this far at all, with a feeling of confused drifting in a dark or murky void—a sort of "twilight zone."[5] In any event, our respondents' accounts strongly suggest that the suicide-related near-death experience does not reach completion; instead, it tends simply to fade out *before* the transcendent elements characteristic of the core experience make their appearance. When one also takes into account the fact (see Table 11A, Page 106) that the highest proportion of nonrecall (67%) is found among suicide attempters, it is tempting to conclude that suicide-induced death experiences tend to be different both in form and frequency from those occurring in conjunction with either illness or accident.

Closer examination of this matter, however, will show that such a conclusion is by no means established by the data I have referred to. Instead, I will argue, the interpretation of our suicide-related data has to contend with a number of problematic factors.

At this point, I need only remind the reader that our sample of suicide attempters is by no means comparable to our other respondents, if only on the grounds of self-selection and source of referral. As a group, they also differ from illness and accident victims in a number of additional ways. The effect of each of these differences, singly or combined, would seem to reduce the likelihood of undergoing a complete core experience.

First of all, all but two of our suicide attempters used drugs or drugs and alcohol in their effort to kill themselves. This means that, as a group, their near-death episode was very much more likely to be contaminated by these substances than our other respondents. Since it has already been shown that near-death experiences are negatively correlated with drug-related conditions,[6] it could be that this common mode of suicide attempt either interferes with the unfolding of the core experience or its recall, or both. It has also been suggested[7] that some of the specific drugs often used by our suicide attempters (for example Valium) could induce a state of retrograde amnesia and thus block recall.[8] Consistent with this argument is the fact that the two individuals who attempted suicide in nondrug related ways (either through hanging or drowning) as well as the young man who was accidentally knocked unconscious while on his way to commit suicide by jumping, all had deep experiences. The number of cases here is obviously too small to be more than suggestive, but they are congruent with Rosen's findings, referred to earlier, describing the experiences of individuals who survive suicide leaps. Thus, the totality of evidence (our own and others') and informed medical opinion on this point inclines me to believe that it may be *mainly drug-related* suicide attempts that tend either to lead to aborted core experiences or that interfere with their unfolding or recall. The study of a large sample of nondrug-induced suicide attempts that bring the individual close to death is clearly necessary to clarify this issue.

Even if the mode of suicide attempt proves not to be a significant factor, there are still other intercondition differences that could account for the low incidence of core experiences and the form these experiences take among our suicide attempters. For example, it will be recalled that our near-death ratings indicate that, on the average, suicide attempters had the lowest scores here by a statistically significant margin (see Table 14). Although the correlations between near-death ratings and near-death experiences were not very high (see Table 15), the truncated range of the near-death ratings themselves and the *relative* unreliability of these ratings render unjustified any inclination to dismiss closeness to death as a possible factor. In my judgment, at least, intercondition differences on this variable are *probably* responsible for at least some of the difference between conditions in regard to the frequency and form of the core experience itself.

A third factor of conceivable relevance here has to do with the psychiatric state of our suicide attempters. Though by no means true of everyone in this condition, quite a few of the suicide attempters had obviously suffered or, in some cases, were suffering still from a variety of problems requiring some sort of psychiatric or therapeutic intervention. A fair number of men and women in this category had either received psychiatric help or were in treatment at the time of our interview; still others appeared to be in need of such help. Because no systematic information along these lines was gathered in this study, it is, of course, not possible to make any legitimate comparisons among conditions in this respect. Still, I think I would be remiss if I did not offer my own *opinion* here that, based on my impressionistic observations only, the suicide attempters, as a group, did appear to be substantially more afflicted by psychiatric problems than our other respondents. Such a conclusion, at any rate, would hardly be surprising given the fact of *how* they happened to come close to death. The relevance of this conclusion—if it is valid—is that there has been some evidence offered[9] that the likelihood of having a peak or mystical experience (which I am assuming bears a fairly close relation to the core experience) is correlated with indices of "mental health." If this is so, then perhaps some of the intercondition differences in the core experience can be ascribed to this factor. Again, to settle the point, we need a study specificially designed to gather the necessary information.

For all these reasons, I believe the only conclusion warranted by our interview materials with suicide attempters is that our data are inconclusive. If we could somehow control all of the possibly implicated factors, either through sampling or statistically, it *might be* found that the suicide-related core experience is indistinguishable in its essential features from naturally occuring ones. Certainly none of our data can be taken as precluding this possibility, and transcendent experiences induced by suicide attempts may well yet be found.

At the same time—and I wish to emphasize this point—it must be borne in mind that our data on suicide-related near-death experiences *are* very weak in transcendent elements. For whatever reasons, few suicide attempters can recall any profound experiences when they were close to death and most recall nothing at all. Although *why* this is so cannot be resolved at this point, *the fact itself cannot and should not simply be dismissed for all that.* Despite all the possible factors and qualifications, it may, of course, also be that subsequent research will demonstrate that there is "something different" about the experience of dying when induced by a suicide attempt—at least in some cases. There is even a hint in some of our own data, to be presented in a moment, that suicide victims can expect that their experience on dying will *not* conform to the Moody pattern.

All this is simply to give both sides of the issue a fair treatment. On one hand, we do not yet know whether suicide-related near-death episodes preclude transcendent experiences; on the other hand, just because we cannot take our data at face value here does not mean that the face value interpretation won't one day be upheld.

In any event, merely because the evidence is inconclusive with regard to the invariance or null hypothesis (that is, that the core experience is *not* a function of the mode of near-death onset) should not be taken to mean that we cannot learn from them. The interviews from suicide attempters are, in fact, sometimes as fully absorbing as those from other respondents and are very much worth quoting. In order to acquire a more concrete sense of the qualitative aspects of suicide-related experiences, it will be helpful to present excerpts from two of our most extensive cases. Doing so will also suggest the subtle ways in which the suicide-induced experience *may* prove different from core experiences triggered by illness or accident.

I have already mentioned that suicide attempters seem never to penetrate further than a murky darkness. In one case, a young man who had attempted to hang himself found himself in a completely black space. In an excerpt already quoted (see page 46) he describes seeing himself from a dual perspective: He sees his hanging physical body and he *also* sees himself walking into this black space. This kind of "double" vision is of course unusual, but the entrance into the dark region seems typical of stage III phenomena.

Before losing consciousness, however, something else happened that isn't usual: He heard a voice but it was a *female* voice. And it was from no one in the room.

> While I was tying the noose, I kept hearing a voice. It was a lady's voice, I would say a middle-aged woman's voice, maybe in her forties, but it was kind of low-pitched and it kept saying, "Go ahead, go ahead," telling me, "It's all right, you'll be okay, go ahead." . . . The sound of that voice I can remember perfectly. And it's no one I've ever heard before, at least no one I can remember hearing. It was real soothing. Like I said, it was an older lady. . . . When I heard the voice, it sounded like it was coming from behind me, but it sounded like it was coming out of the back of my head, *not* from in back of me. I looked around to see if anyone was there; no one was there. It was comforting, it was convincing. . . . So I tied the noose and jumped off the chair *(100)*.

Again, we encounter familiar elements, and, again, with a difference. It is, as we know, not rare to hear a voice, but this experience is one of only two in my entire collection of cases in which a voice speaks while the respondent is conscious. Similarly, it is the only instance in which the voice encourages an individual to attempt to kill himself.[10] It also was reported *prior to* the core experience itself. Finally, the voice is identified as a woman. In cases where a gender has been linked to a voice before, it has always been a *male* voice. Context, message, timing, and gender all serve to make this "voice effect" unique in our sample.

Because the number of core experiencers among failed suicides is so small, there is no one case that can be said to be representative of the group as a whole. So rather than quoting brief excerpts from several interviews, I think it will prove most useful to focus on our fullest case. I believe this can be justified on the grounds that if one wishes to examine the qualitative aspects of different modes of nearly dying, then the richest cases can be taken to provide the most instructive basis for a comparative analysis. In making this comparison, however, it must be remembered that, at least among instances of attempted suicide, rich cases are by no means typical.

A young man tried to kill himself by taking an assortment of pills—Librium, Demerol, Valium, Dilantin. As a result of this ingestion, he remained unconscious for four days. He remembers finding himself in a "gray area":

> The only thing that I can remember about this is just *grayness*. Like I was in gray water or something. I couldn't really see anything. I couldn't see myself there, either. It was just like my *mind* was there. And no body.

While he was in this state, he felt good:

> Normally, I'm a very anxious, a very nervous person—a lot of fears and things like that. And during this, all the fear was gone. I had no fear whatsoever. Almost an adventurous feeling. Excitement. (*Did you want to stay in that condition?*) Yeah. It was a very good feeling.

He also was aware of music:

> I also heard music—different music. (*Tell me what it was like.*) It was usually like classical music; I like classical music. It wasn't *exactly* the music I've heard, but it was along that line. (*Do you recall how the music made you feel?*) It made me *relaxed*. The fears went away when I listened to it. Again, the feeling of *hope*, that there's something *better* somewhere else.

He also reported that everything, including the music, sounded "hollow and metallic—echoey" and that these acoustical sensations were associated with the watery grayness. He felt the grayness going *through* him, filling him and this felt good to him. After a while, he became aware of a voice:

I think [it was] a woman's voice, but [pause] I didn't recognize the voice. *(Do you recall now what she said to you?)* No. I just remember that it was a *soothing* voice. I kind of remember that with the grayness—her voice kind of *calling*, my moving toward it. *(This was a friendly voice, a reassuring voice in some way?)* Yeah. *(. . . and you felt [drawn] to it?)* Yeah. Right. Like that was the place to be.

He tried to get to where the voice was:

It seemed like I kept trying to *get* to where the voice was, but something was *holding* me back. I *know* I *wanted* to be there; I knew once I was there everything would be fine. I was sure of this. No question about it. But there was still like something holding me back from getting there.

During his experience he had seen images of people he knew. These people somehow seemed to represent the possibility of a good life; they seemed to care. He described this as "like playing back a recording of my life." The issue was joined:

It felt like the woman's was *stronger*. I wanted to get there but there was just some part of me that wanted to [pause] go back with these images.

And resolved:

The thing I remember most is a *falling* feeling. Like I was coming down really fast and then *hit*. And then I woke up with a *jolt*.

And afterward:

When I woke up, the first thing I thought was Oh, God. Thank you. I made it, and I was *extremely* happy. [He had been severely depressed before his suicide attempt.] I was just sitting there *thinking* about it and I felt this—I don't know—*warmth* filling my body. I was very happy, very excited, but then [pause] it was *more* than contented—it was rapture, I guess. But I couldn't explain it to anybody at the time. It was just beyond words. *(99)*

These passages sum up the essential features of his experience. In the course of his interview, he also indicated that although he never clearly saw his physical body on the bed, he did have a sense of bodily detachment and felt he had no weight at all—he was just "pure mind." Neither did he have any sense of time. When he momentarily returned to body consciousness (before drifting back into the grayness), he found the sensory world greatly enhanced—the colors were clearer and more vibrant. The only thing scary about his experience was his fear (which was eventually vanquished) of returning to his body. His experience "in the grayness" was decidedly pleasant and, judging from its immediate aftereffect, very positive and powerful in its emotional impact.

This time we can observe many features in common with the core experience: drifting throught a vast space, feeling good, hearing music and a comforting voice, hearing sounds magnified, seeing a series of flashbacks of one's life, and so forth. But again there are some features that are not commonly found: the environmental vastness is gray (only one other person reported this coloration) rather than dark or black; it has a watery aspect—a unique descriptor among our respondents; it is a *woman's* voice that is heard (the previous case—also suicide-related, obviously—the only other one in the sample where one is reported) rather than a man's. The basic pattern *is* unmistakably similar, and yet there do appear to be some differences. The sheer lack of fully detailed suicide-induced experiences, however, must leave this issue open: There is a *hint* of qualitative difference here *within* the familiar pattern, but more evidence is badly needed before any clarification can be achieved.

Before leaving this case, I want to reiterate one general finding; in my sample, no one who had attempted suicide and who had some recall of the experience reported that it was predominantly unpleasant.[11] The only possible exception is that a few people did describe some unsettling hallucinatory images, but these appear to have been qualitatively different from the feeling-tone of the core experience itself. Certainly, no one felt that he was either in or was on his way to hell. The "worst" perception was a feeling of wandering or drifting in a vast space, but this was a perception that was also reported by respondents who came close to death in other ways. This is not to say that suicide attempts *never* lead to unpleasant experiences, only that there is no strong evidence for this proposition among our cases. Indeed, the affective tone seems to be preponderantly pleasant—at least as much as a limited core experience can afford.

Of course, we are speaking here of *failed* suicide attempts. Our data, obviously, are based solely on the testimony of those who survive the act of self-destruction. But what of those who succeed? Is there any way we can say anything about the experience of those whose suicidal intention is realized?

At first it would appear that there is no way this question can be addressed without entering the world of purported mediums, spiritualists, and clairvoyants, whose allegations about the fate of suicides can obviously not be evaluated scientifically. It turns out, however, that there is another route to this destination, and it is one to which we have access through the accounts of our own respondents.

Just as Moody reports for his interviewees, so some of our respondents who came close to death in ways unrelated to suicide felt that their near-death experiences vouchsafed them certain insights about the probable fate of successful suicides. In most cases, the statements or implications from these respondents seemed to be derived from the "content" of their own experiences rather than from preexisting beliefs or religious views, although this matter is difficult to establish with certainty. Obviously, these assertions cannot be tested any more than can those coming from mediums, but they nevertheless do constitute findings of considerable interest. The fact that—as will be shown—near-death survivors *independently* tend to take very much the same (doubtful) view of the wisdom of suicide seems to me a most significant finding and one that is unlikely to be a coincidence. Again, this is not to imply that near-death survivors have necessarily been privy to a "higher knowledge" regarding suicides; it is to say, however, that their comments on this point, because of their consistency, deserve to be evaluated as part of our effort to determine whether the suicidally induced near-death experience does have certain unique features that differentiate it from the prototypic model.

The woman who had perhaps the deepest experience of all (WCEI = 24) said on this point:

I know one thing: I think that anyone who tries to commit suicide [pause] that suicide is a devastating thing. *(Why is that?)* Because it's like killing a plant or a flower before it's full-grown or before it's served its purpose. It is not [pause] it is not [pause] not right. Something that is very overt to me is that I know that there are murders and that there are deaths in war and there are accidents and so on, but I think that this is by far a karmic experience. I think that to take one's *own* life, I think that it's very, very [pause] very, very [pause] a terrible thing to do. *(Is this something that you've come to as a result of your experience?)* Yes. Yes. Very, very strongly. *(Not as a result of anything you've read elsewhere?)* No. No. No. *(What do you think a person would experience if he or she tried to commit suicide? And came close to death, as you did?)* I have *no* idea. I mean, the only thing that I can think and comprehend is that [pause] to try and understand reincarnation. That somehow, instead of evolving, you would regress. *(20)*

A woman who nearly died as a result of an automobile crash and had a deep experience reflected:

> I would never take my life. *(Why not?)* Because if it were self-induced, I don't think I would get the state that I want . . . [it would be] sheer panic and it would be [pause] where I would just die—without any of the effects of peace. *(You mean, it would be like blackness?)* Yes. . . . Right. It would be aloneness, blackness—not cared for. *(So it would be a negative experience, an opposite kind of experience from—)* I think it would be a *fearful* experience. I don't see any goodness in it at all. If it comes about naturally, then it would be okay. *(64)*

These same sentiments were voiced by the woman who, on nearly dying, received paranormal information about her newly delivered baby and felt she had to come back:

> I feel very strongly that it has to be a natural death, in other words, suicide or something that you're going to try to alter it, I would never consider because I think the reaction would be bad. In other words, this feeling that I had that told me I had to come back, had some kind of control over what I was going to do. So I feel that there is something that controls what we do. And if we want to change it in any way, we are not allowed to do that. If I were going to say, "Now I'm going to do it," it wouldn't work. I don't think it would be allowed. I'd fear the consequences, that would be the only fear I'd have. *(Do you think that if someone took his or her own life, would it be the same experience as yours or would it be different?)* It would be very different. That's what I was trying to say. I feel it would not be good; it would be just the opposite. I just have the feeling that they would be punished. *(25)*

Sometimes a feeling of doubt is only vaguely implied rather than clearly articulated, as in the case of a young man who nearly died in an automobile crash:

> Personally, I think at this point that death is an *up* state from our life, that it's a better state. Suicide—I don't know *what* to think about suicide . . . that's a tricky one. I don't know about that. *(71)*

Another idea expressed by some respondents is that even a successful suicide leaves the individual in the same state his suicide was an attempt to end. Another accident victim put it this way:

> When I was twenty, I was put in a mental instiution because I tried to commit suicide. But see, I hadn't got to the place where I am now [at thirty-two]. Two years ago I came to the place where I realized that it's ridiculous to commit suicide because you're just going to have to go through the same kinds of things, the same pain, 'cause that's what brings you to your progression. *(77)*

The same theme—that of the unavoidability of one's destiny—was also sounded by a former suicide victim (who had, incidentally, no core experience):

> I think probably if you commit suicide, you'll probably have the same problems as you do now. If you die a natural death, then everything will be okay. I think if you die a natural death, there's something good waiting for you—I don't know what it is. I also think that to die a natural death you have to accomplish something here, whatever that something is, small or large or whatever. . . . If you kill yourself, you can't accomplish that thing, so, therefore, you're going to be punished. *(87)*

This whole issue of the violation of one's "life plan" through suicide and its potentially negative consequences was summed up dramatically for the young man who hit his head on a rock while intent on making a suicidal leap. He is describing a portion of a conversation (in thought) he had, while unconscious, with what he took to be God.

> . . . then He said, "Do you want to go back?" And He goes, "Finish your life on earth." And I go, "No, I want to die." And He goes, "You are breaking my laws to commit suicide. You'll not be with me in *heaven* if you die." And I say, "What will happen?" And then after this I started coming to. So I don't know what happened after this. So I think that God was trying to tell me that if I commit suicide I'm going to go to hell, you know? So, I'm not going to think about suicide anymore [laughs nervously]. *(79)*

These opinions from near-death survivors, if taken seriously, obviously put the suicidally induced death in a different, more negative, category from those deaths that occur naturally. These respondents suggest that even if the suicidal death experience is not unpleasant, the ultimate consequences will be.

Life at Death

The evidence bearing on the qualitative aspects of suicide-induced near-death experiences is clearly complex, but it leads to a number of interesting conclusions. First, the descriptions from our suicide attempters tend, relative to other categories, to be weakest in core experience elements: No recall is greatest here, and when experiences do occur, they do not penetrate beyond stage III. Second, there are, however, a number of factors that make the suicide attempters noncomparable to other respondents in such a way as to lower the likelihood of the occurrence of core experiences. Third, therefore, the data on qualitive aspects of suicide-related experiences are ambiguous and inconclusive. Fourth, nevertheless, some evidence suggests that certain transcendent features associated with the core experience may occur in suicide attempts, although these features may manifest themselves in distinctive ways. Fifth, when recall exists, the suicide-related death experience tends to be reported as predominantly pleasant. Sixth, the death experiences of a number of nonsuicide attempters (and the opinion of one suicide attempter) all implied that the consequences of a successful suicidal act were likely to be unpleasant.

Can these six conclusions themselves be interpreted to point to a general conclusion? Probably not—our data are simply too fragmentary and contaminated to warrant any single conclusion. However, I want to offer my own opinion here in the hope that it might lead to further research that will eliminate some of the ambiguity surrounding this issue. If the offending factors could be eliminated or sufficiently reduced to provide comparability among conditions, I would speculate that the *initial* stages of the core experience would be invariant across modes of near-death onset. I would also hypothesize, however, that there would come a point when the suicide-induced experience would begin to show a distinctive qualitative difference. This would, according to my view, come during the decision-making phase, when there would be no hint of transcendent glory (for example, the light phenomenon) or of immediate reunion with loved ones. If an individual were to pass *beyond* this stage, either because he was, in some sense, "permitted to" or because his suicide attempt was successful, I am tempted to believe that the admonitions expressed at the end of this section might prove warranted. This aspect of my opinion can, of course, never be evaluated scientifically, but its other components *could* be in an adequately designed study. If such an investigation were undertaken, it might not only be able to resolve some of the empirical issues, but it would also furnish us with a more extensive basis from which to extrapolate the later stages of the core experience when it is induced by suicide.

Summary of Near-Death Experiences as a Function of the Manner of Near-Death

In this chapter, I have presented our findings relating the way in which a person almost dies to his experience of dying. The underlying question here has been whether the core experience is *independent* of the way a person nearly dies.

In general, we found evidence that elements of the core experience were found in all three categories, but that both the incidence and depth of this experience tended to be greatest for illness victims, moderate for accident victims, and weakest for suicide-attempt victims. Analysis of the core experience by stages was also, on the whole, consistent with this rank order. Nevertheless, this main effect was strongly qualified by a gender-related interaction that indicated that core experiences associated with illness occurred disproportionately among women, whereas men were more likely to have had them in conjunction with accidents and suicide attempts. An examination of a possible factor for this interaction effect, namely, closeness to death, proved unavailing, even though it was shown that there was a modest positive overall correlation between near-death ratings and (depth of) near-death experiences. Qualitative analyses of core experiences associated with different modes of near-death onset suggested that there might be some noteworthy intercondition differences. Thus, accident victims appeared somewhat more likely to experience the life review phenomenon than did respondents in the other two conditions, though this effect was not a strong one statistically. Suicide victims were never found to have had experiences beyond stage III, and the experiences they did report tended to depart somewhat from the prototypical pattern, though the number of cases here proved too few to legitimize any conclusions. A speculative, but partially researchable, opinion was offered concerning possible differences between the suicide-induced core experience and those brought about by nonintentional means.

The complexity of our data, together with some of its inconclusiveness, makes any straightforward conclusion difficult to state, but my own reading of the evidence leads me to this tentative formulation: In general, I believe that the *form* of the core experience *is* invariant across modes of near-death onset, but that its *frequency* may well vary as a function of both manner of nearly dying and sex of respondent and their interaction. In short, the experience of dying itself appears to be much the same, no matter how one comes close to death. Some qualifications are also necessary. I believe, and not only on the basis of my own data, that accidental near-deaths are more likely to elicit a panoramic life review than are other modes of nearly dying. I am also inclined to believe that the experience of dying through an ultimately unsuccessful suicide attempt is likely to conform to the basic pattern only until the decision-making phase is reached, at which time it may diverge. More research is needed on this point, however, before *any* conclusion may safely be drawn.[12] Thus, this statement of my beliefs is based more on hunch than on fact. Taken as a whole, however, I believe our data are *broadly* consistent with the claim that the *experience* of *dying*—that is, the core experience—is largely independent of the means that bring it about.

A question we have still to ask, however, is whether this experience is independent of other antecedent factors that might be assumed to influence it—factors such as a respondent's prior degree of religious-ness or his familiarity with other accounts of near-death experiences.

S E V E N

A Search for Correlates

In the last chapter I considered one possible *situational* determinant of the core experience, namely, the means of near-death onset. Here, however, I want to examine the role of several personal factors that could significantly shape the experience. In all, there are four categories of such antecedent variables: (1) demographic characteristics, (2) religious denominational affiliation, (3) religiousness, and (4) prior knowledge of near-death experience research findings.

Demographic characteristics. Is the core experience correlated with any of the usual demographic categories, such as social class, marital status, race, etc.? Table 16 provides the answer.

Table 16

A Demographic Comparison Between
Core Experiencers and Nonexperiencers

Social Class Index	*Core Experiencers*		*Nonexperiencers*	
	No.	*%*	*No.*	*%*
1	1	2	1	2
2	11	22	10	21
3	35	71	34	68
4	2	4	8	10
Race				
White	48	98	49	92
Black	1	2	4	8
Marital Status				
Married	23	47	24	45
Single	16	33	16	31
Separated/Divorced	7	14	9	16
Widowed	3	6	4	8
Age at interview	42.12		43.83	
Age at incident	34.06		41.28	

Even a casual inspection of this table is sufficient to reveal that the demographic features are quite similar for core experiencers and nonexperiencers. The only hint of a significant difference is found on the age at incident factor (t = 2.09, p <.05), which shows that core experiencers tended to be somewhat younger at the time of their near-death episode. It should be noted, however, that this difference is due in part to a couple of extreme cases. Overall, the two groups are notable for their demographic similarity rather than for any disparity.

Religious denominational affiliation. Does religious affiliation relate to the likelihood of having a core experience? The relevant data are presented in Table 17.

Table 17
_____

Religious Denomination Data for
Core Experiencers and Nonexperiencers

Religious Denomination	Core Experiencers		Nonexperiencers	
	No.	%	No.	%
Catholic	17	35	20	38
Protestant	13	27	21	40
None*	15	31	6	11
Other*	2	4	1	2
Agnostic/Atheist	2	4	5	9

*These two categories include at least four Jews.

Again, we see that except for the None category (which was quite heterogeneous), which is larger for core experiencers, denominational affiliation seems unrelated to the likelihood of core experiences. The experience itself is obviously not disproportionately associated with either of the two major divisions of Christian belief nor is it limited to believers.

Religiousness. One of the obvious questions left unanswered by Moody's research had to do with the role of religiousness (as distinct from religious affiliation) as a factor influencing the core experience. Since most people can be assumed to be at least nominally religious, perhaps the crisis of apparent imminent death triggers a set of religious images that represent a *visual* projection of an individual's religious belief system and expectations. If this is so, we might expect that this effect would be more likely or stronger for those who were more religious. In any event, it seems important to determine whether degree of religiousness is in any way correlated with the core experience. In the extreme case, if we were to find that this kind of experience tended to occur predominantly among people with a religious orientation, our interpretation of this phenomenon would be radically affected.

To assess this matter of religiousness, the interviewer asked a series of questions at the end of the interview designed to elicit some information about the respondent's religious beliefs prior to and after his near-death episode. The subject of each specific question and its category of fixed alternatives may be found in Table 18.

Table 18
_____

Religious Beliefs and Preferences Form

Religious	Before	After	Belief in God	Before	After
Very	———	———	Absolute	———	———
Quite	———	———	Strong	———	———
Fairly	———	———	Fairly Strong	———	———
Not too	———	———	Not too Strong	———	———
Not at all	———	———	Not at all	———	———

Life after death	Before	After	Belief in Heaven	Before	After
Completely convinced	———	———	Yes	———	———
			No	———	———
Strongly convinced	———	———			
Tended to believe	———	———			
Not sure	———	———	Belief in Hell	Before	After
Tended to doubt	———	———	Yes	———	———
Not at all	———	———	No	———	———

On the basis of a respondent's answers to these questions, a straightforward *religiousness index* could be calculated as follows: The first two items were scored 0–4, with a score of 4 denoting the strongest religious orientation; the third item was scored 0–5, and the last two 0–1. The scores were then summed for each respondent, with the combined score on the heaven and hell items being multiplied by a factor of two so as to make these two items, taken together, roughly comparable in weight to the remaining three. Thus, the range of possible scores on the religiousness index was 0–17. Since we were interested here in a respondent's religiousness *prior to* his incident, only the answers given to the "before" portion of each question were used to comprise the religiousness index.

To determine the relationship between religiousness and the death experience, it was merely necessary to correlate the religiousness index with the weighted core experience index (WCEI).

This correlation was −.04, demonstrating that there was essentially no relationship between these two factors. In short, how religious one felt himself to be before one's near-death episode (as measured by our religiousness index) was not related to the depth of one's near-death experience.[1]

Two other analyses using religiousness index measures supported this initial finding.

Close inspection of the data suggested that the items dealing with belief in heaven or hell were particularly likely to have been interpreted in heterogeneous ways and thus might be only weakly related to the overall religiousness index. Accordingly, a new index was constructed which eliminated the scores for the heaven and hell items. Using this "purified" religiousness index, the correlation with the WCEI was still negligible: −.01.

Finally, it was necessary to determine whether the likelihood (as distinct from the depth) of a core experience was associated with religiousness. For this purpose, a biserial correlation[2] was calculated between the presence or absence of the core experience and the "purified" religiousness index. This correlation, too, was consistent with the others: −.08.

Thus, the conclusion from these several analyses seems to be that religiousness is *unrelated* either to the likelihood or to the depth of a core experience. Of course, our measure of religiousness is crude and it may be that a more precise and sophisticated index would have evinced some relationship, but I tend to doubt it. My impression during the course of this investigation, and before I came to analyze these data, was that a respondent's religiousness, like other personal and demographic factors, just didn't seem to make much of a difference. It certainly wasn't my judgment that this experience was more likely to be vouchsafed to persons who had been religious all along. Rather, it seems—and this is consistent with what other investigators[3] have found or suggested—that religiousness as such mainly affects the *interpretation* of a near-death experience, not its occurrence. In short, those who are religious seem to be more inclined to give a religious construction to their experience, but they are not necessarily more likely to have one in the first place.

Both our data and my impressions formed in the process of carrying out this study incline me toward the conclusion that religiousness as such plays no determinative role in the core near-death experience. Whether it can be regarded as an *outcome* of passing through the core experience, however, is altogether another question and one we shall come to consider soon in another context.

Prior knowledge of near-death phenomena. Raymond Moody had one advantage in conducting his research on near-death experiences: He did it during a time when few people were knowledgeable about such phenomena. We, however, had to collect ours in the wake not only of Moody's best seller (more than three million copies sold in the United States alone), but also in the aftermath of the publicity surrounding Elisabeth Kübler-Ross and the attention given to near-death phenomena in such popular periodicals as the *The National Enquirer* and *Reader's Digest*. And, as if this weren't bad enough (from a methodological standpoint), during the last few months of our interviewing, a popular pseudodocumentary film, *Beyond and Back*, dealing with near-death experiences, was featured around Connecticut. In view of all the information about near-death experiences that was potentially available to our respondents, one has to wonder to what extent the accounts we were given were influenced or contaminated by prior knowledge of these phenomena.

To assess this factor, we routinely asked each respondent at the end of the interview a series of questions concerned with the degree of his prior (and subsequent) knowledge of near-death experiences. These questions dealt with such matters as books and articles on the subject, television programs or movies concerned with it, conversations with others about such experiences, and so forth. In this way, we were able to evaluate prior knowledge of near-death experiences as a possible contaminant of our findings.

Altogether, we found that twenty-eight respondents, or 28.6% of all respondents questioned about these matters,[4] had some degree of prior knowledge concerning near-death phenomena. Of these persons only a handful had read Moody's books; most had heard about them through reading popular accounts. An additional twenty-five persons, or 25.5%, had learned something about these experiences after their own near-death incident had taken place.

The question of interest to us, however, is whether prior knowledge of near-death experiences is in any way *associated* with the recall of core experience elements. Specifically, are core experiencers overrepresented among those who were already familiar with Moody-type phenomena at the time of their near-death episode? The answer is found in Table 19.

Life at Death

Table 19

Knowledge of Near-Death Experiences

	Core Experiencers	Nonexperiencers	
Some prior knowledge	9	19	28
Subsequent knowledge only	18	7	25
No knowledge	20	25	45
	47	51	98

$X^2 = 9.04$ (p < .02)

This table reveals a significant difference between core experiencers and nonexperiencers in prior knowledge, but it is a difference *opposite* to that which a contamination factor would have led us to anticipate. In brief, what this table shows is that among core experiencers, only 19% had prior knowledge of such experiences compared to 37% of nonexperiencers.[5] It would appear, therefore, that prior knowledge of this kind of experience not only does not increase the likelihood of reportage of a core experience, but, if anything, decreases it.[6] *Afterward,* however, core experiencers are more likely to acquire knowledge relating to their own experience (38% to 14%). The percentage of respondents remaining ignorant of these phenomena is about the same for both categories (43% for core experiencers, 49% for nonexperiencers).

Even though core experiencers are definitely not overrepresented among those with prior knowledge of such phenomena, it is still possible that such knowledge would nevertheless influence the reports of those core experiencers who *were* knowledgeable. If this were the case, we might expect, for example, that the knowledgeable core experiencers would have higher WCEI scores. Accordingly, I compared knowledgeable and unknowledgeable core experiencers on this index, classifying them on the basis of any knowledge whatsoever (that is, before or afterward). The means for knowledgeable and unknowledgeable respondents were 11.11 and 10.93 respectively—a nonsignificant difference. This result shows that knowledge of Moody-type phenomena does *not* affect the depth of the core experience reported. Knowledgeable and uninformed respondents recount substantially the same experience.

Clearly, there is no support for the fear that knowledge of near-death experiences significantly influences, distorts, or contaminates the reporting of such incidents. Additional evidence will later support this assertion.

Summary of Findings on Personal Antecedents

The data presented in this chapter can be summarized in one word: negative. The likelihood or depth of a core experience does not seem to be significantly related to standard demographic measures, religious affiliation, religiousness, or prior knowledge of near-death phenomena—except possibly in the last instance, where it may be related negatively. Recalling the last chapter, it may also be noted here that the form of the core experience appears to be largely independent of the manner of nearly dying as well. Thus, the thrust of all the evidence presented in these last two chapters points to one conclusion: At least with respect to the possible antecedents examined here, the core experience appears to be a remarkably *robust* phenomenon, cutting across a variety of situational, individual, and demographic factors. Aside from the sheer physical conditions necessary to induce it, it appears to have no obvious determinants or correlates. Clearly, since systematic work on this question has just begun, it is too early to draw any hard conclusions. It will be interesting, however, to see whether subsequent research is able to establish that there are some antecedent factors that are significantly related to the likelihood or depth of the core experience.

EIGHT

Aftereffects I: Personality and Value Changes

It takes no imagination to conceive that the effects of coming close to death leave a profound impact. Someone who survives a core experience usually reports that the experience was so striking and so singular that the passage of time does nothing to dim its vividness. Nevertheless, such experiences, however dramatic, rarely remain "just" memories; they tend to exert a powerful effect on a person's motivations, values, and conduct. Even those respondents—whom we have so far largely neglected except in passing—who recall nothing while they were close to death, report that afterward their lives were altered in significant and drastic ways by the sheer fact of approaching death. As this and the next chapter will amply demonstrate, however one chooses to interpret near-death phenomena, they are unquestionably real in their effects.

In making this investigation, one of our aims was to document systematically the nature of these changes, which previously had been mainly reported in anecdotal form. We wanted to know whether certain changes could be attributed chiefly to the fact of having come close to death *per se*, quite apart from whether or not a Moody-type experience occurred. And, of course, we wanted to determine whether some changes seemed to depend on having had a certain kind of experience while close to death.

To this end, we asked a series of open-ended questions near the close of our interviews that were concerned with whether the person had noticed any changes in himself that he felt he could trace to his near-death episode. After putting the question in its most general form, we moved on to the following specifics: (1) attitude toward life; (2) religious beliefs; (3) fear of death; and (4) conception of death. In some interviews, but not systematically, we asked about value changes, if any. We also had a series of fixed alternative questions designed to determine whether changes in religious convictions had taken place. Finally, we sought to find out whether individuals had attempted to acquire information about near-death experiences.

Here I will present our findings on the personal and value changes that occur after coming close to death. Then I will move on to discuss changes in religious orientation and attitude toward death. As before, I will offer a combination of quantitative data and interview excerpts to underscore the fact that the consequences of nearly dying are fully as absorbing and provocative as the event itself.

138

Personal and Value Changes

Men and women who have survived near-death episodes—whether or not they had a core experience at the time—usually report that their brush with death has changed them in some way and, as a rule, has affected them *positively*. The kind of changes described tend to fall into certain specific categories, and on the whole appear to be similar for experiencers and nonexperiencers alike. Table 20 presents a summary of the reported changes that have to do mainly with personal and value orientations. I have grouped these data somewhat arbitrarily into four principal categories: (1) attitude toward life; (2) sense of personal renewal; (3) personality changes; and (4) attitude toward others.

Table 20

Personal and Value Changes for
Core Experiencers and Nonexperiencers

Change	Core Experiencers No.	%	Nonexperiencers No.	%*
Increased appreciation of life	18	37	14	29
Live life to full extent	3	6	4	8
More afraid of life	2	4	2	4
Renewed sense of purpose	12	24	6	12
Sense of rebirth	2	4	2	4
Stronger person	10	20	4	8
More curious	1	2	1	2
More depressed	1	2	1	2
More death-oriented	1	2	1	2
More loving, caring	12	24	10	20
More compassionate	5	10	5	10
More tolerant	4	8	3	6
More patient, understanding	5	10	0	0
Want to help others	4	8	0	0
Miscellaneous	20	41	14	29
Not ascertained	0	0	4	—

*Percentages for nonexperiencers exclude "not ascertained" respondents
ents

Several points need to be made concerning the data in Table 20. First, it should be noted that most of the changes reported, as remarked earlier, are positive. This is a particularly noteworthy effect when one remembers that many of these respondents experienced severe pain or psychological dislocation for a long period following their near-death episode. Despite such factors, however, many respondents report that the incident left them with a more positive outlook on life and with stronger feelings of self-worth. Second, the basic pattern of changes is similar for both experiencers and nonexperiencers—parallels outweigh contrasts here, at least for these kinds of changes. Finally, where quantitative differences do occur, they tend to favor core experiencers, but the differences in most cases are suggestive rather than striking. One weak quantitative difference not shown in the table is a tendency for experiencers more often to report multiple changes (more than three changes spontaneously mentioned), but this effect is not significant. ($X^2 = 3.33$, $.05 < p < .10$).

Despite the overall quantitative similarity between experiencers and nonexperiencers reflected in Table 20, it remains my personal conviction that there are some important *qualitative* differences between the two groups that are not obvious from the table. This impression is based mainly on my personal experience in interviewing respondents and on my reactions to hearing the taped interviews of all respondents. I must say emphatically that I have no hard data with which to support this contention, but perhaps by the time the reader finishes this section on aftereffects he may also be able to detect this quality from reviewing the interview excerpts.

For what it is worth, then, I believe that core experiencers are more likely to show a heightened sense of what I can only vaguely call "spiritual awareness" and this quality seems to pervade the other changes that they report. They also seem, more often, to radiate a certain serenity or peace or acceptance of life. The dangers of subjective error in assessing such intangible qualities are very great, indeed, and I do not want to make too much of them here. Yet I think I would be remiss to omit mention of this altogether. Perhaps subsequent research could buttress these impressions by approaching the matter more systematically. In any event, in what follows we must be content to allow the respondents from both categories merely to speak for themselves.

Attitude Toward Life

One common sentiment expressed by near-death survivors was a heightened appreciation of life, especially of the world of nature and of other people.

A female suicide-attempt victim commented:

[Something] that I don't know quite how to put into words is a greater appreciation of people, things, places, particularly beautiful things and beautiful places and nice things that happen. They seem more vivid; they seem to mean more. . . . I think the whole thing has made me more aware of life and more curious about it. *(82)*

A woman who survived a high fever during which time she felt that God spoke to her said:

I thoroughly enjoy life. Every day of it. As far as dying, if I were to die tomorrow that wouldn't bother me. But there is more of a thrill to life, each day of living . . . there is an inner feeling that life is terrific, great, fantastic—even on down days. *(26)*

One man who came close to death as a result of contracting cerebral malaria while in Africa, and whose near-death experience did *not* conform as a whole to the Moody pattern, reflected:

One should consider [being alive] fantastic. [Life] is an absolute miracle. *(49)*

The woman who nearly died of a ruptured appendix said emphatically:

I'll tell you one thing. I have no fear of letting people know how I feel about them now. The ones I really care about. I used to be very standoffish. I remember two or three years ago [that is, after her near-death experience] telling my brother how much I loved him. You know? And, uh, he was really amazed. It was an unspoken kind of thing that we had. But [I had to] tell him. I let him know. I let him know . . . now, I have a real sense of beauty.

Before, you'd be out in the summertime, and there'd be things that you'd take for granted. I no longer do that. I sit now and I [pause] watch just nature. Natural things. You know, beauty. *(30)*

A woman who was nearly killed by an automobile explosion but who had no recall whatever for any experience at the time or afterward told me:

My priorities have definitely changed. [After the accident] my parents arrived from Colorado. My father is a very wealthy man and I know that when he got the phone call from my sister saying, "She's not going to make it; the next phone call you get, she'll be dead," my mother reported to me that he smashed his hand through a window or something like that. I just sort of realized that he would have given up his entire amount of money for me to live. Not that I was that overly concerned with money, but it suddenly made me realize that nothing is important unless you have people around you that you love. . . . Now I feel that I *feel* more for people. Just a greater concern for living and how to make people appreciate of their surroundings, or something like that. I just feel that I have a greater appreciation of being here. *(58)*

A woman who had suffered a number of near-death crises owing to an unusual respiratory condition, and who, during one of them, heard a voice, which she took to be God's, assuring her that she would "suffer but the kingdom of heaven will be yours," clearly articulated the view that life is a precious gift:

Well, I appreciate things more. And I should tell people I love them more than I do. Life is precious. And it is a gift of God. Every day I've got is a gift. *(15)*

A former racing car driver who had a stage V experience following an accident at a track one night, summed it up this way:

I would say I appreciate life more because I realize that when it's your time to go, they'll let you go, but when it's not your time to go, possibly the Man Upstairs, in my own thinking, let me see what was beyond, but told me I had more work to do here and come back. *(73)*

Finally, let me quote a little more generously from an interview with a respondent who nearly died from a severe automobile crash, and who had a deep core experience while in a coma. Her comments really epitomize the feelings expressed thus far:

> [Afterward] I enjoyed being with the people more. And I enjoyed just the outdoors. Nature. And *trees* budding. I *still* have a thing for spring. And it was where everything started coming alive. And I *enjoyed* it. (*Do you* [still] *feel some of these same feelings?*) Oh, yeah. Spring is my most favorite time of the year. Just to see everything bursting out—it is just beautiful! The green is beautiful. And snow. I love snow. Because I think it's beautiful. . . . And a spring day like today really makes me happy. To see the buds on the trees and the green grass. It really makes me happy. (*Did you always feel like this or was there something that was accentuated because of the experience?*) I think—I think I *noticed* it more [afterward]. I think that before—before, I used to take spring for granted. But I have the feeling that I'm *looking* more and more—and seeing life. It's really nice. (*Do other people pick up on this? Your children?*) Oh, yes. They can't wait for spring. I think I passed this down to them. *(64)*

One corollary to the enhanced appreciation of life and other people is a decreased emphasis on money and material things generally. This view was explicit in the comments of a number of respondents, including some of the individuals just quoted.

From the same woman:

> I value people more. I don't think I value worldly goods that much. *(64)*

A young man who had been involved in a serious automobile accident, which had triggered a deep near-death experience, found that he developed an:

> . . . awareness that something more was going on in life than just the physical part of it. . . . It was just a tqtal awareness of not just the material and how much we can buy—in the way of cars and stuff, or food or anything. There's more than just consuming life. There's a point where you have to *give* to it and that's real important. And there was an awareness at that point that I had to give more of myself *out* of life. That awareness has come to me. *(71)*

The woman quoted earlier who said that she realized how unimportant money was if you didn't have people around to love, went on to elaborate:

Well, I think I used to be much more concerned with how the restaurant is doing, how well we did in one day, and blah-blah-blah. Now I feel that I *feel* more for people. *(58)*

Finally, the woman who had the highest WCEI score commented in passing:

And I feel totally different about home, house—material things. They're so unimportant to me. *(This is a change from how you felt before?)* Yes. Yes. *(20)*

Another theme that seems related to an enhanced appreciation of life focuses on an increased appreciation of solitude. In some cases this may be related to the long recovery period following many near-death incidents, but the desire for intervals of quiet reflection seems to persist beyond the recuperation time.

The young man who had an out-of-body experience in conjunction with his fever-induced near-death episode, one of some half-dozen who reported on solitude, told me that where he formerly would habitually seek out the company of his friends, now:

I enjoy my solitude a lot more, I enjoy being alone. I've learned to respect my time alone and get something out of it. Life is very valuable and yourself, myself, I'm very valuable too. *(45)*

The young man quoted a moment ago who observed that there was more to life than it's physical, materialistic side, also said:

From that accident, I've become more of a loner person. You know, I used to be at race tracks [he, too, was a former racing car driver] with ten thousand people around me, in the stands and everything. And at this point in my life [a few years later], it's just the total opposite of it in that I spend more time reflecting, walking on beaches, and things of this nature. [He then goes on to describe one typical instance when, while walking on a beach, he was led to some important insights on the impermanence of things and the nature of eternity.] *(71)*

Implicit, if not stated, in many of these accounts are certain individual value changes which the respondent feels can be attributed to the near-death episode itself or its secondary effects. Again and again, allusions to the same values recur: love, compassion, giving and, more rarely, knowledge-seeking. Although the following quotations could be cited with equal usefulness in some of the sections to follow, it is, I think, helpful to introduce them here by way of summing up the essence of the life changes that, to a large extent, underlie the excerpts already given.

I had just asked the previous respondent whether he felt the information disclosed to him during his near-death experience had been "given" to him for a reason. His response was unequivocal:

> Oh, definitely. Definitely. . . . Somehow we have a more important *mission* while we're here. Okay. That's it. We have a more important mission in our lives than just the material end of it in trying just to get material gains. There are more important things. It showed me the spiritual side in that, basically that—it is important, I guess. That's all I can say. That [pause] that [pause] that *love* is important and that *every human being* on the earth is just as equal to each other. They're all the same. It sort of brought that aspect out in my life. I don't know. It's something I wasn't too aware of before. Before I had a lot more prejudice. *(71)*

Another man who had had a profound near-death experience as a result of a diving accident tried to articulate what values deriving from his experience had become important for him to actualize in his own life.

> *Love.* Not necessarily romantic love from a woman or a man. Love. Fulfilling yourself with that love by—by *giving*. As much as by getting. Which are two separate things. And, not really *thinking*, but just in the way of recognizing that—that we're all in the same boat and we all have weaknesses and we all have strengths, and to help is where it's at. Those three things, I'm telling you, are the way of *being* that I spoke about, that I came back here and I gained. The way of being was, like, those three things. *(77)*

Finally, let me quote at length from a woman who had been badly injured in an automobile crash. Although I interviewed her a year and a half after her accident, she was not yet recovered and spoke with difficulty. She had had no conscious Moody-type experience. Indeed, though she had never read Moody's books, what she had heard about such purported experiences had left her feeling extremely skeptical. Shortly after the interview began, she reflected on what her experience had taught her:

> In my opinion, there are two things in life which keep a person going, or, I should say, which are important. To me, they are the most important things. And that is *love* and *knowledge*. And what I

experienced when I was in intensive care, not only once but several times, when I went out of my consciousness, was a closeness of another human being—the love I was treated with from everybody, including the doctors and including the nurses and most of all, my family, my kids, my children. And I think a lot of people who are very religious or so will say they more or less experienced God, whatever God *I* believe in, right? And love was one of the things I felt [when] I was closer to them. I got more of it than others. And I could *give* more of it, too. I felt very much loved and I felt that I loved everybody. I did not only tell one time that I loved my doctor and I still feel that way because they [pause] they gave me life back again. I think that this is worthwhile, to love somebody, because life is the most precious thing. And I think you don't realize that before you actually almost die. . . . [And] the more knowledge you have the better you will understand why certain things have to be this way and why I have—for an example, a friend who was in, well, he was on a dying list, too. And he never believed in doctors, in nurses, or anything like that. And he is *still* ill, and this is over a year now and he's still ill, very ill. And [pause] I think that's very important that you *know* that certain people love you and care for you. You've got to *know* that; that's a little knowledge. You have to know that certain people love you and not only certain people but *most* people love other people. . . . There may be some people, and one hears about it, that they live in hatred, but I think they don't have the knowledge that it is *so important to love* and to understand what life is all about because I think that's the main thing—that's what it's all about. . . .

I asked her if she had felt that way before her accident:

I did, but I did not feel as strong as I do now. The accident, as bad as it was and as much as I suffered and as much as I will probably never be exactly the same as I was before, but mentally I think I grew. I grew a lot. I learned the value of life more than I did before and I gained actually by this experience. It's very important to me. That itself makes life worthwhile for me, to go on and do whatever is in store for me, you know, and to live to the full extent. *(54)*

As we shall see, the feelings, sentiments, and values characteristic of the passages cited in this section dominate and pervade the other aftereffects yet to be described. Indeed, it is important to remember that, like the core experience itself, the various changes reported here and in the following pages are best understood as all of a piece; the separate sections focus on individual aspects of this totality and are justified only on the grounds of narrative convenience, not fidelity to the changes *as experienced.* The sections to follow, then, reflect different angles from which to review the totality of these aftereffects. Consider, first, the sense of renewed purpose that often animates the lives of near-death survivors, and then the insight emphasized in the last passage—the importance of the search for knowledge.

Personal Renewal and the Search for Purpose

Persons who survive a near-death episode sometimes assert that afterward they felt a sense of rebirth:

I felt like I was a new person. I felt I finally had a sense of direction. *(30)*

I found it to be like a rebirth, an awakening. *(7)*

Well, I *realized* then that I had been *given* a second chance. *(24)*

Almost always, however, there is an implied or explicit sense that one has been spared *for a reason*—that one has been given a renewal of life for a purpose. This sense that one's life is meant to fulfill some objective is fairly common, as Table 20 reveals, and is found with or without a conscious sense of rebirth.

The woman I last quoted, who appears to have been clinically dead for nearly three minutes as a result of a heart attack, later amplified her comment on her sense of having been given a second chance:

I *knew* that I had a second chance at life and that God had given it to me. . . . I think at the time I thought it was because he wanted me to raise my children. As I get older, and I hope a little wiser, I have a feeling that each one of us has a *little* something to do, to pass on, that God wants us to do. It may not even register in our minds and it may even be very insignificant. But it *definitely* is part of what God wants us to do. And I feel that that's what I *have* to do. He gave me my chance, because *I* have to *do* something. *(24)*

Another woman who nearly died during childbirth said:

I thought of it since it happened that God must have let me go back—must have said, "Go back, there's something more for you to do." I was worried about my husband and my son; I wanted to get back to them. *(29)*

Just like the woman first quoted here, however, this respondent, as we shall learn in a moment, also came later to feel that her "life's task" encompassed more than taking care of her family.

The young man who stumbled on a rock while intent on suicide reflected on the possible reasons he was "spared" in this way:

> I keep thinking about my girl friend and my future daughter. And I think my daughter will do something very important. That she'll do something for the world or maybe she'll find a cure for cancer. And if I would have died, I'd have had no daughter! So something very important is coming from my existence. It might not be my generation. But—it might be my *kids. (So you think that you were spared for a reason?)* Yeah. I think there is a *reason* for my being on earth. *(79)*

Sometimes it seems that the sheer improbability of one's having survived a dangerous near-death incident is sufficient reason—albeit subjective—to infer a purpose to one's life. This kind of view is nowhere better exemplified than in the reflections of the respondent who quite miraculously survived a parachute leap from 3,500 feet when his chute failed to open:

> *(Did you think that you were spared in some way?)* Let me ask you that. Let me ask you that. All right, out of all the orange groves that were there, there's a row here of all orange trees, right [diagramming the physical layout of the orchard into which he fell]? Then there's an irrigation ditch with water in it. Then another row of oranges, then *another* row of oranges, then an irrigation ditch, and I mean, this went on for acres and acres of land. Out of all those orange groves and trees and water there was one irrigation ditch that broke down that morning and all the water went out of it and there was only about three or four inches in it and the guy that owns it said that it has never been that low since they dug the irrigation ditch out. Now you take this: I was going to jump out of the door—my instructor told me to—but I said, "No, I want to make one more jump under the wing off to the side." Now, the timing was right. If I jumped where I was supposed to jump, I wouldn't have landed where I did. But, I mean, out of all the ditches and trees and everything that was there, I landed—they measured it—exactly a foot from the top of

the bank and slid down. If there was water in there, I would have drowned. I dunno, it was as if something just [pause] guided [trails off] . . . I'm just saying, in my opinion, I don't feel it was just luck, really. I feel that someone wanted me around for something. *(70)*

This sense of purpose is usually only vaguely apprehended. Typically, it is in the nature of an inference, rather than a given of the experience. Most (though not all, as case *79,* above, shows) people, when asked what they feel this purpose is, find that they cannot clearly articulate it—it is something to be discovered in the course of seeking it.

Nevertheless, this sense of renewed purpose seems sometimes to manifest itself initially as a motivational force that both energizes a respondent's life and alters its direction. This kind of change is found in both experiencers and nonexperiencers alike. The woman quoted earlier, who nearly died in childbirth, found that her life acquired a very definite aim:

I have suffered from depression. And there were times when I felt, gee, there wasn't really anything to live for. You know, just very depressed. This [experience] started a whole different life style for me. After this experience, I decided, you know, I'm wasting my life by sitting here feeling sorry for myself and do something. So I went back to school, got my high school diploma and a year ago decided that I was going on to nursing school. . . . And it was really strange because when I was in high school teaching and nursing were the last things I wanted to do. *(Do you attribute these changes to this experience?)* My whole life definitely was—I was going nowhere. Then, all of a sudden, I decided, this was foolish. I've only got this one life and why not do something with it? Which is probably why I decided to go into nursing, because I feel that it is a very rewarding career to help people. I feel a whole lot better about myself. That I am a person who can do something in my life. *(29)*

Sometimes the change, galvanized by a near-death episode, leads a person away from a helping profession in order to concentrate on actualizing his own inner potentials and talents. The young man who nearly died of a high fever observed:

It [his experience] made me give up a profession I've had for seven years [as a pulmonary technologist]. I think I started putting a little more value after that experience on my own life. At one time I was easily stepped on . . . but all in all I think I'm a little more concerned about *my* life, what I want to get out of my life, for me, and me alone. Not in a selfish manner, but, I look at that time as being when I died, I was alone, and I had nobody else around me and it was like the same feeling I have now, that what I have to do in my life has gotta be for me, because when everyone else has gone, if all my loved ones leave me, I'm still going to be me myself and there is more in life for me to do. [He then describes some of the new things he's done or has contemplated doing: He has learned how to renovate houses; he has moved away from home; he has started to write a book; he has started a program of physical conditioning; he has embarked on a regular meditational practice; he has made plans to travel, and so forth.] What makes me happy is, if the experience I had was a death, then I should be very happy that I've been given another chance to live and I should be able to live that life to the utmost. *(45)*

When, a few months after my interview with him, I endeavored to reach him by phone, I found that he had left the state and was traveling in California.

Sometimes a near-death episode seems to engender *both* personal growth *and* a career change, as in the case of the following woman, who was badly injured in an automobile accident but who had no core experience:

(Did your coming close to death change you in any way?) Dramatic. Dramatic. That's all I can say. It's like somebody had taken a meat cleaver, a big, fat, strong, sharp meat cleaver. The shit went over there. What's important came *clearly* into focus. It was once I realized what a close call that was, it was really an extremely profound experience, a magnificent growing experience. At the time of the accident, it just happened that I was not in a very good frame of mind—at the time, I didn't care whether I was alive or dead. I just as soon had been dead. I was really, in retrospect, very depressed, unhappy about my life and whatnot. And had thought many times, "Wouldn't it be nice if my car just went off the cliff and that was the end of it?" But never had acted on it. But then when I realized—I guess in the intensive care unit—solely what had happened and how close I'd come, I was very, very glad to be alive. Just enormously glad. . . . Right after the accident, I remember feeling much more alive than I ever had for years. I wanted to live more, I wanted to live. I realized that I had been wasting my life. . . . And it was a real turning point in my life. [She goes on to discuss how she entered into therapy, went back to school and eventually changed her occupation from that of a

secretary to a vocational counselor, a job she finds much more satisfying because of the contact it affords with people.] *(61)*

Occasionally, this increased tendency to live life more fully and purposively is intensified by the conviction (which may be realistic) that one's life could be cut short. The victim of an automobile accident is aware that, because of the injuries she sustained, she may, in fact, not have more than ten years to live:

> It [her near-death episode] changed my philosophy in life. From being a kind of passive person to a more assertive person. It made me look at things differently. . . . I became restless. I wanted to do everything at once. That's the only negative thing. Now I want to travel. It's got to be now. I want to go back to school. [She has, in fact, enrolled in a graduate program.] It's got to be now. I want my doctorate. It's got to be now. I don't have much longer. *(62)*

More rarely, and particularly for people who have had very deep experiences, this sense of purpose manifests itself in still a different way—as a desire to learn more about the significance of the experience and to find a way to live in accord with the values (see page 139) it seems to inculcate or strengthen. Sometimes I had the feeling that this was what a person was *attempting* to say but didn't quite know how to put it. Again, the possibility of overinterpretation here on my part cannot be discounted. Perhaps the clearest statement of this kind of knowledge-seeking came from the woman who had the highest WCEI score:

> . . . I think that my greatest desire is to develop greater cosmic consciousness, greater awareness. And I feel more and more all the time in myself what I call "centering"—being in *here* and being able to look out at things that I used to find disturbing or upsetting or would be concerned about, now are so unimportant. And I feel that I'm being drawn closer to something meaningful. And I have such a *hunger* to teach or to tell someone about it or to make them aware of it. . . . I feel that I'm *going* somewhere. I feel that I'm *reaching* something . . . [and] in the past eight months, I've been meeting people who are asking the same questions I am; it's like I'm being attracted to those with similar vibrations or wavelengths. [She then mentions several books she has sought out to learn more about this subject.] *(20)*

Although it is rarely so intensely felt, this desire for further knowledge of near-death experiences and their implications is found among many survivors, but it is particularly strong for core experien-

Life at Death

cers. At the same time, the behavior patterns here are not always similar, even among core experiencers, who are sometimes more inclined than others to *avoid* exposing themselves to this kind of knowledge. Table 21 will clarify these apparent inconsistencies. The question here was whether, subsequent to a near-death episode, a respondent either sought out or avoided material dealing with the subject of near-death experiences.

Table 21

_____

Near-Death Experience Information-Seeking or
Avoidance Subsequent to a Near-Death Episode

	Core Experiencers	Nonexperiencers	
Subsequent information sought	19	11	30
Subsequent information avoided	9	0	9
All other categories	19	40	59
	47	51	98*

$x^2 = 18.48$, p $<.001$

*Not ascertained for four respondents

What the data seem to suggest is that material on near-death experiences is, motivationally speaking, more important to core experiencers. They, as a group, are more likely *either* to seek out *or* to avoid knowledge of this subject (indeed, avoiders come exclusively from core experiencers). Thus, this information seems more highly charged—positively or negatively—for core experiencers. Nonexperiencers show a much lower level of interest. These differences, incidentally, are independent of the incident-interview interval; they are just as strong for people interviewed within two years of their incident as for those whose near-death episode occurred years earlier.

Confining ourselves to core experiencers, then, we need to ask: What underlies the patterns of knowledge-seeking or knowledge-avoidance? Most knowledge seekers have straightforward and understandable motives, claiming either that they wished to learn more about such experiences (for example, how common they were, how their own experiences compared to others, and so forth) or they were anxious to put to rest any fears that they might have just "imagined it" or that they were "crazy" or "off-the-wall." Almost invariably, people with such motivations found that reliable information on this score (usually Moody's first book or an excerpt from it) answered many of their questions and erased any lingering doubts. For several, reading Moody's book proved, as might be expected, a great relief.

What about avoiders? Although there was one core experiencer who said she was unable to read Moody's book because it bothered her ("It was too close"), this was not the usual reason mentioned. In most cases, where an indication was given, the reason generally had to do with the person's desire to retain his memory of the experience in an un-distorted form. Such people didn't wish to read of similar experiences lest their own become somehow contaminated. Such avoidance, then, was a way of remaining maximally faithful to one's own experience. A typical expression of these sentiments was the following:

(Did you ever read Moody's book, [Life After Life]*?)* No. I never read that *on purpose.* I thought that it would bias my—my discussions about my own experience. *(77)*

Thus, it appears that the patterns of information seeking and avoidance are not so contradictory as might have been thought. Instead, they point to a common and high valuation of the experience, about which either more knowledge is sought or knowledge is avoided *in order* to keep one's memory of it intact.

All the material presented in this section suggests that, for many respondents, the near-death episode is a pivotal one in their lives, leading to diverse manifestations of a heightened sense of purpose. Although this sense of purpose is usually vague and seldom articulated clearly, it is nevertheless obvious that coming close to death is in itself often sufficient to jar a person into a mode of life that is richer in experience, stronger in feeling, and deeper in meaning than it had been before. It is difficult to resist the conclusion that nearly dying is a good device for "waking up" to life.

Personality Changes

As Table 20 makes clear, most of the personality changes reported by near-death survivors were positive ones, suggesting that coming close to death may bring about an enhancement of self-esteem. The comments of several people cited in the two preceding sections could easily have been placed here to illustrate such a change. For example, the young man who nearly died of a high fever, after recounting a number of positive changes in his life, concluded, "Myself, I'm very valuable, too." *(45)* Similarly, the woman who decided to go into the nursing profession said, "I feel a whole lot better about myself." *(29)* Or, consider the woman who had no core experience but who was badly injured in an automobile accident. Prior to this incident, she said, she was very depressed and prone to suicidal thoughts. Now:

> I don't have many, or any, of those passive feelings that I wished that I could die. I'm much less afraid. I'm much more able to be close to people. . . . I'm much more comfortable with myself. I'm not as depressed. I'm less anxious. I really was living with a lot of anxiety and depression all the time, struggling to keep my head above water. Very often I felt it was going over my head. I don't feel that way [now]. *(61)*

Often, this change in self-concept is expressed very pithily, without elaboration. A woman who had an illness-related death experience said:

> I think it's enriched me. I think I'm a stronger person. *(28)*

Another woman who had a deep experience declared simply:

> [Afterward] I felt this tremendous confidence in myself, that I could do anything, which was a very good feeling. *(7)*

Sometimes, this increased sense of self-worth leads one to become more assertive. The woman who suffered a cardiac arrest stemming from a flawed tonsillectomy procedure, spoke of her attitude toward her church:

> I'm *not* sure I'm such a *follower* of the church anymore. Like they say, "You *have* to do this; you have to do that." I don't do that. Because *I* have to do what *I* think is right now. I rely more on *my* feelings than on *their* commands. I don't believe in their commands. I do what I have to do—and *no one* will ever say to me, "You're excommunicated," because *no one* can take *my* church away from me because no one's got the power but God. This is what I mean—it has made me believe in myself and what I believe in, what I feel. . . . I've become more of an individual thinker. I'm not a follower. I'm a thinker. *(24)*

In one case the effect was to eliminate all fear of physical danger:

Of course, you know when I was in the navy, I was in a very dangerous branch of the service [submarine service]. My life was on the line constantly. But when I came out of this [near-death] experience, I figured anything that I live after this has to be gravy. I just wasn't afraid of anything. [He admitted to being afraid during the war.] Afterwards, I became a race driver, I flew airplanes, I've done everything that a person could get killed very easily at. . . . In that time [afterward], I have been shot at, depth charged, bombed, you name it, I've had it—and it never bothered me one bit. I always remained more or less calm because I figured I had it once and they didn't want me then and I don't think they want me this time and that's just the way I feel about it. *(51)*

In rare instances, an enhanced sense of self-esteem seems to be attributable in part not merely to surviving a near-death episode or having a core experience, but to various physical changes that have occurred following the incident. The young man who was knocked unconscious while intent on suicide provides an example:

When I was younger, I had surgery on my hips and they had been bothering me quite a bit. And now I go jogging and everything and it's quite cleared up. Once in a while, it's sort of like arthritis, on rainy days you have a little bit of pain. But otherwise, it's quite cleared up. And I had ulcers back when I was in the hospital, and I've had hardly any problem at all. Like, if I drink I have problems, but I mean, eating regularly and whatnot I don't have any problems. And when I catch colds now they clear up a lot faster than they used to. I can't attribute this to the experience, but it's only happened *since* then so I don't know what to say. *(79)*

Although most of the personality and self-concept changes reported are positive, there are some exceptions. One such instance comes from a woman who had an out-of-body experience while undergoing an exploratory examination prior to surgery. In the course of this examination her lung was inadvertently punctured, bringing about a near-death crisis.

I had a definite personality change. Where I did a definite slide downwards. Where death became an increasing preoccupation and multiple suicide attempts took place after that. . . . Going through that [experience] and coming that close to death and seeing that it wasn't necessarily that painful, that I could discount pain in coming close to dying—it made it [death] more appetizing. *(22)*

Attitude Toward Others

Many people, particularly those who recalled a core experience, felt that their near-death episode definitely altered their relationships with others. In general, they felt that they loved others—strangers as well as friends and relations—more than they did before; that they were more compassionate and empathetic; that they were more tolerant and less judgmental; and that they were more desirous of helping others. Some of these attitudes have already been expressed in various contexts. Here, all that seems necessary to round out the picture is to present a representative sampling of these changes in interpersonal orientation:

It's given me tolerance. It's made me less judgmental. *(28)*

I think I'm a better person. I try to help people more than I ever did before. That might always have been a part of my nature, but now I realize that I *want* to help. *(4)*

I don't know if I've succeeded, but I *try* more to be a caring person. I think I try more to show that I care for people. *(82)*

I think I was more patient [afterward]. I think I am more understanding. I think I have more tolerance. *(6)*

I also feel I am a very compassionate person because I've known great suffering . . . because all of this happened to me. . . . I've had a great opportunity to help other people—people tell me things that they won't talk to their psychiatrist about. It happens to me continually. *(16)*

There was more compassion there [in his relationships with others afterward]. *(71)*

[Afterward] my husband and I had a really good relationship. It just changed me. It made me more open—to a lot of things . . . it kept me really nice, glowing—very open to people, stuff like that. *(64)*

Love. Not necessarily romantic love from a woman or a man. Love. Fulfilling yourself with that love by—by *giving*. As much as by getting. Which are two separate things. And, not really *thinking*, but just in the way of recognizing that—that we're all in the same boat and we all have weaknesses and we all have strengths, and to help is where it's at. *(77)*

I think I'm becoming much more tolerant, patient. I've always been a very compassionate person, but I think . . . the compassion is deeper . . . it seems to be directed with purpose now. *(20)*

I love people now . . . I've never had the ability to love before. I have a *great* capacity for listening to people. I think I *accept* people—most of all—*as they are.* I don't give them *my* rules to live by . . . the ability to accept people *as they are* and to *love* them for *what* they are and not for what you *want* them to be, this has all come about—and I think that God has done this for me. And it's made *me* richer. *(24)*

Clearly, the effect of nearly dying on one's interpersonal relations is a powerful one. Perhaps the overall effect can be summed up by saying that near-death survivors become more *unconditionally accepting* of others. Other people are appreciated and loved more for what they are. Indeed, we have here come full circle on these personal changes because this attitude toward others appears to be still another manifestation of the *heightened sense of appreciation of life* with which we began. All life is appreciated more—including other people. As I observed earlier, the changes following near-death are really all of a piece anyway, and the different aspects I have distinguished here need to be understood as holistically organized.

Summary of Personal and Value Changes

As with the prototypical account of the core experience given earlier, it is necessary to bear in mind that this summary of personal and value changes, in aiming for generality, will lack a sense of nuance and particularity, and will obviously not correspond to any one individual case, though it will read like one.

The typical near-death survivor emerges from his experience with a heightened sense of appreciation for life, determined to live life to the fullest. He has a sense of being reborn and a renewed sense of individual purpose in living, even though he cannot articulate just what this purpose is. He is more reflective and seeks to learn more about the implications of his core experience, if he has had one. He feels himself to be a stronger, more self-confident person and adjusts more easily to the vicissitudes of life. The things that he values are love and service to others; material comforts are no longer so important. He becomes more compassionate toward others, more able to accept them unconditionally. He has achieved a sense of what is important in life and strives to live in accordance with his understanding of what matters.

NINE

Aftereffects II: Attitudes Toward Religion and Death

In addition to triggering personal and value changes, coming close to death tends to bring about a changed outlook on some of life's perennial issues, such as religion and death itself. Before exploring these more "philosophic" (rather than strictly personal) reorientations, one striking fact should be noted. Where the personal changes reviewed previously tended to be found for core experiencers and nonexperiencers alike, the reorientations in world views are characteristic chiefly of those who report a core experience.

Religious Changes

Do near-death survivors *become* more religious afterward? We have already seen that prior religiousness is not a *determinant* of the core experience, but we have yet to discover whether it might be an *effect*. The answer we shall come to, after reviewing a considerable body of testimony, is that indeed they do—but only if they have had a core experience on approaching death. The evidence needs to be presented first, of course, and, as always, certain qualifications will have to be made before we are through, but the same outcome will be found to pervade all our results here: Core experiencers tend to become more religious, whereas nonexperiencers tend to show no systematic change. To determine the extent of religious changes, we asked our respondents a series of related questions. One was, Before this experience, how religious a person would you say you were? The respondent was asked to reply in terms of the following categories: very, quite, fairly, not too, not at all. In most cases, we explained that "religious" should not be understood in a narrow sense to mean church-going per se, but rather should be taken to refer to an "inward" sense of religious feeling. After a respondent replied to this question, we then asked him to answer it according to how religious he felt himself to be at the present time. The difference between the two ratings we used to assess change in religiousness and the results of the corresponding statistical analysis are presented in Table 22.

Life at Death

Table 22

Pre- and Post-Religiousness Scores According to
Core Experience Status and Sex of Respondent*

	Women	Men	
Core Experiencers	.833 (24)	.710 (19)	.772
Nonexperiencers	.345 (29)	.292 (24)	.318
	.589	.501	

*A positive score means an increase in religiousness.

ANOVA

Source	SS	df	ms	F	p
Sex	0.25	1			
Experience	5.25	1	5.25	4.65	< .05
S x E	0.00	1			
Error	104.00	92	1.13		

The data here demonstrate that where all categories of respondents show a net increase in religiousness, the effect is substantial, on average, *only* for core experiencers. The analysis of variance confirms this impression: core experiencers show a significantly greater increase on this variable and nonexperiencers show only a negligible rise overall. The effect of the core experience here is obviously independent of sex—the effect is the same for both sexes. Although the level of statistical significance here (p <.05) is not terribly strong, subsequent analyses will provide much more compelling evidence, both statistical and qualitative, for the effect noted in Table 22.[1] There was, incidentally, no significant difference on *initial* religiousness between core experiencers and nonexperiencers.

As a part of our formal interview, we also asked (most of) our respondents whether in their own judgment their near-death episode affected their religious feelings in any way. The results of these self-ratings are presented next.

Table 23

Religious Changes: Self-Ratings

Women
Religiousness

	Increased	Remained the Same or Decreased	
Core Experiencers	18	10	28
Nonexperiencers	8	16	24
	26	26	

$x^2 = 3.79, p \cong .05$

Men
Religiousness

	Increased	Remained the Same or Decreased	
Core Experiencers	7	13	20
Nonexperiencers	8	10	18
	15	23	

P = ns

The findings here are consistent with those of the first question for women but not for men. Although the probability level is borderline, significantly more women core experiencers stated that their religious feelings increased afterward, compared to nonexperiencers. For men, there was no difference between categories. There are two conceivable reasons for this small discrepancy from the data presented in Table 22. First, since the data here are nonparametric (that is, based on frequencies rather than averages) rather than parametric, as they were in Table 22, it may be that the average *increase* in religiousness for male core experiencers is greater although the *number* who increase is no greater, compared to nonexperiencers. A second possibility is that since there are more missing cases here, the earlier effect is obscured. In any event, however, it may be helpful at this point to mention that further data to be presented will amply support the assertion that the religiousness changes observed for core experiencers are fully as strong for men as for women. Thus, the self-ratings here for men constitute the only slight exception to the general pattern.

So far, we have examined some evidence that core experiencers tend to evince a higher degree of religiousness than nonexperiencers following a near-death incident. It is obvious on reflection, however, that religiousness is a very broad term, capable of a variety of meanings and shadings. Of these nuances we know nothing as yet, and they turn out to be critical to our understanding of just how the religious views of core experiencers tend to be affected by their coming close to death. These changes, as we shall now see, are both subtle and powerful, and the quantitative data we have reviewed to this point do scant justice to either of these dimensional aspects.

Qualitative Changes in Religiousness Among Core Experiencers

Although there are some exceptions to this generalization, increased religiousness among core experiencers does not as a rule take the form of more frequent church attendance or other modes of formal religious observances. Rather, it is that a *heightened inner religious feeling* reveals itself afterward, and this feeling does not seem to require a formal channel of religious ritual in order to express itself; indeed, some people actually assert that organized forms of religious observance tend to interfere with the expression of this inner religious impulse. In general, then, core experiencers tend to state that they feel closer to God afterward rather than closer to their church; they are more prayerful and privately religious than religious in an external, denominational way. In some cases this kind of religious feeling fades after a few months or years, but for most respondents it appears to represent a lasting transformation of their religious orientation.

Several distinctive aspects of this heightened religious feeling together constitute its principal features. A number of respondents mentioned that they became more prayerful afterward and/or felt a greater awareness of God's presence.

I did find that for a while after the experience I *did* become more religious. I was praying a lot. [Eventually, she ceased to pray so frequently, but she remained more religious than she had been before her near-death experience.] *(7)*

[Afterward] I never prayed so much in my life. *(6)*

My faith in there being a power higher and greater that is somehow controlling my life has been heavily reinforced. *(82)*

I rely a great deal more on God. I know that very definitely He's there. *(26)*

I have become very religious since this experience. More and more so. I spend a great deal of time in prayer every morning. *(4)*

Well [afterward], I felt closer to a—a God. Which I had not for years. [Before] I was an agnostic, I didn't know. *(Do you now feel you know?)* I feel much closer that I know. I find myself praying sometimes to [pause] an unknown Force. *(19)*

It's more or less that there's something in me that I can call on. I almost feel like there's a supreme being in each one of us that we can call on. Whether that's God or not, I don't really know. [She described herself, however, as being much more religious afterward.] *(29)*

It's kind of strange, after leaving the hospital, it started crossing my mind to go into religion. I don't know. I'll tell you one thing: I find myself praying or maybe thinking of God or a Superior Being more often now than I have in the past. *(45)*

After the incident I felt like I had more faith, a *lot* more faith than before. [This change lasted only a couple of months, however.] *(99)*

I've become a *lot* more religious. I pray every night. I've been asking for other visions in my prayers. *(79)*

Another component of the religious attitude of core experiencers has to do with a feeling that organized religion may either be irrelevant to or interfere with the expression of this inward sense of religiousness.

[Before I was] fairly religious, but in a superficial way. I was more or less caught up in the *ritual* and the *trappings* of religion. And afterwards, for the short period after, I realized that the ritual and all that [pause] really meant nothing. It was the faith and the deep-down *meaning* that was of importance. *(99)*

It [the experience] gave me a lot of questions, a lot of questions. I began to question the need for church. [She went on to elaborate that she no longer feels the need of a *building* to be religious. A minister told her that she carries a church within her.] [Now] I don't need the church. *(30)*

I'm *not* such a *follower* of the church anymore. Like they say, "You *have* to do this; you have to do that." I don't do that. Because *I* have to do what *I* think is right now. I rely more on *my* feelings than on *their* commands. I don't believe in their commands. *(24)*

I've always had difficulty with religions anyway. And, after this experience, as time went on, as this progression was going on, I found that the need to go to communion, confession, go to a place to pray, observe Good Friday, or any of these kinds of things, not only weren't necessary, but they were *blocking* what was really supposed to be happening. So that's why I have no affiliation. *(77)*

Although indifference or even contempt for organized religion is sometimes expressed by core experiencers, it is usually stated within a context that implies an overall religious tolerance for all ways of worship. From this point of view, there is no one religion or religious denomination that is superior or "true"; rather, all religions are expressions of a single truth. It is the smug sectarian quality of some religious groups to which core experiencers tend to object, not to the basics of religious worship itself:

All of the religions are more or less blending in together now. The little minor points—you don't believe in this saint or this bless-ing—these things are really very insignificant. *(24)*

I don't think of religion as *a* religion any more. God is above all religions. God is the religion, so, therefore, the various religions have no effect whatsoever on me. *(28)*

I'm not really involved in any *one* religion. I think they *all* have something in common. I'm not really an advocate of any one of them in particular. *(99)*

I believe in the *basics* of *all* religions. They're *all* connected as far as I'm concerned. *(77)*

I feel welcome in any church. But . . . no one certain church. . . . Each person is judged by his own doings. So there's not any man that's going to walk up to me and tell that, say, the Baptists are going to be the only people who will ever see heaven. *(68)*

I know that I can go to a Catholic church, an Episcopalian church, a Baptist church, I don't care *where* you go, it's all the same. There's no difference. It's just a different word. *(20)*

Sometimes the sense of the underlying similarity of all religions goes beyond an articulation of a view of all-embracing religious tolerance and is then phrased in terms of something that transcends mundane forms of religious worship. What seems to be implied here is a "cosmic" view of religion for which no theological doctrines are adequate. One respondent who struggled to put this insight into words summed it up this way:

Yeah—there's—I just can't explain it because I don't know how to explain it in words. But it's just that everything is *infinite* and this has all been going on, in my mind, the universe has been going on forever. I just can't explain it. . . . Somehow we have a more important *mission* while we're here. Okay. That's it. We have a more important mission in our lives than just the material end of it in trying just to get material gains. There are more important things. It showed me the spiritual side in that basically that—it is important, I guess. That's all I can say. That [pause] that [pause] that *love* is important and that *every human being* on the earth is equal to each other. They're all the same. *(71)*

Again, these changes in religious attitude cannot be viewed in isolation from other personal changes triggered by a near-death episode. The increased prominence of an inner sense of God, the weakening or abandonment of outward religious forms, the spirit of religious tolerance and a dim sense of a cosmic religion—all these changes dovetail with a generalized value reorientation that stresses the importance of love and the role of spiritual values in everyday life.

Life at Death

Indeed, my own feeling is that it would be more accurate to claim that experiencers tend to become more *spiritual* rather than religious (in any conventional sense) following their near-death episode. Unfortunately, the term *spiritual* is even vaguer than *religious* and is perhaps of little descriptive value here. Nevertheless, as I have earlier observed, my personal interaction with many core experiencers left me with the impression that a spiritual awakening had definitely occurred in a number of them and that the term *spiritual,* though ambiguous, is nevertheless the most apt to characterize this quality. This impression, of course, is fostered through direct interaction with these respondents and may not be so apparent from the excerpts from their interviews.

It is important to point out here that although an increase in religiousness is the rule among experiencers it is by no means inevitable. A number reported no change in their religious views. None, however, showed a *decline* in religious feeling.

Belief in God

We also asked our respondents about their belief in God, prior to and following their near-death incident. The alternatives we offered them were: absolute, strong, fairly strong, not too strong, and no belief at all. The data from this question are presented in summary form in Table 24.

Table 24

Pre- and Post-Belief in God Scores According to Core
Experience Status and Sex of Respondent*

	Women	Men	
Core Experiencers	.654 (26)	.429 (21)	.553
Nonexperiencers	.232 (28)	.136 (22)	.190
	.435	.279	

*A positive score means an increase in strength of belief in God. No significant effects.

Although the trend is the same as before (that is, favoring the core experiencers), the difference between categories does not reach an acceptable level of statistical significance. If one examines the *percentage* of increasers for both categories (47% for core experiencers versus 28% for nonexperiencers), the difference again fails to attain statistical significance ($X^2 = 2.91$ with 1 df; p <.10).

This result, however, is not too surprising in light of our qualitative data. Strength of *belief* in God is relatively stable (most respondents indicate no change); it is one's degree of religious *feeling* that tends to increase—at least for core experiencers. Obviously, one's belief as such may remain constant even when one's religious sense quickens. In addition, a number of experiencers, in responding to this question, stated or implied that they found the abstract term *God*, too full of conventional meanings for it to be a reliable reference word for their religious orientation. In other cases, core experiencers implied a qualitative increase in belief without being able to express this change quantitatively. For example, one woman said that whereas before she "thought" her belief was absolute, afterward she was "sure" that it was *(7)*. Another stated: "Well, I always believed that there was *something*. Now, it's not like I believe *more*, now I *live* like there is." *(77)* For these reasons, the failure to obtain a stronger difference between core experiencers and nonexperiencers on this item is, at least post hoc, perhaps understandable.

Only one core experiencer showed a decline in belief in God. This was a woman who had an out-of-body experience while close to death. In her case, however, the reason for this decline seems to stem, not from her core experience itself, but rather from the period afterward, when she was recovering in the hospital:

(*Did this experience change your religious view in any way?*) Yes, that was another negative factor. *Not my own personal experience* [italics added] because I went in basically an agnostic. But I came out an atheist. . . . What I saw in the hospital [during the time of her recovery] I couldn't understand. I used to talk with the doctors, "How could you believe in God after what you see every day?" I watched someone that I had become good friends with in the hospital—we became such good friends. She used to come in and bring me flowers and just talk to me and she had a brain tumor. And finally when I got to the stage where I could walk, she got bad and she died four days later. And I watched her die. It was my first time watching somebody die. And that was the point when she didn't know my name anymore—and after that, I became so bitter. And then I went to the pediatrics ward and I would see severely burned children that were just so hideous to look at. And I said, "What kind of a God could make people this awful?" I mean, I knew He was punitive, but this was really sadistic. . . .

And there's nothing you can do, and there's cancer and, oh! I used to see that every day . . . and watching them go, and the suffering and the yelling, the pain, the screaming. When you're in a hospital and have nowhere to go, you do a lot of thinking about things like that. *(62)*

Even this powerful indictment of a "sadistic God" (so reminiscent of Ivan's argument in *The Brothers Karamazov* and of the views of many death camp victims) does not, of course, preclude a heightening of this respondent's *spiritual* sensitivity. Indeed, by becoming more aware of life's tragic dimension, she, too, reveals one of the characteristic concerns of core experiencers—compassion for the suffering of others. Thus, while it is true she has become less a believer in God, she has apparently shown the same kind of value change expressed by those whose religiousness has increased. Such an outcome, then, only reinforces the view that changes in religiousness must be understood as part of a large context of value change; it also would seem to support my contention that it may be that core experiences tend to stimulate spiritual awareness rather than religious belief *per se*.

Belief in Life After Death

Still another question had to do with the conviction that there was such a thing as life after death. In this case, we provided six possible categories of response: completely convinced, strongly convinced, tend to believe, not sure, tend to doubt, and no belief at all. As with our other questions, we asked our respondents to answer in terms of their pre- and post-incident beliefs. Table 25 furnishes the data.

Table 25

Pre- and Post-Life-After-Death Scores According to
Core Experience Status and Sex of Respondent*

	Women	Men	
Core Experiencers	1.585	2.075	1.798
Nonexperiencers	0.268	0.286	0.276
	0.902	1.159	

*A positive score means an increase in conviction in the belief that there is life after death.

ANOVA

Source	SS	df	ms	F	p
Sex	1.40	1			
Experience	56.06	1	56.06	25.60	< .001
S x E	1.40	1			
Error	199.22	91	2.19		

There is a huge effect here—one of the strongest of the entire investigation. Core experiencers increase on the average 1.8 scale units—from an average position of "not sure" to "strongly convinced"— where nonexperiencers show virtually no change. Comparison of preliminary scores on this item, incidentally, reveals that although experiencers were somewhat less inclined to believe in life after death to start with, compared to nonexperiencers (the means were 2.10 versus 2.73, respectively), they are significantly more inclined to believe in it afterward (3.93 versus 3.03; t = 3.18, p <.01). Thus, it is not "merely" coming close to death that tends to convince one that there is life after death; it is, apparently, the core experience itself that proves decisive.

The testimony here is unambiguous. A woman who suffered a heart attack said as a result of her experience:

I believe beyond any question of a doubt that there is something beyond [this life]. *(4)*

A man who was badly injured in a racing car accident said his experience changed his view of death:

My attitude toward death is that death is not dying; death is being reborn. You're reborn to a new peaceful life that when you die, you'll be able to experience. *(73)*

A man who suffered a cardiac arrest during surgery stated:

I would say—and not being religious at all—that there must be something after death, which I never believed in before. I always believed that when you were dead, they put you in the ground and you stayed there. But I'm not too sure about that anymore. *(48)*

A man who appears to have died "clinically" during open heart surgery also became convinced in life after death through this experience:

Well, it [his experience] gave me the idea that I think there's life after death. I believe that now. Before I believed that if you died, you were just dead. But now I really believe that there is some kind of life after death. *(33)*

The woman who had a cardiac arrest when undergoing a tonsillectomy said that prior to her operation:

I had a doubt. *(How do you feel about it now?)* Oh, I'm positive now. Completely convinced. *(24)*

Finally, a man who nearly died in a diving accident said that before his accident:

I thought it was all a bunch of baloney. . . . *(how about now—is there life after death?)* Sure. Definitely. *(77)*

As Table 25 implies, comments like these are quite typical of core experiencers. For most, the idea of life after death becomes not merely highly probable, but a veritable certainty. Nonexperiencers, on the other hand, are not only significantly less convinced that life after death is a reality, but remain relatively unaffected by their near-death episode in this regard.

Global Index of Religiousness Changes

As an overall index of change in religiousness, difference (that is, pre and post) scores for the three items having to do with religious feelings, belief in God and belief in life after death were summed for each individual. (These items make up our "purified" religiousness index previously discussed [see pages 133–134] in connection with our data on religiousness as an antecedent of the death experience.) This overall score obviously represents a *composite* index of religious changes and as such is probably more reliable than any one difference score taken by itself. The data, based on this index, are presented in Table 26.

Table 26

Pre- and Post-Global Religiousness Scores According to
Core Experience Status and Sex of Respondent*

	Women	Men	
Core Experiencers	2.74	2.76	2.75
Nonexperiencers	0.95	0.80	0.89
	1.79	1.70	

*A positive score means an increase in global religiousness.

ANOVA

Source	SS	df	ms	F	p
Sex	0.00	1			
Experience	76.10	1	76.10	11.46	< .005
S x E	0.22	1			
Error	570.99	86	6.64		

The results prove clear-cut. On this measure of global religiousness, experiencers show a much greater increase following their episode, compared to nonexperiencers (p <.005). Furthermore, the means for male and female core experiencers are virtually identical. Although the "life after death" item plainly contributes a disproportionate share of the variance here, the other two items, it will be remembered, did provide data indicative of the same overall effect. Thus, all our religious indicators converge on a single conclusion: Core experiencers become more religious following their near-death episode than do nonexperiencers.

Beliefs in Heaven and Hell

As a final inquiry into our respondents' religious views, we asked them two simple yes/no questions having to do with their belief in heaven and hell. As I noted earlier, these questions ultimately proved *too* simple since they tended to elicit a variety of questions in response such as, What do you mean by heaven (or hell)? Since the interpretation of these terms were quite variable, the interpretation of the data based on them is necessarily hazardous. With this caution in mind, we can, however, examine these data for whatever dim light they may furnish on the question of near-death survivors' religious beliefs.

The first point that needs to be made is that beliefs in heaven and hell tend to be relatively stable: 71% of all respondents showed no change in belief patterns. (Belief in heaven, by the way, was more common than belief in hell—62% to 44%). Nevertheless, core experiencers were significantly more likely to change their beliefs in some way following their incident than were nonexperiencers (41% versus 19%, p <.05). The preponderance of changes among core experiencers was in a positive direction, that is, either a postincident belief in heaven or a lack of belief in hell, or both. Seventy-two percent of the directional changes among core experiencers conformed to this pattern. Among nonexperiencers, there were only seven persons altogether who showed a directional change; of these four were positive, three negative. The number of cases were too small here for a statistically significant difference to emerge.

Thus, the data here suggest that although beliefs in heaven and hell are quite stable, core experiencers are more likely to change their (in a positive direction) than are nonexperiencers. Nevertheless, the ambiguity of the questions themselves and the small proportions of changers render this conclusion highly tentative.

This section will close with a few representative comments by core experiencers who did demonstrate a postincident change.

A woman who nearly died during surgery was asked:

Interviewer: Before, did you believe in heaven?
Respondent: Yeah.
Interviewer: What about now?
Respondent: Now I definitely do.
Interviewer: What about hell, before?
Respondent: Not really. No.
Interviewer: What about now?
Respondent: I don't believe in it now at all. (7)

The woman who nearly died of a cardiac arrest during surgery for a tonsillectomy had this to say:

Interviewer: Heaven, before?
Respondent: I did, but I was *hoping* it was there. Now of course I *know* it's there.
Interviewer: Hell?
Respondent: Yes, I did. I always believed in hell.

Interviewer: Do you believe in it now?
Respondent: Oh, yes.
Interviewer: What is hell?
Respondent: I don't know how to explain it. To me, it's more of life. It's feeling pain, seeing people you love suffer.
Interviewer: So hell is here then.
Respondent: I don't think it's here, but it's like here. It takes place on the other side of life. *(24)*

A number of core experiencers, however, are quite insistent that there was no such "place" as hell. One woman put it this way:

I don't believe there's a hell. I just feel that when your spirit leaves you, it just goes into a spirit world and that's where it remains. *(Do you mean that this spirit world is like heaven?)* Yeah. *(64)*

A man who experienced a presence and who saw scenes from his life, which he viewed "like a movie," summed up his convictions on the existence of hell as follows:

I don't actually believe there's a hell in the sense of fiery pits. Actually, I'll say this and this is what I believe: God is an All-Loving Source and I don't believe He's up there twisting people's fingers. I had the feeling that it was complete comfort and even things I did wrong, on viewing them, weren't wrong. *(71)*

Summary of Religiousness Changes

In general, core experiencers tend to become more religious following their near-death episode, nonexperiencers do not. The way in which postincident religiousness reveals itself among core experiencers is primarily in terms of an inward sense of religion: They feel closer to God, are more prayerful, are less concerned with organized religion and formal rituals, and express a sense of religious tolerance and religious universalism. It isn't clear that their belief in God *per se* grows stronger, although it is clear that their religious *feeling* does. Following their incident, they are significantly more inclined than nonexperiencers to be convinced there is life after death. Their views on heaven and hell, though usually not affected by their experience, tend to become more positive (that is, a stronger belief in heaven or a weaker belief in hell, or both) when change does occur.

All these changes can more aptly be described by the term *spiritual* rather than *religious*. It seems to me that the core experience tends to trigger or intensify one's sense of spiritual awareness, whereas coming close to death, *without* an accompanying core experience, tends to leave religious views and spiritual values largely intact.

Attitude Toward Death

We also asked our respondents whether their coming close to death had had any effect on their attitude toward death. Most respondents replied in terms of their *fear* of death and those who didn't were usually then asked specifically whether their fear of death had been altered through their near-death episode. The responses to this question fell into six main categories and the full data are presented in Table 27.

Table 27

Effects on Fear of Death
According to Core Experience Status

Effect	Core Experiencers			Nonexperiencers*		
	No.	%		No.	%	
Increased it	1	2		5	13	
No change	3	6	20%	4	11	71%
Never afraid	6	12		18	47	
Decreased it	9	18		3	8	
No fear of death	15	31	80%	8	21	29%
Lost all fear	15	31		0	0	

*15 nonexperiencers were coded in an irrelevant category (most of these representing a "not ascertained" status).

It is clear that the patterns of response to this question vary dramatically as a function of core experience status. The extent of this difference can be more easily grasped by examining the following chi-square analysis.

Table 28

Chi-Square Analysis of
Effects of Fear of Death

	Lost it No fear Decreased	Never afraid No change Increased	
Core Experiencers	39	10	49
Nonexperiencers	11	27	38
	50	37	87

$x^2 = 20.43$, p $<.0005$

The data in Table 28 clearly demonstrate that core experiencers, as a group, tend to show a sharp decline in fear where no such pattern is evident for nonexperiencers. Nevertheless, the form of the question itself is such that the resultant data need to be more closely inspected before these findings can be properly interpreted.

The problem arises from the fact that several response categories used here are ambiguous. For example, the "no change" category does not permit a statement of how afraid of death the respondent was (or is); it is conceivable, therefore, that some in this category could well be placed in other categories of Table 27. Similarly, the "never afraid" category could conceivably be classified with the "no fear of death" respondents. And this last category may very well contain some persons who "lost all fear."[2] For these reasons, the placement of individual respondents into certain categories is somewhat arbitrary and often depends on the particular phrase a respondent happens to use. Not only that, but the lumping of several particular categories into one overall classification is itself a bit arbitrary. Besides these matters of response categories and their classification, it must be remembered that fifteen nonexperiencers do not appear in Tables 27 and 28 and we have no way of knowing whether these respondents' data, if we have had them, would have changed the pattern of findings in a significant way.

Nevertheless, despite these methodological and interpretative problems, there remains little doubt that core experiencers, on the whole, show a drastically different pattern of response to this question than do nonexperiencers. For example, the *only* persons—and there were fifteen of them—who testified that they lost all fear of death were found

Life at Death

among core experiencers. Indeed, 62% of all core experiencers said that they now had no fear of death whatever, compared to 21% for nonexperiencers. If one examines the patterns of increased or decreased fear, the same result obtains: Among experiencers, there are nine respondents reporting a decline and only one who says that fear has increased; among nonexperiencers, the corresponding figures are three and five, respectively.

Additional data, not fully reflected in Tables 27 and 28, further buttress the sharp differences between groups. The modal response among nonexperiencers was the avowal that they had never been afraid of death, but this was often said very matter-of-factly, and, at least in some cases, the inflection did not impress me with its conviction. The response of core experiencers was, as a rule, very different. They would often comment on this matter *before* I (or other interviewers) had asked them about it (for example, "I'll tell you one thing, doctor: I'm not afraid of death any longer"), and when they addressed themselves to this point, it was often with great emphasis and emotion, as though it was no mere "intellectual conviction," but rather a deeply felt truth. Overall, my subjective impression throughout the course of this investigation was that the loss or decrease in the fear of death among core experiencers was one of the strongest points of difference between them and nonexperiencers.

I believe the reader will come to share this impression if he examines the comments from core experiencers on this point which I have arrayed below in some profusion.

(Do you fear death?) Not at all. *(Did you before?)* Yes, as far as anyone else would. *(26)*

(Did this change your attitude toward death?) Yes, it has. Yes, it has. Because I had a fear—I didn't want to talk about it. A real genuine fear of death. I used to get *preoccupied* with it. I used to get preoccupied with it. . . . I don't have that anymore. I'm not afraid of it. I'm not ready for it right now—I got things to do. But when it comes, I'm not afraid of it. *(30)*

I can kind of sum it [his experience] up: I'm not afraid of dying anymore. I guess I've made up my mind that this is the way dying is going to be like and, if this is the way it is going to be, then don't be afraid of it or don't be scared because what I experienced was [pause] almost happiness. *(Had you been afraid of dying before?)* Yes. *(45)*

Well, one thing I most distinctly remember is that it left me, where

I had been terrified by death before, it now left me with a total *lack* of fear of death. *(4)*

Well, I certainly no longer have any fear of death. *(82)*

I'm not afraid of death at all. *(29)*

I have no fear of dying, I don't to this day. I have no fear of it at all. It's as if I've been there and know what it's like and I am not afraid of it. I'm just not, you know. *(16)*

If that is what death is like, then I'm not afraid to go. . . . If that's any way like the hereafter is, then I'm not afraid to go at all. I have absolutely no fear at all. . . . I'm convinced. I think I had just a peek into it. *(10)*

(Has this eliminated your fears of death, then?) Yes, yes, definitely. *(25)*

(Did this experience change you in any way?) I should say it has. I have no fear of death [said with decided emphasis]. *(53)*

I'm not afraid of dying. I'm really not afraid and I used to be scared to death. *(23)*

It's a very peaceful feeling, believe me. That's why I tell people I have no fear of death. I mean, I have no fear of death. *(Because of these experiences?)* Aw, sure. *(38)*

I'm not afraid of death. This is the point I'm at right now. I'm not afraid of death at all. *(71)*

[Before] I looked at death—let's say I was scared of death. Frightened. So much. When I was a child. Now I find it as a beautiful experience. One of peace, calm . . . *(It doesn't sound as though you're afraid of death.)* No. I think death is a necessary part of living. *(This view of death that you have—is this something that changed as a result of this experience?)* Oh, yeah. *(64)*

Basically . . . death is not frightening the way we *think* it's frightening. . . . It can be a very *beautiful* experience. *(70)*

(Are you afraid of death?) No. I'm not afraid of death at all. *(77)*

(Did it [his experience] change your attitude toward death in any way?)

Yes! I used to be *afraid* of death. Now, it seems like that, you know, it was a little scary at first, the *wandering* aspect, but *talking* to God and the *warmth* I felt when I was with Him, you know—it was really—Oh! I just get the chills thinking about it, it was so GOOD, you know? And I feel that when my time for death comes, that I won't be afraid to go. *(79)*

(Would you say that this experience has in any way affected your attitude toward death?) I'm not *scared* of it. I'm just wondering when [laughs]. *(68)*

(Do you fear death?) Absolutely not! I have no fear of death *at all.* *(20)*

Perhaps the strongest statement concerning the loss of fear of death was made by the woman who was apparently clinically dead for three minutes from a surgically related cardiac arrest. Both to conclude and to sum up these comments in a single quotation, I shall draw from a portion of her account:

I was afraid of death. I remember as a young woman when I had my two children, sometimes I'd wake up crying in the middle of the night and my husband would hold me, because it would *hit* me in the middle of the night and . . . [my husband] would just hold me and talk to me and I would get over it. But, I was *always* afraid of death. Which they say is quite common. Well, I faced death those three weeks I was in the hospital. They never knew whether my heart would stop or not. And they told me this [that her heart could stop at any moment] and I knew this and was aware of it, and yet I had *no fear at all.* First time in my life that I was actually *face to face* with death, that I knew that I would close my eyes and not wake up again and I wasn't afraid. Because I remember the *feeling.* I just remember this *absolute beautiful feeling.* . . . And ever since then I've never been afraid of death. *(24)*

These accounts, as I'm sure the reader will agree, offer powerful testimony for the assertion that having a core experience at the point of apparent imminent death provides a potent antidote to the fear of death. Not only that, but the effect of such an experience seems to be permanent and not merely transitory. No such systematic changes, and certainly not the emphatic and emotionally charged statements on this matter, are found for nonexperiencers. Again, it is *having a core experience* itself that appears to be crucial here, not merely the fact of coming close to death.

There is one last issue, however, that needs to be raised here. How do near-death episodes affect suicide attempters' fear of death?

The first point that needs to be made is that well over half the suicide attempters respond to the question on fear of death with the phrase (or a variant of it), "I never was afraid of death." In their case, perhaps their actions suggest that such statements are more than empty bravado. Most others report no change; two report an increase in fear of death. Only three suicide attempters report a decrease.

As we have already observed, most of our suicide attempters recall no experiences or only an aborted one. Nevertheless, it is important to look at those cases where some kind of suicide-related core experience did occur in order to determine whether core experiences induced in this way also result in a decrease in fear of death.

Actually, two of the persons already quoted in this section *(79* and *82)* who were involved in suicide-related near-deaths[3] resulting in deep experiences have indicated that they lost their fear of death through their brush with death. Another suicide attempter who had a deep experience also felt he was no longer afraid to die:

> The way I feel now is, I don't want to die. But I'm not afraid to die now. Before I was afraid to die, well, not really, but I was afraid to die. But now I'm not afraid to die. I feel that I know what it's all about. *(100)*

Several other suicide attempters who had partial experiences said they didn't fear death and never had. But not all, however. A possible exception—it is, at least, a mixed case—to the general effect of the core experience on the fear of death comes from a suicide attempter who had a deep, though somewhat atypical, experience. Whether it is a real exception the reader can judge for himself:

> *Interviewer:* Did this experience have any effect on your attitude toward death? On your fear of death?
> *Respondent:* Yeah, when I think about dying, it *bothers* me. Let's see. For some time I haven't had any faith in Christianity. And so that makes it even worse, thinking that you're going to die— because you don't think that you're going to *go* anywhere. Before, I thought that there would be a heaven or something. But *now* I—I don't know—you go into limbo or something like that.
> *Interviewer:* You think you go into a state of a sort of—a no place, a nothing?
> *Respondent:* Yeah.
> *Interviewer:* So in terms of its effect on your attitude toward death,

it's less positive than it was before, less hopeful or something.
Respondent: Yeah.
Interviewer: Would you say that you're more or less afraid of it?
Respondent: [Pause] I'm afraid of it, but not for the same reason.
Before, I was afraid of something *unknown.* Now I think I'm
afraid of just leaving people behind. I don't have the same fear.
Interviewer: You don't have a fear for yourself personally, but you
have a fear for the survivors of your death.
Respondent: Yeah. *(99)*

Another important related issue is whether coming close to death
through suicide, particularly when one does have a core experience,
acts as a deterrent to further attempts.

Most suicide attempters without any core experience either denied
that they would try again to kill themselves or thought it was unlikely;
several, however, could conceive of the possibility and several had, in
fact, already made multiple attempts. Merely coming close to death
through suicide attempt—as we know from other investigations—
doesn't necessarily vanquish self-destructive urges.

What about when one has a core experience? Here, the evidence is
again mixed. Most of those who had an experience state with varying
degrees of emphasis that they would not attempt to kill themselves now:

I decided that I have to wait. . . . I figure God's going to take me
when he's ready and it doesn't appear that He is. . . . If I came
that close to dying and didn't, it's 'cause I wasn't supposed to. *(81)*

(Has it changed your attitude to suicide?) Yes, I think suicide is useless.
You know, it's nothing to it. It really doesn't do anything for
you. . . . The way I feel now is, I don't want to die. *(100)*

So I think that God was trying to tell me that if I commit suicide
I'm going to hell, you know. So I'm not going to think about
suicide anymore [nervous laughter]. *(That did it, then?)* Yeah, I
think that did the trick about thinking about suicide. *(79)*

On the other hand, one respondent who had a core experience as a
result of a faulty preoperative procedure made multiple attempts to kill
herself afterward, precisely because death was no longer terrifying:

. . . coming that close to death and seeing that it wasn't necessarily
painful, that I could discount pain in coming close to dying, it
became more appetizing. *(22)*

It should be added here, however, that this respondent's suicide-related near-death episode was very "cloudy and vague" compared to her illness-related one and that she suffers from a variety of severe physical and psychological problems.

Thus, the evidence on the deterrent power of suicide-related core experiences is only suggestive. It is perhaps relevant to note here that the three cases where a suicidal intent or act was *not* associated with either drugs or alcohol *(79, 82* and *100)* were the *only* ones where a loss of fear of death was reported.[4]

In general, then, the core experience acts as a powerful reducer of the fear of death in cases involving near-death through illness or accident and *may* have a like effect on suicide-related cases. (More research on the final point is necessary, however, before any firm conclusion can be reached.)

Conception of Death

From all that has been written so far, it is obvious that having a core experience at the point of apparent imminent death must have an effect on one's *conception* of death. Indeed, it can be assumed that changes in attitude toward or fear of death are mediated by a changed understanding of death. In order to inquire into this, toward the end of our interviews, we would usually ask our respondents to tell us, in effect, what death meant to them. The answers, as can be imagined, were quite variable, but we were able to group them into nine major categories as shown in Table 29.

Life at Death

Table 29

Conceptions of Death According to Core Experience Status

	Core Experiencers		Nonexperiencers	
Conception	*No.*	*%**	*No.*	*%*
Annihilation, finality	2	4	6	11
Something beyond	17	35	8	15
Transition, new beginning	14	29	8	15
Peace, beauty, bliss	18	37	4	8
Heaven/hell	1	2	1	2
Reincarnation notions	12	24	2	4
Other	2	4	5	9
No idea	7	14	11	21
Not ascertained	1	2	12	23

*Percentages total more than 100 because many respondents gave more than one answer.

As can be seen, core experiencers tend to hold more definite, more positive views on the nature of death than do nonexperiencers. Among core experiencers, the notion is particularly strong that not only does life continue after death, but that it is likely to be very pleasant. Another point of difference between core experiencers and nonexperiencers is the former's greater openness to reincarnation concepts. It is not, however, that core experiencers necessarily come to profess a belief in reincarnation; it is rather that the underlying idea of reincarnation no longer appears altogether implausible. These differences are highlighted in Table 30.

Table 30

Conceptions of Death
—Selected Comparisons—
According to Core Experience Status

	Annihilation, finality	Peace, beauty, bliss	
Core Experiencers	2	18	20
Nonexperiencers	6	4	10
	8	22	

$$x^2 = 6.16, p < .02$$

	Reincarnation mentioned	Reincarnation not mentioned	
Core Experiencers	12	36	48
Nonexperiencers	2	39	41
	14	75	

$$x^2 = 5.32, p < .02$$

Since both comparisons presented here are completely ad hoc, the results can at best be taken only as suggestive; nevertheless, they do point to some possible dimensions of conceptions of death where core experiencers and nonexperiencers may differ sharply.

The following succinct statements dramatically convey the affective associations death has to core experiencers:

If there is a life after death, I think it's going to be very beautiful, if the brief experience I had is an example of what it is going to be. *(48)*

My attitude toward death is that death is not dying; death is being reborn. You're reborn to a new, peaceful life that, when you die, you'll be able to experience. *(73)*

(Your idea of death, then?) Well, it means utterly at peace. *(6)*

(Is it true to say that death does not represent in your mind any feeling of annihilation or finality?) Absolutely! *(What does it represent?)* Peace! *(4)*

These next passages speak of a sense of continuance:

I was wrapped up in the whole conventional belief in death: "Oh, God, what am I going to do when I die? What is going to happen? [Now] I *know* what is going to happen. It's just going to be another life somewhere else. Maybe in a different form, but I'll still have my soul. *(66)*

(What is your understanding of what death is?) With this experience [pause] there is no such thing. To me, it's just a passing phase, to get someplace else. I don't know what the other place is, but I know that it's all right. *(25)*

Something *will* happen. You *will* go *somewhere*. It's not the end. Just like your life is not the end. *(79)*

The next respondents reveal an openness to reincarnation:

[If you die by suicide], you'll die, but you're going to come back as another creature somewhere else and start all over again and you're going to have the same problems sooner or later. *(100)*

Interviewer: What do you think happens at death?
Respondent: You leave your physical body and you're transformed into your spiritual body. I think that's right.
Interviewer: Have you any idea what happens after that?
Respondent: I would say that we go to a school of learning of some type where we're just—it's just like we walk out of this one class and we're going into this other thing and—just a *very intense learning process*. Then I would just guess a place of comfort and from there either to being reborn again to go on to something else that there is out there that I don't know about.
Interviewer: Is reincarnation an idea that makes sense to you?
Respondent: I think that people are born again if they *choose* to or if they have something that has to be worked out.
Interviewer: Just like you were having a choice at the point where you could have—
Respondent: Right. My actual feeling at that point was that if I didn't [choose to come back], I'd have to start all over again. *(71)*

In concluding this discussion of conceptions of death—and at the same time this entire segment presenting the basic findings of our study of near-death experiences—perhaps it is fitting to give the final words here to the woman who, according to the WCEI, had the most profound experience of anyone:

> *Interviewer:* What do you understand death to be?
> *Respondent:* [Long pause] I really believe that death is just part of a continuous cycle. I think when you are born, consciousness is enveloped with a body. And you grow and you develop and you learn. And I believe that you try to attain—whether you are aware of it or not—you develop a greater awareness of higher consciousness. I feel that with each death, it's like taking off an old coat and putting on another one to grow further and further in consciousness until you become one with God, or with Creation, or with whatever it is. Whatever this great thing is.
> *Interviewer:* So death is just a change in the cycle?
> *Respondent:* Yes. Yes, it's a continual thing. I think of it as just a cycle. Not an end *at all.* Not an end at all. I know that whenever I have another grandchild, I look at him and think, Could you be papa? Could you be mama? *Who* could you be? [She laughs.] And it's very exciting! Very exciting. *(20)*

Summary

Religious changes. Core experiencers, as a group, became more religious after their experience; the religiousness of nonexperiencers remained about the same. The increased religious feeling on the part of the core experiencers involved a sense of being closer to God, feeling more prayerful, taking less interest in formal religious services, but expressing greater tolerance for various forms of religious expression and endorsing an attitude of religious universalism. These changes might be regarded as representing a heightened spiritual awareness rather than religiousness. Although a global index of religiousness demonstrated that core experiencers were significantly more religious afterward than nonexperiencers, the strongest difference here was based on a conviction in life after death: Core experiencers showed a large increase in belief in life after death; nonexperiencers showed a negligible change.

Attitude toward death. Although the data here were marked by some

Life at Death

interpretative problems, they seem to show that the effect of a core experience is to significantly reduce or eliminate one's fear of death. Nonexperiencers tended to state that they never feared death in the first place, but there was no strong evidence suggesting that merely coming close to death in itself had much of an impact on fear of death. The suicide-related core experience also seemed to reduce a respondent's fear of death (and possibly the inclination to kill oneself), but the number of relevant cases was too few to draw any definite conclusion.

Conception of death. While both core experiencers and nonexperiencers tended to express belief in some form of an afterlife, core experiencers were both more definite and positive about it. Core experiencers' conceptions of death were more likely than nonexperiencers' to emphasize the peace and beauty of death and to reflect a greater openness toward a reincarnation view of life after death.

TEN

The Principal Findings and Some Comparisons

Now that all the findings from this investigation have been fully presented, we are ready to consider what they have to tell us. This task will occupy us for the next several chapters and will begin here with a comparison of our results with those described elsewhere in the medical and professional literature. In making this comparison, I will, of course, be particularly concerned with evaluating the extent to which our own data support Moody's prior findings. In the following chapters, after considering various explanations that have been proposed, I will offer my own provisional interpretation of the core experience based on a recent scientific model of consciousness that is capable of handling transcendental experience. I will also attempt to explain various specific features of the core experience, using some concepts that may or may not prove scientifically testable. My *preference* will be to articulate a scientific framework for the understanding of near-death phenomena, but I will not be reticent to *speculate* about possibilities currently outside the accepted paradigm of science if contemporary scientific theorizing about states of consciousness seems inadequate. Finally, in light of whatever understanding of near-death phenomena I can provide, I want to conclude by considering the significance of these experiences and by assessing what implications, if any, they may have for what has traditionally been called "the survival problem," that is, whether one's personality, or some aspect of it, can be said to survive bodily death.

The Form of the Core Experience

Juxtaposing two quotations from Moody's first book furnishes us with his challenge:

All I ask is for anyone who disbelieves what he reads here to poke around a bit for himself.[1] . . . it has been my experience that anyone who makes diligent and sympathetic inquiries . . . about the occurrence of such experiences will soon have his doubts dispelled.[2]

Life at Death

Although I myself did not really doubt Moody's findings or his integrity, I can at least aver that our own findings offer an impressive degree of independent corroboration for his. And while we have somewhat different conceptions of how these near-death phenomena are organized, as I will make clear, there is no substantive disagreement over the form of the core experience itself. I myself have no doubt that Moody and I have had the *same* phenomenon described to us by our respective respondents.

Not only that, but since the publication of Moody's original work, we have had further independent confirmations of his prototypic description of the core experience by other medical and scientific researchers.[3] Aspects of these investigations will be considered later, but for now it is sufficient to note that there has already accumulated an impressive array of findings generally supportive of Moody's original publication (as well as the findings publicly reported by Kübler-Ross). At this point there seems to be little doubt about the authenticity and reliability of the phenomenon.

This much noted, there are still some minor differences in findings and interpretation between Moody and myself which do require comment.

Perhaps the most obvious of these has to do with what Moody calls "a being of light." According to his prototypical description:

> . . . a loving, warm spirit of a kind he has never encountered before—a being of light—appears before him. This being asks him a question, non-verbally, to make him evaluate his life and helps him along by showing him a panoramic, instantaneous playback of the major events of his life.[4]

The experiences described here are, of course, already familiar to us from the abundant interview excerpts presented earlier—with one exception: None of my respondents ever reported *seeing* "a being of light." True, many did perceive a light and most described it as a warm, loving and comforting light; and many also described an undeniable sense of a "presence." Yet, no respondent ever explicitly wedded these two phenomena into "a being of light" and none ever used that term to characterize his experience.

What are we to make of this discrepancy?

In my judgment, not much. First of all, other researchers besides Moody have reported this phenomenon,[5] so it doesn't rest on the word of a lone investigator. Second, the same *elements* comprising the "being of light" seem to be present in our study also; they just didn't quite come together in the way that some of Moody's respondents described. Third, it may be that the "being of light" phenomenon tends to occur mainly in cases of rather extended clinical death experiences,[6] of which my own study had no such certified instances. Finally, even if the last speculation proves unfounded, it may still be that, though authentic, this is a *rare* phenomenon. If, say, it tends to occur in fewer than 5% of core experiences, it is patently conceivable that merely through sampling error no such instance turned up among my respondents. Indeed, as I have already mentioned, several of the phenomena cited by Moody in his prototypic description appeared to be quite infrequent (for example, hearing a noise, feelings of loneliness, sensing a "second" body, traveling through a "tunnel," approaching a border, and so forth) and it is perfectly reasonable, it seems to me, to conjecture that the "being of light" feature is also rarely instanced. This, at any rate, is my own provisional conclusion and the research of others will likely soon afford us a better basis for evaluating. In the meantime, I do not consider this discrepancy a serious one.

Another set of minor differences between Moody's findings and my own have to do with what appear to be, in the main, *differences in incidence* of various near-death phenomena. Since Moody's work is descriptive but not statistical, however, it is impossible to determine whether the low incidence in our reports of the Moody features just reviewed represents a real discrepancy. Since our investigation does not provide a sound sampling basis for inferring the incidence of these phenomena in the population of near-death survivors, further, more comprehensive, parametric research will have to be undertaken to settle this question. My own conclusion, therefore, is that where there is little doubt that these features do sometimes occur in conjunction with near-death episodes, how *often* they occur cannot now be estimated with any real accuracy. As with "the being of light," however, it may be that extended clinical death cases may provide a greater abundance of these elements.

The relative rarity of these features was, in fact, one of the reasons that lead me to propose a conception of the core experience cast in terms of *stages* rather than *elements per se*, as Moody's description would have it. Although these stages do not always unfold in the strict sequence in which I have arranged them, they do appear to accord reasonably well with the chain of events described in Moody's prototypic account. Since we also found that their relative incidence over the entire sample decreased systematically with increasing depth of the core experience, as shown in Figure 1 (see page 40) we can say that this "logical" ordering has a measure of empirical support from our own data.

While I believe that this framework represents an improvement over Moody's "element-conception" approach, it is not without its drawbacks. Any scheme that seems to impose a "logical" temporal ordering on the core experience does a certain violence to it, because, as we have seen, the experience itself tends to occur in connection with a state of consciousness in which time is not a meaningful construct. To speak of stages, then, contradicts the nature of the experience itself. A wholly different paradigm is therefore required to deal adequately with this problem to which we shall return in Chapter Twelve, when we take up the structure of one such possible paradigm. In the meantime, we have to regard the notion of "dividing" the core experience into "stages" as a matter of convenience for narrative purposes and not a strict experiental reality.

Finally, there is one more empirical point that results in a conceptual disagreement between Moody's prototypical account and our interpretation. Moody's description suggests that the near-death experiencer encounters both the "spirits" of loved ones and "the being of light":

> . . . soon other things begin to happen. Others come to meet and to help him. He glimpses the spirits of relatives and friends who have already died, and a loving warm spirit of a kind he has never encountered before—a being of light—appears before him.[7]

Our own evidence, however, indicates that this kind of conjunction between "ordinary spirits" and what I have called a "presence"[8] rarely, if ever, happens. Instead, the accounts of our respondents imply that this tends to be an either/or feature of the experience: Either one sees relatives *or* one encounters a presence, but not both. Furthermore, the qualifications from the last paragraph notwithstanding, the presence phenomenon appears to come "earlier" in the experience and to obviate the "functional need" for spirits. This last statement, however, requires some explanation.

Recall that when a presence is encountered or a voice heard, the respondent usually feels it is up to him to *choose* whether to return to life. And when this choice is offered or seems necessary, the man or woman, sometimes with reluctance, elects to live. This decision usually terminates his experience at that point. Spirits, on the other hand, are glimpsed and heard almost invariably by respondents who never felt the sense of a presence and who, therefore, experienced no urgency to choose. The spirits, however, usually tell the individual, in effect, that he *must* "go back," that "his time" hasn't come yet, thus effectively usurping the power of choice. It is almost as though the individual has "inadvertently" trespassed into a "region" which he is not yet qualified to enter and the spirits, rather like gatekeepers, must usher him out. However one may choose to interpret this phenomenally real event, spirits seem to perform, in these cases, a "fail-safe" function: If the presence doesn't manifest itself or if the individual doesn't himself choose to return to life, the spirits tend to appear to send him back. This "functional" interpretation implies that there should be no *need* for both a presence *and* spirits in a given instance, and that, of course, is consistent with our data. It is in this respect, then, that our understanding of the near-death experience is at variance with Moody's.

Having reviewed some minor points of difference—both empirical and conceptual—with Moody's findings, it would perhaps be well to conclude this section with a reminder of my opening observation: On the whole, Moody's depiction of the near-death experience seems to accord very well indeed with the composite account that I have constructed from the interviews with our own respondents.

The Incidence of the Core Experience

One of the questions to which the present study was addressed was concerned with the relative frequency of core experiences. Although Moody states in *Reflections on Life After Life* that he has talked to many near-death survivors who had no recall, he gives no approximate figures. Of course, since his interviewees are highly self-selected, even if Moody did provide statistical information of this kind it would be impossible to interpret for purposes of parametric estimation.

In the present study, which was plagued with sampling problems of its own, our core experience incidence level was 48% overall and 39% for all medical or hospital referrals. Since our data also suggest that core experience incidence may vary as a function of manner of near-death, our sample values themselves are obviously difficult to interpret. Even if they are reasonably representative of the "true" parameter value, a different study with a different "mix" of near-death survivors could easily arrive at a substantially different incidence level. In addition, since we used a specific criterion (based on the WCEI) for determining the presence and depth of a core experience, studies using different or unspecified criteria could also reach very different conclusions regarding the incidence rate. From our study alone, all that one can apparently conclude is that in a somewhat haphazard collection of near-death cases, the core experience is *not rare*.

Fortunately, however, the present study is not the only one on which to base these estimates. Concurrently with our study, Sabom and Kreutziger were independently conducting a very similar investigation, using a format not unlike our own. Sabom has since continued this investigation on his own and has kindly shared his preliminary findings with me. Before presenting them, it is necessary for me to report that, as a cardiologist, Sabom has interviewed mostly cardiac arrest patients (they constitute approximately 70% of his sample of 107 patients). Most of the remainder were illness-related, comatose patients. Twenty-nine were referred to him because they related an experience. The figures I shall report are based on what Sabom calls his "prospective" patients, namely, those who were "known only to have had an episode of unconsciousness and near-death prior to interview."

To insure comparability, Sabom analyzed his data using the WCEI and he also adopted the same criterion as I had used for assessing the presence of a core experience (that is, WCEI ⩾6). Arrived at in this way, the core experience incidence level for Sabom's seventy-eight prospective patients was 42%, a figure very close to our value of 39% for our fifty-nine hospital- or medically-referred interviewees.

Thus, two independent studies can be said to have found an incidence rate of about 40% for the core experience if one restricts oneself to what Sabom called "prospective patients." Both studies also found abundant cases in which the core experience occurred in others. The impressive agreement between these studies bolsters our confidence that this phenomenon may be fairly common in an unselected sample of near-death survivors. More systematic studies are obviously necessary to address the matter more definitively, but Sabom's work and our own combine to suggest that other investigators should have no difficulty in finding many experiencers among samples of near-death survivors on which to base these estimates.[9]

Hell and Judgment

There is one point of correspondence with Moody's data that requires some commentary: the *absence* of any hellish experiences. According to Moody's most recent publication,

> . . . it remains true that in the mass of material I have collected no one has ever described to me a state like the archetypal hell.[10]

His failure to obtain any such accounts was duplicated in the present investigation, as I have noted earlier. Although people sometimes reported feeling scared or confused near the beginning of their experience, none felt that they either were on their way to hell or that they had "fallen into" it. On the contrary, as I have repeatedly emphasized, both the affective tone and the visionary aspects of the near-death experience tend to be predominantly and highly positive. Even in suicide-related cases, no one described a mainly unpleasant or hellish experience.

What about other studies? Sabom has also reported a complete failure to obtain any cases suggestive of a hellish experience. In the cross-cultural work of Osis and Haraldsson, which dealt with deathbed visionary experiences in the United States and India, of 112 cases of "afterlife visions" only one was indicative of a "hell." Even here, however, the authors are inclined, on the basis of information they had about this person, to interpret this "vision" in psychodynamic terms. Consistent with our own data from respondents who reached stage V, Osis and Haraldsson found the afterlife vision to consist of stereotypic "heavenly" scenes of surpassing beauty. Other accounts, both scientific and anecdotal, of documented or purported near-death experiences suggest that hellish experiences are extremely rare.[11]

Nevertheless, as Moody himself remarks, "nothing [that he found] precludes the possibility of a hell" and the few cases that have been reported, even though they represent only a tiny fraction of all near-death experiences, cannot be dismissed entirely out of hand.

Indeed, recently a cardiologist, Dr. Maurice Rawlings, has contended that on the basis of his own examination of near-death cases, hellish experiences may be a good deal more common than previous research had indicated.[12] While he has found numerous examples of the classic positive near-death experience, he has also alleged that as many as *half* the cases he has uncovered have had hellish elements.[13] Since his claims are dramatically different from our own findings as well as from those of a number of other investigators, his work deserves a careful assessment.

Rawlings argues that his discovery of many "hellish" cases derives from the minimal time gap between the near-death episode itself and the gathering of information about it. As a cardiologist whose specialty is resuscitation, Rawlings is often able to be present at the scene of a near-death episode so that he is in a position to *observe* as well as to interview the patient immediately afterward. He states that at least one of his patients exclaimed at the time of a series of cardiac arrests that "he was in hell," but that afterward he had *no memory* of this experience! Instead, the patient related only positive elements of his experience, such as being out of his body and encountering deceased relatives in "a gorge full of beautiful colors." This apparently selective recall suggested to Rawlings that perhaps *many* persons might *repress* hellish aspects of near-death experiences. If so, this would help to explain the discrepancy between his findings and those of others. Since most researchers (including myself) tend to interview near-death survivors some time after their episode, the processes of repression and selective recall would already have operated to bias favorably the respondent's account.

Rawlings's thesis, though plausible, suffers, however, from a number of weaknesses, both conceptual and methodological.

In the first place, legitimate questions can be raised concerning the data base on which Rawlings's argument is built. From his account, it is far from clear just how many people he himself has actually interviewed who have had hellish near-death experiences. Like Moody, Rawlings presents no statistics and relies on selected case histories he has assembled from a variety of sources.[14] He is also vague about just how many cases his conclusions actually rest on. In my judgment, his evidence by itself is too amorphous to evaluate.

A second factor may be more worrisome. A reading of Rawlings's book shows that it is not really an objective survey of near-death experiences but is essentially a proselytizing Christian tract. Rawlings himself, through his study of near-death experiences, has become a "born again" Christian, and his book is unabashedly written from that point of view. His interest is, in part, to convince the reader that near-death experiences provide empirical support for a Christian conception of both heaven *and* hell and that to experience the former and avoid the latter it is necessary to follow Jesus. This is obviously an issue that is outside the scope of science, but Rawlings does not even pretend he is writing a scientific book. Indeed, he has told me that he can no longer "be impartial."[15] However that may be, Rawlings's evangelizing use of his near-death material plainly is a potential source of bias that must be borne in mind when assessing his work.

Third, there is no direct evidence to support Rawlings's "repression" theory. Rawlings claims that the reason hellish near-death experiences have been so rarely reported is that the usual interview-incident interval is long enough to allow repression to occur. "If," he says, "patients could be *immediately* interviewed, I believe researchers would find bad experiences to be as frequent as good ones."[16] There are several reasons, however, to question the validity of this.

One fact that tends to undermine Rawlings's claim is that both Moody[17] and Sabom[18] have told me that they *have* occasionally interviewed patients directly after a cardiac arrest (Sabom, like Rawlings, is himself a cardiologist), but have never been told of a hellish experience. A second fact that tends to cast doubt on Rawlings's claim is the experience of persons who take powerful psychedelics, such as mescaline or LSD.[19] Experiences triggered by these psychedelic agents sometimes include extremely frightening hellish visions, but such scenes are usually recalled vividly afterward rather than being repressed. Since there appear to be some notable similarities between near-death experiences and some LSD induced states,[20] the lack of immediate repression of frightening features of such "drug trips" would not seem to be in accord with Rawlings's hypothesis. A third point relates to Rawlings's implicit assumption that if repression does occur, it would tend to cause "selective forgetting" of negative aspects of one's near-death experience. That this is not necessarily the case was shown by some of my own data. In at least two instances of which I am aware, patients were reported by witnesses to have apparently glimpsed beautiful visions at the time of their near-death episodes (as evinced by these patients' remarks and gestures), yet they had no recall of such visions when interviewed later. Thus, no "repression" in the traditional Freudian sense seems to have operated here. Such evidence, scanty as it is, inclines me to believe that unreported near-death experiences are not necessarily likely to be unpleasant, as Rawlings implies.

Finally, though it is true that some near-death survivors state that various aspects of their experience were frightening, such features appear to have been, in the main, *hallucinatory visions*, which were *qualitatively discriminable* from the core experience itself. For example, one woman *(20)* recounted a disturbing "dream" about Mephistopheles in which various orgiastic rites took place. She said she "dreamed that Mephistopheles had somehow taken me captive and was trying to scare the hell out of me." Yet this same woman denied emphatically that this "dream" was anything like her death experience: "That [the latter] was very different; really, no comparison. No comparison at all. . . . The [other] was part of an hallucination or dream or whatever one goes through when they are regaining consciousness." Thus, it may be that at least some of Rawlings's cases involve experiences that are, in fact, different in *quality* as well as content from the core experience itself.

In view of all the questions one can raise about Rawlings's data and his interpretations of them, I believe that a fair judgment of his thesis at this stage of our knowledge of near-death phenomena is: *not proven.*

Notice that I did not say *false,* because I am very far from believing that hellish near-death experiences *never* or *cannot* occur. In my opinion, the weight of *all* the evidence suggests that they do, in fact, take place, but probably far more rarely than Rawlings alleges. In short, though I believe the value of Rawlings's work is seriously vitiated by the deficiencies I have listed, I do not think it is legitimate to dismiss all his case history material. Indeed, I am myself persuaded there is something to Rawlings's contention, even though I am equally convinced that he has probably exaggerated its magnitude.

If we admit that hellish near-death experiences may occur, even if they are not frequent, we obviously need to account for such a possibility in our theoretical interpretation of near-death phenomena. Accordingly, I will shortly propose a theoretical formulation that can both subsume hellish experiences (as well as the core experience) and explain their relatively infrequent incidence. At this point, however, our interest is primarily comparative rather than interpretative, and on that basis all we need say here is that hellish near-death experiences appear very rarely in the literature and, in that connection, our investigation is consistent with the bulk of other findings.

We turn now to a related issue: Is there a sense of judgment when one undergoes a near-death episode?

The testimony most relevant to this question comes from those who underwent what I called a "decisional crisis," particularly those who reported a panoramic life review in conjunction with that phase of their core experience. It was their common testimony that, if a judgment was passed, it was one *they* made of *themselves*. Even when someone was aware of a presence or voice and interpreted it as a "being" external to himself, there was no sense of being judged by it. Instead, love, comfort, and acceptance tended to be felt; *that* was the emotional context in which a self-assessment was often made.

Even when no external presence was felt, there was still no sense of judgment other than self-judgment. The following comments from a suicide attempter were typical:

> The only thing I felt *judged* by would be *myself*. Like in the very beginning, when I thought about these things, all these terrible things, then I thought about the good things, then it felt like I'd just run through my life and I'd think of all the stupid things . . . all the mistakes I've made. I think the judging was mainly myself judging myself. *(99)*

Clearly, the drift of our findings here are perfectly congruent with those originally reported by Moody and with the implications he later ascribed to them. A sense of (external) judgment is not a typical feature of the core experience, but a self-assessment is frequently made when one comes close to death.

Antecedents of the Death Experience

Since very little other research has been addressed to this issue, we shall be limited here to a sketchy comparison of our findings with those reported by other investigators. Where appropriate, provisional interpretations of our own data will be offered so that future research may be directed to them.

The underlying question here, of course, was whether or not the near-death experience is uniform over different modes of nearly dying. The answer to this question—within the very considerable methodological and empirical limits of this investigation—was what might be described as a whispered, hesitant, and provisional endorsement of the invariance hypothesis. As will be recalled, it appeared that the *form* of the experience was constant, though its *frequency* varied according to mode of near-death onset. It hardly needs saying that a larger scale and more rigorously conducted investigation is necessary to establish this tentative generalization.

The limits of the invariance hypothesis were, however, severely strained by three findings in particular, which now need to be discussed: (1) the disproportionate occurrence of the life-review phenomenon in conjunction with accidental near-deaths; (2) the aborted core experience in conjunction with suicide attempts; and (3) the gender-related interaction in incidence and depth of the death experience.

The Life Review in Accidental Near-Deaths

Although the life-review phenomenon occurred for about a quarter of our experiencers, I earlier noted that it was statistically more common in accident victims (where it was found in over half the cases) than among people in other categories. This was not a strong difference, on the basis of the raw figures involved, but, in light of other research, it is a suggestive one and needs to be lingered over for a moment.

Albert Heim, a nineteenth-century Swiss geology professor and inveterate mountain climber, who himself several times experienced near-fatal falls, was apparently the first person to interview many who had come close to death through accidents of various kinds, including warfare. He was particularly interested in accidental falls, however, and in a translation of his work provided by Noyes and Kletti, Heim states that "in many [such] cases, there followed a review of the individual's entire past."[21]

Following up on Heim's initial findings, Noyes and Kletti obtained information from 205 respondents concerning 215 life-threatening incidents. They found that, overall, 29% of their sample reported the panoramic life-review phenomenon. Although, ironically, this effect occurred in only 9% of their sample who nearly died from falling (thus apparently disagreeing with Heim's findings), the percentage of positive instances was quite high in conjunction with both near-drownings (43%) and auto accidents (33%). From the breakdown given by Noyes and Kletti, however, it is unfortunately impossible to determine whether the panoramic life-review phenomenon was, in fact, *more* common in these latter two modes of accidental near-death than in illness-related episodes, but it appears that this could possibly have been the case.

The form of these experiences, incidentally, appears to be identical with those described in this book, including an intimation of a flash-forward, as well as flashback effect.

Obviously, neither Heim's original investigation nor Noyes and Kletti's more recent study does more than hint at the possibility, suggested by our own findings, that accidental near-deaths may be more likely to generate a panoramic life review. If further research does not uphold this relationship, of course, there is "nothing special" that needs to be accounted for—in the sense that no one condition of near-death onset is differentially associated with this phenomenon.[22]

Suppose, however, that accidental near-deaths are more likely to stimulate a life review. Why should this be so?

My own hunch is that one determinant of this effect would be the *suddenness* or *unexpectedness* of the near-death crisis. Many illnesses, obviously, have a long period of onset before bringing the individual to the threshold of death. Suicide attempts are also usually premeditated, at least to a degree. Accidents, however, by definition, are those events that catch the individual unprepared. Such a condition, when the prospect of death suddenly flashes like a lightning bolt of inevitability, might well unleash the life-review effect as a means of *condensing* one's experience into the shortest possible time frame. Subjective time may lengthen tremendously but clock time is, apparently, preciously short. If a core experience is to occur, events need to be compressed in the most drastic way and the life review does exactly that. Just *how* it does it is a question we shall take up later.

This line of thinking implies that it is not the accidental nature of the near-death incident itself that is crucial, but the *suddenness* and *unexpectedness* of the event. It follows, therefore, that in illnesses that occur without warning (for example, a cardiac arrest) or in cases of impulsive suicide attempts, one would expect to find a fairly high incidence of the life review. Obviously, such an interpretation need not remain speculative; it can easily be tested by well-designed research.

Finally, it should be added that this hypothesis specifies only one possible determinant of the life-review phenomenon. Doubtless, there are other factors that may play a part in facilitating it. Noyes and Kletti themselves consider still other possibilities, but we shall not detail them here.

The Suicide-Related Near-Death Experience

We have already considered at great length the complex and ultimately inconclusive data on the experiences of failed suicides. The basic finding here, which suggests a possible departure from the invariance hypothesis, has to do with the fact that suicide attempters seem not to progress beyond stage III. Thus, their death experiences appear to be aborted or truncated, compared to other categories of near-death survivors. In addition, the testimony of several experiencers converges on the belief that successful suicides would *not* experience positive transcendental states. A review of all this evidence left us in doubt whether the suicide-related experience represented a true deviation from the modal death experience.

Other data bearing on this question have been hard to obtain, but the work of a San Francisco psychiatrist, David Rosen, is directly relevant here. He was able to interview six of the eight survivors of suicide leaps from the Golden Gate Bridge and one of the two people who survived a jump from the Oakland–San Francisco Bay Bridge. What Rosen found, in brief, proves quite instructive. A number of these suicide attempters did indeed report elements consistent with the core experience and also were found to show aftereffects similar to those characteristic of our experiencers. Interestingly, one phenomenon they did *not* report was the life review, a finding in keeping with our own hypothesis.

Although Rosen's sample is highly selective and very small, his findings imply support for the invariance hypothesis. Recall that the clearest suicide-related cases consistent with the death experience from the present study were those (few) that did not entail the use of drugs or drugs and alcohol. Rosen's data, coupled with our own, suggest that *drug-free* suicide attempters may well have deep core experiences— certainly in comparison to those who attempt to kill themselves by overdoses of one sort or another. *This conclusion, however, is by no means established* and further research along these lines is urgently needed if the invariance hypothesis is to be established. Such cases are also particularly germane to Rawlings's thesis. Indeed, in my opinion, of all the unanswered questions concerning near-death phenomena, the experience of failed suicides still seems to be the most pressing, on both practical and theoretical grounds.[23]

The Gender-Related Interaction

The last threat to the invariance hypothesis is comprised by the unexpected finding that women are disproportionately likely to have a near-death experience in connection with illness, where men tend to have theirs as a result of accident or suicide attempt. As will be recalled, this difference was a statistically strong one.

No other investigation, to my knowledge, has systematically examined this set of variables in relation to the core experience, and no explanation was readily available from an analysis of our own data. Furthermore, I confess that I cannot think of any explanation that intuitively strikes me as plausible.

Accordingly, though it is probably unbecoming to do so—since it is obviously an easy out—I prefer to abandon the search for an explanation for this relationship until it is replicated in further research. My own inclination is to regard it as a kind of sampling error, (that is, an alpha error) in the absence of any cogent interpretation for this unanticipated effect. This is an unsatisfactory state of affairs, to be sure, but I am prepared to put up with it until I have reason to change my mind.

To conclude this section, it seems fair to say that although much more research needs to be done on the invariance hypothesis, the evidence from our own investigation as well as that from other work leads decisively to the affirmation that the core experience is a highly *robust* phenomenon. That is, across a variety of conditions, it tends to manifest itself in very much the same form. I have not, of course, demonstrated that the experience is itself *strictly* invariant across different ways of near-death onset, but I believe that its basic similarities have proved much more evident than its differences. In sum, it appears that the experience of dying is *essentially* the same, regardless of how that experience is brought about.

Correlates of the Core Experience

Of the various possible correlates of the death experience, the one of greatest potential theoretical significance is religiousness. In the introduction I stated that one of my concerns in undertaking this investigation was to determine the role of an individual's religious belief system in shaping his near-death experience. If religiousness was highly correlated with the likelihood or depth of the near-death experience, that would suggest that the "religious ambiance" of that experience might have its roots in the individual's religious belief system. The crisis of apparent imminent death, then, would merely serve to trigger a visual projection of images consistent with an individual's expectations about the afterlife.

This possible interpretation of the core experience, however, found no empirical support whatever from our data. As will be recalled, neither the likelihood nor the depth of the core experience was related to various measures of individual religiousness. That is to say, religious people were no more likely to report phenomena indicative of the core experience than were the nonreligious. What about the findings of other researchers on this issue?

In the investigation most similar to our own—Sabom's—the findings were virtually identical. Among the seventy-eight prospective patients, those reporting a core experience had a mean religiousness index of 2.1; this index for those not reporting a core experience was 2.4. The difference was not significant. Although Sabom's index was based primarily on frequency of church attendance rather than inward feelings of religiousness, his findings are obviously consistent with ours in suggesting that religiousness per se is not a determinant of the death experience.

Sabom's work, however, is not the only evidence leading to this conclusion. Osis and Haraldsson's cross-cultural study of deathbed visions also affords data consistent with the small role of religiousness and religious beliefs in shaping the core experience:

> Belief [in life after death] did not significanly change the frequency of experiences of beauty and peace and the frequency of images of another world. Apparently, the belief in life after death changes very little of the afterlife images themselves, but rules the religious emotions and sharply increases positive valuation of death.
>
> Patients' personal involvement in religion did not affect the subject matter of visions at all. Deeply involved patients saw gardens, gates, and heaven no more often than those of lesser or no involvement. Experiences of great beauty and peace were also independent of the degree of patients' involvement in religion.[24]

In short, religiousness as such does not appear to affect either the likelihood or content of the core experience; but, as Osis and Haraldsson suggest, it probably does play a role in shaping the *interpretation* the individual gives to that experience. This accords with my own view, based on our own interview data, that an individual's religious belief

Life at Death

system is more likely to serve a filtering function *after,* rather than before, the near-death experience. For many persons, the experience *is* a religious experience, but its *content* appears to be independent of one's prior religiousness.

As was the case with religiousness itself, so also were various standard demographic factors unrelated to the incidence or depth of the core experience. Sabom has also reported that the same demographic factors we assessed were completely unrelated to near-death experiences in his own investigation. Much the same picture, by and large, is drawn by Osis and Haraldsson, with the provision that their study is demographically much more complex because of its cross-cultural character. Even Heim stated that his findings were independent of the educational level of his respondents.

No one to my knowledge has yet published an investigation charting the *personal* correlates of near-death experiences, so that we cannot as yet say whether these experiences are systematically related to any individual difference variables, such as level of ego strength or repressive or denial tendencies.

This is not to say, of course, that such relationships will not one day be uncovered, but thus far the seeming independence of the core experience of situational demographic factors as well as individual religious belief systems again suggests its robustness. Still, we do know that not everyone who comes close to death reports a core experience, and the question therefore lingers: Why do some people have the experience and others not?

I once put this question to Raymond Moody, who has perhaps interviewed more near-death survivors than anyone else, with the exception of Kübler-Ross. I distinctly remember his pithy answer: "Ken, I haven't got a clue!"[25]

It remains to be seen whether further research will offer any.

There was, in fact, only one factor found in this investigation that did seem to relate, albeit in a puzzling way, to the core experience: People who had already been familiar with the findings of near-death research at the time of their crisis were *less* likely to report an experience. This was a strong effect statistically (p $<.02$) with nearly twice as many nonexperiencers having heard of Moody-type experiences as experiencers (37% versus 19%). These data clearly show that prior knowledge of this kind of experience was not a contaminant in this study, but what is curious, of course, is why there should be a difference in the *opposite* direction from the one that had been methodologically feared. That is, why should people knowledgeable about the Moody-type experience be less likely to have one?

One might be tempted to regard this as a "fluke" difference except for one additional fact that has recently come to light: Sabom has found the same paradoxical effect in his research. In his case, this difference was also highly significant (p <.01). That two independent investigations should furnish evidence for the same apparent "knowledge-inhibiting" effect is certainly striking, though how it is to be interpreted remains a mystery. If this finding is to be taken seriously, it is almost as though vicarious knowledge of this phenomenon is functionally equivalent to the direct experience itself. Such a conclusion, of course, seems extremely far-fetched, but the matter must remain tantalizingly unresolved until further research offers some clarity.

Aftereffects of the Near-Death Experience

Most of the research that has dealt anecdotally with near-death experiences has suggested that their aftereffects are profoundly transforming, particularly in regard to the loss of the fear of death. In the present investigation, both through the interview transcripts and through our statistical findings, abundant evidence has been offered to support the contention that surviving a near-death episode does indeed lead to profound personal changes for many. It is, furthermore, one of the specific contributions of this investigation to disclose which of these changes are apparently dependent on the core experience itself and which are a function of a near-death episode. In this section, we shall be largely concerned with the former category, though since these changes are all of a piece, the entire cluster reported by experiencers must be considered.

Why does the experiencer show the particular *pattern* of changes that we have earlier reviewed? First of all, it is necessary to remember that these changes are mediated by the individual's *interpretation* of his experience and that for him the experience is, above all, *real*. Second, it is for many an experience with definite spiritual or religious overtones. Third, the experience is usually interpreted to mean that there is a life after death *and* that it is a joyous, pain-free life. Fourth, one has apparently been given "a second chance" to live. Fifth, all these impressions have been transmitted in a way so as to make them extremely vivid, compelling, and subjectively authentic. Is it really surprising then, that experiencers resume life by living it more fully, loving more openly, and fearing death less, if at all? Is it surprising that their life seems more grounded in a sense of purpose and is more consciously shaped by the spiritual values of love, compassion, and acceptance? If the implications of the core experience are regarded as *true* by those who have undergone the experience itself, then one would expect, I think, precisely these kind of changes.

A person who has survived a death experience has been, to a variable degree, "spiritualized" and his postincident life is a continuing testimony to the profundity of the event that has marked him. Although it is true that not all the changes last and that many other factors have contributed to them, nevertheless, what is impressive is the power of the core experience to compel positive change. Its effect seems to be to reorganize the person's life around a new "center," which affords direction, purpose, and energy. Indeed, this effect has been described to me by one respondent as akin to "receiving a seed." And so, the experience must not be regarded as merely a "beautiful but frozen memory," but rather it is, for many, a continuing, active force that seeks to manifest itself in life-affirming ways. In this sense, it may certainly be likened to a religious conversion and, I think, most—but not all—our experiencers would not take exception to that expression as long as it was not defined too narrowly.

If we now turn to the question of how well some of the specific changes reported by our experiencers have been corroborated by other researchers, we can, once again, profitably examine Sabom's investigation point by point for each of the three major changes associated with the death experience: (1) increase in conviction of belief in life after death; (2) loss of fear of death; and (3) increase in religiousness.

Increase in conviction of belief in life after death. Our finding was that experiencers showed a dramatic postincident increase in this belief, where nonexperiencers showed virtually none ($p < .001$). Sabom's (1978a) results were identical ($p < .001$).

Loss of fear of death. Our findings, despite some methodological ambiguities, strongly suggested a marked decrease for experiencers, where nonexperiencers tended to show no systematic change ($p < .0005$). Again, Sabom's findings revealed the same effect ($p < .001$) and, in his case, were methodologically clean. In addition, he has gone on to show[26] that this effect persists for up to two years after the respondent's near-death crisis (this was the time limit for his follow-up measure).

Increase in religiousness. Our study demonstrated that experiencers tend to increase in religiousness ($p < .05$ to $p < .005$ for different measures). Sabom summarizes his findings here as follows: "Because of the near-death experience, many patients expressed a new or renewed fervor in religious activity, which was not observed in non-experiencers."[27] Again, the responses of our two samples of experiencers seem similar.

Perhaps this is the place to call attention to the remarkable overall similarity between Sabom's findings and our own. Not only in this section but throughout this discussion the various parallels between our independently conceived and executed studies will have been evident to the attentive reader. Whether in regard to the death experience itself, its correlates, or its aftereffects, it is as though we are referring to a *common* sample. This set of similarities is all the more remarkable when one takes into account that we each began our research with opposite biases[28] yet found the same thing. Again, the *robustness* and reliability of the core experience is underlined by these comments.

Altogether, the material from my own investigation and the corroborative evidence from Sabom's work dealing with the aftereffects of the core experience combine to produce a fairly clear image of this aspect of near-death phenomena. Neither the changes themselves nor their underlying dynamics are particularly puzzling or problematical. They are, to be sure, dramatic and striking in many cases, but they represent, on the whole, one of the few features of near-death experiences that do not confound our attempts to understand them.

We come now to the task that we have so long postponed: How to interpret the core experience itself. This is obviously the *key* question on whose answer the final assessment of this extraordinary phenomenon may hinge. The underlying question, of course, has really been with us from the start: Does the core experience have more than a *subjective* validity? And whatever the answer to this question may be, how, if at all, can we *explain* this singular experience?

ELEVEN

Some Possible Interpretations of the Near-Death Experience

The interpretative issue now rises before us like an indomitable peak and the question becomes: Will the near-death experience yield its secrets to a scientific explanation? Up to this point, the near-death experience has been surrounded by mystery and tinged with numinous qualities, but need it remain so? We need to know whether the theories of science can provide us with a satisfactory interpretation of the phenomena of dying. If they can, and the near-death experience is susceptible to a naturalistic explanation, we will have to view this extraordinary patterning of events as little more than the result of understandable psychological or neurological mechanisms set off by the apparent onset of death. To be sure, even if this proves the case, the *aftereffects* will remain authentic—the near-death survivor's behavior and attitude changes *are* real, whatever the ultimate explanation of the experience itself may be. On the other hand, if scientific explanations are not convincing, we may find ourselves driven to one of two alternatives: (1) to enlarge our concepts of science so as to subsume this phenomenon or (2) to employ another framework in an attempt to understand what the near-death experience represents.

In either event, the *meaning* of the core experience is critically dependent on the interpretation we are justified in giving it.

Obviously, there are a number of *categories* of explanations that are potentially relevant here. Psychological, pharmacological, physiological, parapsychological, and religious interpretations have all been suggested as possibilities. And these perspectives are not necessarily mutually exclusive. For example, a psychological explanation may actually be dependent on a specific physiological condition, say, cerebral anoxia (or insufficient oxygen to the brain). These explanations would, then, reflect different but compatible explanatory *levels*. Another complication is that not all these potential explanations are susceptible to disproof. Some parapsychological and, presumably, all religious explanations cannot be evaluated by scientific methods. That being so, my approach will be to give preference to verifiable scientific explanations in this discussion. Only if *all* such explanations seem inadequate are we justified, I believe, in entertaining interpretative possibilities presently outside the scope of science.

Let us begin, therefore, with several explanations that seek to understand the core experience as a reflection of psychological conditions assumed to be present at the point of (apparent) death.

Psychological Explanations

Depersonalization

Noyes and Kletti have been prominent (but not alone) in advancing a "depersonalization" interpretation to explain reactions to the perception of impending death. Studying mostly accidental near-deaths, they have proposed that the prospect of death initiates a defensive psychological reaction, which serves to allow a person to cope with highly stressful, life-threatening situations. From this perspective, the phenomena associated with the prospect of impending death, such as a sense of peace and well-being, feelings of bodily detachment, a panoramic life review, and mystical transcendence are all to be understood as ego-defensive maneuvers to insulate the individual from the harsh realities of imminent annihilation by providing a cocoon of compensatory fantasies and feelings. In other words, the perception of death results not in physical ejection from one's body, but in *psychological detachment* from one's (apparent) fate. In this respect, their interpretation is obviously patterned after Freud.[1] However, aspects of the experience (for example, the panoramic life review, to the understanding of which Noyes and Kletti have made a significant contribution), are given a neurological underpinning *as well as* a psychodynamic rendering.

Despite its surface plausibility, there are several difficulties with Noyes and Kletti's position that argue for its rejection.

First of all, the classic description of depersonalization they quote differs, as the authors themselves admit, in many ways from the psychological state of near-death survivors. In order to force the near-death experience into the procrustean bed of depersonalization, they have to make numerous ad hoc assumptions for which there is little support. Both Osis and Haraldsson and Sabom have for these, and other reasons, found Noyes and Kletti's thesis either unconvincing or irrelevant.

Second, the depersonalization interpretation is completely unable to handle one rare, but extremely significant, aspect of near-death experiences: the perception of a deceased relative whom the dying person does not know is dead. Several such cases were reported and documented by early psychical researchers[2] and, more recently, Kübler-Ross has mentioned further episodes of this kind.[3] After my own investigation was completed, I heard of such a case myself. A woman respondent informed me that her father, as he lay dying, saw a vision of two of his brothers, one of whom had been dead for years while the other had died only two days previously—a fact unknown to her dying father. The father, however, decided to "return" when he heard his (living) wife call to him and only afterward learned of his brother's recent demise. If near-death experiences are merely elaborate denial reactions, it is hard to see how they could provide the basis for such extraordinary accurate perceptions.

Finally, Noyes and Kletti fail to consider that where stress may indeed trigger a defensive reaction to begin with, the transcendental realities that appear to an individual confronted with death may represent a higher dimension of consciousness and not just a symbolic fantasy rooted in denial. In this respect, Noyes and Kletti seem to fall prey to the well-known tendency of orthodox psychoanalysis toward facile reductionism. In this respect, it might be more important to listen carefully to the testimony of near-death survivors than to follow the predilections of Freud.

For these reasons, the psychoanalytic attempt to explain away near-death experiences as depersonalization seems both forced and inadequate.

Wishful Thinking

A milder version of the depersonalization thesis is the assumption, considered (and rejected) by Moody that near-death experiences are a product of wishful thinking. Since near-death experiences tend to be not merely positive but exceedingly pleasant, it might seem that they would derive from the desire to turn the finality of death into a death-defying "peaceful journey."

Again, this position does not seem to stand up to scrutiny—and for some of the same reasons I rejected the depersonalization view. For example, it, too, would be unable to explain instances where a deceased relative whose death was not known to the near-death survivor was seen.

Moreover, as Kübler-Ross has pointed out, this view would imply that small children who are dying would ordinarily fantasize their parents—the human beings who would be most significant to ones so young.[4] Yet, she reports, they *never* do—unless one or both are dead. Instead, they appear to see *other* relatives or religious figures.

The wishful-thinking hypothesis also has difficulty in dealing with cases where a near-death survivor encounters a relative whom she never knew in life, such as (7), reported in this study. Such a perception could hardly be ascribed to wish fulfillment.

Still other factors are incompatible with the wishful-thinking hypothesis. For one, the *consistent patterning* of the core experience across different people is itself evidence against the hypothesis. Presumably, people *differ* in their wishes in regard to a hoped-for afterlife, yet the sequence of experiences they go through on coming close to death is remarkably alike. It is also noteworthy that the experiences of non-believers and suicide attempters also tend, on the whole, to conform to the general patterning of the core experience—yet one would imagine they would wish for the cessation of consciousness.

In sum, the wishful-thinking explanation appears to be . . . wishful thinking!

Psychological Expectations

If the wish isn't father to near-death visions, perhaps it is the thought—in the form of expectations of one's imminent death or of an afterlife.

Expectational determinants, however, seem not to bear any systematic relationship to near-death experiences.

Osis and Haraldsson for example, found that a number of people who expected to live—and were given excellent prognoses by their physicians—nevertheless had powerful near-death visions after which they died.

In regard to expectations of the afterlife based on religious teachings, Moody observed in his original study that ". . . many people have stressed how unlike their experiences were to what they had been led to expect in the course of their religious training."[5] No one, he said, referred to conventional images of heaven or hell in relating their experiences; indeed, no one in his sample (or mine) described anything like an archetypal hell, even though one may suppose that at least a few of our respondents might have feared "going there" when they died.

It should also be noted that since Sabom and I both found that core experiences are independent of religiousness, it can hardly be contended that religious-based expectations shape near-death experiences (although they do influence individual interpretations given them). Thus, religious-minded men and women are no more likely to have core experiences than are the religiously indifferent.

Finally, if expectations tended to structure near-death experiences, one would suppose that those already familiar with Moody-type experiences at the time of their own near-death episodes would be more likely to report such experiences. Instead, as the reader will recall, the *reverse* was true: Uninformed respondents described proportionately more core experiences.

We can conclude, therefore, that psychological expectations also fail to provide an explanatory foundation for near-death experiences.

Dreams or Hallucinations

We have previously considered whether near-death experiences have the quality of either dreams or hallucinations, and concluded that they do not. Instead, according to the testimony of survivors, these experiences were perceived as "real." This characteristic has been noted by other researchers as well,[6] and Moody himself is also very definite on the matter:

> [my informants] report what they underwent as they came near death, not as dreams, but as events which happened to them. They almost invariably assure me in the course of their narratives that their experiences were not dreams, but rather were definitely, emphatically real.[7]

In addition, both Sabom and I have found that our respondents who reported both hallucinations and a core experience could clearly distinguish between them.

Although our data here are limited to self-reports, the testimony is extremely consistent: Core experiences do not seem like a dream or an hallucination—either at the time of their occurrence or afterward.

Thus, the effort to explain (away) the core experience by reference to such psychological concepts as depersonalization, wishful thinking, prior expectations, dreams, and hallucinations has proved unsuccessful. The explanation will have to be sought elsewhere.

Pharmacological Explanations

Anesthetics

Moody has noted that occasionally the use of anesthetics is associated with phenomena that bear some similarity to the core experience. Can anesthetics alone, then, trigger the core experience, independent of the near-death state? Theoretically, this could occur if the administration of anesthetics brought about an elevation of carbon dioxide, a condition known to be capable of triggering visionary experiences.

First, though anesthetics vary, properly administered they have no specific effect on carbon dioxide levels.[8] Furthermore, in cases of cardiac arrests during surgery, the anesthetic is shut off and the patient is given oxygen instead.

Second, there is some evidence that anesthetics may actually interfere with the occurrence of near-death experiences. For example, Moody relates a case of a woman who "died" twice. The first time she did not have an experience, the lack of which *she* attributed to her anesthetized state. In the second instance, where no drugs were involved, Moody reports that she had a complex experience. This observation is also consistent with Miller's findings that the typical anesthetized patient has no recall of any kind afterward.[9]

Third, where—in an atypical case—some experience *is* described, Moody contends that the experience usually deviates in obvious ways from the core experience pattern.[10]

Finally—and most telling—not only in my study, but also in Moody's and in Sabom's, some of our respondents who described core experiences were never given any anesthetics whatever and, in some cases, did not even receive any medical treatment. Obviously, if the effect is sometimes observed in the absence of the putative cause (that is, anesthetics), that cause is not a sufficient one.

Therefore, we conclude that although anesthetics may not preclude phenomena associated with near-death experiences, such experiences cannot be explained by them.

Other Drugs

If anesthetics are not responsible for inducing the core experience, what about other drugs?

From what has already been noted, it is clear that in many instances no drugs of *any* kind were either used by or given to respondents who related core experiences. Indeed, there are a number of reasons to think that many drugs might actually interfere with, rather than facilitate, the occurrence or the recall of a core experience.

First, both Moody and Sabom have pointed out that the effects associated with drug usage in medical settings are *variable*, where the core experience itself, as we know, tends to adhere to a common format. For example, Sabom cites an instance where a core experiencer could clearly distinguish his near-death episode from a delusional hallucination stemming from the use of a medical narcotic. In this case, the near-death experience was described as "being clearer, not distorted, more 'real', and associated with a calm and peace not previously encountered." [11]

Second, in the present study, we have already noted that suicide attempters represented the category of respondents with the highest incidence of nonrecall (67%). This fact is relevant here because all but two of our suicide attempters used drugs or a combination of drugs and alcohol in an attempt to kill themselves. These drugs obviously did nothing to facilitate recall and probably induced instead a state of retrograde amnesia. Indeed, the few suicide-related cases where the deepest experiences were found tended to be those in which no drugs were used.

Finally, Osis and Haraldsson went to considerable trouble to determine the relationship between various medical factors and aspects of the near-death experience. Although their cross-cultural research was focused on mood changes and visionary (stage V) experiences occurring at the point of death, their findings are completely consistent with the thrust of this section: Drug-related conditions were associated with an *impairment* of the near-death experience. In fact, they found that fully 80% of both terminally ill and recovered patients had a visionary experience that definitely could *not* be ascribed to medication; most of these were under no medication whatever at the time of their episode. I will elaborate on these important findings later. For now, however, it will suffice to reiterate: Pharmacological factors cannot serve to explain the core experience. [12] Indeed, the evidence suggests that drug usage tends to be negatively associated with the experience. [13]

Physiological and Neurological Explanations

Since as one nears death a state of physiological deterioration sets in, revealing in itself such conditions as blood pressure decreases and interference with or stoppage of cardiac and respiratory functions, it is reasonable to suppose that the depleted physiological state of the individual may in some specific way trigger the core experience. Although there are a variety of theoretical mechanisms and biochemical changes that might be suspected of being involved here, the two that have so far been considered most seriously are temporal lobe seizurelike firing patterns and cerebral anoxia.

Temporal Lobe Involvement

Noyes and Kletti have proposed that some aspects of the core experience (for example, the panoramic life review) might be traceable to seizurelike neural firing patterns in the temporal lobe. Moody and Sabom have also considered this kind of mechanism, however, and both have found it inadequate to explain the *entire range* of near-death phenomena. Although some similarities exist between experiences induced by temporal lobe stimulation or associated with temporal lobe seizures on the one hand, and the core experience on the other, many *differences* between the two are also apparent, as Sabom clearly points out. The evidence at the present time, then, seems clearly to rule out neurological interpretations linking the core experience with abnormal temporal lobe patterns.

Cerebral Anoxia

The most common physiological speculation offered for the core experience suggests that it can be understood as resulting from insufficient oxygen to the brain (or, correlatively, the buildup of carbon dioxide). Since heart rate decreases and respiratory failures would tend to bring about precisely these effects, it is obvious that, at first glance, this is a plausible mechanism.

It is true that the overwhelming majority of our core experiencers were, so far as we know, unconscious or comatose at the time of their experience, though it seems extremely doubtful that *all* these people would, on that account alone, have experienced significant hypoxia. In Moody's investigations, it was possible for him to be even more definitive on this point. He explicitly rejects this interpretation because "... all of the phenomena [of the core experience] ... have been experienced in the course of near-death encounters in which this cutoff of blood flow to the brain never took place"[14] Again, we have a state of affairs where a postulated cause is sometimes absent from instances where the effect has been observed.

Doubt on the cerebral anoxia hypothesis is also cast by Osis and Haraldsson. They were able to demonstrate that visionary aspects of the core experience were often found in nonhallucinating, *conscious* patients whose experience occurred well before the final slide into the coma which typically precedes death. In fact, they state that "the majority of the patients who had these visionary experiences were in a normal, waking state of consciousness."[15] Such data are obviously difficult to interpret from the standpoint of cerebral anoxia.

In addition to empirical evidence that tends to undermine the cerebral anoxia interpretation, there is another argument that can be raised against it. Suppose, for a moment, that anoxia *was* the trigger to the core experience. One would still have to explain just how that condition could bring about all the *specific effects* reported by core experiencers which comprise the experience. And how would the cerebral anoxia theory explain the knowledge that core experiencers sometimes have of the status of a loved one whose death has not been disclosed to them? Examined in this light, the trouble with the anoxia theory is that it tends to be embraced too glibly and leaves most of the *specific* effects of the core experience still unaccounted for.

That at least is the case when this interpretation is used in an effort to explain away the core experience as a physiological by-product. There is, however, another, more subtle version of this theory, which does not involve using it in a *reductionistic* way, and before concluding this section it will be worth considering it.

Grof and Halifax, in drawing the parallels between naturally occur- ring near-death experiences and psychedelically induced "death" expe- riences, suggest that the underlying mechanism may be the same: disruption of oxygen transfer on an enzymatic level. In embracing this version of the cerebral anoxia hypothesis, they are still unable, of course, to rebut the empirical objections suggested by Moody's and Osis and Haraldsson's work, but their views are of interest to us because of a conceptual twist they give. According to them, the oxygen-deficient condition of the individual induces an *altered state of consciousness,* which, in turn, activates "unconscious matrices" (possibly associated with archaic parts of the brain) containing the "elements" that comprise the core experience. In other words, Grof and Halifax are suggesting that at the moment of actual or psychologically imminent death, a "stored program" (the phrase is my own) is released, which tends to unfold and to be experienced as the coherent unity I have labeled the core experience. It is imperative to note, however, that this matrix or program is associated with an *altered state of consciousness* that corre- sponds to an *alternate reality,* access to which is not normally available in one's ordinary waking state.

Thus, what Grof and Halifax seem to be proposing is that the onset of apparent or psychological death first induces certain critical phys- iological changes which then permit the individual to "slip into" another reality—a reality that becomes available only through the activation of an unconscious "program."

This is obviously a vastly different conception of the role of cerebral anoxia than the version we have already rejected. Here the alleged physiological changes do not explain away the core experience but merely enable the individual to undergo a transformation of consciousness which sensitizes him to a "new reality." The core experience itself is seen as a perception of that reality and not merely as a by-product of the individual's physiological state.

While this interpretation cannot be reconciled with all the findings so far reported by near-death researchers, the idea of a stored program, released at the point of apparent death, nevertheless, is a provocative one that warrants further attention.

Other Physiological or Neurological Explanations

It is, of course, possible to speculate on other physiological or neurological mechanisms that could play a role in shaping the near-death experience. It has, for example, been suggested that because there are some phenomenological similarities between near-death experiences and those occasioned by sensory isolation procedures[16] the same underlying mechanisms may be involved. This is certainly a reasonable hypothesis since both situations entail a severe reduction of sensory-based input to the brain; in addition, kinesthetic cues are minimal, if not absent. The only problem with this line of thinking, as Moody himself points out, is that there is very little consensus on how to interpret the visions associated with sensory isolation. For this reason, the problem would merely be shifted rather than solved: Instead of having to account for near-death visions, we would now be compelled to explain those occurring under sensory isolation. Even assuming that the visions under the two circumstances are identical—which is doubtful—one would still be left wondering whether such visions reflect the unfolding of a stored program or merely the imagistic representation of basic neurological activities in the brain. Between those alternatives is, of course, precisely where we *now* find ourselves in regard to near-death experiences.

This is not to say that sensory isolation research shouldn't be pursued with the *specific aim* of identifying experiential parallels between visions occurring in that setting and those stemming from near-death episodes. If one could, for example, artificially induce the core experience through sensory deprivation procedures, it might prove possible to gain a much clearer view of its determinants and, conceivably, its underlying neurological mechanisms. It might also turn out that nearly dying and sensory isolation "merely" represent two different but equivalent means of transcending sensory-based reality and entering into other states of consciousness, which would have to be explained in their own right. At this point, it is impossible to decide the issue, and one can only hope that some enterprising researcher will take the hint.

Another neurological possibility relevant to the near-death experience has to do with certain neurotransmitters, notably those called endorphins. These chemicals are associated with certain analgesic effects and a sense of psychological well-being,[17] conditions which, as we know, occur in the initial stages of the core experience. Perhaps coming close to death unleashes increased endorphin production in the brain, thus providing a neurological underpinning for at least the beginning of the core experience. Perhaps. No one, to my knowledge, has investigated this question. Again, we must await further research to see if this possibility represents anything more than an untested, if plausible, speculation.

In general, this is the status of proposed physiological or neurological explanations. Either research has rendered them unlikely or, as with the last two possibilities, the research remains to be done. In the meantime, all we can do is to keep an open mind on the question. Simply because no one has yet found the neurological key to unlock the mysteries of the near-death experience doesn't mean that none exists. Near-death experiences are complex phenomena and the search for a satisfactory neurological explanation, if one is diligently pursued, is likely to be demanding.

In this regard, I would like to advise any neurologically minded researcher interested in investigating this issue of one important constraint: Any adequate neurological explanation would have to be capable of showing how the *entire complex* of phenomena associated with the core experience (that is, the out-of-body state, paranormal knowledge, the tunnel, the golden light, the voice or presence, the appearance of deceased relatives, beautiful vistas, and so forth) would be expected to occur in subjectively authentic fashion as a consequence of specific neurological events triggered by the approach of death. It is not difficult—in fact it is easy—to propose naturalistic interpretations that could conceivably explain some aspect of the core experience. Such explanations, however, sometimes seem merely glib and are usually of the "this-is-nothing-but-an-instance of" variety; rarely do they seem to be seriously considered attempts to come to grips with a very puzzling phenomenon. A neurological interpretation, to be acceptable, should be able to provide a *comprehensive* explanation of *all* the various aspects of the core experience. Indeed, I am tempted to argue that the burden of proof has now shifted to those who wish to explain near-death experiences in this way.

In the meantime, I think it is fair to conclude that physiological or neurological interpretations of near-death experiences are so far inadequate and unacceptable. The definitive physiological or neurological explanation remains to be articulated. Now that the phenomenon itself has been established as a reliable feature of the dying experience, we can only applaud serious scientific research and theorizing in this direction.

While we wait for a plausible interpretation of this kind, we are obviously free to explore other categories of explanations. As we so far have found none of those stemming from the conventional sciences to be arguably adequate, we seem to be driven to consider the less conventional scientific viewpoints. Thus, we find ourselves at the threshold of the scientific study of "impossible" events—parapsychology.

Perhaps those scientists who are used to pondering impossible matters will have the conceptual tools to demystify the "impossible" event with which this book is concerned.

TWELVE

Beyond the Body: A Parapsychological-Holographic Explanation of the Near-Death Experience

As I mentioned in the first chapter, psychical researchers—the forerunners of today's parapsychologists—were among the first scientists to concern themselves with death-related experiences. Although the results of their investigations were never widely accepted by the scientific community, many of their conclusions have been upheld by more recent investigations of near-death experiences, both within and outside the field of contemporary parapsychology. It may profit us, then, to see whether parapsychological concepts can help us understand how the core experience comes about and what mechanisms underlie it.

Before that, however, I want to make a few personal observations concerning both the utility and the drawbacks of the parapsychological perspective.

In my opinion, this perspective offers us the most convincing conceptual framework for understanding the dynamics of the core experience. I say this not as a parapsychologist—for I am not one—but as a psychologist who has spent the last two years sifting through various interpretative possibilities. I will, therefore, want to linger over this approach in order to make the case for its utility as cogent as I can. Of course, I recognize that future research may undermine the value of this kind of interpretation or lead to its abandonment altogether. But, I would submit, at the present rudimentary state of our knowledge, it represents our best hope for getting an exploratory handle on this otherwise enigmatic phenomenon.

That said, it is necessary to be equally frank about the limitations and disadvantages of using the parapsychological perspective in this way. Four problems occur here. First, the empirical foundation underlying this approach is often embarrassingly weak. Although the field of parapsychology was accepted in 1969 as a member in good standing by the American Association for the Advancement of Science, and the methodological sophistication of modern parapsychological research has received high praise by knowledgeable outsiders,[1] much of the early work—to which we must sometimes refer—is often anecdotal in nature and not amenable to direct verification. It is only the impressive *convergence* of parapsychological data—both "hard" and "soft"—that

218

justifies our reference to materials that would otherwise have no place in a book of this kind. In any event, where such questionable data need to be cited, they will be qualified accordingly.

The second point centers on the nature of parapsychological *concepts*. Historically, many of these concepts, such as telepathy, clairvoyance, precognition, psychokinesis, and so on, have simply been unacceptable to the scientific and medical community at large chiefly because they seemingly could not be accommodated within the prevailing scientific paradigm that governs the practice of what the philosopher of science, Thomas Kuhn, calls "normal science."[2] Actually, as the writer Arthur Koestler has pointed out, such concepts are not nearly as mind-boggling as those in modern quantum physics, which even physicists sometimes confess they can't understand.[3] In fact, physicists, and often Nobel laureates at that, have played a leading role in parapsychology from the outset, and the parallels between the two fields have often been noted.[4] This somehow suggests a kind of double standard by which the writings of physicists dealing with such speculative possibilities as quarks and tachyons are treated with respect, where the writings of parapsychologists on out-of-body experiences or reincarnation phenomena go unread or are simply dismissed.

There is evidence, however, that this cavalier attitude toward parapsychology is softening somewhat as scientists themselves become aware of a revised perspective in science, called a paradigm shift,[5] in which the concept of consciousness seems now to be emerging as central to work in many fields (for example, the neurosciences, medicine, physics, and psychology). In the present context, I will have to make a plea similar to that which has traditionally been sounded by parapsychologists themselves: for openness to concepts that remain generally unacceptable to the scientific community. It is my opinion that without such concepts the near-death experience simply cannot be understood. If it is true that a paradigm shift is underway, perhaps now there will be a greater openness to parapsychological concepts and my request will prove unnecessary.[6]

A third problem is perhaps more serious than mere unfamiliarity with or hostility to parapsychological ideas. I am referring here to the difficulty in establishing rigorous scientific procedures for determining the existence and effects of certain parapsychological phenomena. Although some of those I will be discussing have been studied in laboratory settings,[7] such study is not always possible. In many cases, one needs to exploit unusual circumstances or exceptional people in order to examine a given phenomenon at all. Sometimes, in order to investigate a problem, special instrumentation has to be used, the readings from which may be inaccurate, misleading, or subject to various interpretations. And, of course, parapsychological phenomena

are notoriously unstable and variable. All these handicaps have contributed to the low esteem in which much parapsychological work has
traditionally been held. For the time being, there is not much that we
can do but to recognize these limitations as serious ones and to hope
that future research, coupled with a paradigm shift, may be able to
improve this state of affairs somewhat. I am not going to pretend that
those matters can be ignored here. But I will try to document my case as
best I can and will suggest some ways in which aspects of my
interpretation could be tested. Perhaps if there are a few testable
features of this interpretation that can be repeatedly confirmed, it will
not be too difficult to suppose that other aspects of the interpretation—
which can be checked only indirectly or not at all—might also be true.

Finally, I want to indicate that the parapsychological framework I will
employ, though important, is not by itself fully adequate to deal with all
the aspects of the core experience that need to be explained. For this
reason, I mean to graft a *states-of-consciousness* component onto the body
of the parapsychological interpretation I will propose. This component
will be based, in large measure, on recent developments in neuroscience
and is usually referred to as the *holographic theory* or paradigm.[8] This
theory, as I will show, has specific implications for the changes in
consciousness that are reported in connection with the core experience,
explanations for which are not available using parapsychological concepts alone. Therefore, the explanation I will be advancing will actually
involve a hybrid parapsychological-holographic model. In my view,
these two components together can furnish an account of virtually
every aspect of the core experience to which science is capable of
speaking.

In presenting this interpretation, it seems best to start by trying to
account for each of the major stages of the experience. Various specific
features (for example, the life review) that are not necessarily coordi-
nated to any one stage of the core experience will, however, also be
dealt with in the course of this examination. For the purpose of this
discussion, I will be condensing the five stages of the experience into
three clusters: peace and out-of-the-body components (stages I and II);
the tunnel and the light (stages III and IV); and "the world of light"
(stage V).

Peace and Out-of-Body Components

I begin with the hypothesis that the first two stages actually represent
an out-of-body experience, whether or not the individual is aware of it.

That is, I believe that what happens when an individual is near the point of apparent death is a *real*, and not just a subjective, *separation* of "something"—to be specified shortly—from the physical body. It is this "something" that then perceives the immediate physical environment and then (on subsequent stages of the core experience) goes on to experience events outside of the time-space coordinates of ordinary sensory reality.

What is it that splits off from the physical body at the point of apparent death? For the present, there are two possibilities. One is that it is a person's *consciousness* that has detached itself from his body. The other is that it is actually a *second* body of some kind. This "body" has been called by various terms, but since it is usually described by those who claim to see it as a *replica* of the physical body, let us simply use the term *the double* to refer to this alleged second body. Of course, these two possibilities need not exclude one another: It may be that what happens during a near-death episode is that one's consciousness itself shifts its "locus" from the physical body to the double, or that one's consciousness is contained within the double all along.

At this point, perhaps it is wise not to settle on a particular interpretation of what this hypothesized split actually represents. After we consider the evidence bearing on this matter, we will be in a better position to do so. Nevertheless, for the time being, just to have a way of talking about it, suppose we adopt the convention that it is one's consciousness only that leaves the body during a near-death episode.

If this is so, then all the attributes of stage I fall neatly into place. If consciousness is no longer in the body, the individual is suddenly free of all input from body-based cues; he exists as *disembodied* consciousness or consciousness (temporarily) without a body. When people report feelings of extraordinary peace, lightness, painlessness, quiet, and so forth, it certainly implies that they are free from all bodily based sensations. While such reports hardly prove that one's consciousness has left the body, these are—as we will shortly see—precisely the kinds of self-reports we would expect under such conditions. The fact that core experiencers sometimes claim to be out of their bodies obviously does nothing to lower the probability of this hypothesis.

The implication of this hypothesis, then, is that the feelings associated with stage I of the core experience are dependent on being out of body. They are, in fact, as will be shown, the affective concomitants of the out-of-body condition. To anticipate somewhat, I will argue that the entire range of core experiences actually represents an *extended* out-of-body experience and that all the phenomena associated with dying cohere impressively as soon as one begins to build on this assumption.

So much for the postulated origins of the core experience. We now need to ask: What is the *independent* evidence in support of this hypothesis? Specifically, we need to ask: (1) What are the data suggesting that out-of-body experiences are real events? (2) What are the subjective attributes associated with an out-of-body condition and what are its effects? (3) Has anyone ever seen the alleged double and, if so, under what conditions?

The answers to these questions will serve to lay the empirical foundation for a comprehensive understanding of the core experience.

It is no exaggeration to claim that in the parapsychological literature the evidence for the reality of out-of-body experiences is abundant. Crookall's work[9] alone represents an analysis of thousands of cases collected, albeit somewhat indiscriminately, from all over the world. Celia Green, and English parapsychologist, has reported the results of a survey of some four hundred out-of-body experiences,[10] providing us with a most valuable body of evidence we will be considering shortly. Charles Tart has conducted several laboratory studies of out-of-body experiences[11] and has, in addition, hundreds of cases in his own collection. Osis has also done considerable laboratory work dealing with such experiences[12] and has already reported the results of a new, extensive survey similar to Green's.[13] Much of the well known anecdotal literature on out-of-body experiences as well as most of the scientific studies conducted by parapsychologists through 1974 are described by Herbert Greenhouse,[14] a journalist. Beyond the investigators already mentioned (and this is far from a complete list), our understanding of out-of-body experiences has been deepened by the detailed descriptions of such experiences by individuals who have learned to leave their bodies virtually at will. Among the best known of these accounts are those provided by Robert Monroe, Sylvan Muldoon, and Muldoon and Hereward Carrington, Oliver Fox, Yram, and Vincent Turvey.[15]

Although interpretations of these experiences vary, the many similarities in the reports of those who claim to have been out of their bodies leave little doubt that such episodes represent a distinctive category of human experience. Obviously, I cannot do justice here to the voluminous literature I have cited dealing with such experiences, but I would invite any reader still skeptical or even curious about them to examine it with some care. Doing so will suffice, I think, to convince all but the most diehard materialists of the reality of out-of-body experiences.

If we can take the existence of such experiences as established, we next need to inquire into their attributes and effects. Here Green's work is particularly relevant. Her research evidence unequivocally demonstrates that what her informants (many of whom had their experiences in the absence of any physical trauma) report is *precisely* what our respondents relate in connection with the first two stages of the core experience.

Let me give some specific examples of this unmistakable correspondence.

One of the most striking and characteristic features of the ecsomatic state [Green's term for what I have called an out-of-body experience] is that of autoscopy—i.e., the subject apparently viewing his own body from the outside.

If the ecsomatic experience takes place indoors, the subject frequently refers to his ecsomatic position as being near the ceiling, e.g., "suspended against the ceiling." Again, the corner of the ceiling is often specified.

Sometimes the subject appears to view his surroundings from a height greater than that of the room in which his physical body is located.

Subjects sometimes report that their sensory acuity is increased in the ecsomatic state, saying that their senses were "heightened" or "enhanced."

Many subjects comment on the "brightness" or "vividness" of colors in the ecsomatic state.

There is rarely any indication that the information about his environment, which is conveyed to the subject by his perceptions in an ecsomatic state, is in any way erroneous. For example, if the subject describes his physical body as having a certain appearance while he is observing it from the outside, his description is in accordance with the observations of independent observers, if any are present.

Subjects usually report that their intellectual faculties were unimpaired in the ecsomatic state; indeed, their reports often suggest a greater than usual degree of mental clarity.

Subjects characteristically report their experiences of the ecsomatic state as being distinguished by sensations of naturalness, completeness, reality, lightness, freedom, vitality, and health.

Nearly one in ten of single subjects [that is, individuals relating a single experience] report feelings of excitement, elation, exaltation, and the like.

Subjects characteristically emphasize that they were not frightened, worried or anxious; observing, for example: "I looked at
myself without concern," "I was not the slightest afraid," or "I
certainly was not worried." On the contrary, subjects describe
themselves as being calm, relaxed, detached, or indifferent.[16]

Many additional citations could be quoted, but they would only be
redundant to the point I am trying to establish: the parallels between
Green's description of the ecsomatic state and the initial stages of the
core experience. Can there be *any* reasonable doubt that the core
experience begins (at least in many instances) with an out-of-body
episode?

Not only are the qualities Green describes characteristic of our
accounts of the beginnings of the core experience, but some of the
aftereffects coincide with those observed for our sample. Although
Green apparently didn't investigate this issue, we have it on Tart's
authority that

> The effect on a person of having an OOBE [i.e., out-of-body
> experience] is enormous. In almost all cases, his reaction is
> approximately, "I no longer believe in survival after death—I *know*
> my consciousness will survive death because I have *experienced* my
> consciousness existing outside my physical body."[17]

Consistent with our findings, Tart also observes that

> In almost all reported OOBES, the person is totally convinced that
> this was a "real" experience, not some sort of dream or hallucina-
> tion.[18]

If the core experience begins with a process of separation from the
physical body, we still need to know just *what* it is that separates. Here
we return to the question we set aside earlier: Is there a second body—a
double—that splits off at this point, or is it consciousness itself that
somehow detaches itself from the physical body? If there is a double,
has anyone ever seen it and, if so, under what circumstances? This
question can be approached from a dual perspective: that of the
"disconnected" individual himself and that of the external witness to
the process of separation.

According to Moody, most of his respondents, while subjectively out
of their physical body, found themselves to be "in" another body.
Typically, however, his interviewees found it difficult, if not impossible,
to describe this body. It is, of course, weightless and invisible, but

sometimes it seems to have a human shape and is capable of at least visual and auditory perception. Moody remarks that this second body is usually characterized by such terms as a *mist, cloud, vapor, energy pattern,* or the like. He felt that the term that best epitomized its quality was the *spiritual body.*

Kübler-Ross has taken a similar position.[19] According to one report:

> Patients who "died" perceived an immediate separation of a spirit-like self-entity from their bodies. This spirit then became aware of its former body lying in bed.

On the other hand, most of our respondents implied or stated that they were *not* aware of a second body, but rather felt as though it was simply "themselves" or "their mind" that was conscious while out of the body. Our data agree with those of Green, who found that 80% of her subjects reported that they appeared to be a "disembodied consciousness" rather than inhabiting a second body. Nevertheless, she also found some instances where a second body *was* experienced and it is sometimes described as a duplicate or replica of the physical body.

From these several sources, then, about all we can conclude is that the *perception* of a second body—the double—is *sometimes* reported by persons having an out-of-body experience, but it is by no means always the case.

Perhaps the perspective of the witness to another's death will provide us with a clearer picture of what happens at death. Is the double ever seen by observers and, if so, how is it described?

It goes without saying, of course, that if such perceptions were common we should all know about them. A diligent search of the literature, however, is sufficient to establish that glimpses of a second body splitting off from the physical at death have occasionally been reported and that independent accounts reveal a strong overall similarity.

Let me begin with a suggestive instance—one which, admittedly, by itself, is hardly more than a secondhand bit of curious lore from another culture. I have taken this account from Greenhouse, although the original source is to be found in Muldoon and Carrington. According to a nineteenth-century missionary, the Tahitians believe that at death

> . . . the soul [is] drawn out of the body, whence it was borne away, to be slowly and gradually united to the god from whom it had emanated. . . . The Tahitians have concluded that a substance, taking human form, issued from the head of the corpse, because

among the privileged few who have the blessed gift of clairvoyance, some affirm that, shortly after a human body ceases to
breathe, a vapour arises from the head, hovering a little way above
it, but attached by a vapoury cord. The substance, it is said,
gradually increases in bulk and assumes the form of an inert body.
When this has become quite cold, the connecting cord disappears
and the dis-entangled soul-form floats away as if borne by invisible
carriers.[20]

Is there any reason to regard this belief as anything more than a bit of
anthropological exotica? If we can trust Crookall's (and others') investigations of death-bed perceptions, the answer may well be: yes.

In one of Crookall's books,[21] he presents roughly a score of such
reports from Western observers, but I will mention only two instances
here.

Estelle Roberts described her husband's transition. "I saw his spirit
leave the body. It emerged from his head and gradually molded
itself into an exact replica of his earth-body. *It remained suspended
about a foot above his body, lying in the same position* i.e., *horizontal, and
attached to it by a cord to the head. Then the cord broke and the spirit-form
floated away, passing through the wall.*"[22]

The similarity between this description and the Tahitian belief
concerning what happens at death is unmistakable. Here is a second,
more extended, example of the perception of the formation of a
double, as given by Crookall. The account was furnished by a twentieth-
century physician, R. B. Hout, who apparently witnessed a number of
such occurrences. In this case, he is describing the death of his aunt.

My attention was called . . . to something immediately above the
physical body, suspended in the atmosphere about two feet above
the bed. At first I could distinguish nothing more than a vague
outline of a hazy, foglike substance. There seemed to be only a
mist held there suspended, motionless. But, as I looked, very
gradually there grew into my sight a denser, more solid, condensation of this inexplicable vapor. Then I was astonished to see
definite outlines presenting themselves, and soon I saw this foglike
substance was assuming a human form.

Soon I knew that the body I was seeing resembled that of the
physical body of my aunt . . . the astral body [Hout's term] hung
suspended horizontally a few feet above the physical counterpart
. . . I continued to watch and . . . the Spirit Body [again, Hout's

term] now seemed complete to my sight. I saw the features plainly. They were very similar to the physical face, except that a glow of peace and vigor was expressed instead of age and pain. The eyes were closed as though in tranquil sleep, and a luminosity seemed to radiate from the Spirit Body.

As I watched the suspended Spirit Body, my attention was called, again intuitively, to a silverlike substance that was streaming from the head of the physical body to the head of the spirit "double." Then I saw the connection-cord between the two bodies. As I watched, the thought, "The silver cord!" kept running through my mind. I knew, for the first time, the meaning of it. This "silver cord" was the connecting-link between the physical and the spirit bodies, even as the umbilical cord unites the child to its mother . . .

The cord was attached to each of the bodies at the occipital protuberance immediately at the base of the skull. Just where it met the physical body it spread out, fanlike, and numerous little strands separated and attached separately to the skull base. But other than at the attachments, the cord was round, being perhaps an inch in diameter. The color was a translucent luminous silver radiance. The cord seemed alive with vibrant energy. I could see the pulsations of light stream along the course of it, from the direction of the physical body to the spirit "double." With each pulsation the spirit body became more alive and denser, whereas the physical body became quieter and more nearly lifeless . . . By this time the features were very distinct. The life was all in the astral body . . . the pulsations of the cord had stopped . . . I looked at the various strands of the cord as they spread out, fanlike, at the base of the skull. Each strand snapped . . . the final severance was at hand. A twin process of death and birth was about to ensue . . . the last connecting strand of the silver cord snapped and the spirit body was free.

The spirit body, which had been supine [horizontal] before, now rose . . . The closed eyes opened and a smile broke from the radiant features. She gave a smile of farewell, then vanished from my sight.

The above phenomenon was witnessed by me as an entirely objective reality. The spirit-forms I saw with the aid of my physical eye.[23]

Besides the cases furnished in Crookall's book, there are other, similar, ones described in Sir William Barrett's pioneering book on deathbed visions and further instances are recounted by Greenhouse. It would be easy to multiply examples of these visions of a second

Life at Death

body separating from the physical at death, but it is not likely that additional accounts would measurably increase our understanding of this phenomenon.

What, then, can we say concerning such reports?

First, it must be acknowledged that, despite the basic similarity of these visions and the apparent sincerity and clearheadedness of the witnesses who provide them, their evidential value is very weak. This is an instance of the point I made previously, concerning the anecdotal nature of much of the data collected by psychical researchers, especially the early investigators. Many similar cases are better than a few, of course, but anecdotal data *at best* can only be suggestive.

Second, it appears that these visions tend to be seen chiefly, if not exclusively, by persons with clairvoyant sight, with "astral vision," as it were. Typically, only a single observer (of several) will report such a vision, but occasionally multiple witnesses seem to agree on essential details. If modern researchers were to reinvestigate this deathbed phenomenon, a possible strategy would be to station (with the knowledge and consent of the dying individual, of course) two or more psychics or clairvoyants in the room and ask them each to describe or sketch what they saw as death approached. If there was a correspondence in the perceived timing and formation of a spirit double among the reports of such observers, that would certainly be a valuable, if less than thoroughly convincing, corroboration of the separation hypothesis. There are claims in the literature that the second body has been successfully photographed, but due to the notorious difficulty in establishing photographic proof of paranormal events, this kind of "evidence" is highly suspect. Whether any modern photographic techniques could ever provide convincing documentary evidence for the existence of the double is, in my opinion, an open question.

Third, if, for the moment, we entertain these data seriously—if only for the purpose of hypothesis formation—they could provide us with a possible explanation for the discrepancies in the self-perceptions of a second body. Recall that some people sense or see themselves in a second body, whereas others do not. The clairvoyant visions I have cited, however, all suggest that the formation of a second or duplicate body *takes time*, that it does not appear all at once. If that is so, then it becomes understandable why only some people would feel that they were "in" such a body; presumably those who failed to report such perceptions were at an earlier stage of the dying process, a pre-second body stage, to be exact. Whether this alleged second body is actually an objective reality (albeit in another set of dimensions to which some clairvoyants are presumably sensitive) or is nothing more than what esotericists call a "thought-form" (that is, a mind-created reality in the physical space-time with which we are all familiar) is a question that we must leave unanswered. It may even be that it is not a terribly helpful way of phrasing the alternatives.

The last point that needs to be made here is perhaps the most important one. Not only is there a high level of agreement across independent witnesses concerning the formation of a spirit double at death, but their descriptions accord, on the whole, very neatly with the accounts provided by near-death survivors themselves! That is, both the *external* perspective of the witness and the *direct* testimony of the individual close to death converge on what is occurring during the *initial* stages of death: There is a splitting-off process that takes place during which one's center of self-awareness is freed from the constraints of the physical body.

Nevertheless, there is one difference of degree we should note between these two perspectives: The outside observer usually provides a more *detailed* description of these death-related events. The second body is clearly observed forming; the connecting cord is not only perceived but is usually reported to be pulsating; the cord seems to snap or be severed at the point of physical death; and so on.

Obviously, from the data presented earlier in this book, such detailed perceptions are *not* typical in the accounts of near-death survivors. Perhaps it is understandable that someone caught up in this extraordinary process would not be as sensitive to some of these detailed features as would someone observing it from the outside. In addition, since some of these alleged phenomena occur at the point of death, not all of our *near*-death survivors would have got far enough into the experience to be able to observe them. Nevertheless, one can still ask whether there are *any* cases in the literature on near-death experiences where such precise details are recounted.

Although there may well be other accounts with which I am not familiar, I was able to locate only one. Fortunately, it is a well-documented case, though not a recent one, and it was thoroughly investigated by two of the leading and most respected early researchers of the British Society for Psychical Research—Richard Hodgson and F.W.H. Myers, whose book *Human Personality and Its Survival of Bodily Death* is a classic.

The case involves a certain A. S. Wiltse, a medical doctor, who nearly died of typhoid fever in 1889. Wiltse obtained sworn depositions from the witnesses, including his own physician, concerning his medical condition and the actions that took place during his coma. In reading his testimony, the accounts I have just finished relating—especially the one provided by Dr. Hout—should be borne carefully in mind. In presenting this case, I am drawing on a summary provided by Moss.

Feeling a sense of drowsiness come over me, I straightened my stiffened legs, got my arms over my breast, and soon sank into utter unconsciousness.

I passed about four hours in all without pulse or perceptible heart beat as I am informed by Dr. S. H. Raynes, who was the only physician present. [During that time] I came again into a state of conscious existence and discovered that I was still in the body, but the body and I had no longer any interests in common.

With all the interest of a physician, I beheld the wonders of my bodily anatomy, intimately interwoven with which, even tissue for tissue, was I, the living soul of that dead body. By some power, apparently not my own, the Ego was rocked to and fro, laterally, as a cradle is rocked, by which process its connection with the tissues of the body was broken up. . . . I felt and heard, it seemed, the snapping of innumerable small cords. When this was accomplished, I began slowly to retreat from the feet, toward the head. . . . As I emerged from the head, I floated up and down and laterally like a soap bubble attached to the bowl of a pipe until at last I broke loose from the body and fell lightly to the floor, where I slowly rose and expanded into the full stature of a man. I seemed to be translucent, of a bluish cast and perfectly naked. . . . As I turned, my left elbow came in contact with the arm of one of two gentlemen, who were standing at the door. To my surprise, his arm passed through mine without apparent resistance, the severed parts closing again without pain, as air re-unites. I looked quickly up at his face to see if he had noticed the contact, but he gave no sign—only stood and gazed toward the couch I had just left. I directed my gaze in the direction of his, and saw my own dead body. It was lying just as I had taken so much pains to place it. . . .

Without previous thought and without apparent effort on my part, my eyes opened. Realizing that I was in the body, in astonishment and disappointment, I exclaimed: "What in the world has happened to me? Must I die again?"[24]

The detailed correspondences of Wiltse's description with the accounts given earlier are obvious and remarkable. Perhaps the parallels are so marked in his case because of the apparent extraordinary length of his clinical death. In any event, such cases, though rare, strongly support the observations provided by clairvoyant witnesses to deathbed scenes, as well as enlarge our knowledge of the details of the splitting process.

Although the evidence I have already presented—from both the external and the internal perspective—argues strongly for some kind of separation hypothesis, it may be worthwhile to consider briefly one additional class of observations bearing on the initial stages of the core experience.

I have so far scrupulously avoided drawing on esoteric writings on death (of which there is, needless to say, an unwelcome overabundance). Esoteric writers often have interesting ideas to offer, of course, but since they are usually presented *ex cathedra,* one is usually left in an intellectual quandary over how to evaluate them. Since they are generally untestable anyway, such ideas usually are of little value for scientific inquiry.

Nevertheless, I want to relax my standards here just for a moment in order to consider a few passages from a little book called *The Transition Called Death.* It was originally published in 1943 and was written by Charles Hampton, a man about whom I know nothing except that from the contents of his book I infer that he was both a priest and a clairvoyant. His book is written in the usual authoritative style common among esotericists.

The reason I wish to cite it here, however, is because what Hampton claims happens at death accords astonishingly well with the empirical evidence I have just finished presenting. Consider, for example, this passage concerning the silver cord at the moment of death:

> As the rest of the body becomes negative and dead, the heart and brain become more alive because all of the forces of the body are now concentrated in the upper part of it. When a dying person says: "Everything is becoming clear; my mind is more lucid than it has ever been," we may know that the transition is taking place. The head becomes intensely brilliant; it is like a golden bowl. All this time the silver cord also becomes more alive; etheric matter flows over it like a rapidly moving fluorescent light, but imperceptibly extracting the life force more and more, somewhat as a suction. Where the silver cord joins the main nerve ganglia it consists of thousands of very fine threads. As the life forces flow back into the higher world, those threads begin to break.[25]

Later on, he has these comments to make on the [etheric] double:

> During earth life the etheric double is coterminous with the nervous system as well as enveloping it. In outline, in form and feature, it is a replica or double of the physical body in matter finer and more tenuous than the finest gaseous substance, yet it is still physical matter. . . . The etheric double disintegrates or dematerializes once it is abandoned. It never was intended to be a vehicle of consciousness. Its function was to convey vitality to the

Life at Death

body through the nervous system. . . . Its appearance is that of a bluish-white mist. . . . Death means that the etheric double is disunited from the nervous system, but the double is no more to be preserved than the physical is; it is part of the physical and will disintegrate. Immediately on awakening in the astral world the etheric matter fades out like mist.[26]

What to make of these uncanny parallels is hard to say. It certainly sounds as though Hampton was basing himself on our case material—or material like it. The extent of which his pronouncements are actually rooted in his own direct clairvoyant perceptions, however, is unfortunately never made clear. Despite his old-fashioned terminology and didactic style—elements not likely to endear him to the scientifically minded—Hampton's observations obviously express at least one esotericist position congruent with the empirical data on the separation hypothesis.

Conclusion

In making my case for an out-of-body interpretation for the initial stages of the core experience, I have argued that there is abundant empirical evidence pointing to the reality of out-of-body experiences; that such experiences conform to the descriptions given by our near-death experiencers; and that there is highly suggestive evidence that death involves the separation of a second body—a double—from the physical body. I want to reiterate here that this interpretation is subject to all the weaknesses associated with the parapsychological approach and should be evaluated in that light.

There is one implication in this separation hypothesis that needs to be brought out. Some readers may think that I have tried to sneak in the concept of the soul through the back door, even though I have steadfastly avoided this term. Certainly, talking about "something" leaving the body at death sounds suspiciously like soul-talk even if another expression is used. For my part, it might be well to remember that the root meaning of psychology—my own field—is "the study of the soul" or psyche, even though this is *not* a definition one tends to find in the textbooks. Osis and Haraldsson are even more insistent on this point when, in speaking of psychology, they observe "it is time to consider the concept of 'soul' if empirical facts demand it." Clearly, their opinion is that the facts *do* demand it. Moody seems to take a similar position.[27]

My preference, however, is to continue to eschew the word *soul* on the grounds that it is entirely too religiously tinged to be helpful in scientific work. In this respect, I find myself totally in accord with Tart's views, which are stated with admirable concision:

> . . . *soul* is not simply a descriptive term but one that has all sorts of explicit and implicit connotations for us because of our culture's religious beliefs. Even though a person may have had no formal religious training or may have consciously rejected his early training, such an emotionally potent concept as soul can have strong effects on us on a subconscious level. Since a prime requirement of scientific investigation is precise description and clear communication, a word like *soul* is difficult to deal with scientifically because of the deep, hidden reactions it may evoke in the human practitioners of science.[28]

Instead, I would content myself with saying that out-of-body experiences provide us with an empirical referent for the possible origin of the concept of soul. As such, I favor restricting its use to religious contexts. On the basis of the separation hypothesis, however, I do endorse the proposition that consciousness (with or without a second body) may function independently of the physical body.

Finally, there is the so-far-neglected issue of the "mechanisms" underlying the separation of consciousness (or the double) from the physical body. An answer to this question could only take us into the wilds of esoteric speculation, where I have no wish to roam. Even the assumption of a connecting cord of energy that breaks at death does not get us very far. What exactly is this cord? Of what is it composed? How does it function? Is there only one such cord? These and similar questions present a thicket of problems that I wish to sidestep with a polite, "No, thank you." Other explanations I have heard proposed, for example, that out-of-body experiences are triggered by the excitation of a subtle biological energy, usually called kundalini,[29] are similarly speculative and unverifiable at the present time. For me, it is sufficient to postulate that a separation can take place. Just *how* it occurs is a problem I must leave to scientists more imaginative and daring than I.

To account now for the later developments of the core experience we will have to go beyond the approach of parapsychology and employ a different but compatible framework, based, in part, on an emerging paradigm in contemporary scientific thought: holographic theory.

The Tunnel and the Light

We are now at the stage of the core experience where the individual's consciousness is assumed to have split off from his physical body and is continuing to function independently of it (possibly now having its locus in the double). And it is here that events far more puzzling than the out-of-body experience itself begin to take place. For an individual now becomes aware of traveling through a dark tunnel or void toward a brilliant golden light. Part of this experience may also entail an encounter with a "presence" or the hearing of a "voice," at which time one comes to take stock of his life in an effort to decide whether one should live or die. Part of this assessment—which is sometimes consciously linked with the presence or voice—may involve a rapid, almost instantaneous life review.

How may we understand what these extraordinary phenomena represent?

My own interpretation rests on the assumption that these experiences reflect psychological events associated with a shift in *levels of consciousness*. The intermediate stages of the core experience can be understood as initiating a transition from a state of consciousness rooted in "this-world" sensory impressions to one that is sensitive to the realities of another dimension of existence. When consciousness begins to function independent of the physical body, it becomes capable of awareness of another dimension—let us, for ease of reference, simply call it for now a fourth dimension. Most of us, most of the time, function in the three-dimensional world of ordinary sensory reality. According to the interpretation I am offering, this reality is grounded in a *body-based* consciousness. When one quits the body—either at death or voluntarily, as some individuals have learned to do—one's consciousness is then free to explore the fourth-dimensional world. This means, as we will see, that the elements of the core experience with which we are here concerned are *not* unique to near-death states but are potentially available to *anyone* who learns to operate his consciousness independent of the physical body. *Any* trigger that brings about this release may induce such experiences. It happens that coming close to death, for reasons that are obvious, is a reliable trigger effecting this release of consciousness. But to repeat: *Anything* that sets consciousness free from the body's sensory-based three-dimensional reality is capable of bringing about an awareness of the fourth dimension. There are numerous accounts of these experiences by individuals who have entered into this realm—without dying.[30]

It may strike some readers that I have rather abruptly abandoned my scientific orientation to embrace a vague mystical conception of the core experience. This is not so, however. These aspects of the core experience can be interpreted in scientific terms if one uses some of the postulates of holographic theory, which will be presented shortly. In fact, the exciting thing about this approach, which had its origins in both the neurosciences and physics, is that it offers a means to make good theoretical sense of the mystical world view. Many writers have, in fact, already contended that science and mysticism meet in holographic theory and can be seen to represent two divergent "methodological" paths leading to a common vision of the nature of the universe.[31] If these writers prove correct, holographic theory may turn out to be one of the most significant intellectual developments in the history of modern thought, because, through it, a profound synthesis of knowledge may be achieved. This is its promise, but, of course, it is entirely too soon to determine whether this promise will be realized.

In the meantime, however, we can make use of this approach to develop an interpretative framework for the understanding of the core experience.

Although holographic theory can be exceedingly complex and technical, it is possible to present a simplified version of it for our purposes here and then apply it to the core experience.

Holography is actually a method of photography—photography without a lens. In holography, the wave field of light scattered by an object—say, an orange—is recorded on a plate as an interference pattern. The idea of an interference pattern can be illustrated by imagining that one drops three pebbles simultaneously into a shallow pan of water. The resultant waves will crisscross one another. If one were then to quick-freeze the surface ripples, one would have a record of the interference pattern made by the waves. When the interference pattern is then illuminated by a laser beam, the orange reappears as a three-dimensional image. This image is a hologram.

The photographic plate itself is a jumbled pattern of swirls. These swirls—the interference pattern—store the information, however, and release it in response to a coherent light source (the laser beam).

One of the most extraordinary properties of the interference pattern is that any part of it contains information about the whole. That means that if one broke off a portion of the pattern storing information about the orange and illuminated *only* that portion, an image of the *entire* orange would appear.

What is the relevance of holography to an understanding of the states of consciousness presumably involved in near-death experiences? Just this: It has been proposed by Karl Pribram, the well-known neurosurgeon and holographic theorist, that the brain itself functions holographically by mathematically analyzing interference wave patterns so that images of objects are seen.[32] "Primary reality" itself is said to be composed of frequencies only. Different cells of the brain respond to different frequencies, and the brain functions like a *frequency analyzer,* breaking down complex patterns of frequencies into their components. These frequencies are then converted into our familiar object world by a process analogous to the illumination of an interference pattern by a laser beam. Thus, in Marilyn Ferguson's explication of Pribram's theory:

> Our brains mathematically construct "concrete" reality by interpreting frequencies from another dimension, a realm of meaningful, pattern primary reality that transcends time and space.[33]

There is apparently a fair amount of empirical support for the theory, although it remains controversial. It has proved helpful in illuminating long-standing problems in psychology, such as how memory is distributed in the brain. Consideration of this aspect of the theory, however, would take us off the track we need to follow.

To make the connection between near-death experiences and holographic theory, we must emphasize the properties of what Pribram calls the *frequency domain*—the primary reality composed of frequencies only. Of this realm Pribram has said:

> The frequency domain deals with density of occurrences only; time and space are collapsed. Ordinary boundaries of space and time, such as locations of any sort, disappear . . . in a sense, everything is happening all at once, synchronously. But one can read out what is happening into a variety of co-ordinates of which space and time are the most helpful in bringing us into the ordinary domain of appearances.[34]

From this statement it is only a short step to the implications of direct relevance to us. Pribram, who, from his own statements, appears not to have had any mystical experiences himself, nevertheless has observed:

> As a way of looking at consciousness, holographic theory is much closer to mystical and Eastern philosophy. It will take a while for people to become comfortable with an order of reality other than the world of appearances. But it seems to me that some of the

mystical experiences people have described for millenia begin to make some scientific sense. *They bespeak the possibility of tapping into that order of reality* [that is, holographic reality] *that is* behind *the world of appearances.* . . . Spiritual insights fit the descriptions of this domain. They're made perfectly plausible by the invention of the hologram.[35]

Indeed, parapsychologists and students of mysticism have not been slow to discern the implications of Pribram's holographic theory for their respective domains of interest. If one assumes that paranormal events (such as telepathy or synchronicity—meaningful patterns of "coincidence" without apparent causal connections) or mystical experiences are manifestations of a holographic reality—where, remember, time and space are collapsed and where, therefore, causality can have no meaning—then a great deal that was formerly puzzling or paradoxical in these domains falls neatly into place, as we will see.

By now, the direction I am taking here will be evident, but let me spell it out clearly. I assume that the core experience *is* a type of mystical experience that ushers one into the holographic domain. In this *state of consciousness,* there is a *new order* of *reality* that one becomes sensitive to—a frequency domain—as time and space lose their conventional meaning. The act of dying, then, involves a gradual *shift* of consciousness from the ordinary world of appearances to a holographic reality of pure frequencies. In this new reality, however, consciousness still functions holographically (without a brain, I must assume) to interpret these frequencies in object terms. Indeed, as Pribram himself has argued—and he is not alone in this—the universe itself seems to be organized holographically.

Access to this holographic reality becomes *experientially* available when one's consciousness is freed from its dependence on the physical body. So long as one remains tied to the body and to its sensory modalities, holographic reality *at best* can only be an intellectual construct. When one comes close to death, one experiences it directly. That is why core experiencers (and mystics generally) speak about their visions with such certitude and conviction, while those who haven't experienced this realm for themselves are left feeling skeptical or even indifferent.

Such, at least, is my general interpretation of the core experience.

At this point, it becomes necessary to see whether this holographic conception can help us to make sense of any of the *specific* aspects of the core experience of concern to us here. While this may not always be the case, where holographic theory seems relevant I will try to indicate just how it is. In any event, from this point onward, it will be useful to bear the holographic perspective in mind.

Now, we must return to the specific phenomena of the core experience mentioned at the outset of this section. Let us begin with the sense of *moving through a dark tunnel or dark void.*

There are, of course, many possible interpretations of this effect. They range from assumptions that it reflects decreased blood flow or impaired respiration to speculations that tunnel "perceptions" actually represent the flow of the "vital force" through the connecting cord. Between these purely physiological and unverifiable esoteric interpretations, however, is a psychological one that has recently been suggested to me. Since it tends to square with my states of consciousness interpretation, I will offer it here.

According to Itzhak Bentov, another prominent holographic theorist and consciousness researcher, the tunnel effect

> Is a psychological phenomenon whereby the consciousness experiences "motion" from one "level" to the other. It is the process of adjustment of the consciousness from one plane of reality to another. It is usually felt as movement. This is so only for people . . . for whom this is new. For people who are used to going into the astral or higher levels, this tunnel phenomenon does not happen anymore.[36]

Thus, what Bentov appears to be saying is that the tunnel or darkness is an intermediate or transitional zone occurring between levels of consciousness. It is as though one's awareness is "shifting gears" from ordinary waking consciousness to a direct perception of the frequency domain. The gap in *time* while this shift is being effected is experienced as movement through (a dark) *space.* What is actually "moving," however, is awareness itself—or mind without a body—and what it is moving "through" is the gateway to holographic, or four-dimensional, consciousness. This is why Bentov can imply that when this shift becomes habitual it occurs instantaneously. Tunnel effects, then, are merely the mind's experience of transitions through states of consciousness.[37]

Another argument in support of a psychological interpretation of the tunnel phenomenon is based on occasional reports one can find in the literature where people claim to be aware of "others" in the tunnel. To illustrate this, let me simply relate an anecdote recently told me by Raymond Moody.[38] After one of Moody's talks, a woman approached him in order to recount her own near-death experience. Part of it involved her moving through the tunnel toward the brilliant golden light. What was unusual in her case, however, is that as she was moving through the tunnel, she saw a friend of hers coming back! As they drew nearer, somehow the friend conveyed the thought to her that he had been "sent back." Later, according to what Moody was told, it developed that her friend had actually suffered a cardiac arrest at the approximate time of the woman's own experience. At this writing, Moody is attempting to verify the details of this case and to find out whether the friend himself had any awareness of the woman informant in the tunnel. In any event, if authenticated, this is certainly a provocative, and, to my knowledge, unique case.

Finally, the tunnel effect is not restricted by any means to near-death circumstances. This phenomenon has been reported in out-of-body episodes not associated with death, where a transition in consciousness was subjectively taking place.[39] Such occurrences are again consistent with a psychological interpretation of the kind that I am advancing and also reinforce the point made earlier that aspects of the core experience may occur whenever consciousness can be detached from the body.

The next phenomenon that manifests itself is, of course, *the brilliant golden light*, which is sometimes seen at the end of the tunnel and at other times appears independent of a tunnel experience. Sometimes, as we have noted, people report that it envelops them rather than being seen as though at a distance.

What is this light? In my own view, it represents *two* distinct, but related, phenomena.

One interpretation is that it represents the "light" associated with the state of consciousness one enters after death. At this level of consciousness—where we are no longer constrained by the sensory systems of the physical body—we are presumably sensitive to a higher range of frequencies, which appear to us as light of extraordinary brilliance and unearthly beauty. In many traditions, this is spoken of as the light of the "astral" world or plane, and it is said that, for most people, this is the realm to which one "goes" after death. Of course, there is no way of providing acceptable scientific evidence for such statements, but it is perhaps at least noteworthy that virtually every description that purports to convey a sense of "the next world" depicts "a world of light." This is true not only for ancient esoteric traditions,[40] but is also found in the accounts of accomplished individual mystics, both historical[41] and contemporary.[42] Not only that, but the extensive popular literature on "life after death" is replete with descriptions from a great diversity of sources which accord with this conception of an astral realm. None of this material, however voluminous, would be evidential in the courts of science, but it still seems reasonable to ask: Could they *all* be in error?

In my own opinion, the idea of an astral reality—or call it whatever else you will—to which we may become sensitive at the point of death is not an outlandish notion, even if it can never be established scientifically. In any event, my own provisional conclusion is that one interpretation of the light phenomenon reported by our respondents is that it represents a glimpse of this astral reality.

In this context, it might also be recalled that holographic theory also postulates a primary reality defined as a "frequency domain." One can wonder whether one *level* of this frequency domain might correspond to what has traditionally been called the "astral plane."

I said before that, in my judgment, the perception of the brilliant golden light actually represents *two* separate but related phenomena. If "astral light"—as a range of frequencies to which we are sensitive in a fourth dimension, or holographic reality—is one aspect of the light effect, we still need to know what the other is.

And at this point, we must enter boldly, if with considerable trepidation, into the heart of the interpretative mystery of near-death experiences. What we will find there, however, will not so much resolve the mystery as it will enlarge our sense of it.

Moody spoke of a "being of light," and though none of our respondents used this phrase some seemed to be aware of a "presence" (or "voice") in association with the light. Often, but not always, this presence is identified with God. However this may be, I want to consider what the light represents when it is conjoined with the sense of a presence or with an unrecognized voice.

Here we must, I think, make a speculative leap. I submit that this presence/voice is actually—oneself! It is not merely a projection of one's personality, however, but one's *total self*, or what in some traditions is called the *higher self*. In this view, the individual personality is but a split-off fragment of the total self with which it is reunited at the point of death. During ordinary life, the individual personality functions in a seemingly autonomous way, as though it were a separate entity. In fact, however, it is invisibly tied to the larger self structure of which it is a part. An analogy would be that the individual personality is like a child who, when grown up, completely forgets his mother and then fails to recognize her when they later meet.

What has this to do with the light? The answer is—or so I would say— that this higher self is so awesome, so overwhelming, so loving, and unconditionally accepting (like an all-forgiving mother) and so *foreign* to one's individualized consciousness that one perceives it as *separate* from oneself, as unmistakably *other*. It manifests itself as a brilliant golden light, but it is actually *oneself*, in a higher form, that one is seeing. It is as though the individual, being thoroughly identified with his own limited personality, asks: "What is that beautiful light over there?" never conceiving for a moment that anything so magnificent could possibly be himself in his complete—and, we need to add here, divine—manifestation. The golden light is actually a reflection of one's own inherent divine nature and symbolizes the higher self. The light one sees, then, is one's own.

The higher self, furthermore, has total knowledge of the individual personality, both past and future. That is why, when it is experienced as a voice, it seems to be an "all-knowing" one (to use the phrase of one respondent).[43] That is why it can initiate a life review and, in addition, provide a preview of an individual's life events. At this level, information is stored holographically and is experienced holographically—simultaneously or nearly so. In fact, the life review *is* a holographic phenomenon par excellence; I have even heard a couple of individuals, who knew about holograms, characterize their life reviews in this way. In Pribram's words, in holographic consciousness, "everything is happening at all once, synchronously."[44]

From this perspective, it is easy to understand why so many interpret this kind of experience as "a conversation with God" or simply "being with God" and, in a sense, they are right. If one can accept the idea of a higher self, it is not difficult to assume that that self—as well as the individual himself—is actually an aspect of God, or the Creator, or any such term with which one feels comfortable. Since most people are used to thinking dualistically of God as somehow "up there" while they remain "down here," they can be expected to interpret their experience with their higher self as a direct encounter with God. The idea of "God" is, after all, more familiar to most people than is the notion of a higher self.

This is perhaps not the appropriate context to get deeply into this issue, but readers familiar with various spiritual traditions will know that the point of many spiritual disciplines, such as meditation and prayer, is precisely to cultivate an awareness of one's higher self in order to align one's individual personality with it. It is believed that in this way one can live more fully in accordance with the total being of which one's personality is but an expression. In this light, one might argue that the onset of apparent death may trigger this kind of awareness directly and involuntarily. It is interesting to observe that, as we have previously seen, such experiences tend to bring about "a spiritualization of consciousness" in some near-death survivors, similar to that expressed in the lives of those who are already consciously following some kind of "spiritual" path. Thus, one may speculate that the near-death experience may represent, at least for some, a *sudden* means of awakening to a higher spiritual reality. This kind of interpretation, however, lies outside what science itself can establish.

There is one further feature of the core experience that we must consider in connection with the higher-self interpretation I have advanced: the decisional crisis. If the higher self does indeed have total knowledge of the individual personality, both past and future, that knowledge must include the "programmed" time of death for the personality. Thus, when an individual is told that he is being "sent back" or that "his time has not yet come," this presumably reflects the "life program" of that person's life.[45] The "spirits" who sometimes give these injunctions also seem to have access to this information.[46] It will be recalled, however, that the majority of individuals who report that a decision was made about their fate feel that *they* made it themselves— that they were given a *choice*. In such instances, we must either assume that the "life program" of an individual is modifiable after all—at least in certain states of consciousness—or that the higher self knows all along what choice the individual himself will make. At this level, we can only speculate whether the sense of choice individuals feel they have is real or illusory. For my part, I would like to believe that it is real, but it is difficult to see how we could ever know this.

There are *hints*, however, in the literature on near-death experiences. Moody, for example, cites an extensive case in which a man first learned from a voice that he was to die, only to be allowed to live after all. This is how the man in question described this aspect of his experience. Before this, he had been very worried about the welfare of his adopted nephew:

> And again I felt this presence, but I didn't see any light this time, and thoughts or words came to me, just as before, and he said, "Jack, why are you crying? I thought you would be pleased to be with me." I thought. "Yes, I am. I want to go very much." And the voice said, "Then why are crying?" I said, "We've had some trouble with our nephew, you know, and I'm afraid my wife won't know how to raise him. I'm trying to put into words [he was in the midst of writing a letter when the presence manifested itself] how I feel, and what I want her to try to do for him. I'm concerned, too, because I feel that maybe my presence could have settled him down some."
>
> Then the thoughts came to me, from this presence, "Since you are asking for someone else, and thinking of others, not Jack, I will grant you what you want. You will live until you see your nephew become a man."[47]

Such a case makes it appear that the "life plan" can indeed be altered but that it may be the higher self that must consent to the change.

In considering such matters, perhaps it is best not to try to be too definitive concerning what the "rules" are! As always, the reader is free to ponder this material and arrive at his own conclusions.

I have been so far assuming, of course, that the higher-order entity which seems to be in charge of things is actually the individual's higher self, but there are certainly other interpretations. Here, however, I want to consider one possible alternative. Just as the concept of the double (the second body) may suggest to the religious-minded the idea of the soul, so the concept of the presence may appear to some to represent the idea of the "guardian angel." Before one dismisses this notion as a fancy worthy only of Sunday school classes, let me refer to a portion of a near-death experience that suggests that we should not be too quick to reject it after all.

John Lilly, a scientist best known for his research with dolphins, relates a powerful near-death experience in his autobiographical work, *The Center of the Cyclone.* In the course of his experience, he became aware of two "sources of radiance, of love, of warmth." These conveyed to Lilly a series of "comforting, reverential, awesome thoughts" and instructed him in a number of spiritual matters. Lilly's entire experience is far too complex to condense here, but at its end, these beings identify themselves:

> They say they are my guardians, that they have been with me before at critical times and that in fact *they are with me always,* but I am not usually in a state to perceive them. I am in a state to perceive them when I am close to the death of the body.[48] (My italics.)

Lilly's account certainly squares with a common understanding of the concept of "guardian angel," and other near-death testimony is consistent with this interpretation. Despite such instances, however, I am not convinced that the concept of guardians or guardian angels cannot be reconciled with that of the higher self. In fact, at this point I am inclined to believe that such guardians themselves represent an *aspect* of the higher self and not "entities," which are somehow separate and independent of it. Furthermore, a closer examination of Lilly's own account affords some evidence for this more inclusive interpretation.

Recall, first of all, that the guardians conveyed to Lilly that they were with him always. Then consider carefully these additional excerpts from Lilly's description:

> Their magnificent deep powerful love overwhelms me to a certain extent, but I finally accept it. As they move closer, I find less and less of me and more and more of them in my being. They stop at a critical distance and say to me that at this time I have developed only to the point where I can stand their presence at this particular distance. If they came any closer, they would overwhelm me, and I would lose myself as a cognitive entity, merging

with them. They further say that I separated them into two, because that is my way of perceiving them, but that in reality they are one in the space in which I found myself. They say that I insist on still being an individual, forcing a projection onto them, as if they were two. They further communicate to me that if I go back to my body as I developed further, I eventually would perceive the oneness of them and of me, and of many others.[49]

It seems to me that the whole thrust of this paragraph is consistent with the assumption that these guardians actually represent an aspect of the total self of which Lilly's personality is only a part. He finds that they threaten to overwhelm his very (individual) essence; that he is in danger of "merging with them"; that they are not two, but one essence, together with Lilly; that they tell him that he still insists on being an individual; and so on. To me, this sounds as though it is really the higher self speaking and that is is *perceived* by Lilly in the form of two guardians.

In view of Lilly's early religious training, this makes sense. He was reared a Catholic and says that as a child he was strongly influenced by his Church's imagery regarding angels, cherubim and seraphim and the like. Since it has already been noted (see footnote 43, page 295) that the higher self tends to speak in an idiom consistent with the respondent's style, it is reasonable to suppose that it may also reveal itself in a form congruent with an individual's early religious training and belief system. This interpretation would also apply to Craig Lundahl's investigations of the near-death experiences among Mormons, where guardian angels are also sometimes mentioned.

I am inclined to conclude, therefore, that the guardian angel interpretation, rather than constituting an alternative to the one based on the concept of the higher self, is actually only an alternative *manifestation* of the latter.

We have now considered most of the major phenomena associated with the tunnel/light stages of the core experience. In my opinion, the holographic perspective provides an interpretative framework that helps to make sense of some of these phenomena, though not all of the concepts I have employed (for example, the higher self) in my explanation derive from holographic ideas. Nevertheless, in evaluating this framework's utility, we must always bear in mind that since *we* are not functioning in a holographic reality right now, we cannot reasonably expect to be in a position to judge definitively the appropriateness of this framework. In this respect, those few people who are *both* conversant with holographic theory and have had a near-death experience would seem to have the best qualifications for assessing the relevance of this kind of interpretation here.

Before turning to the last stage of the core experience, however, it may be helpful to make explicit one further aspect of the core experience that *is* easily understandable in holographic terms. I have in mind the perception of time and space. We have already seen in Chapter Six that the modal near-death experience is one in which the concepts of time and space have no meaning. This is precisely what we should expect if the experience takes place in a holographic state of consciousness, since in that state

> . . . time and space are collapsed. Ordinary boundaries of space and time, such as locations of any sort, disappear. . . .[50]

This is not only the common testimony of our own near-death survivors, but has also been indicated in the near-death narratives of famous scientist-mystics as well.

Lilly's own account, for example, ends with the lines:

> In this state, there is no time, there is an immediate perception of the past, present and future as if on the present moment.[51]

Carl Jung, a psychiatrist noted for his explorations of the deep unconscious, had an extraordinary near-death experience when he was about seventy. In describing it in his autobiographical work, *Memories, Dreams, Reflections,* he comments:

> . . . I can describe the experience only as the ecstasy of a non-temporal state in which present, past and future are one. Everything that happens in time had been brought together into a concrete whole. Nothing was distributed over time, nothing could be measured by temporal concepts. . . . One is interwoven into an indescribable whole yet observes it with complete objectivity.[52]

Later, in discussing the possibility of life after death, Jung goes on to say:

> . . . the psyche at times functions outside of the spatio-temporal law of causality. This indicates that our conceptions of space and time, and therefore of causality also, are incomplete. A complete picture of the world would require the addition of still *another dimension;* only then could the totality of phenomena be given a unified explanation. . . . I have been convinced that at least a part of our psychic existence is characterized by a relativity of space and time. This relativity seems to increase, in proportion to the

Life at Death

distance from [normal] consciousness, to an absolute condition of timelessness and spacelessness.[53]

Clearly Jung is describing a holographic conception of reality and is doing so, as he concedes, partly on the basis of his own near-death experience.

This conception, then, seems to fit the experiences of both gifted students of the inner life and those whose near-death experience was their first conscious encounter with a world beyond time and space. It is on the basis of such correspondences as these that holographic theory seems to me to offer the best hope of providing a scientific underpinning for an understanding of the core experience.

We will see further evidence of its applicability when we examine some of the features associated with the final stage of the experience.

"The World of Light"

The last stage of the core experience seems to fulfill the promise implied by the encounter with the brilliant golden light. Here one appears to move *through* that light and into a "world of light." At this point, the individual perceives a realm of surpassing beauty and splendor and is sometimes aware of the "spirits" of deceased relatives or loved ones.

What is this world?

In holographic terms, it is another frequency domain—a realm of "higher" frequencies. Consciousness continues to function holographically so that it interprets these frequencies in object terms. Thus, another "world of appearances" (just as the physical world, according to holographic theory, is a world of appearances) is constructed. At the same time, this world of appearances is fully "real" (just as our physical world is real); it is just that *reality is relative to one's state of consciousness.*

In esoteric terms, this is the—or one—level of the so-called astral plane. As I have already mentioned, the esoteric literature is replete with descriptions of this world of light.

If one reads the literature that purports to describe this realm or if one simply rereads the accounts of stage V provided by our respondents (or some of Moody's in *Reflections on Life After Life*), one quickly forms the impression that everything in this world is immeasurably enhanced in beauty compared to the things of our physical world. That is why it is often characterized as a world of "higher vibrations."

That such talk isn't mere metaphor was suggested by the comment of one of our respondents *(20)*, who, in attempting to describe the music of this realm, likened it to "a combination of vibrations . . . many vibrations." Of course, music *does* consist of vibrations, but it isn't ordinarily spoken of in that way. Such observations again hint that those near-death survivors who reach this stage are responding directly to a frequency (vibratory) domain of holographic reality.

But in just what sense is this realm a holographic domain? Just where do the landscapes, the flowers, the physical structures, and so forth *come from?* In what sense are they "real"?

I have one speculative answer to these questions to offer—a holographic interpretation of the astral plane. I believe that this is a realm that is created by *interacting thought structures.* These structures or "thought-forms" combine to form patterns, just as interference waves form patterns on a holographic plate. And just as the holographic image appears to be fully real when illuminated by a laser beam, so the images produced by interacting thought-forms appear to be real.

There might appear to be a serious imperfection in this holographic analogy: The pattern produced on the physical holographic plate is, after all, only a meaningless swirl. It only becomes coherent when a coherent beam of light (that is, a laser) is used to illuminate the swirl. What, then, is the equivalent of the laser in the stage V realm?

The logic of my speculation seemingly leads to a single conclusion: It is the mind itself. If the brain functions holographically to give us our picture of physical reality, then the mind must function similarly when the physical brain can no longer do so. Of course, it would be much simpler if one merely assumed, as some brain researchers (for example, Sir John Eccles[54] and Wilder Penfield[55]) appear to have done, that the mind works *through* the brain during physical life but is not reducible to brain function. If the mind *can* be supposed to exist independent of the brain, it could presumably function holographically *without* a brain. If one is not willing to grant this assumption, one would seem forced to postulate a *non-physical* brain of some kind that operates on this "astral" level. At this point, we would have passed over the limit of tolerable speculation. In my view, it is preferable merely to assume that sensorylike impressions at this level are functionally organized in a way similar to sensory impressions of the physical world, that is, holographically.

If we can assume this (leaving the question of the "mechanism" open), then the attributes of stage V would fall neatly into place. Since individual minds "create" this world (out of thoughts and images), this reality reflects, to a degree, the "thought-structures" of individuals used to the world of physical reality. Thus, the "forms" of the stage V world are similar to those of the physical world. *However,* since this is a realm that is also (presumably) composed of minds that are more clearly

Life at Death

attuned or accustomed to this higher frequency domain, those minds can shape the impressions of the "newly arrived." The holographic result—an interaction of these thought patterns—thus tends to create a "higher gloss" to the perceived forms of this realm—that is, they are experienced in an enhanced way. One is tempted to say that *what* is seen is, at least at first, largely determined by preexisting schemata of near-death survivors, but that *how* (finely or beautifully) it appears is influenced primarily by minds used to that frequency domain.

The gist of this speculative holographic interpretation, then, is that "the world of light" is indeed a mind-created world fashioned of interacting (or interfering) thought patterns. Nevertheless, that world is fully as real-seeming as is our physical world.[56] Presumably—and this is an admitted and obvious extrapolation—as one becomes increasingly accustomed to this holographic domain and to "how it works," the correspondences between the physical world and this realm grow increasingly tenuous. Eventually one would suppose that an individual's consciousness would become anchored in the four-dimensional reality of the holographic domain and the familiar structures of our world would be radically changed there in ways we can only surmise.

The holographic interpretation can obviously also be used to account for the perception of "spirit-forms," a common feature of stage V experiences and deathbed visions. Just as object-forms are, theoretically, from a holographic point of view, a function of interacting mind patterns, so, too, are encounters with "persons" in "spirit bodies." Such "entities" are, then, the product of interacting minds attuned to a holographic domain in which thought alone fashions reality. The fact that communication between the near-death survivor and the "spirit-form" is usually said to be telepathic in nature again points to a world of existence where thought is king. From this angle, one can easily see that the manifestations in this high order of reality could easily transcend the forms of our sensory world. As individuals whose consciousnesses are rooted in the natural world, we can only speculate on the levels of mind that may be able to influence perceptions in the frequency domain associated with stage V experiences.

Before concluding our discussion of this domain, we must return to an issue we raised but did not resolve earlier: the matter of hell.

Stage V experiences, as we have seen, are almost always described in terms of paradisical imagery; the individual appears to enter a world of incomparable delight. Yet, in discussing Rawlings's work, we saw evidence that near-death survivors sometimes have hellish experiences. The bulk of the evidence plus the methodological shortcomings and tendentiousness of Rawlings's research led us to conclude that such experiences are probably very much rarer than Rawlings himself claims, but that they sometimes do occur.

The question is how to account for them.

Rawlings's own interpretation is that hellish experiences simply reflect a lack of a personal commitment to Christ. In this respect they serve as a warning of the ultimate consequences of failing to make such a commitment.

Without wishing to get entangled in theological issues, I must confess that I find this interpretation too simplistically doctrinaire for my taste. But quite apart from my personal opinion, even some of Rawlings's own evidence fails to square with his interpretation. For example, Rawlings cites the case of one man, described as "a staunch Christian, the founder of a Sunday school, and a lifelong supporter of the church,"[57] who had multiple near-death experiences, the first of which was hellish while the remaining two conformed to the Moody pattern. That kind of variation is not explicable on the basis of Rawlings's interpretation. Neither is the fact that, according to Osis and Haraldsson's cross-cultural research, Hindus have very much the same kind of paradisical (or stage V) deathbed visions as do Christians.

My own interpretation, naturally, is quite different. Rawlings is not the only investigator to find evidence of an occasional near-death experiential sequence that begins unpleasantly and ends well. Robert Crookall has also described this sequence (sometimes, however, in connection with out-of-body experiences only) and so has Moody. In addition, Ritchie has recounted a detailed personal example of this kind.[58] The sequence, in fact, when it is reported, *always* seems to be from "bad to good." My interpretation of hellish near-death experiences is predicated on this particular sequence.

In my view, what is happening in these cases is that the individual is "passing through" a lower frequency domain (although he may occasionally—temporarily—"get stuck" there). This domain is also a holographic reality and is organized in precisely the same way as the paradisical realm we have already considered. The principal difference is in the nature of the minds that are interacting to create this reality.

Even if this kind of interpretation is correct, however, there would still seem to be a problem. Why is this domain so rarely reported compared to the paradisical realm? One proposal has it that the tunnel phenomenon serves as a shield to protect the individual from an awareness of this domain.[59] It will be recalled that the tunnel effect itself was interpreted as representing a *shift in consciousness* from one level to another. Functionally, this state of affairs can be compared to a traveler riding a subway *underneath* the slums of a city: the subway tunnel prevents him ever being directly *aware* of his surroundings although the slums are there. Instead, like the typical near-death survivor, he begins his trip in darkness and emerges into the light.

That this is no mere fanciful analogy is suggested by one of Moody's cases. One woman, who was believed to be "dead" for fifteen minutes, reported that during one stage of her experience she became aware of what Moody calls a "realm of bewildered spirits." In describing this realm she says that:

> . . . what I saw was after I left the physical hospital. As I said, I felt I rose upward and it was in between, it was *before* I actually entered this tunnel . . . and before I entered the spiritual world where there is so much brilliant sunshine [that I saw these bewildered spirits].[60]

In my opinion, then, the near-death survivor is usually kept from having a direct awareness of this realm, just as, for perhaps different reasons, he usually has no recall for his "return trip." Hell may exist as a "lower frequency domain," but most near-death survivors never seem to encounter it and, if they do, only a tiny fraction seem to "get stranded" there. What may happen *after* the initial stages of death— something this research cannot speak to—remains an open question.

Conclusions

So much for the interpretation of the core experience. Since I have taken up so much space in presenting my parapsychological-holographic formulation, I will make only a few brief comments here before concluding this chapter.

First of all, by no means do I want to leave the impression that I feel that I have totally "explained" the core experience in a theoretically satisfactory way. There are many loose threads still lying about, as any perceptive reader undoubtedly will have noticed. For example, the whole question of whether the core experience is really in the nature of a "stored program" that is released at the point of death (or perhaps in other ways), as Grof and Halifax have proposed, was never resolved. The relevance of the possible neurological basis of near-death experiences is likewise still largely an uncharted territory. I can only hope that my discussion of such issues and my own interpretation will motivate other researchers to probe these matters more deeply.

Of course, it is at this point an unanswerable question whether the mysteries of the near-death experience can ever be fully understood through scientific investigation alone. Such experiences may well have an infrangible or nonphysical quality that will prevent us from providing a truly comprehensive scientific accounting of them. Try as we may (and I believe, should) to articulate such an understanding, it may finally prove to be the case that science can take us only so far in shaping that understanding.

These observations bring us, finally, to the role of religious and spiritual concepts in the interpretative matrix of the near-death experience. It is obvious that my own interpretation, though I tried to keep it grounded in scientific theory and research, occasionally was forced to stray into the spiritual realm. I confess that I did so with considerable intellectual reluctance, but also with a sense that it would have been intellectually cowardly to *avoid* doing so. In my opinion—and I could be wrong—there is simply no way to deal with the interpretative problems raised by these experiences without confronting the spiritual realm. Indeed, Pribram himself says, in a passage already quoted, that:

> Spiritual insights fit the description of this [holographic] domain. They're made perfectly plausible by the invention of the holo-gram.[61]

In my view, not only plausible but *necessary*. In the paradigm shift (which I have previously alluded to) that seems to be leading to a recognition of the primary role of consciousness, the world of modern physics and the spiritual world seem to reflect a *single* reality. If this is true, no scientific account of *any* phenomenon can be complete without taking its spiritual aspect into account.

This position, of course, is hardly new. It has been espoused in one form or another, not only by mystics, but by large numbers of in-fluential scientists and intellectuals as well. I could list many names of well-known men and women to buttress this point, but instead let me conclude simply by quoting the most eminent scientist of our century. To me, his attitude suggests not only the proper spirit in which to approach the study of near-death experiences but also its likely effect on the world view of those who do explore them.

Perhaps it is ironically fitting that Albert Einstein himself did not believe in life after death, but his words nevertheless speak to the emotions kindled by familiarity—either direct or vicarious—with the near-death experience itself:

> The most beautiful thing we can experience is the mysterious. It is the source of all true art and science. He to whom this emotion is a stranger, who can no longer pause to wonder and stand rapt in awe, is as good as dead: his eyes are closed. This insight into the mystery of life, coupled though it be with fear, has also given rise

to religion. To know what is impenetrable to us really exists, manifesting itself as the highest wisdom and the most radiant beauty which our dull faculties can comprehend only in their most primitive forms—this knowledge, this feeling, is at the center of true religiousness.[62]

THIRTEEN

Implications and Applications of Near-Death Experience Research

We have now approached the limit of knowledge of the near-death experience that can be disclosed to us through scientific inquiry alone. We have seen what it is like to die and what happens in the lives of people who somehow manage to survive their encounter with death. We have also examined a variety of theoretical explanations that provide some clues concerning how such near-death experiences might occur in the first place.

But now we reach questions to which science itself is unable to speak: What is the *meaning* of these experiences? What are their implications for our lives? What do they reveal to us about the nature of reality? What is their relevance to religious and spiritual issues? In short, just what—as human beings, not merely scientists or scholars—are we to make of all this?

These are the kinds of questions that most readers of this book will, I am sure, have pondered throughout. However objective and scientific we may strive to be in our work and thinking, we naturally find ourselves dwelling on these matters, especially when we are confronted with experiences that *inherently* trigger such concerns. All of us ultimately must deal with these larger meanings, which form a context for our lives, and with the underlying values that give them direction. And these issues, as the philosopher Huston Smith has pointed out, are precisely what science, as presently constituted, cannot by its nature address.[1] For our answers here we must turn to other sources: religion, philosophy—or ourselves.

Questions such as those I have raised explicitly here admit of no certainties. There are no pat answers to be found and no consensus to be expected. Each of us must quest after these answers individually and arrive at his own conclusions. Scientific data or the pronouncements of scientists may *help* in that search, but, at bottom, it is up to each inquiring individual to achieve his own understanding through extra-scientific means.

Here, of course, our common experience has been our study of near-death experiences and their aftereffects. Each reader, accordingly, will have arrived at *some* kind of assessment of their meaning, even if it is one that is largely intuitive or implicit. Naturally, too, I have my own view—which is important chiefly for myself, not for others. If I choose to share it, it is obviously not because I give it any special weight and certainly not because I think it is compelled by our data, but only because I believe that some readers may genuinely wish to know what I myself make of these materials.

So for the next few pages, I will, in a sense, remove my white lab coat and describe my own beliefs—for what they may be worth. I feel somewhat (but not entirely!) comfortable in doing so now only because I trust that by trying not to obtrude my own opinions earlier, readers of this book will have had the opportunity to arrive at their own views uninfluenced by mine.

One of the first questions I am generally asked, following my talks on near-death experiences, is whether I believe that they are indicative of a "life after death." Usually—still having on my scientific garb—I remind my audiences that what I have studied are *near*-death experiences, not *after*-death experiences. The persons I have talked with have been close to death and, in some cases, may have survived the initial stages of death, but they have not *actually* died. Therefore, one can only extrapolate—if one is so inclined—from these experiences, what, if anything, might occur after death. There is obviously no guarantee either that these experiences will *continue* to unfold in a way consistent with their beginnings or indeed that they will continue at all.

That, I believe, is the correct *scientific* position to take on the significance of these experiences. But my questioners can usually figure that out for themselves, and that answer is not really responsive to the implicit question that I sense behind the words. *That* question is better phrased as: Well, you must have given all this plenty of thought. What do you *personally* make of it? Do *you* think there is life after death?

Here, I no longer have the floor of science to support me and must, therefore, support myself. This time, however, I would like to go beyond a simple statement of my own beliefs by outlining the framework within which they fall.

I *do* believe—but not just on the basis of my own or others' data regarding near-death experiences—that we continue to have a conscious existence after our physical death and that the core experience does represent its beginning, a glimpse of things to come. I am, in fact, convinced—both from my own personal experiences and from my studies as a psychologist—that it is possible to become conscious of "other realities" and that the coming close to death represents one avenue to a higher "frequency domain," or reality, which will be fully accessible to us following what we call death. Let me be clear, however, that it would be exceedingly naive for anyone to believe this on the basis of my say-so (or anyone else's), nor would it be justified to claim that the findings I have presented in this book in any way *prove* this assertion. What I do hope is that the material I have offered here will initiate or contribute to a personal search aimed at the exploration of such issues as "life after death." The "proof" of this matter is, in any case, not something one will find in books.

My own understanding of these near-death experiences leads me to regard them as "teachings." They are, it seems to me, by their nature, *revelatory experiences*. They vouchsafe both to those who undergo them *and* to those who hear about them an intuitive sense of the transcendent aspect of creation. These experiences clearly imply that there is something more, something *beyond* the physical world of the senses, which, in the light of these experiences, now appears to be only the mundane segment of a greater spectrum of reality. In this respect, core experiences are akin to mystical or religious experiences of the kind that William James discusses so brilliantly in his classic lectures on the subject.[2] Anyone who makes the effort to inform himself of the nature and consequences of genuine mystical or religious experiences will soon become convinced that the core experience is itself a member of this larger family.

Why do such experiences occur? Surely, no one can say with any certainty, but I have one speculative answer to offer, though I admit it may sound not only fanciful but downright playful. I have come to believe that the universe (if I may put it in this fashion) has many ways of "getting its message across." In a sense, it wants us to "wake up," to become aware of the cosmic dimensions of the drama of which we are all a part. Near-death experiences represent one of its devices for waking us up to this higher reality. The "message"—for the experiencing individual at least—is usually so clear, potent, and undeniable that it is neither forgotten nor dismissed. Potentially, then, those who have these experiences become "prophets" to the rest of us who have fallen back to sleep or have never been awake. From this point of view, the voices we have heard in this book are those of prophets preaching a religion of universal brotherhood and love and of divine compassion. This, obviously, is no new message; it acquires its significance chiefly from the unusual experiential circumstances that give rise to it—the state of consciousness associated with the onset of apparent death.

Of course, the experiences we have discussed in this book happen, for the most part, to ordinary men and women, who have neither the inclination nor, usually, the charismatic gifts to become religious prophets in any serious, sociological way. Indeed, the typical near-death survivor will disavow any such ambition and will usually say that his religious or spiritual understanding is not one he wishes to impose on others. We have already seen that some of these men and women have been, in fact, reluctant to discuss their experiences at all, much less to broadcast them indiscriminately. Certainly, no "new" religion has yet grown up around these experiences, nor is it easy to see how or why one would; there is nothing new here.

For these reasons, I prefer to think of these experiences as *seed* experiences. The individual to whom a core experience happens is given a *chance* to awake; the seed may or may not take root. If it does, it shows itself by developing the individual's spiritual sensitivity in ways that are obvious to others. As with a mystical experience, a core experience in itself is not *necessarily* transformative. Much depends on how the experience is interpreted and integrated.[3] Nevertheless, the seed experience rarely remains just a treasured memory, like a flower chastely preserved in glass. On the contrary, it appears to be a *dynamic* structure, *like* a seed, in that its nature is to unfold and flower within the individual in such a way as to manifest itself without. It is in this sense that it seems to represent a *potential* for development and self-actualization. In any event, for at least some near-death survivors, it becomes a central motif in their lives, governing the direction of their spiritual development. Such lives—where the seed potential is realized—then become lives lived in accordance with the vision one has had of what we can call Greater Life.

Another question I am often asked is why some people have (or can recall) this experience where others remember nothing on coming close to death. There has not yet been enough research directed to this question for me to give any reliable answers here. Nevertheless, in line with my own personal interpretation, I could perhaps suggest one possibility (although there is, as far as I can see, no way to test it). *If* these experiences occur in order to provide a means of awakening to a "higher reality," then perhaps those who report such experiences somehow "needed" them to provide a catalyst to their own development. If we allow ourselves the dubious luxury of a teleological argument for a moment, it may be worth pointing out that many near-death experiencers appeared to suggest that *following* their experience their lives took on a meaningfulness and direction that was formerly lacking. By the same kind of reasoning, perhaps this is why those who are previously informed about Moody-type experiences are less likely to have them: The universe has already got its message across; the seed of awakening has already been planted in a different way.

I hope it will be understood that I am offering these ideas only as personal speculations and that I myself regard some of them very doubtfully, since they are obviously based on a logic that cannot really be intellectually defended. It is certainly possible to dismiss them totally while accepting the general interpretative framework presented in the last chapter. Still, while we are on the topic of impossible questions, let me consider just one more that is sometimes put to me.

How is it, questioners will ask, that all of a sudden we are hearing so much about these near-death experiences? Haven't people always had these experiences?

In normal contexts, I usually reply that there are a number of factors responsible for this development: the liberating climate for this research provided by Kübler-Ross's work and the thanatological movement generally; improvements in resuscitation technology; the effect of Moody's work in facilitating discussion of these experiences on the part of those who formerly would not have divulged them; and so on. Typically, I also mention selected historical examples of these experiences so that my audiences will know that they are by no means only a phenomenon of modern times.

In *this* context, however, I want to mention a different kind of answer to this question, one that speaks to a different level of meaning and is quite beyond our capacity to evaluate by any formal standards. Again, it is offered only in the spirit of speculative food for thought.

I think everyone realizes that the closing decades of this century already give us grave cause for uneasiness concerning the destiny of the human race on this planet. Predictions of widespread, even global, calamities are plentiful, and though the scenarios differ, all of us have heard enough of them for them to have become real *as possibilities*. Could it be, then, that one reason why the study of death has emerged as one of the dominant concerns of our time is to help us to become globally sensitized to the experience of death precisely because the notion of death on a *planetary scale* now hangs, like the sword of Damocles, over our heads? Could this be the universe's way of "innoculating" us against the fear of death? Even if planetary catastrophes should befall us in the next decades (and of course I am not *predicting* that they will), resulting in deaths on a massive scale, we could never be certain why the thanatological movement arose when it did. But our gloomy global prospects certainly help make our interest in death understandable. The connection between these two developments is, of course, interpretable in many ways (and at several levels), of which my suggestion is merely one speculative possibility.

Now, assuming that the world *is* going to endure for a while after all, I want to turn our attention to quite different matters: new directions in near-death research and the possible applications to be derived from research in this field.

New Directions in Near-Death Research

This investigation and other similar, already-published explorations of near-death phenomena hardly constitute the last word on this important subject. In fact, it is closer to the truth to say that so far research devoted to these experiences has done little more than establish the existence of the core experience. Many questions remain to be answered concerning the factors and effects associated with it before we can say we have any real understanding of it. Accordingly, I would like to take a few moments here to suggest what lines of research seem most worthwhile to pursue, given our present level of knowledge of near-death phenomena.

First, it seems to me, we need more extensive and rigorous studies of near-death experiences in different populations. Perhaps the foremost question to be answered through this research is this: Is the core experience a *universal* phenomenon? Osis and Haraldsson's study, though highly significant in itself, is only a promising beginning in the cross-cultural work on near-death phenomena. We need much more evidence here before we can conclude anything concerning the extent to which the core experience pattern is transcultural. Also falling into this category would be studies of near-death experiences of children, prisoners who have committed serious crimes (for example, murder) and suicide attempters who have not used drugs to kill themselves. The special circumstances of these three groups would contribute significantly to our understanding of the possible limits associated with the core experience. Another interesting group to study, as Moody also pointed out, would be mothers who during or immediately after childbirth may have had a near-death experience. My impression from our study is that many unusual experiences may be found among this population.

Second, there are still a host of questions revolving around the issue of why some people recall this experience while close to death where others do not. As we have seen, it may be that at one level this issue cannot really be addressed through scientific procedures, but at other levels it is clearly amenable to scientific study. At this point, all we know is that demographic variables tend to be unrelated to recall, but there may be individual personality factors that might be predictive. For example, it could be that persons high in defensiveness or repressive tendencies might be less likely to remember such experiences where people gifted with psychic ability or ease of dream recall might be more likely. In any event, studies focusing on such individual characteristics might be able to shed some light on these questions. Of course, it would be provocative if *no* relationship whatsoever between such factors and core experience recall was uncovered! Another aspect of this issue to which further research should be directed is the question of the effect of prior knowledge on recall of a core experience. Both Sabom and I, in our independent investigations, found an unexpected and statistically significant *negative* relationship here. Future research should be geared to determining if this is indeed a consistent relationship and, if it is, how it is to be interpreted.

Third, the study of aftereffects is one richly deserving of further attention. More systematic work needs to be done documenting the changes that can be attributed to the near-death experience itself. In this work, it is also necessary to go beyond the self-report measures used here; perhaps behavior rating scales (to be filled out by family members) or direct observational investigations could be undertaken as a first step in supplementing our knowledge here. Particularly promising would be studies aimed at detecting the development of psychic abilities (which may be enhanced following core experiences) and those concerned with the measurement of belief and attitudinal shifts (for example, openness toward the idea of reincarnation, fear of death, and so forth).

A fourth set of research possibilities centers around direct observational studies of the dying. Too much of our data comes from *ex post facto* accounts and, correspondingly, not enough from on-the-scene witnesses. Such investigations are particularly crucial to assessing such notions as Rawlings's repression hypothesis and the hypothesis that the double separates from the physical body at death. Obviously, such research presents many formidable problems quite apart from the ethical issues involved, which are themselves considerable. Perhaps some public- and private-duty nurses could be enlisted to serve as unobtrusive observers, as could some chaplains. If some of these men and women were also gifted with clairvoyant sight, the possibilities for significant observations would, of course, be that much richer. In any event, some attention can and ought now be given to working out the procedures for such observational studies so as to rebut the criticisms that will stigmatize such work as "ghoulish" or "coldly clinical." Along these lines, I have some suggestions that I will put forward in Appendix IV of this book.

Finally, there is a clear need for neurologically trained investigators to undertake the kinds of studies that will speak to some of the neurological and physiological speculations outlined in Chapter Eleven. So far we have almost nothing *but* speculative possibilities that have been proposed in an offhand way to account for the core experience. Although I myself remain unconvinced that a neurological interpretation will be found that will serve to "explain away" the core experience, nevertheless, I strongly feel that the search for this level of explanation should be intensified by those who feel "the answer" may be found here. No avenue that holds out some hope for insight into this phenomenon should go untraveled—even if it contains the possibility of totally undermining one's prior convictions.

It remains to be seen what course near-death research will actually follow as it develops, but whatever work may be undertaken to enlarge our theoretical understanding of the core experience, it will run concurrently with an allied aspect of this endeavor: application. And this work is already beginning.

Applications

Granted that there is still much to be learned about near-death phenomena, we cannot delay our consideration of how the knowledge we have already gained can best be used in dealing with death and dying. Indeed, as I have just observed, the applications stemming from this research are not just matters of potential; they are, in some cases, already fact.

In my opinion, the applications tend to fall into three rather distinct categories: (1) those aimed at individuals who are close to death, either as a result of illness or psychological inclination (that is, suicidal individuals); (2) those that pertain to individuals who have recently survived a near-death incident; and (3) those directed toward individuals who have not been close to death themselves, but who may be concerned with another's actual or possible death—or their own. In what follows, I will consider each of these categories of application in turn.

Individuals Close to Death

Many people fear death and many fear it unnecessarily. We have seen how having a near-death experience, however, tends to eliminate or drastically reduce that fear of death. If one could transmit, even vicariously, the *effect* of the near-death experience to those who are about to die, could we not expect a reduction of apprehension in these men and women as well?

Sabom and Kreutziger have evidence that just hearing about these experiences tends to reduce one's fear of death. Thus, it seems that the widespread dissemination of the findings of this research would in itself tend to bring comfort to the last days of those who are about to die. But one could do more than this—much more.

If a dying person were open to it, it might be possible to play for him specially prepared audio or video tapes in which near-death survivors describe their own experiences when close to death. In other cases, it should be possible to bring together, directly, dying individuals with those who have almost died; the near-death survivor's experience could serve as a powerful reducer of death anxiety. Indeed, my colleagues and I have already made a start toward doing this work on an informal basis here in Connecticut, with gratifying results.

Of course, I do not mean to imply that such procedures, or elaborations of them, will, in themselves, dissolve all fears of death or necessarily lessen the pain often associated with dying. But they will, I feel sure, help the dying person become better prepared for death and approach it with a heightened awareness of its transcendent possibilities.

Such an approach could easily be adopted in settings where professionals work with the dying, for example, in hospices (community-oriented hospitals for the dying), in general hospitals with units for the terminally ill, and in private homes. It could also be the basis for an entirely new kind of facility that is especially designed for dying individuals—a Center for the Dying Person. I offer my thoughts on this particular topic in Appendix IV.

I have so far discussed applicational ideas that are targeted to those who know that they are soon likely to die. But what about those who *wish* to die by their own hand? Can near-death research help in deterring suicide attempts?

My own belief—which research could easily be undertaken to confirm or refute—is that the findings in such books as Moody's and my own (and, I trust, from other books that are not yet published at this writing) would tend to discourage a person from taking his own life. In my own study, it was not that suicide-related near-death experiences were in themselves unpleasant that would tend to give one pause. Indeed, they were *not* unpleasant, but merely abridged when there was any recall at all. Rather, it was the testimony of *other* near-death survivors, which tended to imply that a *successful* suicide would probably regret his action, that might serve as a deterrent. The message in Moody's books is, of course, much the same.

In fact, it has *already* been shown that exposure to near-death research findings can apparently be helpful in reducing the likelihood of suicide. Psychologist John McDonagh practices what he calls "bibliotherapy" with his suicidally minded patients. He simply has them read Moody's book *Life After Life*. His findings? It works.

Of course, we need more research than this to buttress the point, but it already seems clear that near-death research can be beneficial to those bent on suicide as well as those who will soon die as a result of disease.

Near-Death Survivors

Knowledge about near-death experiences should prove useful to those who find themselves dealing professionally with individuals who have recently survived such an episode. Particularly for physicians (including psychiatrists, of course), nurses, chaplains, and social workers whose work brings them into contact with people who have been close to death, it is highly desirable to have some familiarity with and understanding of these experiences. I am not thinking of such obvious matters as realizing that a patient may be able to hear, while comatose, a conversation taking place among the members of a medical team or that he may even be able to see his own operation taking place—from a position outside his body. These possibilities are evident from our (and others') data and medical personnel should become familiar with them—if only to save themselves from later embarrassment!

What is more consequential here is not simply awareness of these possibilities at the time of a near-death episode, but *how that episode is handled afterward.* Even if one chooses not to regard a core experience as "real," it must be recognized that to most individuals it *is* real. And, more than that, it is a psychologically powerful event with a rich potential, as we have seen, for deep personal transformation. For these reasons alone, it is extremely important for professionals working with individuals who have had this kind of experience to be alert and sensitive to the immediate psychological state of the individual following a close confrontation with death. Although I do not believe that it is necessarily wise to inquire directly as to whether the individual has had any kind of experience (such question *may* be appropriate in some cases, however), the professional should remain open to the possibility that one has occurred and that the patient may wish to talk about it. He may also be confused, afraid, or deeply disappointed (at least at first) upon finding himself still alive. An understanding of the nature and dynamics of near-death experiences is, accordingly, essential if a professional is to be able to relate sensitively to a person who has survived such an incident. In my opinion, a professional ignorant of this kind of experience can sometimes inadvertently prove an obstacle to a patient's attempt to understand and integrate it.

Moody, who is, of course, himself a medical doctor, has recently advocated a similar approach.[4] The implication here for the training of those who work with the dying is fairly straightforward: At a minimum, it involves the dissemination of information about near-death experiences. Along with other near-death researchers, I have been attempting to do precisely this in my talks to professionals in medical settings.

Individuals Concerned with Death

Of course, the vast majority of those who learn about near-death experiences are neither terminally ill nor near-death survivors. They are instead united by a single characteristic: One day they too will die. Everyone, then, has a stake in understanding what it is like to die since no one is exempt from it, however far away it may seem psychologically. Let us therefore ask: What can we—who are not confronting (so far as we know) an imminent death—learn from the study of near-death experiences? Are there lessons here that we can apply to our own lives?

Some lessons are so clear, it seems to me, that hardly any discussion is needed for them beyond merely pointing them out. *If*, for example, we take these experiences to be authentic intimations of what death itself will be like (and, as I pointed out earlier, such a view is *not* strictly warranted by our data, but represents an extrapolation from them), then our view of death *must* be affected by this interpretation. Like near-death survivors themselves, we will probably come to think of death as representing a very beautiful and joyous transitional state. This may make it a good deal easier not only to accept our own deaths, but the death of loved ones, especially those who have died pre-maturely. One of the profoundly gratifying experiences I have had in the aftermath of this work is to hear people tell me, following one of my talks, that they can now readily accept the death, say, of a child, in the light of these experiences. Such statements are not usually made out of intellectual conviction only, of course; they are usually expressed in a heartfelt way, sometimes accompanied by tears. These moments (and I am not claiming they are frequent episodes) bring home to me just how profound the implications of this work can be for the living.

There are, of course, other applications as well. To the extent that we, too, can live *as if* we have almost died, then the ways of being in the world evinced by our near-death survivors become *our* ways, their perceptions, our perceptions, and their values our own. To live in the shadow of death, as if each day might be our last, can clearly promote a quickening of one's spiritual sensitivity. Pettiness and selfishness re-cede; expressions of love and compassion are natural to this state. If you actually thought—right now, this minute—that this was really the last time you were going to be able to see your spouse, your mother, your child, this world, how would you act? Near-death survivors have been there; they almost "left" without being able to say good-bye. Since returning, many of them have had occasion to think about "what might have been." And their subsequent lives are a powerful testimony to our common ability to live more deeply, more appreciatively, more lovingly, and more spiritually. In these near-death experiences are lessons in living that apply to all of us. As one near-death survivor commented, "I somehow feel that *everyone* should have this experience one time in their life. Maybe the world would be a happier place."

Well, obviously, not everyone *can* have the experience. But everyone *can* learn from it—if he chooses to. In their book, *The Human Encounter with Death*, Grof and Halifax quote a seventeenth-century monk: "The man who dies before he dies, does not die when he dies." This aphorism speaks not only to death, however; it is a prescription *for* life. If only through the power of imagination, we can all now experience what it is like to die in order truly to live.

These reflections bring me to a final point. As I remarked in the last chapter, near-death experiences are *not* uniquely associated with the moment of apparent death; that is simply one of the more reliable pathways to them. Instead, they seem to point to a higher spiritual world, and confer the possibility of a greater spiritual awareness for those who wish to nourish the seed that they have been given. But one does not have to nearly die in order to feel the beginnings of spiritual insight. There are many paths leading to spiritual awakening and development. The people we have studied in this book all happened to have stumbled onto a common path, which some followed further than others. That is their way. What our way may be is for each of us to discern. But perhaps another lesson we can glean from the study of near-death experiences is to realize that there is indeed a higher spiritual dimension that pervades our lives and that we will discover it for ourselves in the moment of our death. The question is, however: Will we discover it in the moments of our lives?

APPENDIX I

Interview Schedule

Date(s) of interview_____

Name of interviewer_____

Name of interviewee_____

Condition of the patient at time of interview_____

Circumstances of the interview (other persons, noise, interruptions, and so forth)_____

_____

_____

(In introducing yourself to the patient, you should explain the purpose of the interview pretty much as follows. These initial comments should be as standardized as possible across interviewers and hospitals.)

Hello, my name is_____. I'm a [graduate student, professor] at_____. How are you feeling today? [Take whatever time necessary to establish rapport with patient.] I believe_____[name of contact] told you a little about why I wanted to speak with you. Some associates and I at the University of_____ are working on a project concerned with what people experience when they undergo a life-threatening situation, like having a serious illness or accident. I understand that you recently may have experienced such an occurrence. Is that right? [Wait for patient to respond.] Naturally it is extremely helpful to us to be able to speak with people who have had this kind of experience themselves; that's why I'm grateful to you for being willing to talk to me about this. So, in a few minutes I'd like to ask you some questions that I've prepared for this purpose, but first let me mention a few things that may help us.

The first thing I should say is that some people—not necessarily everyone, though—appear to experience some unusual things when they have a serious illness or accident or when they come close to dying. Sometimes these things are a little puzzling and people are somewhat hesitant to talk about them. [Be a little jocular here; try by your manner to put the patient at ease.] Now please don't worry about this in talking with me! I just want you to feel free to tell me *anything* you can remember—whether it makes sense to you or not. O.K.? [Wait for patient to respond.]

Now let me assure you about one further thing. These interviews will be held in strictest confidence. When we analyze our results, any information you may furnish us will never be identified by name. Since we can guarantee that these interviews will be kept anonymous and confidential, you can feel free to tell me whatever you wish without having to worry that others may learn of your private experience.

265

As you may remember from the informed consent sheet you signed, Mr. [Mrs., Ms.]_____, we are going to tape-record this interview. This is standard practice in these studies and makes it possible to have an absolutely accurate record of what you say without my having to try to write everything down. Naturally, the tape-recorded material will also be available *only* to my associates.

Hopefully we'll be able to complete this interview today, but if you should grow tired, please let me know and we shall complete it another time. After we're finished, I would be happy to answer any [further] questions you may have, but I think it would be best if I spoke with you first.

[Turn tape cassette on at this point—*and make sure to check it for sound level;* an inaudible or poorly audible recording is useless to us.]

INTERVIEW PROPER BEGINS HERE:
Now, Mr. [Mrs., Ms.]_____, I first need to ask you just a few questions about yourself. First of all, may I know your *age*, please? What is your *occupation*? What is the *highest grade* you completed in school? May I know your *religious preference* or affiliation, please, if you have one? [Also make a note of *race, sex*; if apparently foreign, get nationality. All this information should be written down on the prepared form even though it is on tape.] Are you *married*? [If not, find out what marital status is: Widowed? Divorced? Single? Separated?]

Now, according to_____ [name of contact], you recently_____ *[specify condition,* for example, attempted suicide, had a serious accident, illness, experienced cardiac arrest, and so forth]. Can you tell me how this came about? [Let patient narrate this as much as possible in his/her own words, but probe, as necessary, for pertinent details if not otherwise forthcoming: date, location, circumstances, witnesses, and so on. Try to get patient to describe circumstances as specifically as possible.]

Sometimes people report experiencing certain things during an incident like yours. Do you remember being aware of anything while you_____ [specify condition]. Could you describe this for me? [Probe here, if necessary, for any feelings, perceptions, imagery, visions, and so forth. Try to make the patient aware that you understand that some aspects of his/her experience may be difficult or impossible to put into words. If you think it would facilitate matters, give patient a paper and pencil in case he/she would prefer to depict some aspect of his/her experience visually. But again, allow the patient to describe the experience in his/her own words as much as possible.]

Now, I'd like to ask you certain more specific questions about your experience. [For those patients who report no awareness during their episode, say, "Even though you don't recall anything specific from this time, let me just ask you whether any of these things rings a bell with you."]

[Modify this section, as necessary, depending on what a patient has previously said.]

1. Was the kind of experience difficult to put into words? [If yes:] Can you try all the same to tell me why? What was it about the experience that makes it so hard to communicate? Was it like a dream or different from a dream? [Probe]

2. When this episode occurred, *did you think you were dying or close to death? Did you actually think you were dead?* [Important questions to ask!] Did you hear anyone actually say that you were dead? What else do you recall hearing while in this state? [Ask these questions in turn.]

3. What were your feelings and sensations during the episode?

4. Did you hear any noises or unusual sounds during the episode?

5. Did you at any time feel as though you were traveling or moving? What was that experience like? [If appropriate:] Was this experience in any way associated with the noise (sound) you described before?

6. Did you at any time during this experience feel that you were somehow separate from your own physical body? During this time, were you ever aware of *seeing* your physical body? [Ask these questions in turn. Then, if appropriate, ask:] Could you describe this experience for me? How did you feel when you were in this state? Do you recall any thoughts that you had when you were in this state? When you were outside your own physical body, where were you? Did you have another body? [If yes:] Was there any kind of connection between yourself and your physical body? Any kind of link between the two that you could see? Describe it for me. When you were in this state, what were your perceptions of time? of space? of weight? Is there anything you could do while in this state that you could not do in your ordinary physical body? Were you aware of any tastes or odors? How, if at all, were your vision and hearing affected while in this state? Did you experience a sense of loneliness while in this state? How so? [Ask these questions in turn.]

7. During your episode, did you ever encounter other individuals, living or dead? [If affirmative:] Who were they? What happened when you met them? Did they communicate to you? What? How? Why do you think they communicated what they did to you? How did you feel in their presence?

8. Did you at any time experience a light, glow, or illumination? Can you describe this to me? [If affirmative:] Did this "light" communicate anything to you? What? What did you make of this light? How

did you feel? [Or how did it make you feel?] Did you encounter any religious figures such as angels, guardian spirits, Christ, and so forth? Did you encounter any frightening spirits such as demons, witches, or the devil? [Ask questions in turn.]

9. When you were going through this experience, did your life—or scenes from your life—ever appear to you as mental images or memories? [If so:] Can you describe this to me further? What was this experience like? How did it make you feel? Did you feel you learned anything from this experience? If so, what? [Ask questions in turn.]

10. Did you at any time have a sense of approaching some kind of boundary or limit or threshold or point of no return? [If so:] Can you describe this to me? Did you have any particular feelings or thoughts that you can recall as you approached this boundary? [Ask questions in turn.] Do you have any idea what this boundary represented or meant?

11. [If patient has previously stated that he/she *came close to dying,* ask:] When you felt close to dying, how did you feel? Did you want to come back to your body, to life? How did it feel when you did find yourself conscious again in your own body? Do you have any recollection of how you got back into your physical body? Do you have any idea why you didn't die at this time? Did you ever feel judged by some impersonal force? [Ask questions in turn.]

12. This experience of yours has been (very) recent but I wonder if you feel it has changed you in any way. Do you think so or not? If it has changed you, in what way? [If necessary and appropriate, then ask:] Has this experience changed your attitude toward life? How? Has it altered your religious beliefs? If so, how? Compared to how you felt before this experience, are you more or less afraid of death, or the same? [If appropriate:] Are you afraid of death at all? [If patient had attempted suicide, ask:] How has this experience affected your attitude toward suicide? How likely is it that you might try to commit suicide again? [Be tactful.] [Ask these questions in turn.]

13. [If this has not been fully covered in question 12, then ask, if patient has stated that he/she has come close to dying:] As one who has come close to dying, can you tell me, in your own way, what you now understand death to be? What does death now mean to you?

14. Is there anything else you'd like to add here concerning this experience or its effects on you?

Religious Beliefs and Practices

Now, I have just a few more brief questions to ask you and then we'll be done. This time I'd like you to answer these questions from two points of view: How things were *before* this incident occurred and how things were *afterward.* Do you understand? [Make sure patient does.] If you feel that something *remained the same afterward* as it had been before, just say "same," O.K.? [Record responses on the appropriate form.]

1. Before this incident occurred, how religious a person would you say you were: very religious? quite religious? fairly religious? not too religious? not religious at all? [If patient selects last alternative, ask him/her if he/she would call him/herself an atheist or nonbeliever.] How would you classify yourself now? [If patient has previously classified him/herself as a nonbeliever, ask him/her if this has remained the same.]
2. Before, how strongly would you say you believed in God: absolute belief in God? strong belief? fairly strong belief? not too strong belief? no belief at all? How about now?
3. Before, how convinced were you that there was such a thing as life after death: completely convinced? strongly convinced? tended to believe there was? not sure? tended to doubt it? didn't believe it at all? How about now?
4. Before, did you believe in heaven? in hell? How about now? [If patient's views have changed, encourage him/her to say why. We are especially interested in his/her conception of *hell* here, so try to solicit his/her views on that especially.]
5. Before, had you read, thought or heard about the kind of experience you came to have? Do you recall seeing anything about this sort of thing on TV, in books and magazines, and so forth. [Try to find out *specifically* what patient has seen or read.] [If appropriate:] Have you had time or the inclination to look into this matter since your own experience? Have you talked with anyone besides me about the experience? Who? When was this? Do you remember what you talked about? [Ask these questions in turn.]

(This ends the formal portion of the interview.)

Well, Mr. [Mrs., Ms.]_____, that's all the questions I have. Do you have any you'd like to ask me? [Answer these questions in however much detail the patient seems interested to hear no matter how long it takes—even if you have to make an extra trip back to do so; consider it part of your job.]

[When this is done] Mr. [Mrs., Ms.]_____, I want to thank you very much for your willingness to grant us this interview. Your comments will be of great help to us in our research and if you're interested, we'd be happy to send you a brief report of our findings when our research is completed. Would you be interested in this? [If patient expresses interest, obtain an address where the report can be sent.]

Now, if for any reason, Mr. [Mrs., Ms.]_____, you should wish to get in touch with me, this is my name and phone number—or you can write to me at this address. [Give either home address or university address. Have *cards* typed or printed up for distribution.]

I'll gather my things together now. Thank you again for helping us out. [If it applies:] We'll send you a copy of our report when our preliminary work is finished—probably in the late summer of 1978. [If appropriate, wish the patient a speedy recovery or good health—or at least—diminished pain. *Don't leave, however, until you've done all you can, if necessary, to relieve any stress or anxiety the interview may have occasioned.]*

APPENDIX II

Factors Affecting Category Comparability

The three categories of near-death survivors studied in this investigation are not directly comparable to one another for a variety of reasons. The principal differences among them are considered in this appendix.

A total of 208 names of potential interviewees was submitted to us during the course of our project; 156 of them were hospital-based referrals. Of the 52 persons who came to our attention either through nonmedical referrals or self-referrals (including responses to our ads), 48, or almost all, were interviewed. With hospital-referred cases, however, our success rate was only slightly better than one in every three. A complete breakdown of these data, for hospital referred cases only, is presented in Table A (see p. 272).

In the upper part of the table it will be seen that we had our best success (proportionately speaking) with accident victims, our least with suicide attempt victims, and illness cases falling in between. The relatively high rate (24%) of physician refusals is attributable mainly to a judgment that the patient or individual would not be sufficiently recovered from his near-death incident to be able to discuss it coherently; relatively few physicians were flatly uncooperative with the aims of this study. Potential respondent refusals, on the other hand, were motivated by a variety of reasons and excuses. If we restrict ourselves to the individuals who were genuinely available for us to interview (by eliminating those who died or could not be reached), we arrive at the figures displayed in the lower half of Table A. There it will be seen that the percentage of refusal varies widely according to condition of classification. Accident victims, though few in number, were almost always agreeable to an interview, whereas four of every five suicide attempters were either not available to us or refused on their own, as might have been expected. With illness victims, the most plentiful category, it was essentially a fifty-fifty split.

These differences in category availability and category refusal rates led us to seek out other sources to be considered in conjunction with issue of respondent selectivity. Table B (see p. 273) gives the relevant figures.

271

Life at Death

Table A

Summary of Hospital Referral Data

Condition	No. referrals	Died	Physician refusal	Respondent refusal	No contacts made	Interviewed
Illness	101	16	18	17	14	36
Accident	17	1	1	0	4	11
Suicide attempt	38	0	18	9	4	7
Totals	156	17	37	26	22	54

Refusal Rate Data

Condition	No. possible	Physician refusal	Respondent refusal	Total refusals	% Refusals
Illness	71	18	17	35	48.7
Accident	12	1	0	1	8.3
Suicide attempt	34	18	9	27	79.4
Totals	117	37	26	63	53.8

Table B

Source of Respondents by Condition

Condition	Hospital/ Physician	Nonmedical	Self	Advertisement	Totals
Illness	38	8	4	2	52
Accident	12	7	1	6	26
Suicide attempt	9	1	1	13	24
Totals	59	16	6	21	102

Life at Death

Inspection of Table B discloses, as the preceding discussion implied, that the source of referral is confounded with the condition of the respondent. Specifically, most (73%) illness victims were referred by medical sources; accident victims were referred by medical sources less than half the time (46%); while suicide attempters were predominantly obtained from those who replied to our ads (54%).

Taking into account all the data on category availability, source of referral, and refusal rates, it is clear that a very different pattern of selectivity was operative for each of the three conditions of near-death onset represented in our study. Illness victims were (relatively speaking) plentiful, generally referred to us by medical sources, but only available for interviews on a fifty-fifty basis. Accident victims were difficult to locate, were recruited from a number of different sources, but were almost always willing to consent to an interview when contacted. Suicide attempters were also difficult to locate, were recruited mainly by ads, and had a very high refusal rate. The net effect of these differences in selectivity is that the three principal categories of near-death onset are obviously not directly comparable for the purpose of estimating the frequency of the core experience parameter in the population from which they can be assumed to be (nonrandomly) drawn. In this regard, the illness category appears to be the most representative, owing to its size and source features, though its refusal rate is a clearly troublesome matter. One way of minimizing, but not eliminating, the problem of self-selection, is to analyze some of the frequency data according to source of referral and this I will do. This issue will be considered again following the presentation of my findings, but it was necessary to raise it here, in what may seem a premature way, in order to alert the reader to sources of noncomparability and nonrepresentativeness across categories.

APPENDIX III
TAPE RATING FORM

Respondent _____   Rater _____

Coding symbols and instructions:
Use + + if a characteristic is present *and* strong, vivid, stressed, or otherwise compelling.
Use + if a characteristic is present.
Use ? if a characteristic might have been present.
Use − if a characteristic has been inquired about *and* is either denied or not present.
Make no mark next to a characteristic that is not mentioned.

In the space for comments, write down any memorable quotes verbatim or indicate that there is good, quotable material by writing a large Q in the relevant space. Also use this space to note anything pertinent to your ratings or to the comments of the respondent.

With regard to uncertainty concerning the proper section to note *feelings or sensations,* when in doubt make your entries in Section D, along with any appropriate comments.

CHARACTERISTICS	RATING	COMMENTS
A. Ineffability of experience		
B. Subjective sense of dying		
C. Subjective sense of being dead		
D. Feeling and sensations at time of near-death experience (use 22.–25. to specify others)		
1. Peacefulness		
2. Calmness		
3. Quiet		
4. Serenity		
5. Lightness		
6. Warmth		
7. Pleasantness		
8. Happiness		
9. Joy, exaltation		

CHARACTERISTICS	RATING	COMMENTS
10. Painlessness		
11. Relief		
12. No fear		
13. Relaxation		
14. Resignation		
15. Curiosity		
16. Anxiety		
17. Fear		
18. Anger		
19. Dread		
20. Despair		
21. Anguish		
22.		
23.		
24.		
25.		
E. Unusual noise(s); if +, describe		
F. Sense of movement, location		
1. Quality of movement, experience		
a. Walking		
b. Running		
c. Floating		
d. Flying		
e. Movement w/o body		
f. Dreamlike		
g. Echoic		
h.		
i.		
2. Feelings on moving		
a. Peaceful		
b. Exhilarating		
c. Struggling		
d. Fearful		
e. Panicky		
f.		
g.		
3. Sensed features of location		
a. Dark void		

CHARACTERISTICS	RATING	COMMENTS
b. Tunnel		
c. Path, road		
d. Garden		
e. Valley		
f. Meadow		
g. Fields		
h. City		
i. Illumination of scene		
j. Vivid colors		
k. Music		
l. Human figures		
m. Other beings		
n.		
o.		
p.		
G. Sense of bodily separation		
1. Felt detached from body, but did not see it.		
2. Able to view body		
3. Sense of time		
a. Undistorted		
b. No sense of time		
c. Timelessness		
d.		
4. Sense of space		
a. Undistorted		
b. No sense of space		
c. Infinite, no boundaries		
d.		
5. Feeling bodily weight		
a. Ordinary bodily weight		
b. Light		
c. Weightlessness		
d. No sense of body		
e.		
6. Sense of loneliness		
H. Presence of others		
1. Deceased relative(s); if +, specify		
2. Deceased friend		

CHARACTERISTICS	RATING	COMMENTS
3. Guide, voice		
4. Jesus		
5. God, the Lord, a higher power, etc.		
6. Angels		
7. Evil spirits, devil, etc.		
8. Living person(s); if +, specify		
I. Light, illumination		
1. Color(s)		
2. Hurt eyes?		
J. Life flashbacks		
1. Complete		
2. Highpoints		
3. Other (specify)		
4. Sense of sequence		
K. Threshold effect		
L. Feelings upon recovery		
1. Not relevant		
2. Anger		
3. Resentment		
4. Disappointment		
5. Shock		
6. Pain		
7. Relief		
8. Peace		
9. Happiness		
10. Gladness		
11. Joy		
12.		
13.		
M. Changes		
1. Attitude toward life		
a. Increased appreciation		
b. More caring, loving		

CHARACTERISTICS	RATING	COMMENTS

c. Renewed sense
     of purpose
   d. Fear, feeling of
     vulnerability
   e. More interested, curious
   f.
  2. Religious beliefs/attitudes
   a. Stronger
   b. Weaker
   c. Other (specify)
  3. Fear of death
   a. Greater
   b. Lesser
   c. None		

N. Idea of death
  1. Annihilation
  2. Body dies, soul survives
  3. Transitional state
  4. Continuance of life
    at another level
  5. Merging with universal
    consciousness
  6. Reincarnation ideas
  7. Peace
  8. Bliss
  9. A beautiful experience
 10. A journey
 11. No idea
 12. Nothing, nothingness
 13.
 14.		

APPENDIX IV

A Proposal for a Center for the Dying Person

I have in mind the establishment of a facility where terminally ill individuals would live while being prepared to die with full awareness of the transcendent potentialities inherent in the process of dying.

Research by Raymond Moody, Elisabeth Kübler-Ross, Karlis Osis, and many lesser-known investigators has clearly established a common pattern of transcendent experiences that appears to be triggered by the onset of death. The effect of these experiences for those who survive such near-death episodes is a virtual elimination of the fear of death, coupled with a feeling of certainty that physical death is followed by a profoundly beautiful transformation in consciousness. Through their experiences such men and women are admirably prepared to face death not only fearlessly but joyously.

It is time to draw on the implications of these experiences in order to assist others to make their life-death transition a fully transcendent one.

Toward this end, I am proposing the creation of a Center for the Dying Person. Its principal aim would be to prepare the terminally ill to die aware of what death really is: a passage into another dimension of life. This kind of preparation would have three components:

1. *The alleviation of pain.* It is hard to focus on anything while experiencing pain. The first task of the center's medical personnel would be to minimize pain. In this respect, our center would function like a hospice.

2. *The working through of fears about death.* To clear the way for an easeful death, various fears would need to be expressed and discharged and all "unfinished business" taken care of. Trained counselors and therapists would work with the patient and his family to achieve this sense of closure.

3. *Preparation for the death experience.* Dying individuals need to know what it is like to die. This information can be provided in a number of ways: (a) by discussing the findings of near-death research; (b) by playing audio and video tapes of persons describing their own near-death experiences; (c) by encouraging direct interaction between dying patients and those who have survived near-death episodes; (d) by the staff sharing their own experiences with other dying individuals; and eventually (e) by showing the dying patient (through journals, audio tapes, photographs, and so forth) how other patients at the center approached and experienced their own death.

Thus, the patient-focused program at the center would consist of *medical,* *therapeutic,* and *educational* features combined and blended in such a way as to facilitate a pain-free and fear-free transition into life after death.

In addition to its principal task of helping patients to die in the manner just described, the center would be designed to accomplish two other objectives:

The first would be to serve as a *training institute*. Since only a small number of patients could live and die at the Center, it would be necessary to expose professionals concerned with dying people to our procedures. In this way, our approach to death could be used in other facilities, for example, in hospitals, hospices, homes, and so forth. Thus a training program for interested professionals is a necessary adjunct to our primary work with patients at the center.

The second objective would be for the center to function as a *research facility*. Patients would understand that it is necessary to study the process of dying and to witness the moment of death if we are to help others die more easily. In this way, our patients would be "donating their deaths" to medicine just as others bequeath bodily organs. Patients thus become our teachers as they share their experience of dying with us. Accordingly, to the extent a patient's health allows, we would ask him to keep a journal, record his feelings and reactions on tape, and to participate in periodic, informal interviews. Since staff and patients would be coparticipants in the endeavor to contribute to our understanding of dying and death, the research phase of our work should not be marred by a "clinical" orientation on the part of those concerned with this aspect. *Collaborative* research is the keynote here.

The center I envisage would be small, perhaps six to ten beds. Personnel required for the operation of the center would include administrative staff, medical personnel, researchers, and therapists (including those who have had near-death experiences themselves) and religious personnel. It is possible, of course, that a given member of the staff would fall into more than one of these categories.

Eventually, if this idea proves workable, various centers could be constructed, all serving the aim of helping persons to die peacefully and joyfully. In fact, our role would be to create not only a new institution for the dying, but a new variety of midwife—one who assists not in the process of birth, but in the process of rebirth. All of us connected with this undertaking, however, would be participants in a sacred rite of passage, marking the transition from life to Greater Life. In the acting out of our respective parts, we should be always mindful that this is a journey each of us must one day take.

APPENDIX V

The Association for the Scientific Study of Near-Death Phenomena

In order to reach the objectives discussed in the last chapter, an association was recently formed to bring together all those who share an interest in this work. Reproduced below is the association's statement of purpose, which further describes its activities and long-range plans.

THE ASSOCIATION FOR THE SCIENTIFIC STUDY OF NEAR-DEATH PHENOMENA
Statement of Purpose

This association is intended to serve the interests of professionals and lay persons concerned with the scientific study of near-death phenomena and with the judicious clinical application of knowledge derived from such study in appropriate settings. The association proposes to:

1. Sponsor and promote further scientific inquiry into near-death experiences and related paranormal phenomena.
2. Encourage the exchange of ideas and the communication of findings among individuals concerned with the systematic investigation of near-death phenomena.
3. Disseminate information about near-death phenomena to the media and to the general public directly.
4. Provide a forum for those who have had near-death experiences or other peak experiences of a related nature.
5. Facilitate the application of knowledge emerging from near-death research in appropriate settings, that is, in hospitals, hospices, nursing homes, funeral establishments, and so forth.

Pursuant to these objectives, the association will conduct the following activities.

1. It will publish a quarterly newsletter to keep readers abreast of significant developments regarding near-death research and the application of near-death research findings.
2. It will sponsor both small-scale conferences for scholars/researchers and larger symposiums for the general public related to the topic of near-death experiences and related phenomena.

3. It will provide opportunities for near-death survivors to meet one another and share their mutual experiences.
4. It will provide a roster of speakers and workshop leaders for those organizations interested in learning more about near-death phenomena.
5. It has plans to incorporate and actively pursue financial support for near-death research and its applications.

If any reader is interested in joining this association or otherwise supporting its work, please write to Mr. John Audette for more information. His address is: Association for The Scientific Study of Near-Death Phenomena, P.O. Box 2309, East Peoria, Illinois 61611.

NOTES

Preface

1. Such research has recently begun to appear. After my own project was underway, the important cross-cultural work of Osis and Haraldsson, *At the Hour of Death,* on deathbed visions was published. In addition, Sabom and Kreutziger's studies of near-death experiences—whose findings are impressively congruent with my own—appeared during this time. These investigations will be cited later in the book.

One

1. I. Stevenson, "Research into the Evidence of Man's Survival After Death," pp. 152–70.
2. R. Noyes, Jr., and R. Kletti, "The Experience of Dying From Falls," pp. 45–52.
3. Noyes, "The Experience of Dying," pp. 174–84; Noyes and Kletti, "Depersonalization in the Face of Life-Threatening Danger: A Description," pp. 19–27; "Depersonalization in the Face of Life-Threatening Danger: An Interpretation," pp. 103–14; "Panoramic Memory," pp. 181–93.
4. I have omitted reference to still other investigators and authors interested in near-death phenomena on the grounds that their work, though sometimes useful, is of questionable relevance, either because it is unsystematic, unreliable, or intended for popular audiences. Included here are books by Crookall, Hampton, Wheeler, Matson, and Tralins, among others. Nevertheless, some of the theoretical speculations presented by some of these authors appear to have possible merit and will be considered at a later point in this book.
5. R. A. Moody, Jr., *Life After Life,* pp. 23–24.
6. I have omitted the postexperience effects Moody includes in his original list.
7. D. H. Rosen, "Suicide Survivors: A Follow-Up Study of Persons Who Survived Jumping from the Golden Gate and San Francisco–Oakland Bay Bridges," pp. 289–94; "Suicide Survivors: Psychotherapeutic Implications of Egocide," pp. 209–15.

Two

1. This report was sent in August 1978.
2. My thanks to Charlene Alling for her contributions.
3. Our two most extreme cases were persons having had a close brush with death forty-five years and fifty-one years ago, respectively.

4. For the sake of readers not familiar with statistical terminology, the phrase "statistically significant" refers to a difference that is unlikely to have occurred by chance. For example, if one reads that a difference is (statistically) significant at the .01 level, written p <.01, it means that such a difference would occur less than one time in a hundred by chance. Similarly, if a difference is said to be "nonsignificant," it may be regarded as a chance fluctuation.
5. I have assigned each respondent an identification number so as to make possible for the interested reader the comparison of remarks made by respondents who are multiply quoted. These identification numbers will usually appear at the conclusion of an interview excerpt.
6. I have rearranged some of the quoted remarks for the sake of expositional coherence, but the changes do not alter the substance of this respondent's account.

Three
1. All of the data in this chapter are based on the ratings of the taped interviews. Each tape was independently rated by three judges, including the author, who were familiar with the project. In order for any given characteristic (such as peacefulness) to be coded positively, at least two raters had to agree on its presence. Thus, our criterion is a conservative one in that it probably slightly underestimates the proportion of persons exemplifying any given experimental feature. Data bearing on interrater reliability will be presented later in this book. The tape rating form itself will be found in Appendix III.
2. R. A. Moody, Jr., *Life After Death,* p. 90.
3. It should be noted that these cases are unusual only in the context of my sample. Many such cases have been reported in the extensive literature on out-of-body experiences. (See Crookall, *Out-of-the-Body Experiences;* Green, *Out-of-the-Body Experiences;* Greenhouse, *The Astral Journey;* Monroe, *Journeys Out of the Body;* Tart, in *Psychic Exploration.*)
4. Moody, *Life After Life,* p. 90.
5. Ibid., p. 84.
6. C. Hampton, *The Transition Called Death.*
7. R. Crookall, *Out-of-Body Experience,* p. 23.
8. I have been told by those who profess to have some knowledge of this phenomenon, that in order to see the alleged connecting cord, one must "turn around" while in the hypothetical second body so that one is looking back at one's physical body. Even if this is so, it is still not obvious why, if this cord does exist, more persons did not

report it, since many of my respondents did claim to have a clear view of their physical body.

9. This respondent's account is unusual in that she reports having been aware of whitish-smoky coloration in the "funnel." It is of interest that a classic manual for the dying—*The Tibetan Book of the Dead*—alludes to a smoky white light in connection with the postmortem state. The respondent herself was not familiar with this book.

10. This respondent was, however, familiar with Moody's work (from a *Reader's Digest* excerpt) *before* his near-death episode. Nevertheless, some findings to be presented later in this book indicate that such knowledge did *not* serve to bias or contaminate the accounts from informed respondents.

11. Only one respondent implied that the illumination hurt his eyes. All others denied that this was the case—usually emphatically.

12. A few others described a similar phenomenon—seeing a dazzling and rapidly changing array of beautiful rainbowlike colors—but they are not included in the figure given here.

13. The phenomenology associated with the transition from stage III to stage IV of the near-death experience appears to bear an unmistakable resemblance to certain features of the psychedelically induced "perinatal experience" as described by Grof, in which an individual seems to relive some of the events of his own birth. In these perinatal episodes, there is often a subjectively compelling experience of dying, which is, according to Grof, always followed by a sense of rebirth. The rebirth phase is said to be accompanied by "visions of blinding white or golden light" (*Realms of the Human Unconscious*, p. 139). I will discuss these parallels in Chapter Eleven.

14. There were only three such instances in my sample.

15. However, it is possible in this case that the individual received an injection of nitrous oxide at the time öf his tooth extraction. He is not sure and the dentist's records are not available.

16. Two other persons used the same biblical phrase to describe their experience of a "valley."

Four

1. This term was used by a number of my respondents and seems as phenomenologically appropriate as any.

2. I did not systematically ask about the gender associated with a presence who spoke until after a couple of respondents volunteered that "it was a man's voice." Altogether six respondents identified the voice they heard as a "man's voice" or a "male voice." The voice is never recognized as belonging to anyone the respond-

ent knows or has known, though quite a few people identify the presence with God and feel they are communicating directly with Him. In two instances—both related to suicide, incidentally, unlike any of the six cases just mentioned—the respondents reported hearing a woman's voice, but the nature of the communication in these cases seemed to be qualitatively different from and a good deal less specific and vaguer than the six cases involving a distinct sense of a male presence. In the two instances where an unrecognized female voice was reported, then, it is not clear whether it is the same phenomenon as in the six nonsuicide related cases.

3. In a few cases here counted as positive, the respondent did not actually use the term *presence* or *person* or *God* to externalize the source of the communication, but the phenomenological features associated with this event were otherwise in keeping with the description given here.

4. In fact, the experience of the presence and that of encountering deceased loved ones were almost always mutually exclusive—a respondent would encounter either one or the other, *but not both.* The sole exception to this pattern is a woman who felt she "had a conversation with God" but who also claimed to have had a vague sense of deceased others. Her perception of them, however, was very indistinct compared to most of the instances where an encounter with a loved one was claimed.

5. There are some exceptions.

6. A check of her medical records reveals that the arrest was mentioned, but not its duration.

7. In this respect, this respondent was very unusual. As will be discussed later, most persons who recall a core experience are quite clearly unconscious or comatose during the time it takes place. To my knowledge, only one other woman in my sample was conscious at the time of her experience—and she, too, was aware of a light.

8. This case is very similar to that of a woman who was interviewed by some students of mine as part of a course project on near-death experiences. This woman had accidentally nearly suffocated after giving birth and found herself feeling very peaceful and light and "speaking with God." She relates: "I got there and I said, 'Gee, you know, I just couldn't die at this particular point because I had one small child at home and was about to have another one and I just had to take care of this child. And next time, I'd be very happy [laughs] to come, but at this point, it was just impossible for me and that really is the end of it.'" The next thing she knew she had regained consciousness and was talking to her incredulous husband about her experience.

9. Later in this report, in connection with accidental near-deaths, more material will be furnished concerning one of the aspects of the core experience perhaps insufficiently described here—the life review phenomenon.

Five

1. As my own case histories suggest, however, it may be that through the publication of books like Moody's, the publicity given to Kübler-Ross's work, and the films and television documentaries dealing with near-death research, near-death survivors will no longer be as hesitant to share their experiences with others.
2. H. B. Greenhouse, *The Astral Journey*, p. 54.
3. After completing this study, I did informally interview one near-death survivor who said that she was being ferried across the River Styx when she decided to come back. She also claimed her physician later told her she was clinically dead for five minutes.
4. The panoramic life review, which is an aspect of the decisional process, is, of course, imagistic, but the images do not conform to the features enumerated by Moody in connection with the threshold phenomenon.

Six

1. As it happens, the trends in the accident and suicide attempt categories are sufficiently similar that they can be safely combined. The sex ratios for these two categories (that is, illness and accident/suicide attempt) are also very similar: twenty-nine women fall into the illness category, twenty-eight into the combined accident/suicide attempt category; for men, the respective figures are twenty-three and twenty-two. Therefore, it seems justified to conduct a chi-square test for core experiencers only, according to sex and condition.
2. For readers not familiar with statistical analysis, ANOVA is the conventional abbreviation for a statistical procedure called analysis of variance. The results of this procedure disclose whether differences among a set of means are statistically significant.
3. A statistical procedure similar to an analysis of variance in which a possible "contaminating variable" can be statistically controlled for and its influence assessed.
4. R. Noyes, *Panoramic Memory*, pp. 181–93.
5. I need to emphasize that this description is based solely on my limited sample of twenty-four cases. I have heard, *secondhand*, of at least two cases where a tunnel phenomenon was apparently experienced and of one case where a light was alleged to have been

seen, but I have been unable, despite persisting efforts, to interview these people. Rosen has also obtained some intriguing data from a small sample of suicide attempters who survived leaps from either the Golden Gate or the San Francisco–Oakland Bay bridges. His findings suggest that this mode of suicide attempt may lead to certain more positive and transcendent features—if one is lucky enough to survive, that is!

6. K. Osis and E. Haraldsson, *At the Hour of Death,* p. 71.
7. By Dr. Michael Sabom, a cardiologist, who also has done an extensive near-death study; in personal communication.
8. Where this condition was specifically noted in the case of several accident victims, no recall of core experience elements was ever recounted.
9. A. M. Greeley, *Ecstasy: A Way of Knowing,* p. 46.
10. Even this fact is ambiguous, however. If one considers this voice that of a "lower order entity" (see Van Dusen, *The Natural Death in Man),* one may perhaps properly interpret its remarks as goading the individual to commit a self-destructive act. If, on the other hand, one understands this voice to represent a "presence" or a "higher order entity," the remarks acquire a different meaning, namely, "even if you try to kill yourself, you won't succeed and [thus] it will be all right." The rest of the interview gives us no real basis to favor one interpretation over the other nor does it exclude other more conventional explanations.
11. This flatly *disagrees* with Moody's statement in the Afterword of his first book, but I believe the case histories on which his assertion rests were quite few in number.
12. Research in progress, undertaken by Stephen Franklin and me, has already made it clear that in at least some cases of attempted suicide a full core experience *does* occur even when it is associated with drug ingestion. As a result of these new research data, I am now prepared to argue that the suicide-related near-death experience is substantially the *same* as that which is induced by illness or accident. The full report of this investigation is forthcoming.

Seven

1. Sabom and Kreutziger, using a slightly different religiousness index, also failed to find any difference between core experiencers and nonexperiencers in religiousness.
2. A biserial correlation measures the relationship between a dichotomous variable and a continuous one.
3. B. Greyson and I. Stevenson, "Near-Death Experiences: Characteristic Features," p. 7.
4. We failed to ask these questions of 4 of our 102 respondents.

5. This unanticipated difference may not be a fluke. In a study of seventy-eight survivors of near-death episodes, Sabom found that only 12% of his core experiencers had prior knowledge of near-death research whereas 60% of nonexperiencers had such knowledge, a highly significant difference (p<.01).

6. It might be thought that perhaps proportionately more core experiencers had their experience before the work of Moody, Kübler-Ross, and others, was well known, thus giving rise to an artifactual rather than a "true" difference. However, analysis shows that this difference *cannot* be attributed to differences between core experiencers and nonexperiencers in incident-interview intervals. The difference between groups is just as marked for those whose near-death incident was recent (within two years of interview) as for those whose incident took place before publicity about near-death experiences was widespread.

Nine

1. The reader may rightly infer from the numbers appearing in this table (and others to appear in this section) that data from a few respondents are missing. In these cases, the relevant question was simply not asked, owing to interviewer error.

2. All these ambiguities could have been avoided, of course, if we had asked a simple pre/post form of the question, as we did with religiousness items. Unfortunately, the correct form of the question only occurred to me when the study was halfway completed. Future researchers, take note!

3. In fact, case *79*—the young man who smashed his head on a rock while contemplating suicide—is officially classified as an accident.

4. Unfortunately, the number of cases here is just too small to make much of this finding. Nevertheless, the work by David Rosen and Stanislav Grof and Joan Halifax is consistent with it and with the proposition of the deterrent role of suicide-related transcendental experiences. Accordingly, I will consider it in the interpretative portion of this book.

Ten

1. Moody, *Life After Life*, p. 10.
2. Ibid., p. 93.
3. Greyson and Stevenson; Osis and Haraldsson, *At The Hour of Death;* C. Lundahl, "The Near-Death Experiences of Mormons"; M. B. Sabom, *The Near-Death Experience: A Medical Perspective;* Sabom and S. A. Kreutziger, "Physicians Evaluate the Near-Death Experience," pp. 1–6; Fred Schoonmaker, article in *Anabiosis,* (July 1979), pp. 1–2.

4. Moody, *Life After Life*, pp. 23–24.

5. Russell Moors. Personal communication; Sabom, *The Near-Death Experience*.

6. G. Ritchie, *Return From Tomorrow*.

7. Moody, *Life After Life*, p. 23.

8. Though the terms *spirits* and *presence* are used throughout this paragraph, this usage should not be taken to imply that such "entities" necessarily exist in some external sense. These terms are used for narrative convenience and because respondents themselves tended to speak in this way; this usage, however, does not imply any ontological acceptance of such entities as self-existent.

9. It has recently been reported in a newsletter of the Association for the Scientific Study of Near-Death Phenomena (see Appendix V) that a Denver cardiologist, Fred Schoonmaker, has been quietly amassing data on near-death survivors since 1961. Although his research has not yet been published, it appears that better than 60% of his more than 2,300 cases have disclosed to him Moody-type near-death experiences.

10. Moody, *Life After Life*, p. 36.

11. R. Bayless, *The Other Side of Death;* Grof and J. Halifax, *The Human Encounter with Death;* R. Tralins, *Buried Alive*.

12. M. Rawlings, *Beyond Death's Door*.

13. Rawlings. Personal communication.

14. Indeed, one of the "cases" Rawlings cites—that of a Christian minister who had had a hellish near-death experience prior to entering the ministry—was previously made known to me by a correspondent who sent me a brochure written by this minister describing his experience. As might be expected, the minister makes use of this experience in a hortatory way to support a Christian belief system.

15. Rawlings. Personal communication.

16. Rawlings, *Beyond Death's Door*, p. 66.

17. Moody. Personal communication.

18. Sabom. Personal communication.

19. Grof, *Realms of the Human Unconscious;* R.E.L. Masters and J. Houston, *The Varieties of Psychedelic Experience*.

20. Grof and Halifax.

21. Noyes, "The Experience of Dying," p. 174–84.

22. Of course the phenomenon itself—quite apart from its triggers—would have to be explained in any case. This is a question we will address later in this book.

23. The data from the forthcoming study by Stephen Franklin and me (see footnote 12, chapter 6) strongly support the invariance hypothesis.

24. Osis and Haraldsson, p. 173.
25. Moody. Personal communication.
26. Sabom and Kreutziger, pp. 1–6.
27. Ibid.
28. Sabom was skeptical of Moody's findings whereas I was persuaded that they were authentic. Sabom undertook his work to "disprove" Moody, I, to corroborate him.

Eleven

1. S. Freud, *Civilization and Its Discontents.*
2. Bayless; F.W.H. Myers, *Human Personality and Its Survival of Bodily Death;* J. H. Hyslop, *Psychical Research and the Resurrection.*
3. E. Kübler-Ross. Interview on the *Tomorrow Show* (February 14, 1978).
4. Ibid.
5. Moody, *Life After Life,* p. 98.
6. Sabom, *The Near-Death Experience;* Osis and Haraldsson.
7. Moody, *Life After Life,* p. 119.
8. Nancy Miller. Personal communication.
9. Ibid.
10. Moody, *Life After Life,* p. 110.
11. Sabom and Kreutziger, "Physicians Evaluate the Near-Death Experience," p. 5.
12. This is not to assert, of course, that some drugs can't artificially induce experiences that may be similar or even identical to the core experience. This is, in fact, precisely the thesis of the book by Grof and Halifax, which holds that LSD is one such agent. Although their argument is not without its weaknesses, there is clearly some support for it. I myself have talked to (though not yet interviewed formally) two people who claim to have had deep core experiences as a result of using LSD.
13. This does not mean that the use of, say, narcotics or antidepressants, would always *prevent* such an experience. As with anesthetics, such drugs can sometimes be associated with its occurrence, even if they do not initiate the experience.
14. Moody, *Reflections on Life After Life,* p. 109.
15. Osis and Haraldsson, p. 71.
16. J. C. Lilly, *The Center of the Cyclone;* R. E. Byrd, *Alone.*
17. *Mind/Brain Bulletin,* p. 8.

Twelve

1. T. X. Barber. Address at the Parapsychology Association annual convention, 1978.
2. T. S. Kuhn, *The Structure of Scientific Revolutions.*

3. A. Koestler, *The Roots of Coincidence.*
4. Koestler; L. LeShan, *The Medium, the Mystic and the Physicist;* K. R. Pelletier, *Toward a Science of Consciousness.*
5. Pelletier.
6. This may provide only cold comfort to my more scientifically minded skeptical readers, but I might add here that I came tentatively to embrace the parapsychological interpretation offered here only with reluctance and because I simply could find nothing else that seemed to fit the explanatory requirements.
7. Tart; J. Mitchell, "Out of the Body Vision"; Osis, "Out-of-the-Body Experiences: A Preliminary Survey"; Greenhouse.
8. *Re-Vision;* entire issue.
9. R. Crookall, *The Study and Practice of Astral Projection; The Techniques of Astral Projection; More Astral Projections; The Mechanisms of Astral Projection; Out-of-the-Body Experience; Casebook of Astral Projection; The Supreme Adventure.*
10. C. Green, *Out-of-the-Body Experiences.*
11. Tart.
12. Greenhouse.
13. Osis, "Out-of-the-Body Experiences."
14. Greenhouse.
15. R. A. Monroe, *Journeys Out of the Body;* S. Muldoon, *The Case for Astral Projection;* Muldoon and H. Carrington, *The Projection of the Astral Body;* O. Fox, *Astral Projection;* Yram, *Practical Astral Projection;* Turvey, *The Beginnings of Seership.*
16. Green, pp. 33, 40, 41, 72, 73, 75–76, 85, 90, 93, 104.
17. Tart, p. 353.
18. Ibid., pp. 355–56.
19. Kübler-Ross. Article in *The Hartford Courant* (March 30, 1975).
20. Greenhouse, p. 26.
21. Crookall, *Out-of-the-Body Experiences.*
22. Ibid., pp. 161–62. Crookall's italics.
23. Ibid. Crookall's italics and ellipses.
24. T. Moss, *The Probability of the Impossible,* pp. 289–90.
25. Hampton.
26. Ibid.
27. Moody, *Life After Life,* p. 98.
28. Tart, p. 368.
29. G. Krishna, *Kundalini;* R. L. Peck, *American Meditation.*
30. Lilly; Swedenborg; Monroe; I. Bentov, *Stalking the Wild Pendulum.*
31. *Re-Vision:* Bentov, *Stalking the Wild Pendulum;* M. Ferguson, "A New Perspective on Reality," pp. 3–7; Pelletier; F. Capra, *The Tao of Physics.*

32. K. H. Pribram, *Languages of the Brain;* "Problems Concerning the Structure of Consciousness"; Address at the American Psychological Association annual convention, 1978; "What the Fuss is All About," pp. 14–18; Interview in *Psychology Today* (February 1979), pp. 70–84.

33. Ferguson, p. 3.

34. Pribram. Interview in *Psychology Today,* p. 84.

35. Ibid., pp. 83–84. My italics.

36. Bentov. Personal communication.

37. There is one feature of the tunnel experience that may not be conformable to this states-of-consciousness interpretation. Individuals sometimes describe the trip through the tunnel or void as an *ascent.* Likewise, one may have the feeling that the light is coming from *above.* At one level, these may be mind images that symbolically represent the shift from a *lower* to a *higher* state of consciousness. On the other hand, some might wish to argue that these perceptions *actually* reflect the experiences of the double as it traverses bands of space in dimensions to which it alone is sensible. To add a note of paradox to this puzzle, it must be recalled that since we are talking about experiences that *transcend* both space and time, almost any spacelike interpretation is bound to be false or drastically distorted.

38. Moody. Personal communication.

39. See, for example, Greenhouse, pp. 41–42.

40. R. Fremantle and C. Trungpa, eds., *The Tibetan Book of the Dead.*

41. Swedenborg.

42. Bentov, *Stalking the Wild Pendulum.*

43. Perhaps it is also worth noting here that although the voice may appear to be all-knowing, it always seems to speak in a style consistent with the respondent's own speech patterns. This is another feature that suggests that the voice or presence is an aspect of the individual's (higher) self, rather than the "voice of God" Whom we would not expect to be so colloquial!

44. Interestingly, both Grof and Halifax and Keith have interpreted the life review in holographic terms. Bentov also claims that at this level "knowledge comes in a nonlinear way . . . in large chunks, imprinted on the mind in a fraction of a second" (p. 80).

45. Advanced yogis, Zen masters, and other spiritual adepts are sometimes said to be able to forecast the time of their death, often well in advance of the actual date. Perhaps the best-known documented case of this kind in the West is that of the famous eighteenth-century scientist-seer, Emanuel Swedenborg, who told John Wesley in February 1772 that he, Swedenborg, would not be

able to meet him later that year since he was to die on March 29—
which he did. Presumably, such information is available by making
contact with the higher self *before* the moment of death.

46. Craig Lundahl's work on near-death experiences among Mormons
gives some particularly striking examples of this kind.
47. Moody, *Life After Life*, p. 75.
48. Lilly, p. 28.
49. Ibid., pp. 26–27.
50. Pribram. Interview in *Psychology Today*, p. 84.
51. Lilly, p. 27.
52. C. G. Jung, *Memories, Dreams, Reflections*, p. 296.
53. Ibid., pp. 304–5. My italics.
54. J. C. Eccles, *The Understanding of the Brain.*
55. W. Penfield, *The Mystery of the Mind.*
56. This interpretation is obviously consistent with "the doctrine of
correspondences" as taught by Swedenborg and similar ideas which
can be traced back to Plato and the hermetic tradition. The aspect
of that teaching relevant here is that the physical world is merely a
reflection of a higher world and that everything in this world has its
correspondent *there*. It seems reasonable to suppose that visionary
"after-life" experiences (for which Swedenborg was famous during
his lifetime) may have contributed the experiential foundation to
this doctrine.
57. M. Rawlings, *Beyond Death's Door*, p. 118.
58. Ritchie.
59. Bentov. Personal communication.
60. Moody, *Reflections on Life After Life*, p. 20. Moody's italics.
61. Pribram. Interview in *Psychology Today*, p. 84.
62. A. Einstein, *Living Philosophies*, p. 6.

Thirteen

1. H. Smith, *Forgotten Truth.*
2. W. James, *The Varieties of Religious Experience.*
3. That is one reason why it is so important that medical and religious
professionals in particular be knowledgeable concerning these
experiences. If they are, they can help the seed to take root just
through their understanding rather than inadvertently destroying
it through ignorance. My hope is that this book might contribute
something toward that end. In any event, we will return to this
matter toward the close of this chapter.
4. Moody, "Near-Death Experiences: Some Clinical Considerations."

BIBLIOGRAPHY

Barber, T. X. Address at the Parapsychology Association annual convention, St. Louis, Mo., August 1978.

Barrett, W. *Death-Bed Visions*. London: Methuen, 1926.

Bayless, R. *The Other Side of Death*. New Hyde Park, N.Y.: University Books, 1971.

Bentov, I. *Stalking the Wild Pendulum*. New York: E. P. Dutton, 1977.

———. Personal communication, 1979.

Byrd, R. E. *Alone*. New York: Ace Books, 1938.

Capra, F. *The Tao of Physics*. Berkeley: Shambhala, 1975.

Crookall, R. *The Study and Practice of Astral Projection*. London: Aquarian Press, 1961.

———. *The Techniques of Astral Projection*. London: Aquarian Press, 1964.

———. *More Astral Projections*. London: Aquarian Press, 1964.

———. *The Mechanisms of Astral Projection*. Moradabad, India: Darshana International, 1968.

———. *Out-of-the-Body Experiences*. New York: University Books, 1970.

———. *Casebook of Astral Projection*. New Hyde Park, N.Y.: University Books, 1972.

———. *The Supreme Adventure*. Greenwood, S.C.: Attic Press, 1975.

Eccles, J. C. *The Understanding of the Brain*. New York: McGraw-Hill, 1973.

Einstein, A. *Living Philosophies*. New York: Simon and Schuster, 1931.

Ferguson, M. "A New Perspective on Reality." *Re-Vision*, 1 (1978): 3/4, 3–7.

Fox, O. *Astral Projection*. London: Rider and Co., 1939.

Fremantle, R., and Trungpa, C., eds. *The Tibetan Book of the Dead*. Berkeley: Shambhala, 1975.

Freud, S. *Civilization and Its Discontents*. Garden City, N.Y.: Doubleday, 1958.

Greeley, A. M. *Ecstasy: A Way of Knowing*. Englewood Cliffs, N.J.: Prentice-Hall, 1974.

Green, C. *Out-of-the-Body Experiences*. New York: Ballantine, 1968.

Greenhouse, H. B. *The Astral Journey*. New York: Avon, 1974.

Greyson, B., and Stevenson, I. "Near-Death Experiences: Characteristic Features." University of Virginia, unpublished manuscript, 1978.

Grof, S. *Realms of the Human Unconscious*. New York: Viking, 1975.

———, and Halifax, J. *The Human Encounter with Death*. New York: Dutton, 1977.

Gurney, E. et al. *Phantasms of the Living*. London: Trubner and Co., 1886.

Life at Death

Hampton, C. *The Transition Called Death*. Wheaton, Ill.: The Theosophical Publishing House, 1972.

Heim, A. "Notizen ueber den Tod durch Absturz." *Jahrbuch des Schweizer Alpenklub* 27 (1892): 327–337.

Hyslop, J. H. *Psychical Research and the Resurrection*. Boston: Small, Maynard and Co., 1908.

James, W. *The Varieties of Religious Experience*. New York: Mentor, 1958.

Jung, C. G. *Memories, Dreams, Reflections*. New York: Vintage Books, 1961.

Keith, F. "Of Time and Mind: From Paradox to Paradigm." In J. White, ed., *Frontiers of Consciousness*. New York: Harper & Row, 1976.

Koestler, A. *The Roots of Coincidence*. New York: Vintage Books, 1972.

Krishna, G. *Kundalini*. Berkeley: Shambhala, 1971.

Kübler-Ross, E. "Doctor Says Death is 'Pleasant.'" Article in *The Hartford Courant*, March 30, 1975.

———. Interview in *People*, November 24, 1975.

———. Address at the annual conference of the Association for Transpersonal Psychology. Stanford, California, July 1975.

———. Interview in *Psychology Today*. September 1976.

———. Public lecture. Harvard Divinity School, Cambridge, Mass. December 1, 1977.

———. Interview on the *Tomorrow Show*. February 14, 1978.

Kuhn, T. S. *The Structure of Scientific Revolutions*. Chicago: University of Chicago Press, 1962.

LeShan, L. *The Medium, the Mystic and the Physicist*. New York: Viking, 1974.

Lilly, J. C. *The Center of the Cyclone*. New York: Julian Press, 1972.

Lundahl, C. "The Near-Death Experiences of Mormons." Paper read at the American Psychological Association annual convention. New York, September 1979.

Maslow, A. *Toward a Psychology of Being*. New York: Van Nostrand, 1968.

Masters, R.E.L., and Houston, J. *The Varieties of Psychedelic Experience*. New York: Delta, 1966.

Matson, A. *Afterlife*. New York: Tempo Books, 1976.

McDonagh, J. "Bibliotherapy with Suicidal Patients." Paper read at the American Psychological Association. New York, September 1979.

Miller, N. Personal communication, 1979.

Mind/Brain Bulletin. 14 (1979): 8.

Mitchell, E., ed. *Psychic Exploration*. New York: Putnam's, 1974.

Mitchell, J. "Out-of-the-Body Vision." *Psychic*. April 1973.

Monroe, R. A. *Journeys Out of the Body*. New York: Doubleday, 1971.

Moody, R. A., Jr. *Life After Life*. Atlanta: Mockingbird Books, 1975.

————. *Reflections on Life After Life.* Atlanta: Mockingbird Books, 1977.

————. Personal communication, 1979.

————. "Near-Death Experiences: Some Clinical Considerations." Paper read at the American Psychological Association annual convention. New York, September 1979.

Moors, Russell. Personal communication, 1978.

Moss, T. *The Probability of the Impossible.* Los Angeles: J. P. Tarcher, 1974.

Muldoon, S. *The Case for Astral Projection.* Chicago: Aries Press, 1936.

————, and Carrington, H. *The Projection of the Astral Body.* London: Rider and Co., 1929.

Murphy, G., and Ballou, R. O., eds. *William James on Psychical Research.* New York: Viking, 1969.

Myers, F.W.H. *Human Personality and Its Survival of Bodily Death.* London: Longmans, Green, 1903.

Noyes, R., Jr. "The Experience of Dying." *Psychiatry,* 35 (1972): 174–184.

————, and Kletti, R. "The Experience of Dying From Falls." *Omega,* 3 (1972): 45–52.

————. "Depersonalization in the Face of Life-Threatening Danger: A Description." *Psychiatry,* 39 (1976): 19–27.

————. "Depersonalization in the Face of Life-Threatening Danger: An Interpretation." *Omega,* 7 (1976): 103–114.

————. "Panoramic Memory." *Omega, 8* (1977): 181–193.

Osis, K. *Deathbed Observations by Physicians and Nurses.* New York: Parapsychological Foundation, 1961.

————. "Out-of-the-Body Experiences: A Preliminary Survey." Paper presented at the Parapsychology Association annual convention, St. Louis, Mo., August 1978.

————, and Haraldsson, E. *At The Hour of Death.* New York: Avon, 1977.

Peck, R. L. *American Meditation.* Windham Center, Conn.: Personal Development Center, 1976.

Pelletier, K. R. *Toward a Science of Consciousness.* New York: Delta, 1979.

Penfield, W. *The Mystery of the Mind.* Princeton, N.J.: Princeton University Press, 1976.

Pribram, K. H. *Languages of the Brain.* Englewood Cliffs, N.J.: Prentice-Hall, 1971.

————. "Problems Concerning the Structure of Consciousness." In C. G. Globus et al., eds. *Consciousness and the Brain.* New York: Plenum, 1976, pp. 297–313.

————. Address at the American Psychological Association annual convention, New York, September 1978.

————. "What the Fuss is All About." *Re-Vision*, 1 (1978): ¾, 14–18.

————. "Holographic Memory"; interview in *Psychology Today*. 12 (February 1979): 70–84.

Rawlings, M. *Beyond Death's Door*. Nashville: Thomas Nelson, 1978.

————. Personal communication, 1979.

Re-Vision, 1 (1978): ¾, entire issue.

Ritchie, G. *Return From Tomorrow*. Waco, Texas: Chosen Books, 1978.

Rosen, D. H. "Suicide Survivors: A Follow-Up Study of Persons Who Survived Jumping from the Golden Gate and San Francisco–Oakland Bay Bridges." *Western Journal of Medicine*, 122 (1975): 289–294.

————. "Suicide Survivors: Psychotherapeutic Implications of Egocide." *Suicide and Life-Threatening Behavior*. 6 (1976): 209–215.

Sabom, M. B. Personal communication, 1979.

————. *The Near-Death Experience: A Medical Perspective*. Philadelphia: J. B. Lippincott, in press.

————, and Kreutziger, S. A. Personal communication, 1977.

————. "Physicians Evaluate the Near-Death Experience." *Theta*, 6 (1978): 1–6.

Schoonmaker, Fred, "Denver Cardiologist Discloses Findings After 18 Years of Near-Death Research," Article in *Anagiosis*, 1 (July 1979): 1–2.

Smith, H. *Forgotten Truth*. New York: Harper & Row, 1976.

Stevenson, I. "Research into the Evidence of Man's Survival After Death." *Journal of Nervous and Mental Disease*, 165 (1977): 152–170.

Swedenborg, E. *Heaven and Its Wonders and Hell*. New York: Citadel, 1965.

Tart, C. T. "Out-of-the-Body Experiences." In Mitchell, E., ed. *Psychic Exploration*. New York: Putnam's, 1974, pp. 349–373.

Tralins, R. *Buried Alive*. North Miami Beach: Argent Books, 1977.

Turvey, V. *The Beginnings of Seership*. New Hyde Park, N.Y.: University Books, 1969.

Van Dusen, W. *The Natural Death in Man*. New York: Harper & Row, 1972.

Wheeler, D. *Journey to the Other Side*. New York: Tempo Books, 1976.

Yram [pseud.] *Practical Astral Projection*. London: Rider and Co., 1935.

Index